ASIAN DEVELOPMENT OUTLOOK 2019
STRENGTHENING DISASTER RESILIENCE

APRIL 2019

ASIAN DEVELOPMENT BANK

 Creative Commons Attribution 3.0 IGO license (CC BY 3.0 IGO)

© 2019 Asian Development Bank
6 ADB Avenue, Mandaluyong City, 1550 Metro Manila, Philippines
Tel +63 2 632 4444; Fax +63 2 636 2444
www.adb.org

Some rights reserved. Published in 2019.

ISBN 978-92-9261-560-4 (print), 978-92-9261-561-1 (electronic)
ISSN 0117-0481 (print), 1996-725X (electronic)
Publication Stock No. FLS190070-3
http://dx.doi.org/10.22617/FLS190070-3

The views expressed in this publication are those of the authors and do not necessarily reflect the views and policies of the Asian Development Bank (ADB) or its Board of Governors or the governments they represent.

ADB does not guarantee the accuracy of the data included in this publication and accepts no responsibility for any consequence of their use. The mention of specific companies or products of manufacturers does not imply that they are endorsed or recommended by ADB in preference to others of a similar nature that are not mentioned.

By making any designation of or reference to a particular territory or geographic area, or by using the term "country" in this document, ADB does not intend to make any judgments as to the legal or other status of any territory or area.

This work is available under the Creative Commons Attribution 3.0 IGO license (CC BY 3.0 IGO) https://creativecommons.org/licenses/by/3.0/igo/. By using the content of this publication, you agree to be bound by the terms of this license. For attribution, translations, adaptations, and permissions, please read the provisions and terms of use at https://www.adb.org/terms-use#openaccess.

This CC license does not apply to non-ADB copyright materials in this publication. If the material is attributed to another source, please contact the copyright owner or publisher of that source for permission to reproduce it. ADB cannot be held liable for any claims that arise as a result of your use of the material.

Please contact pubsmarketing@adb.org if you have questions or comments with respect to content, or if you wish to obtain copyright permission for your intended use that does not fall within these terms, or for permission to use the ADB logo.

Corrigenda to ADB publications may be found at http://www.adb.org/publications/corrigenda.

Notes:
In this publication, "$" refers to US dollars.
ADB recognizes "China" as the People's Republic of China and "Vietnam" as Viet Nam.

Cover design by Anthony Victoria.

Contents

Foreword   v
Acknowledgments   vi
Definitions   vii
Abbreviations   viii

ADO 2019—Highlights   xi

Part 1   Challenges from rising headwinds   1
Softening growth amid prolonged trade tensions   4
Exchange rates affect domestic financial conditions
    through trade and financial channels   35
Annex: Dimming global growth prospects   43

Part 2   Strengthening disaster resilience   55
Natural hazards putting Asia's prosperity at risk   59
Disaster impacts and how they propagate   72
Investing in development with disaster resilience   89
Prepared to build back better after a disaster   110

Part 3   Economic trends and prospects in developing Asia   139

Central Asia   141
Armenia   143
Azerbaijan   148
Georgia   153
Kazakhstan   158
Kyrgyz Republic   164
Tajikistan   169
Turkmenistan   174
Uzbekistan   178

East Asia   183
Hong Kong, China   185
Mongolia   190
People's Republic of China   194
Republic of Korea   203
Taipei,China   208

South Asia   213
Afghanistan   215
Bangladesh   219
Bhutan   226
India   231
Maldives   240
Nepal   245
Pakistan   249
Sri Lanka   255

Southeast Asia   263
Brunei Darussalam   265
Cambodia   268
Indonesia   271
Lao People's Democratic Republic   277
Malaysia   280
Myanmar   285
Philippines   288
Singapore   294
Thailand   298
Viet Nam   303

The Pacific   309
Fiji   311
Papua New Guinea   314
Solomon Islands   319
Timor-Leste   322
Vanuatu   327
North Pacific economies   330
South Pacific economies   335
Small island economies   340

Statistical appendix   345

Foreword

Developing Asia seems to be on a path of moderating growth as a recovery in global trade and economic activity that began in 2017 loses steam. Estimated regional growth remains robust but slowed in 2018 to 5.9% and is expected to slow further to 5.7% this year and 5.6% in 2020. Minus the newly industrialized economies, regional expansion at 6.4% in 2018 is envisaged softening to 6.2% this year and 6.1% in 2020. Although regional inflation crept up slightly to 2.5% last year on rising oil prices and currency depreciation, it remains well below the 10-year historical average of 3.2%. Headline inflation is forecast to remain at 2.5% in the next 2 years.

Persistent trade tensions continue to weigh on the region and pose the biggest risk to the forecast. Uncertainty over trade can deter consumption and investment. Other potential shocks that could buffet the region include a sharper slowdown in the advanced economies or the People's Republic of China. Fortunately, policy makers in the region are vigilant and ready to respond to shocks. When problems in Argentina and Turkey threw some emerging market currency exchanges into turmoil last year, many countries in the region gave their exchange rates room to move while tightening policy rates as guardrails against large and disruptive currency movements. As a result, currency adjustments were orderly, exchange rates eventually stabilized, and many currencies have since recovered. This kind of flexibility with vigilance is the necessary response to avoid disaster in an uncertain economic environment.

Another kind of disaster that nations must prepare for are those posed by natural hazards like cyclones and earthquakes. As documented in the theme chapter from which this report takes its name, developing Asia suffered from, 2000 to 2018, an annual average of nearly 38,000 disaster fatalities. As development patterns and climate change intensify the risks posed by natural hazards, their effects can spread across borders through migration and supply chain links. As a region that routinely lives with natural hazards—the home to more than four-fifths of the people affected by disasters globally in the past 2 decades—Asia must prioritize strengthening its disaster resilience. This can be done in various ways: integrating disaster risk reduction into national development and investment plans, spending more on prevention for a better balance with spending on response, and pooling risk through insurance and reinsurance, among other strategies.

Asian Development Outlook 2019 proudly marks 30 years as a publication providing Asian Development Bank economic analysis, forecasts, and policy advice tailored to its developing member countries. We in ADB hope to continue influencing the global discourse toward finding lasting solutions to the challenges we share and building resilience that will benefit us all.

TAKEHIKO NAKAO
President
Asian Development Bank

Acknowledgments

Asian Development Outlook 2019 was prepared by staff of the Asian Development Bank (ADB) in the Central and West Asia Department, East Asia Department, Pacific Department, South Asia Department, Southeast Asia Department, and Economic Research and Regional Cooperation Department, as well as in ADB resident missions. Representatives of these departments constituted the Regional Economic Outlook Task Force, which met regularly to coordinate and develop consistent forecasts for the region.

The authors who contributed the sections are bylined in each chapter. The subregional coordinators were Kenji Takamiya, Lilia Aleksanyan, and Fatima Catacutan for Central Asia, Akiko Terada-Hagiwara for East Asia, Lei Lei Song for South Asia, Thiam Hee Ng and Dulce Zara for Southeast Asia, and Rommel Rabanal and Cara Tinio for the Pacific.

A team of economists in the Economic Research and Regional Cooperation Department, led by Abdul Abiad, director of the Macroeconomics Research Division, coordinated the production of the publication, assisted by Edith Laviña. Technical and research support was provided by Shiela Camingue-Romance, Cindy Castillejos-Petalcorin, Suzette Dagli, Rhea Manguiat Molato, Nedelyn Magtibay-Ramos, Pilipinas Quising, Aleli Rosario, Dennis Sorino, Priscille Villanueva, and Mai Lin Villaruel. Additional research support was provided by Emmanuel Alano, Zemma Ardaniel, Kristina V. Baris, Donald Jay Bertulfo, John Arvin C. Bernabe, Paul Neilmer Feliciano, Jesson Pagaduan, Rene Cris Rivera, and Michael Timbang. The support provided by Sandile Hlatshwayo, Fahad Khan, and Mahinthan J. Mariasingham are much appreciated. The economic editorial advisors Robert Boumphrey, Joshua Greene, Srinivasa Madhur, Richard Niebuhr, and Reza Vaez-Zadeh made substantive contributions to the country chapters and regional outlook.

In addition to the contributors named in the byline and the authors of the background papers, the theme chapter benefited from inputs by Emma Allen, Yurendra Basnett, Ananya Basu, Preety Bhandari, Maria Vicedo Ferrer, Shikha Jha, Thomas Kessler, Sameer Khatiwada, Kijin Kim, Junkyu Lee, Xianfu Lu, Noelle O'Brien, Arghya Sinha Roy, Frank Thomalla, Hannah Usimaa, and James Villafuerte. The valuable support and guidance of Yasuyuki Sawada, Joseph E. Zveglich, Jr., Edimon Ginting, Juzhong Zhuang, and the ADB Climate Change and Disaster Risk Management Division of the Sustainable Development and Climate Change (SDCC) department is gratefully acknowledged. Margarita Debuque-Gonzales provided editorial advice on the theme chapter.

Peter Fredenburg advised on ADB style and English usage. Alvin Tubio handled typesetting and graphics generation, in which he was assisted by Heili Ann Bravo, Fermirelyn Cruz, Elenita Pura, and Priscille Villanueva. Art direction for the cover design was by Anthony Victoria. Critical support for the printing and publishing of the report was provided by the Printing Services Unit of the ADB Office of Administrative Services and by the publications and web teams of the ADB Department of Communications. Fermirelyn Cruz, Angel Love Alcantara Roque, and Rhia Bautista-Piamonte provided administrative and secretarial support. The Department of Communications, led by Vicky Tan and Karen Lane, planned and coordinated the dissemination of *Asian Development Outlook 2019*.

Definitions

The economies discussed in *Asian Development Outlook 2019* are classified by major analytic or geographic group. For the purposes of this publication, the following apply:

- **Association of Southeast Asian Nations** comprises Brunei Darussalam, Cambodia, Indonesia, the Lao People's Democratic Republic, Malaysia, Myanmar, the Philippines, Singapore, Thailand, and Viet Nam.
- **Developing Asia** comprises the 45 members of the Asian Development Bank listed below.
- **Newly industrialized economies** comprise Hong Kong, China; the Republic of Korea; Singapore; and Taipei,China.
- **Central Asia** comprises Armenia, Azerbaijan, Georgia, Kazakhstan, the Kyrgyz Republic, Tajikistan, Turkmenistan, and Uzbekistan.
- **East Asia** comprises Hong Kong, China; Mongolia; the People's Republic of China; the Republic of Korea; and Taipei,China.
- **South Asia** comprises Afghanistan, Bangladesh, Bhutan, India, Maldives, Nepal, Pakistan, and Sri Lanka.
- **Southeast Asia** comprises Brunei Darussalam, Cambodia, Indonesia, the Lao People's Democratic Republic, Malaysia, Myanmar, the Philippines, Singapore, Thailand, and Viet Nam.
- **The Pacific** comprises the Cook Islands, the Federated States of Micronesia, Fiji, Kiribati, the Marshall Islands, Nauru, Palau, Papua New Guinea, Samoa, Solomon Islands, Timor-Leste, Tonga, Tuvalu, and Vanuatu.

Unless otherwise specified, the symbol "$" and the word "dollar" refer to US dollars. *Asian Development Outlook 2019* is generally based on data available up to **8 March 2019**.

Abbreviations

AAL	average annual loss
ADB	Asian Development Bank
ADO	Asian Development Outlook
APEC	Asia-Pacific Economic Cooperation
ASEAN	Association of Southeast Asian Nations
BBB	build back better
BER	bilateral exchange rate
CBA	cost–benefit analysis
CPEC	China–Pakistan Economic Corridor
DDR	disaster risk reduction
DFI	development financial institution
DRM	disaster risk management
EM-DAT	Emergency Events Database
EEU	Eurasian Economic Union
EU	European Union
FCB	foreign commercial bank
FDI	foreign direct investment
FSM	Federated States of Micronesia
FY	fiscal year
GDP	gross domestic product
GST	goods and services tax
GVC	global value chain
IMF	International Monetary Fund
IT	information technology
Lao PDR	Lao People's Democratic Republic
Libor	London interbank offered rate
LNG	liquefied natural gas
M1	money that includes cash and checking accounts
M2	broad money that adds highly liquid accounts to M1
M3	broad money that adds time accounts to M2
mbd	million barrels per day
MPU	monetary policy uncertainty
MSEs	micro and small enterprises
NEER	nominal effective exchange rate
NFRK	National Fund of the Republic of Kazakhstan
NGO	nongovernment organization
NIE	newly industrialized economy
NPL	nonperforming loan
OECD	Organisation for Economic Co-operation and Development
OPEC	Organization of the Petroleum Exporting Countries
PCB	private commercial bank
PMI	purchasing managers' index
PNG	Papua New Guinea
PRC	People's Republic of China
Q	quarter

R&D	research and development
RMI	Republic of the Marshall Islands
ROK	Republic of Korea
RPC	Regional Processing Centre (Nauru)
saar	seasonally adjusted annualized rate
SCB	state-owned commercial bank
SMEs	small and medium-sized enterprises
SNG	subnational government
SOE	state-owned enterprise
SOFAZ	State Oil Fund of Azerbaijan
SSC	social security contribution
TFY	transitional fiscal year (Myanmar)
TPU	trade policy uncertainty
TVET	technical and vocational education and training
UK	United Kingdom
UN	United Nations
US	United States of America
VAT	value-added tax
WTO	World Trade Organization

ADO 2019—Highlights

Despite increasing headwinds, developing Asia posted strong growth in 2018, albeit moderating from 2017. Growth in the region is projected to soften to 5.7% in 2019 and 5.6% in 2020. Excluding Asia's high-income newly industrialized economies, growth is expected to slip from 6.4% in 2018 to 6.2% in 2019 and 6.1% in 2020.

As oil prices rose and Asian currencies depreciated, inflation edged up last year but remained low by historical standards. In light of stable commodity prices, inflation is anticipated to remain subdued at 2.5% in both 2019 and 2020.

Risks remain tilted to the downside. A drawn-out or deteriorating trade conflict between the People's Republic of China and the United States could undermine investment and growth in developing Asia. With various uncertainties stemming from US fiscal policy and a possible disorderly Brexit, growth in the advanced economies could turn out slower than expected, undermining the outlook for the People's Republic of China and other economies in the region. Though abrupt increases in US interest rates appear to have ceased for the time being, policy makers must remain vigilant in these uncertain times.

Disaster risk from natural hazards is a growing threat to the development and prosperity in the region, and the consequences tend to be more severe in developing countries, affecting poor and marginalized people disproportionally. Home to more than four-fifths of the people affected by disasters globally in the past 2 decades, developing Asia must prioritize strengthening its disaster resilience. Governments should integrate disaster risk reduction into national development and investment plans. Spending more on prevention would bring a better balance with spending on response and provide better protection to people at risk. Pooling risk through insurance and reinsurance promises to be cost-efficient.

Yasuyuki Sawada
Chief Economist
Asian Development Bank

Challenges from rising headwinds

Growth softens as trade tensions persist

- **Developing Asia posted strong but moderating growth in 2018.** Despite rising headwinds, growth in aggregate gross domestic product (GDP) slowed only slightly from 6.2% in 2017 to 5.9% in 2018 as global trade and economic activity decelerated at the end of the year, affecting many economies in the region. With growth in the People's Republic of China (PRC) continuing to moderate, regional growth will soften further to 5.7% in 2019 and to 5.6% in 2020. Excluding the newly industrialized economies, growth will slow from 6.4% in 2018 to 6.2% in 2019 and to 6.1% in 2020.

  » **A slowdown from late 2018 will continue in the advanced economies.** Aggregate growth in the three major advanced economies—the United States, the euro area, and Japan—slowed from 2.3% in 2017 to 2.2% in 2018. The slowing trend will likely reach 1.9% in 2019 and 1.6% in 2020 under less accommodative fiscal and monetary policies in the US, uncertainty surrounding Brexit in the United Kingdom and the European Union, and the trade conflict between the PRC and US.

  » **PRC moderation reflects structural factors and financial tightening.** With the economy maturing, growth in the PRC slowed from 6.8% in 2017 to 6.6% in 2018 as the government sought to reduce corporate leveraging and control financial risks. Growth will moderate further to 6.3% in 2019 and 6.1% in 2020 as restrictions on housing markets and shadow banking continue and as the trade conflict with the US weakens exports.

  » **India is set to see growth pick up as consumption strengthens.** Growth slowed from 7.2% in fiscal 2017 to 7.0% in 2018, with weaker agricultural output and consumption growth curtailed by higher global oil prices and lower government expenditure. Growth is expected to rebound to 7.2% in 2019 and 7.3% in 2020 as policy rates are cut and farmers receive income support, bolstering domestic demand.

  » **Southeast Asia will sustain growth at close to 5% this year and next.** Strengthening domestic demand will offset weaker export growth. Strong consumption—spurred by rising incomes, subdued inflation, and robust remittances—should boost economic activity in the subregion. Export demand, on the other hand, is likely to soften in 2019 in line with the weaker global environment and a muted forecast for semiconductor exports, before picking up slightly in 2020.

  » **Growth will recover in the Pacific but moderate in Central Asia.** Growth in the Pacific is set to rebound from a meager 0.9% in 2018 to 3.5% in 2019 as liquefied natural gas production in Papua New Guinea, the subregion's dominant economy, returns to full capacity following an earthquake in 2018. Meanwhile, lower oil prices and slower growth in the Russian Federation will weigh on economies in Central Asia. Growth in the subregion is projected to decelerate to 4.2% in both 2019 and 2020 as slowdowns in Kazakhstan and Turkmenistan more than offset higher growth elsewhere.

- **Financial conditions in Asia tightened in 2018, but have since improved.** Jitters over emerging markets sparked by Argentina and Turkey in 2018 caused regional currencies to depreciate against the US dollar, with the Indian rupee, Indonesian rupiah, and Philippine peso most sharply hit. Partly in response, many central banks in the region hiked their policy rates during the year. Then a pause in the tightening of US monetary policy, and some dissipation of concern about Asian emerging markets, allowed many regional currencies and equity markets to recover. Capital flows have stabilized.

- **Inflation edged up in 2018 but remains low by historical standards.** On the heels of rising oil prices and currency depreciation, inflation in developing Asia picked up slightly from 2.2% in 2017 to 2.5% in 2018. Despite the increase, inflation remains well below the 10-year historical average of 3.2% for the region. It is expected to remain subdued in the coming years. With stable commodity prices, headline inflation is forecast unchanged at 2.5% in 2019 and 2020.

- **In a cloudy outlook, risks remain tilted to the downside.** The primary risks still center on the US–PRC trade conflict. Uncertainty is heightened by protracted negotiations and disagreements, which could curtail investment and growth in the region. A possible upside risk to the outlook is that negotiations readily bring agreement and lower trade barriers. Beyond the trade conflict, growth in the advanced economies and the PRC may slow by more than expected if Brexit is disorderly, for example, or fiscal policy uncertainty persists in the US. On the other hand, the risk from the US abruptly raising the policy rate has subsided compared with 2018, but the risk of financial volatility remains.

Exchange rates affect domestic financial conditions through financial and trade channels

- **Exchange rate uncertainty may bear on regional financial conditions.** Local currency depreciation and heightened exchange rate volatility in 2018 could affect borrowing costs for economies in the region. High reliance on funding denominated in US dollars renders countries vulnerable to changing global financial conditions. Changes to the exchange rate and the sovereign bond spread, a measure of domestic financial conditions, closely correlated in emerging Asia in 2018. The exchange rate influences financial conditions in emerging markets through two competing effects: As a currency depreciates, the trade channel tends to loosen domestic financial conditions by improving external competitiveness, while the financial channel tends to tighten financial conditions by worsening the economy's balance sheet.

- **Trade and financial channels both affect domestic financial conditions.** Empirical analysis of selected economies in emerging Asia shows that changes in exchange rates affect sovereign credit risk premiums, which can further influence financial conditions through domestic lending rates. Changes to bilateral exchange rates against the US dollar affect financial conditions largely through the financial channel, while movements in nominal effective exchange rates act via the trade channel. However, the relative dominance of these two effects depends on circumstances specific to each economy, so policy prescriptions should be tailored individually.

- **Domestic financial resilience can mitigate adverse external influences.**
An appropriate policy mix and regional policy dialogue can strengthen domestic financial resilience and limit the impact of shocks from external funding conditions. Ensuring domestic financial stability is a challenge when external funding conditions are unfavorable. Monetary and macroprudential policies need to consider the effects the exchange rate has through both financial and trade channels. More broadly, it is important to cultivate an investor base at home and deepen capital markets in the region, in particular by further developing local currency bond markets. These policies should go hand in hand with strengthened policy dialogue across borders to monitor macro-financial conditions. Further, capital flow management measures must be considered to mitigate disruptive spillover in an increasingly interconnected global financial system.

Outlook by subregion

- **Growth will moderate in 2019 across most of developing Asia.** Only 20 of 45 individual economies are projected to see growth accelerate in 2019. By subregion, aggregate growth rates in Central Asia, East Asia, and Southeast Asia are expected to decelerate, while South Asia and the Pacific will bounce back from slowdown in 2018. South and Southeast Asia will grow more quickly in 2020 than in 2019.

- **East Asia slows as the global economy and trade weaken.** Economic growth in East Asia decelerated by 0.2 percentage points to 6.0% in 2018, weighed down by weakening external trade and moderating investment in the People's Republic of China (PRC) but sustained by resilient domestic consumption. Growth moderated to 6.6% in the PRC as policies to control risk in the financial sector and housing market dampened investment. Unique in the subregion, growth in Mongolia accelerated to 6.9% on large mining investment. Expansion in the PRC should moderate to 6.3% in 2019 and 6.1% in 2020 as global growth slows and economic policy targets a more sustainable growth trajectory. Growth will slow in the rest of the subregion as well in tandem with slower expansion in exports. Economic growth in the whole subregion will thus slide to 5.7% in 2019 and 5.5% in 2020. Inflation edged up last year as food prices and rents rose in most subregional economies. It will trend down from 2.0% in 2018 to 1.8% in 2019 and 2020 as oil prices moderate and rents and food prices stabilize.

- **South Asia bucks the trend of slowing growth in Asia.** Growth is expected to edge up by 0.1 percentage point, from 6.7% in 2018 to 6.8% in 2019 and again to 6.9% in 2020. Subregional averages in South Asia reflect heavy weighting for India, where growth slipped from 7.2% in 2017 to 7.0% in 2018 as agriculture and government expenditure both experienced slower growth and as global oil prices rose. Growth in India is forecast to pick up a bit to 7.2% in 2019 and 7.3% in 2020 on recovery in agriculture and stronger domestic demand, with reform having strengthened the health of banks and corporations, and as the implementation of a value-added tax makes domestic firms and products more competitive. Most other countries in South Asia are expected to maintain or slightly improve on their high growth rates, with Bangladesh expected to achieve 8.0% growth in 2019 and 2020. Pakistan and Sri Lanka, however, are currently reining in fiscal and external imbalances by implementing a broad range of economic reforms. Inflation in South Asia was stable at 3.7% in 2018 with benign food inflation and despite higher global oil prices. Subregional inflation is expected rise to 4.7% in 2019 and 4.9% in 2020 under pressure from currency depreciation and India's upward adjustment of some agricultural procurement prices to cover higher input costs.

- **Southeast Asia holds steady with some growth moderation.** Subregional growth was marginally lower at 5.1% last year as strong domestic demand countered slowing exports. With weakening global growth, slowing trade, and softer commodity prices, export prospects dim further for these highly trade-engaged economies. Continued strength in domestic demand should nevertheless support growth at 4.9% this year and 5.0% next year. In half of the 10 subregional economies, growth is forecast to slow this year, while Indonesia and the Lao People's Democratic Republic will be unchanged, and Brunei Darussalam, Myanmar, and the Philippines will post higher growth. Strong consumption, spurred by rising incomes, stable inflation, and robust remittances, is underpinning growth in Indonesia, Malaysia, the Philippines, Singapore, and Thailand, as is foreign investment in Cambodia and Viet Nam and large infrastructure projects elsewhere. Inflation in the subregion will dip marginally this year before returning to last year's 2.7%, broadly held in check by slowing growth and lower international oil prices, even as some countries hike administered prices.

■ **Central Asia will slow again after growth picked up in 2018.** Average growth in the subregion rose from 4.2% in 2017 to 4.4% last year as higher oil prices restored growth to Azerbaijan and expansion accelerated in Tajikistan and Uzbekistan, the latter reflecting the authorities' revision of statistics in prior years. Growth remained unchanged in Georgia and Kazakhstan and slowed in Armenia, the Kyrgyz Republic, and Turkmenistan, the last reflecting fiscal tightening. Growth in the subregion is forecast to slow to 4.2% in both 2019 and 2020 with lower average oil prices trimming expansion in Kazakhstan, and despite improvement in Azerbaijan, Georgia, the Kyrgyz Republic, and Uzbekistan. With tight monetary policy reducing inflation in Kazakhstan and particularly in Azerbaijan, where the exchange rate stabilized, average inflation in the subregion fell from 9.0% in 2017 to 7.9%, despite acceleration in Armenia, Turkmenistan, and Uzbekistan. Inflation is projected to slow further to 7.8% in 2019 and 7.2% in 2020 with further tightening of fiscal policy in Turkmenistan and monetary policy in Kazakhstan, as well as slower credit growth in Uzbekistan.

■ **The Pacific continues to lag behind other subregions.** Low growth at 0.9% in 2018 once again reflected developments in Papua New Guinea, the predominant economy in the subregion, which grew by a mere 0.2% following an earthquake in February that hit output of gold and liquefied natural gas. Timor-Leste, the third largest economy in the subregion, contracted for a second successive year as political uncertainty continued to hamper government spending. Nauru also contracted because of downsizing at the Regional Processing Centre for asylum seekers. With recovery in Papua New Guinea and Timor-Leste and continued growth in the other economies, subregional growth is forecast at 3.5% in 2019 and 3.2% in 2020, still the lowest in developing Asia. Inflation eased slightly to 4.0% in 2018 as slower price rises in Papua New Guinea and Tonga, the economies with the highest inflation, outweighed significant increases reflecting in large part higher fuel prices in several of the remaining economies, notably Timor-Leste and Fiji, the second largest economy in the subregion. Inflation is expected to slow to 3.7% in 2019 and then bounce back to 4.0% in 2020, primarily reflecting movements in international fuel and food prices.

Strengthening disaster resilience

Summary

- **Disaster risk and costs are rising, and Asia is particularly vulnerable.**
  - Rapid socioeconomic development is converging with worsening threats from natural hazards to pose unprecedented risk from catastrophes in developing Asia.
  - While the direct, immediate impacts of disasters tend to be local and short term, new evidence presented in this report shows how these effects can spill over to other places and last for a lifetime.
  - Suitable policy interventions are required to keep disaster losses from spiraling into the future and across the region.
- **Disaster risk management has improved, but gaps remain.**
  - Governments should continue to integrate disaster risk reduction into broader development policies and public investment strategies. They can build resilience from the ground up by facilitating climate change adaptation through enhanced disaster-resilient infrastructure, supporting the development of market mechanisms, and investing directly in communities.
  - Asia has led progress on these fronts in recent years, but positive trends need reinforcement. Spending on disaster prevention continues to lag far behind disaster response. Access to credit, insurance, and remittances remains sparse and uneven, limiting the coping strategies available to households affected by disasters. Immediate humanitarian response could be better coordinated with subsequent interventions for long-term recovery.
- **Managing disaster risk can enhance equity, resilience, and sustainability.** A greater focus on strengthening disaster resilience and preparing for recovery can ensure that rebuilding in the wake of disasters—building back better—emphasizes safety, timeliness, social equity, and the full realization of economic potential.

Natural hazards putting Asia's prosperity at risk

■ **Disasters are worse when vulnerable populations are exposed to hazards.** The upshot is harm to people and their physical assets such as property and infrastructure. Hazards can be natural, like hurricanes and earthquakes, or man-made, like industrial accidents and nuclear meltdowns. This report focuses on disasters that emerge from natural hazards, including severe weather events, geophysical disturbances, and epidemics. They can occur suddenly with little or no warning, or they can build slowly over the span of days, weeks, months, or years.

- **Development and climate change alter disaster risk.** On the one hand, rising incomes enable communities to cope with disasters. On the other, rapidly expanding coastal megacities, for example, create greater exposure to natural hazards. As the frequency and intensity of extreme weather events worsen because of climate change and associated sea level rise, coastal areas and island states across Asia face increasingly dire threats.

- **More than four in five people affected by natural hazards live in Asia.** From 2000 to 2018, developing Asia was home to 84% of the 206 million people affected by disasters globally on average each year. With nearly 38,000 disaster fatalities annually in that period, the region accounted for almost 55% of 60,000 disaster fatalities worldwide, and it suffered 26% of the $128 billion in economic damage. In Asia, 82% of disasters ensued from extreme weather events such as floods, storms, and droughts.

- **Those who suffer most are poor, marginalized, and isolated.** Surveys after severe flooding in Indian cities found that poor and migrant families were the worst affected, with some losing more than they earned in a year. Many small businesses fell into financial distress, some having to sell their assets and close down. Further, surveys of communities heavily exposed to flooding across five Asian countries found that, among rural households surveyed, 90% had suffered in the past decade either loss of life or significant damage to assets from floods, and their financial recovery took more than three times longer than for urban households. Pacific island economies are especially vulnerable to severe hazards, reflecting their isolation, limited economic diversification, and extreme exposure.

Disaster impacts and how they propagate

- **Immediate impacts on local economic activity can be substantial.** New evidence on the economic impacts of tropical storms in the Philippines shows that each of these events reduced local economic activity in that year by 1.7% on average but by as much as 23% after the most severe storms. More extreme events can have much larger impacts. Cyclone Pam in 2015—the second most intense tropical cyclone ever recorded in the South Pacific—caused damage in Vanuatu equal to 64% of annual GDP. Events that fall short of catastrophic typically affect economic activity for a year or less, allowing households that temporarily migrate away in the aftermath of a disaster to return to their land and livelihoods.

- **Beyond immediate loss of life and wealth, effects can persist over time.** More than a decade after the 1995 Kobe earthquake in Japan, for example, income per capita in Hyogo Prefecture was 12% lower than it otherwise would have been. Case studies of flooding in Indian cities show that, in the absence of social protection, disaster-hit families deplete their savings or borrow at high interest rates from informal sources, pushing them into indebtedness and poverty traps. Recent research reveals that disasters can affect victims for decades as reduced household spending on food, medicine, and education, for example, stunts a child's potential well into adulthood.

- **Effects can spread and link up with epidemics, conflict, and other risks.**
Disruption to supply chains, as occurred in 2011 after floods in Thailand and the Tohoku earthquake and tsunami in Japan, can transmit disaster impacts to firms and customers not directly hit by the event. Spatial transmission of impacts happens as well when people are forced to leave a stricken area, creating a displaced population. East, Southeast, and South Asia accounted for over 60% of the estimated 19 million people displaced by disasters in 2017—some briefly, others for much longer. The number of internal climate migrants is projected to increase rapidly. Disaster-induced migration can expose migrants to flooding, landslides, heat stress, and other hazards. It may also facilitate the spread of disease and even spark social disorder in urban areas, as suggested by new evidence on flood-induced migration.

Investing in development with disaster resilience

- **Asia has achieved substantial mainstreaming of disaster risk management.**
Many countries in the region are adapting the Sendai Framework for Disaster Risk Reduction, 2015–2030 for national needs and thereby effecting a notable policy shift in disaster response from reactive to proactive. Escalating losses from disasters suggest that these positive trends require reinforcement to translate plans into actions and to address the causes of social vulnerability and the drivers of disaster risk.

- **Greenfield investment is a natural entry point for disaster resilience.**
Developing Asia is estimated to need $26 trillion in infrastructure investment from 2016 to 2030, or $1.7 trillion per year. Planning for and investing in climate-friendly and disaster-resilient infrastructure from the start can help avoid locking in further exposure to disaster risk and is a particularly cost-effective way to reduce future losses from disasters.

- **Spending on prevention needs to catch up with spending on response.**
Globally, governments in developing countries receive seven times more assistance for responding to disasters after they occur than for preparing in advance for rapid recovery and, where possible, taking measures to keep hazards from developing into disasters. In Asia, this spending gap has narrowed slightly over the past few years but remains large. Further closing the gap will yield multiple dividends, especially when investments have development benefits aside from reducing disaster risk. Examples include stable water resource management that integrates flood risk considerations, the construction of cyclone-safe multipurpose evacuation centers that serve daily as classrooms or community centers, the reestablishment of sustainable mangrove forests to absorb storm impacts and prevent coastal erosion, or hydroponic projects that diversify incomes in normal times and safeguard food security when disaster strikes.

- **Risk shared through commercial credit or insurance is manageable risk.**
Across Asia including Japan, just over 8% of catastrophe losses since 1980 were covered by insurance. Recent years have seen an increase in programs that offer insurance coverage, especially across developing Asia. New studies show that

two-thirds of them offer micro-insurance to cover agriculture losses, and over 80% depend on subsidies or other financial support. The benefits of insurance are clear: pooling risk to preserve human welfare, facilitating investment by containing risk, and making post-disaster support more predictable. While traditional indemnity insurance models are difficult to scale down to the needs of individual households in poor communities, more innovative insurance models such as index-based risk-transfer products (such as drought insurance linked to rainfall) offer potential, and government and international support for reinsurance allows broader pooling of risk.

- **Hiring victims can help, as can informal support networks and remittances.** Labor market interventions can gainfully employ some disaster-affected people in reconstruction after disasters. Informal risk-sharing arrangements such as through private transfers within communities can effectively cope with shocks to individual households but not with shocks to whole communities from large disasters. Public transfers can help, as can remittances from outside the affected area. In the Philippines, for example, remittances compensated for nearly 65% of income lost in shocks caused by rainfall deviation. The poorest of the poor, however, often lack the social and financial networks necessary to allow family members to migrate and remit.

- **Community action must complement national efforts.** Communities are themselves the first responders to disasters, often with little or no immediate external support, and are key to ensuring sustained recovery and reconstruction. New evidence from flood resilience surveys across 88 communities in Asia shows that community investments can build resilience while delivering broader development benefits, such as better education, transportation, and food supply. Proper waste management, for example, can prevent the spread of disease and keep rivers and drains clear to carry away floodwaters, while benefiting communities more broadly day to day. Recent experience after major earthquakes and tropical cyclones in Asia highlights the role of local communities as custodians of local knowledge and experience that enables the dissemination of early warning messages and timely evacuation, and that can guide the effective delivery of humanitarian response and recovery assistance.

- **Development agencies support disaster resilience in many ways.** Countries have received concessional loans and grants from development agencies to strengthen disaster resilience. Multilateral and regional lenders support the establishment of disaster-contingent financing arrangements designed for quick disbursement. An ADB $6 million contingent financing loan to Tonga, for example, was fully disbursed in just 3 days after that Pacific island country was struck by Tropical Cyclone Gita in February 2018. Other multilateral assistance from ADB has designed and piloted innovative insurance programs, notably a disaster insurance pool for city governments in the Philippines that was a world first. Meanwhile, international efforts continue to provide to poor countries access to finance through more traditional emergency assistance loans and grants offered in response to disasters.

- **Enhanced financial arrangements enable better disaster management.**
Delayed or insufficient financing for relief, early recovery, or reconstruction exacerbates the economic and social consequences of direct physical damage, extending the time required to rebuild infrastructure, render it fully functional, and deliver the services that depend on it. Such shortcomings stymie efforts to build back better. Governments increasingly recognize this and work to enhance both sovereign and nonsovereign financing instruments with support from development partners. The Government of the Philippines became the first to position these instruments in a wider framework by establishing in 2015 a national financing strategy for disaster risk to promote a comprehensive approach. The Government of Indonesia launched a similar strategy in 2018, and such strategies are currently under development in Myanmar and Pakistan.

Prepared to build back better after a disaster

- **Humanitarian response is a prelude to recovery and reconstruction.**
Sustainable recovery must overcome operational challenges and bridge the gap between urgent humanitarian response and longer-term recovery and reconstruction. The efficient and equitable allocation of private and public resources in response to disasters is often challenged by deficiencies in governance. Even after finances are secured, reconstruction projects face local implementation challenges such as a lack of skilled personnel, unclear land tenure, transportation bottlenecks, and sudden increases in wage rates and prices for construction materials. Case studies of the 2015 earthquake in Nepal and Cyclone Pam in Vanuatu the same year indicate that successful long-term recovery requires broad collaboration involving central and local governments, civil society, and affected communities. The roles and responsibilities of all stakeholders must be clear, and responsible parties must have the experiential knowledge and capacity necessary to absorb and effectively apply the large influxes of resources that materialize after disasters.

- **Build back better to equitably realize social and economic potential.**
Building back better means ensuring that recovery is not only complete but superior to the status quo before the disaster. While building back fast often takes precedence in the immediate aftermath, it must be balanced against other objectives. Strengthening resilience under future hazards should be central to recovery and reconstruction. Crucially, this entails integrating measures that mitigate disaster risk when restoring infrastructure and social capital, as well as ensuring that reconstruction restores and renews economic opportunity and dynamism. Finally, public planning for recovery and building back better must be inclusive and fair to vulnerable segments of society.

GDP growth rate and inflation, % per year

	GDP growth				Inflation			
	2017	2018	2019	2020	2017	2018	2019	2020
Central Asia	4.2	4.4	4.2	4.2	9.0	7.9	7.8	7.2
Armenia	7.5	5.2	4.3	4.5	1.0	2.5	3.5	3.2
Azerbaijan	0.1	1.4	2.5	2.7	12.9	2.3	4.0	5.0
Georgia	4.8	4.8	5.0	4.9	6.0	2.6	3.2	3.0
Kazakhstan	4.1	4.1	3.5	3.3	7.4	6.0	6.0	5.5
Kyrgyz Republic	4.7	3.5	4.0	4.4	3.2	1.5	3.0	3.5
Tajikistan	7.1	7.3	7.0	6.5	6.7	5.4	7.5	7.0
Turkmenistan	6.5	6.2	6.0	5.8	8.0	9.4	9.0	8.2
Uzbekistan	4.5	5.1	5.2	5.5	13.7	17.9	16.0	14.0
East Asia	6.2	6.0	5.7	5.5	1.6	2.0	1.8	1.8
Hong Kong, China	3.8	3.0	2.5	2.5	1.5	2.4	2.3	2.3
Mongolia	5.3	6.9	6.7	6.3	4.3	6.8	8.5	7.5
People's Republic of China	6.8	6.6	6.3	6.1	1.6	2.1	1.9	1.8
Republic of Korea	3.1	2.7	2.5	2.5	1.9	1.5	1.4	1.4
Taipei,China	3.1	2.6	2.2	2.0	0.6	1.3	1.1	1.2
South Asia	6.9	6.7	6.8	6.9	3.9	3.7	4.7	4.9
Afghanistan	2.7	2.2	2.5	3.0	5.0	0.6	3.0	4.5
Bangladesh	7.3	7.9	8.0	8.0	5.4	5.8	5.5	5.8
Bhutan	6.3	5.5	5.7	6.0	4.3	3.6	3.8	4.0
India	7.2	7.0	7.2	7.3	3.6	3.5	4.3	4.6
Maldives	6.9	7.6	6.5	6.3	2.8	-0.1	1.0	1.5
Nepal	7.9	6.3	6.2	6.3	4.5	4.2	4.4	5.1
Pakistan	5.4	5.2	3.9	3.6	4.2	3.9	7.5	7.0
Sri Lanka	3.4	3.2	3.6	3.8	7.7	2.1	3.5	4.0
Southeast Asia	5.3	5.1	4.9	5.0	2.8	2.7	2.6	2.7
Brunei Darussalam	1.3	-1.0	1.0	1.5	-0.2	0.1	0.2	0.2
Cambodia	7.0	7.3	7.0	6.8	2.9	2.5	2.5	2.5
Indonesia	5.1	5.2	5.2	5.3	3.8	3.2	3.2	3.3
Lao People's Dem. Rep.	6.9	6.5	6.5	6.5	0.8	2.0	2.0	2.0
Malaysia	5.9	4.7	4.5	4.7	3.8	1.0	2.0	2.7
Myanmar	6.8	6.2	6.6	6.8	4.0	7.1	6.8	7.5
Philippines	6.7	6.2	6.4	6.4	2.9	5.2	3.8	3.5
Singapore	3.9	3.2	2.6	2.6	0.6	0.4	0.7	0.9
Thailand	4.0	4.1	3.9	3.7	0.7	1.1	1.0	1.0
Viet Nam	6.8	7.1	6.8	6.7	3.5	3.5	3.5	3.8
The Pacific	2.4	0.9	3.5	3.2	4.2	4.0	3.7	4.0
Cook Islands	6.8	7.0	6.0	4.5	-0.1	0.4	1.0	1.5
Federated States of Micronesia	2.4	2.0	2.7	2.5	0.1	1.0	0.7	1.5
Fiji	3.0	3.0	3.2	3.5	3.3	4.1	3.5	3.0
Kiribati	0.3	2.3	2.3	2.3	0.4	2.1	2.3	2.2
Marshall Islands	3.6	2.5	2.3	2.2	0.0	0.7	0.5	1.0
Nauru	4.0	-2.4	-1.0	0.1	5.1	3.8	2.5	2.0
Palau	-3.7	0.5	3.0	3.0	0.9	1.1	0.5	1.5
Papua New Guinea	3.0	0.2	3.7	3.1	5.4	4.5	4.2	4.7
Samoa	2.7	0.9	2.0	3.0	1.4	3.7	2.0	1.5
Solomon Islands	3.2	3.0	2.4	2.3	0.1	3.3	2.5	2.5
Timor-Leste	-5.4	-0.5	4.8	5.4	0.6	2.1	3.0	3.3
Tonga	2.8	0.4	2.1	1.9	7.4	5.3	5.3	5.3
Tuvalu	3.2	4.3	4.1	4.4	4.4	1.8	3.4	3.5
Vanuatu	4.4	3.2	3.0	2.8	3.1	2.2	2.0	2.0
Developing Asia	6.2	5.9	5.7	5.6	2.2	2.5	2.5	2.5
Developing Asia excluding the NIEs	6.6	6.4	6.2	6.1	2.3	2.6	2.6	2.6

Note: The newly industrialized economies (NIEs) are Hong Kong, China; the Republic of Korea; Singapore; and Taipei,China.

1
CHALLENGES FROM RISING HEADWINDS

Challenges from rising headwinds

Developing Asia posted strong but moderating growth in 2018, and this trend will continue into 2019 and 2020. Growth weakened slightly from 6.2% in 2017 to 5.9% in 2018 as global trade and economic activity softened and as trade tensions persisted. The region's two largest economies, the People's Republic of China (PRC) and India, both saw growth dip slightly to still-robust rates thanks to strong consumption growth. Inflation in the region edged up from 2.2% in 2017 to 2.5% on rising food and oil prices but remained low by historical norms. Trade growth remained strong in the first half of 2018 but slowed toward year-end as global economic activity softened and trade tensions between the United States and the PRC escalated (Figure 1.0.1).

The outlook for developing Asia is for continued deceleration. The region is expected to grow by 5.7% in 2019 and 5.6% in 2020 (Figure 1.0.2). Growth in the PRC is expected to continue moderating to 6.3% in 2019 and 6.1% in 2020 as the economy matures and as measures to control financial risks are maintained. In India, growth is expected to pick up to 7.2% and 7.3% in response to more accommodative policies. For most subregions except the Pacific, growth is expected to stay flat or decline slightly.

The main risk to the outlook is still the ongoing trade conflict, as heightened trade policy uncertainty can negatively affect investment and manufacturing activity. A sharper slowdown in the advanced economies or the PRC is another risk. A rapid hike in the US policy rate is now less likely. But the risk of financial volatility remains, and this can affect domestic financial conditions. In sum, persistent headwinds that slowed growth in 2018 will continue to shape the region's economic performance in 2019 and 2020.

This chapter was written by Valerie Mercer-Blackman, Sameer Khatiwada, Abdul Abiad, Shiela Camingue-Romance, Junkyu Lee, Arief Ramayandi, Peter Rosenkranz, Benno Ferrarini, Madhavi Pundit, Nedelyn Magtibay-Ramos, Pilipinas Quising, Dennis Sorino, Michael Timbang, and Priscille Villanueva of the Economic Research and Regional Cooperation Department, ADB, Manila. Contributions from Jill Adona, Lilia Aleksanyan, Donghyun Park, Irfan Qureshi, Shu Tian, Cindy Castillejos-Petalcorin, and Mai Lin Villaruel are gratefully acknowledged.

1.0.1 Global activity indicators

World trade weakened in 2018 as global economic activity slowed and trade tensions between the US and the PRC escalated.

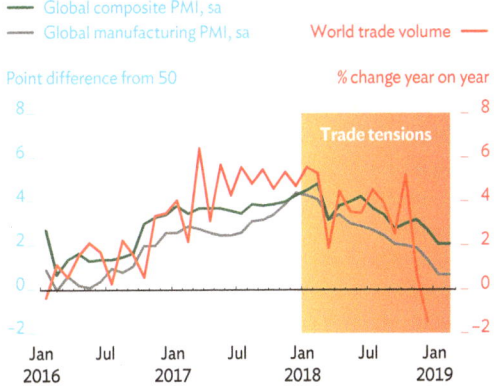

PMI = purchasing managers' index, PRC = People's Republic of China, sa = seasonally adjusted, US = United States.
Sources: CEIC Data Company; CPB Netherlands Bureau for Economic Policy Analysis. https://www.cpb.nl/en/worldtrademonitor (both accessed 8 March 2019).

1.0.2 GDP growth outlook in developing Asia

The growth outlook for the next 2 years is continued deceleration, with the PRC moderating to a more sustainable growth rate while growth in India picks up in the next 2 years.

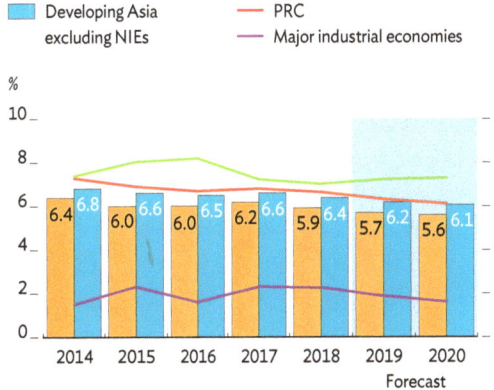

Major industrial economies = the euro area, Japan, and the United States, NIEs = newly industrialized economies (Hong Kong, China; the Republic of Korea; Singapore; and Taipei,China), PRC = People's Republic of China.
Sources: *Asian Development Outlook* database; ADB estimates.

Softening growth amid prolonged trade tensions

After stellar growth in 2017 at 6.2%, developing Asia slowed slightly to 5.9% in 2018 as rising trade tensions generated stiffening headwinds. This slowdown occurred in tandem with a slowdown in the major industrial economies of the US, the euro area, and Japan, where composite growth moderated slightly from 2.3% in 2017 to 2.2%. Expansion in the two largest economies in developing Asia decelerated, with growth in the PRC declining from 6.8% in 2017 to 6.6% in 2018 and in India from 7.2% to 7.0%. Excluding the newly industrialized economies (NIEs), GDP growth in 2018 was down from 6.6% in 2017 to 6.4%. Growth decelerated in 28 economies in the region, or 62% of them, and accelerated in 14, or 31%, with Bangladesh leading the pack as growth at 7.3% in 2017 accelerated to 7.9%. Solid growth momentum in the first 3 quarters of 2018 started to fade in the last few months, the weakness most evident in exports (Figure 1.1.1A). This trend was clearest in the PRC, the NIEs, and five larger economies in the Association of Southeast Asian Nations (ASEAN-5). Growth in industrial production also showed some signs of weakening (Figure 1.1.1B).

Key drivers of growth

Much of the impetus for growth in 2018 on the demand side came from consumption, while export growth slowed. On average, the consumption contribution to growth rose from 3.4 percentage points in 2017 to 3.7 points in 2018 (Figure 1.1.2). Net exports subtracted from GDP growth in 7 of the 11 larger economies in the sample, reflecting slowing export growth as the external environment weakened, as well as rising imports with higher oil prices.

Investment spurred growth in some economies but dragged on growth in others. In 2018, the contribution of investment to growth picked up in Indonesia; the Philippines; Taipei,China; and Thailand (Figure 1.1.3). This reflected increased public investment as governments launched initiatives for infrastructure and new technology, as well as private investment funded by foreign direct investment (FDI), particularly in Indonesia and Thailand (Section 1.1.6). Meanwhile, the contribution to growth from investment declined notably in Malaysia, the Republic of Korea (ROK), and Singapore.

1.1.1 Growth in exports and industrial production, selected economies

Export growth in developing Asia was strong in 2017 and most of 2018 but lost momentum in the last months of 2018...

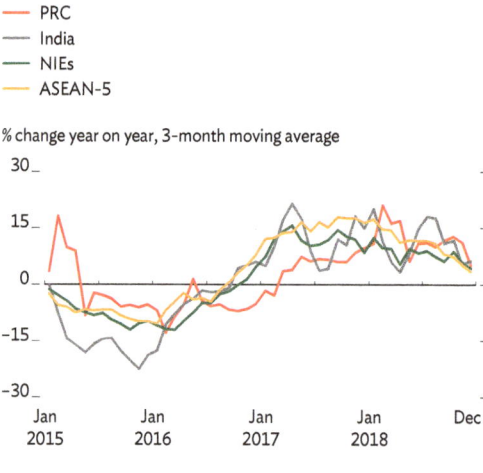

...while growth in industrial production moderated.

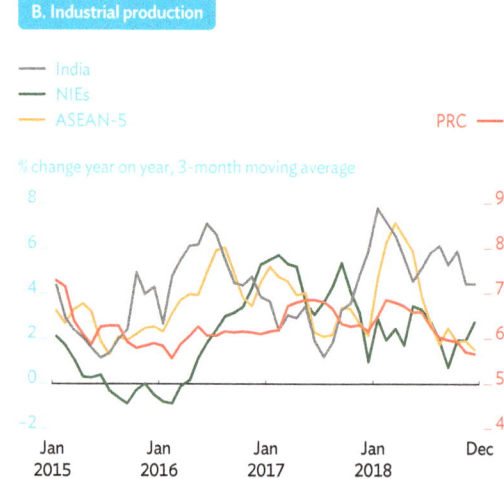

ASEAN-5 = five larger economies in the Association of Southeast Asian Nations (Indonesia, Malaysia, the Philippines, Thailand, and Viet Nam), NIEs = newly industrialized economies (Hong Kong, China; Republic of Korea; Singapore; and Taipei,China), PRC = People's Republic of China.

Source: CEIC Data Company (accessed 16 March 2019).

1.1.2 Demand-side contributions to growth, selected economies

The impetus for growth in 2018 came from consumption, while net exports subtracted from growth in most economies.

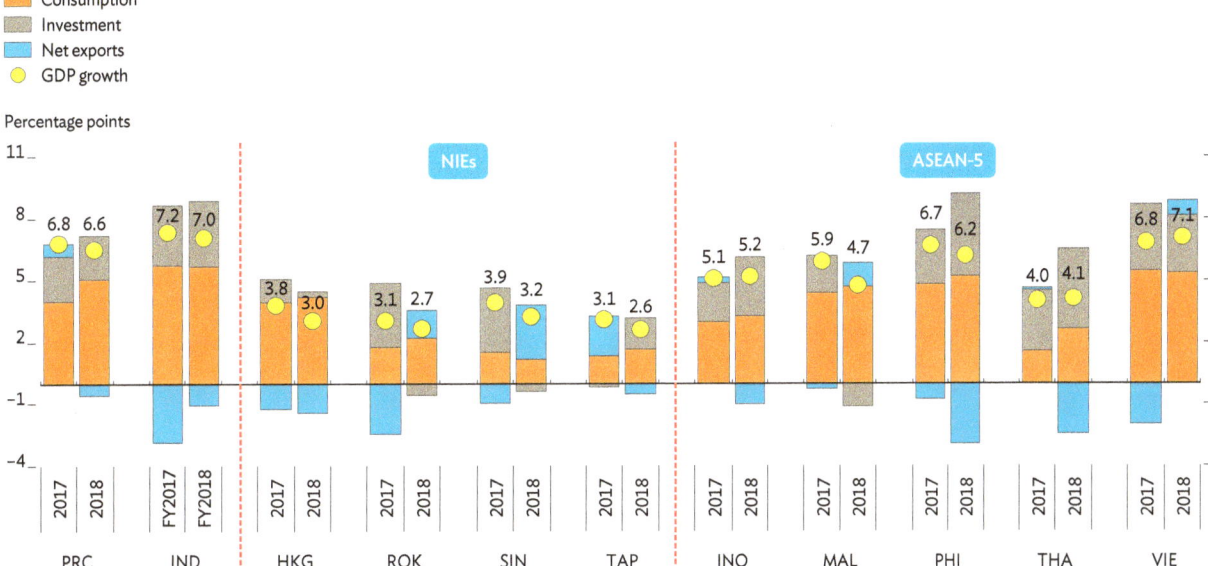

ASEAN = Association of Southeast Asian Nations, FY = fiscal year, HKG = Hong Kong, China, IND = India, INO = Indonesia, MAL = Malaysia, NIEs = newly industrialized economies, PHI = Philippines, PRC = People's Republic of China, ROK = Republic of Korea, SIN = Singapore, TAP = Taipei,China, THA = Thailand, VIE = Viet Nam.
Notes: Data for India are in fiscal years ending 31 March of the next year. Components do not sum to GDP growth because statistical discrepancy was excluded.
Sources: Haver Analytics (accessed 25 March 2019); ADB estimates.

In Malaysia, the investment decline resulted partly from private investors waiting out an election and partly from some major public investment projects being put on hold. In the ROK and Singapore, a slowdown in private investment was the main factor, reflecting a decline in confidence as the external environment weakened.

The loss in momentum during 2018 was evident in consumer confidence and retail sales and also in business confidence in several economies. Consumer confidence declined through most of 2018 in the PRC, the ROK, and Taipei,China (Figure 1.1.4A). Lower consumer confidence in East Asia manifested itself in retail sales, which followed a similar pattern (Figure 1.1.4B). In Southeast Asia, however, growth in retail sales held steady or increased in 2018, except in Singapore. Rising consumer confidence in India played a key role in raising domestic demand and creating a positive outlook for 2019.

1.1.3 Change in the investment contribution to growth, 2018 versus 2017

Investment boosted growth in some economies but dragged on growth in others.

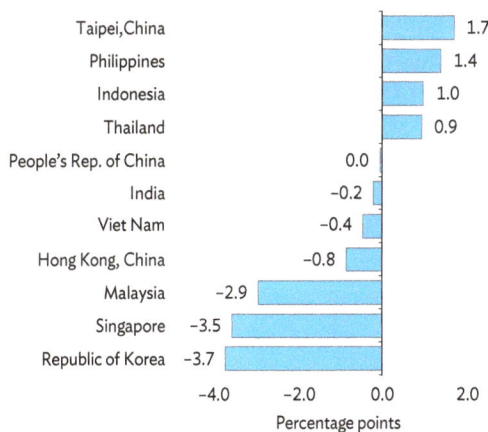

Sources: Haver Analytics (accessed 8 March 2019); ADB estimates.

1.1.4 Consumer confidence and retail sales, selected economies

Fading momentum was evident in consumer confidence in East Asia, but less so in Southeast Asia...

...and trends in consumer confidence were mirrored by retail sales, with slower growth in the second half of 2018.

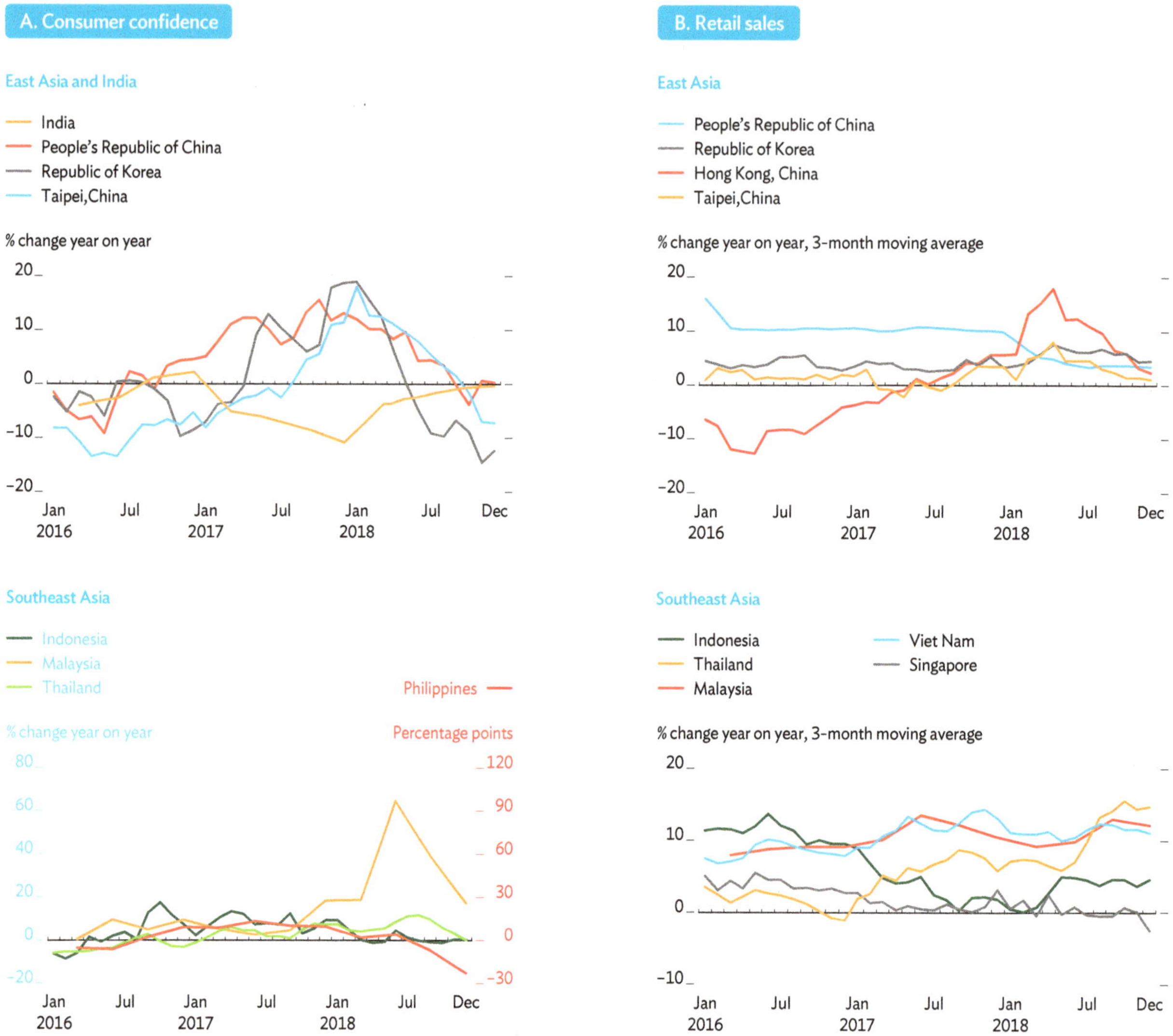

A. Consumer confidence

East Asia and India
— India
— People's Republic of China
— Republic of Korea
— Taipei,China

% change year on year

Southeast Asia
— Indonesia
— Malaysia
— Thailand
— Philippines

% change year on year / Percentage points

B. Retail sales

East Asia
— People's Republic of China
— Republic of Korea
— Hong Kong, China
— Taipei,China

% change year on year, 3-month moving average

Southeast Asia
— Indonesia — Viet Nam
— Thailand — Singapore
— Malaysia

% change year on year, 3-month moving average

Note: Data unavailability and inconsistency exclude Central Asia, the Pacific, and some other smaller economies from this analyses, as well as South Asia except for India's inclusion in consumer confidence. Data are quarterly for India, Malaysia, and the Philippines, for the last of which the consumer confidence index measures positive or negative consumer household expectations.
Sources: Haver Analytics; CEIC Data Company (both accessed 31 January 2019).

Reflecting trends in consumer confidence and retail sales in 2018, business expectations deteriorated in East Asia but not in Southeast Asia (Table 1.1.1). In the PRC, the ROK, and Taipei,China, the purchasing managers' index (PMI) was its lowest in 2 years, with muted business plans reflecting weaker external demand and an ongoing downcycle in electronics. Meanwhile, Southeast Asia showed signs of continued expansion in manufacturing, with a PMI over 50 in the latest available quarter. In India, the only economy in South Asia for which PMI data are available, continued strength in manufacturing was evident throughout 2018.

1.1.1 Markit Manufacturing Purchasing Managers' Index, selected economies

Meanwhile, business expectations deteriorated in East Asia, while in Southeast Asia they remained buoyant.

Economy	2017a												2018a												2019a	
	Q1 2017		Q2 2017		Q3 2017		Q4 2017		Q1 2018		Q2 2018		Q3 2018		Q4 2018		Q1 2019									
India	50.4	50.7	52.5	52.5	51.6	50.9	47.9	51.2	51.2	50.3	52.6	54.7	52.4	52.1	51.0	51.6	51.2	53.1	52.3	51.7	52.2	53.1	54.0	53.2	53.9	54.3
Indonesia	50.4	49.3	50.5	51.2	50.6	49.5	48.6	50.7	50.4	50.1	50.4	49.3	49.9	51.4	50.7	51.6	51.7	50.3	50.5	51.9	50.7	50.5	50.4	51.2	49.9	50.1
Malaysiab	51.6	52.4	52.5	53.7	51.7	49.9	51.3	53.4	52.9	51.6	55.0	52.9	53.5	52.9	52.5	51.6	50.6	52.5	52.7	54.2	54.5	52.2	51.2	49.8	50.9	50.6
PRC	51.0	51.7	51.2	50.3	49.6	50.4	51.1	51.6	51.0	51.0	50.8	51.5	51.5	51.6	51.0	51.1	51.1	51.0	50.8	50.6	50.0	50.1	50.2	49.7	48.3	49.9
Philippines	52.7	53.6	53.8	53.3	54.3	53.9	52.8	50.6	50.8	53.7	54.8	54.2	51.7	50.8	51.5	52.7	53.7	52.9	50.9	51.9	52.0	54.0	54.2	53.2	52.3	51.9
Rep. of Korea	49.0	49.2	48.4	49.4	49.2	50.1	49.1	49.9	50.6	50.2	51.2	49.9	50.7	50.3	49.1	48.4	48.9	49.8	48.3	49.9	51.3	51.0	48.6	49.8	48.3	47.2
Taipei,China	55.6	54.5	56.2	54.4	53.1	53.3	53.6	54.3	54.2	53.6	56.3	56.6	56.9	56.0	55.3	54.8	53.4	54.5	53.1	53.0	50.8	48.7	48.4	47.7	47.5	46.3
Thailand	50.6	50.6	50.2	49.8	49.7	50.4	49.6	49.5	50.3	49.8	50.0	50.4	50.6	50.9	49.1	49.5	51.1	50.2	50.1	49.9	50.0	48.9	49.8	50.3	50.2	49.9
Viet Nam	51.9	54.2	54.6	54.1	51.6	52.5	51.7	51.8	53.3	51.6	51.4	52.5	53.4	53.5	51.6	52.7	53.9	55.7	54.9	53.7	51.5	53.9	56.5	53.8	51.9	51.2

PRC = People's Republic of China, Q = quarter.
a seasonally adjusted.
b For Malaysia, the series is adjusted by adding 3 points as historical experience suggests that values above 47 are consistent with expansion.
Note: Reddish color indicates contraction (<50). White to green indicates expansion (>50).
Source: CEIC Data Company (accessed 1 March 2019).

Growth by subregion

Growth in East Asia remained broadly in line with expectations, moderating from 6.2% in 2017 to 6.0% in 2018 (Figure 1.1.5). Tighter financial conditions and trade tensions between the PRC and the US weighed on economic activity in the subregion's major economies. The PRC, which accounts for three-fifths of the subregion's economic activity, saw continued moderation to a more sustainable growth rate that reflected efforts to contain financial risk and restrictions to cool the housing market—but also uncertainty about trade policy and prospects. The ROK grew at a slower pace in 2018, down from 3.1% in 2017 to 2.7%, with a decline in fixed investment and tighter property financing to cool the real estate market. In Hong Kong, China, growth decelerated from 3.8% in 2017 to 3.0% as private spending and external demand weakened. Taipei,China continued to bear the brunt of the slowdown in the PRC and of heightened trade tensions between the PRC and the US, with growth slowing from 3.1% in 2017 to 2.6%. Mongolia, on the other hand, was buoyed by strong investment and posted robust growth acceleration from 5.3% in 2017 to 6.9% in 2018.

In South Asia, growth decelerated slightly from 6.9% in 2017 to 6.7% as all economies in the subregion except Bangladesh and Maldives expanded more slowly. Growth in India slipped by 0.2 percentage points to an estimated 7.0% with weaker private consumption. Meanwhile in Sri Lanka, continued fiscal and structural reform slowed growth from 3.4% in 2017 to 3.2%.

1.1.5 Growth by subregion, 2016 to 2018

With the exception of Central Asia, growth in 2018 edged downward across the region.

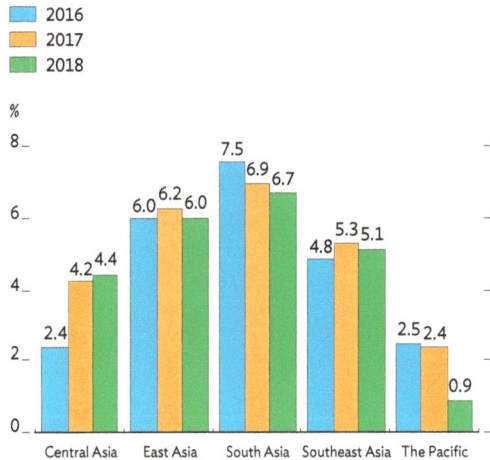

Source: *Asian Development Outlook* database.

Growth in Pakistan edged lower from 5.4% in 2017 to 5.2% as the country continued to grapple with its large current account deficit. Growth in Nepal slowed from 7.9% in 2017 to 6.3% in 2018 as agriculture suffered under poor weather. In Bangladesh, however, growth remained buoyant, accelerating from 7.3% in 2017 to 7.9% in 2018 on strong domestic demand and growth in remittances.

Southeast Asia ended 2018 on a fairly solid footing with average growth coming in at 5.1%, lower than in 2017. Strong exports and domestic demand pushed growth up to 7.3% in Cambodia and 7.1% in Viet Nam. By contrast, weaker exports and domestic demand dragged down growth in Malaysia from 5.9% in 2017 to 4.7% and in Myanmar from 6.8% to 6.2%. Meanwhile, robust domestic demand more than offset weaker exports to drive growth higher to 5.2% in Indonesia and 4.1% in Thailand. Elsewhere in the subregion, weaker external demand trimmed growth in the Philippines from 6.7% in 2017 to 6.2% and in Singapore from 3.9% to 3.2%, while domestic factors slowed growth in the Lao People's Democratic Republic.

Growth in Central Asia exceeded expectations in 2018, rising from 4.2% in 2017 to 4.4%, thanks to a recovery in energy and mining that boosted expansion in Azerbaijan and Uzbekistan. Expansion in Tajikistan accelerated from 7.1% in 2017 to 7.3% thanks to continued strong public investment and higher remittances. However, growth in Armenia slowed from an exceptionally strong 7.5% in 2017 to 5.2% with lower industry production and contraction in agriculture. In the Kyrgyz Republic, lower output in mining and manufacturing slowed growth to 3.5% in 2018. In Turkmenistan, growth slowed as fiscal consolidation trimmed expansion outside of the large hydrocarbon economy. Growth was unchanged in Georgia at 4.8% and in Kazakhstan at 4.1%.

In the Pacific, growth fell from 2.4% in 2017 to 0.9% in 2018 after a devastating earthquake slashed growth in Papua New Guinea, the dominant economy in the subregion, to only 0.2%. Growth slowed as well in Solomon Islands as log exports and fish catches slumped. Timor-Leste contracted again in 2018, though less than in 2017. Meanwhile, Fiji was able to maintain 3.0% growth thanks to robust tourism receipts.

India continues to outpace the PRC

The region's two largest economies continued their robust growth in 2018, albeit at slightly lower rates than in 2017. Domestic demand remains the main growth driver in both the PRC and India, with consumption contributing about 5 percentage points to growth in each country in 2018 (Figure 1.1.6).

Economic growth in India slowed to 7.0% in fiscal 2018 (FY2018, ended 31 March 2019), slightly down from 7.2% in FY2017. The slowing reflected subdued agriculture, which grew by only 2.7%, the lowest in 3 years. Food grain production was robust but slightly below the harvest in the previous year, mainly from a shortfall in cereals and pulses. Services also slowed to 7.4%,

1.1.6 Demand-side contributions to growth: India versus the PRC

Among drivers of growth, domestic demand remains key in both India and the PRC.

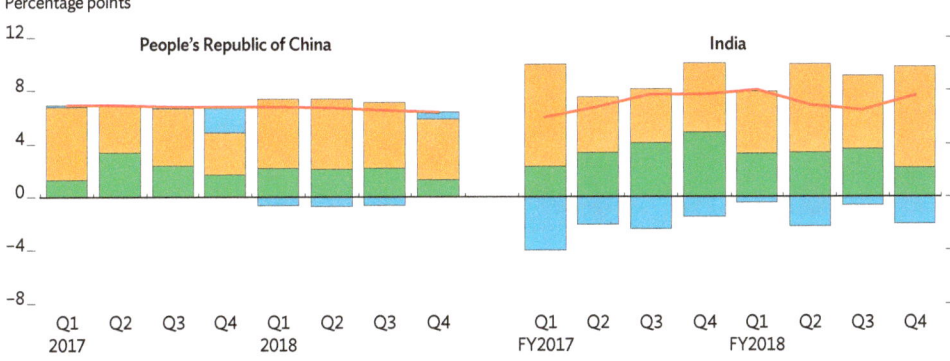

FY = fiscal year, PRC = People's Republic of China, Q = quarter.
Note: Data for India exclude statistical discrepancy and are for fiscal years that end 31 March of the following year.
Source: *Asian Development Outlook* database.

their lowest growth rate in 7 years. Small and medium-sized enterprises, which account for a large part of this sector, may have struggled to comply with new regulations under the goods and services tax (GST), undermining the sector's performance. In contrast, growth in industry sharply increased to 7.7% in FY2018, owing to strong manufacturing, construction, and utilities.

On the demand side, private consumption was the main driver of India's growth in FY2018. It grew by 8.3%, the highest rate in 7 years, despite rural consumption remaining sluggish under subdued crop prices, slow growth in rural wages, and stress on nonbank lenders. Consumption is likely to have received impetus from reduced GST rates across a wide range of commodities during the year and a cut in key monetary policy rates. Government consumption slowed, as expected, because of tightened finances. Gross fixed capital formation grew by a robust 10% in FY2018, sustained by 20.3% growth in central government capital expenditure as investment in roads, railways, and urban infrastructure remained strong. Private investment is estimated to have increased a bit, reflecting a pickup in lending to industry, an uptick in capacity utilization, and increased production of capital goods.

The PRC saw growth slow from 6.8% in 2017 to 6.6% in 2018, in line with the government's growth target of around 6.5%. Growth moderation is partly structural as the PRC economy matures. But it also reflected rising trade tensions with the US combined with domestic efforts to manage risks in the financial sector as well as tighter fiscal policy in the first half of the year.

Consumption growth accelerated from 7.5% in 2017 to 9.6% in 2018, supported by a rapid increase in government social spending, a cut in personal income tax, and solid growth in household disposable income. But the contribution of investment to growth slipped, as local governments tightly controlled expenditure, both on budget and off budget, in the first 9 months of 2018. Growth in infrastructure investment plummeted from 19.0% in 2017 to 3.8% in 2018. Exports rose in the PRC partly because shipments were frontloaded ahead of the imposition of tariffs, but growth in merchandise imports accelerated even more, so that net exports subtracted 0.6 percentage points from growth.

On the supply side, services remained the main driver of PRC growth, despite slowing from 7.9% growth in 2017 to 7.6% last year. Growth was strong in transport, in leasing and commercial services, and in information technology services, while financial and real estate services remained weak. Growth of industry including construction and mining moderated marginally from 5.9% in 2017 to 5.8% in 2018. Strong increases in consumer, high-tech, and export-oriented manufacturing partly offset deceleration in mining and raw materials, where retrenchment targets reined in production.

The PMI, which is a forward-looking indicator of health in manufacturing, suggests the trajectories of the two economies may be diverging (Figure 1.1.7). The most recent data for India indicate that India's PMI surged to a 14-month high of 54.3 in February 2019, distinguishing it from the rest of developing Asia (Table 1.1.1). In the PRC, by contrast, the PMI declined for much of 2018, as export growth slowed, to reach its lowest reading in 34 months, though still averaging 50.7 in the whole of 2018, slightly above the threshold at 50 indicating expansion.

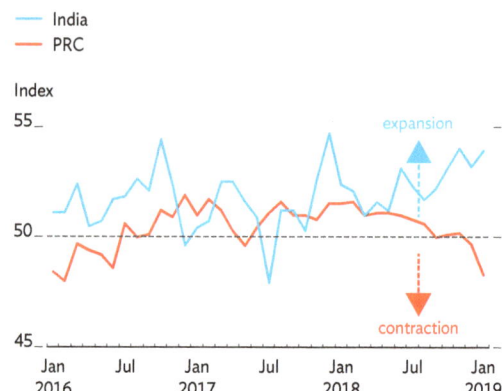

1.1.7 Purchasing managers' index: India versus the PRC

Manufacturing activity is diverging in India and the PRC.

PMI = purchasing managers' index, PRC = People's Republic of China.
Source: CEIC Data Company (accessed 13 February 2019).

Tighter monetary policy in response to currency depreciation

Many currencies in developing Asia depreciated against the US dollar in 2018. This reflected a steady increase in the federal funds rate set by the US Federal Reserve and jitters in emerging markets caused by problems in Argentina and Turkey. Currencies that experienced especially deep depreciation against the US dollar were the Indian rupee, Indonesian rupiah, and Philippine peso (Figure 1.1.8). The Indonesian rupiah hit a 20-year low against the US dollar, and the Philippine peso a 13-year low. By late 2018, most currencies had stabilized, and since then several have appreciated, but bouts of currency turmoil could recur (Box 1.1.1). In response to currency depreciation against the US dollar, many central banks in developing Asia raised policy rates during the year, with India, Indonesia, and the Philippines raising their benchmark interest rates the most (Table 1.1.2).

1.1.8 Exchange rate against the US dollar in selected economies, January 2018 = 100

Many countries in developing Asia saw their currencies depreciate sharply against the US dollar, though with some reversal toward the end of 2018...

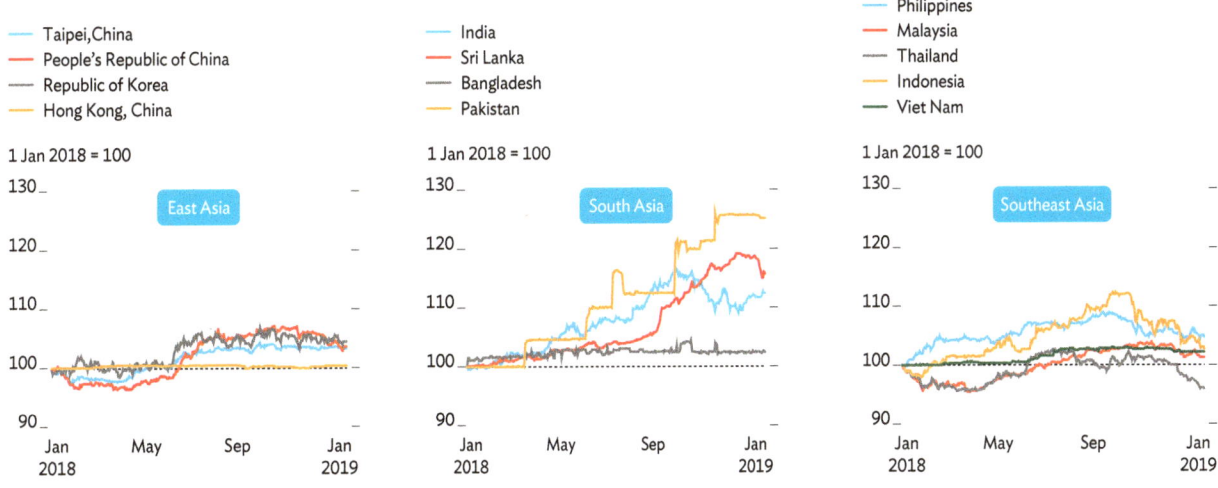

Source: Bloomberg (accessed 2 February 2019).

1.1.2 Policy rates, selected economies in developing Asia

... Partly in response to this, countries in the region tightened their monetary policies.

Countries	Latest policy rate (as of 31 Dec 2018)		Change from 2017, same period		
	% per annum	Date of decision	Percentage points	Direction of change	Number of adjustments
Hong Kong, China	2.75	20 Dec 2018	1.00	▲	4[a]
India	6.50	19 Dec 2018	0.50	▲	2[b]
Indonesia	6.00	20 Dec 2018	1.75	▲	5[c]
Japan	−0.10	19 Dec 2018	0.00	■	0
Kazakhstan	9.25	4 Dec 2018	−0.50	▼	4[d]
Malaysia	3.25	8 Nov 2018	0.00	■	0
Pakistan	10.00	30 Nov 2018	4.00	▲	4[e]
Papua New Guinea	6.25	30 Sep 2018	0.00	■	0
People's Republic of China	4.35	27 Dec 2018	0.00	■	0
Philippines	4.75	13 Dec 2018	1.75	▲	5[f]
Republic of Korea	1.75	30 Nov 2018	0.25	▲	1[g]
Singapore	127.19	12 Oct 2018	1.53	▲	2[h]
Sri Lanka	8.00	27 Dec 2018	0.75	▲	1[i]
Taipei,China	1.38	20 Dec 2018	0.00	■	0
Thailand	1.75	19 Dec 2018	0.25	▲	1[j]

■ = no change, ▲ = increase, ▼ = decrease.

[a] Hong Kong, China increased its rate by 25 basis points on 22 Mar 2018, 14 Jun 2018, 27 Sep 2018, and 20 Dec 2018.
[b] The Reserve Bank of India hiked its policy rate by 25 basis points on 6 Jun 2018 and 1 Aug 2018.
[c] Bank Indonesia hiked its policy rate by 50 basis points on 17 May 2018 and 29 Jun 2019 and 25 points on 15 Aug 2018, 27 Sep 2018, and 15 Nov 2018.
[d] Kazakhstan shaved 25 basis points from its policy rate on 5 Mar 2018, 16 Apr 2018, and 4 Jun 2018 but added 25 points on 15 Oct 2018.
[e] Pakistan increased its rate by 50 basis points on 25 May 2018, 100 points on 14 Jul 2018 and 29 Sep 2018, and 150 points 30 Nov 2018.
[f] The Philippines added 25 basis points on 10 May 2018, 20 Jun 2018, and 15 Nov 2018 and 50 points on 9 Aug 2018 and 27 Sep 2018.
[g] Bank of Korea raised the policy rate by 2 basis points on 30 Nov 2018.
[h] Singapore manages monetary policy by tweaking the exchange rate, rather than with the interest rate, letting the nominal effective exchange rate rise or fall within an undisclosed policy band. It adjusted upward its policy rate on 13 Apr 2018 and 12 Oct 2018.
[i] Sri Lanka hiked its policy rate by 75 basis points on 13 Nov 2018.
[j] Thailand increased its policy rate by 25 basis points on 19 Dec 2018.

Sources: Haver Analytics; CEIC Data Company; and Central bank websites (all accessed 8 March 2019).

1.1.1 Are emerging market currencies out of the woods?

Last year witnessed a great deal of instability in foreign exchange markets, epitomized by sharp depreciation of the Turkish lira and Argentine peso. The instability, driven by the US Federal Reserve's repeated interest rate hikes, raised concerns about broader risk aversion toward emerging markets. In recent months, a measure of stability has returned to emerging markets, but it remains unclear how long the calm will last.

Emerging market currencies on the rebound

The Turkish lira and Argentine peso have both stabilized since the fourth quarter (Q4) of 2018. Forceful interest rate hikes by the Central Bank of Turkey seem to have restored investor confidence in that economy. In Argentina, expansion and acceleration of an International Monetary Fund loan package and the government's commitment to fiscal consolidation arrested the peso's fall. Despite clear improvement in investor sentiment toward both economies, they still suffer under substantial macroeconomic imbalances and remain vulnerable to shocks. In line with the stabilization of the lira and peso, the currencies of emerging markets as a whole have performed noticeably better since Q4 of 2018 (box figure 1). Broadly speaking, emerging market currencies fell sharply during Q2 of 2018, bottomed out in Q3, and rebounded in Q4. To a large extent, according to the International Institute of Finance, depreciation reflected correction of exchange rate misalignment that prevailed at the beginning of the year. Since misalignment has been largely corrected, emerging market currencies are now showing greater stability.

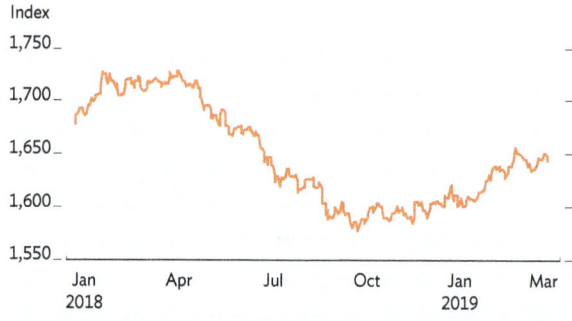

1 MSCI Emerging Markets Currency Index

MSCI = Morgan Stanley Capital International.
Notes: MSCI Emerging Market Currency Index measures the total return of 25 emerging market currencies relative to the US dollar where the weight of each currency is equal to its country weight in the MSCI Emerging Markets Index. Data are from 1 January 2018 to 1 March 2019.
Source: Bloomberg (accessed 2 March 2019).

2 Indian rupee and Indonesian rupiah versus the US dollar

Note: Data are from 1 January 2018 to 1 March 2019.
Source: Bloomberg (accessed 2 March 2019).

Emerging Asian currencies recover as well

Relatively strong fundamentals are giving a fillip to emerging market currencies. Emerging Asian economies in particular enjoy relatively healthy fundamentals and are thus well positioned to withstand shocks. For example, inflation is below 4% in the two major Asian markets that came under the most pressure during emerging market currency turmoil in 2018: India and Indonesia. The same two economies also suffered the most volatility during the "taper tantrum" of 2013. In line with broader recovery of emerging market currencies, both the Indian rupee and Indonesian rupiah rebounded since Q4 of 2018 (box figure 2). Although India and Indonesia are still burdened with twin deficits in their fiscal and current accounts, the magnitude of these deficits is manageable. In addition to relatively strong fundamentals, the two economies have benefited from decisive policy action to stabilize financial markets. The Reserve Bank of India and Bank Indonesia each aggressively hiked their benchmark interest rates in Q2 and Q3 of 2018 to defend their currencies and stave off inflationary pressures.

Fragile but improving outlook for financial stability in developing Asia

Notwithstanding a notable trend toward more stable emerging market exchange rates since Q4 of 2018, global financial markets remain febrile and vulnerable to shocks. Global trade tensions, especially tensions between the PRC and the US, the world's two biggest economies, have not yet been resolved, casting a shadow over the global economic outlook

continued next page

1.1.1 Continued

and financial stability. Although the effects of trade tensions seem to be limited so far, their persistence creates uncertainty and thus may yet harm economic growth. Uncertainty over trade and more generally global growth prospects contributed to severe volatility in the US stock market in December. Risk aversion toward emerging markets is therefore likely to remain elevated. As noted above, the most vulnerable emerging markets still suffer from imbalances. Lingering vulnerability helps explain why emerging market credit spreads remain elevated even though they are trending down (box figure 3).

Therefore, in light of the heightened uncertainty surrounding global growth prospects partly because of the unsettled status of the US–PRC trade conflict, and considering the unsettling effect this is having on global financial markets, it is premature to say that emerging markets are completely out of the woods. Furthermore, going forward, there is a great deal of uncertainty surrounding the trajectory of US monetary policy, which may destabilize emerging-market exchange rates (Box 1.1.5). Nevertheless, on balance, the foreign exchange markets of emerging economies, including those in Asia, are unlikely to be as volatile in 2019 as they were in 2018. One reason for confidence is that the most vulnerable economies have implemented various measures to promote financial stability, including fiscal consolidation and monetary tightening. The stabilizing effects of such confidence-building measures will persist into the near future.

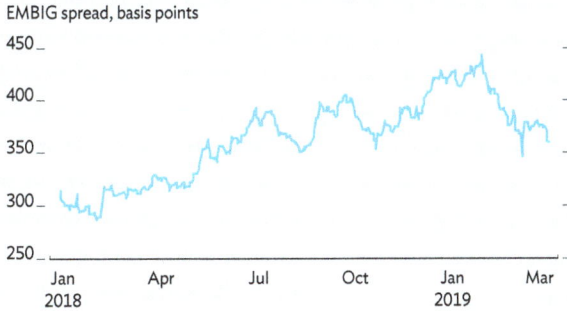

3 Emerging markets sovereign bond spreads

EMBIG = Emerging Markets Bond Index Global.
Notes: EMBIG is JP Morgan's index of US dollar-denominated sovereign bonds. It tracks total returns for traded external debt instruments issued by sovereign and quasi-sovereign entities in emerging markets. Widening spreads mean investors are shying away from riskier investments in emerging markets, and narrowing spreads mean investors are warming to them. Data are from 1 January 2018 to 1 March 2019.
Source: Bloomberg (accessed 2 March 2019).

Perhaps more importantly, there are growing signs that the US Federal Reserve will slow the pace of its normalization of monetary policy. Although the US monetary tightening cycle is probably incomplete, the frequency and total magnitude of interest rate hikes are likely to be less in 2019 than in 2018. To conclude, although emerging-market exchange rates have gained a measure of stability since Q4 of 2018, the potential for volatility remains.

Major equity markets across the region declined in 2018 (Figure 1.1.9). The worst performing equity markets were in the PRC, as the major indexes in Shanghai and Shenzhen suffered annual losses of close to 25%. All 10 sectors in Shanghai stock index declined in 2018, with some of the sharpest drops in the technology sector. The story was different in India, where equity markets were among the best performers among emerging markets.

Subdued inflation despite rising oil prices

Despite rising oil prices and currency depreciation, inflation remained subdued in developing Asia at 2.5% in 2018 (Figure 1.1.10). A recent spike in food prices and higher prices for health care, education, and rent all put upward pressure on consumer prices in the PRC, which pushed up inflation in East Asia from 1.6% in 2017 to 2.0% in 2018.

1.1.9 Equity indexes, selected economies

Major equity markets across the region declined in 2018, with the exception of India, where equities performed relatively well.

ASEAN-5 = five larger economies in the Association of Southeast Asian Nations (Indonesia, Malaysia, the Philippines, Thailand, and Viet Nam), NIEs = newly industrialized economies (Hong Kong, China; the Republic of Korea; Singapore; and Taipei,China).
Source: Bloomberg (accessed 2 February 2019).

Inflation declined in other subregions, most notably from 9.0% to 7.9% in Central Asia.

The subregion with the highest inflation rate, Central Asia, saw inflation slow in 2018 because of decreases in Azerbaijan and Kazakhstan (Figure 1.1.11). In Kazakhstan, Central Asia's biggest economy, inflation decelerated from 7.4% in 2017 to 6.0% in 2018 as food price inflation slowed sharply from 8.6% in 2017 to 5.1% and increases for other goods slowed from 8.4% to 7.8%. In Azerbaijan, inflation plunged from 12.9% in 2017 to 2.3% in 2018 as higher oil prices and monetary tightening stabilized the exchange rate, thereby minimizing pass-through to domestic prices.

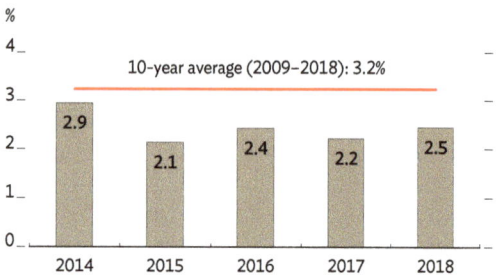

1.1.10 Inflation in developing Asia

Inflation remains below the 10-year historical average despite edging up slightly in 2018 to 2.5%...

Source: *Asian Development Outlook* database.

Trade remained buoyant but lost momentum at the end of 2018

Following a sharp rise in 2017, external demand moderated in 2018. Excluding the newly industrialized economies (NIEs), growth in both exports and imports was higher, reflecting how the US–PRC trade conflict and the global down cycle in the semiconductor industry depressed business sentiment in the NIEs. About 40% of aggregate NIE exports in 2018 went to the PRC and the US, while as much as two-thirds of their global exports were in electronics, one of the industries hardest hit by the trade conflict.

Growth in exports across the region moderated in most economies (Figure 1.1.12). Exports began strong in the first half of 2018 in most economies—partly reflecting frontloading ahead of tariff hikes—but moderated toward the end of the year as export orders and manufacturing slowed. On balance, growth in regional exports slowed from 11.3% in 2017 but still expanded by 7.9% in 2018. Exports slowed in every subregion except the Pacific. Export growth held up well in Central Asia, continuing double-digit expansion recorded in 2017, as commodity exporters benefited from the rise in global fuel prices and notable recovery in the Russian Federation, the subregion's largest trade partner. It decelerated in East Asia from 9.9% to 7.6% largely from the downturn in electronics, which caused declines in Hong Kong, China; the ROK; and Taipei,China. Growth in PRC exports accelerated from 6.5% in 2017 to 8.5% on higher exports of manufactures, particularly machinery and transport equipment, partly reflecting frontloading ahead of the imposition of tariffs. Exports surged in the first half of 2018 in Southeast Asia as manufacturers ramped up production and shuffled their production networks to the region ahead of escalating US–PRC trade tension. However, this growth trend reversed in the second half as factory activity declined and some

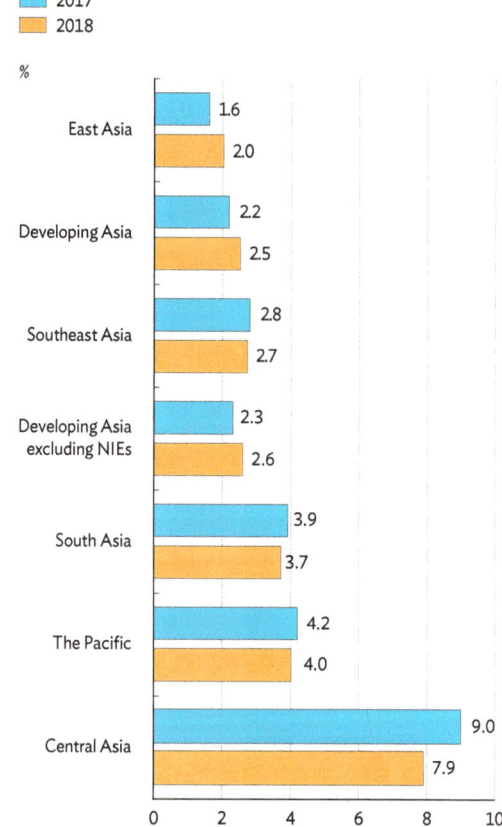

1.1.11 Change in inflation between 2017 and 2018

...except in Central Asia, where inflation slowed from 9.0% in 2017 to 7.9% in 2018.

NIEs = newly industrialized economies (Hong Kong, China; the Republic of Korea; Singapore; and Taipei,China).
Source: *Asian Development Outlook* database.

1.1.12 Nominal change in exports and imports in developing Asia, selected economies

Following a strong 2017, trade expanded at a more moderate pace in 2018.

- 2016
- 2017
- 2018

Exports | Imports

Note: 2018 data to September for Brunei Darussalam and May for Tajikistan.
Source: CEIC Data Company (15 March 2019).

large economies suffered supply interruptions. Deceleration in South Asia, from 11.7% to 7.9%, reflected lower exports from Pakistan and soft recovery in India. By product, exports of manufactures remained steady, while shipments of commodities and primary goods halved in 2018 despite a huge bump in mid-2018 (Figure 1.1.13).

As in exports, growth in imports decelerated across the region from 15.1% in 2017 to 11.5% in 2018, reflecting waning imports to the region's largest economies.

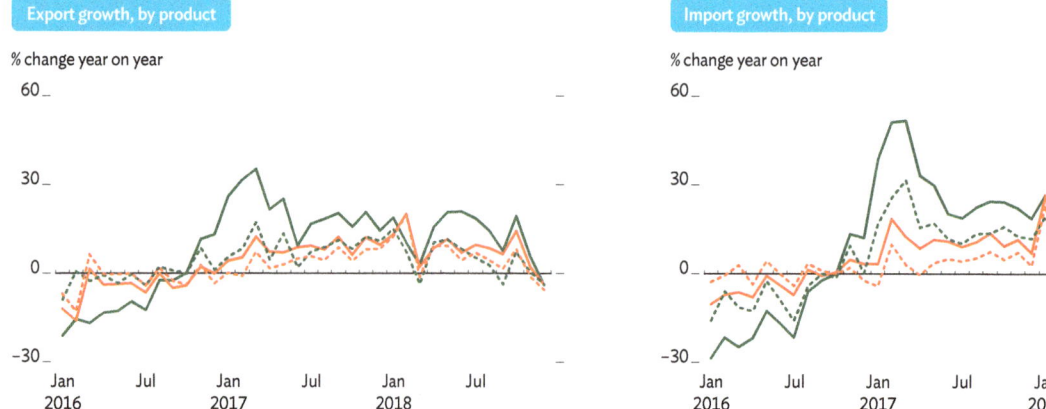

1.1.13 Developing Asia's exports and imports of primary and manufactures, real versus nominal growth

A slowdown is more evident in primary products, which generally serve as inputs to production, and to some extent in manufactures.

Notes: Product groupings follow the Standard International Trade Classification, Revision 3 (SITC, Rev. 3). Export and import data are deflated using available export and import indexes for each economy. For Indonesia, Malaysia, and Singapore, trade data are first deflated by type of commodity, then summed to get total real values for each major commodity. Data in real terms for India were computed using interpolated monthly data. Primary products include SITC Rev. Codes 0–4; manufactured goods are SITC Rev. 3 Codes 5–9.
Source: CEIC Data Company (accessed 15 March 2019).

Much of the deceleration reflected lower imports of commodities and primary products—particularly in the 10 large economies of East, South, and Southeast Asia that produce about 90% of regional output—though these products were only about 30% of all regional imports in 2018. Imports of manufactures, the bulk of imports to these 10 economies, remained strong, expanding by 10.3%, almost unchanged from 2017. The drop in imports of primary goods to the PRC came largely from a significant decline in imported mineral fuels. Elsewhere, external demand exhibited a similar trend, in line with deceleration in global trade volume from 4.7% in 2017 to 3.3% in 2018, except in Central and Eastern Europe, where exports maintained steady growth in 2018, buoyed by strong shipments in oil-exporting economies (Figure 1.1.14).

Growth outlook moderates

Developing Asia is projected to grow by 5.7% in 2019 and 5.6% in 2020. Excluding the NIEs, growth will taper from 6.4% in 2018 to 6.2% in 2019 and 6.1% in 2020. The declines in trade, sentiment, and activity seen in the fourth quarter (Q4) of 2018 will continue affecting the most open economies in the region, the NIEs and ASEAN countries in particular.

1.1.14 Real growth in exports and imports, by selected regions

Slower trade toward the end of 2018 was evident in other parts of the world as well, in both nominal and real terms.

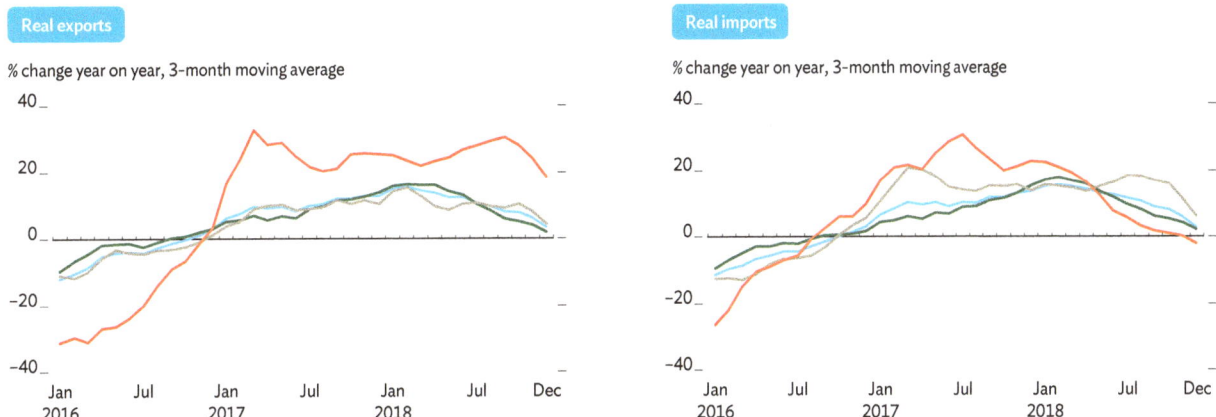

Notes: Export and import volume and price per unit values in US dollars are indexed to 2010 (2010 = 100). The advanced economies are Australia, Bulgaria, Canada, Croatia, the Czech Republic, Denmark, the euro area, Hungary, Iceland, Japan, New Zealand, Norway, Poland, Romania, Sweden, Switzerland, Turkey, the United Kingdom, the United States, and the Former Yugoslav Republic of Macedonia. Central and Eastern Europe are Belarus, Kazakhstan, the Russian Federation, and Ukraine. Emerging Asia are Hong Kong, China; India; Indonesia; Malaysia; Pakistan; the People's Republic of China; the Philippines; the Republic of Korea; Singapore; Taipei,China; Thailand; and Viet Nam.
Source: CPB Netherlands Bureau for Economic Policy Analysis. https://www.cpb.nl/en/worldtrademonitor (accessed 15 March 2019).

Declining oil prices will affect oil exporters directly—and other Central Asian economies indirectly through lower growth in the Russian Federation—and will likely weigh on growth in that subregion throughout 2019. Growth in Q1 of 2019 is expected to be further muted but will recover somewhat toward the latter half of 2019 and in 2020. Private consumption will continue to be the driver of growth in most of developing Asia's large economies.

The baseline assumes that external demand will continue to weaken over the outlook period as growth slows in the advanced economies. Aggregate growth in the advanced economies should moderate from 2.2% in 2018 to 1.9% in 2019 and 1.6% in 2020 (Table 1.1.3), with slower global trade acting as a drag. The US will slow the most, from 2.9% in 2018 to 2.4% in 2019 and 1.9% in 2020, in part as the impact of fiscal stimulus in 2018 wears off, though consumption growth should remain healthy as wage income rises. In the European Union, growth will slow slightly amid weaker economic sentiment. In Japan, a slight pickup in consumption demand ahead of higher taxes will boost growth slightly in 2019, but the trade slowdown will weigh on manufacturing growth. Inflation in the advanced economies will remain steady at 1.9% over the outlook period.

1.1.3 GDP growth in the major advanced economies

Growth in advanced economies to slow.

	2017	2018	2019	2020
	Actual	Actual	ADO 2019 Projection	
Major industrial economies[a]	2.3	2.2	1.9	1.6
United States	2.2	2.9	2.4	1.9
Euro area	2.5	1.8	1.5	1.5
Japan	1.9	0.8	0.8	0.6

ADO = Asian Development Outlook, GDP = gross domestic product.
[a] Average growth rates are weighed by gross national income, Atlas method.
Sources: US Department of Commerce, Bureau of Economic Analysis, http://www.bea.gov; Eurostat, http://epp.eurostat.ec.europa.eu; Economic and Social Research Institute of Japan, http://www.esri.cao.go.jp; Consensus Forecasts; Bloomberg; CEIC Data Company; Haver Analytics; World Bank, Global Commodity Markets, http://www.worldbank.org; ADB estimates.

The resulting slowing growth in external demand will weigh on developing Asia's expansion, but growth will remain robust. Domestic demand is expected to remain strong and offset much of the slowdown in external demand. Despite their high trade dependence, many East and Southeast Asian countries have reached a stage of development where household consumption can be a stable and leading driver of growth (Figure 1.1.2).

Much of the expected slowdown in regional growth in 2019 reflects growth moderation in the PRC. The downward trend in GDP growth is expected to persist as uncertainties pertaining to trade tensions with the US continue to weigh on consumption, investment, and trade. Growth in the PRC should slow to 6.3% in 2019 and moderate further to a more sustainable 6.1% in 2020, reflecting ongoing efforts to contain risks in the financial sector. Fiscal policy should remain supportive through greater social expenditure, targeted programs to support employment, and lower value-added tax rates for manufacturers, transportation firms, and utilities, among others. On the demand side, private consumption will remain the main driver of growth, but less so as growth in household income slows. Relaxed real estate restrictions expected in 2019, and continued industrial upgrading, should help keep investment in manufacturing growing but at a slower pace, owing to declining profits in manufacturing and less dynamic external trade. Accommodative PRC monetary policy so far in 2019 will continue, aiming to prevent any sharp deceleration in growth, even if the tradeoff is a lower growth rate than in 2018. While restrictions on shadow bank financing—the main alternative financing vehicle for small and medium-sized enterprises—are expected to continue through 2019 and 2020, they may be relaxed to allow a more gradual reduction in the volume of outstanding shadow credit.

In India, growth is poised to pick up over the outlook period, as South Asia's largest economy is less exposed than other Asian economies to the slowdown in manufacturing trade. Growth is projected to step up from 7.0% in 2018 to 7.2% in 2019 and 7.3% in 2020, with domestic demand still the main driver. Rural income and consumption will enjoy policy boosts from enhanced income support to farmers and hikes in procurement prices for food grains, while interest rate cuts and soft food and fuel prices will bolster consumption in urban areas. Consumer sentiment will remain strong, and private sector investment will likely grow at a healthy pace, as business surveys indicate upbeat trends in confidence and credit availability. Net exports are expected to drag less on growth as lower oil and commodity prices restrain import growth and a more competitive exchange rate helps exports.

Growth in the higher-income economies of East Asia and large Southeast Asian economies will slow in 2019 in tandem with slower growth in the PRC and lower trade in manufactures. Semiconductor producers and users with large high-tech manufacturing bases—such as Malaysia; the ROK; Singapore; Taipei,China; and Viet Nam—already saw exports drop in late 2018 and early 2019 after some frontloading of sales ahead of tariff increases in 2018. All these countries are fully engaged in electronics value chains and are large suppliers to high-tech companies in both the PRC and the US. Private investment is also in a lull as firms await the resolution of trade negotiations that directly affect their exports. Growth in East Asia including the PRC will step down from 6.0% in 2018 to 5.7% in 2019 and 5.5% in 2020.

In Southeast Asia as a whole, growth is expected to moderate slightly as external demand falls a little more quickly than domestic demand grows. Some economies will pick up in 2020, while others see continued growth moderation. Growth is projected to dip from 5.1% in 2018 to 4.9% in 2019, recovering to 5.0% in 2020. A downturn in the global electronics trade cycle, and a slowdown in world trade more generally, will dampen the investment and export prospects of this highly open subregion in 2019—though investment approvals and FDI figures in late 2018 in Malaysia and Viet Nam suggest that investment will pick up later in the outlook period as uncertainty is resolved. Business surveys show plans heavily affected by uncertainty, both domestic and external, while purchasing managers' indexes in the main ASEAN economies have been generally falling since mid-2018 (Table 1.1.1). Even as external demand softens, strength in domestic demand should provide some cushion to subregional growth both this year and next.

Accelerating domestic investment and buoyant consumption will boost growth in the Philippines in 2019 and in Indonesia both this year and next. Growth will strengthen on improved prospects for tourism and FDI in Myanmar and as oil refineries come back online in Brunei Darussalam. Viet Nam and Thailand should see growth stabilize in 2020, and Malaysia should see a pickup as investment and resulting exports regain strength with intermediate trade redirected from the tariff-affected PRC and US, as well as from continued strong domestic demand. In Singapore, a more mature economy, growth in private consumption may have already reached its peak. The remaining smaller Southeast Asian economies will continue to grow at rates of 6%–7% in 2019 and 2020.

Meanwhile, growth will rebound in South Asia and the Pacific and, with lower external demand, moderate only slightly in Central Asia. South Asia will remain the fastest-growing subregion in the world, projected to grow by 6.8% in 2019 and 6.9% in 2020, led by Bangladesh at 8.0% in both years. In contrast, Pakistan's outlook is for a sharp drop in growth as, following a pronounced widening of its balance of payments deficit in 2018, it likely embarks on austerity measures supported by the International Monetary Fund. Some oil-exporting Central Asian countries will see a small drop in growth from 4.4% in 2018 to 4.2% in 2019 and 2020 as oil prices moderate. Sluggish growth in the Russian Federation will limit the rise in income from remittances in the Kyrgyz Republic, Tajikistan, and Uzbekistan. Country-specific factors will have effects, with higher natural gas production boosting growth slightly in Azerbaijan and a recovery in gold production doing the same in the Kyrgyz Republic, offsetting slowing factors in Uzbekistan. Currency woes in 2018 in neighboring Turkey spilled over into Central Asia, particularly Azerbaijan and Georgia, where strong economic links with the troubled regional power are calculated to have shaved about 0.6 percentage points off GDP (Box 1.1.2). By contrast, growth in the Pacific is expected to recover from near stagnation at 0.9% in 2018 to 3.5% growth in 2019. This is largely the result of liquefied natural gas facilities coming back online in Papua New Guinea after suffering earthquake damage in 2018. Growth in the Pacific is forecast to ease to 3.2% in 2020.

Inflation will remain low and stable

Headline inflation in developing Asia is forecast unchanged at 2.5% in 2019 and 2020, assuming that commodity prices stabilize. Brent crude oil prices are projected to fall from an average of $71/barrel in 2018 to $62/barrel in 2019 and 2020. This will keep energy-related inflation under control. Moreover, fuel subsidies in many larger economies will dampen pass-through effects. Price changes for other commodities in developing Asia—such as copper, steel, natural gas, timber, and palm oil—are exported mainly to markets outside of developing Asia, so they generally have little impact on inflation in the region, but they have important direct effects on export growth in exporting countries. On the other hand, prices for food, particularly rice,

1.1.2 Turkey's economic impact on Central Asian economies

Sustained rapid economic growth has turned Turkey into a regionally significant economy. Turkey's economic presence is felt in the Balkans, the Middle East, the Caucasus, Central Asia, and other regions. Among ADB developing member countries, the three Caucasus republics and the five Central Asian republics enjoy the closest historical, cultural, and economic links with Turkey. Given Turkey's relative economic weight—in 2017, its GDP was twice the combined GDP of the eight economies in the Caucasus and Central Asia—it is bound to have a substantial economic impact on them (box figure 1).

Turkey has served in the past as an engine of growth for most countries in Central Asia. However, in recent years, growth in Turkey has slowed. Further, in 2018, Turkey suffered severe financial stress from country-specific factors and from interest rate hikes by the US Federal Reserve. At one point, the Turkish lira lost more than half its value against the US dollar, and inflation reached 25%, its highest in 15 years. Although decisive monetary tightening by the Central Bank of Turkey restored a measure of financial stability in Q4 of 2018, growth remains subdued. It slowed sharply from 7.4% in 2017 to only 2.6% in 2018 because of monetary tightening, fiscal consolidation, and weak domestic demand. Although Turkey's financial markets have stabilized somewhat, they remain fragile and vulnerable to shocks. The *World Economic Outlook Update, January 2019* of the International Monetary Fund projects a large economic contraction in Turkey in 2019 because of monetary policy tightening and unfavorable external financing conditions, followed by a slow recovery in 2020.

The lira's steep depreciation made Turkish goods cheaper in Central Asia but, at the same time, made Central Asian goods more expensive in Turkey. Slower economic growth also reduces Turkish demand for imports, including imports from Central Asia. In the first 11 months of 2018, growth in Central Asian exports to Turkey slowed from the same period in 2017 for all the economies except Georgia (box figure 2).

1 Gross domestic product, Turkey and the Central Asian economies, 2017

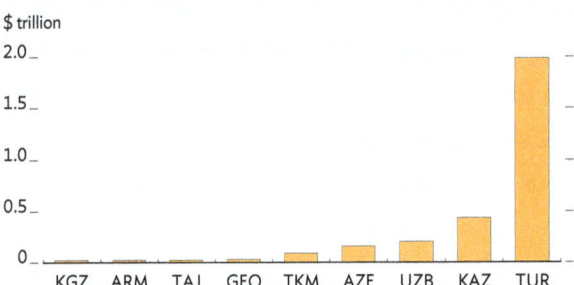

ARM = Armenia, AZE = Azerbaijan, GEO = Georgia, KAZ = Kazakhstan, KGZ = Kyrgyz Republic, TAJ = Tajikistan, TKM = Turkmenistan, TUR = Turkey, UZB = Uzbekistan.
Note: GDP is expressed in 2011 constant international dollars.
Source: IMF World Economic Outlook database October 2018.

The primary economic link between Turkey and Central Asia is trade, but investment and remittances also come into play. Turkey's importance as a trading partner varies across Central Asia. It is an especially important export market for Azerbaijan, receiving 12% of its exports, and for Tajikistan, receiving 30%. Meanwhile, Georgia has the highest share of imports from Turkey, valued at the equivalent of 9% of GDP, and relies heavily on Turkey for machinery, chemicals, and metals. Azerbaijan, the Kyrgyz Republic, and Turkmenistan also import substantially from Turkey, amounts equal to about 3% of their GDP. Since 2003, about 37% of Turkish FDI in Central Asia went to Azerbaijan, while another 54% went to Georgia, Kazakhstan, and Turkmenistan. Azerbaijan is the main Central Asian investor in Turkey, providing 95% of FDI from the subregion into Turkey since 2003.

2 Growth of exports from Central Asia to Turkey

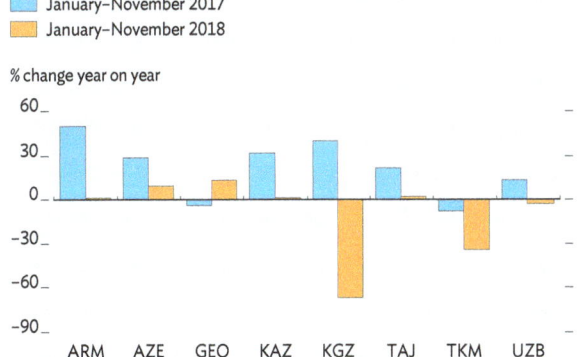

ARM = Armenia, AZE = Azerbaijan, GEO = Georgia, KAZ = Kazakhstan, KGZ = Kyrgyz Republic, TAJ = Tajikistan, TKM = Turkmenistan, UZB = Uzbekistan.
Note: Using mirrored imports data from Turkey.
Sources: IMF Direction of Trade Statistics; Haver Analytics; ADB estimates.

continued next page

1.1.2 Continued

By contrast, imports from Turkey into Central Asia increased for all the economies except Kazakhstan and Turkmenistan.

In 2018, FDI flows from Turkey markedly contracted from 2017, by 76% to Azerbaijan and by 86% to Kazakhstan, though they picked up to Georgia. Further, remittances sent from Turkey to Georgia have been falling since August 2018. Azerbaijan's financial exposure to Turkey can become a concern in the event of default by Turkish borrowers because Azerbaijan had $4 billion of its sovereign wealth fund deposited in Turkish banks in 2017 and more than $2 billion in outstanding private sector loans to financial and nonfinancial borrowers in Turkey in 2018.

To more formally assess spillover from Turkey's growth slowdown on Central Asia, the impact of Turkey's growth on Central Asian economies was separately estimated using a vector autoregression analysis for Azerbaijan, Georgia, Kazakhstan, and Tajikistan. The vector of endogenous variables contains the economy's own GDP growth, inflation, and real effective exchange rate; the GDP of Turkey; and the GDP of Russian Federation, using quarterly data from Q1 of 1998 to Q4 of 2018, where available.

Impulse response functions show how an exogenous growth shock in Turkey spills over to selected Central Asian economies. Impulse responses from positive growth shocks of one standard deviation to Turkey's growth is highest after 1 year in Georgia at 1.2 percentage points, 3 quarters in Tajikistan at 0.5 percentage points, and 2 years in Azerbaijan at 1.1 percentage points (box figure 3). Spillover is almost nonexistent in Kazakhstan. These effects are statistically significant at 95% confidence bands for Georgia and Tajikistan.

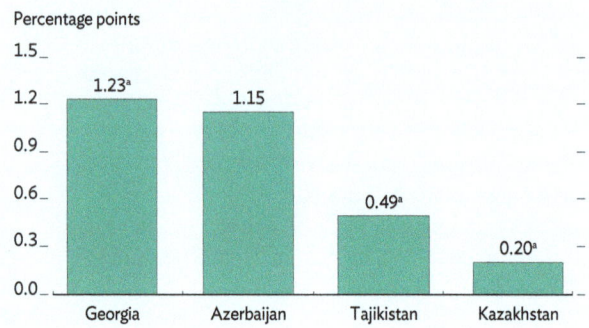

3 Maximum impulse response from one standard deviation increase in Turkey's GDP growth on GDP growth of selected economies in Central Asia

GDP = gross domestic product.
a Significant effect at 95%.
Source: ADB estimates.

The effects linger for about 6 quarters in Georgia, with maximum cumulative impact of 4.6 percentage points, and for about 3 quarters for Tajikistan, with maximum cumulative impact of 1.2 percentage points.

The implication of these results is that a decline in Turkey's GDP growth adversely affects Central Asia's growth, though the effects differ considerably across the eight economies. Reduced financial stress in recent months provides some grounds for optimism about Turkey's growth prospects beyond the very short term. In the meantime, Central Asian economies should continue to pursue policies that strengthen their fundamentals and insulate them from the risk of contagion, from Turkey or elsewhere.

---

significantly affect the welfare of low-income urban households in developing Asia. They are expected to remain flat in 2019 and rise by a moderate 1.5% in 2020 as global food prices stay broadly stable under forecasts for generally favorable weather (Figure 1.1.15).

Domestic inflationary pressures vary, but regional inflation will remain well anchored below the 10-year average of 3.2% (Figure 1.1.16). In the PRC, inflation is expected to remain moderate at 1.9% in 2019 and 1.8% in 2020, in line with slightly slower economic growth. Inflation in India is expected to climb to 4.3% in 2019 and 4.6% in 2020 as food inflation accelerates with upticks in procurement prices paid to farmers, wages paid to agricultural workers, and prices for fertilizer.

Further, Indian rupee depreciation in 2018 adds inflationary pressure with a lagged effect. More broadly in South Asia, inflation will rise slightly in response to domestic demand pressures. Average inflation in Southeast Asia this year and next will remain near the 2.7% recorded in 2018. Administered domestic fuel prices may prevent lower oil prices being passed on to consumers.

Inflation in Central Asia will rise on one-time price jumps in Azerbaijan, the Kyrgyz Republic, and Tajikistan. Inflation in Turkmenistan and Uzbekistan will remain high on average but should ease over time with fiscal reform, especially in Turkmenistan, and as monetary and exchange rate reform takes hold. The same holds true for their southern neighbor Afghanistan. Inflation in the Pacific will moderate from 4.0% in 2018 to 3.7% in 2019 and then return to 4.0% in 2020 as country-specific effects offset pass-through from import prices.

A cloudy external outlook

The trade outlook will be shaped by the US–PRC trade conflict and a forecast general deterioration in external demand in 2019 and 2020. Trade growth will be much lower than it has been lately, and some global supply chain reallocations will occur in response to the trade conflict. The outlook assumes that some headway is made on removing technology restrictions, but also that some sticking points, such as digital trade issues and technology transfer modalities, will continue to affect investment decisions in the first half of 2019.

The deterioration of developing Asia's current account balance will continue into 2019 and 2020 (Figure 1.1.17). In 2018, it dropped to the equivalent of 0.8% of GDP in 2018, the lowest it has been since the Asian financial crisis of 1997–1998. This largely reflects a new focus in the PRC on its domestic economy, as well as lower global demand and muted export activity spurred by the trade conflict. The current account surplus for the region will narrow further to 0.4% in 2019 and 0.3% in 2020, reflecting significantly narrower gaps in the PRC, and in some other larger economies in East and Southeast Asia. South Asia will continue to incur a current account deficit to the forecast horizon, the Central Asian deficit will narrow, and East and Southeast Asia and the Pacific will see their current account surpluses shrink. In Southeast Asia, aside from trade policy uncertainty, softer global fuel prices will exert downward pressure on commodity exports despite likely higher volumes shipped, while higher imports for intermediate and capital goods to supply manufacturers and public projects will likely balance some of the gains the Philippines and Viet Nam garner in higher exports.

1.1.15 Global oil and food prices

Stabilizing global commodity prices...

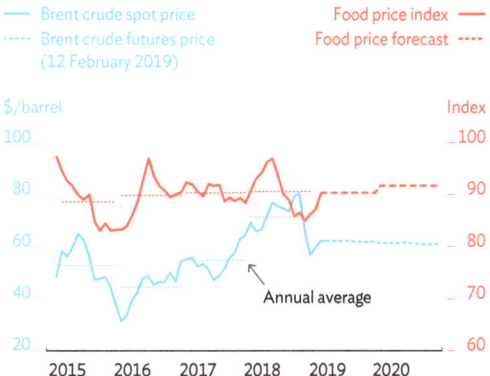

Sources: Bloomberg (accessed 8 March 2019); ADB estimates.

1.1.16 Subregional contributions to inflation, developing Asia

... will likely keep currently tame headline inflation unchanged.

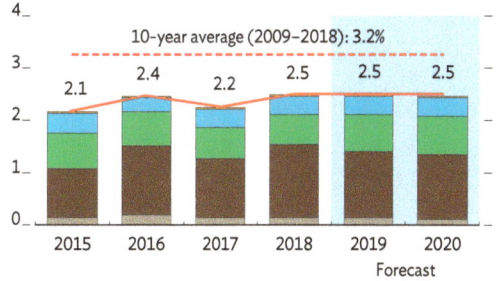

Source: *Asian Development Outlook* database.

1.1.17 Current account balance, developing Asia

Most subregions will see current account balances narrow in 2019 and 2020 ...

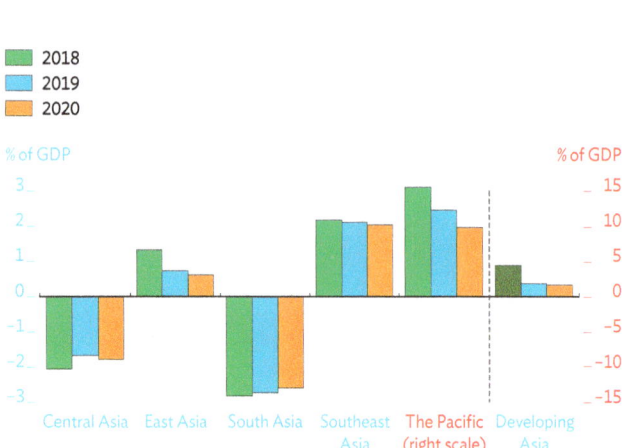

GDP = gross domestic product.
Source: *Asian Development Outlook* database.

1.1.18 World current account balance

...shrinking the regional surplus with the rest of the world to the equivalent of 0.1% of global GDP in 2019, even as the US deficit widens.

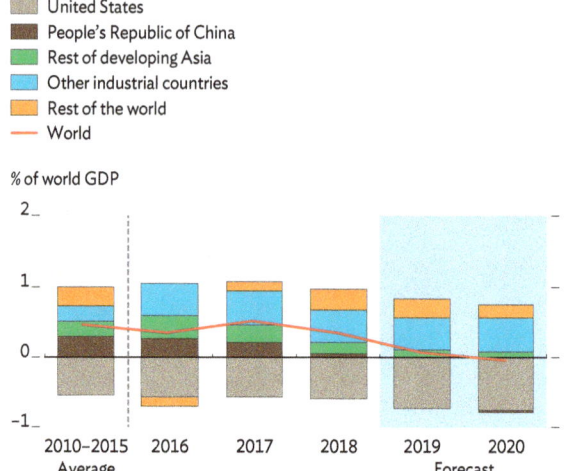

GDP = gross domestic product.
Sources: Haver Analytics (accessed 16 March 2019); *Asian Development Outlook* database.

With declining global growth tempering export demand and a service deficit persisting, the PRC current account surplus is forecast to disappear in 2019 and become a thin deficit in 2020. The surpluses of the other economies in East Asia are expected to weaken further to the forecast horizon as the impact of frontloading of exports across the region during mid-2018 reverses, and as trade policy uncertainty continues to hamper external demand.

Inter- and intraregional trade patterns in developing Asia look likely to shift more quickly than usual in 2019 and 2020 as global production relocates in response to the trade conflict. Some relocation will reflect a long-term trend toward greater reliance on domestic demand, given large structural changes in the past 2 decades, particularly in the PRC. And some will reflect new trade agreements such as the Comprehensive and Progressive Agreement for Trans-Pacific Partnership signing in early 2019. Slower trade this year and next should narrow the regional current account surplus with the rest of the world (Figure 1.1.18). With the reallocation within the region of production for some US–PRC trade, the pattern of trade is likely to show an increased share of trade within Asia. In addition, demand in the PRC and the US for imports from the rest of developing Asia will rise, slightly widening the US trade deficit with developing Asia excluding the PRC (Figure 1.1.19).

1.1.19 US trade deficit with developing Asia, excluding the PRC

Trade redirection in response to the US–PRC trade conflict should increase demand in US for imports from the rest of developing Asia.

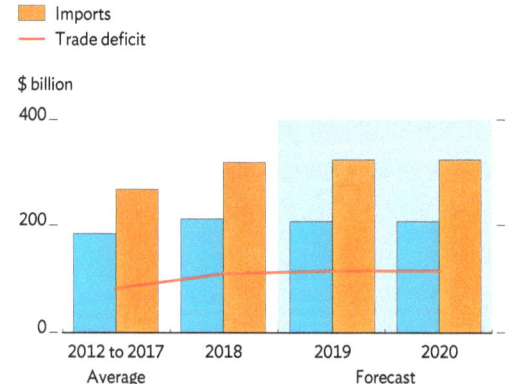

PRC = People's Republic of China, US = United States.
Sources: ADB estimates using data from Haver Analytics; ADB Multi-regional Input–Output Table (MRIOT) Database, and updates from Abiad et al. (2018).

Current trade negotiations to affect more than just tariffs and trade

Very little can be predicted at this stage about the outcome of trade negotiations between the PRC and the US. Without a clear end date for the negotiations, estimates of the effects of foregone trade are difficult to calculate, and they provide only one aspect of the far-reaching impact of the trade conflict. The baseline scenario assumes that tariffs remain at current levels throughout 2019 and 2020, with additional tariffs avoided by some agreement—perhaps requiring the PRC to wind back some regulatory restrictions on high-tech investment, for example, or to ease some financial restrictions. A step in this direction is a new investment law the PRC passed on 15 March 2019 that addresses priority issues for foreign investors regarding the protection of intellectual property rights. This scenario would have a relatively benign impact over the medium term, much of which may already have been priced in by global markets.

The outcome of the negotiations is likely to influence broad areas of developing Asia's economy beyond its effects on tariffs and trade. As discussed in *Asian Development Outlook 2018 Update* last September, the tariffs enacted last year will likely suppress and redirect trade, affecting employment. Estimates of these effects have since been updated to reflect the assumed continuation of existing tariff rates into 2019 and 2020. Relative to there being no trade conflict (the situation in December 2017), global GDP is estimated to be 0.05% lower by the end of 2020. The PRC comes out as worst hit, with GDP 0.25% lower than in a no-conflict scenario, but the US also suffers a net loss of 0.13% of GDP. On the other hand, the NIEs may see a net gain of 0.06% of aggregate GDP, and the ASEAN-5 a gain of 0.04%, if trade redirection materializes (Figure 1.1.20). These are very small percentages; for the NIEs, falling external demand more than offsets this effect, causing growth in the outlook period to underperform 2018. Taipei,China, for example, will see growth drop from 2.6% in 2018 to 2.2% in 2019 and 2.0% in 2020 as business confidence suffers heavily under both the trade conflict and the slowdown in external demand.

Employment in key areas of the protagonists' economies suffers the most. Losses are not limited to tradable sectors but extend to services that support export sectors. According to the model estimates, the PRC loses about 1.76 million jobs relative to a no-conflict scenario—equal to 0.21% of 2017 employment over both years—with the largest losses occurring in agriculture, community and social services, retail trade, electrical and optical equipment, and machinery. The US may lose 194,000 jobs over both years compared with a no-conflict scenario, with the largest losses in agriculture, business services, metals,

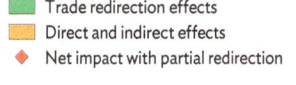

1.1.20 GDP impact of the trade conflict by economic region, current scenario

The impact of tariffs imposed so far is small but hits the PRC and the US the hardest with both countries losing small percentages of GDP.

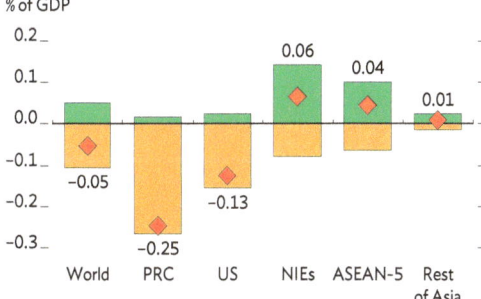

ASEAN-5 = five large economies in the Association of Southeast Asian Nations (Indonesia, Malaysia, the Philippines, Thailand, and Viet Nam), GDP = gross domestic product, NIEs = newly industrialized economies (Hong Kong, China; the Republic of Korea; Singapore; and Taipei,China), PRC = People's Republic of China, Rest of Asia = Bangladesh, Bhutan, Brunei Darussalam, Cambodia, Fiji, India, the Lao People's Democratic Republic, Maldives, Mongolia, Pakistan, and Sri Lanka, US = United States.
Sources: ADB estimates using data from ADB Multi-regional Input–Output Table (MRIOT) database and Abiad et al. (2018).

transport equipment, and food and beverages. With lower exports and lower imports, the US–PRC trade imbalance will narrow over the outlook period very marginally from its record gap of $419.2 billion in 2018 (Figure 1.1.21).

Foreign direct investment (FDI) flow patterns between the PRC and the US suggest that the trade conflict can affect production links (Figure 1.1.22). Current investment flows provide some clues about trade and growth patterns 1–2 years from now. For 2018 as a whole, US FDI outflows to the PRC surged, particularly toward the end of 2018, and especially into auto components and chemical products. These goods are subject to US import tariffs, suggesting that some investment may have been motivated by the desire to circumvent tariffs on future exports or in expectation of future investment restrictions. Still, the PRC receives on average only about 12% of total FDI from the US. In contrast, FDI flows from the PRC to the US barely rose, and now constitute only 7% of the PRC's total FDI flows compared to 11% on average in 2011–2017. All flows of FDI into the PRC slowed sharply in Q4 after having increased in the first 3 quarters of 2018, owing mainly to the unresolved trade conflict.

The PRC has been tightening its investment links with the rest of developing Asia in recent years, but the trend seems to have accelerated under the trade conflict in 2018, just as intraregional trade links strengthened. This trend is expected to continue to the forecast horizon (Figure 1.1.23). Greenfield FDI from the PRC to the rest of developing Asia soared by 198% in 2018, with the region's share climbing from 40% of the PRC total in the previous 8 years to 60%. Investment went to diverse sectors, such as renewable energy in Indonesia; oil, gas, and metals in the Philippines; software and electronics in Singapore; real estate in Hong Kong, China; leisure and entertainment in the ROK; and even high-tech textile production in Kazakhstan. Investment approval data indicate that FDI into machinery and electronic components is poised to grow in Malaysia and Viet Nam, though actual investment has been slow so far in 2019. FDI from the US to developing Asia excluding the PRC also rose, by 71% in 2018 to reach its highest since the global financial crisis of 2008–2009, though it is still less than 20% of all US outbound FDI.

Going forward, the outcome of the negotiations has the potential to shape FDI flows into high-tech over the medium term. The FDI index of regulatory restrictions sheds light on this issue (Figure 1.1.24). The most protected areas are not high-tech and typically involve non-traded services other than air travel. Nevertheless, taking into account restrictions in all areas, the PRC is generally more restrictive than most of the advanced economies. Moreover, according to data available for 13 economies in developing Asia that together account for 87% of regional income, the PRC is the second-most-restrictive economy in the region, after the Philippines. It is particularly restrictive in high-tech services.

1.1.21 US trade deficit with the PRC

US–PRC bilateral trade will shrink, but the bilateral trade deficit will hardly change.

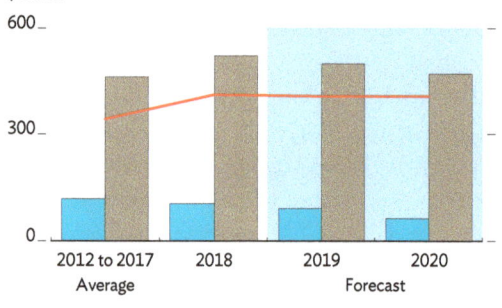

GDP = gross domestic product, PRC = People's Republic of China, US = United States.
Sources: ADB estimates using data from Haver Analytics; ADB Multi-regional Input–Output Table (MRIOT) database; and Abiad et al. (2018).

1.1.22 PRC and US outbound greenfield investment by host region

Greenfield investment—defined as equity investment into new projects—from the PRC and the US rose in 2018 despite some tightening of restrictions at the end of 2018...

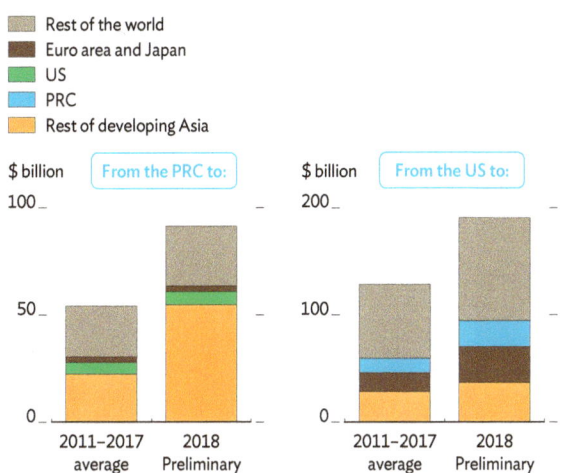

PRC = People's Republic of China, US = United States.
Sources: ADB estimates using data from Financial Times, fDi Markets. https://www.fdimarkets.com/ (accessed 16 March 2019). See https://aric.adb.org/pdf/AEIR_FDI_Database.pdf for data description and methodology.

1.1.23 Greenfield investments to developing Asia by source

... but there was an even sharper pickup of investment into developing Asia from all regions, particularly the PRC.

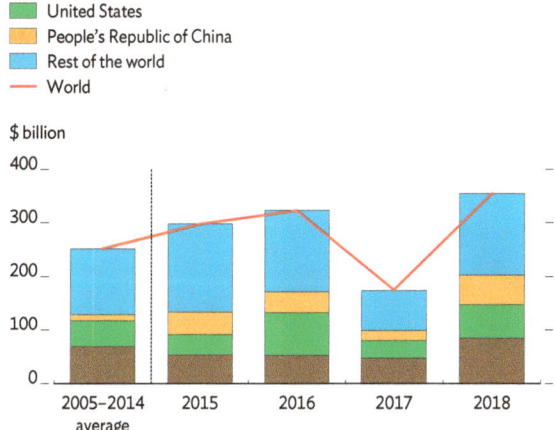

1.1.24 FDI regulatory restrictiveness, 2017

The index of FDI regulatory restrictiveness—indicating more restrictions—is high in developing Asia, especially in the telecommunications sector in the PRC...

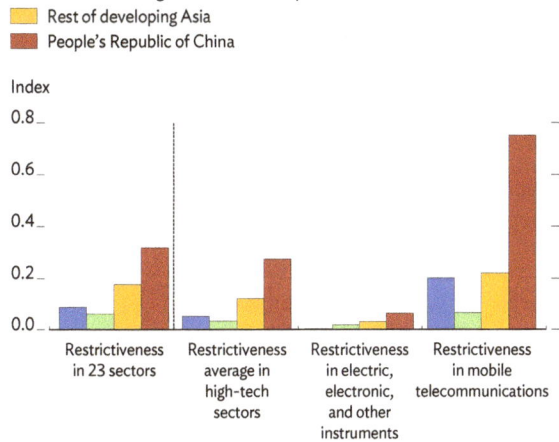

FDI = foreign direct investment, OECD = Organisation for Economic Co-operation and Development.
Note: The FDI regulatory restrictiveness index indicates greater restriction with a higher number. A score of 1 indicates an economy that is highly restrictive, and a score of 0 indicates an economy that is open.
Source: Organisation for Economic Co-operation and Development. https://www.oecd.org/investment/fdiindex.htm.

1.1.25 Outward greenfield investment to key technology sectors by destination, 2014–2018

... but FDI between the PRC and the US is small in the sectors targeted by US negotiators: aerospace equipment, energy, biotechnology, engineering services, the internet of things, and defense.

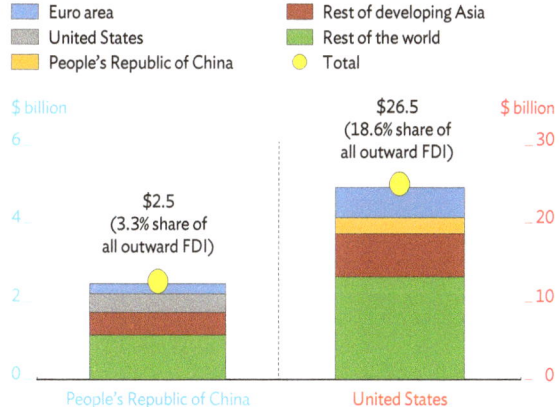

FDI = foreign direct investment.
Note: The key technology sectors affected by negotiations are aerospace, biotechnology, industrial machinery and equipment, software and information technology services, semiconductors, and space and defense.
Sources: ADB estimates using data from Financial Times, fDi Markets. https://www.fdimarkets.com/ (accessed 16 March 2019). See https://aric.adb.org/pdf/AEIR_FDI_Database.pdf for data description and methodology.

More broadly, the outcome of the negotiations may influence the pace and pattern of technology transfers within the region. Underlying the negotiations are issues around "winning the technology race," particularly for advanced technologies in manufacturing, robotics, 5G cellular mobile communications, artificial intelligence, biotechnology, aerospace, and the internet of things. These areas do not loom particularly large in their share of FDI flows, as they are mostly between the US and other advanced economies. Over the 5 years to 2018, these sectors accounted for 18.6% of all FDI inflows from the US, and the amount of those sectors bound for PRC was only 1.6% of all US outward FDI; and 3.3% of total outbound FDI from the PRC was in those sectors, but only 0.6% bound to the US (Figure 1.1.25). Nevertheless, one potential casualty of new restrictions would be the semiconductor industry. At the end of 2018, the industry was forecast to grow by a meager 2.6% in 2019, following 2 years of double-digit growth. Now estimates are for sales to contract by 3.0% this year (Figure 1.1.26). Production may be thwarted because of the national security concerns of European Union, PRC, and US governments that geopolitical rivals may inappropriately use semiconductors in high-tech defense applications. However, semiconductors are also used in mass consumer goods. Semiconductor production for mass applications is thus likely to be lower as well (Figure 1.1.27). Small businesses in high-tech sectors globally—which tend to be highly innovative but rely on open source technologies—could suffer disproportionately if protracted negotiations continue to affect semiconductors.

1.1.26 Semiconductor trends and forecast

Semiconductor sales are expected to disappoint...

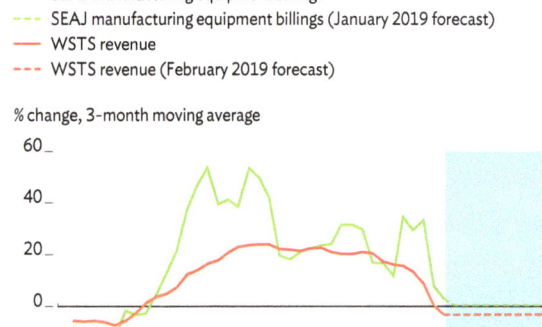

SEAJ = Semiconductor Equipment Association of Japan, WSTS = World Semiconductor Trade Statistics.
Sources: Semiconductor Equipment Association of Japan. http://www.seaj.or.jp/; WSTS news release, February 2019. https://www.wsts.org/.

1.1.27 Semiconductor revenue, by type

...affecting their use in many other commercial and consumer applications, possibly thwarting innovation.

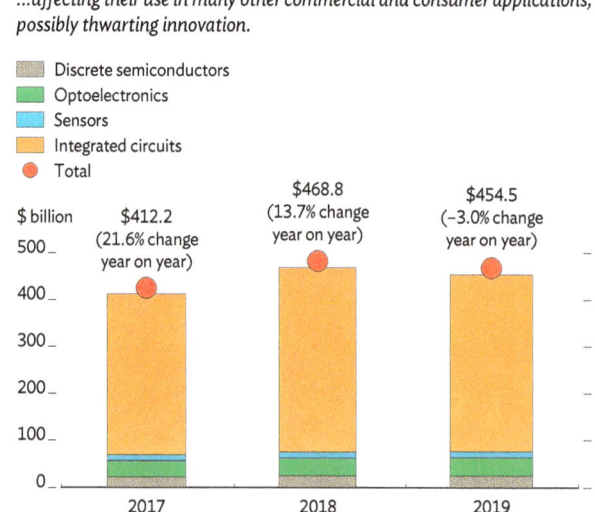

Source: World Semiconductor Trade Statistics News Release February 2019. https://www.wsts.org/.

The outlook cloudy, the risks tilting to the downside

The greatest risks to the outlook arise from the US–PRC trade conflict. Tariff hikes that were originally scheduled to take effect in January were postponed as negotiations continued. This development suggests that the risk of tariff escalation has subsided somewhat since the September publication of *Asian Development Outlook 2018 Update*. But the risks still tilt to the downside. The sluggish pace of negotiations, and fluctuating views about whether a resolution is on the horizon or not, have expanded the cloud of uncertainty for businesses, particularly those engaged in trade. With the possibility of protracted negotiations and periodic announcements of tightening regulations governing high-tech investment, uncertainty could deepen and spread to other sectors of the economy beyond those directly affected. A news-based indicator of trade policy uncertainty finds investor perceptions of trade policy uncertainty at an all-time high (Box 1.1.3). Uncertainty is particularly damaging to investment, which depends heavily on investors' view of the future. Greater uncertainty can cause investors to delay costly and irreversible investment. Box 1.1.3 provides evidence that spikes in trade policy uncertainty like the current one can reduce PRC investment by about 1%. A possible upside risk, though, is that negotiations will quickly bring an agreement that lowers existing tariffs. Recent announcements can be read as gestures of good faith on both sides, raising the possibility of an agreement being reached, at which time trade and investment barriers may be reduced.

1.1.3 Trade policy uncertainty: trends and impact

Analysis in the September *Asian Development Outlook 2018 Update* showed how economies and their sectors in developing Asia would be affected by tariffs already imposed and under various scenarios of escalated tariffs. A potentially important and distinct concern is uncertainty about trade policy. Trade policy uncertainty (TPU) may cause firms to postpone investment decisions until the uncertainty is resolved. The literature has found that investment can sometimes pick up in periods of TPU, when, for example, the uncertainty is over a country's negotiations to join a trade agreement (Hlatshwayo forthcoming). This analysis provides new measures of TPU pertinent to Asia, documents trends in these measures, and provides initial evidence of uncertainty's impact on investment.

To measure TPU, a useful resource is the news-based index developed in Baker, Bloom, and Davis (2016). The indicator utilizes the number of news articles that mention TPU and captures the degree of uncertainty that the public perceives about trade policy actions and their consequences. Box figure 1 plots the measure of US TPU using the index. Readings peaked in the early 1990s during negotiations on the North American Free Trade Agreement but have been rising again over the past 2 years. Box figure 2 plots a newly constructed variant of this index that captures US TPU vis-à-vis Asia. This is at an all-time high.

TPU indicators can also be constructed for individual economies in the region. Box figure 3 plots the TPU indicator for the PRC, constructed in Hlatshwayo (forthcoming), from January 1995 to January 2019. The indicator was high in 1995 during a US–PRC trade conflict over intellectual property rights. It was also elevated in the late 1990s and early 2000s when the PRC was negotiating to join the World Trade Organization. The indicator began rising again in 2017 and 2018 when the US and the PRC started threatening to impose tariffs on each other's products. The PRC TPU indicator is now at an all-time high.

continued next page

1.1.3 Continued

1 US trade policy uncertainty index
US trade policy uncertainty has increased over the past 2 years...

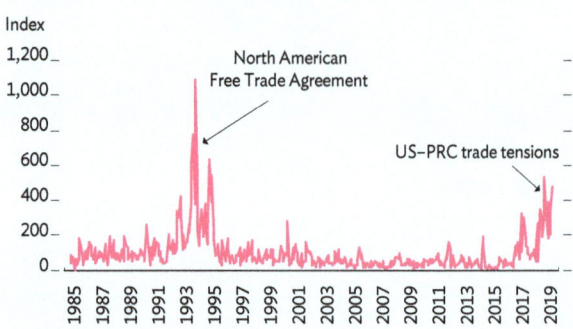

2 US trade policy uncertainty index vis-à-vis Asia
...and US TPU vis-à-vis Asia is at an all-time high.

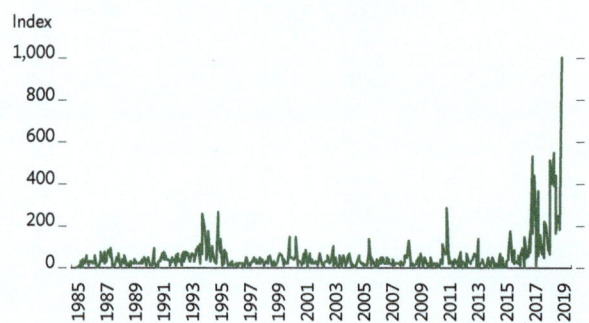

PRC = People's Republic of China, US = United States.
Sources: ADB estimates; Economic Policy Uncertainty. www.policyuncertainty.com (accessed 1 March 2019).

3 PRC trade policy uncertainty, 1995-2019
Trade policy uncertainty in the PRC is also at all-time highs...

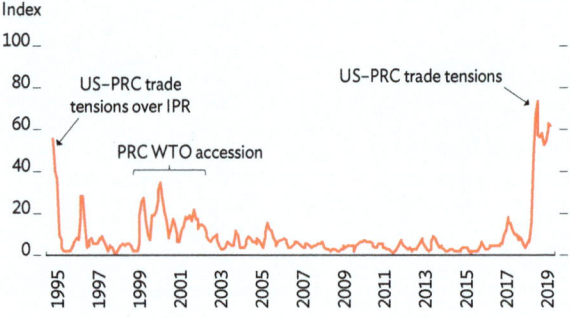

4 Estimated effect of TPU shocks on investment in the PRC
...which can have adverse effects on investment.

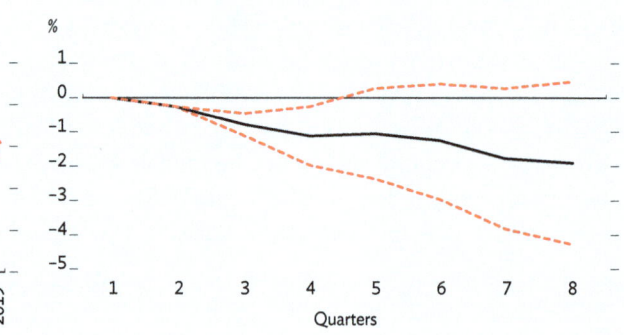

PRC = People's Republic of China, TPU = trade policy uncertainty, US = United States, WTO = World Trade Organization.
Note: Chart on the right shows investment response to trade policy uncertainty shocks, based on a vector autoregression and using the local projections method as in Jordà (2005) while the dotted lines plot the 10% and 90% percentile of the confidence intervals. See Abiad et al. (forthcoming).
Source: ADB estimates based on methodology in Hlatshwayo (2018).

To analyze the effects of high TPU on investment, a vector autoregression model similar to that in Baker, Bloom, and Davis (2016) was estimated.[a] Box figure 4 shows that periods of high TPU—similar to those observed in 1995, the early 2000s, and at present—have statistically significant and measurable effects on investment in the PRC. Spikes in TPU tended to depress investment by 1% in the third quarter after the shock. There was no significant effect beyond the third quarter. The analysis confirmed that TPU causes a temporary decline in investment, probably because firms postpone investment decisions until the uncertainty is resolved.

[a] The vector autoregression includes the log of fixed asset investment, TPU, the money market rate, and the stock market index using quarterly data from Q1 of 1996 to Q4 of 2018. To focus on the effects of high TPU on investment, the vector autoregression uses dummy variables that identify periods where TPU is more than one standard deviation above the mean.

References:
Abiad, A., J. Adona, S. Hlatshwayo, and I. Qureshi. Forthcoming. *Trade Policy Uncertainty: Trends and Impact*. Asian Development Bank.
Baker, S. R., N. Bloom, and S. J. Davis. 2016. Measuring Economic Policy Uncertainty. *The Quarterly Journal of Economics* 131(4).
Hlatshwayo, S., Forthcoming. *Unpacking Policy Uncertainty: Evidence from European Firms*. International Monetary Fund.
Jordà, Ò. 2005. Estimation and Inference of Impulse Responses by Local Projections. *American Economic Review* 95(1).

An additional downside risk is the possibility of disappointing growth in the major economies. Triggers for such a scenario include heightened fiscal uncertainty deepening the slowdown of economic activity in the US, or a disorderly exit of the United Kingdom from the European Union causing a sharper slowdown there. The direct effects of Brexit on developing Asia through trade channels are likely to be small. Even for countries like Sri Lanka—for which the United Kingdom is an important trade partner, and which benefits from tariff-free entry of its products into that market—the forecast effects of Brexit are small (Box 1.1.4). But a disorderly Brexit might roil global financial markets, worsen uncertainty, and raise risk aversion, which would affect developing Asia more broadly. Within the region, while the PRC is working both to support growth and to reduce financial risks, various external or internal shocks could still materialize, making it a challenge for the authorities to continue to engineer controlled growth moderation.

1.1.4 How might Brexit affect developing Asia? Evidence from Sri Lanka

The United Kingdom (UK), a member of the European Union (EU) since 1973, held a referendum on 23 June 2016 on whether to withdraw from the EU. The decision to leave the EU, or Brexit, passed by a narrow margin. On 29 March 2017, the UK invoked Article 50 of the Lisbon Treaty, which provides 2 years to negotiate an exit from the EU. As *Asian Development Outlook 2019* goes to press, the deadline to close negotiations looms large, and UK parliamentary deliberations are in full swing to either approve a plan already agreed with the EU, extend the negotiations, or institute measures to manage a "hard Brexit." Uncertainty over the fate of the negotiations poses a downside risk to the economy of the UK and the EU, and the global economy at large, including developing Asia. There are many channels through which Brexit could have an economic impact on the rest of the world, including confidence channels that are difficult to anticipate and quantify. This analysis sheds light on the economic impact of Brexit by examining the trade channel closely, using Sri Lanka to illustrate.

One of the special bilateral trade arrangements that some developing economies have with the EU is the Generalised Scheme of Preferences Plus (GSP+), a preferential tariff system that grants full tariff removal on more than two-thirds of EU tariff lines.[a] With Brexit, the UK will no longer be covered by GSP+. Sri Lanka and other exporters can be directly affected by Brexit because they lose access to the UK market through the EU GSP+ program, and what replaces GSP+ is still unclear. Currently, the UK is Sri Lanka's second-largest trading partner, taking 8.3% of Sri Lanka's exports.[b]

Analysis of the economic impact of Brexit employs two scenarios, both of which influence trade flows through changes in tariffs. The first scenario is no-deal Brexit, which assumes that trade between the UK and the EU will be reduced by higher tariffs post-Brexit. The second scenario is tariff escalation between Sri Lanka and the UK, which extends the analysis to explore potential impacts if Sri Lanka's exports to the UK become subject to a tariff when the UK is no longer party to the GSP+. In both scenarios, the tariff change from the baseline is assumed to be equal to the average most-favored nation rate of 5.62% imposed by the UK and the EU on manufactured goods.[c] Assuming that the UK reaches the Brexit date without a deal with the EU or other countries, trade between the UK and the EU, as well as bilateral trade between Sri Lanka and the UK, will then be subject to tariff rates charged by the EU in its common customs tariff or the most-favored nation rates.

The effects on Sri Lanka's economy through the trade channel are small (box figure). There are no direct effects from increased tariffs between the UK and the EU, and indirect effects through international supply chains shave 0.06% off Sri Lanka's GDP. The adverse indirect effects may even be offset by a potential gain of 0.08% of GDP if trade redirection to accommodate new tariffs between the UK and EU allowed Sri Lanka to provide more agricultural and industrial exports. If these gains from trade redirection materialized—and it should be stressed that they are neither automatic nor assured—the net impact would be small but positive at 0.01%. If Sri Lanka faced higher tariffs when the UK exits the EU and its GSP+ program, the direct effects of those tariffs would be

continued next page

1.1.4 Continued

Impact of Brexit on Sri Lanka

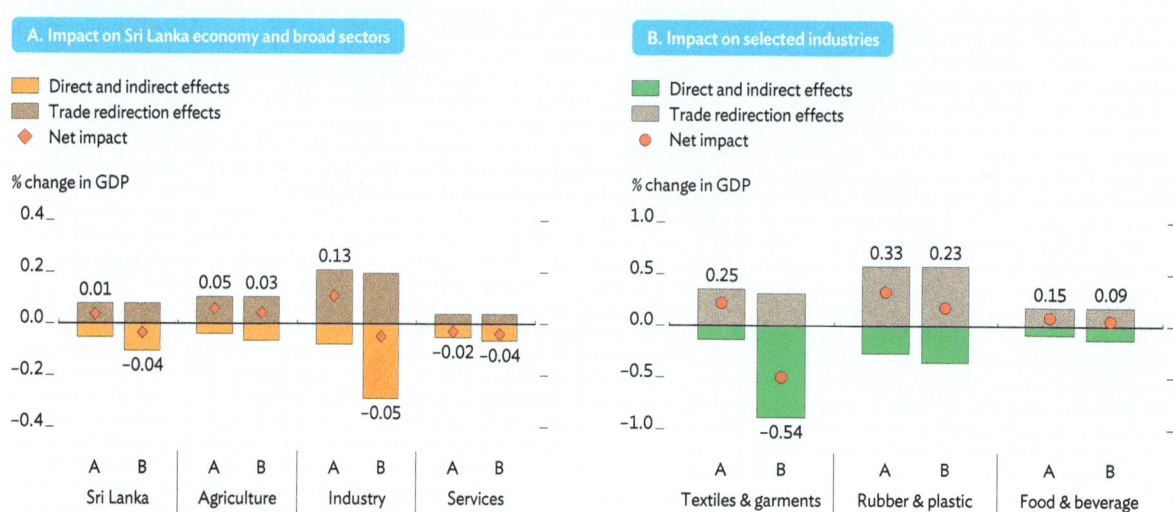

A = No-deal Brexit, B = United Kingdom–Sri Lanka.
Sources: ADB estimates using data from ADB Multi-regional Input-Output Table (MRIOT) database and Abiad et al. (2018).

to decrease Sri Lankan exports to the UK by 3.1% and overall exports by 0.4%, and Sri Lanka's GDP would be lower by 0.11%. Trade redirection would potentially offset 0.07% of the loss.

Under both scenarios, industry appears to be the sector most affected, with certain segments like textiles and garments suffering significant losses. The combined effects of higher tariffs and disrupted supply links could hit industry gross value added by as much as 0.08%–0.28%, though this could be offset by trade redirection. The effects on agriculture and services are smaller. In a scenario where tariffs escalate between Sri Lanka and the UK, textiles would be hurt the most. The direct and indirect effects would reduce textile and garment exports to the UK by 7.7%, and textiles and garments gross value added by 0.85%. Trade redirection would attenuate but not completely offset these losses.

In sum, the economy-wide effects of Brexit through trade channels are small even for Sri Lanka, which has strong trade ties with the UK and risks losing a preferential trade arrangement if the UK leaves the EU. This suggests that the effects through trade channels on developing Asia more broadly are likely to be small as well. This updated assessment is consistent with analysis in the July 2016 *Asian Development Outlook Supplement*, which assessed the impact on developing Asia to be small. An important caveat is that a disorderly Brexit could significantly affect growth prospects in the EU, as highlighted in the main text of this chapter, as well as rattle global financial markets. These channels are harder to quantify and could have more significant implications for developing Asia.

[a] GSP+ provides tariff exemptions to vulnerable developing countries from the more general rules of the World Trade Organization (WTO) on exports to the EU. The European Commission states that it has three main objectives: to contribute to poverty reduction by expanding exports from poorer countries, to promote sustainable development and good governance, and to ensure that EU financial and economic interests are safeguarded.

[b] Other ADB member countries covered by GSP+ are Armenia, the Kyrgyz Republic, Mongolia, Pakistan, and the Philippines.

[c] Under most favored nation (MFN) rule of the WTO, the UK cannot decrease tariffs for any country unless a trade deal has been agreed with it. In 2018, the UK submitted WTO schedules of goods tariffs following its withdrawal from the EU, which is pending approval by the WTO. In the absence of this information, a no-deal scenario is assumed wherein the UK applies rates close to the MFN rates to avoid damaging trade effects. Therefore, this study applies the average MFN rate of 5.62%.

One risk that has subsided since the publication of *Asian Development Outlook 2018 Update* is the possibility of interest rates rising faster than anticipated. Weakening global and US economic activity in late 2018 and early 2019 motivated the US Federal Reserve to bring to a pause its monetary tightening, and the previous view that the Fed would hike rates three or four times in 2019 no longer holds. Despite this, the risk of financial volatility remains. There is now also greater uncertainty regarding US monetary policy, and estimates show that this is associated with greater exchange rate volatility for Asian currencies (Box 1.1.5). And, while the jitters evident in emerging markets in 2018 have abated for now, this could reemerge, with consequences for domestic financial conditions.

1.1.5 Impact of US monetary policy uncertainty on Asian exchange rates

Analysis here examines the impact of uncertainty about US monetary policy on the exchange rates of Asian countries. Currency turmoil in mid-2018—during which Turkey and Argentina suffered large currency depreciation in the wake of the US Federal Reserve steadily raising its interest rates since 2017—underlined the role US monetary policy can play in shaping exchange rate behavior in emerging markets. Regional currencies, including the Indian rupee and Indonesian rupiah, have recovered fairly well since Q4 of 2018. In light of slowing US and global growth, the future trajectory of US monetary policy is increasingly uncertain. The Fed is now expected to take a more cautious and gradual approach to monetary policy normalization, but how cautious and how gradual is the subject of much debate.

Uncertainty about US interest rates may affect exchange rates in emerging markets independently of what the rates actually are. Systematic analysis of news reports confirms that the public is becoming increasingly unclear about the exact trajectory of US monetary policy. Recent research finds that searching for relevant text can deliver useful information on uncertainty about economic policy. Baker, Bloom, and Davis (2016) constructed a news-based index of US monetary policy uncertainty (MPU) that attempts to capture the degree of uncertainty that the public perceives about the Fed's actions and their effects. The MPU index for the US remains elevated, most likely reflecting the uncertain effect of global trade tensions and global growth slowdown on the Fed's policy calculus.

The box figure plots data on monetary policy uncertainty based on Baker, Bloom, and Davis (2016) from January 1985 to January 2019. It shows large spikes occurred around times of uncertainty: Black Monday in October 1987, the 11 September attacks, the March 2003 invasion of Iraq, the Lehman Brothers collapse in September 2008, prior to the October 2015 Federal Open Market Committee meetings to discuss interest rate liftoff from the zero lower bound, Brexit, and the November 2016 election in the US. Another spike seems to be brewing recently, presumably in response to the issues surrounding trade uncertainty and US federal government shutdown.

Park, Qureshi, Tian, and Villaruel (forthcoming) examined the effect of uncertainty about US Fed monetary policy on exchange rate fluctuations in 10 Asian economies using monthly data from 2006 to 2019. The study combined the news-based measure of monetary policy uncertainty with a measure of actual exchange rates and the interest rate spread using a country-specific model of exchange rate returns and volatility called the GARCH model (Bollerslev 1986). This framework enabled the capture not only of time variance in the exchange rate market but also extracted the impacts of MPU on both exchange rate values and variance of return.

Monthly data on the US federal funds rate, exchange rates against the US dollar, and policy interest rates in the selected Asian economies were collected from Bloomberg. Data availability limited the sample period to February 2006–January 2019 in India; Indonesia; Japan; Malaysia; the PRC; the Philippines; the Republic of Korea; Singapore; Taipei,China; and Thailand. In the analysis, the monthly percentage change in MPU and exchange rates are constructed using log difference between levels in the current and previous month. The interest rate spread was defined as the difference between each Asian economy's policy interest rate and the

continued next page

1.1.5 Continued

Monetary policy uncertainty index for the United States

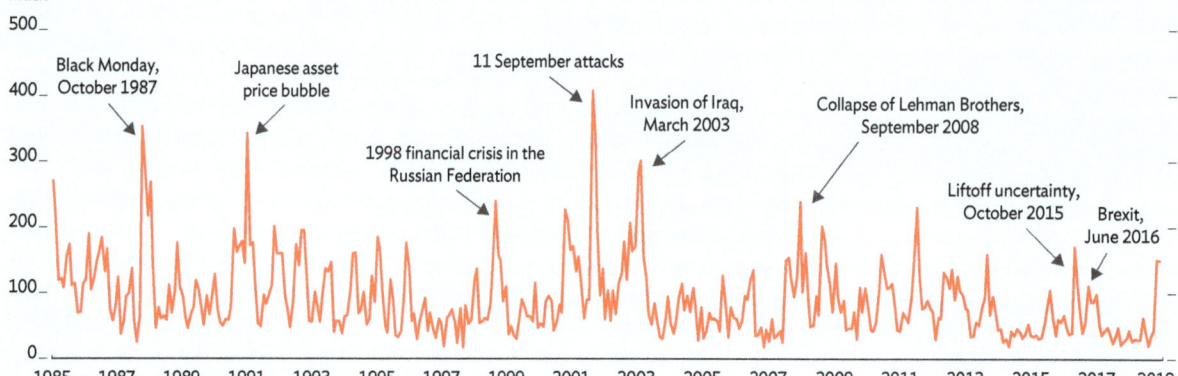

Note: The figure plots data on monetary policy uncertainty based on Baker, Bloom, and Davis (2016).
Sources: ADB estimates; Economic Policy Uncertainty. www.policyuncertainty.com (accessed 1 March 2019).

US federal fund rate. The econometric analysis then examined how US monetary policy uncertainty would affect return patterns in exchange rates in Asian economies, in terms of both values and variances.

The empirical results indicated that uncertainty about US monetary policy affected exchange rate variability but not the exchange rate levels of Asian countries. The box table reports the estimated effect of uncertainty about US monetary policy on the variance of exchange rate in the 10 Asian economies. The effect was uniformly positive. It appeared that greater uncertainty about the path of US interest rates generated greater diversity of belief about exchange rates among participants in foreign exchange markets. More diverse beliefs meant more diverse trading and hence more volatile exchange rates. The magnitudes varied across economies. For example, during the sample period, the average monthly increase in MPU was 0.59%, which was associated with an increase in exchange rate return variance of 0.02 in the Philippines. When the MPU rose sharply in 2018 by 14%, variance increased by 0.50. Similarly, exchange rate return variance rose by approximately 0.30 in Indonesia in 2018.

Analysis suggested that periods of heightened uncertainty about US monetary policy tended to be periods of heightened volatility in Asian exchange rates. This strengthens the case for more closely monitoring exchange rates when there is less clarity about the Fed's course of action. Although heightened volatility strengthens the case for measures to stabilize exchange rates, a great deal of caution is advised because US monetary policy uncertainty is just one of many factors that affect exchange rates.

References:

Baker, S. R., N. Bloom, and S. J. Davis. 2016. Measuring Economic Policy Uncertainty. *The Quarterly Journal of Economics* 131(4).

Bollerslev, T. 1986. Generalized Autoregressive Conditional Heteroskedasticity. *Journal of Econometrics* 31(3).

Park, D., I. Qureshi, S. Tian, and M. L. Villaruel. Forthcoming. *Impact of US Monetary Policy Uncertainty on Asian Exchange Rates*. Asian Development Bank.

Impact of US monetary policy uncertainty on the variance of exchange rates in 10 Asian economies

Dependent variable: actual exchange rate (t)	PRC	INO	IND	JPN	ROK	MAL	PHI	SIN	THA	TAP
Variance equation										
MPU (t-1)	0.261	2.039***	0.707	1.461**	0.479	1.079	3.531**	1.257**	0.0853	0.447
	(4.3760)	(0.4350)	(1.7380)	(0.6690)	(0.5560)	(1.2710)	(1.6020)	(0.5670)	(0.0896)	(0.4290)
Observations	154	154	154	154	154	154	154	154	154	154
chi-squared	31.94	0.00842	2.603	1.353	1.925	1.948	0.321	0.473	8.836	4.318

IND = India, INO = Indonesia, JPN = Japan, MAL = Malaysia, MPU = monetary policy uncertainty, PRC = People's Republic of China, PHI = Philippines, ROK = Republic of Korea, SIN = Singapore, TAP = Taipei,China, THA = Thailand.
Note: For the Philippines and Taipei,China, GARCH (1 2) is employed to fit particular time series attributes. Standard errors in parentheses.
*** denotes significance at 0.01, ** at 0.05, and * at 0.10.
Source: Park, Qureshi, Tian, and Villaruel, forthcoming.

Exchange rates affect domestic financial conditions through trade and financial channels

Many economies in developing Asia saw their currencies depreciate in 2018, reversing the appreciating trend in 2017 (Figure 1.2.1). This resulted from a confluence of factors including a steady rise in US policy rates that caused a shift in market sentiment away from riskier assets in the region. Those factors, woven with trade tensions, led investors to reevaluate their emerging market portfolios more generally. Indeed, some regional currencies depreciated significantly against the US dollar in 2018.

By late 2018, most regional currencies had stabilized, and since then several have appreciated. As Box 1.1.1 makes clear, however, regional exchange rates are not out of the woods; local currency depreciation and challenging financial market conditions could recur. With the recent subsiding of the earlier risk that the US Federal Reserve would raise its rates more quickly than expected, the path for normalizing monetary policy in the US has become less certain. And, as analysis in Box 1.1.5 shows, periods of heightened US monetary policy uncertainty are associated with greater volatility in bilateral exchange rates vis-à-vis the US dollar.

As the present analysis documents, exchange rate fluctuations can have significant effects on domestic financial conditions in many open economies. These effects can work through two distinct channels with opposing effects: the trade channel and the financial channel, as described in more detail below. Recent years have seen more analysis of these effects, most notably in a Bank of International Settlements study (Hoffman, Shim, and Shin 2017). The present analysis explores these issues in the context of ADB developing member countries. It provides quantitative estimates of the relative strength of the trade and financial channels' effects on domestic financial conditions, examines whether the strength of these channels varies across selected economies in developing Asia, and discusses how exchange rate fluctuations in 2018 affected domestic financial conditions in the region. It considers the role of the US dollar in global liquidity conditions and illustrates how exchange rate changes can have significant impacts on sovereign credit risk premiums.

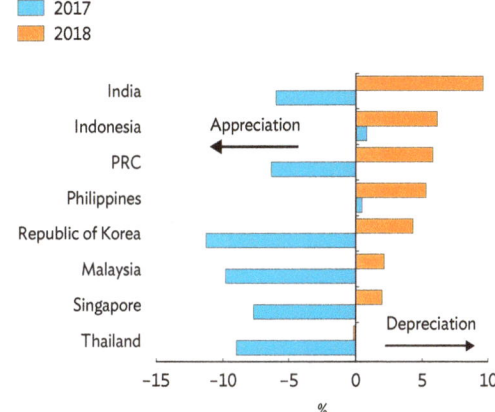

1.2.1 Change in nominal exchange rate against the US dollar

PRC = People's Republic of China, US = United States.
Note: Because all currency units are smaller than $1, negative values indicate appreciation and positive values indicate depreciation.
Source: ADB estimates using data from Bloomberg (accessed 13 February 2019).

Exchange rates and the transmission of global financial conditions

One of the main causes of the Asian financial crisis of 1997–1998 was currency and maturity mismatches in the debt held in many economies in the region. Large amounts of short-term debt denominated in foreign currency were used to finance long-term investments that yielded revenue in local currency. Deteriorating values of local currencies in 1997, despite closely managed exchange rates in the region at the time, triggered the crisis by inflating external debt to unsustainable levels and prompting large capital outflows.

Today, financial systems in the region have generally become more resilient, thanks to a wide range of reforms implemented after the Asian financial crisis. However, the US dollar remains the major funding currency for the region's growing external debt. In recent years, the value of outstanding US dollar-denominated international debt securities has increased as a percentage of total external debt in a number of Asian economies (Figure 1.2.2). The concentration of foreign borrowing in a single currency leaves the region's financial systems vulnerable to external shocks through unexpected changes in global currency liquidity conditions and related capital flow reversals, with significant implications for domestic financial and macroeconomic conditions.

In this regard, the bilateral US dollar exchange rate can transmit global dollar funding conditions into emerging economies. Recent data suggest that exchange rates movements—both the bilateral US dollar exchange rate (BER) and the trade-weighted nominal effective exchange rate (NEER)—correlated throughout 2018 in most economies in emerging Asia with changes in sovereign bond spreads (Table 1.2.1). The bond spreads are measures of domestic financing conditions relative to global conditions, as they show the yield premium between domestic and foreign bonds.

In 2018, the correlation between changes in the spread and exchange rates was highest in Malaysia and lowest in the Republic of Korea. Meaningful correlation was observed in other economies. Positive correlation indicates that currency depreciation tended to come in tandem with a widening spread, or a tightening of domestic financing conditions, and currency appreciation with a loosening of domestic financing conditions as the spread narrowed. Correlation coefficients tended to be higher and more consistent for the BER than for the NEER, as the sign of the latter's coefficient tended to vary more across economies.

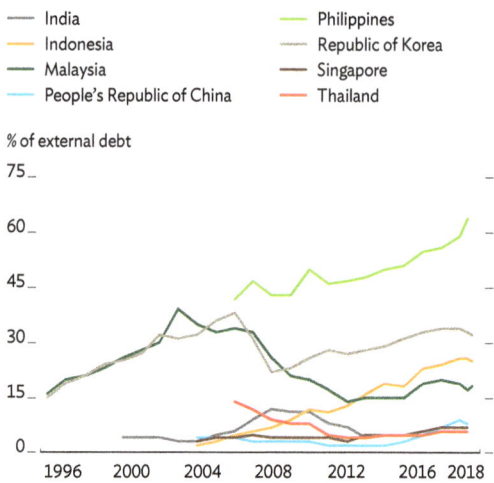

1.2.2 US dollar-denominated international debt securities as a percentage of external debt

Source: ADB estimates using data from the Bank for International Settlements and CEIC Data Company (accessed 20 December 2018).

1.2.1 Correlation between changes in sovereign bond spreads and exchange rates in 2018

Country	BER	NEER
People's Republic of China	0.35	0.40
India	0.38	0.35
Indonesia	0.67	0.20
Republic of Korea	–0.02	–0.11
Malaysia	0.85	0.70
Philippines	0.24	–0.02
Singapore	0.40	–0.16
Thailand	0.69	0.10

BER = bilateral exchange rate, NEER = nominal effective exchange rate.

Note: Positive signs indicate a positive correlation between currency depreciation and changes in the sovereign bond spread, the latter defined as the change month on month in the difference between the 5-year local currency sovereign yield and the 5-year US Treasury yield, following the definition used in Hofmann, Shim, and Shin (2017).

Source: ADB estimates.

These observations suggest that the exchange rate may play a role as a transmission channel influencing domestic financial conditions in emerging markets. Variation in the correlation sign, however, raises the possibility of contrasting channels through which exchange rates affect domestic financial conditions. In theory, the exchange rate may affect domestic financial conditions positively through the trade channel and negatively through the financial channel.[1] In the trade channel, currency depreciation improves international competitiveness, which boosts net exports and eventually improves the current account, which loosens domestic financial conditions. However, currency depreciation can also work through the financial channel by inflating the size of foreign currency-denominated debt, thereby tightening domestic financial conditions and worsening the economy's balance sheet. Depending on which of the two channels dominates, the effect of exchange rates on domestic financial conditions can vary across economies.

Evidence from the region

The trade and the financial channels both seem to influence domestic financing conditions in the region. Empirical findings from Lee, Rosenkranz, and Pham (forthcoming), summarized in Box 1.2.1, showed that changes in exchange rates affected sovereign credit risk premiums, which could then influence domestic financial conditions. Changes to BERs against the US dollar affected financial conditions largely through the financial channel, as depreciation worsened the balance sheets of indebted economies and hence tightened their financial conditions. In contrast, movements in NEERs acted more through the trade channel, as depreciation improved competitiveness and therefore improved financial conditions. On average, the analysis found that 1% bilateral depreciation against the US dollar tended to widen sovereign bond spreads[2] by approximately 4.2 basis points, while 1% depreciation in NEER terms tended to narrow local currency spreads by approximately 7.2 basis points.

To illustrate, the following paragraphs decompose the factors behind the actual changes in the sovereign bond spread in 2018, based on the estimates reported in Box 1.2.1. Figure 1.2.3 shows the decomposition of the average monthly changes to the sovereign bond spread in 2018 in eight emerging market economies in Asia: India, Indonesia, Malaysia, the Philippines, the PRC, the Republic of Korea, Singapore, and Thailand. The red dots show the average of monthly changes in spread for each economy in 2018, which are decomposed into the average effects contributed by changes to the BER, the NEER, and other factors explaining movements in the spread.

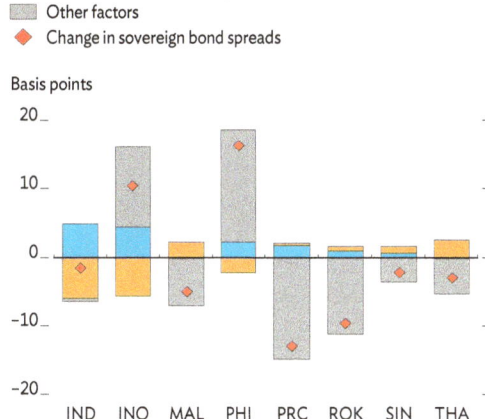

1.2.3 Average changes in spread in 2018

IND = India, INO = Indonesia, MAL = Malaysia, PHI = Philippines, PRC = People's Republic of China, ROK = Republic of Korea, SIN = Singapore, THA = Thailand.

Notes: ADB computation based on Lee, Rosenkranz, and Pham (forthcoming). Regression analysis using monthly data from December 2006 to August 2018.

Source: ADB calculations using data from the Bank for International Settlements; Bloomberg; Haver Analytics; International Monetary Fund (accessed 10 January 2019).

1.2.1 The influence of US dollar funding conditions on Asian financial markets

In a panel analysis of 20 emerging market economies, Hofmann, Shim, and Shin (2017) found that local currency appreciation against the US dollar improved a country's balance sheet as the value of dollar-denominated liabilities decreased relative to assets. Appreciation also increased foreign fund flows into sovereign bonds, suppressed yield spreads between bonds denominated in local currency and foreign currency, and lowered an economy's credit risk premium, thereby loosening financial conditions. Avdjiev, et al. (2018) found evidence that a stronger dollar was associated with lower growth in dollar-denominated cross-border bank flows and lower real investment in emerging market economies. These findings support the view that a stronger US dollar can have real macroeconomic effects in the opposite direction to effects from the standard trade channel.

Focusing more on evidence from emerging economies in Asia, Lee, Rosenkranz, and Pham (forthcoming) estimated a dynamic panel model for eight such economies—India, Indonesia, Malaysia, the People's Republic of China, the Philippines, the Republic of Korea, Thailand, and Viet Nam—with monthly data from December 2006 to August 2018. The following equation was estimated using Anderson-Hsiao's instrumental variable estimation (Anderson and Hsiao 1982), which also addressed possible endogeneity problems.

$$(1) \quad \Delta y_{i,t} = \alpha + \delta \Delta y_{i,t-1} + \beta_1 \Delta BER_{i,t-1} + \beta_2 \Delta NEER_{i,t-1} + \gamma_1 \Delta CPI_{i,t-1} + \gamma_2 \Delta IP_{i,t-1} + \gamma_3 \Delta r_{i,t-1} + \eta_1 \Delta VIX_{t-1} + \eta_2 \Delta CPIUS_{t-1} + \eta_3 \Delta IPUS_{t-1} + \eta_4 \Delta MMUS_{t-1} + \varepsilon_{i,t}$$

The dependent variable was defined as the change month on month in local currency sovereign bond spread,[a] whereby an increase indicated tightening domestic financial conditions. The main control variables were the change month on month in the BER against the US dollar and the change month on month in the NEER. Other variables included were the change month on month in the volatility index; change in the domestic and US consumer price index year on year; change in the domestic and US industrial production index year on year; change in the domestic lending rate month on month, which was defined as the average 1-year lending rate of domestic commercial banks; and change month on month in the 3-month money market rate in the US. Regression results are presented in the box table.

The results point to two opposing channels of the exchange rate being in play. While changes in BERs against the US dollar primarily affected financial conditions through the financial channel, changes in NEERs acted more through the trade channel.

Estimation results dynamic panel regression

Dependent variable: change month on month in the local currency sovereign bond spread			
$\Delta y_{i,t-1}$	0.403***	$\Delta r_{i,t-1}$	-0.00165***
$\Delta BER_{i,t-1}$	0.0424***	ΔVIX_{t-1}	0.00114**
$\Delta NEER_{i,t-1}$	-0.0723***	$\Delta CPIUS_{t-1}$	0.000522
$\Delta CPI_{i,t-1}$	-0.000180	$\Delta IPUS_{t-1}$	-0.0231
$\Delta IP_{i,t-1}$	0.00149	$\Delta MMUS_{t-1}$	-0.00255

*** = significant at 1%, ** = significant at 5%, * = significant at 10%, ΔBER = log change month on month in the bilateral exchange rate against US dollar (an increase indicates local currency depreciation), ΔCPI, $\Delta CPIUS$ = change year on year in the domestic and US consumer price index, ΔIP, $\Delta IPUS$ = change year on year in the domestic and US industrial production index, $\Delta MMUS$ = change month on month in the 3-month money market rate in the US, $\Delta NEER$ = change month on month in the nominal effective exchange rate (an increase indicates local currency depreciation), Δr = change month on month in the lending rate (defined as the average 1-year lending rate of domestic commercial banks), ΔVIX = log change month on month in the Chicago Board Options Exchange volatility index, US = United States.

Sources: Lee, Rosenkranz, and Pham, forthcoming.

Estimation results suggested that, on average, 1% bilateral depreciation against the US dollar tended to increase sovereign bond spreads by approximately 4.2 basis points, while 1% currency depreciation in NEER terms tended to decrease sovereign bond spreads by approximately 7.2 basis points. Qualitatively, the regression results aligned with the findings of Hofmann, Shim, and Shin (2017). The findings suggested a significant relationship between US dollar funding and domestic financial conditions in selected emerging Asian economies and highlight the vulnerabilities that stem from the region's high reliance on US dollar-denominated external funding.

[a] The difference between the 5-year local currency sovereign bond yield and the 5-year US Treasury yield, following the definition used in Hofmann, Shim, and Shin (2017).

Background Paper

Lee, J., P. Rosenkranz, and H. Pham. Forthcoming. *The Influence of US Dollar Funding Conditions on Asian Financial Markets*. Asian Development Bank.

References

Anderson, T. and C. Hsiao. 1982. Formulation and Estimation of Dynamic Models Using Panel Data. *Journal of Econometrics* 18(1).

Avdjiev, S., V. Bruno, C. Koch, and H. S. Shin. 2018. The Dollar Exchange Rate as a Global Risk Factor: Evidence from Investment. *BIS Working Papers* No. 695. Bank for International Settlements.

Hoffmann, B., I. Shim, and H. S. Shin. 2017. Sovereign Yields and the Risk-taking Channel of Currency Appreciation. *BIS Working Papers* No. 538. Bank for International Settlements.

Figure 1.2.3 suggests that variations in exchange rates explained part of the spread variations for sovereign bonds in 2018. In India, Indonesia, and the Philippines, currencies depreciated in both BER and NEER terms on average throughout the year. As a result, the two opposing channels for the exchange rate effects on the spread were in play, with a tightening effect from the BER and a loosening effect from the NEER. In contrast, the PRC and Singapore saw their BERs and NEERs move in different directions in 2018, with the BER showing currency depreciation and the NEER appreciation. Therefore, instead of causing contrasting effects, the two channels worked in the same direction, tightening domestic financial conditions.

In addition to changes in exchange rates, other factors, both domestic and external, were in play driving the actual direction of the changes in sovereign bond spreads, as captured by the gray portion of the bars. However, for explaining the differences in spread movements across economies, what matters are the country-specific drivers of the spreads, which included a wide range of variables from domestic macroeconomic indicators—such as prices, production activity, and lending rates—and other factors that might affect investors' and consumers' confidence domestically, such as political uncertainty and disasters. These other factors were generally in play to explain the dynamics of spread movements in most regional economies in 2018.

The relative importance of exchange rate movements in explaining changes in sovereign bond spreads also varied depending on the conditions experienced within a year. The monthly decomposition of the region's average spreads in 2018 showed that, within the year, exchange rate changes tended to dictate the movements in sovereign bonds spread, especially in Q3 of 2018, when regional currencies were under pressure to depreciate against the US dollar (Figure 1.2.4). Similar observations on the opposing channels of the exchange rate effects on domestic financial conditions appeared in the months when the average changes in both BER and NEER were pointing at the same direction.

Figure 1.2.3 highlights heterogeneity in the relative importance of factors explaining the spreads across economies—and therefore cautions against drawing general conclusions. A closer look at individual country analyses explained in Box 1.2.2 further supports this observation. The role of exchange rates in explaining variations in sovereign bond spreads differed across economies. For example, effects on economies' country risk premiums associated with a stronger US dollar were found to be prominent in the Philippines but less so in India. Effects from depreciation in NEER terms tended to be heterogeneous across economies but with a general tendency to loosen domestic financial conditions.

1.2.4 Decomposition of average monthly changes in sovereign bond spreads in emerging Asia in 2018

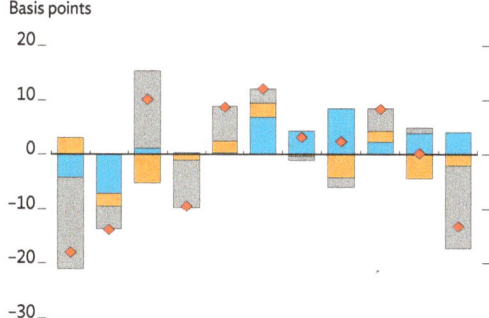

Notes: ADB computation based on Lee, Rosenkranz, and Pham, forthcoming. Regression analysis of eight economies in emerging Asia—India, Indonesia, Malaysia, the People's Republic of China, the Philippines, the Republic of Korea, Singapore, and Thailand—using monthly data from December 2006 to August 2018.

Source: ADB calculations using data from the Bank for International Settlements; Bloomberg; Haver Analytics; International Monetary Fund (accessed 10 January 2019).

Analysis in Box 1.2.2 further suggests the important positive link between the sovereign bond spread and the domestic lending rate, which highlights the connection between the spreads and domestic financial conditions. In general, widening spreads translates into a tightening of domestic credit conditions. However, heterogeneity in country estimates presented in Box 1.2.2 suggests that applying a one-size-fits-all approach for policy prescriptions may not be appropriate, calling instead for country-specific action.

What can the region do?

Despite heterogeneity by country, there are still some general approaches to policy that can be adopted to limit the influence of adverse external conditions on domestic financial systems. Ensuring domestic financial stability is a challenge, especially when external funding conditions are clouded with uncertainty. Experience from past crises like the Asian financial crisis of 1997–1998 and the global financial crisis of 2008–2009 repeatedly highlights the importance of strengthening domestic financial resilience to mitigate negative spillover from changes in global funding conditions.

The analysis here points to the role of smoothing exchange rate fluctuations to reduce uncertainty regarding domestic financial conditions. To this end, both monetary and macroprudential policies need to take into consideration the effects exchange rate movements have on domestic financial conditions through both the financial channel and the trade channel. As such, domestic policies should be coordinated to ensure that they are effective, avoiding potential conflict and undesirable outcomes.

More broadly, further developing and deepening capital markets in the region can provide a better environment for maintaining healthy domestic financial conditions. Expanding the investor base at home and further developing local currency bond markets can dampen unwanted effects from the global financial environment.

To promote better domestic financial resilience and dampen the impact of external funding conditions on domestic financial markets, all these policies should go together with strengthened policy dialogue across borders to monitor macrofinancial conditions, identify systemic risks, and improve regional financing arrangements. Capital flow management measures should also be considered to mitigate disruptive spillover of capital flows in an increasingly interconnected global financial system.

1.2.2 Checking for a feedback effect from sovereign bond spreads

The results from Lee, Rosenkranz, and Pham (forthcoming) reported in Box 1.2.1 was based on a single equation estimation that explained how changes in exchange rates affected sovereign bond spreads. The estimation considered the potential for solving the endogeneity problem and dealt with it through an instrumental variables approach. Therefore, while the analysis reflected how exchange rates affected sovereign bond spreads, it dealt only implicitly with feedback loops to other variables considered in the estimation.

To uncover the feedback to other variables, the present analysis extended the approach in Lee, Rosenkranz, and Pham (forthcoming) by estimating the following vector autoregression with exogenous variables (VAR-X), which is specified exactly according to the logic of equation (1) in Box 1.2.1:

$$Y_t = A(L)Y_t + BX_t + Cu_t$$

Y_t is a vector of domestic endogenous variables that include the change month on month in the local currency sovereign bond spread, the change month on month in the BER against the US dollar, the change month on month in the NEER, consumer price inflation year on year, growth year on year in industrial production, and changes month on month in the domestic lending rate. X_t is a vector of exogenous external indicators used in equation (1) of Box 1.2.1, and u_t is a vector of six residuals that represent relevant shocks to Y_t. The VAR-X is estimated for each of the eight emerging Asian economies considered in Box 1.2.1, and the impulse responses to shocks that alter the exchange rates are identified based on Cholesky decomposition approach, which in this case is insensitive to variable ordering.

On average, an exogenous shock that depreciated the local currency in BER terms by 1% tended to tighten financial conditions by widening sovereign bond spreads by 3.5 basis points in a following month (box figure 1). By contrast, an exogenous shock that depreciated the local currency in NEER terms by 1% was followed by a spread narrowing by 2.0 basis points and a consequent loosening of domestic financial conditions (box figure 2). Qualitatively, this confirmed the results reported in Box 1.2.1, which said that the BER effects on spreads in emerging Asia were dominated by the financial channel, and those of the NEER were dominated by the trade channel. Box figures 1 and 2 highlight, however, differences in the magnitude of effects in different economies. First, effects on sovereign bond spreads following a shock to the US dollar exchange rate tended to be more uniform across economies, with the Philippines having the most pronounced effect. Second, effects resulting in shocks on the NEER appeared to be more heterogeneous across economies. On average, however, results aligned with the single equation estimation. Vector autoregression analysis also highlighted that an exogenous increase in sovereign bond spreads tightened domestic lending conditions by increasing lending rates.

1 Change in the spread between local currency and US bonds following a shock to bilateral exchange rate

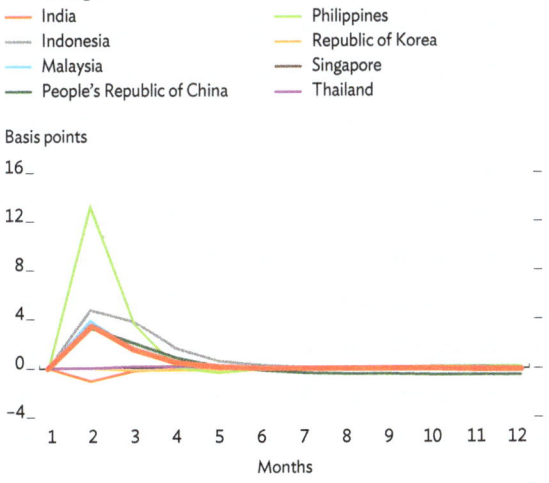

2 Change in the spread between local currency and US bonds following a shock to nominal effective exchange rate

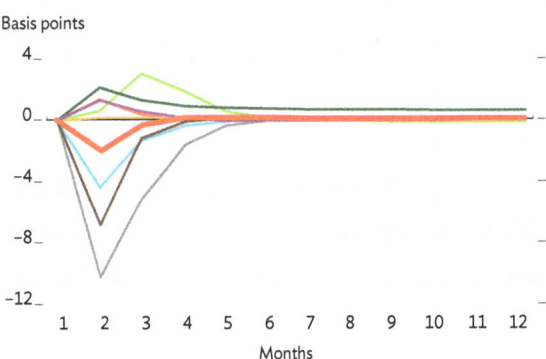

Source: ADB estimates.

Endnotes

1. Traditional analysis of the mechanisms underlying exchange rate movements points to the positive effect of currency depreciation making exports more competitive and encouraging their growth, thereby positively affecting the current account and thus improving domestic financial conditions (Fleming 1962, Mundell 1963). More recent analysis, however, highlights an alternative financial channel. Through it, currency appreciation pushes down the size of foreign debt denominated in local currency, effectively loosening domestic financial conditions and consequently improving the economy's balance sheet position (Borio and Lowe 2002, Reinhart and Reinhart 2009).
2. Sovereign bond spread is defined as the difference between the 5-year sovereign local currency bond yield and the 5-year US Treasury yield (Box 1.2.1).

References

Abiad, A., K. Baris, J. Bernabe, D. Bertulfo, S. Camingue-Romance, P. Feliciano, J. M. Mariasingham, and V. Mercer-Blackman. 2018. The Impact of Trade Conflict on Developing Asia. *ADB Economic Working Paper Series* No. 566. Asian Development Bank. https://www.adb.org/sites/default/files/publication/471496/ewp-566-impact-trade-conflict-asia.pdf.

Borio, C. and P. Lowe. 2002. Assessing the Risk of Banking Crises. *BIS Quarterly Review*. December. Bank for International Settlements.

Fleming, J. M. 1962. Domestic Financial Policies under Fixed and under Floating Exchange Rates. *IMF Staff Papers* 9(3). International Monetary Fund.

Hoffmann, B., I. Shim, and H. S. Shin. 2017. Sovereign Yields and the Risk-taking Channel of Currency Appreciation. *BIS Working Papers* 538. Bank for International Settlements.

Lee, J., P. Rosenkranz, and H. Pham. Forthcoming. The Influence of US Dollar Funding Conditions on Asian Financial Markets. Asian Development Bank.

Mundell, R. A. 1963. Capital Mobility and Stabilization Policy under Fixed and Flexible Exchange Rates. *The Canadian Journal of Economics and Political Science* 29(4).

Reinhart, C. M. and V. R. Reinhart. 2009. Capital Flow Bonanzas: An Encompassing View of the Past and Present. *NBER Working Paper* 14321. National Bureau of Economic Research.

Annex: Dimming global growth prospects

Aggregate growth in the major industrial economies of the United States, the euro area, and Japan moderated somewhat from 2.3% in 2017 to 2.2% in 2018 despite a growth pickup in the US (Table A1.1). Growth is set to continue slowing to the forecast horizon, to 1.9% in 2019 and further to 1.6% in 2020, as less accommodative monetary policy in the US, uncertainty surrounding Brexit, and continued trade tensions weigh on growth. A weakening external sector and waning domestic consumer and business sentiment cloud prospects in Japan.

A1.1 Baseline assumptions on the international economy

	2017	2018	2019	2020
	Actual		ADO 2019 Projection	
GDP growth (%)				
Major industrial economies[a]	2.3	2.2	1.9	1.6
United States	2.2	2.9	2.4	1.9
Euro area	2.5	1.8	1.5	1.5
Japan	1.9	0.8	0.8	0.6
Prices and inflation				
Brent crude spot prices (average, $/barrel)	54.4	71.2	62.0	62.0
Food index (2010 = 100, % change)	0.6	0.3	0.0	1.5
Consumer price index inflation (major industrial economies' average, %)	1.7	2.0	1.9	1.9
Interest rates				
United States federal funds rate (average, %)	1.0	1.8	2.6	2.9
European Central Bank refinancing rate (average, %)	0.0	0.0	0.0	0.0
Bank of Japan overnight call rate (average, %)	-0.1	-0.1	-0.1	-0.1
$ Libor[b] (%)	1.1	1.8	2.6	2.9

ADO = Asian Development Outlook, GDP = gross domestic product.
[a] Average growth rates are weighted by gross national income, Atlas method.
[b] Average London interbank offered rate quotations on 1-month loans.
Sources: US Department of Commerce, Bureau of Economic Analysis, http://www.bea.gov; Eurostat, http://ec.europa.eu/eurostat; Economic and Social Research Institute of Japan, http://www.esri.cao.go.jp; Consensus Forecasts; Bloomberg; CEIC Data Company; Haver Analytics; and the World Bank, Global Commodity Markets, http://www.worldbank.org; ADB estimates.

Recent developments in the major industrial economies

United States

Economic growth greatly accelerated from 2.2% in 2017 to 2.9% in 2018. All components of domestic demand in the US contributed positively to growth, with consumption contributing 1.8 percentage points, investment 1.1 points, and government spending 0.3 points. Thus, domestic demand overwhelmed a slight drag on growth by 0.3 points from net exports. GDP growth in the fourth quarter (Q4) of 2018 was still healthy at a seasonally adjusted annualized rate (saar) of 2.6% but slowed from even higher expansion at 3.4% saar in Q3 (Figure A1.1).

Supporting this strong economic performance, consumption held up well throughout 2018. After disappointing 0.5% expansion in Q1, it jumped by 3.8% in Q2 and 3.5% in Q3, before slowing to 2.8% in Q4. The trend in consumer confidence also turned positive during the year, particularly in the second half, when in October it reached 133.4, its highest reading since September 2000 (Figure A1.2). Retail sales also rose through much of the year, with the index hovering above 130.0.

Private investment growth slowed in Q4 with slower expansion in private inventories. Fixed investment expanded further, as nonresidential fixed investment increased by 6.2% in real terms in Q4 on high growth in equipment and double-digit growth in intellectual property products. The purchasing managers' index (PMI) echoed strong investment figures throughout the year with values well above 50, indicating continued expansion in manufacturing (Figure A1.2). In addition, the industrial production index shows a positive trend and continues to hover above readings recorded in 2007.

However, economic activity tended to decelerate toward the end of 2018. PMI readings declined from as high as about 60 in September–November to 57.6 in December. The decline continued further to 56.7 in January 2019, but the PMI bounced back to 59.1 in February, putting into question the belief of many that production growth was starting to slow in the US. A similar pattern was observed on the consumption side. Retail sales slowed in December 2018 in tandem with declining consumer confidence. The consumer confidence index continued to decline to 117.7 in January 2019 but sharply reversed to 127.1 in February. The PMI and consumer confidence figures still suggest, therefore, continuing expansion of private spending in the US, at least to Q1 of 2019, particularly in view of a relatively strong recent outturn in the labor market.

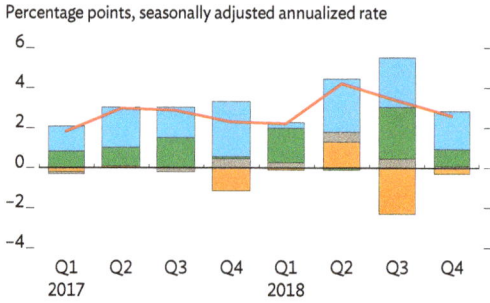

A1.1 Demand-side contributions to growth, United States

Q = quarter.
Sources: US Department of Commerce. Bureau of Economic Analysis. http://www.bea.gov; Haver Analytics (both accessed 1 March 2019).

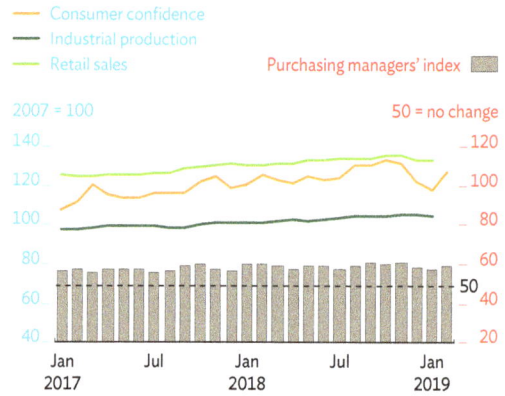

A1.2 Business activity and consumer confidence indicators, United States

Note: A purchasing managers' index reading <50 signals deterioration, >50 improvement.
Source: Haver Analytics (accessed 12 March 2019).

The labor market trended positive throughout 2018 and into 2019, though nonfarm jobs increased by only 20,000 in February after surging to 227,000 in December 2018 and 311,000 in January 2019. A rapid increase in labor force participation beginning in December 2018 took unemployment to 4.0% in January 2019, but the rate eased back to 3.8% in February. The average duration of unemployment remained at 20–22 weeks in the 3 months to February 2019, an improvement from 23–24 weeks a year earlier (Figure A1.3). Average worker earnings also rose steadily in the first 2 months of 2019. All in all, current trends suggest that continuing income growth will lend support to further expansion in domestic spending.

Inflation continued to ease as lower energy prices brought headline inflation down from 1.9% in December 2018 to 1.6% in January 2019. Meanwhile, core inflation has remained above 2.0% (Figure A1.4). Headline inflation may pick up with dissipation of the effects of lower oil prices, though, and somewhat higher core inflation may persist given current low unemployment and rising wages. That said, the inflation rate is not seen rising significantly in the near future, especially as slowing global growth may sap some momentum in the US.

In this situation, the Federal Reserve is seen to have less appetite for raising its benchmark policy interest rate, suggesting a more gradual increase this year than last. The already higher interest rate will, with the waning of fiscal stimulus and slower growth prospects for the global economy, at least tap the brakes on US growth in the months ahead. However, continuing strong consumer confidence, wage increases, and further expansion in production as suggested by the PMI support a growth forecast of 2.4% in 2019—still strong but considerably down from 2018, perhaps partly reflecting the 35-day partial government shutdown from 22 December 2018. Growth is projected to slow further to 1.9% in 2020. This suggests more moderate inflation to the forecast horizon, projected to average 2.2% in 2019 and 2.1% in 2020. Risks to growth projections are mostly on the downside.

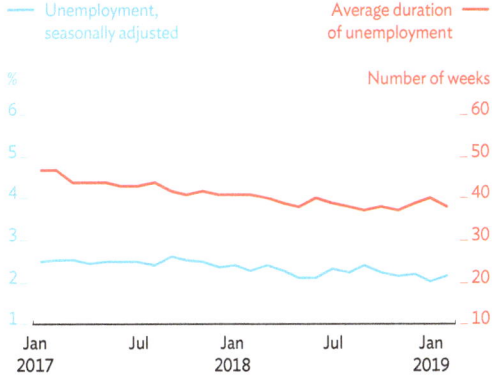

A1.3 Unemployment rate and average duration, United States

Source: Haver Analytics (accessed 12 March 2019).

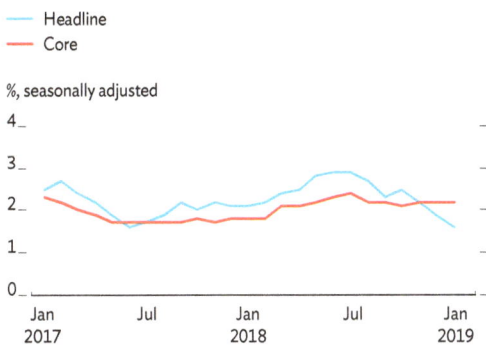

A1.4 Inflation, United States

Source: Haver Analytics (accessed 1 March 2019).

Euro area

After growth slowed to 0.9% saar in Q4, full-year data confirm that growth in the euro area slowed from 2.5% in 2017 to 1.8% in 2018. The slowdown reflects a broad decline in most GDP components. Fixed investment was the exception as supportive financing conditions propelled its growth from 2.9% in 2017 to 3.1% in 2018, when it contributed 0.6 percentage points to growth. Growth in private spending weakened from 1.8% in 2017 to 1.3%, restrained by cautious consumer sentiment, but it still contributed 0.7 percentage points to growth.

Growth in government consumption also softened, from 1.2% to 1.0%, for a contribution of 0.2 percentage points. Externally, a firm euro and slower global trade in the past year weighed on growth in net exports, which dropped from 22.4% in 2017 to 4.7% in 2018, also contributing 0.2 percentage points to GDP growth (Figure A1.5).

Consistent with the weaker outturn for the whole euro area, economic growth is marked down for several economies within it. In Germany, GDP growth dropped from 2.5% in 2017 to 1.5% in 2018 under drag imposed by the external sector. In Italy, growth softened from 1.7% in 2017 to 0.8% in 2018, mainly because of weak domestic demand and higher borrowing costs. In France, economic expansion slowed from 2.3% in 2017 to 1.5% against a difficult political backdrop. Other economies in the region also slowed as both Spain and the Netherlands shaved half a percentage point off their 2017 growth rates to expand by 2.5% in 2018. Economic growth weakened in Portugal from 2.8% to 2.1%, and in Belgium from 1.7% to 1.4%.

The growth forecast for the euro area as a whole is downgraded to 1.5% in both 2019 and 2020, weighed down by weakening economic sentiment, less favorable external developments, and sluggish growth in key trade partners. Domestic demand looks set to support continued growth, albeit at a lower rate than in 2018. Consumer spending will go some way toward sustaining activity, shored up by a tighter labor market and a more positive jobs outlook. Investment is also set to drive growth, buoyed by favorable financing conditions. Continuing accommodative monetary policy and expansionary fiscal measures—notably in France and Germany—will help buttress economic activity in the European currency bloc.

Early indicators suggest the euro area entered 2019 on a sour note. The downbeat data observed in the past year has persisted into 2019, signaling a slower growth path for the region. Surveys of economic sentiment remained in positive territory but deteriorated notably throughout 2018, ending the year at 107.4 in December and weakening further to 106.3 in January and to 106.1 in February. The PMI improved slightly from 50.7 in January, the lowest reading since July 2013, to 51.4 in February (Figure A1.6). After its sharpest plunge in over 2 years in November 2018, industrial production rebounded slightly in December but continues to indicate contraction. And, indeed, broad-based contraction was observed in November in 11 euro economies, including the 4 largest (Figure A1.7).

A tightening labor market is providing some lift to aggregate demand in the euro area. The unemployment rate fell to 7.8% in January, the lowest since the global financial crisis of 2008–2009. Unemployment rates fell in France, Germany, and Spain but inched up in Italy and Portugal.

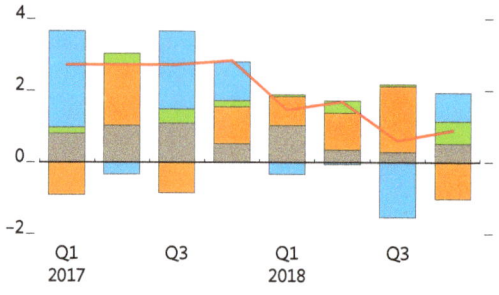

A1.5 Demand-side contributions to growth, euro area

Source: Haver Analytics (accessed 8 March 2019).

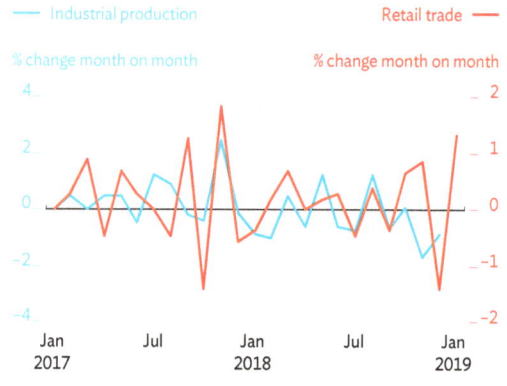

A1.6 Selected economic indicators, euro area

Source: Haver Analytics (accessed 8 March 2019).

Wage growth increased from 2.3% in Q2 of 2018 to 2.5% in Q3, which may spur inflation over the coming months.

Headline inflation cooled from 1.5% year on year in December 2018 to 1.4% the following month as the effects of higher oil prices in the past year faded. Core inflation inched up from 1.1% year on year in December to 1.2% in January. Consumer price inflation averaged 1.7% in 2018, well within the European Central Bank target of below 2.0%. The central bank left interest rates unchanged in January and reiterated guidance that it will keep rates at current levels until the end of summer in Q3 of 2019. Even so, inflation is seen to pick up only gradually as the year progresses, not enough to raise the inflation forecast for 2019 and 2020 above this year's rate of 1.7%.

Risks to the outlook tilt to the downside. Economic prospects in the region are muted by trade policy uncertainty and weakening sentiment in financial markets. The threat of new tariffs remains a possibility that could make net exports an even heavier drag on growth in the euro area. Disruption from a no-deal Brexit, or prolonged uncertainty if the matter is further delayed, became more likely as British lawmakers voted down the Prime Minister's proposals for a withdrawal agreement three times in January and March. The specter of a populist surge in May 2019 elections for the European Parliament raises the possibility of a Europe disunited over some members' quest for radical changes to institute more flexible rules.

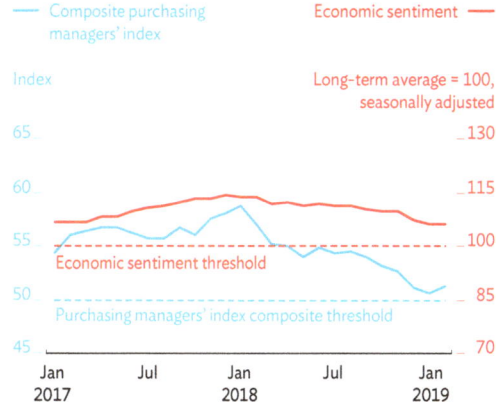

A1.7 Economic sentiment and purchasing managers' indexes, euro area

Sources: Bloomberg; Haver Analytics (both accessed 8 March 2019).

Japan

A growth streak continued, however modestly, at 0.8% in 2018. The year ended on a positive note on the back of a recovery in domestic demand, but output contractions in Q1 and Q3 dragged annual growth down from the 1.9% rate recorded in 2017 (Figure A1.8). The performance was enfeebled by weakness in the all-important external sector, with net exports weighing on growth in the last 3 quarters, and by natural disasters that disrupted activity in Q3. Private consumption and investment were choppy as slumps in 2 quarters alternated with rebounds in the others. While government consumption boosted growth to a limited extent, public investment dragged it down throughout the year.

Other recent indicators suggest that a recovery in domestic demand is fragile, particularly in business investment. Industrial production fell for a third consecutive month in January 2019, by a steep 3.7% (Figure A1.9). Further, the Nikkei manufacturing PMI fell sharply from 50.3 in January to 48.9 in February. This sends the index below the 50-point threshold that indicates contraction in manufacturing and is the lowest reading since July 2016.

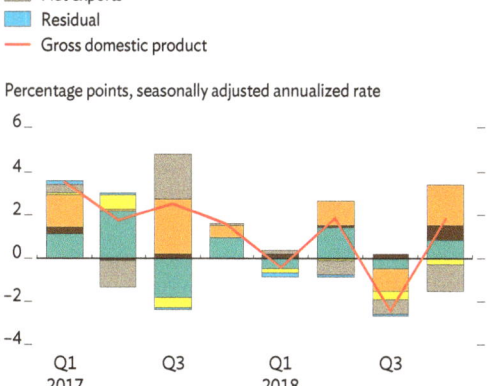

A1.8 Demand-side contributions to growth, Japan

Q = quarter.
Source: Economics and Social Research Institute, Cabinet Office, Government of Japan. http://www.esri.cao.go.jp (accessed 8 March 2019).

Contraction in January in core machinery orders, considered a leading indicator for capital expenditure over a couple of quarters, similarly suggests that recent gains in investment may be slipping away.

On the consumption side, seasonally adjusted retail sales declined in January by a sharp 2.3% month on month, reversing a 0.9% increase in the previous month. The consumer confidence index, having shown a weakening trend since the start of 2018, fell further in February to a 2-year low of 40.9 on a scale of 0–100 measuring consumers' expectations for their living standards over the next 6 months. Sluggish spending and a pessimistic outlook could reflect concerns about job prospects, as the January unemployment rate edged up slightly to 2.5%. While sales may surge ahead of a planned sales tax hike in October, and may enjoy additional support from expenditure related to the 2020 Olympics, prevailing consumer thrift could be exacerbated by the end of the year as consumers cut back on purchases after the higher sales tax takes effect.

Despite a tight labor market, wage gains have been lackluster, and price pressures have built only slowly. Consumer price inflation was steady at 0.2% year on year in January 2019, while core inflation excluding energy and fresh food crept up in the same month from 0.1% in December to 0.3% in January. With inflation remaining well below the target of 2.0%, the Bank of Japan decided at its last meeting to continue expanding the monetary base and keep its policy rates low, with the short-term rate at −0.1% and the yield of the 10-year government bond within a narrow band around zero.

Merchandise exports declined in January 2019 for a third consecutive month, by 6.9% year on year, the sharpest decline in 36 months (Figure A1.10). This reflected low demand for machinery and transport equipment in the People's Republic of China (PRC). Import growth also weakened in the same month, to 1.0%, and the trade deficit ballooned from $496 million in December 2018 to $13.0 billion.

The Japanese economy having headed into 2019 with a slow start amid concerns over a global slowdown, full-year growth is expected to moderate. Consumption demand in early 2019 may improve ahead of the upcoming tax hike from 8% to 10% in October, but the impact is expected to be smaller than from a hike in April 2014, which was by a full 3 percentage points. The government plans to implement measures to counter the negative impact of the hike and to bolster spending in 2020, which may avoid a sharp plunge as was seen after the 2014 hike. Nonetheless, as trade tensions continue to threaten global trade and growth, and as domestic business sentiment wanes, the forecast for 2019 is a cautious 0.8%, downgraded to 0.6% for 2020.

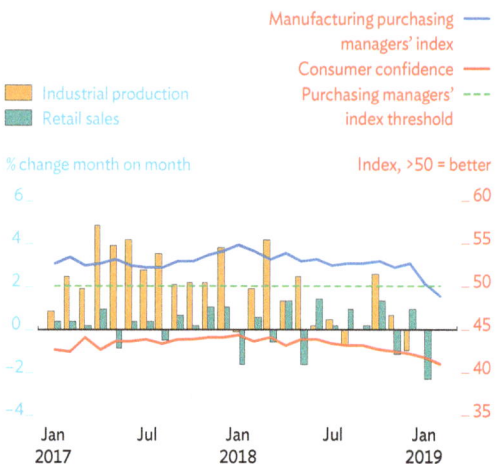

A1.9 Consumption and business indicators, Japan

Notes: A purchasing managers' index reading <50 signals deterioration, >50 improvement. A consumer confidence reading >50 signals better conditions. Data on industrial production are in quarters.
Sources: Haver Analytics; Bloomberg (both accessed 7 March 2019).

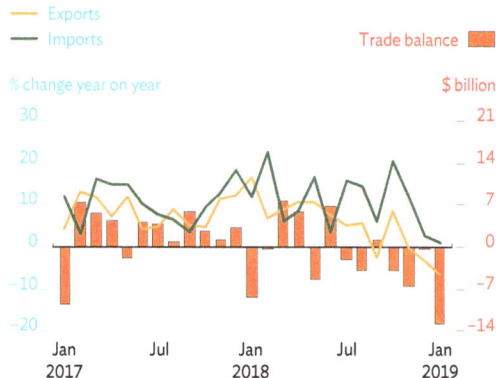

A1.10 Trade indicators, Japan

Sources: Haver Analytics; Bloomberg (both accessed 7 March 2019).

Recent developments and outlook in other economies

Australia

GDP slowed from 1.1% saar in Q3 of 2018 to 0.7% in Q4 of 2018 because of weak demand at home and abroad (Figure A1.11). Consumption was the largest contributor to growth, adding 2.3 percentage points. Changes in inventory contributed 0.6 points as fixed capital formation subtracted 1.0 point and net exports subtracted another 0.7 points. Seasonally adjusted retail sales grew in January 2019 by 0.1% month on month, down from average monthly growth of 0.2% in 2017 and 2018. The consumer sentiment index stayed in 2018 above the 100-point threshold that indicates optimism, slipped marginally to 99.6 in January, then recovered to 103.8 in February. The business confidence index, which subtracts the percentage of pessimists from that of optimists, fell in December to a 12-month low of 2.7, still above the zero threshold and improving to 3.6 the following month. The seasonally adjusted unemployment rate improved from an average of 5.6% in 2017 to 5.3% in 2018. The Australian Industry Group's manufacturing performance index ended 2018 at the threshold of 50 that separates expansion in manufacturing from contraction, but it climbed in the next 2 months to 54 in February.

Inflation declined steadily from 2.1% in Q2 to 1.8% in Q4, moving below the target range of 2.0%–3.0% set by the Reserve Bank of Australia, the central bank. In its 5 March 2019 monetary policy meeting, the board of the central bank decided to leave the cash rate unchanged at a low 1.50% to continue to support the economy. With income tax cuts approved by the Senate in mid-June, positive consumer sentiment, and a significant increase in employment sustaining private spending, consumption is expected to continue as the main driver of economic growth. Indications of stable economic growth include expansion in manufacturing, measures of business confidence reflecting optimism about future economic conditions, and a robust labor market. FocusEconomics panelists predict GDP to expand by 2.7% in 2019 and 2.6% in 2020, bolstered by robust commodity exports and favorable financing conditions to support stronger business investment outside of the large mining industry.

A1.11 Demand-side contributions to growth, Australia

Consumption
Change in inventories
Gross fixed capital formation
Net exports
— Gross domestic product

Percentage points, seasonally adjusted annualized rate

Q = quarter.
Source: CEIC Data Company (accessed 7 March 2019).

New Zealand

Economic expansion slowed from 4.4% saar in Q2 of 2018 to 1.9% in Q3 with weaker exports and contraction in government consumption and fixed capital formation. Consumption was the top contributor to growth, adding 1.7 percentage points while net exports contributed 0.7 points. Change in inventories subtracted 1.2 points, and fixed capital formation deducted 0.9 points (Figure A1.12). Retail sales expansion accelerated from 4.0% in Q3 to 4.5% in Q4. The seasonally adjusted performance of manufacturing index slipped from 54.8 in December 2018 to 53.1 in January 2019 but still indicated expansion by staying above the threshold of 50. The business confidence index sank deeper into negative territory, from –24.1 in December to –30.9 in February. However, consumer confidence climbed from 103.5 in Q3 of 2018 to 109.1 in Q4, both values above 100 and indicating optimism.

Inflation was stable at 1.9% in the last 2 quarters of 2018, still within the target range of 1.0%–3.0% set by the Reserve Bank of New Zealand, the central bank. The seasonally adjusted unemployment rate rose from 4.0% in Q3 of 2018 to 4.3% in Q4. On 13 February 2019, the central bank announced that the official cash rate would remain at a record low of 1.75%. Consumer optimism, a low policy interest rate, and only moderate inflation continue to boost private consumption, as shown by increasing retail sales. Potential dampening factors are the rise in unemployment and a projected slowdown in fixed investment under tighter financial conditions and imminent changes to bank capital requirements. FocusEconomics panelists forecast growth at 2.7% in 2019, slowing to 2.5% in 2020, with exports expected to be weaker in the near term as slowing in the PRC reduces demand for dairy products, New Zealand's major export.

Russian Federation

In developing Asia's vast northern neighbor, GDP growth accelerated from 1.6% in 2017 to 2.3% in 2018, the highest rate in 6 years (Figure A1.13). This reflected thriving construction at home and an improved external sector, with net exports reversing 44.1% contraction in 2017 to grow by 27.4% in 2018. All demand components contributed positively to growth, with consumption in the lead, adding 1.3 percentage points, as net exports contributed 0.8 points and capital formation 0.4 points. Industrial production improved on 2.1% growth in 2017 with 2.9% expansion in 2018. Although the Markit manufacturing PMI declined from 51.7 in December 2018 to 50.9 in January, it remained above the threshold of 50 indicating expansion. The average consumer confidence reading in 2018 was negative, but only a quarter as bad as the worst-ever reading in Q4 of 1998. Retail sales also reflect improving consumer sentiment as growth more than doubled from 1.2% in 2017 to 2.6%.

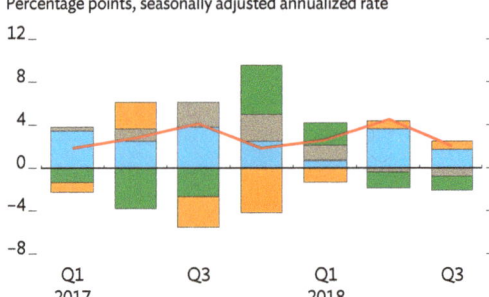

A1.12 Demand-side contributions to growth, New Zealand

Q = quarter.
Source: CEIC Data Company (accessed 7 March 2019).

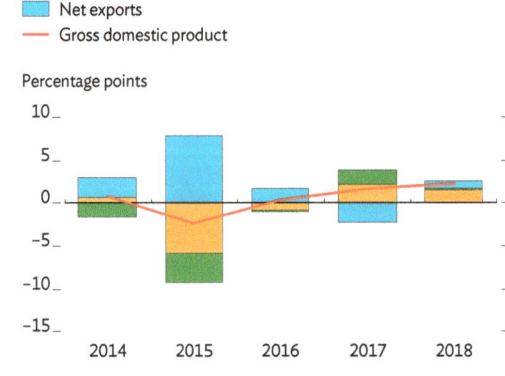

A1.13 Demand-side contributions to growth, the Russian Federation

Source: CEIC Data Company (accessed 7 March 2019).

Average inflation eased from 3.7% in 2017 to 2.9% in 2018, and unemployment improved from 5.2% to 4.8%. On 14 December 2018, the Central Bank of the Russian Federation raised its key policy rate from 7.50% to 7.75% on the expectation that prices could spike in the wake of ruble depreciation and a 2019 hike in the value-added tax. In 8 February 2019, the central bank decided to keep the key rate unchanged as the balance of risks remained tipped toward inflation. FocusEconomics panelists expect growth to moderate to 1.4% in 2019 with constrained oil production, the value-added tax hike, tight financial conditions, and uncertainty over economic sanctions. The panels predict growth recovering to 1.7% in 2020.

Commodity prices

Average commodity prices continued to rise in 2018, albeit at a much slower pace than in the previous year. Economic and geopolitical developments caused wide fluctuations in oil prices in 2018, taking them to 4-year highs in early October before they started declining again in November. Oil prices are forecast to remain below $70/barrel as upward price pressure stemming from reduced output by members of the Organization of the Petroleum Exporting Countries (OPEC) is tempered by downward pressure from higher output outside of OPEC and by global growth concerns. The food price index is expected to be little changed in 2019 and to rise by just under 2% in 2020, owing mainly to lower energy costs and adequate supply.

Oil price movements and prospects

Brent crude finished 2018 at $53/barrel, or almost $14/barrel lower than at the end of 2017 (Figure A1.14). The US decision to allow eight countries to continue purchasing Iranian oil after its implementation of sanctions on 4 November 2018 sent oil prices into a downward spiral. At the same time, the world's top three oil producers—Saudi Arabia, the Russian Federation, and the US—pumped volumes close to all-time highs, placing further downward pressure on prices. On the demand side, concern over anemic growth prospects in the euro area, Japan, and the PRC weighed on prices.

A1.14 Price of Brent crude

Sources: Bloomberg; World Bank. Commodity Price Data (Pink Sheet). http://www.worldbank.org (both accessed 8 March 2019).

After brief respite toward the end of last year, crude oil prices increased throughout January and February and into March as global oil stocks shrank. Brent crude oil breached the $60/barrel mark in mid-January and has stayed above it since then. The Brent crude average in the year to the first week of March was $61.90/barrel. According to the International Energy Agency, oil price increases are not yet alarming because the market is still getting rid of surpluses built up in the second half of 2018, when global supply exceeded demand by an estimated 1.3 million barrels/day (mbd).

In 2018, global oil supply rose by 2.6 mbd, more than 5 times the increase in 2017. As in the previous year, the US accounted for most of the increase as its crude oil production grew by 1.6 mbd (with rounding) from 9.4 mbd in 2017 to 10.9 mbd in 2018, while supply from OPEC fell by 0.1 mbd. Meanwhile, growth in world oil demand slowed by a quarter, from a 1.6 mbd increase in 2017 to 1.2 mbd in 2018. With oil supply increasing faster than demand, global oil inventories increased by 0.8 mbd in 2018, reversing year's inventory drawdown.

The International Energy Agency report *Oil 2019* predicted a gradual rebalancing of the oil market in 2019. Growth in global oil demand is forecast to be 1.4 mbd in 2019, or 0.1 mbd higher than estimated growth in 2018. For world oil supply, the swing factor will still be US production. The US Energy Information Agency forecasts US crude oil production to average 12.4 mbd in 2019 and 13.2 mbd in 2020. According to the agency, growth in domestic production will offset forecast decreases in OPEC production to the forecast horizon. Meanwhile, OPEC continues its efforts to drain the global oil glut and support prices. OPEC's oil output fell in February to a 4-year low as member countries, especially Saudi Arabia, overdelivered on the group's cutback agreement. Meanwhile, output from Venezuela and Iraq continued to decline, and 0.3 mbd remained offline in Libya because of a shutdown at El Sharara, the country's largest oilfield.

Opposing factors will keep Brent crude oil prices volatile. Support for oil prices will come from the forecast increase in global oil demand, agreed oil production cuts, and economic and geopolitical tensions that impinge on oil production and trade. Upward price pressure will come as well from the implementation of the International Maritime Organization's 0.50% global sulfur cap for marine fuels on 1 January 2020, especially for Brent and West Texas intermediate crude, which have relatively low sulfur content. Upward pressure on Brent crude prices will be tempered, however, by concerns about slowing global economic growth, further strengthening of the US dollar, the resumption of oil production in Libya from El Sharara, and higher US crude oil production. The futures market shows Brent crude trading above $60/barrel to the forecast horizon (Figure A1.15). Barring major supply disruptions, the price of Brent crude is forecast to average $62/barrel in both 2019 and 2020.

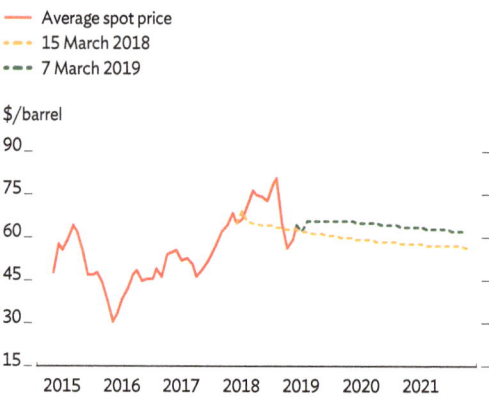

A1.15 Brent crude futures and spot prices

Sources: Bloomberg; World Bank. Commodity Price Data (Pink Sheet). http://www.worldbank.org (both accessed 8 March 2019).

Food price movements and prospects

Food prices, as measured by the World Bank food price index, increased by 0.3% in 2018 (Figure A1.16). Apart from grain, the other two indexes used to calculate the index fell in 2018.

The retreat in the edible oil index came primarily as international palm oil prices dropped by 15% because of persistently large inventories in the leading exporters. At the same time, soybean oil values weakened with abundant supplies across the European Union, the US, and several emerging markets, as well as positive production prospects near the Black Sea. Similarly, the "other food" category fell by 3.2% in 2018 with a continued glut-driven decline in the price of sugar, the commodity with the highest weight in the index, and an easing of meat prices because of increased production.

Meanwhile, grain prices increased by 10.2% last year. The grain index trended upward in 2018, with wheat and maize prices higher in Q4. Wheat prices benefited from weather disturbances, especially in Australia, the Russian Federation, and Ukraine, as did maize prices from robust demand. By contrast, rice prices dropped in the second half of 2018 as bountiful harvests, competition among exporters, and currency movements weighed on them. These price movements have continued into 2019, pushing the food price index down by 5.0% year on year in the first 2 months of the year.

The latest forecasts in a March 2019 report from the US Department of Agriculture show global grain production reaching 2,606.5 million tons in the current 2018/19 crop season, which is lower than the previous crop year estimate but still higher than the 5-year average. The outlook for edible oil remains favorable, with the US Department of Agriculture forecasting higher production and exports in 2018/19 and higher stocks at the end of the year.

According to a 26 February update from the World Meteorological Organization, there is a 50%–60% chance that El Niño will recur by May 2019, though it is expected to be not as strong as in 2015 and 2016. In any case, it is notable that current and past El Niño weather disturbances show only a weak link with global food prices, as reported in *ADO 2016*: Food prices first dropped by 16.6% in 2015 before rising by 1.3% in 2016. With ample supplies of major agricultural commodities and energy prices low, the forecast El Niño is unlikely to cause global food prices to spike. In view of recent deep declines in food commodity prices, and of mostly subdued oil prices, the food commodity price index is forecast to remain unchanged in 2019 before rising by 1.5% in 2020.

There are several risks to the forecasts, key among them more adverse weather, oil price volatility, worsening trade frictions, domestic support policies, and further currency depreciation hitting commodity exporters.

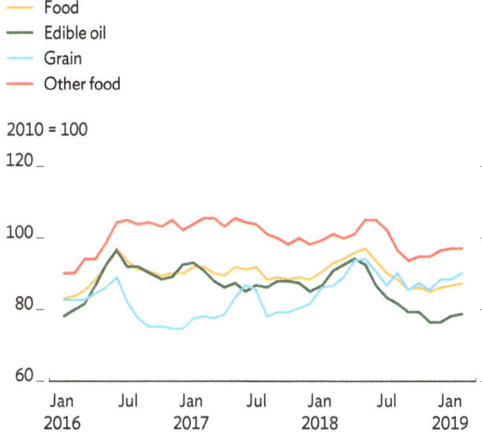

A1.16 Food commodity price indexes

Source: World Bank. Commodity Price Data (Pink Sheet). http://www.worldbank.org (accessed 8 March 2019).

2 STRENGTHENING DISASTER RESILIENCE

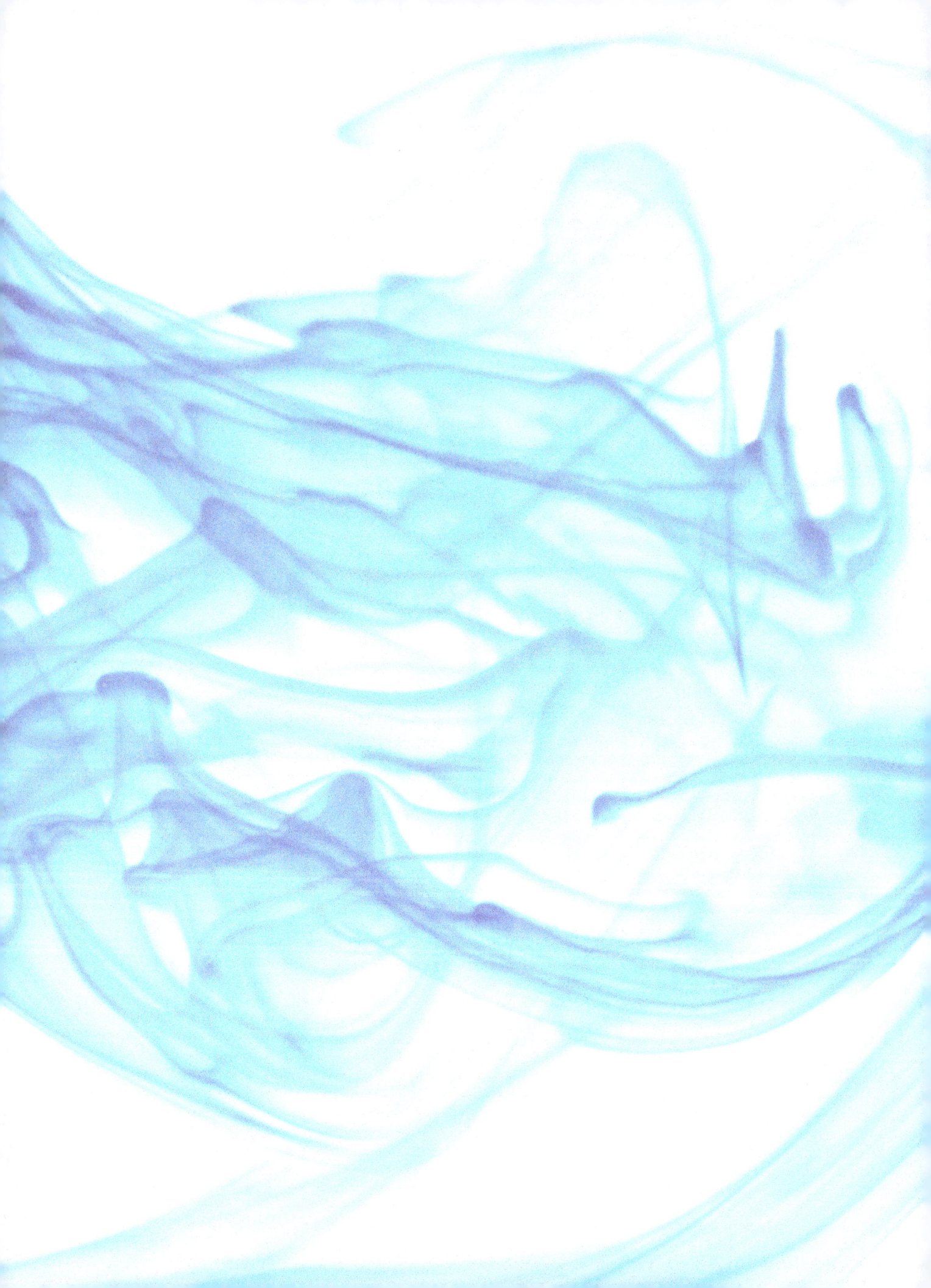

Strengthening disaster resilience

Over the past half century, developing Asia has transformed from one of the world's poorest regions to its center of economic gravity. Almost all Asian economies are now at least middle income, yet they are also among the most heavily affected by natural hazards that become disasters and the most exposed to the consequences of climate change. More than four in five people affected by such disasters from 2000 to 2018 lived in developing Asia.

Although advanced and developing countries alike are exposed to various types of disaster risk, the consequences tend to be more severe in developing countries, where disasters disproportionally affect the poor and marginalized. Understanding and addressing disaster risk in developing Asia, where it has become a growing threat to development and prosperity, has thus become a critical challenge in research, policy, and practice.

The causes and consequences of disasters do not exist in isolation, however, but are bound up instead in the ongoing dynamics of the economy, society, and environment in which they occur. As such, comprehensively understanding the impact of disasters requires understanding their complexity.

The context in which disasters occur tends to be highly dynamic. Disasters are the result of the complex interactions between human actions and natural hazards. Many of the drivers of vulnerability and exposure to natural hazards can be found in underlying socioeconomic attributes and trends: poverty and inequality, demographic change, urbanization, governance structures, infrastructure investments, and the unsustainable use of natural resources and ecosystems. Climate change and climate variability intensify disaster risk by changing the frequency, intensity, and timing of extreme events, as well as the size of the area affected (IPCC 2012).

This chapter was written by Benno Ferrarini of the Economic Research and Regional Cooperation Department, ADB, Manila; Thomas McDermott of the National University of Ireland–Galway; and Ilan Noy of Victoria University of Wellington. It draws on the background papers listed at the end of the chapter. The contribution from Charlotte Benson of the Sustainable Development and Climate Change Department is gratefully acknowledged. Other contributions are listed in the Acknowledgments section.

The impacts of disasters are highly diverse. They affect different individuals and social groups in different ways, and they may extend well beyond the here and now. When disaster impacts spill across space and time, they may be either restrained or amplified through social and economic networks, migration, remittances, and production supply chains. They may be influenced by market mechanisms that operate through insurance or supply chains; government action in the form of infrastructure investment, early warning systems, and recovery assistance; and the actions of individuals as they relocate and migrate; or of communities as they reinforce social networks and build social capital.

Looking on the bright side in the aftermath of a disaster, the recovery phase is often a window of opportunity to learn from experience, mitigate future vulnerability and exposure, and enhance resilience. It is important, in a world where extreme weather events are expected to become more frequent and severe, that policy makers and affected communities resolve to "build back better." As this chapter shows, a new approach to opportunity in the wake of a disaster distinguishes four main objectives: building back for a safer community, building back faster to sustain individual and community well-being, building back more inclusively for a fairer society, and building back for more social and economic potential in the future.

Natural hazards putting Asia's prosperity at risk

Developing economies across Asia are among the most dynamic in the world. However, they are also among the most vulnerable to natural hazards, such as storms, floods, droughts, tsunamis, and earthquakes, and to the impacts of climate change, such as sea-level rise, coastal erosion, and extreme temperatures.

The impacts of disasters—either direct effects that cause fatalities, render people homeless or displaced, and wreak economic damage, or indirect effects that hamper economic growth, development, and poverty reduction—all exhibit distinct relationships with the underlying drivers of disaster risk: hazard types, the exposure of population and assets, vulnerability, and socioeconomic resilience (Box 2.1.1).

2.1.1 Disasters are hazards combined with a society's exposure and vulnerability

A disaster occurs when a hazard interacts with an exposed and vulnerable population, harming people and damaging physical assets such as property and infrastructure (box figure). Hazards can be natural, such as tropical storms and earthquakes, or man-made, such as industrial failures and nuclear accidents. This chapter focuses on disasters that are triggered by natural hazards. They can occur with little or no warning, or they can occur slowly over a span of days, weeks, months, or years. A hazard by itself need not constitute a disaster, as it must combine with a society's exposure and vulnerability to turn into a disaster. As such, no disaster is purely natural.

Disaster impacts can be direct and indirect. Direct impacts include damage to fixed assets and capital, including inventories; lost raw materials, crops, and natural resources; and death, injury, and disease. Indirect impacts are lost economic activity, in particular the production of new goods and services that will not take place following a disaster. Losses can be further divided between the short term, from a few months up to several years, and the long term, until reconstruction and recovery are complete.

Types of disaster impact

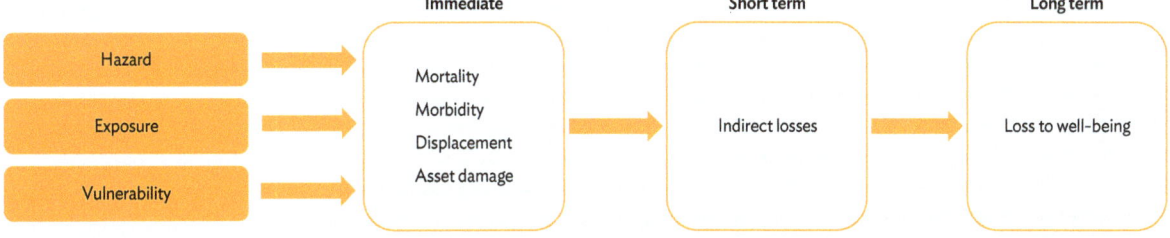

Notes: **Hazard** refers to the physical phenomena that can trigger disasters, including such weather-related phenomena as temperatures, rainfall, wind speed, and storm surges, or such geophysical phenomena as seismic activity. **Exposure** refers to the population and economic, social, cultural, and environmental assets located in areas that experience these physical hazards. **Vulnerability** refers to the outcomes experienced in terms of human, social, and economic impacts from a given hazard and degree of exposure to hazards. Higher vulnerability permits a more adverse outcome for the same intensity of hazard and exposure.
Source: Noy, Ferrarini, and Park, forthcoming, based on Noy 2016a.

2.1.2 Indonesia's three large disasters in 2018

In July and August 2018, the island of Lombok in West Nusa Tenggara Province of Indonesia experienced weeks of tremors before suffering a series of devastating earthquakes. Hundreds of people died, and thousands more were injured and displaced. In September, a magnitude 7.4 earthquake in a different part of Indonesia triggered a tsunami that struck the coast of Central Sulawesi. The earthquake triggered landslides and soil liquefaction in several densely populated districts, burying entire villages. In December, Anak Karakatoa, a small volcano in the Sunda Strait, erupted and generated a sudden tsunami that hit the densely populated coasts of Java and Sumatra on either side of the strait.

In these three events, more than 3,000 people were confirmed dead and more than 700,000 people were injured or displaced (box table). Homes, schools, hospitals, irrigation systems, and hundreds of kilometers of roads suffered extensive damage. Along the coasts of Central Sulawesi, Java, and Sumatra, tsunamis destroyed fishing vessels, ports, warehouses, and refrigeration facilities. Initial damage reports from the National Disaster Management Agency indicate damage and losses of $950 million for Central Sulawesi and $1.3 billion for West Nusa Tenggara. Damage in the Sunda Strait disaster was estimated at $22.7 million by Maipark Indonesia Reinsurance Data, a reinsurance company.

Initial estimates suggest that growth in Central Sulawesi's 2018 gross regional product slowed by 3.6 percentage points, cutting growth by half. In West Nusa Tenggara, the effects of the earthquakes are estimated to have cut the gross regional product growth rate by 1.6 percentage points (box figure, left panel). In both cases, the local economies are expected to take several years to recover to pre-disaster trends.

The incidence of poverty is expected to increase in both areas, to 16.4% in Central Sulawesi and 16.8% in West Nusa Tenggara, reversing the trend toward lower poverty incidence in the affected provinces before the disasters (box figure, right panel). The disasters will likely push the poor deeper into poverty, as job prospects are significantly reduced in the wake of the disaster. In Central Sulawesi, the number of jobs in agriculture, fisheries, and mining shrank, driving more workers into the informal economy. Primary irrigation channels were damaged, with immediate consequences for farmers. Wide stretches of coastline were rendered unusable for aquaculture, and marine life will be slow to recover. The Lombok earthquakes had major adverse effects on tourism and the people employed in the industry either formally and informally.

Fiscal adjustments will be required nationally and locally to meet disaster recovery needs. The economic and social costs of the recent disasters, which could exceed $2.8 billion, have significantly intensified fiscal pressure on the Government of Indonesia. It immediately mobilized resources for relief and rescue efforts, but funding recovery in the affected areas will be more fiscally challenging as it competes with other spending priorities. The government is seeking to address a remaining gap in the annual budget allocation for disaster response and is evaluating sustainable options for disaster risk mitigation and financing.

Disasters, damage, and losses

Effects	Lombok	Central Sulawesi	Sunda Strait
Deaths	515	2,081	437
Injured	7,733	11,000	14,059
Missing	0	1,309	16
Displaced	431,416	206,494	33,719
Damaged houses	76,765	68,451	2,752
Damaged health facilities	360	45	...

... = data not available.
Sources: Asian Development Bank; ASEAN Coordinating Centre for Humanitarian Assistance on disaster management (AHA Centre). https://ahacentre.org/ (accessed 21 February 2019).

Simulated impact on regional economic growth and poverty rates (%)

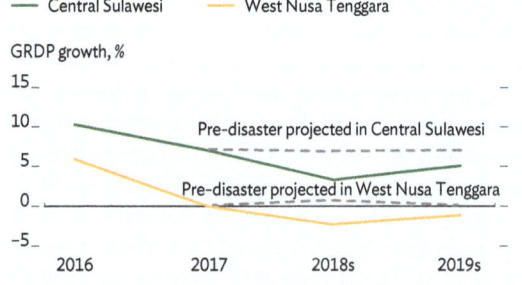
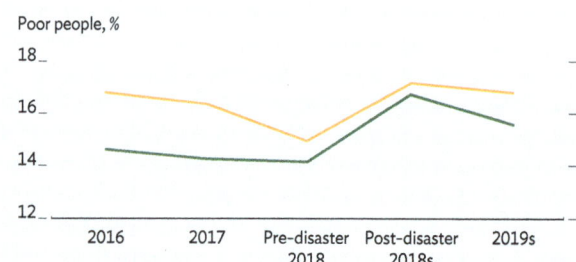

GRDP = gross regional domestic product, s = simulation.
Source: Based on ADB 2018a, with updates.

The high human cost of disasters

In absolute terms, disaster impacts are concentrated in larger, higher-income, hazard-exposed economies, where there are greater concentrations of people and economic assets in locations exposed to hazards. However, higher incomes and better-quality institutions tend to reduce vulnerability (Fankhauser and McDermott 2014), with the benefits of higher income particularly pronounced in reduced mortality (Kahn 2005).

While advanced and developing countries alike are exposed to various types of disaster risks, the consequences—particularly in terms of fatalities and economic impacts—tend to be much more severe in developing countries, affecting poor and marginalized people disproportionately. This was borne out most recently through the experience of three Indonesian disasters in 2018 (Box 2.1.2).

These general observations are reflected in the data from the Emergency Events Database (EM-DAT) on recent disaster impacts across developing Asia, which is by far the world region most heavily affected by disasters in terms of human impact (Box 2.1.3). From 2000 to 2018, developing Asia was home to 84% of the 206 million people affected by disasters globally on average each year. It also accounted for almost 55% of 60,000 disaster fatalities worldwide. The most catastrophic disasters since 1990 have caused fatalities in almost every corner of Asia, but especially in East and South Asia (Figure 2.1.1). Even in global aggregates, catastrophes in Bangladesh in 1991, Indonesia in 2004, Pakistan in 2005, Myanmar in 2008, and the People's Republic of China in 2008 account for a disproportionate share of total mortality (Figure 2.1.2). Asia also suffers 26% of the $128 billion in economic damage recorded annually on average.

2.1.3 The Emergency Events Database

The Emergency Events Database (EM-DAT), compiled by the Centre for Research on the Epidemiology of Disasters, provides comprehensive information about the frequency, type, and intensity of disasters in terms of human and material losses, with nearly global coverage. EM-DAT records the number of people killed by a disaster, the number of people affected, and the amount of direct damage to property, crops, and livestock. "Affected" is broadly defined in the database as encompassing everything from severe physical injury to a temporary need to relocate because of periodic flooding that otherwise does little damage. However, data can be scant, especially on damage, being available for less than 40% of the disasters reported in developing Asia since 1980. More generally, disaster records before 2000 are presumed not to be very reliable, especially in developing countries, because the reporting of events and damage is incomplete and inconsistent across countries and time.

EM-DAT defines "disasters" as situations or events for which at least one of the following criteria holds true: 10 or more people are killed, 100 or more people are reported affected, a state of emergency is declared, or international assistance is requested. Data users are cautioned that these thresholds are the same whether an event reaches a threshold in a territory as vast as India or as tiny as the Marshall Islands. As a result, events of significance to a small country may fall through the cracks and go unreported (Noy 2015).

Included in EM-DAT are disasters triggered by weather-related hazards such as floods, storms, extreme temperatures, droughts, and wildfires; geophysical hazards such as earthquakes and volcanic eruptions; and biological hazards such as epidemics and insect infestations. Also included, but not featured in this report, are wholly man-made disasters such as industrial and transport accidents.

EM-DAT data and a full description can be obtained at https://www.emdat.be.

2.1.1 Death toll from the most devastating disasters in Asia since 1990

- 2015: Nepal — Earthquake — 8,969 deaths
- 2010: PRC — Earthquake — 2,977 deaths
- 2008: PRC — Earthquake — 87,564 deaths
- 1996: PRC — Flood — 4,091 deaths
- 1998: PRC — Flood — 4,250 deaths
- 2005: Afghanistan, India, Pakistan — Earthquake — 74,653 deaths
- 2011: Japan — Earthquake and tsunami — 19,848 deaths
- 1995: Japan — Earthquake — 5,297 deaths
- 1991: Bangladesh — Cyclone Gorky — 138,987 deaths
- 2007: Bangladesh — Cyclones: Akash, Sidr — 4,275 deaths
- 1990: Philippines — Earthquake — 2,417 deaths
- 2001: India, Pakistan — Earthquake — 20,017 deaths
- 1991: Philippines — Cyclone Thelma — 6,083 deaths
- 1998: India — Gujarat cyclone — 3,471 deaths
- 2013: Philippines — Cyclone Haiyan — 7,415 deaths
- 2013: India — Flood — 6,453 deaths
- 2018: Indonesia — Earthquake and tsunami — 3,989 deaths
- 1993: India — Earthquake — 9,748 deaths
- 1999: India — Odisha cyclone — 10,378 deaths
- 2006: Indonesia — Earthquake — 6,592 deaths
- 1998: Papua New Guinea — Earthquake and tsunami — 2,182 deaths
- 2004: Indian Ocean — Tsunami — Over 200,000 deaths
- 2008: Myanmar — Cyclone Nargis — 138,366 deaths

PRC = People's Republic of China.

Sources: Based on ADB. 2019. Recent Significant Disasters in the Asia and the Pacific Region. Infographic. https://www.adb.org/news/infographics/recent-significant-disasters-asia-and-pacific-region (accessed 4 February 2019), with updates using Centre for Research on the Epidemiology of Disasters. The Emergency Events Database. https://www.emdat.be/ (accessed 6 February 2019).

2.1.2 Deaths from disasters, 1990–2018

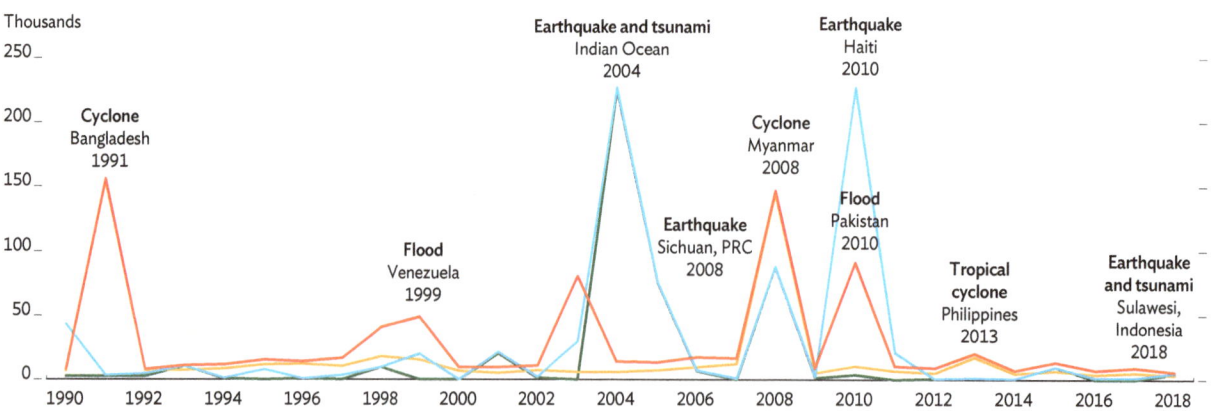

PRC = People's Republic of China.

Source: ADB estimates using Centre for Research on the Epidemiology of Disasters. The Emergency Events Database. https://www.emdat.be/ (accessed 6 February 2019).

Diverse response strategies for diverse disasters

Hazards and their resulting disasters differ in their frequency and the intensity of their effects. They can thus be seen to represent different risk layers. Weather-related hazards such as storms, floods, and droughts are by far the most frequently recorded hazards in developing Asia, accounting for 82% of all events recorded in the EM-DAT database for the region over the past 2 decades (Figure 2.1.3). Geophysical hazards—including earthquakes, tsunamis, volcanic activity, and movements of dry mass—account for a further 12% of EM-DAT entries for the region. Biological hazards, either epidemics or insect infestations, make up the remaining 6%.

Weather-related hazards were responsible for 97% of people affected in the region since 2000. On the other hand, geophysical hazards caused 61% of disaster fatalities in developing Asia, well more than the 37% of fatalities in weather-related hazards (Figure 2.1.4).

2.1.3 Disaster occurrence by type, 2000–2018

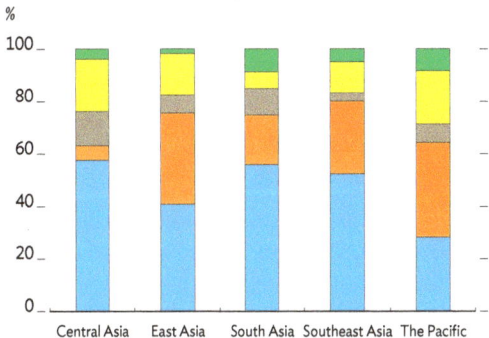

Source: ADB estimates using Centre for Research on the Epidemiology of Disasters. The Emergency Events Database. https://www.emdat.be/ (accessed 6 February 2019).

2.1.4 Disaster impact in developing Asia, 2000–2018 (%)

Impact	Share to world total	Disaster type		
		Weather-related[a]	Geophysical[b]	Biological[c]
Death toll	55	37	61	2
Number of affected	84	97	3	0
Damage	26	79	21	...
Total occurrences		82	12	6

... = No data reported in EM-DAT.
Notes:
[a] Weather-related hazards include storms, droughts, floods, landslides, extreme temperatures, and wildfire.
[b] Geophysical hazards include earthquakes, volcanic activity, tsunami, and movement of dry mass.
[c] Biological hazards include epidemics and insect infestations. Data on epidemics are underreported because EM-DAT is not designed to capture events that develop slowly.
Source: ADB estimates using Centre for Research on the Epidemiology of Disasters. The Emergency Events Database. https://www.emdat.be/ (accessed 6 February 2019).

Of the estimated $644 billion in damage from disasters across the region from 2000 to 2018, weather-related hazards caused the greatest share, at $507 billion or 79%, and geophysical hazards accounted for the remaining $137 billion or 21% (Figure 2.1.4). Weather-related hazards usually have a much bigger footprint than geophysical hazards, which tend to be more localized. This may explain part of the difference in the distribution of damage. However, the differing composition of damage to assets, and of fatalities and the number of people affected, associated with different disaster types may be attributable as well to differing frequency and predictability.

Weather-related hazards are fairly predictable, facilitating preparation and effective early warning. Riverine floods, for example the 2011 flood in Thailand, can be predicted well in advance, sometimes by more than a month, and landfall for a tropical cyclone is usually known days before it happens. In these cases, lives can be saved by evacuating people out of harm's way and using specially constructed shelters. The construction of cyclone shelters and the introduction of early warning systems in Bangladesh, for example, has dramatically reduced the number of casualties in these events (Haque et al. 2012). In principle, deaths in weather-related hazards should be almost fully preventable. Those that occur are appropriately perceived as revealing a policy failure, especially as the costs of prevention are not prohibitive. In many cases, early warning systems have the added benefit of reducing asset damage by enabling people to defend some assets or move them out of harm's way.

Disasters triggered by geophysical hazards are relatively rare, so populations and governments may tend to underappreciate them and underprepare for them. Volcanic eruptions are becoming increasingly predictable, albeit only by several days but enough to allow the authorities to issue evacuation orders before they occur. Earthquakes, by contrast, are essentially unpredictable, even as the general seismic risk profiles of particular geographical regions become known. As such, mortality and damage from earthquakes is largely preventable only to the extent that construction standards are made robust enough for buildings and other infrastructure to withstand ground movement. This is a costly and challenging undertaking.

Early warning systems for tsunamis are feasible, but how much in advance warnings can be sounded depends on the distance of threatened areas from the epicenter of the geophysical event that generated the tsunami. More generally, warnings are conditional on scientists' limited ability to predict tsunamis precisely. The three deadly disasters in Indonesia in 2018 (Box 2.1.2) hit the coast without any advance warning despite the introduction, after the catastrophic 2004 tsunami in Aceh, of an early warning system in the Indian Ocean. While technically more challenging and more costly than early warning systems for weather events, tsunami alert systems date back to 1949, when the

Pacific Tsunami Warning Center was founded in Hawaii and began providing alerts throughout the Pacific Ocean.

Early warning is best done through a collective approach. Regional neighbors establish and maintain an integrated warning system as a regional public good that reduces cost while boosting efficacy. An integrated system can avoid duplication of components and enable effective coordination in the deployment of detection equipment, while participating countries' interdependence and mutual oversight provide incentives to maintain the system.

Bigger impact on smaller economies

Even for larger weather events, their geographic scale is typically smaller than most countries they hit, and their direct impacts in terms of human and economic losses are dwarfed by the population, territory, and gross domestic product (GDP) of affected countries. Partly for this reason, the impacts of disasters tend to be more eye-opening in smaller economies, such as those in the Pacific, when expressed relative to national population or GDP. From 2000 to 2018, 11% of the residents of Pacific island economies were affected by disasters, and economic losses equaled 7% of GDP. Economic damage to countries in other subregions of Asia ranges from 1% to 6% of GDP (Figure 2.1.5).

The 15 developing member countries of the Asian Development Bank (ADB) in the Pacific, with a combined population of 12.5 million people, are located in one of the most disaster-prone regions on earth. Many of these countries are exposed to tropical cyclones, frequent seismic and volcanic activity, and recurrent floods and droughts. In addition, they face growing threats from climate change as rising sea levels and deteriorating coral reef ecosystems exacerbate their vulnerability to tropical cyclones and storm surges. Disaster impacts are further compounded by these economies being small, remote, and undiversified.

Since 2000, disasters have affected 5.6 million people in Pacific developing member countries of ADB, causing close to 1,500 reported deaths. They have cost these countries $1.9 billion in reported damage (EM-DAT). A global estimate of life-years lost per capita to disasters from 1980 to 2012 found Tuvalu and the Cook Islands most badly affected, followed in order by Samoa, Tonga, Vanuatu, and Fiji (Noy 2016b). Less exposed in per capita terms, but nevertheless still very exposed, were Papua New Guinea and the island states in the North Pacific. Tonga, Vanuatu, and several other countries in the Pacific top the World Risk Index, which assesses exposure to natural hazards, structural vulnerability, and coping and adaptation capacity (Heintze et al. 2018).

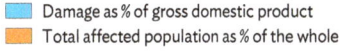

2.1.5 Disaster impacts normalized by GDP and population, 2000–2018

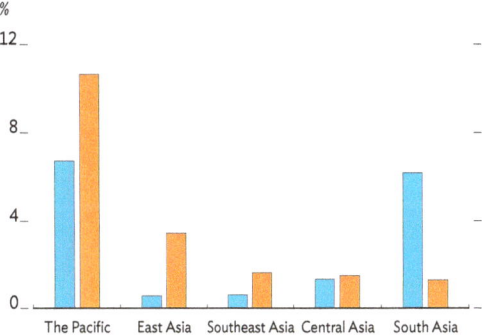

Note: In EM-DAT, "total affected" is the sum of those injured, left homeless, or otherwise affected after a disaster. "Affected" refers to people requiring immediate assistance during an emergency, either urgent medical assistance and other basic survival needs such as food, water, shelter, and sanitation.

Sources: ADB estimates using Centre for Research on the Epidemiology of Disasters. The Emergency Events Database. https://www.emdat.be/ (accessed 6 February 2019); World Bank. World Development Indicators online database (both accessed 6 February 2019).

2.1.4 Vanuatu and Cyclone Pam

In March 2015, Tropical Cyclone Pam left a trail of destruction through the South Pacific. The effects of the category 5 cyclone left Kiribati, Solomon Islands, and Tuvalu with significant damage, even though it passed far to the side from them. The worst impact was in Vanuatu, where the cyclone made landfall in the evening of 13 March 2015. Sustained wind speeds were recorded as high as 270 kilometers per hour, with a reported maximum gust reaching 320 kilometers per hour (Handmer and Iveson 2017).

Eleven people were killed during the storm, which was fewer than predicted given the storm's ferocity, in part because of timely and accurate hazard warnings and community responses (Handmer and Iveson 2017). As the cyclone approached, the Vanuatu Meteorology and Geohazards Department sent warnings by text message, direct phone call, shortwave radio, and the internet. Damage was most widespread on the larger islands of Efate, Erromango, and Tanna. Approximately 65,000 people were displaced from their homes. Estimates were that 17,000 buildings had been damaged or destroyed, including houses, schools, public health clinics, and other medical facilities. The tropical cyclone destroyed the vast majority of crops and compromised the livelihoods of at least 80% of Vanuatu's rural population. The tourism industry was badly affected. Arrivals by air from March to June dropped by 26% below the previous year, and cruise ship arrivals by 52%, though arrivals swiftly recovered in the second half of the year (ADB 2016).

Estimated damage and losses to the Vanuatu economy exceeded the equivalent of 64% of GDP (ADB 2016). GDP growth fell from 2.3% in 2014 to 0.2% in 2015, rebounding to 3.5% in both 2016 and 2017 (ADB 2016, 2018b). GDP was initially projected to decline by more, but the large influx of external grants and loans, and accompanying post-disaster operations, softened the impact on the economy, allowing evidence of a significant economic recovery to emerge in less than a year (Mohan and Strobl 2017). The trade deficit in goods and services widened by almost half from the equivalent of 25% of GDP in 2014 to 36%, driven up by cyclone damage to export facilities and higher imports to compensate for domestic shortages and to supply post-disaster operations. The budget recorded a surplus equal to 1.4% of GDP because the bulk of the cyclone reconstruction was financed by development partners, allowing fiscal expenditure to rise only slightly.

Insurance from the Pacific Catastrophic Risk Assessment and Financing Initiative, which pools sovereign disaster risks across several Pacific island economies, paid the national government $1.9 million within 10 days of the cyclone. Subsequent financing and international support, however, was far more substantial. External grants rose to $75 million in 2015, and overall financial support from development partners—including ADB, the International Monetary Fund, the World Bank, and bilateral partners—exceeded $147 million. Recovery financing went predominantly to large infrastructure projects, notably to rebuild airports and roads. As the economy rebounded, recovery and reconstruction projects continued, with many communities still feeling the impact of the cyclone almost 4 years later.

The most severe events can have catastrophic implications for small island countries. For example, Cyclone Pam in 2015, one of the most intense tropical cyclones ever experienced in the South Pacific, caused damage and losses in Vanuatu equal to 64% of that country's annual GDP (Box 2.1.4). More broadly, cross-country growth regressions suggest that severe disasters slowed annual rates of economic growth in the Pacific by 1.4 percentage points on average from 1980 to 2017. Little or no comparable evidence is found for developing Asia as a whole or its other subregions (Dagli and Ferrarini, forthcoming).

Severe disasters can affect the fiscal and external balance sheets of affected countries. Consumption-smoothing in the aftermath of disasters can generate temporary current account deficits. Similarly, disasters often temporarily reduce output growth even as they spur increased public investment for reconstruction and higher public expenditure as well for disaster relief (Obstfeld and Rogoff 1996, Felbermayr and Gröschl 2013).

Samoa experienced a catastrophic tsunami in September 2009 that killed 147 people and affected 5,585 others. International partners provided $26.7 million for tsunami reconstruction, and Samoa managed to raise $20.5 million from its own fiscal resources for disaster response. This equaled 9% of all government expenditure in fiscal year 2014 and left a large funding gap. As a report by the Government of Samoa noted, the recovery plan, spread over 3 years, would cost over $100 million (Noy and Edmonds 2019).

With sufficient funding, recovery efforts are likely to be successful. This is illustrated by Vanuatu's recovery from devastation caused by Cyclone Pam, which triggered substantial international financial support. The disaster proved timely, as it occurred just as the Sendai Framework for Disaster Risk Reduction was being signed in March 2015 by most United Nations member countries in a conference in Sendai, Japan.

Average annual losses view disaster costs over time

The historical record of disaster losses is limited and can fail to capture extremely rare events. A 50-year historical record, for example, may very well not include an earthquake that occurs only once in 400 years. An alternative way of expressing disaster impacts, rather than isolating losses from a particular event or summing up the measured losses over a particular period, is through average annual losses (AALs). These are total expected losses annualized over a projected time frame of up to thousands of years. AALs are therefore the predicted amount that countries would have to set aside each year to cover the cost of future disasters, assuming they received no international support. Another way to put it is that AALs approximate the actuarially fair annual cost of insuring against these disasters.

As with other metrics for measuring disaster impacts, AALs expressed in absolute terms concentrate in larger and higher-income economies that are exposed to hazards. However, expressed as a percentage of exposed assets, they are significantly higher for smaller and low-income countries. AALs are estimated at around 0.8% of exposed assets for low-income countries in developing Asia, compared with 0.2% for those with lower-middle incomes, 0.1% for those with upper-middle incomes, and 0.2% for high-income countries. In terms of regional distribution, ratios of AALs to exposed assets in the Pacific subregion are, at over 0.6%, more than twice as high as those for any other subregion in developing Asia (Figure 2.1.6).

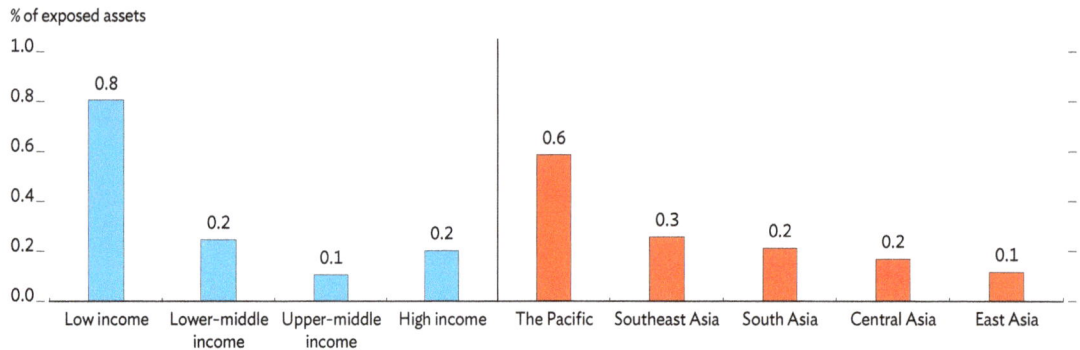

2.1.6 Average annual losses in developing Asia, by income group and subregion

Low income: Afghanistan, Bangladesh, Cambodia, Myanmar, Nepal, and Tajikistan. **Lower-middle income:** Armenia, Bhutan, Federated States of Micronesia, Georgia, Indonesia, Kiribati, the Kyrgyz Republic, the Lao People's Democratic Republic, Mongolia, Pakistan, Papua New Guinea, the Philippines, Samoa, Solomon Islands, Sri Lanka, Timor-Leste, Uzbekistan, Vanuatu, and Viet Nam. **Upper-middle income:** Azerbaijan, Fiji, Kazakhstan, Malaysia, Maldives, Marshall Islands, Palau, the People's Republic of China, Thailand, Tonga, Turkmenistan, and Tuvalu. **High income:** Brunei Darussalam; Hong Kong, China; Singapore; and Taipei,China. **The Pacific:** Excludes Cook Islands and Nauru. **East Asia:** Excludes the Republic of Korea.
Source: UNISDR 2015.

AALs for earthquakes and tropical cyclones affecting Pacific island countries, based on a different risk modeling analysis, are detailed in Table 2.1.1. Also shown are expected losses from events that have a 10% chance of occurring in the next 50 years. Both lists emphasize the elevated risk to these countries in terms of both human and property losses.

2.1.1 Expected losses from earthquakes and tropical cyclones in the Pacific

Country	Average annual losses from earthquakes and tropical cyclones ($ million)	Minimum cost threshold of events deemed to have a 10% chance of occurring in the next 50 years	
		Losses ($ million)	Casualties
Marshall Islands	3.0	>160	>150
Fiji	79.0	>1,500	>2,100
Solomon Islands	20.0	>520	
Tonga	15.8	>437	
Palau	2.7	>247	>175
Vanuatu	48.0	>540	>2,150
Kiribati	0.3	>40	>200
Timor-Leste	5.9	>530	>2,100
Tuvalu	0.2	>9	>50
Nauru	0.0[a]	>0.2	= 0
Papua New Guinea	85.0	>1,400	>11,500
Cook Islands	4.9	>268	
Samoa	10.0	>315	
Federated States of Micronesia	8.0	>470	>600

[a] $20,000.

Source: Pacific Catastrophic Risk Assessment and Financing Initiative. http://pcrafi.spc.int/documents/?limit=100&offset=0&doc_type__in=presentation (accessed 23 November 2018).

Bringing 'extensive disaster risk' out of the shadows

Globally, most disaster mortality is concentrated in very intensive disasters, as noted above (Figure 2.1.2). More than 45% of global disaster mortality since 1990 has been concentrated in just six events. However, the United Nations Office for Disaster Risk Reduction has argued that mortality associated with what is referred to as "extensive disaster risk" is almost unmeasured but also on the rise (UNISDR 2013). Events that pose extensive risk are not very dramatic or severe but happen frequently: mainly flash floods, landslides, urban flooding, storms, and other localized weather events. Electrical storms and lightning are notable for increasingly causing losses from extensive risk, by sparking wildfires (UNISDR 2015).

Global risk modeling rarely captures extensive risk. The losses incurred from extensive risk are rarely reported internationally but simply absorbed locally by low-income households, small businesses, and municipal governments (UNISDR 2009). Yet deaths and economic losses from extensive risks are mounting in low- and middle-income countries, as measured on the database of the United Nations Office for Disaster Risk Reduction. In the past decade, losses to extensive risk in 85 countries and territories came to $94 billion.

Extensive disaster risk typically worsens inequality and poverty by slowly eroding development assets such as houses, schools, health facilities, roads, and other local infrastructure (Gall, Borden, and Cutter 2009). As is intensive risk, it is made worse by the usual adjuncts of inequality and poverty: weak governance, badly planned and managed urban development, and rural livelihoods made even more vulnerable by environmental degradation. As extensive risk rises, it undermines efforts to reduce poverty and to achieve many of the Sustainable Development Goals, while the accumulating losses associated with extensive disaster risk highlight that understanding and practicing disaster risk reduction has not been effective at avoiding risk generation and accumulation (UNISDR 2015).

Evidence is mounting about the social and economic costs of widespread, high-frequency natural hazards such as changing rainfall patterns and temperature fluctuations. They constrain human mobility (Barrios, Bertinelli, and Strobl 2006; Henderson, Storeygard, and Deichmann 2014) and human capital accumulation (Maccini and Yang 2009, Hyland and Russ 2019), and can even cause conflict (see literature cited in Dell, Jones, and Olken 2014).

These different types of disaster risk call for different response strategies that follow a "risk layering" approach. For example, financing response to disaster risk through insurance may be the most viable mechanism for large residual risks that cannot be reduced or managed otherwise. In the case of extensive risk, the most effective responses may be investment in improved and disaster-resilient infrastructure, education and social strengthening to build community resilience, and improved access for vulnerable groups to market mechanisms such as finance and remittances. Generally, disaster risk reduction is the most effective first action to tackle disaster risk, both extensive and intensive. These are central themes in the remainder of this chapter.

Escalating risk of disaster losses

Across developing Asia, losses from disasters are substantial and continue to impede development. They would seem to indicate that rising incomes and efforts toward adaptation and disaster risk reduction have been insufficient to balance the worsening of hazards and greater community exposure to them.

Exposure to disaster risk in developing Asia is rising rapidly. This is partly just a function of population and economic growth, as there are more people and built structures in harm's way, but it is also a function of trends that concentrate population and assets in high-risk locations, such as the spread of coastal megacities. Some of these trends are particularly pronounced in developing Asia.

The most striking recent illustration of such trends and their consequences was flooding in the second half of 2011 that hit Thailand, specifically Greater Bangkok. According to EM-DAT, this was the costliest flood ever recorded globally. World Bank (2012) estimated that there were 800 fatalities and $46.5 billion in losses. The direct loss of property and infrastructure to the flood was estimated to equal nearly 13% of the annual GDP of Thailand. The flood affected many provinces, including commercial and industrial districts outside of Bangkok. It started with very heavy rains in late July and early August. Flooding started in the north of the country, causing the south-flowing Chao Phraya, the main river bisecting Greater Bangkok, to overflow its banks. Most of the flood impact was experienced in the last quarter of 2011, with the high water bulge reaching Greater Bangkok in early November. While the wet monsoon of 2011 was indeed exceptional, a lot of the damage was traceable to the recent construction of many industrial estates in flood-prone areas on the edges of Bangkok and the consequent lack of flood-water retention areas (known in Thai as *kaem ling* or monkey's cheeks).

In addition to rising exposure, worsening disaster risk can be traced to the effects of climate change and the rise in sea level that is threatening coastal cities and island states across Asia and the Pacific. Many coastal cities in the region are experiencing increased flood risk from other causes as well, notably from land subsidence, in part a result of uncontrolled water abstraction; upriver deforestation, which reduces the capacity of the soil to hold water; and the paving of once-permeable surfaces in urban areas.

Many studies project large increases in economic damage from disasters in the near future. Some studies project annual global damage from floods to increase ninefold from $6 billion in 2005 to $52 billion by 2050, this increase arising from projected socioeconomic change alone (Hallegatte et al. 2013). Recent research into the effects of future sea-level rise on coastal cities highlights the potential economic and population losses for global megacities. One dramatic prediction for Ho Chi Minh City is that it will lose 41% of its area, 22% of its population, and 22% of its real gross regional product (Desmet, Nagy, and Rossi-Hansberg 2018). Other metropolitan areas that stand to lose an important share of their population include Bangkok, Shanghai, and Tianjin. Similarly, studies of future damage to coastal cities around the world from storm surges predict very large losses in absolute terms, concentrated in large Asian megacities. Many Asian cities risk losses equal to 2% or more of their GDP from events that threaten each city with a 5% probability of occurring by 2030 (Abadie, Galarraga, and de Murieta 2017).

Projections of future global losses from tropical storms indicate large increases in economic damage caused mainly by increased exposure arising from socioeconomic trends. In some cases, higher intensity comes from higher temperatures in the ocean. Economic damage from tropical cyclones in countries that are not wealthy members of the Organisation for Economic Co-operation and Development (OECD) is forecast to be doubled or trebled by 2100 by socioeconomic change alone, soaring from the current $6.7 billion per year to $13 billion–$18 billion by 2100. The projected increase reflects the estimated historical positive elasticity of cyclone damage with respect to incomes (Bakkensen and Mendelsohn 2019).

Factoring in the effects of climate change increases the projection for cyclone damage in non-OECD countries by a further 8% on average. By contrast, fatalities from cyclones are projected to decline by as much as three-quarters with socioeconomic change, dropping from 8,000 per year currently in non-OECD countries to just over 2,000 per year by 2100. The decline reflects the estimated historical trend toward fewer cyclone fatalities with rising income, as well as significant improvements in early warning systems.

Disaster impacts and how they propagate

Local effects

Some large, geographically widespread disasters are particularly memorable. In 2013, Typhoon Haiyan swept from the Federated States of Micronesia through Palau, the Philippines, Viet Nam, the People's Republic of China, and Taipei,China. More often, though, disasters are localized events with economic impacts largely concentrated in the affected area. Studies that rely on regional or national indicators to estimate the economic impacts of disasters are therefore often prone to underestimate the true local impact in the localities hardest hit.

The immediate impacts of disasters on local economic activity can be significant. New analysis of the local economic impacts of tropical cyclones in the Philippines showed that the local effects of these storms could be substantial (Box 2.2.1).

2.2.1 The local economic impacts of tropical cyclones in the Philippines

Much of the existing literature on the impact of tropical cyclones has tended to focus on national or regional effects. While insightful, these macroeconomic studies provide little useful information for formulating policies to build resilience locally. More specifically, tropical cyclones are, like most natural hazards, inherently local in nature, but local impact becomes diluted if averaged out over a large regional unit of analysis. A number of recent papers investigated this aggregation problem when measuring the impact of tropical storms and found that aggregate data tended to underestimate the true impact of these extreme weather phenomena on local economies (Strobl 2011, Elliott, Strobl, and Sun 2015).

Strobl (forthcoming) used nightlight intensity derived from satellite images, illustrated in box figure 1, as a proxy for economic activity (Henderson, Storeygard, and Weil 2012) and combined it with actual storm tracks and a wind field model to investigate the local economic impact of typhoons in the Philippines. The Philippines is one of the most storm-prone countries of the world, with an average of 7.5 typhoons having made landfall annually since 1970 (Blanc and Strobl 2016).

Results from this analysis show that exposure to tropical cyclones significantly disrupts economic activity in the Philippines. After a storm of average intensity in the sample, local economic activity was

1 Night light intensity in the Philippines in 2013

Source: Strobl, forthcoming.

continued next page

2.2.1 Continued

reduced by 2%. After the most severe storm in the sample, local economic activity was reduced by 23%. On average, these effects on local economic activity appeared not to persist beyond the year of the storm.

The findings can be used to construct a distribution of losses using the full set of storms hitting the Philippines from 1950 to 2013. This enables an estimate of expected damage from typhoon intensities with different return periods, or from storms occurring with different probabilities. The results of this exercise are illustrated in box figure 2 for national losses.

Relatively frequent storms, those with a 5-year return period, should be expected to produce losses equal to about 1% of national economic activity. This rises as one considers less frequent events. For example, a storm with a 50-year return period is expected to cause a reduction of national economic activity exceeding 2% in the year of the storm.

At a regional level, the expected losses vary substantially. For instance, in Region VIII on the southern island of Mindanao, typhoons with 50-year return periods caused losses in economic activity exceeding 20%. In contrast, losses were relatively modest in the National Capital Region and northern Luzon. For the capital, a storm with a 20-year return period is not likely to cause more than a 1% reduction in economic activity. The regional analysis, and the variation of results across regions, underlines the need to take into account the local and regional impacts of disasters in disaster risk management and disaster preparedness, to identify hot spots for expected damage and stress-test response and recovery plans against more extreme scenarios.

2 N-year return period national losses

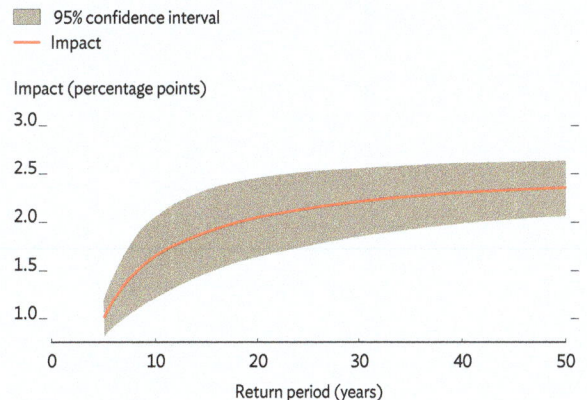

Source: Strobl, forthcoming.

These estimates illustrate the magnitude of losses that should be expected from tropical storms occurring in the Philippines, both nationally and regionally. However, the expected losses estimated here are based on historical observations. The impacts of tropical storms may be expected to increase in the future as storms likely become more severe under climate change and as communities become more exposed. Moreover, approximating GDP using nightlight intensity reflects only some forms of economic activity, such as services and manufacturing, and likely underrepresents other activities, particularly agriculture, which is very vulnerable to weather.

After a storm of average intensity in the sample, local economic activity was reduced by 2%; after a storm of the highest intensity, local economic activity was reduced by 23%. The cumulative impact of these events in the Philippines since 1992 is estimated to have exceeded $11.6 billion.

These findings on the Philippines correspond to other recent evidence on the local economic impacts of flooding, which found that large floods in urban areas reduced local GDP by 2%–8% in the year of the event (Kocornik-Mina et al. forthcoming). As is observed with cyclones, GDP in affected cities appears to be fully restored in the year following the flood.

It is important to note that GDP, even when measured locally, is itself an aggregation and may therefore obscure impacts on particular groups or individuals. This is especially problematic if the impact is not distributed evenly across various groups and affects specific groups more intensely.

Further, by focusing on measures of economic activity, this analysis omits any social, cultural, or environmental impacts that do not materially affect the economy.

The relatively quick restoration of economic activity observed in these studies may partly reflect that, in many cases, households that temporarily migrate away in the aftermath of disasters subsequently return to their land and livelihoods. Of course, this rapid restoration of population and economic activity to affected areas may or may not be interpreted as a sign of disaster resilience. In particular, if disasters tend to reoccur, hitting the same locations with high frequency—as for example with monsoonal flooding—then restoring activity to these vulnerable locations may simply put people and economic assets back in harm's way.

These concerns are reinforced by the anticipated effects of climate change on the risk of extreme weather events. Climate change will increase natural hazard risk for particular locations. An important part of adaptation to climate change, at least in the long run, may involve moving people away from locations with worsening hazards, with consequent reductions in productivity (Desmet and Rossi-Hansberg 2015, Desmet, Nagy, and Rossi-Hansberg 2018).

The evidence available to date indicates that such adjustment is likely to be slow because current and future patterns of spatial development tend to follow paths laid down by earlier development, and it is costly to deviate from them (Bleakly and Lin 2012, Michaels and Rauch 2018). Cities in particular have been found to persist even in the aftermath of devastating shocks, including wartime devastation (Davis and Weinstein 2002, Miguel and Roland 2011) and large-scale flooding (Kocornik-Mina et al., forthcoming).

Persistent effects of disasters

Empirical evidence of the effects of disasters on growth is strongest in relation to small island developing states, where major events can wipe out a large part of the economy and destroy critical infrastructure such as airports and harbors (Heger, Julca, and Paddison 2008, Lee, Zhang, and Nguyen 2018, Dagli and Ferrarini, forthcoming). However, the broader empirical literature on disasters and economic growth is far from conclusive.

While most disaster impacts on economic activity appear to be short-lived, in some cases the effects may persist for a long time. (Recent empirical evidence on the short- and long-run impacts of disasters in developing countries is reviewed in Sawada and Takasaki [2017].) For example, a decade on from the 1995 Kobe earthquake in Japan, local income per capita in Hyogo Prefecture was still depressed by 12% because of lost employment opportunities. This reflected a regional shift from manufacturing to services that was directly attributable to the earthquake. A significant share of heavily damaged factories failed to resume operations in Kobe, and there was a shift in employment from Kobe to nearby Osaka. As a result, the earthquake caused a permanent loss of economic opportunity (duPont et al. 2015, Cole et al. 2018).

There is also evidence that poor countries can experience prolonged, slow, and incomplete recovery in the aftermath of severe disasters. In particular, small island states are the most vulnerable because of their diminutive size relative to the hazards' footprint, their geographic isolation, and their lack of economic diversity. These factors mean not only higher aggregate damage but less hope of recovery in the short or long term (ADB 2018c). The 2010 earthquake in Haiti, for example, was so catastrophic that it was found to have undermined the long-term development prospects of the Haitian economy (Best and Burke 2017).

Macro impacts through market prices

Disaster effects can spread across time because of permanent shifts in market forces. They can, for example, cause lasting distortions through market concentration and collusive price hikes. Recent research on the impact of the 2011 Thailand flood on the hard disk drive industry, for instance, suggests that the disaster enticed market-distorting collusion in certain segments of the industry (Box 2.2.2).

Disasters may affect location choices for households and businesses, thus influencing real estate prices. In efficient real estate markets, prices provide market signals about property value and its many determinants. However, there is substantial evidence that real estate markets are far from efficient in reflecting disaster risk in their prices. A large number of empirical investigations in several countries demonstrated how past experience of floods and flood risk affected house prices relatively little and not for long. Meta-analysis established price effects ranging from –7% to +1% (Beltrán, Maddison, and Elliott 2018).

The weak sensitivity of real estate markets to disaster risk has been attributed to their lack of liquidity, which limits price movements. This and other frictions in land and real estate markets kept commercial and residential land prices from declining despite substantial damage from the 2011 flood in Thailand (Sawada et al. 2018, Wong 2008).

By contrast, there is ample evidence that, where market frictions are small, real estate rental and asset prices may reflect disaster risk well. Research on earthquake risk aversion in the Tokyo metropolitan area, for example, found that housing rents were substantially lower in risky areas than in safer ones (Nakagawa, Saito, and Yamaga 2007).

2.2.2 Impact of the 2011 Thailand flood on the hard-disk drive industry

To examine the impacts of the 2011 Thailand flood on the hard disk drive (HDD) industry, Nakata, Sawada, and Wakamori (2019) analyzed the quarterly data of individual firms on HDD shipments and the average prices for the nine market segments of the HDD industry from the first quarter of 2006 to the fourth quarter of 2015. In relation to the consumer 2.5-inch segment, it found evidence that the three biggest manufacturers colluded after the floods. The evidence was higher shipments after the production plunge caused by the floods (box figure 1a). Meanwhile, the average price declined by only a limited extent and remained higher than it was before the flood (box figure 1b).

By contrast, shipments of the desktop 3.5-inch segment did not recover from the large drop triggered by the floods, and the average price returned to its previous level. Even in this segment, the study could not preclude that HDD manufacturers became more collusive after the flood by collectively controlling shipments.

The 2011 Thailand flood was thus found to have had an impact on the HDD market structure against the interests of consumers. This evidence illustrates the need for public policy intervention to keep firms from unduly benefiting from disasters and thereby restore their incentive to invest in risk prevention.

Hard disk drives shipments and average price

Source: Nakata, Sawada, and Wakamori 2019.

Similarly, there was evidence of a 20% discount on nonresidential land prices for every kilometer closer to the Uemachi fault line passing east of Osaka Prefecture in Japan, after the 1995 Kobe earthquake highlighted for residents and policy makers earthquake risk along faults (Gu et al. 2018).

A study on companies' location choices following the 2011 Thailand flood shows that firms in affected regions became more aware of flood risk following the event, but some were unable to relocate for one reason or another (Sawada et al. 2018). Land prices in unflooded areas increased relative to those in flooded areas, but this was driven mainly by new entrants choosing less risky locations. While industrial land prices were affected, there was no evidence of effects from flooding on residential or commercial land values.

Other studies found similar short-term moderate price declines for houses that were associated with earthquake risk (Hidano, Hoshino, and Sugiura 2015, Timar, Grimes, and Fabling 2018a).

Real estate markets may fail to reflect disaster risk for a number of reasons. One is incomplete information on existing risk, as suggested by studies showing sharpened risk perceptions following extreme events. For example, Gallagher (2014) found that insurance take-up in the US spiked the year after heavy floods and steadily declined thereafter. Another is the moral hazard associated with government interventions to provide protective infrastructure and disaster recovery. A typical trade-off involves public money spent to reduce risk to people living in flood-prone areas, which makes them more reluctant to relocate away from risky areas (Kocornik-Mina et al., forthcoming).

It is notable that, despite limited liquidity and other frictions in the real estate market, once the government intervenes to clearly define and constrain the risk, the impact on real estate prices can be significant. For example, prices for buildings in Wellington, New Zealand, fell by an average of 45% after they were officially declared earthquake-prone and in need of remediation to meet earthquake safety standards (Timar, Grimes, and Fabling 2018b).

Macro impacts through small businesses

Disasters can disrupt businesses by, for example, increasing costs for their inputs. Smaller firms in particular will struggle to cope with direct damage to their buildings, equipment, and inventory and with other interruptions to their operations. In the aftermath of flooding in Mumbai in 2005, for example, a survey was carried out on a randomly selected group of 627 retail outlets in six flood-prone wards. Only 2% of surveyed businesses filed insurance claims for flood-related losses, and the average compensation received by those that did was only about ₹35,000. Insurance claims compensated for no more than one-third of the losses on average, and only for the small minority of businesses that filed insurance claims (Patankar, forthcoming).

Further evidence from surveys and interviews with flood-affected small and medium-sized enterprises (SMEs) in Chennai found that the businesses worst affected were those with annual turnover of less than ₹100 million (Idicheria and Neelakantan 2016). Most of the losses incurred by these businesses were damage to fixed assets like physical infrastructure, with manufacturers the worst affected. Many lost as well important business documents, including electronically stored documents along with the electronic equipment. Business services were disrupted by flood damage to infrastructure. On average, firms made do without electricity for 13 days and without water supply for 12 days. Solid waste and sewage issues persisted for more than 15 days.

The flood exposed how very much smaller businesses rely on informal financing channels like friends and unlicensed moneylenders. Most smaller businesses had invested their own money or borrowed from private sources to set up their enterprises. They typically had slim profit margins and limited credit. Losses to the flood were amplified for such businesses by their lack of access to emergency funds or additional finance through official lending institutions. Although some had insurance, the payouts were very low and in some cases were not paid for months. With production shut down, perhaps for lack of inputs and clients, many firms suffered significant financial distress. Many could not repay their loans and were forced to shut down and sell their assets (Patankar, forthcoming).

Low insurance penetration is a problem not only for firms in developing countries. Disaster insurance uptake by firms is low even in developed countries like Japan, where the participation rate for disaster insurance is only 47% for SMEs (Sawada et al. 2017).

Micro impacts on households and health

The direct effects of disasters disproportionately hit poorer households and the more vulnerable members of society, as is well recognized. Particularly in rural areas, disasters can trap households in poverty, rendering them unable to take advantage of opportunities for growth. In many cases, poorer households are forced to migrate to cities in the hope of escaping an adverse economic shock. Responding to community surveys conducted in areas vulnerable to flooding across five Asian countries, 90% of rural households surveyed reported that they had suffered loss of life or significant damage to assets from flooding within the past decade. These rural households took more than three times longer than urban households to recover financially from damage caused by flooding, 27 weeks versus 7–8 for urban households (Figure 2.2.1) (Laurien and Keating, forthcoming).

Household surveys following severe flooding in Indian cities showed that, in the absence of social protection, disaster-hit families used up savings or borrowed at high interest rates from informal lenders, pushing them further into indebtedness and poverty. Poor households were disproportionately affected by disasters in that they are more likely to be hit by a disaster than wealthier households and, when hit, suffered greater losses relative to their income (Box 2.2.3) (Patankar, forthcoming; see also Winsemius et al. 2018, Hallegatte et al. 2016a and 2017, Sakai et al. 2017). Compounding these vulnerabilities, poorer households had difficulty accessing the mechanisms that were typically used to cope with income shocks, notably financial services such as insurance and credit (Castells-Quintana, Lopez-Uribe, and McDermott 2018).

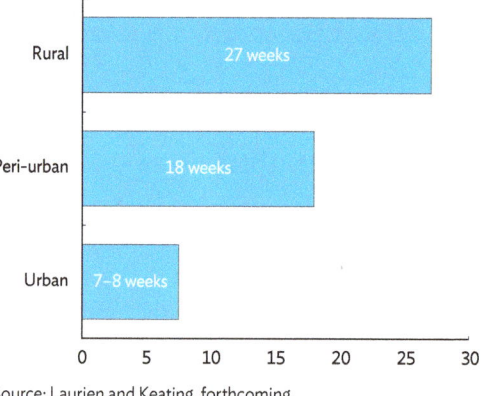

2.2.1 Financial recovery time from last severe flood

Source: Laurien and Keating, forthcoming.

2.2.3 The impact of floods on households—evidence from India

Mumbai

In a case study of severe flooding in the Indian city of Mumbai in 2005, the administrative wards worst affected by flooding featured high population density, at 4–5 times the city average of 27,150 per square kilometer, and many households in tenements, slums, and other poor living conditions. The percentage of slum-dwelling households in these wards was 21%–46%. Of the households randomly selected in affected wards for inclusion in the survey, 71% were classified as poor and 16% as living below the poverty line. Most households surveyed lived in badly constructed dwellings.

Poorer households reported higher intensity of flood impacts, and the losses they reported were more substantial relative to income (box figure 1). Families below the poverty line suffered losses exceeding a year's income from damage to assets they owned, while the losses of households classified as poor equaled about 5 months of their income. Others reported the cost of repairing or replacing damaged assets equal to 1–2 months of income. Almost all surveyed families covered losses out of their own pockets.

In the absence of adequate support mechanisms such as social protection or insurance coverage, disasters have the potential to push poor families into debt traps and chronic poverty. Reported indirect impacts suggest potential knock-on effects from the disaster on household welfare, health, and ability to access basic services. For example, many households surveyed in the aftermath of the flooding reported fuel shortages, garbage inside their homes, problems getting electricity and clean water, food shortages, price rises, and a lack of transport (box figure 2).

Compensation for damage from flooding came through government relief in what it called gratuitous relief assistance, amounting to ₹5,000 for affected families to cover such immediate requirements as food and clothing. The amount was uncorrelated with actual losses reported by families, and it covered only a small proportion of losses: 13.5% for families below the poverty line and 10.4% for poor families. In fact, the government carried out no needs assessment after the disaster to capture information about losses suffered by families. Compensation per capita was slightly lower for the poorest households than for others because they tended to have larger families.

Chennai and Puri

When Chennai and Puri suffered severe flooding in late 2015, the houses of many poor and migrant families were washed away or partly damaged. Most families reported work losses ranging from 15 to 45 workdays and an average loss in wages at ₹250–₹500 per day. Some lost their jobs because they could not report to work for more than 2 weeks, including families working as domestic help in richer homes in Chennai. Many people had to temporarily leave their damaged homes, sheltering in the homes of relatives or returning to their villages and so losing workdays or their jobs altogether.

Families reported that they lost important identification, bank, or insurance documents and certificates. Identification documents were required to claim relief for damage or establish ownership of houses and other assets. In addition, migrant families were denied shelter and relief by government officials if they lacked voter or ration cards to establish their identity as residents.

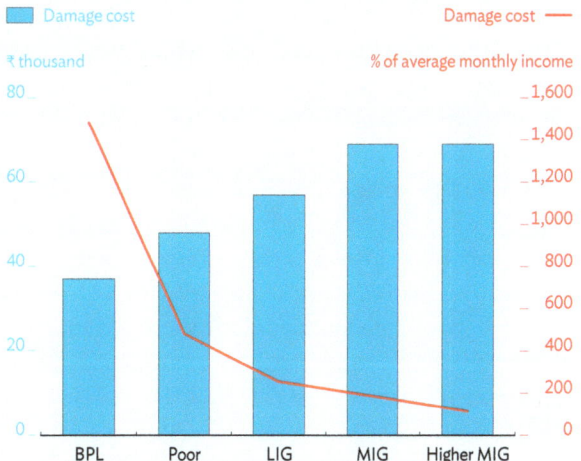

1 Cost of asset repair and replacement after flooding in Mumbai

BPL = below poverty line of ₹5,000, Poor = ₹5,000–₹15,000, LIG = lower-income group earning ₹15,000–₹30,000, MIG = middle-income group earning ₹30,000–₹45,000, Higher MIG = earning more than ₹45,000.

Source: Patankar, forthcoming (calculations based on primary data).

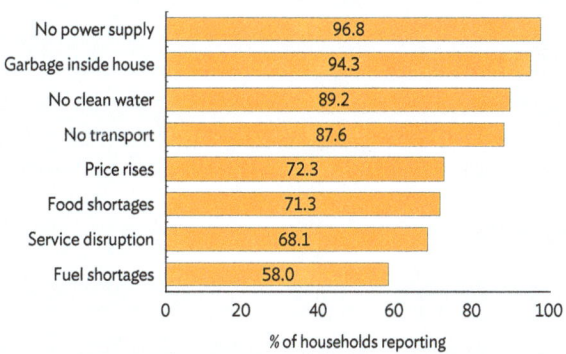

2 Indirect impacts of floods (% of households)

- No power supply: 96.8
- Garbage inside house: 94.3
- No clean water: 89.2
- No transport: 87.6
- Price rises: 72.3
- Food shortages: 71.3
- Service disruption: 68.1
- Fuel shortages: 58.0

Source: Patankar, forthcoming (calculations based on primary data).

A growing body of evidence documents how the long-term effects of disasters that occurred during victims' childhood and infancy, or even when they were in utero, affected their subsequent achievements in adult life (Almond and Currie 2011, Almond 2006). Considering drought, for example, rainfall in the year and location of birth significantly correlated with adult outcomes for Indonesian women born in 1953–1974, with more bountiful rainfall in infancy associated with better health and higher educational attainment and household wealth in adulthood (Maccini and Yang 2009). In the Philippines, typhoons were linked to higher infant mortality for baby girls up to 2 years after a typhoon (Hsiang and Anttila-Hughes 2013). Hurricane risk appeared to have a significantly negative impact on educational achievement in the Caribbean (Spencer, Polachek, and Strobl 2016). Among children who lost parents in Indonesia to the 2004 Indian Ocean tsunami, the older ones subsequently completed fewer years of school, either because they had to assume parental responsibilities or because of trauma associated with the loss (Cas et al. 2014). Younger children were less affected.

Even more troubling are findings from studies on the potential for intergenerational transmission of adverse disaster impacts. Research showed that women who were exposed in utero to a catastrophic Peruvian earthquake in 1970 bore children decades later who suffered lower educational attainment than their peers whose mothers had not been similarly exposed (Caruso and Miller 2015).

Another recent study found that women in sub-Saharan Africa who were exposed to drought in rural areas during their early childhood received fewer years of formal education, were significantly less wealthy as adults, and, if the drought was extreme, grew to be shorter in stature (Hyland and Russ 2019). Moreover, evidence in this study suggested again that effects might be transmitted to the women's offspring, with the children of affected women more likely to be born with low birth weight.

As can be seen from these examples from Peru and sub-Saharan Africa, the vulnerability of the poor is compounded by marginalization along various dimensions, including gender. Existing patterns of discrimination against women can be exacerbated by climate stress transmitted through income shocks (Miguel 2005, Sekhri and Storeygard 2014).

Natural hazards can stymie the formation of human capital through their effects on health. Extremes of both flooding and drought have been associated with higher incidence of malaria and with outbreaks of other vector-borne diseases such as plague, Lyme disease, and hantavirus pulmonary syndrome, as well as outbreaks of various waterborne diseases including cholera, typhoid, and other diarrheal diseases (Hales, Edwards, and Kovats 2003).

Epidemics in particular arise from complex interaction between physical, ecological, and social mechanisms. The trigger can be an extreme weather event that leaves in its wake deficient or contaminated water supplies, malnutrition because of disrupted food supply, human displacement, increased pressure on local infrastructure and health care facilities, or physical conditions favorable for pathogens and their carriers to breed.

Reported health impacts affecting households surveyed in the aftermath of severe flooding in India included a notable rise in reported cases of diseases such as gastroenteritis and leptospirosis, as well as increased incidence of malaria, dengue, and typhoid. These impacts came immediately following the flood, measurably exceeding their already high prevalence during a normal monsoon season (Patankar, forthcoming).

Thus, while disasters may usually appear to deliver transient shocks at the macroeconomic scale, their effects at the micro scale may persist over the long term, with potential to disrupt markets, push poorer households into debt and poverty, and diminish educational attainment, future earning potential, and long-term health outcomes.

Impact on institutions, governance, and conflict

Disasters may similarly have indirect effects on longer-term development trajectories through their effects on institutions, governance, and conflict, though the evidence is difficult to establish and suggests heterogenous effects (Castells-Quintana, Lopez-Uribe, and McDermott 2017). In some cases, disasters can actually improve institutions and governance by generating dissatisfaction with the status quo.

There is a growing literature on the relationship between weather shocks and conflict. It generally finds that weather shocks—particularly droughts, extremely high temperatures, and deviation in rainfall patterns—can make conflict more likely and, when it occurs, more intense (Dell, Jones, and Olken 2014). Most of the studies linking climate and conflict focus on the effect of weather shocks on rural incomes. A drought, for example, that removes jobs and hurts rural incomes may increase the supply of willing combatants.

It has been suggested as well that disaster shocks can create windows of opportunity for democratic development as affected populations become more motivated to contest power (Burke and Leigh 2010, Brückner and Ciccone 2011). Some historical accounts suggest that the Meiji Restoration in Japan, for example, was triggered by a series of devastating earthquakes in 1854–1855 (Clancey 2006). However, disaster shocks are also associated with a higher likelihood of irregular or extralegal leadership transitions, including military coups, setting back democratic development and economic growth

(Dell, Jones, and Olken 2012). The Islamic revolution in Iran, which caused a dramatic decline in incomes, may have been triggered by the devastating 1978 earthquake in the southern city of Tabas (Cavallo et al. 2013).

The findings from the literature remain controversial because the determinants of conflict are highly complex, and the potential effects of weather shocks or disasters on institutions, for better or worse, appear to depend heavily on the socioeconomic, political, and institutional characteristics of the affected country (Waldinger 2016, Castells-Quintana, Lopez-Uribe, and McDermott 2017).

Pervasive effects of disasters

Disaster effects can spread across wide geographic areas through, for example, damage to market mechanisms, such as disruption to supply chains, and the movements of employers, employees, or affected populations more generally. When disaster strikes and impacts propagate through production networks or supply chains, the shock is felt not only by companies in the affected region, but also by those outside it and sometimes very far away. This happened in the aftermath of the Tohoku earthquake in March 2011, for example, and the Thailand flood later that year. Both events imposed severe shortages on firms in the US and Europe that used inputs from the affected regions in their production processes. The customers of the Japanese and Thai firms directly hit by the disaster had to slow or even stop their own production for lack of parts and components.

Negative spillover through supply chains

Recent empirical literature has found strong evidence of these supply-chain ripple effects, using data on firms in Japan and the US and on multinational companies in global supply chains. For example, research on idiosyncratic shocks from disasters to firms in the US since the mid-1980s found that affected suppliers imposed heavy output losses on downstream users, especially when they produced unique inputs (Barrot and Sauvagnat 2016). This then translated into significant losses that spilled over to other suppliers within production networks. Similarly, studies on the upstream and downstream impacts of the 2011 Japan earthquake and tsunami on suppliers and consumers found that the transmission of the shock through input–output linkages caused a 1.2% decline in Japan's gross output in the year after the earthquake (Carvalho et al. 2016).

Supply-chain interdependencies, especially if coupled with cost-effective just-in-time delivery of components, potentially create greater indirect exposure to natural hazards for firms not directly exposed or even located in hazard zones.

Moreover, the propagation of impacts can occur quickly and widely in modern supply chain networks (Inoue and Todo 2018). But the role of supply chains in either propagating or mitigating business disruptions from disasters appears to depend on the characteristics of the supply chain. Specifically, the propagation effect is larger when inputs are more specific and cannot be easily substituted (Barrot and Sauvagnat 2016).

Some research looking at international spillover found that these supply chain effects were typically confined within the affected country. Several studies observed neither downstream nor upstream propagation beyond national borders. For instance, using firm-level and supply-chain data on more than 100,000 major firms around the world, Kashiwagi, Todo, and Matous (2018) found the propagation effect on US firms to be smaller for larger firms and for those linked into international supply chains. International firms can find substitutes for damaged suppliers and customers more easily than can firms with purely domestic supply chains, which may explain why the international propagation of shocks is less likely.

Other studies, however, do find evidence that the interruption of supply chains can reverberate internationally. Philippine imports of automobiles and parts from Thailand, for example, were observed to decline by more than 35% from January 2011 to November 2011, after floods disrupted supply chains in Thailand, than in the same period in 2010, when there was no such disruption (Haraguchi and Lall 2014). Sales of new automobiles in the Philippines in the period consequently decreased by up to 140,000 units, a 4.0% decline from the first 11 months of 2010.

The interconnected nature of supply chain networks hints at the potential for government responses to disasters—targeted, for example, at affected firms—to prevent spillover on unaffected firms and regions. Governments can leverage market mechanisms to minimize disruption to supply chains by facilitating and supporting the reconstruction of damaged production facilities, particularly those of smaller enterprises, and by fostering greater cooperation among firms and redundancies in their supply chains.

A role for targeted subsidies?

Firms have incentives to prepare business continuity plans and to cooperate with each other to find substitutes for damaged suppliers after a major disaster, but room still exists to actively encourage and facilitate such cooperation. Government intervention can mitigate the propagation of disaster shocks by, for example, organizing emergency trade fairs to ease supply chain disruptions in both affected and unaffected areas. Similarly, governments may choose to subsidize damaged firms' recovery of key capital goods if those firms are crucial nodes in production supply chains.

One prominent example of this was a policy intervention by which the Japanese authorities funded 75% of costs to repair or reinstall the damaged capital goods and facilities of groups of SMEs after the 2011 earthquake and tsunami. For greater impact, the subsidy was provided only to groups of firms linked through supply chains and located in the same industrial or commercial area. Group subsidy disbursements started within 6 months of the disaster. By 2018, ¥504 billion had been granted through this program to 705 company groups.

Kashigawi and Todo (forthcoming) evaluated the impact of this subsidy and how it filtered through supply chains. The study found that group subsidies particularly benefitted small recipient firms—manufacturers with no more than 20 employees or service providers with no more than 5 employees, in both cases counting employees after the disaster. Crucially, research found that, within the four disaster-hit prefectures, the subsidies also benefitted firms that received no subsidy but had supply chain connections to recipient firms. By contrast, no impact was found for larger recipients, possibly because these medium-sized firms benefited more from the support of stronger industrial, financial, and commercial networks. Nor did the study find indirect supply chain effects beyond the disaster-hit prefectures, possibly because those links entailed support from a larger network of partners.

A simple cost–benefit analysis for this subsidy program, for small firms only, estimated total benefits in excess of ¥299 billion against a total cost of ¥31.8 billion. Considering that ¥217 billion in benefits accrued indirectly to the suppliers of inputs to firms that received the subsidy, these results seem to highlight the need for policy makers to incorporate supply chain considerations when devising disaster recovery policies (Figure 2.2.2).

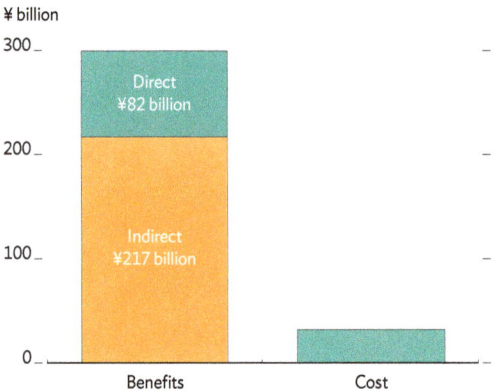

2.2.2 Cost and benefits of the subsidy program

Source: Kashiwagi and Todo, forthcoming.

Migration as an effective coping strategy

From the dawn of humanity, people have coped with risk by migrating away from it. Nowadays, one in three migrants comes from Asia, and the countries with the highest ratio of outward migrants are the hazard-exposed Pacific economies (ADB 2018d). Both international and internal rural–urban migration is often driven by economic pressures and the search for more opportunity. Every year, millions of people around the world are forced to leave their homes after disasters render them unable to sustain themselves in their homes. These pressures are particularly pronounced in developing Asia.

In 2017, more than 18.8 million people were displaced internally (many only temporarily) by sudden-onset disasters worldwide, with East and South Asia accounting for 11.4 million, or over 60% of the total (Figure 2.2.3) (IDMC 2018). At the same time, concern is rising over slow-onset disasters, especially as they relate to climate change. The World Bank has predicted that there will be by 2050 some 140 million internal climate migrants, 60 million of them in South Asia alone, fleeing water scarcity, crop failure, sea-level rise, and more frequent storm surges (Rigaud et al. 2018). IDMC (2019) estimated that the cost of internal displacement associated with Typhoon Haiyan in the 6 months following the storm was $816 million in the Philippines, where Haiyan was named Yolanda.

Not always a stay-or-go dichotomy, migration is often temporary or seasonal, and it is an integral part of household strategies for coping with risk. Migrants often remain closely tied to the home region, for example through remittances. Population movements in response to disasters similarly span a spectrum from forced displacement to voluntary migration, and from temporary and local to permanent and long distance (Figure 2.2.4). For this reason, numbers can be contentious, but it is clear that large numbers of people move in response to disasters. Regardless of the precise numbers, it is who moves and on what terms that is more important in determining the consequences of disaster-related movement.

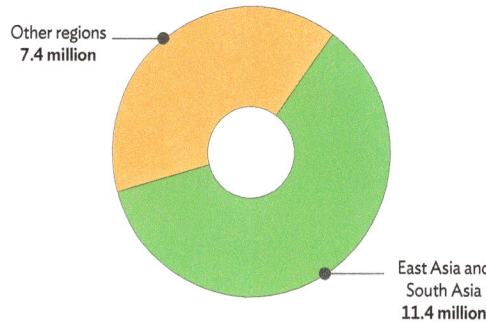

2.2.3 New internal displacement from disasters, in 2017

Other regions 7.4 million

East Asia and South Asia 11.4 million

Source: IDMC 2018.

2.2.4 The spectrum of human mobility and immobility

MOBILITY			IMMOBILITY	
Migration	Relocation	Displacement	Stay	Trapped
People choose to migrate permanently to a distant location, maybe abroad.	People permanently relocate with government assistance to what is hoped is a less risky area.	People evacuate a devastated area and may choose to go back.	People choose to stay.	People cannot move.

Source: Adapted from Ober (forthcoming), originally from Rigaud et al. 2018.

The benefits of migration arise from its use as a mechanism to diversify and smooth household income. In the aggregate, migration can raise average labor productivity—and consequently incomes—when people move to locations where productivity is higher than at home. This is typically so in cities, which are generally more productive than rural areas. In this context, migration more generally has been shown to offer potentially large welfare gains to migrants and their families, as in Gröger and Zylberberg (2016), studying households hit by typhoons in Viet Nam.

Disasters usually motivate internal, localized, and short-term movement. During sudden-onset disasters, people often make decisions quickly and under duress. The decisions whether to move—and who moves, how, when, and to where—are determined by the exposure, vulnerability, and resilience of each household, as well as by the assets they own and can use to finance such decisions. Unfortunately, the people who end up displaced by disasters are often among the most disadvantaged.

On average, the poor are more likely to migrate than other groups when hit by disaster. However, the poorest of the poor may be unable to migrate because they lack the necessary social connections or the resources including credit necessary to finance such a move. They thus becoming trapped and even more vulnerable to future disasters (Black et al. 2011). Droughts in rural Bangladesh, for example, mobilized many households that were not directly affected, while the worst affected were less likely to migrate because their already meager financial resources had been further decimated (Gray and Mueller 2012). The most severe disasters tend to inhibit mobility, as the capacity to move is reduced by the adverse shock to income, credit, and wealth (Robalino, Jimenez, and Chacon 2015). Other factors may stifle the desire to migrate in response to adverse environmental pressures, such as the decision of people in Tuvalu to stay put and advocate change (Noy 2017).

In sum, migration can benefit resilience, and when migration does not happen, the barriers to migration may further victimize those who are unable to move. Support for greater voluntary mobility—specifically to empower individuals and households to move on their own terms—thus constitutes an important but largely neglected policy response to disaster risk.

Risk of unplanned migration and forced displacement

Disasters often displace populations and destroy physical capital including buildings and other infrastructure, heightening vulnerability to the next disaster and creating exposure to other risks. When disasters cause people to migrate to urban areas, for example, they may face additional exposure to flooding, heat stress, and epidemics, particularly in marginal and suburban shantytowns where basic shelter, infrastructure, and sanitation were lacking even before the migrants arrived.

Globally, the observed increase in disaster-exposed populations is being driven, at least in part, by high migration to areas at risk, particularly urban areas in flood-prone coastal zones. Moreover, evidence suggests that migrant families newly arrived in urban areas are particularly vulnerable to hazards. When severe flooding hit the Indian city of Chennai, the houses of poor and migrant families were damaged or even washed away, yet migrant families were denied shelter and compensation for lack of official documentation. Some of the affected migrant families had resettled from other areas vulnerable to hazards (Box 2.2.3). This suggests a role for government in planning and directing voluntary migration toward areas with lower disaster risk, even if only by providing information to migrants on the relative risk at various locations (Waldinger 2016).

Disasters that push migrants to urban areas can create additional problems in the receiving localities if, for example, congestion worsens or competition intensifies in labor markets or for basic amenities, potentially sparking social disorder (Bhavnani and Lacina 2015, Castells-Quintana and McDermott, forthcoming).

Disasters can have diverse impacts on social cohesion. Especially where deep schisms already exist in a society, disasters and migration pressures generated by them can perpetuate these schisms or exacerbate them (Aldrich 2010). Sometimes, though, disasters can improve social relations. Examples of these dynamics are much more prevalent than of worsening schisms, the most notable example in recent times in Aceh, Indonesia. A peace accord between the Government of Indonesia and the Free Aceh Movement in 2005, after 30 years of conflict, came as a direct consequence of the destruction in Aceh wrought by the tsunami of December 2004.

The importance of appropriate policy support

Policy support can make migration more inclusively available as a mechanism for coping with risk. It can minimize the potential for negative spillover caused by displacement.
In particular, information on the potential costs and benefits of migration, and on job opportunities at destinations, can help individuals make more informed choices and improve the outcomes of migration (Bryan, Chowdhury, and Mobarak 2014, Munshi 2003). Lowering other barriers—including credit constraints and institutional issues related, for example, to land tenure security—can help potential migrants make better decisions that are more likely to improve their welfare (Deininger and Jin 2006).

Policy intervention is required to mitigate any negative impacts in both the sending and the receiving region.
In urban areas, additional strains on urban labor markets and infrastructure can alarm local residents when a rapid increase in population occurs, particularly if it is caused by a large number of migrants appearing suddenly, as can happen, for example, when drought hits a nearby rural area.

Where arriving migrants have difficulty accessing labor markets, public services, accommodation, and other amenities, economic and social problems can ensue (Castells-Quintana and McDermott, forthcoming). Government policies that aim to manage the flow of displaced people and strengthening absorptive capacity at migrant destinations can help ensure that migration is a risk coping strategy that broadly enhances the welfare of all concerned.

More fundamentally, policy responses that build disaster resilience promise to reduce the extent of forced displacement and enable individuals and households to make choices about migration that are informed and voluntary—choices that improve outcomes in terms of livelihoods and well-being today and that strengthen disaster resilience in the future.

Investing in development with disaster resilience

Resilience begins with risk reduction, which alleviates vulnerability and exposure to natural hazards that threaten to become disasters, ranging from localized events to major catastrophes. Disaster risk cannot be eliminated entirely, though, and unavoidable disasters can place significant budgetary pressure on governments, businesses, and individual households. Mindful of the social and economic costs imposed by the disasters discussed above, this section turns to the roles that governments and their international partners can play in building disaster resilience.

Tackling the underlying drivers of disaster risk and vulnerability requires a shift in approach toward disaster risk management strategies that emphasize preventative and systemic investments. Resilience is a useful concept in the field because it has the potential to facilitate a shift in perspective and practice toward more forward-looking, comprehensive, and integrated approaches.

In addition to a conceptual shift toward resilience, a parallel need is to explore risk management options available for local communities and individuals. After all, it is within communities that disaster impacts are felt most strongly and a lot of detailed knowledge resides. Therefore, community action to tackle growing disaster risk and mitigate impacts can be very effective.

Much progress has been made on these fronts in recent years, with developing Asia leading the way. Governments should continue to integrate disaster risk reduction (DRR) into broader development policies and public investment strategies. They can seek to build resilience from the ground up by supporting the development of market mechanisms such as insurance and credit facilities, by investing directly in communities, and by emphasizing climate-change adaptation and disaster resilience in infrastructure development.

Progress in dealing with disaster risk

Asia has made substantial progress in mainstreaming disaster risk into development plans. Over the past few decades, governments, populations, and the international community have increasingly recognized the need to reduce risk and enhance financial preparedness for disasters in countries across developing Asia. The Sendai Framework for Disaster Risk Reduction 2015–2030 articulates this need and sets out key goals to this end. It identifies its four priority areas for action as (i) understanding disaster risk, (ii) strengthening disaster risk governance, (iii) investing in DRR, and (iv) enhancing disaster preparedness.

2.3.1 Asian Development Fund financing of disaster risk reduction

Growing international awareness of the need for DRR is illustrated by the establishment of a DRR financing mechanism under the 12th replenishment of the Asian Development Fund (ADF), covering 2017–2020. The ADF is the fund from which ADB provides grants to its 18 lower-income developing member countries.

The DRR financing mechanism was established to strengthen disaster resilience and help spur further investment in DRR by enhancing awareness of disaster risk and opportunities to address it. ADF donors agreed to allocate up to $200 million for this mechanism under the 12th replenishment of the ADF, including grants for lower-income countries normally eligible only for concessional loans.

Additional concessional loans have been made available for DDR with the requirement that recipients provide matching funds, to encourage countries to invest in and mainstream DRR into their broader expenditure. The DRR funds are used to support standalone DRR projects with disaster resilience as their primary objective, DRR components of other grant and loan projects, and the incremental cost in strengthening the disaster resilience of other development infrastructure.

Source:
Asian Development Bank 2019a.

Improved data availability and risk analysis provide the modern knowledge base from which to design effective solutions and inform practical action both to address underlying risk and to enhance financial preparedness. Efforts to address underlying disaster risk center on better mainstreaming of disaster resilience measures into broader development investments (Box 2.3.1). For example, from 2010 to 2018, ADB approved 240 new development projects incorporating measures to strengthen disaster resilience.

Despite recent progress, a large difference remains in disaster spending between ex-post crisis response and ex-ante investment. Globally, assistance to governments in developing countries is about seven times larger for responding to disasters after they occur than for preparing in advance to prevent them from happening (Kellett and Caravani 2013). In Asia, spending on disaster prevention and preparedness has risen in recent years, but the gap is still large between this and spending on emergency response and reconstruction relief and rehabilitation. While data on disaster risk reduction is sparsely available, a rising trend of preventive spending can be observed in relation to humanitarian aid, especially to Southeast Asia and the Pacific (Figure 2.3.1). Further closing this gap will yield multiple dividends, especially when investments have development benefits beyond disaster risk reduction.

Disaster resilience and development

While substantial funds are spent on dealing with disasters, the burden imposed by these events remains heavy in many places, particularly in Asia. Despite ample evidence of disasters' adverse development impacts and of the benefits of reducing risk, it often remains difficult to motivate

2.3.1 Humanitarian aid to developing Asia

- Reconstruction relief and rehabilitation
- Disaster prevention and preparedness
- Emergency response

For disaster prevention, emergency response, and reconstruction

- Central Asia
- East Asia
- South Asia
- Southeast Asia
- The Pacific

For disaster prevention and preparedness by subregion

Note: Humanitarian aid is emergency and distress relief in cash or in kind, including emergency response, relief food aid, short-term reconstruction relief and rehabilitation, and disaster prevention and preparedness.
Source: OECD. Query Wizard for International Development Statistics. https://stats.oecd.org/qwids/ (accessed 20 February 2019).

decision makers in the public sector, private business, and civil society to increase their investments in disaster risk reduction.

International policy debate has made strides since the first and second global conferences on reducing disaster risk in Yokohama and Kobe and has been shaped by three key global agreements in 2015: on DRR in Sendai, on climate change in Paris, and on the Sustainable Development Goals adopted at a United Nations summit in New York. These compacts all emphasize the need to integrate disaster and climate risks with development concerns and thus promote approaches that concurrently reduce disaster risk, adapt to climate change, and pay development dividends.

Figure 2.3.2 shows how international disaster risk discourse has moved over the years, from early perceptions of disasters as "acts of God" to the current understanding of risk in terms of shaping development challenges and opportunities. At the same time, decision makers have been requesting actionable information to close knowledge gaps and generate metrics for grasping the benefits generated from managing risk, fostering climate adaptation, and building resilience (Mechler and Hochrainer-Stigler, forthcoming).

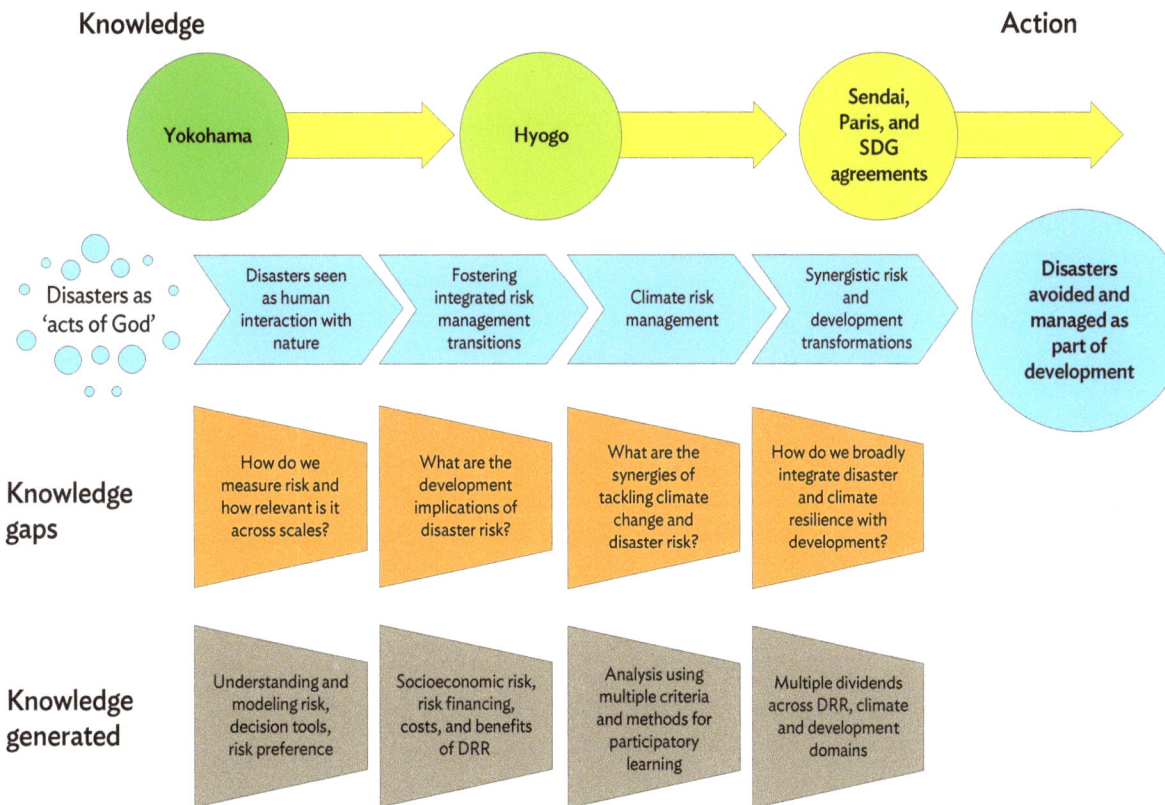

2.3.2 Evolving approaches to disaster risk management

DRR = disaster risk reduction, SDG = Sustainable Development Goal.
Source: Mechler and Hochrainer-Stigler, forthcoming.

The "triple resilience dividend framework" has captured this alignment of discourse and presents a broad business case for DRR, suggesting three types of dividends associated with investments in disaster risk management (DRM): The first dividend is reducing damage and loss of life, livelihoods, and assets; the second is unlocking development; and the third is garnering development co-benefits (Surminski and Tanner 2016). Illustrative examples of each of the three dividends are presented in Box 2.3.2 and its table.

Policy and investment have started to build on the multiple dividend framework, and the DRM and development policy domains are becoming increasingly integrated. In practice this has meant that donor institutions are embedding disaster and climate risks into development projects and programs.

Examples of investments with multiple dividends are becoming more commonplace, and international development nongovernment organizations (NGOs) have taken up this agenda. NGOs that participate in the Flood Resilience Alliance, for example, have reported engaging in various community-led projects across Asia that generate additional dividends in addition to reducing flood risk. One example integrates into early warning systems weather boards that improve preparedness for extreme weather but also generate more routine benefits from better weather forecasting, including improved crop-sowing decisions. Other examples are water resource management that integrates flood risk considerations, the construction of disaster-resilient multipurpose evacuation and community centers, the reestablishment of mangrove forests against storms and coastal erosion, and hydroponics projects that stabilize incomes in normal times and safeguard food security when disaster strikes.

Little detailed information is available about national projects designed to have synergistic multiple dividends. The few countries that release such information rarely take it beyond the first risk reduction dividend. Donors and some NGOs have reported synergistic spending on DRR integrated with climate and development concerns, and countries should follow suit. Some evidence on national spending can be evinced from a recent review of national DRR expenditure in the Lao People's Democratic Republic, Thailand, and Viet Nam in the 4 years to 2014. It found that average DRR-relevant expenditure in the three countries ranged from the equivalent of 0.2% of GDP to 1.7%, and from 4.6% to 8.9% of central government total expenditure (Abbott 2018).

Figure 2.3.3 demonstrates nascent reporting practices by analyzing the reporting done through the Sendai Monitor and as required by all signatories to the Sendai Framework for DRR. Reporting covers only 2017 and the first half of 2018. Countries are required to measure their progress against a benchmark established using 2005–2014 aggregates. Most countries in Asia have yet to establish this benchmark.

2.3.2 Assessing returns on ex-ante investment into disaster risk management

Mechler and Hochrainer-Stigler (forthcoming) reviewed the findings of a global database of 65 cost–benefit analyses of DRR investments, of which 15 studies (11 on Asia) can be considered to have taken a multiple resilience dividend approach, though only one explicitly builds on the triple resilience dividend framework. The dividends, presented as cost–benefit ratios, appear substantial and in line with estimates of benefits across other studies that do not consider benefits beyond the first dividend (with cost–benefit ratios of 2–5:1 on average for various hazards). However, the quantification of benefits in these studies tends to be unreliable, which undermines confidence in their estimates of the multiple resilience dividend.

A focus beyond the first dividend, for which probability-based risk calculations are required, often inspires broader-brush estimates in response to the need to gauge benefits across a number of risk and development variables and to aggregate them. Further, multiple dividend approaches require assessments of interventions with indirect or intangible outcomes, such as recreational, ecological, and social benefits, for which a quantitative cost–benefit analysis (CBA) may be less suitable. The second resilience dividend, indirect economic co-benefits through unlocked development potential, has not been assessed as frequently because data on development processes are collected over longer periods of time, requiring additional effort and resources that are only rarely available.

CBA remains attractive as a tool for deciding technical points in well-defined DRR interventions, such as how high to build flood embankments. Indeed, potential exists to integrate the decision tool with the multiple-dividend logic. IPCC (2012) differentiated between "hard infrastructure-based responses and soft solutions such as individual and institutional capacity building and ecosystem-based responses." Soft investments are even more difficult to assess, especially using CBA. Other tools for specialists, such as cost-effectiveness analysis, and robust decision-making approaches may help with the challenge of monetizing intangible benefits.

Rising demand for "softer" DRM investments has brought to the fore decision support tools with stronger participatory assessments and more inclusive processes for decision-making. Approaches that measure resilience may be used to support actions and decisions at every stage of the project cycle, in contrast with decision-support tools limited to evaluating and selecting options. These approaches focus on capacity, not outcome. Such capacity assessments can serve as decision support for organizations working in local communities to scope out the interactions between development and disaster risk, fostering their understanding of the strengths and weaknesses of existing resilience before actual events, helping them gauge resilience after events, and facilitating affected communities' participation in formulating solutions.

Reported resilience dividends in representative cost–benefit analyses following the 3 dividends framework

Risk management intervention	Dividend 1: Losses and damage avoided and reduced	Dividend 2: Unlocking development	Dividend 3: Co-benefits
Meteorological services	Avoided mortality, improved preparedness from weather extremes		Utility from weather predictions: improved crop-sowing decisions
Alternative flood control approach	Avoided economic, social, and environmental impacts		Recreational benefits, improved public safety, landscape and nature conservation, benefits of system functions of wetlands.
Flood management under climate change	Reduction in damage to crops, livestock, housing, assets, public infrastructure, health, and wages, but suffering costs from waterlogging	Agricultural productivity enhanced	Community grain and seed bank
Drought risk management	Reduced relief expenditure	Stabilization of income and consumption	Benefits from installed irrigation infrastructure
Mangrove afforestation against coastal flooding	Avoided direct and indirect flood damage	Economic benefits to planters' income, increased yields	Ecological benefits: carbon value, nutrient retention, sediment retention, biodiversity habitat
Earthquake-proof construction using straw bale	Reduction in lives lost		Reduced price of building materials, reduced heating and cooling costs, decrease in the child labor common in brickmaking, improved air quality

2.3.3 Overview of 2017 target reporting in the Sendai Monitor

195 countries total

A – Mortality
- 124 not started
- 20 in progress
- 20 ready for validation
- 31 validated

B – People affected
- 135 not started
- 17 in progress
- 26 ready for validation
- 17 validated

C – Economic losses
- 136 not started
- 31 in progress
- 14 ready for validation
- 14 validated

D – Critical infrastructure
- 160 not started
- 9 in progress
- 12 ready for validation
- 14 validated

E – Disaster risk reduction strategies
- 134 not started
- 25 in progress
- 16 ready for validation
- 20 validated

F – International cooperation
- 158 not started
- 17 in progress
- 12 ready for validation
- 8 validated

G – Warning and risk information
- 144 not started
- 29 in progress
- 8 ready for validation
- 14 validated

Progress of target reporting of developing Asian countries, 2017

A – Mortality
- Reports in progress (AZE, BAN, GEO, INO, KAZ, KGZ, SRI, TAJ, THA)
- All indicators validated (AFG, ARM, BHU, CAM, ROK, FIJ, MAL, MYA, MON, NEP, PRC)

B – People affected
- Reports in progress (AZE, BAN, GEO, INO, KAZ, KGZ, TAJ, THA)
- Some indicators validated (ARM, ROK, PRC)
- All indicators validated (AFG, BHU, CAM, FIJ, MAL, MON, MYA, NEP)

C – Economic losses
- Reports in progress (AZE, GEO, KAZ, KGZ, TAJ, TIM)
- Some indicators validated (ARM, CAM, ROK, NEP)
- All indicators validated (AFG, BHU, MAL, MON, MYA)

D – Critical infrastructure
- Reports in progress (ARM, GEO, INO, KAZ, KGZ, TAJ)
- Some indicators validated (CAM, ROK)
- All indicators validated (AFG, BHU, MAL, MON, MYA, NEP)

E – Disaster risk reduction strategies
- Reports in progress (ARM, AZE, BHU, GEO, KAZ, KGZ, TAJ)
- Some indicators validated (ARM, ROK)
- All indicators validated (AFG, MAL, MON, MYA, NEP, THA)

F – International cooperation
- Reports in progress (ARM, GEO, KGZ, TAJ)
- Some indicators validated (BHU, ROK)
- All indicators validated (AFG, MAL, MON, MYA)

G – Warning and risk information
- Reports in progress (ARM, GEO, INO, KAZ, KGZ, TAJ, THA)
- Some indicators validated (AFG, BHU, ROK, MAL, NEP)
- All indicators validated (MAL, MON)

AFG = Afghanistan, ARM = Armenia, AZE = Azerbaijan, BAN = Bangladesh, BHU = Bhutan, CAM = Cambodia, FIJ = Fiji, GEO = Georgia, INO = Indonesia, KAZ = Kazakhstan, KGZ = Kyrgyz Republic, MAL = Malaysia, MON = Mongolia, MYA = Myanmar, NEP = Nepal, PRC = People's Republic of China, ROK = Republic of Korea, SRI = Sri Lanka, TAJ = Tajikistan, THA = Thailand, TIM = Timor Leste.
Source: UNISDR. https://sendaimonitor.unisdr.org/ (accessed 20 February 2019).

Disaster-resilient infrastructure

Significant investments in infrastructure projects are currently under way or planned in countries across developing Asia. Infrastructure investment needs in developing Asia are estimated at $26 trillion from 2016 to 2030, or $1.7 trillion per year including necessary investments in climate-change mitigation and adaptation (ADB 2017, ADB 2019b). These investments need to take into account disaster risk for two reasons. First, some of the projects are themselves likely to be subject to disaster risk, which affects their expected return on investment.

Second, infrastructure investments can influence future exposure to disaster risk by, for example, altering spatial development patterns, especially with the construction of new roads, ports, or other transport infrastructure (Dietz, Dixon, and Ward 2016).

The large scale of anticipated investment needs underscores the potential for these investments to influence future exposure and vulnerability to disaster risk in developing Asia. Many infrastructure projects are irreversible to a greater or lesser extent. This is clearly the case with major physical infrastructure projects designed for long use and bearing a large initial price tag, making them costly to reverse. But it may be true as well for other investments that influence long-term development patterns by creating path dependencies. This is often the case, for example, with urban planning and development, making such investments very expensive to undo (Dietz, Dixon, and Ward 2016, Kocornik-Mina et al., forthcoming).

Greenfield infrastructure investments are natural entry points for including disaster resilience in the planning process from the outset. With such investments, accounting for the likely effects of future exposure to disaster risk promises to be highly cost-effective. A recent study of road investments in Viet Nam, for example, showed that the tendency to favor already densely developed coastal areas had significant costs (Balboni 2018). While the returns on coastal road investments from 2000 to 2010 were positive, a greater concentration of investment inland would have offered higher returns. The risk posed by future sea-level rise further underscored the inefficiency of coastal investments. Welfare gains of some 72% could have been achieved by investment that avoided the most vulnerable regions.

The types of infrastructure investments for which disaster and climate risk assessment is most relevant can be identified using a simple framework that considers the following: the scale of the project; the extent to which the investment can be expected to affect disaster and climate risk by worsening community exposure and vulnerability, either directly or through its outputs; the time horizon of the investment, as longer-term investments require greater scrutiny; and the extent to which the investment is considered irreversible (Ranger and Garbett-Shiels 2012). The framework should also take into account the expected impact of an investment that attracts further development investment into a hazard-prone area. Examples of investment projects that most urgently require consideration of disaster and climate risk include energy generation, urban greenfield developments, water supply and irrigation systems, and transport infrastructure.

While returns on infrastructure investments are substantial, especially in developing Asia, public investment in infrastructure projects generally raises the thorny issue of decision-making rendered deeply uncertain by climate change.

Such uncertainty presents an additional motivation for policy makers to prioritize building adaptive capacity into human resources that is likely to strengthen disaster resilience under a wide range of future climate scenarios. Uncertainty about the effects of climate change on future disaster risk generally shifts the balance of DRM portfolios toward these soft investments, which are less uncertain (see e.g., McDermott 2016, Watkiss 2016).

Financial management of disasters

Delays and financing shortfalls can considerably exacerbate the economic and social consequences of direct physical damage from disasters, extending the time required to bring infrastructure back into use and restart service delivery, as well as stymieing efforts to rebuild for greater disaster resilience and to revitalize livelihoods and the economy—that is, to "build back better," as the literature discusses it. Spending plans and goals can go awry when delayed recovery and reconstruction combine with deteriorating balance sheets caused by unplanned spending on disaster relief, with adverse consequences for long-term development.

Governments are therefore working to enhance financial planning for disasters, seeking to ensure that sufficient financing is available to support timely relief, early recovery efforts, and reconstruction, as well as to promote enhanced financial preparedness in the private sector and the population at large.

Governments can draw on an array of instruments to enhance financial preparedness. A risk-layered approach to disaster risk financing is widely advocated, breaking disaster risk down according to hazards' frequency, or probability of occurrence, and the magnitude of associated losses to identify the most appropriate instruments for each layer of risk (Figure 2.3.4).

These begin with risk retention instruments for more frequent but less damaging events, including annual contingency budget allocations, disaster reserves, and contingent financing arrangements, all of which are established before disasters strike (Benson 2016). In the aftermath of a disaster, governments can reallocate budget lines or increase their borrowing to provide additional resources.

Risk transfer solutions are typically more cost-efficient sources of financing for medium-range risks generating relatively large but less frequent losses. These instruments include insurance and insurance-linked securities, such as catastrophe and resilience bonds, and are taken out in anticipation of potential disasters. In the event of a major disaster, though, risk transfer instruments are rarely sufficient,

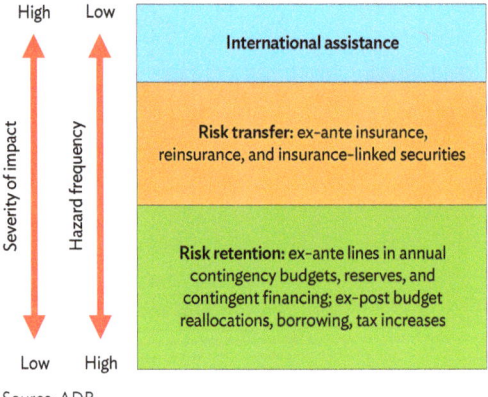

2.3.4 Layered approach to disaster risk financing

Source: ADB.

leaving governments to turn to the international community for assistance. For these solutions to be effective, they need to be accompanied by strong and effective recovery planning and post-disaster budget execution, to ensure that available resources can be mobilized quickly and effectively.

Finally, it is essential that disaster risk financing strategies be designed within a broader context of disaster resilience, placing primary emphasis on risk reduction to stem the trend of rising disaster losses. If not, the cost of post-disaster response will place mounting pressure on government budgets, and disaster risk could ultimately become neither insurable nor transferable. In line with this, opportunities should be exploited to design insurance and other instruments to encourage investments in risk reduction (Box 2.3.3).

2.3.3 Steps to developing a comprehensive disaster risk financing strategy

Steps to enhance financial preparedness begin with disaster risk modeling to quantify the scale of the disaster risk and express it in monetary terms (see e.g., Strobl, forthcoming; Box 2.2.1). Historical records of past disasters provide a starting point but typically extend back over just a few decades and therefore offer no instances of infrequent events not experienced recently. Hazard models overcome these shortcomings, combining the latest scientific knowledge on natural hazards with the historical record to generate catalogs of potential events over many years. These catalogs are then combined with data on the assets and infrastructure exposed to the hazards, and on their vulnerability, to generate loss curves expressed in monetary terms. These loss curves plot probable maximum losses for hazards with varying return periods, ranging from annual events to rare extreme events that occur perhaps only once in 500 years and therefore have a very small probability of 0.2% in any given year. The box figure depicts a typhoon loss frequency curve for the city of Hue in Viet Nam.

Loss frequency curve for typhoon risk in Hue, Viet Nam

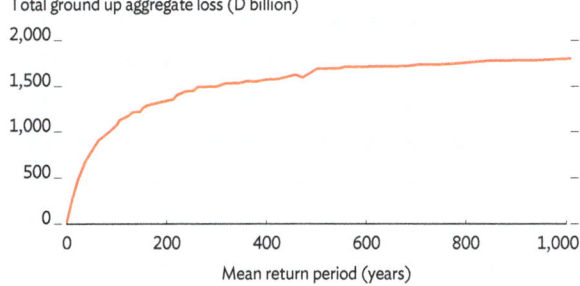

Source: ADB 2015.

With this loss frequency information, governments can determine their associated explicit and implicit contingent liabilities. These liabilities include the repair and reconstruction of public assets and the fulfillment of public guarantees to provide, for instance, financial backing for insurance programs or for lending institutions that are in danger of failing because of disaster-induced defaults. Further, governments sometimes act in the aftermath of a disaster to alleviate poverty, provide housing, or stimulate economic recovery. Predicting and quantifying all these liabilities provides to the government a full account of them and enables it to adequately plan for them.

The most appropriate bundle of instruments for each country and risk profile depends on a range of factors:
- the scale of resources required at each layer of loss;
- the required speed of disbursement;
- the costs and tradeoffs of different financing instruments for particular layers of loss;
- associated incentives or disincentives to address underlying risk and accept residual risk;
- government appetite for risk and expected goals and priorities after a disaster, such as to channel additional resources through social protection programs or to support the recovery of small businesses;
- individual country circumstances, such as indebtedness;
- broader government economic and fiscal goals and objectives;
- access to global credit markets; and
- the market cost of borrowing.

Financial preparedness nationally

In terms of financial preparedness, governments typically make only limited use of disaster risk financing instruments set up in advance for disaster response, beyond practical limits on regular budgetary provision for relief and early recovery and for other unforeseen events (for the first risk layer). In some cases, governments purchase indemnity insurance to cover a portion of public assets (the second layer). Such arrangements have proved to be far from adequate when a major disaster strikes, inevitably requiring unplanned budget reallocations. Such reallocations can take time to secure, particularly if budget realignment can be considered only during scheduled midterm budget reviews and annual budget formulations. Ad hoc arrangements for disaster risk financing, and related uncertainties regarding budget availability, hinder post-disaster planning and the effective use of resources.

Recognizing these limitations, governments have begun to strengthen options for both risk retention (first layer) and risk transfer (second layer) to enhance their financial preparedness. The Sendai Framework specifically calls for the promotion of "mechanisms for disaster risk transfer and insurance, risk sharing and retention and financial protection, as appropriate, for both public and private investment in order to reduce the financial impact of disasters on governments and societies, in urban and rural areas" (UN 2015).

These efforts have included the increased uptake of contingent financing arrangements, under which pre-negotiated lines of financing can be rapidly disbursed in the aftermath of a disaster (Box 2.3.4). Contingent financing arrangements target in particular the layer of disaster risk beyond which a government's own contingency budget lines and reserves are exhausted but before insurance become cost-efficient. The use of sovereign and nonsovereign insurance mechanisms is also growing, though they remain relatively limited.

Governments increasingly recognize the importance of positioning the various initiatives and instruments in a broader strategy for disaster risk financing. In developing Asia, the Government of the Philippines was the first to establish its DRM financing strategy, in 2015. This strategy recognizes that local governments and individuals, as well as the national government, require sound disaster risk financing arrangements. The Government of Indonesia also launched a disaster risk financing strategy, in 2018, and such strategies are under development in Myanmar and Pakistan, both with support from ADB.

It is important to note that disaster risk financing is not a responsibility only for the government. Toward developing a comprehensive financing strategy, action needs to be considered to stimulate commercial insurance markets, including for homeowners, businesses, and agriculture.

2.3.4 Contingent disaster financing and other financing instruments

Contingent disaster financing establishes preapproved lines of credit and grants that can be disbursed in the immediate aftermath of a disaster to provide timely budget support and alleviate fiscal pressures. They come conditional on monitorable actions to enhance long-term disaster resilience, thereby ensuring that underlying disaster risk is addressed. The achievement of required prior actions enables disbursement. However, funds are disbursed in part or in full only in the event of an agreed trigger event, typically the declaration of a state of disaster in accordance with national legislation. Funds can then be spent through the national budget.

ADB has supported the establishment of disaster contingent financing arrangements through policy-based instruments in five island countries in the Pacific to date, with coverage for another four countries expected by the end of 2019. Tonga's $6 million disaster contingent financing from ADB, disbursed in full just 3 days after the country was struck by Tropical Cyclone Gita in February 2018, demonstrated the rapid-disbursement feature of this instrument. The World Bank has supported the establishment of similar arrangements in the Philippines, Samoa, and Sri Lanka. Along similar lines, the World Bank has introduced in a number of its projects contingency emergency response components into which uncommitted project funds can be reallocated to finance urgent needs in the event of a crisis or emergency, including a disaster triggered by a natural hazard.

Development partners have formulated financing instruments to make more resources available for more traditional emergency assistance loans and grants offered in the aftermath of disaster. In Asia and the Pacific, ADB piloted the Disaster Response Facility under the eleventh replenishment of the Asian Development Fund, 2013–2016 and regularized it under the twelfth replenishment. It provides countries eligible for only concessional assistance up to twice their annual country allocation for use in response to disasters triggered by natural hazards. The World Bank offers similar support, including in response to disasters, to the same set of countries through its crisis response window. The International Monetary Fund offers support to the balance of payments, including after a disaster, to all its member countries through its rapid financing instrument and its corresponding rapid credit facility for low-income countries.

Sources:
Asian Development Bank 2019a; IMF 2018, 2019; and World Bank 2017.

This can be achieved through legislative and regulatory measures, improved supervision, financial literacy campaigns, and in some cases direct subsidies. Also useful is support for underlying disaster risk modeling and for technical structuring of insurance products.

Enhancing financial capacity in poorer households

Access to formal financial services remains limited in many economies in developing Asia, especially for the poor. Problems the poor face in accessing financial services impede their adoption of efficient risk coping strategies, with implications for poverty reduction and development more generally, as well as for vulnerability to natural hazards.

While many advance risk management strategies, such as investment in disaster-proof housing or disaster insurance, are cost-effective ways to contain disaster losses (World Bank and United Nations 2010), these mechanisms are often absent in developing countries, or they are available only to people who are better off.

Where advance protection is unavailable, households attempt to smooth consumption following disasters, using a range of coping responses dependent on their own resources and those of their community (Sawada and Shimizutani 2008, Sawada 2007). Self-reliance can mean reducing nonessential consumption expenditure, spending previously accumulated savings, selling physical assets, taking any additional work that is available, using informal credit, obtaining emergency public transfers, and receiving private transfers and credits from the extended family network, friends, and neighbors.

Informal, community-based coping mechanisms are often well developed in poorer communities (Collier, Conway, and Venables 2008, Ligon 2008). These informal risk-coping mechanisms have been shown to be effective in dealing with isolated shocks to individuals, as evidenced by data on households in Viet Nam (Sawada, Nakata, and Kotera 2017).

Similarly, remittances can allow consumption smoothing and finance home reconstruction. In general, remittances are transferred more rapidly and efficiently than formal relief efforts, allowing households to recover more quickly, as illustrated in a number of case studies, including in Pakistan after an earthquake in 2005, in Samoa after a tsunami in 2009, and in Sri Lanka after the 2004 Indian Ocean tsunami. Some of these gains can be substantial, with one study finding that financial remittances compensated for nearly 65% of income lost to rainfall shocks in the Philippines (Yang and Choi 2007).

However, informal coping mechanisms tend to fail in the face of the relatively widespread destruction caused by larger disasters. This is especially true if the coping mechanism relies on neighbors or other households who were similarly hit by the disaster. Some studies found that remittances often reinforced existing inequality, as most remittances reached those in the community who were already better off (Le Dé et al. 2015).

Studies in India, Pakistan, and Thailand showed that financially constrained households employed various coping strategies after disasters struck, some of which were inefficient, such as selling productive assets (Dercon 2002), providing more paid labor only to force down wages (Kochar 1999), sending children to work rather than to school (Jacoby and Skoufias 1997, Sawada and Lokshin 2009), or borrowing at high interest from informal lenders (Banerjee and Duflo 2011). These risk management strategies undermined investment and growth and aggravated poverty (Elbers, Gunning, and Kinsey 2007).

In addition to challenges poorer households face in coping with risk, disasters can affect individual risk perceptions and risk aversion, with consequent effects for long-term development. A number of studies have shown how disaster-hit populations became more risk averse following, for example, the direct experience of a flood or earthquake in Indonesia

(Cameron and Shah 2015) and the 2004 tsunami in Thailand (Cassar, Healy, and von Kessler 2017). Similarly, studies using data from diverse locations and situations—a village in the Philippines that was hit by flooding in 2012 and a city in Japan following the March 2011 earthquake and tsunami—found that being hit by disaster made individuals significantly more focused on the present than were those unaffected by the disaster, favoring payoffs that came sooner out of doubt for the future (Sawada and Kuroishi 2015a, 2015b).

The effects of disasters on individual preferences suggest that one-off shocks can have long-lasting consequences for development and poverty (Sawada 2017). Relaxing credit and financial constraints on the poor could therefore do more than help them cope better with risk, encouraging them to take on riskier investments that have potential to be more productive (Castells-Quintana, Lopez-Uribe, and McDermott 2018). These findings underline the scope for policy intervention to improve access to financial services and to support temporary labor migration, toward distributing more widely the benefits of these effective market mechanisms.

Disaster insurance to manage disaster risk

Insurance against disasters arising from natural hazards is a useful tool to manage climate risk and could, if carefully implemented, make poor and vulnerable communities more resilient. However, access to commercial insurance against disasters is limited and unevenly distributed for several reasons, including the technical challenge of designing insurance products that are affordable and suitable.

In low-income countries, more than 95% of all losses from weather and climate hazards were uninsured (Golnaraghi, Surminski, and Schanz 2016). Just 6% of losses in floods in Kerala in 2018 were insured, for example, while payouts after the 2018 earthquake and tsunami in Sulawesi were reported as negligible despite substantial damage (Aon Benfield 2019). Similarly, more than 90% of the affected families surveyed after floods in Mumbai, Chennai, and Puri did not have any form of insurance, and those who did suffered long delays for paltry settlements (Patankar, forthcoming).

The benefits of insurance are clear: pooling and transferring risks to financial markets, enabling fairly risk-free investment, providing incentives for risk reduction, preventing hardship, and making post-disaster support more predictable. These features of insurance can alleviate the immediate welfare impacts caused by disasters and contain disruption to state budgets (Hallegatte 2014, Clarke and Dercon 2016).

Recent years have seen the introduction of new insurance designs, especially across developing Asia, and a shift from traditional indemnity-based policies toward indexed insurance (Box 2.3.5). Microinsurance and the bundling of insurance with credit can confer additional advantages, as they not only enable better risk management but also render individuals more creditworthy and promote investment in productive assets that may otherwise be too risky.

At the same time, advances in disaster risk modeling facilitate more accurate pricing of risk transfer instruments. As margins of uncertainty built into insurance premiums become narrower, premiums become more affordable. Innovations in parametric insurance—which pays compensation following the tripping of agreed triggers that are readily measured, such as maximum wind speed or millimeters of precipitation, rather than for actual loss—mean lower costs for damage assessment and therefore further reductions in premium prices, as well as quicker settlements.

Progress is being made in establishing regional parametric insurance pools, which offer opportunities to reduce premiums through a number of mechanisms (ADB 2018e):

(i) Diversifying risk reduces volatility in losses experienced by the group.
(ii) Absorbing the first layer of loss from pool reserves reduces the cost of the reinsurance required to protect the pool, as does collective bargaining when negotiating reinsurance.
(iii) Shared administrative costs make the creation and management of the pool more affordable.

A regional sovereign disaster insurance pool was launched under the second phase of the Pacific Catastrophe Risk Assessment and Financing Initiative in 2017. A pool is planned for several countries under the Southeast Asia Disaster Risk Insurance Facility. A city disaster insurance pool is currently under development in the Philippines with support from ADB. Some subnational governments have entered into contracts directly with insurance companies, an example of which is Swiss Reinsurance Company Limited parametric insurance issued to PRC provincial governments in Guangdong and Heilongjiang.

A range of nonsovereign products is also being piloted and launched. The PRC, which has subsidized agricultural insurance since the 1980s, is now one of the world's largest agricultural insurance markets, and a substantial subsidized agricultural insurance market exists in India as well. In Indonesia, insurance companies' compulsory cession of earthquake risk to a specialist earthquake reinsurer has been in force since 2004.

Remaining challenges to greater disaster insurance penetration

While observed trends indicate a growing role for insurance as part of broader DRM strategies, a number of challenges remain. Most straightforward are the standard concerns of traditional indemnity insurers over moral hazard and adverse selection. For example, Adachi et al. (2016) found that commercial property insurance subscription before the 2011 Thailand flood was systematically higher among firms located in the areas directly affected by the flood than elsewhere, indicating adverse selection. Moreover, the study showed that insured firms and those receiving business interruption payouts had lower production and employment after the flood, suggesting a moral hazard. Concerns about adverse selection and moral hazard may be particularly pronounced when coverage for small policyholders, such as farmers and smaller businesses, makes observing mitigation efforts and assessing losses expensive.

Indexed insurance, under which claim payments are triggered by an indexed event such as precipitation below some predefined threshold for drought insurance, offers an alternative as it overcomes concerns about moral hazard while reducing monitoring costs (Clarke and Grenham 2013). Indexed coverage can also facilitate accelerated claim payment, which is important especially for poor households.

Indexed insurance is beneficial, though, only if the index correlates closely with actual damage. Basis risk—a mismatch between the triggering index and actual damage—can be significant, making insurance more like a lottery than a mechanism to transfer risk.

An especially problematic situation is when indexed microinsurance for vulnerable households leaves them uncompensated for damage and disappointed, because the index did not trigger a payment. Significant basis risk of this kind can erode trust in insurance companies and suppress demand for their insurance products.

As disaster insurance takes on large regional risks rather than smaller individual ones, risk can be spread, or reinsured, across wide geographical areas with varying disaster risk profiles. One suggested solution is to combine indemnity and indexed insurance. Community mutual insurance groups could provide indemnity insurance against individual shocks, the system backed by indexed insurance for the community, offering protection against aggregate shocks by transferring the risk to reinsurers (Clarke and Grenham 2013).

2.3.5 Snapshot of active disaster insurance schemes in developing Asia

Surminski, Panda, and Lambert (forthcoming) reported on data from the Grantham Disaster Risk Transfer Scheme Database to describe the landscape of insurance for natural hazards throughout developing Asia. Each entry in this database was referred to as a "scheme," and each scheme was defined by two key properties: the transfer of risk away from entities in low- or middle-income countries, and the use of one or more ex-ante market-based risk transfer instruments. Commercial insurance was sold and purchased, but most schemes in the database included some government involvement.

There were 35 schemes actively transferring risk in 2012, since expanded to 53 schemes operating today. Increases have been notable in Southeast Asia and the Pacific in this period, rising from 8 schemes in 2012 to 22 in 2018 (box figure 1). Many countries in developing Asia now boast multiple disaster insurance schemes, including 15 in India, 8 in the PRC, 8 in the Philippines, 6 in Bangladesh, and 5 in Indonesia.

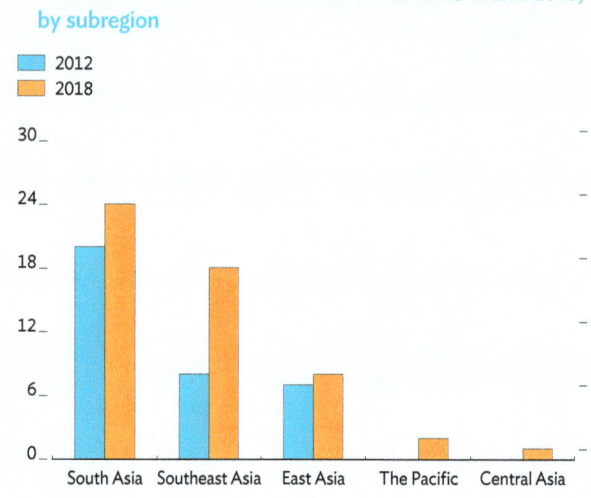

1 Number of active risk transfer schemes in 2012 and 2018, by subregion

Note: The Pacific Catastrophic Risk Assessment and Financing Initiative in the Cook Islands, the Marshall Islands, Samoa, Tonga, and Vanuatu is the scheme for the Pacific. The one for Central Asia is in Kazakhstan.
Source: Surminski, Panda, and Lambert, forthcoming.

continued next page

From the demand side, reaching poorer household with greater insurance penetration is a notable challenge because of some tough constraints: such households' limited perception of risk and willingness to disregard it, particularly risk for events with low probability; the budget constraints that deter poorer households from purchasing insurance; and the tendency among the poor to view insurance as an investment rather than a hedge against risk, encouraging underinsurance. Relatively low take-up for novel indexed insurance by smallholder farmers in particular has been highlighted, for example in Carter et al. (2017) and Surminski, Panda, and Lambert (forthcoming).

In theory, demand for formal insurance may be crowded out by the informal community risk-sharing mechanisms prevalent in many developing countries, for example among groups of smallholder farmers. However, it has been shown that informal risk-sharing can complement formal indexed insurance, with the informal network protecting households from basis risk—which is, as noted above, the mismatch between actual losses and payouts from indexed policies (Mobarak and Rosensweig 2013).

Successful disaster insurance programs implemented to date have tended to rely on some form of public subsidy (Box 2.3.5). Development partners have participated in a number of financing solutions for disaster risk, seeking to provide associated public goods such as data collection and helping to cover fixed establishment costs.

2.3.5 Continued

Of the active schemes, 70% offer microinsurance (box figure 2), and 12% are larger sovereign risk arrangements. The coverage of the schemes ranges from a single country, such as earthquake insurance bonds issued by the Government of the PRC, to regional schemes such as the Pacific Catastrophe Risk Assessment and Financing Initiative, which pools sovereign disaster risks in five Pacific island countries.

Most of the schemes included in the database are delivered by private entities, with international public entities providing 11%, national public entities 30%, and NGOs 5%. Over 80% of the schemes include subsidies or other financial support, and 13% are fully subsidized and free for those covered.

Most active schemes, or 62%, cover agricultural losses. Among these, 74% are indexed, with the risk transfer determined by weather indexes or other indexes such as average crop yield.

A third of the insurance schemes are bundled with credit and compulsory, with loans disbursed only in combination with insurance. The major benefit of credit-linked insurance is the reduced possibility of debtor default as debtors are insuring against catastrophic shocks. In the Philippines, the three most prominent microinsurance schemes are all credit-linked.

2 Number of disaster insurance schemes, by subregion and type

3 Schemes with government financial support, by scheme type

SME = small and medium-sized enterprise.

Notes: Micro schemes facilitate access to disaster insurance for individuals, often to protect the livelihoods of the poor against extreme events. SME schemes are for homeowners, small- and medium-sized enterprises, and public entities. Meso schemes provide cover for risk aggregators such as banks, microfinance institutions, agribusinesses, and municipal actors such as water authorities. Sovereign schemes aim to increase the financial response of governments in the aftermath of disasters while protecting their long-term fiscal balances through risk transfer instruments including insurance. Six schemes span two insurance types, such as microinsurance and meso insurance for farmers and microfinance institutes, and are thus double counted.

Source: Surminski, Panda, and Lambert, forthcoming.

Development partners have provided technical inputs and financing for designing products, developing the underlying disaster risk models, capitalizing insurance pools, and, in some cases, granting subsidies for premiums. The challenge for government is to create new insurance markets, rather than simply replace insurance previously sold by private providers.

Finally, disaster insurance can be designed to encourage risk reduction in addition to its primary goal of transferring risk.

Providing incentives for risk reduction is possible when insurance premiums can be linked accurately to risk, so that premium discounts motivate risk reduction. Measuring the effects of insurance on resilience and risk outcomes remains difficult (Surminski, Panda, and Lambert, forthcoming). Some examples indicated resilience benefits, however, such as indexed livestock insurance in Mongolia, which subsidized insurance for herders and was found to have improved survival rates for the livestock of policy-holding herders (Bertram-Huemmer and Kati 2015).

Strengthening disaster resilience is increasingly important as exposure to natural hazard risk rises, and as climate change continues to alter risk profiles. Risk reduction is necessary to keep some insurance programs viable in the future (Surminski, Panda, and Lambert, forthcoming). Without risk reduction, unviable insurance programs may impose, when they fail, explicit or implicit liabilities on governments. Today, more and more providers of disaster insurance recognize this and include risk reduction targets and objectives. Surminski, Panda, and Lambert (forthcoming) found that explicit support for risk reduction has become more widespread, offered by only one-third of providers in 2012 but by two-thirds in 2018.

A comprehensive approach to disaster risk

Disaster insurance generally requires public backing to provide both financial support and risk modeling. The longer-term sustainability of programs and their success in reaching the poorest and most vulnerable requires coordination with broader risk management and development policies to limit any worsening of exposure to disaster risk and to improve access to credit and financial services.

An integrated approach includes investing directly in disaster resilience within communities, because local residents are the first responders in disasters, often with little or no external support, and are key to ensuring sustained recovery and reconstruction. Thus, strengthening communities' resilience goes some way toward the ultimate goal of strengthening societal resilience.

Quantifiable measures of social and community resilience are critical for multiple reasons: They allow community progress to be tracked over time in a standardized way. They enable the prioritization of measures most needed by the community. And they generate evidence for identifying what characteristics contribute most to community disaster resilience before an event strikes, and what can be done after it strikes.

New evidence from flood resilience surveys shows that community investments can build resilience while delivering broader development benefits, such as better education, transportation, and food supply (Box 2.3.6). Proper waste management, for example, keeps rivers and drains unclogged and reduces the spread of disease after a flood, while benefiting a community more broadly by improving public health and well-being in normal times.

2.3.6 Measuring community resilience—what gets measured gets managed

New evidence from Flood Resilience Measurement for Communities, a conceptual framework and assessment tool developed by the Zurich Flood Resilience Alliance, is beginning to shed light on the factors that contribute to disaster resilience in communities while facilitating the design of innovative DRM strategies.

In developing Asia, this tool has been applied in Afghanistan, Bangladesh, Indonesia, Nepal, and Timor-Leste by five NGOs in seven country programs. Communities were selected based on their flood risk and such socioeconomic indicators as poverty and vulnerability, prioritizing poor or otherwise vulnerable communities perceived to be at high risk of flooding. Baseline studies were conducted in 88 communities in 2016–2017, directly involving more than 4,000 households and indirectly 220,000.

The data show socioeconomic factors such as educational attainment and the type and diversity of livelihood strategies closely correlated with flood resilience. Approximately 20% of sources of flood resilience studied in the framework overlap with sources of community development, the other 80% being more flood-specific. This overlap between community flood resilience and general community development indicators—such as education, transportation, and food supply systems—suggests significant potential for investment with significant collateral benefits.

The survey further found that rural households face greater resilience challenges, with 90% of those surveyed having suffered loss of life or significant damage to assets from flooding in the past decade. Rural households took longer to recover financially from floods than their urban counterparts. The assessment of resilience indicators, aggregated by community type, suggests greater room for improvement in rural areas (box figure 1). Coping strategies appear to be significantly stronger in urban communities, in part because urban residents in the sample are on average wealthier and are less dependent on the local environment, both natural and social, for their livelihoods as a result of higher livelihood diversification.

Across all communities, the factor contributing to flood resilience with the highest grade is often human capital, while financial capital is graded very low. Education, transportation, and water supply are typically among the greatest strengths identified. This may be because NGOs see these services as easy wins and useful entry points for building community flood resilience. It may also be because these services are traditional targets for community development investment.

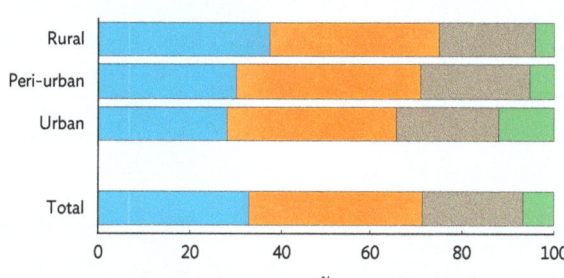

1 Distribution of flood resilience scores, by settlement type

Source: Laurien and Keating, forthcoming.

Another common strength, identified across the communities in the sample, is knowledge and awareness of flood-exposed areas. In fact, this is one of the highest-graded sources of resilience: tenth in urban communities, first in peri-urban, and second in rural communities. It is encouraging to note that efforts by local authorities, community organizations, and NGOs to increase knowledge and awareness of flood risk are found to have enjoyed some success.

A number of significant gaps in flood resilience are also identified, with differences seen across community types. These differences were highlighted in two case studies, one on urban communities in Semarang, Indonesia, and the other on rural communities in the Yawan District in Afghanistan (box figure 2). Both communities showed improvement across all resilience categories over time. Comparing communities, capacity improvement was assessed as stronger across all five types of capital in urban communities in Indonesia than in rural communities in Afghanistan. Financial capital appeared to be the worst weakness in rural Afghan communities, while weak social and natural capital were larger areas of concern in urban Indonesian communities.

These types of findings can inform decisions for DRM, resilience, and well-being by helping to prioritize intervention investments into community or regional programs that, for example, leverage human capital or prioritize financial coping strategies.

continued next page

2.3.6 Continued

The utility of this kind of study is illustrated by the innovative disaster resilience initiatives it has facilitated and by the old adage "what gets measured gets managed." For example, the performance of waste management systems in the event of a disaster, highlighted in Semarang City, and the need to engage in prospective risk reduction were not previously well understood as important by NGOs working in community development and disaster resilience, but became better understood through the use of the tool Flood Resilience Measurement for Communities.

Similarly, in Yawan District in Afghanistan, surveys highlighted vulnerability to transitory disaster-induced food and water insecurity when fuel became unavailable for cooking and boiling water. In response, solar cookers were distributed to the poorest and most vulnerable households in the communities studied. While supporting food and water security, the cookers offered additional benefits by promoting gender equality and environmental sustainability.

2 Distribution of grades of resilience

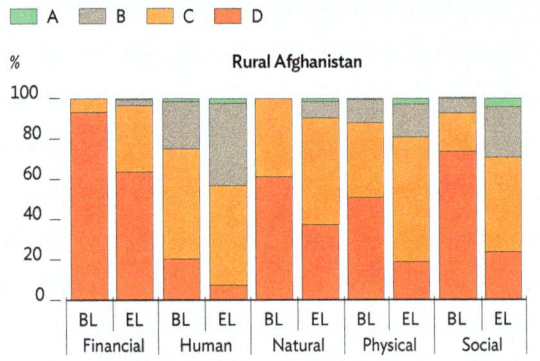
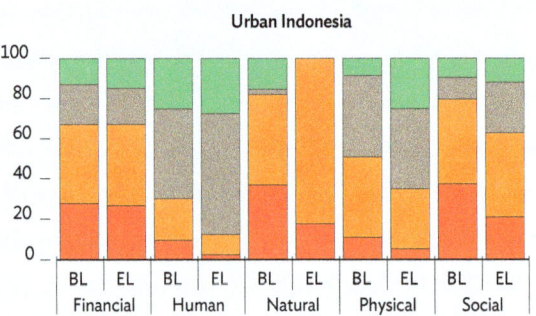

A = best practice in community resilience, B = good resilience standard, no immediate need for improvement, BL = baseline, C = deficiencies, evident room for improvement, D = significantly below good standard, potential for imminent loss, EL = end line.
Source: Laurien and Keating, forthcoming.

The value of local indigenous knowledge

Recent experience after major earthquakes and tropical cyclones in Asia further demonstrates the role of local communities and indigenous groups as custodians of local knowledge and experience relevant to effective DRM. In particular, indigenous groups, with their long history in their home locations, possess better information about severe but very low-frequency events, catastrophes that are all but invisible to modern modeling techniques and observations using short time periods. The most striking recent example of this is from the Indian Ocean tsunami of 2004 and is described in McAdoo et al. (2006).

Examples abound of the ways in which indigenous knowledge and practice was, is, or can be used proactively in DRM. For example, Kelman, Mercer, and Gaillard (2012) identified in communities in the Philippines and Papua New Guinea several ways in which indigenous knowledge pointed to vulnerabilities that were not recognized through more modern scientific knowledge. Another example is traditional building techniques, such as those used to build hazard-resilient vernacular housing in Nepal.

Three observations pertain to indigenous or traditional knowledge:
 (i) Context is important, and this knowledge is only sometimes transferable.
 (ii) Building on knowledge already accepted within an indigenous community helps to align actions with the things that the community values and understands, empowering them to recognize what they can do for themselves.
 (iii) Even indigenous communities are rarely homogeneous, and neither is their body of knowledge. As such, no nugget of knowledge necessarily applies to all members of a community. In any case, even indigenous communities with traditional knowledge may have only limited experience of recovering from catastrophic events over the long term.

These challenges notwithstanding, harnessing indigenous knowledge can help to mainstream disaster risk reduction policies and practice, as well as contribute to their integration with all disaster-related policies and processes, from prevention to recovery.

Prepared to build back better after a disaster

Almost all measurement and discussion of disaster risk focuses on the immediate impact of disasters and the emergency phase. Researchers and practitioners alike pay little attention to the longer-term consequences of these events: how they affect long-term economic trajectories; the longer-term political, cultural, and social perspectives; and their impacts on public health and the environment. In line with the dearth of research on long-term outcomes, policy frameworks and implementation plans almost always emphasize only the short-term and expend less effort planning for the long-term.

In contrast with these gaps in detailed policy research and implementation discussions, the literature is full of aspirational plans to "build back better" and to facilitate recovery from disaster that is more than complete, adding improvements that go beyond the situation before the disaster. The United Nations General Assembly adopted in 2016 a definition of build back better (BBB) that was developed by an intergovernmental expert working group convened by the United Nations Office for Disaster Risk Reduction (Box 2.4.1). In this definition, BBB aims to strengthen resilience in nations and communities and to revitalize livelihoods, economies, and the environment (UN 2016).

As Oscar Wilde observed: "A map of the world that does not include Utopia is not worth even glancing at, for it leaves out the one country at which Humanity is always landing. And when Humanity lands there, it looks out, and, seeing a better country, sets sail. Progress is the realization of Utopias" (Wilde 2009).

2.4.1 What is 'build back better'?

The Sendai Framework for Disaster Risk Reduction was signed in 2015 and endorsed by all ADB members in the Ulaanbaatar Declaration of 2018. Priority 4b.4 in the Sendai Framework calls on its signatories to "institute or strengthen policies, laws, and programs that promote (incentivize), guide (ensure), and support Build Back Better (BBB) in Recovery, Rehabilitation, and Reconstruction."

The United Nations Intergovernmental Expert Working Group on Indicators and Terminology was tasked with clarifying the central concepts that guide the Sendai Framework priorities.

The working group defined build back better as "the use of the recovery, rehabilitation, and reconstruction phases after a disaster to increase the resilience of nations and communities through integrating disaster risk reduction measures into the restoration of physical infrastructure and societal systems, and into the revitalization of livelihoods, economies, and the environment."

In this definition, agreed after wide consultation, there are four goals for building back better: increased resilience, revitalization of livelihoods, revitalization of economies, and revitalization of the environment.

continued next page

2.4.1 Continued

Resilience—maybe the thorniest term of all—is defined by the same working group as "the ability of a system, community, or society exposed to hazards to resist, absorb, accommodate, adapt to, transform, and recover from the effects of a hazard in a timely and efficient manner, including through the preservation and restoration of its essential basic structures and functions through risk management." As such, resilience focuses on what happens over time to a system, community, or society after it has been exposed to a hazard.

The build-back-better paradigm first achieved some prominence after the 2004 Indian Ocean tsunami and was frequently mentioned in recovery planning after that catastrophe. The former US president Bill Clinton was the UN secretary general's special envoy for tsunami recovery, a position he later held in Haiti during and after the earthquake there in 2010. The special envoy outlined 10 *Key Propositions for Building Back Better* (Clinton 2006). Based on the definition from the UN working group and the special envoy's propositions, the concept of build back better can be operationalized through four easily identifiable and distinct aims: safety, speed, inclusiveness, and opportunity (box figure).

The build-back-better paradigm

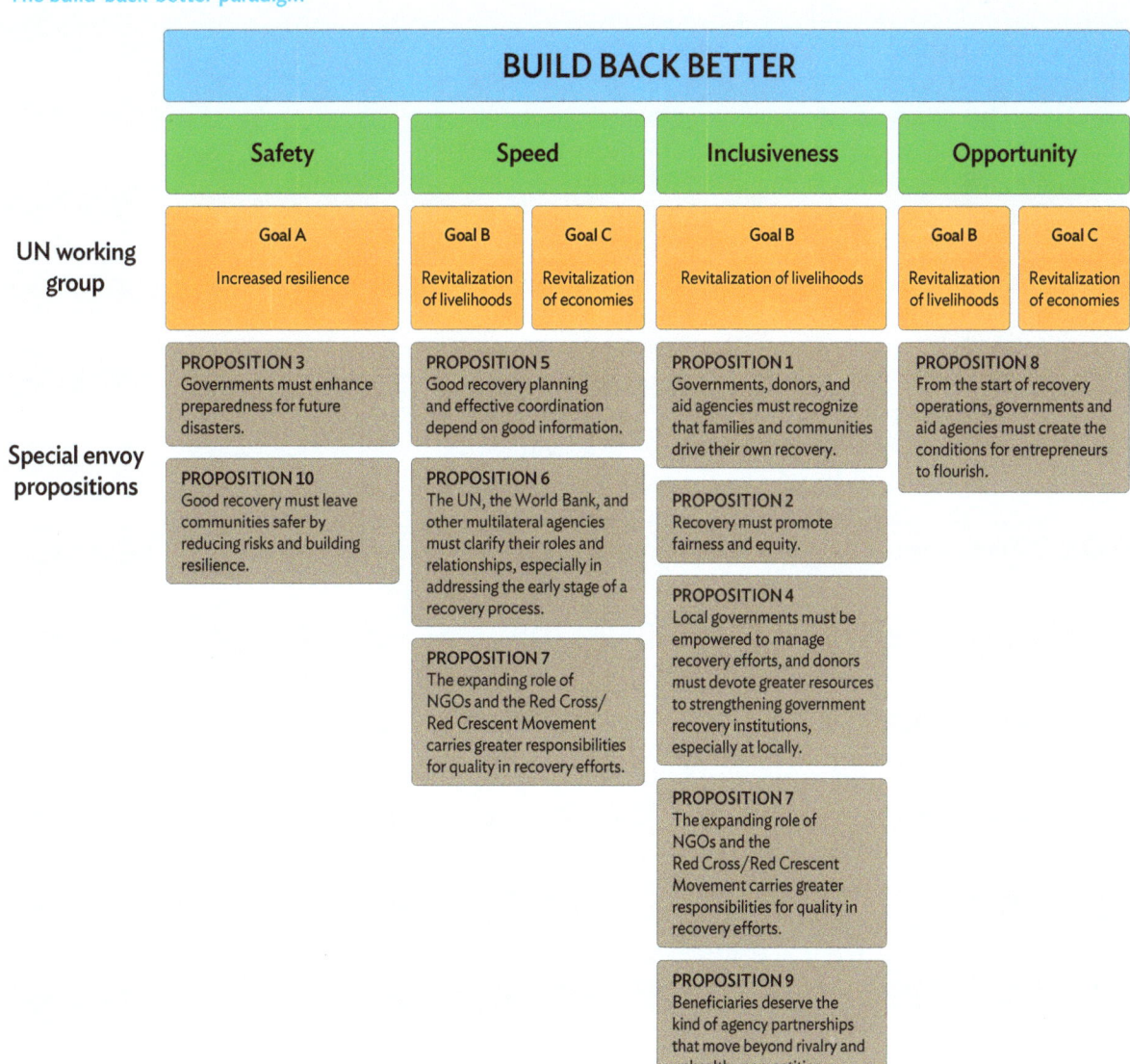

NGO = nongovernment organization, UN = United Nations.
Source: Authors.

While the previous section focused on what is being done, and what more can be done, to reduce the cost of disasters and their immediate aftermath, here the focus is on the aspirations behind BBB. These aspirations may sound utopian, but they are nonetheless achievable, even if only rarely so far. To turn utopia into policy, operationalize BBB.

Governance challenges

Beyond a better definition of BBB, and before any attempt to define the path leading to BBB, it is necessary to address the governance challenges that are typically posed in the aftermath of a disaster.

The recovery phase can be a very fluid time with opportunities poised against the many barriers and obstacles that seem to dominate the landscape. A demand surge for specialized construction services after an earthquake, for example, can nurture the emergence of a thriving seismic engineering knowledge industry that can become a future service export when this knowledge is required elsewhere. However, many of these potential benefits require active policy decisions and mechanisms that facilitate useful developments. Without them, such nascent opportunities will be missed. More fundamentally, overcoming the many barriers and obstacles that are always present in post-disaster recovery equally demands active management of these challenges.

Often, post-disaster financing is at the forefront of planning for reconstruction and recovery. However, such a focus does not adequately address the implementation challenges associated with post-disaster operations. Past experience amply demonstrates that a lack of access to finance is not the only barrier to a swift return to normality (Hallegatte, Rentschler, and Walsh 2018, Mochizuki, Hallwright, and Handmer, forthcoming). Even with financing available, governments, firms, and households often struggle to reconstruct and recover.

The efficient and productive use of disaster risk finance, when it is available, is frequently stymied by the complex governance landscape of post-disaster operations and its multiple actors. Even when agreements clearly define responsibilities, local administrative capacity may be overwhelmed by the due diligence and reporting requirements of a highly fragmented response community.

Overcoming these obstacles requires comprehensive disaster risk financing strategies. They should go beyond developing disaster risk financing instruments by also enhancing budget execution capacity so that financing can be used promptly and effectively. Adequate procedures for appropriating, disbursing, and monitoring the use of post-disaster funding, and capacity to implement them, are essential for successful mobilization and recovery. Adequate emergency procurement regulations and capacity, including advance contracting arrangements, are also key.

In other cases, partly because of failure to consult with local entities, stakeholders, and the people directly affected, governments may underestimate the obstacles and opportunities in the post-disaster environment. Population movements, skills bottlenecks, and inflation in a construction boom can all delay procurement and rebuilding.

In general, it helps tremendously to have the roles and responsibilities of external and internal actors clearly codified in formal frameworks and policy guidelines. That said, without experiential knowledge gained from past recovery processes, and without mutual trust, any predetermined plan for reconstruction and recovery is prone to implementation failure in the chaos of post-disaster operations. If no such plan exists, and the actors lack experience, the governance challenges posed by this process are immense.

One crucial need for building experiential knowledge is to institutionalize lessons from previous events. Disasters are opportunities to develop this knowledge toward better managing the next disaster. Quantitative evidence shows that countries that have experienced frequent smaller disasters are better able to handle large ones.

Preparing for recovery funding

Overcoming all these governance challenges requires enablers that are both explicit and tacit. Explicit enablers facilitate setting up appropriate institutions, getting access to recovery financing, and establishing with clarity participants' roles and responsibilities by drafting pre-disaster plans and frameworks. Tacit enablers provide opportunities for building trust, gaining experiential knowledge through joint simulation exercises, and fostering the operational knowledge and capacity local staff need to handle the complex administrative demands of the post-disaster period. Explicit and tacit enablers are equally important to the success of BBB.

Governing post-disaster operations is a complex undertaking in under-resourced environments. This is partly because the availability of sufficient external assistance is unpredictable, but also because multiple external and domestic actors must be mobilized and coordinated despite varying and potentially conflicting recovery priorities and disagreements over them.

While immediate humanitarian needs are fulfilled through a large variety of funding sources, formal channels for the funds necessary for long-term recovery and reconstruction are typically the product of a post-disaster needs assessment and conferences called in response to requests for external assistance and support from the national government.

Immediate humanitarian relief is typically coordinated nationally and supported internationally through an established protocol using a cluster approach, as was done in Nepal through the National Disaster Response Framework (Box 2.4.2). In contrast, long-term recovery and reconstruction is primarily led by national, subnational, and local governments. These bodies typically operate in a less coordinated fashion, reflecting their limited capacity and experience in designing and implementing complex rebuilding projects (Lloyd-Jones 2006). Clarifying the respective roles of the various government entities, with clear demarcation of responsibilities and decision-making roles, is key to their successful collaboration.

2.4.2 The 2015 earthquake in Nepal—challenges to rebuilding homes and livelihoods

The 2015 earthquake in Nepal, striking on 25 April with an initial shock of magnitude 7.8, caused over 8,790 deaths and 22,300 injuries. It displaced 2.8 million, and the 8 million people who were affected in one way or another amounted to a third of the country's population (Government of Nepal 2015). Fourteen of Nepal's 75 districts were classified as "crisis hit" and received targeted support for rescue and relief (IMF 2015).

Strong international support

On 29 April, a UN flash appeal launched by 78 participating organizations made an initial request for $422 million to use in the following 3 months. A post-disaster needs assessment released 2 months after the initial earthquake estimated that damages and other losses could add up to some $7 billion, equal to a third of Nepal's gross domestic product. Half of the damage was to private homes (Government of Nepal 2015). In the months following the earthquake, the value of remittances increased by 20%–35% (UNOCHA 2015). The International Monetary Fund (IMF) forecast that higher remittances would be offset by lost income from tourism and higher imports needed to supply recovery efforts and reconstruction. The IMF subsequently approved the disbursement of $49.7 million in direct budgetary support under its Rapid Credit Facility (IMF 2015). Within 2 months of the initial shock, ADB approved $200 million in emergency assistance to rebuild and restore schools, roads, and public buildings.

In June, the Government of Nepal hosted an international conference on Nepal's reconstruction. The international community pledged $4.4 billion in grants and loans to support the country's recovery and reconstruction (IMF 2015). This was more than twice the amount requested in the government's initial call for support, but actual disbursement would prove to be much lower and delayed. To facilitate home reconstruction in the hardest hit 14 rural districts, the Nepal Earthquake Housing Reconstruction Program Multi-Donor Trust Fund was established with support from the international community.

In May 2016, the government published a 5-year post-disaster recovery framework outlining five strategic focuses: restore and improve disaster-resilient buildings, strengthen the disaster resilience of communities and individuals and foster social cohesion, restore and improve access to services, restore and develop livelihoods, and build the state's capacity to respond to future disasters (NRA 2016).

Need for better coordination

The National Disaster Response Framework, created in 2013, was tasked with aligning the international humanitarian cluster coordination structure with national line ministries, designating each national ministry as cluster lead and an international humanitarian agency as the co-lead of a streamlined structure with 11 clusters. The framework further provided a detailed timeline and assignment of responsibilities for 62 actions to be taken immediately following a disaster. Surveys conducted after the earthquake revealed that 30 of 62 mandatory emergency operations were performed in accordance with the framework (Bisri and Beniya 2016).

While these pre-disaster activities have certainly helped coordinate immediate response, a number of concerns were raised, one pertaining to a rapid surge of new actors in the cluster system. The shelter cluster, for example, had 10 agencies that regularly participated in it before the earthquake, but the cluster now had 120 agencies that needed to be coordinated (IASC 2016). Another concern was the very limited

continued next page

2.4.2 Continued

inclusion of national NGOs and local actors in the official coordination mechanisms. Of $422 million in the consolidated humanitarian appeal made by 78 organizations, only 0.8% of the funds were directed to Nepali organizations. Further, the National Disaster Response Framework did not address coordinating with the needs of national NGOs and local actors, leaving smaller organizations to continue to work outside of the formal cluster system.

On the ground, relief efforts were hampered by other factors such as a dearth of local knowledge; a lack of local leadership to convey needs from locals and support from international participants; administrative inefficiency; sporadic implementation of national policies that were considered irrelevant in particular local contexts; border tensions, which increased prices for fuel and other goods; and discrimination by social caste. In many instances, isolated by complex topography and bedeviled by implementation challenges, participants had to learn to help themselves (Auerbach 2015, Cook, Shrestha, and Bo 2016, Dahal 2016, Grunewald and Burlat 2016, Hall et al. 2017).

Funding challenges

Despite generous pledges from the international community, Nepal's reconstruction faced numerous funding challenges. As of April 2018, almost 3 years after the earthquake, only 16% of reconstruction pledges had actually been disbursed. Against the official goal of rebuilding 400,000 homes by the end of fiscal 2018 in mid-June of last year, only a quarter had been completed. As is quite typical in post-disaster recovery in many countries, including wealthy ones, the 3-year mark was when frustration with delays started to boil over and trust in the authorities started to erode.

Even when funding was secured nationally, reconstruction projects faced local implementation challenges: a lack of skilled personnel, skills mismatch in labor markets, disputes over eligibility for reconstruction grants, price increases for construction materials and transportation, unclear land tenure, delays in channeling funds through providers of financial services, and even the absence of bank accounts to facilitate transactions.

Two years after the earthquake, more than 60% of people in severely affected districts still lived in temporary shelters. These challenges persisted despite progress in streamlining reconstruction and the publication of guidelines for settlement development, subsidy distribution, and training and deploying personnel, as well as the provision of a design catalogue for earthquake-resistant building prototypes.

The Nepal case study illustrates the common governance challenges of financing and implementing post-disaster operations. According to official statistics published on 2 May 2018, Nepal had achieved mixed progress on reconstruction and recovery: Of 379 public buildings to be rebuilt, 220 had been rebuilt and another 147 were under construction. Of 7,553 educational facilities to be rebuilt, 3,613 had been completed and another 1,719 were under construction, while the rest were still in planning stages.

Meanwhile, of 753 cultural heritage structures to be rebuilt, 100 had been completed and another 329 were under construction. Similarly, many health institutions and drinking water systems still had to be rebuilt, with 581 completed and 795 still under construction (NRA 2018). This illustrates how the victims' full recovery of livelihoods remains elusive for many, especially those living in remote areas or still in temporary shelters.

In addition to the different levels of government, community members providing mutual support, and families receiving remittances, voluntary organizations funded by contributions from private individuals and philanthropic organizations occupy their corner of the reconstruction and recovery ecosystem, as do international NGOs. Coordinating these diverse entities presents considerable challenges to governments and their partners. An important role for the entity in charge of reconstruction, typically an office of the national government, is therefore to work together with funders, local government, the private sector, and civil society. Part of the job is naturally to define the aims of post-disaster recovery and coordinate the assemblage and distribution of resources during the design and implementation phases of the recovery process.

Planning and training as key elements of recovery

Contingency planning for recovery, backed by pre-financing arrangements, can be a useful vehicle to clarify expectations before a disaster hits, and to facilitate setting recovery on a BBB track after it does. Defining governance arrangements and codifying them through legislative action before a disaster strikes is particularly important. While the details will always be specific to particular disasters, the main framework for governing the recovery process should be decided ahead of time.

After a disaster, the assessment of needs has conventionally been implemented as a technical exercise using information on economic damage and the country's access to domestic and external resources. Yet more can be achieved toward facilitating the implementation of post-disaster BBB if, in the needs-assessment phase, a plan for BBB is already incorporated into the decision-making process.

Governments and domestic stakeholders should ensure that roles and responsibilities are clearly defined in all phases of post-disaster operations. In particular, though, they should plan in advance for the recovery and reconstruction phases of the disaster cycle. Emphasis should be placed on setting clear mandates within the ministries of national governments regarding the coordination of financing, operations, and monitoring of disaster response, recovery, and reconstruction. Pre-disaster training and simulations should clarify roles and responsibilities across government departments, as well as units' relationships with international and domestic partners in the private sector and civil society.

Often missing in contingency planning are procedures for a transition from emergency response to recovery and reconstruction over the medium and long term. Setting up explicit rules and systems is only part of what is required, but a part that often plagues post-disaster reconstruction. Local staff and partners should have sufficient training and knowledge before the disaster to effectively follow plans and procedures when pressed for time in the post-disaster phase. Capacity-building programs should therefore target international, national, and local actors alike, including the government, private firms, and civil society, and should elaborate the details of operational processes and any requirements related to external disaster risk financing and ways of preparing domestic financial, accounting, and accountability systems to scale up their operations as necessary after a disaster strikes.

To summarize, the United Nations International Strategy for Disaster Reduction notes that national governments would benefit greatly by creating a functional and productive environment where stakeholders appreciate the importance of a build-back-better mindset after disasters (UNISDR 2017).

This should ideally be supported by national laws and equitably enforced, with all necessary resources—human, financial, and otherwise–made readily available. Able leadership and good governance are essential to provide the support mechanisms needed for such a strategy.

External benefits of post-disaster reconstruction and recovery

Supporting evidence for "creative destruction" dynamics that arise organically in post-disaster reconstruction appears to be limited to several cases, such as the 2008 Wenchuan earthquake in the PRC (Box 2.4.3). Nevertheless these few cases point to what a government can do to improve outcomes. One is to offer generous funding to build resilience. After the 2008 earthquake, the Government of the PRC spent a very large amount of money to build more seismically robust infrastructure.

Another way that recovery can engender favorable BBB outcomes, even if not deliberately, is for reconstruction to create positive externalities that enable development to speed up, bringing benefits that would have come only later, if at all, without reconstruction as a trigger. One vintage example can be found in an analysis of the Great Boston Fire of 1872 (Hornbeck and Keniston 2017). The study found that the reconstruction of individual properties rendered benefits to nearby properties that facilitated their development as well. The fire and the resulting need to reconstruct destroyed buildings, it seems, accelerated urban renewal that otherwise would have taken much longer.

Progress through technological leap-frogging is another possibility, though infrequently realized. Hornbeck and Naidu (2014) found that the Great Mississippi Flood of 1927 accelerated the modernization of agriculture in the area through mechanization that was forced in part by labor shortages occasioned by the outward migration of sharecroppers. According to the study, it was this shortage of labor created by the flood that drove farmers to adopt new technologies.

However, evidence exists that, even in a strong post-disaster recovery enjoying generous financing from domestic and international sources, such as insurance and development assistance, the outcome can be a worsening of structural social inequality. This may happen because households with more income are better able to withstand disasters and to benefit from long-term changes in the post-disaster environment (De Alwis and Noy, forthcoming). This is clearly one aspect of the BBB strategy that must be appropriately addressed.

2.4.3 The 2008 Wenchuan earthquake

On 12 May 2008, a massive earthquake measuring 8.0 on the Richter scale struck Wenchuan County, 92 kilometers northwest of Chengdu, the capital of Sichuan Province in the PRC. Damage was widespread across 116,000 square kilometers of heavily affected areas in Sichuan and the neighboring provinces of Gansu and Shaanxi, but most of the damage by far was in Sichuan (box table).

Damage and loss

Province	Sichuan	Gansu	Shaanxi
Number of affected counties	139	40	40
Deaths	68,708	370	125
Missing persons	17,923		
Injured persons	360,796	10,165	2,970
Damaged housing units (CNY million)	418,830	34,498	11,947
Damaged infrastructure (CNY million)	168,794	11,765	7,577
Agriculture, industry, and services (CNY million)	139,466	2,563	2,309
Land, minerals, cultural heritage, etc. (CNY million)	44,680	1,709	998
Total (CNY million)	771,770	50,535	22,830

Source: ADB 2008.

The most severely affected areas in Sichuan were mountainous, with most of the area at 3,000 meters above sea level. The disaster-affected region included economically less-developed national minority regions and wealthier urban regions, notably the cities of Chengdu, Deyang, and Mianyang. The earthquake destroyed houses, other property, and infrastructure for rail transport, electric power supply, water supply and sanitation, as well as such critical infrastructure as hospitals, roads, and communications systems. The earthquake and aftershocks incurred secondary disasters, notably by creating many large barrier lakes that posed a significant threat of flashfloods to millions of people downstream. The cost of reconstruction was estimated at CNY1 trillion, which was nearly equal to the gross provincial product of Sichuan, or 3.9% of the PRC gross domestic product in 2007. The vast majority of households and businesses had no insurance coverage.

In 2009, in response to a global economic crisis, the government passed a massive CNY4 trillion stimulus package, of which 25% went to earthquake reconstruction. In addition, richer coastal provinces were paired with disaster-affected counties and required to put aside 1% of provincial government revenue—a very large amount of money for the affected counties—to assist reconstruction in partner counties. Shanghai, for example, was matched with Dujiangyan, a city of 600,000, and provided CNY8.3 billion for 117 projects.

The purpose of pairing provinces with affected counties was to overcome the logistical hurdles of managing post-disaster assistance, as it allowed not only the provision of funding but also the mobilization of personnel and knowledge from the coastal provinces. It engendered competition in which provinces were judged by how effectively they assisted reconstruction in affected counties. This matchmaking generated an additional CNY91 billion in assistance for the affected region and more than 4,000 reconstruction projects. By the end of September 2009, the PRC had mobilized CNY79.7 billion in social contributions from individuals and NGOs—an unprecedented amount to that time—from both inside and outside of the PRC.

Sichuan's regional economic indicators showed rapid recovery in aggregate from the earthquake. The massive spending on reconstruction stimulated the region's economy for a few years before the effect began to wane. The largest increase in manufacturing value added was in construction, which grew quickly until 2010, before eventually subsiding (box figure 1).

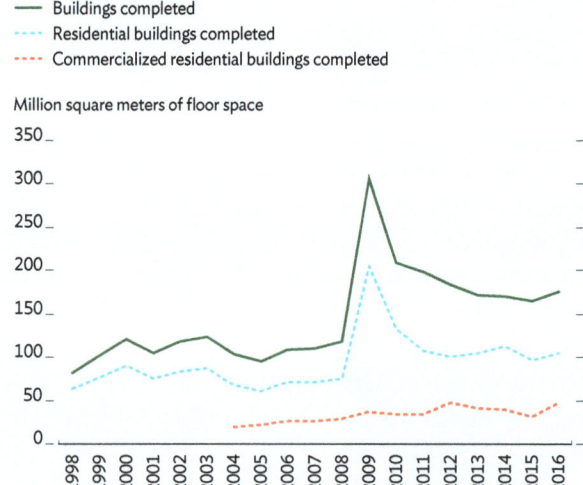

1 Building construction in Sichuan

Source: ADB 2008.

continued next page

2.4.3 Continued

Park and Wang (2017) used data from a survey conducted more than 10 months after the earthquake of 3,000 rural households living in 100 poor villages in 10 counties in the disaster-affected areas. The study found that asset and income losses for surveyed households were substantial, especially in the most severely damaged areas. It described "an overwhelming government response to the disaster," with subsidies provided to households in 2008 that were so large that median income per capita was 17.5% higher in 2008 than in 2007 and the poverty rate declined from 34% to 19%. The extent of government support for victims of the Wenchuan earthquake was unprecedented.

Perhaps reflecting this massive infusion of funding to the affected region, the trajectory of the provincial population seems to have shifted for the better after recovery investment started to bear fruit (box figure 2). The earthquake in Wenchuan is a clear example of a build-back-better recovery, premised on a massive investment in recovery through funding received from both the Government of the PRC and the governments of several provinces.

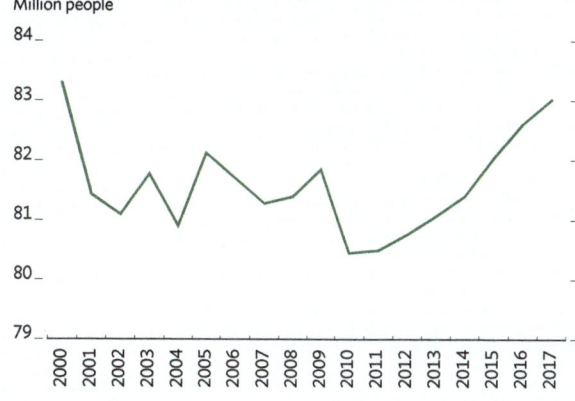

2 Resident population in Sichuan at year-end

Source: ADB 2008.

Migration after a disaster

Outmigration is sometimes perceived as a failure of BBB, but it can be a boon to those who choose to migrate and for their families. An example from Viet Nam is instructive. Rural households in Viet Nam cope with disasters mainly by sending family members into urban areas (Gröger and Zylberberg 2016). As is common in lower-income countries, only selected members of households are able migrate away from disaster-affected areas. Often, those displaced by a storm opt not to return. While the migrants' households benefit from remittances, the affected region ends up with a lower population and therefore less economic activity.

Conversely, disasters can motivate migration *into* the affected region. They may be attracted by spending on reconstruction, by the structural changes brought about by the recovery spending, or even by risk reduction achieved after the disaster. Such dynamics were evident in population increases seen in areas in the Netherlands affected by the North Sea Flood in 1953, for instance, as these places benefited from a large public works program aiming to strengthen flood protection in flood-prone areas (Husby et al. 2014). In-migration can also reflect a surge in job opportunities, particularly in the building industry, that may be only temporary.

Voluntary migration into and out of affected areas can therefore, under certain circumstances, enhance resilience and improve well-being. Governments sometimes try to convince inhabitants of affected areas to relocate away from the most hazard-prone area by, for example, banning home construction within a certain distance of the shoreline.

Much better data is required on the length of post-disaster migration in and out of affected areas to really grasp its drivers and implications. Only then will it be possible to develop appropriate policies and measures to manage migration well and encourage optimal flows of people.

Policy aims of building back better

"Build back safer" may be a better tagline than build back better because "better" can mean many things, some of which may actually worsen risk by, for example, increasing population density. "Safer" provides a clearer goal to focus on during recovery, especially with respect to reconstructing residential and commercial buildings. The thinking behind this emphasis is that safety should trump all other aspirations for post-disaster recovery (Kennedy et al. 2008).

In many cases, however, there are other aims that residents and policy makers hope to achieve with recovery and reconstruction. These aims can impose trade-offs that need to be carefully balanced to avoid jeopardizing the goal of maintaining or strengthening safety. Important questions need to be asked when following BBB principles after a disaster (Kennedy et al. 2008): Will recovery ensure safety and security? What will be the impact on the affected community? Is it fair and equitable, and does it tackle the root causes of vulnerability?

Following this logic, the World Bank has suggested three separate components to building back better: stronger, faster, and more inclusive (Hallegatte, Rentschler, and Walsh 2018). In line with this approach, it has been argued that building back stronger may have a different connotation than, say, building back safer. This would be the case if, for example, safety standards called for construction methods and standards that could reasonably ensure that lives would not be lost as a consequence of a disaster but not necessarily that the buildings would be stronger and continue to be habitable after the disaster. However, even these goals can impose trade-offs that ought to be carefully considered during reconstruction and recovery, especially considering that, ultimately and most fundamentally, the process should end with resilience enhanced enough for the community to survive future disasters and more generally thrive in future circumstances. The number of BBB components can thus be extended to four: safety, speed, fairness and inclusivity, and future social and economic potential.

Building back a safer environment

Reducing the risk of mortality and morbidity in future events is an uncontroversial goal of recovery and reconstruction in the aftermath of any adverse event. One important observation is that, unlike a lot of the other impacts of disasters, mortality and morbidity are irreversible. As such, it is clear why preventing them should be the overriding goal of reconstruction and recovery policies. All things considered, preventing mortality and morbidity is always likely to be the most important goal guiding government policy after a disaster. It seems indisputable that safety should be prioritized because the consequences of unsafe— or less safe—reconstruction would affect harmed individuals and their families for a very long time.

Hallegatte, Rentschler, and Walsh (2018) used the term "stronger" instead of "safer." This implied reconstructing houses, public buildings, and transportation and other infrastructure in ways that make them more able to resist the onslaught of an extreme disaster. If the hazard is an earthquake, for example, this suggests rebuilding with more robust construction methods so that buildings will not collapse when shaken. Safety can also be achieved, however, through softer defenses—the classic example of which is mangrove forests to counter risks from storm surges— or by retreating from dangerous locations altogether (Hino et al. 2017). Improved safety post-disaster can be achieved by other policies as well, ones that do not entail strong, hard, or soft engineering solutions.

Even further from bricks-and-mortar concerns but maybe no less important is the strengthening of social ties within communities. This was found to be important in preventing mortality in the 2011 tsunami in Japan (Aldrich and Sawada 2015). Safety under tsunami risk depends on timely warnings and the ability to evacuate. Social ties allow the timely evacuation of people, such as the elderly, who would find it difficult to evacuate independently. Therefore, one can build back a safer community by establishing mechanisms that strengthen social ties. This can be achieved in many ways, for example through the spatial planning of residential neighborhoods.

Building back faster for well-being

Rebuilding at a faster pace is also a fairly obvious and uncontroversial goal of public policy. All things being equal, a faster recovery is always better than a slower one. Speed is often motivated as well by political and electoral pressures. Surprisingly, though, governments sometimes do not realize that speeding up recovery is achievable and should be seen as an explicit policy goal. For example, many post-disaster situations give rise to complicated legal questions that need to be resolved in court, such as on property rights, insurance liability, and the role of the various branches of government versus the private sector. Governments should make every effort to speed this up and purposely remove any bottleneck that delays reconstruction and recovery.

In Sichuan, the government made a conscious and concerted effort to speed up recovery even as it benefited greatly from the abundant resources made available to finance reconstruction. In many cases, lack of funding is a stubborn bottleneck impeding reconstruction. Indeed, recovery in Sichuan was much faster than in other disaster-affected areas—in Myanmar, for example, in the aftermath of Tropical Cyclone Nargis in 2008, or even in high-income Japan during reconstruction following the 2011 earthquake and tsunami. There are other barriers and hurdles to the process, however, so funding cannot be considered a guarantee of rapid reconstruction.

The more difficult problem is when the desire to speed up recovery conflicts with other explicit aims of the BBB framework. There may even be a trade-off between speed and safety. If, for example, the disaster uncovered vulnerability or exposure that was not recognized before—perhaps with the discovery of a previously unknown seismic fault line— it may take some time to investigate and determine the best corrective action, which may be an appropriate engineering solution. In such cases, building back safer may require a more deliberative process.

The desire for speed clearly conflicts with the desire to consult with the affected local community and seek its participation, and it typically conflicts as well with the desire to carefully consider all plausible development, planning, and reconstruction paths. Many of these alternative paths entail significant planning effort and require reallocating property rights for certain assets, the most difficult of which is almost always land. Alternative paths are challenging to implement in the best of times, and this is clearly one reason why speed does not seem to be a priority in many reconstruction projects. The existence of a trade-off between speed and a carefully considered reconstruction path is undeniable, but, all things being equal, speed should be prioritized. A slow recovery makes achieving a build-back-better recovery more difficult.

Building back inclusively for a fairer community

Recovery should aim to be fair and inclusive in both process and outcome. If recovery does not include consultations with communities and other stakeholders that were affected by the event and will be affected by reconstruction, it is not inclusive in process. While there may be a lot of advantages to having recovery guided by an authority tied to the central government and funded by it, the need to continuously consult with those that are directly affected is not diminished and may even be strengthened.

Without adequate consultation, there will be no buy-in from the local community and no assurance that the right decisions will be made and supported. It is not unusual for recovery to be derailed or delayed when disagreements or tensions arise between affected communities and the authority guiding recovery. The aim of bringing all community stakeholders into the decision-making process is to ensure both that the recovery trajectory is in the right direction and will achieve its stated build-back-better aims, and that community participation will smooth and speed up the process by preventing misunderstandings and miscommunication.

It is well known that affected communities are themselves the first responders in disasters, often with little or no immediate external support. Often overlooked is that local communities are also the key to ensuring sustained recovery and reconstruction. New evidence from flood resilience surveys across 88 communities in Asia shows that community investments can build resilience while delivering broader development benefits, such as better education, transportation, and food supply. Without close community participation, these shared benefits will not be recognized (Box 2.3.6). Recent experience from major earthquakes and tropical cyclones in Asia emphasizes also the importance of local communities and actors as custodians of local knowledge and experience that can be pivotal to the effective delivery of humanitarian response and recovery efforts.

Toward maintaining a fair and inclusive process, it must be monitored carefully to see who might be excluded from it. The benefits of the build-back-better process must be received by all segments of society, especially the most disadvantaged. Noteworthy in this context are the many research projects that have observed recoveries frequently excluding the poorest and most vulnerable (Karim and Noy 2016, Hallegatte et al. 2016b, and Patankar, forthcoming). Given the overwhelming evidence of how recovery often fails to reach the disadvantaged, it is apparent that planning for building back better needs to incorporate ways to ensure that the weakest segments of society are included and are empowered during post-disaster reconstruction.

Building back social and economic potential

Post-disaster recovery should aim to generate potential for improved social well-being and expanded economic opportunity. Without improvement, the quality of life will eventually deteriorate (Sen 2000, Friedman 2006). A fair, fast, and safe recovery does not necessarily mean that the reconstructed city or community will have more social and economic potential or opportunities than it did before. Yet without that social and economic potential, the build-back strategy will fail.

Policy should therefore focus not only on the goals of safety, speed, and fairness but also strive to create conditions that will ensure gainful employment and stronger social ties toward improving community well-being. A cautionary tale might be Kobe, Japan, where reconstruction after an earthquake in 1995 was fast, safe, and most likely fair, but nevertheless brought a reduction in economic opportunity (duPont et al. 2015).

Policy makers at all levels should strive for a reconstruction framework that not only preserves previously available social amenities and economic activity, but aims to move the community toward livelihoods that are sustainable over the long term and toward social relationships that can support the community for many years to come. In many cases, preserving the economic opportunities and social ties that were there before the disaster might not even be feasible any more. In these cases, it is even more important for the authorities to be proactive in identifying and generating conditions that will foster long-term social strength and economic prosperity. Ultimately, without renewed social and economic potential, a sustainable build-back-better recovery is not possible.

Much accomplished, much more to do

The risks posed by the heightened impact of disasters in Asia, especially in the lower-income countries of the region, are manifestly real. Damage and losses can propagate across time and space, causing widespread and prolonged adverse impacts on society and the economy. However, citizens, firms, civil society, governments, and multilateral institutions can do a great deal to mitigate the dangers posed by disasters, avert their consequences, and manage the aftermath. The growing seriousness of problem indicates commensurate room for improvement on all fronts.

Low-hanging fruit is ready to be picked: better early warning systems for disasters; greater investment in protection by, for example, building cyclone or tsunami shelters; contingency funds made automatically available after their triggering events; and more policy attention to planning recovery in advance, rather than having to scramble in the emergency phase.

Plenty more can and should be done to initiate change in the ability of societies to pursue the aims of the Sendai Framework Agreement, which focuses on four priorities for action:

Priority 1. Understanding disaster risk.
Priority 2. Strengthening disaster risk governance to manage disaster risk.
Priority 3. Investing in disaster risk reduction for resilience.
Priority 4. Enhancing disaster preparedness for effective response and to build back better during recovery, rehabilitation, and reconstruction.

Increasing attention has been paid to priorities 1 and 2: understanding disaster risk in developing Asia and dealing with the governance issues that abound in disaster risk management. While this is certainly a welcome development in the region, and though more needs to be done, other aspects of disaster resilience also need to be addressed. As this chapter argues, more attention must now be paid to all four priorities, including 3 and 4: strengthening countries' disaster resilience, improving disaster preparedness, and promoting a more comprehensive strategy for reconstruction. Only then can countries ensure a safer, faster, and more inclusive post-disaster recovery—a recovery that can realize economic and social potential.

Background papers

Abrigo, M. and A. Brucal. Forthcoming. *Aid, Intergovernmental Transfer, and Disaster Recovery: Evidence from the Philippines*. Asian Development Bank.

Castells-Quintana, D. and T. McDermott. Forthcoming. *Climate, Urbanisation, and Conflict: The Effects of Weather Shocks and Floods on Urban Social Disorder*. Asian Development Bank.

Dagli, S. and B. Ferrarini. Forthcoming. *The Growth Impact of Disasters in Developing Asia*. Asian Development Bank.

Kashiwagi, Y. Forthcoming. *Enterprise Resilience to Disasters: Who Needs Public Support?* Asian Development Bank.

Kashiwagi, Y. and Y. Todo. Forthcoming. *Aid, Propagation of Positive Effects of Post-Disaster Policies Through Supply Chains: Evidence from the Great East Japan Earthquake*. Asian Development Bank.

Laurien, F. and A. Keating. Forthcoming. *Evidence from Measuring Community Disaster Resilience in Asia*. Asian Development Bank.

Mechler, R. and S. Hochrainer-Stigler. Forthcoming. *Generating Multiple Resilience Dividends from Managing Unnatural Disasters in Asia? Opportunities for Measurement and Policy*. Asian Development Bank.

Mochizuki, J., J. Hallwright, and J. Handmer. Forthcoming. *Enabling Factors for Financing and Implementing Post-Disaster Operations*. Asian Development Bank.

Noy, I. and S. Shields. Forthcoming. *A Retroactive Examination of the Economic Costs of the 2003 SARS Epidemic*. Asian Development Bank.

Noy, I., B. Ferrarini, and D. Park. Forthcoming. *Build-Back-Better: What is it, and What Should it Be?* Asian Development Bank.

Ober, K. Forthcoming. *The Links Between Climate Change, Disasters, Migration, and Social Resilience in Asia*. Asian Development Bank.

Patankar, A. Forthcoming. *Characterization of Impacts of Natural Disasters on Households and Small Businesses in India with Specific Reference to Extreme Precipitation Events*. Asian Development Bank.

Strobl, E. Forthcoming. *The Impact of Typhoons on Economic Activity in the Philippines: Evidence from Nightlight Intensity*. Asian Development Bank.

Surminski, S., A. Panda, and P. J. Lambert. Forthcoming. *Market-Based Insurance and Building Resilience Against Natural Disasters: Analysis of Insurance Schemes in Asia*. Asian Development Bank.

References

Abadie, L. M., I. Galarraga, and E. S. de Murieta. 2017. Understanding Risks in the Light of Uncertainty: Low-Probability, High-Impact Coastal Events in Cities. *Environmental Research Letters* 12(1).

Abbott, D. F. 2018. Disaster Risk Management Public Expenditure and Institutional Reviews (DRM-PEIR) for Lao People's Democratic Republic, Thailand, and Viet Nam: Discussion Paper on Lessons Learned. United Nations Development Programme. http://www.asia-pacific.undp.org/content/rbap/en/home/library/democratic_governance/drm-cpeir-lao-pdr-thailand-viet-nam.html.

Adachi, D., H. Nakata, Y. Sawada, and K. Sekiguchi. 2016. Adverse Selection and Moral Hazard in the Corporate Insurance Market: Evidence from the 2011 Thailand Floods. *Discussion Papers* No. 16025, Research Institute of Economy, Trade and Industry.

Aldrich, D. 2010. Separate and Unequal: Post-Tsunami Aid Distribution in Southern India. *Social Science Quarterly* 91(4).

Aldrich, D. and Y. Sawada, 2015. The Physical and Social Determinants of Mortality in the 3.11 Tsunami. *Social Science & Medicine* 124.

Almond, D. 2006. Is the 1918 Influenza Pandemic Over? Long-Term Effects of In Utero Influenza Exposure in the Post-1940 US Population. *Journal of Political Economy* 114(4).

Almond, D. and J. Currie. 2011. Human Capital Development Before Age Five. *Handbook of Labor Economics* 4b.

Aon Benfield. 2019. *Weather, Climate, and Catastrophe Insight: 2018 Annual Report*. London.

ADB. 2008. *Providing Emergency Response to Wenchuan Earthquake*. Asian Development Bank.

———. 2015. *Strengthening City Disaster Risk Financing in Viet Nam*. Asian Development Bank.

———. 2016. *Asian Development Outlook 2016*. Asian Development Bank.

———. 2017. *Meeting Asia's Infrastructure Needs*. Asian Development Bank. https://www.adb.org/publications/asia-infrastructure-needs.

———. 2018a. Proposed Loan Republic of Indonesia: Emergency Assistance for Recovery and Rehabilitation from Recent Disasters. Report and Recommendation of the President to the Board of Directors. November 2018. Asian Development Bank.

———. 2018b. *Asian Development Outlook 2018*. Asian Development Bank.

———. 2018c. *Economic and Fiscal Impacts of Disasters in the Pacific*. Asian Development Bank.

———. 2018d. *Asian Economic Integration Report 2018*. Asian Development Bank.

———. 2018e. *Philippine City Disaster Insurance Pool: Rationale and Design*. Asian Development Bank.

———. 2019a. Supporting Disaster Risk Management: Disaster Risk Reduction Financing Mechanism and Disaster Response Facility. Paper prepared for Asian Development Fund 12 Midterm Review Meeting, 27–28 February 2019. Asian Development Bank.

———. 2019b. *Resilient Infrastructure: Building for the Future*. Draft working paper for the G20 Working Group on Climate Sustainability. Asian Development Bank.

Auerbach, P. S. 2015. Preparedness Explains Some Differences Between Haiti and Nepal's Response to Earthquake. *British Medical Journal* 350.

Bakkensen, L. A. and R. O. Mendelsohn. 2019. Global Tropical Cyclone Damages and Fatalities under Climate Change: An Updated Assessment. In J. Collins, ed. *Hurricane Risk*. Springer.

Balboni, C. 2018. *In Harm's Way? Infrastructure Investments and the Persistence of Coastal Cities*. London School of Economics. http://www.lse.ac.uk/economics/phd-job-market/job-market-candidates/Clare-Balboni.

Banerjee, A. and E. Duflo. 2011. *Poor Economics: A Radical Rethinking of the Way to Fight Global Poverty*. Penguin.

Barrios, S., L. Bertinelli, and E. Strobl. 2006. Climate Change and Rural–Urban Migration: The Case of Sub-Saharan Africa. *Journal of Urban Economics* 60(3).

Barrot, J.-N. and J. Sauvagnat. 2016. Input Specificity and the Propagation of Idiosyncratic Shocks in Production Networks. *Quarterly Journal of Economics* 31(3).

Beltrán, A., D. Maddison, and R. J. R. Elliott. 2018. Is Flood Risk Capitalised into Property Values? *Ecological Economics* 146.

Benson, C. 2016. Promoting Sustainable Development Through Disaster Risk Management. *ADB Sustainable Development Working Paper Series* No. 41. Asian Development Bank.

Bertram-Huemmer, V. and K. Kati. 2015. Does Index Insurance Help Households Recover from Disaster? Evidence from IBLI Mongolia. *Discussion Papers of DIW Berlin* No. 1515. DIW Berlin, German Institute for Economic Research. https://EconPapers.repec.org/RePEc:diw:diwwpp:dp1515.

Best, R. and P. J. Burke. 2017. Macroeconomic Impacts of the 2010 Earthquake in Haiti. *Empirical Economics*.

Bhavnani, R. and B. Lacina. 2015. The Effects of Weather-Induced Migration on Sons of the Soil Riots in India. *World Politics* 67(4).

Bisri, M. B. F. and S. Beniya. 2016. Analyzing the National Disaster Response Framework and Inter-Organizational Network of the 2015 Nepal/Gorkha Earthquake. *Procedia Engineering* 159.

Black, R., S. Bennett, S. Thomas, and J. Reddington. 2011. Climate Change: Migration as Adaptation. *Nature* 478(7370).

Blanc, E. and E. Strobl. 2016. Assessing the Impact of Typhoons on Rice Production in the Philippines. *Journal of Applied Meteorology and Climatology* 55(4).

Bleakly, H. and J. Lin. 2012. Portage and Path Dependence. *The Quarterly Journal of Economics* 127(2).

Brückner, M. and A. Ciccone. 2011. Rain and the Democratic Window of Opportunity. *Econometrica* 79(3).

Bryan, G., S. Chowdhury, and M. Mobarak. 2014. Under-Investment in a Profitable Technology: The Case of Seasonal Migration in Bangladesh. *Econometrica* 82(5).

Burke, P. J. and A. Leigh. 2010. Do Output Contractions Trigger Democratic Change? *American Economic Journal: Macroeconomics* 2(4).

Cameron, L. and M. Shah. 2015. Risk-Taking Behavior in the Wake of Natural Disasters. *Journal of Human Resources* 50(2).

Carter, M., A. de Janvry, E. Sadoulet, and A. Sarris. 2017. Index Insurance for Developing Country Agriculture: A Reassessment. *Annual Review of Resource Economics* 9. https://www.annualreviews.org/doi/abs/10.1146/annurev-resource-100516-053352.

Caruso, G. and S. J. Miller. 2015. Long Run Effects and Intergenerational Transmission of Natural Disasters: A Case Study on the 1970 Ancash Earthquake. *Journal of Development Economics* 117.

Carvalho, V. M., M. Nirei, Y. Saito, and A. Tahbaz-Salehi. 2016. Supply Chain Disruptions: Evidence from the Great East Japan Earthquake. *Columbia Business School Research Paper*.

Cas, A., E. Frankenberg, W. Suriastini, and D. Thomas. 2014. The Impact of Parental Death on Child Well-being: Evidence from the Indian Ocean Tsunami. *Demography* 51(2).

Cassar, A., A. Healy, and C. von Kessler. 2017. Trust, Risk, and Time Preferences after a Natural Disaster: Experimental Evidence from Thailand. *World Development* 94.

Castells-Quintana, D., M. Lopez-Uribe, and T. K. J. McDermott. 2017. Geography, Institutions, and Development: A Review of the Long-Run Impacts of Climate Change. *Climate and Development* 9(5).

———. 2018. Adaptation to Climate Change: A Review Through a Development Economics Lens. *World Development* 104.

Cavallo, E., S. Galiani, I. Noy, and J. Pantano. 2013. Catastrophic Natural Disasters and Economic Growth. *The Review of Economics and Statistics* 95(5).

Clancey, G. 2006. *Earthquake Nation: The Cultural Politics of Japanese Seismicity, 1868–1930*. University of California Press.

Clarke, D. J. and S. Dercon. 2016. *Dull Disasters? How Planning Ahead Will Make a Difference*. Oxford University Press.

Clarke, D. J. and D. Grenham. 2013. Microinsurance and Natural Disasters: Challenges and Options. *Environmental Science & Policy* 27.

Clinton, W. J. 2006. Key Propositions for Building Back Better. United Nations Secretary-General's Special Envoy for Tsunami Recovery. United Nations.

Cole, M. A., R. Elliot, T. Okubo, and E. Strobl. 2018. Natural Disasters and Spatial Heterogeneity in Damages: The Birth, Life, and Death of Manufacturing Plants. *Journal of Economic Geography*.

Collier, P., G. Conway, and T. Venables. 2008. Climate Change and Africa. *Oxford Review of Economic Policy* 24(2).

Cook, A. D., M. Shrestha, and Z. Bo. 2016. *NTS Report: International Response to 2015 Nepal Earthquake Lessons and Observations*. Nanyang Technological University.

Dahal, R. K. 2016. Earthquake Recovery Process in Nepal (A Comparative Analysis with Haiti). *International Development, Community, and Environment (IDCE)*. Paper 40. https://commons.clarku.edu/idce_masters_papers/40/.

Davis, D. and D. Weinstein. 2002. Bones, Bombs, and Break Points: The Geography of Economic Activity. *American Economic Review* 92(5).

De Alwis, D. and I. Noy. Forthcoming. Sri Lankan Households a Decade after the Indian Ocean Tsunami. *Review of Development Economics*.

Deininger, K. and S. Jin. 2006. Tenure Security and Land-Related Investment: Evidence from Ethiopia. *European Economic Review* 50.

Dell, M., B. Jones, and B. Olken. 2012. Temperature Shocks and Economic Growth: Evidence from the Last Half Century. *American Economic Journal: Macroeconomics* 4(3).

———. 2014. What Do We Learn from the Weather? The New Climate-Economy Literature. *Journal of Economic Literature* 52(3).

Dercon, S. 2002. Income Risk, Coping Strategies and Safety Nets. *World Bank Research Observer* 17(2).

Desmet, K. and E. Rossi-Hansberg. 2015. On the Spatial Economic Impact of Global Warming. *Journal of Urban Economics* 88.

Desmet, K., D. K. Nagy, and E. Rossi-Hansberg. 2018. The Geography of Development. *Journal of Political Economy* 126(3).

Dietz, S., C. Dixon, and J. Ward 2016. Locking in Climate Vulnerability: Where Are the Investment Hotspots? In Fankhauser, S. and T. McDermott, eds. *The Economics of Climate Resilient Development*. Edward Elgar.

Du Pont, W., I. Noy, Y. Okuyama, and Y. Sawada. 2015. *The Long-Run Socio-Economic Consequences of a Large Disaster: The 1995 Earthquake in Kobe. PLoS ONE* 10(10): e0138714.

Elbers, C., J. W. Gunning, and B. Kinsey. 2007. Growth and Risk: Methodology and Micro Evidence. *World Bank Economic Review* 21.

Elliott, R. J., E. Strobl, and P. Sun. 2015. The Local Impact of Typhoons on Economic Activity in China: A View from Outer Space. *Journal of Urban Economics* 88.

Fankhauser, S. and T. K. J. McDermott. 2014. Understanding the Adaptation Deficit: Why Are Poor Countries More Vulnerable to Climate Events than Rich Countries? *Global Environmental Change* 27(1).

Felbermayr, G. and J. Gröschl. 2013. Natural Disasters and the Effect of Trade on Income: A New Panel IV Approach. *European Economic Review* 58.

Friedman, B. M. 2006. *The Moral Consequences of Economic Growth*. Penguin Random House.

Gall, M., K. A. Borden, and S. L. Cutter. 2009. When Do Losses Count? Six Fallacies of Natural Hazards Loss Data. *Bulletin of the American Meteorological Society* 90.

Gallagher, J. 2014. Learning About an Infrequent Event: Evidence from Flood Insurance Take-up in the United States. *American Economic Journal: Applied Economics* 6(3).

Golnaraghi, M., S. Surminski, and K. U. Schanz. 2016. *An Integrated Approach to Managing Extreme Events and Climate Risks. Towards a Concerted Public–Private Approach*. The Geneva Association.

Government of Nepal. 2015. *Post Disaster Needs Assessment. Volume B: Sector Reports.* https://www.npc.gov.np/images/category/PDNA_volume_BFinalVersion.pdf.

Gray, C. and V. Mueller. 2012. Natural Disasters and Population Mobility in Bangladesh. *Proceedings of the National Academy of Sciences* 109(16).

Gröger, A. and Y. Zylberberg. 2016. Internal Labor Migration as a Shock Coping Strategy: Evidence from a Typhoon. *American Economic Journal: Applied Economics* 8(2).

Grunewald, F. and A. Burlat. 2016. Nepal Earthquake: A Rapid Review of the Response and A Few Lessons Learnt. *Groupe URD*. https://www.urd.org/en/publications-20/humanitarian-aid-on-the-move/Humanitarian-Aid-on-the-move-17/Nepal-earthquake-a-rapid-review-of.

Gu, T., M. Nakagawa, M. Saito, and H. Yamaga. 2018. Public Perceptions of Earthquake Risk and the Impact on Land Pricing: The Case of the Uemachi Fault Line in Japan. *Japanese Economic Review* 69(4).

Hales, S., S. J. Edwards, and R. S. Kovats. 2003. Impact on Health of Climate Extremes. In McMichael, A. J. et al., eds. *Climate Change and Human Health: Risks and Responses*. World Health Organization.

Hall, M. L., A. C. Lee, C. Cartwright, S. Marahatta, J. Karki, and P. Simkhada. 2017. The 2015 Nepal Earthquake Disaster: Lessons Learned One Year On. *Public Health* 145.

Hallegatte, S. 2014. *Natural Disasters and Climate Change: An Economic Perspective.* Springer.

Hallegatte, S., J. Rentschler, and B. Walsh. 2018. *Building Back Better: Achieving Resilience through Stronger, Faster, and More Inclusive Post-Disaster Reconstruction.* World Bank.

Hallegatte, S., C. Green, R. Nicholls, and J. Corfee-Morlot. 2013. Future Flood Losses in Major Coastal Cities. *Nature Climate Change* 3(9).

———. 2016a. *Shock Waves: Managing the Impacts of Climate Change on Poverty.* World Bank.

———. 2016b. *Unbreakable: Building the Resilience of the Poor in the Face of Natural Disasters.* World Bank.

———. 2017. *Unbreakable: Building the Resilience of the Poor in the Face of Natural Disasters.* World Bank.

Handmer, J. and H. Iveson. 2017. Cyclone Pam in Vanuatu: Learning from the Low Death Toll. *Australian Journal of Emergency Management* 32(2).

Haque, U., M. Hashizume, K. Kolivras, H. J. Overgaard, B. Das, and T. Yamamoto. 2012. Reduced Death Rates from Cyclones in Bangladesh: What More Needs to be Done? *Bulletin of the World Health Organization* 90.

Haraguchi, M. and U. Lall. 2014. Flood Risks and Impacts: A Case Study of Thailand's Floods in 2011 and Research Questions for Supply Chain Decision Making. *International Journal of Disaster Risk Reduction* 14(3).

Heger, M., A. Julca, and O. Paddison. 2008. Analysing the Impact of Natural Hazards in Small Economies. *UNU-WIDER Research Paper.* No. 2008/25. United Nations University–World Institute for Development Economics Research.

Heintze, H-J., L. Kirch, B. Kuppers, H. Mahan, F. Mischo, P. Mucke, T. Pazdzierny, R. Prutz, K. Radtke, F. Strube, and D. Weller. 2018. *World Risk Report 2018.* Aachen: Bündnis Entwicklung Hilft and Bochum: Institute for International Law of Peace and Armed Conflict, Ruhr University Bochum.

Henderson, J. V., A. Storeygard, and D. N. Weil. 2012. Measuring Economic Growth from Outer Space. *American Economic Review* 102(2).

Henderson, J. V., A. Storeygard, and U. Deichmann. 2014. 50 Years of Urbanization in Africa—Examining the Role of Climate Change. *World Bank Development Research Group Policy Research Working Paper* No. 6925. World Bank Group.

Hidano, N., T. Hoshino, and A. Sugiura. 2015. The Effect of Seismic Hazard Risk Information on Property Prices: Evidence from a Spatial Regression Discontinuity Design. *Regional Science and Urban Economics* 53.

Hino, M., C. Field, and K. Mach. 2017. Managed Retreat as a Response to Natural Hazard Risk. *Nature Climate Change* 7.

Hornbeck, R. and D. Keniston. 2017. Creative Destruction: Barriers to Urban Growth and the Great Boston Fire of 1872. *American Economic Review* 107(6).

Hornbeck, R. and S. Naidu. 2014. When the Levee Breaks: Black Migration and the Economic Development in the American South. *American Economic Review* 104(3).

Hsiang, S. and J. Anttila-Hughes. 2013. Destruction, Disinvestment, and Death: Economic and Human Losses Following Environmental Disaster. *SSRN Electronic Journal*. https://ssrn.com/abstract=2220501.

Husby, T., H. de Groot, M. Hofkes, and M. Droes. 2014. Do Floods have permanent Effects? Evidence from the Netherlands. *Journal of Regional Science* 54(3).

Hyland, M. and J. Russ. 2019. Water as Destiny—The Long-Term Impacts of Drought in Sub-Saharan Africa. *World Development* 115.

Idicheria, C. and A. Neelakantan. 2016. Transforming Chennai: A Research Report on Building Micro, Small, and Medium Enterprise Resilience to Water-Related Environmental Change. https://www.mercycorps.org/sites/default/files/Transforming_Chennai_Okapi_Mercy_Corps.pdf.

Inoue, H. and Y. Todo. 2018. Firm-Level Simulation of Supply Chain Disruption Triggered by Actual and Predicted Earthquakes. *RIETI Discussion Paper*. 18-E-013. Research Institute of Economy, Trade, and Industry.

Inter-Agency Standing Committee (IASC). 2016. *Preparedness: What Can We Learn from the Nepal Response?* http://www.deliveraidbetter.org/webinars/preparedness/.

IDMC. 2018. *Global Report on Internal Displacement*. Internal Displacement Monitoring Centre.

———. 2019. *The Ripple Effect: Economic Impacts of Internal Displacement*. Internal Displacement Monitoring Centre.

IMF. 2015. *Nepal: Request for Disbursement Under the Rapid Credit Facility*. International Monetary Fund. https://www.imf.org/en/Publications/CR/Issues/2016/12/31/Nepal-Request-for-Disbursement-Under-the-Rapid-Credit-Facility-43173.

———. 2018. *The IMF's Rapid Financing Instrument (RFI)*. International Monetary Fund. https://www.imf.org/en/About/Factsheets/Sheets/2016/08/02/19/55/Rapid-Financing-Instrument.

———. 2019. *IMF Rapid Credit Facility (RCF)*. International Monetary Fund. https://www.imf.org/en/About/Factsheets/Sheets/2016/08/02/21/08/Rapid-Credit-Facility.

IPCC. 2012. Managing the Risks of Extreme Events and Disasters to Advance Climate Change Adaptation. A Special Report of Working Groups I and II of the Intergovernmental Panel on Climate Change. Cambridge University Press. Intergovernmental Panel on Climate Change.

Jacoby, H. and E. Skoufias. 1997. Risk, Financial Markets, and Human Capital in a Developing Country. *Review of Economic Studies* 64.

Kahn, M. 2005. The Death Toll from Natural Disasters: The Role of Income, Geography, and Institutions. *The Review of Economics and Statistics* 187(2).

Karim, A. and I. Noy. 2016. Poverty, Inequality, and Natural Disasters—A Qualitative Survey of the Empirical Literature. *Singapore Economic Review*.

Kashiwagi, Y., Y. Todo, and P. Matous. 2018. International Propagation of Economic Shocks Through Global Supply Chains. *WINPEC Working Paper* No. E1810. Waseda Institute of Political Economy, Waseda University.

Kellett, J. and A. Caravani. 2013. *Financing Disaster Risk Reduction: A 20-Year Story of International Aid*. Overseas Development Institute.

Kelman, I., J. Mercer, and J. C. Gaillard. 2012. Indigenous Knowledge and Disaster Risk Reduction. *Geography* 97.

Kennedy, J., J. Ashmore, E. Babister, and I. Kelman. 2008. The Meaning of 'Build Back Better': Evidence from Post-Tsunami Aceh and Sri Lanka. *Journal of Contingencies and Crisis Management* 16.

Kochar, A. 1999. Smoothing Consumption by Smoothing Income: Hours-of-work Response to Idiosyncratic Agricultural Shocks in Rural India. *Review of Economic and Statistics* 81(1).

Kocornik-Mina, A., T. McDermott, G. Michaels, and F. Rauch. Forthcoming. Flooded Cities. *American Economic Journal: Applied Economics*.

Le Dé, L., J. C. Gaillard, W. Friesen, M. Pupualii, C. Brown, and A. Aupito. 2015. Our Family Comes First: Migrants' Perspectives on Remittances in Disaster. *Migration and Development*.

Lee, D., H. Zhang, and C. Nguyen. 2018. The Economic Impact of Natural Disasters in the Pacific Island Countries: Adaptation and Preparedness. *IMF Working Paper* No. 108. International Monetary Fund.

Ligon, E. 2008. Risk Sharing. In Palgrave Macmillan. *New Palgrave Dictionary of Economics (2nd edition)*.

Lloyd-Jones, T. 2006. *Mind the Gap! Post-Disaster Reconstruction and the Transition From Humanitarian Relief*. Royal Institute of Chartered Surveyors. https://www.preventionweb.net/publications/view/9080.

Maccini, S. and D. Yang. 2009. Under the Weather: Health, Schooling, and Economic Consequences of Early-Life Rainfall. *American Economic Review* 99(3).

McAdoo, B. G., L. Dengker, G. Prasetya, and V. Titov. 2006. *Smong*: How an Oral History Saved Thousands on Indonesia's Simeulue Island during the December 2004 and March 2005 Tsunamis. *Earthquake Spectra* 22(S3).

McDermott, T. K. J. 2016. Investing in Disaster Risk Management in an Uncertain Climate. *World Bank Policy Research Working Paper* No. 7631. World Bank.

Michaels, G. and F. Rauch. 2018. Resetting the Urban Network: 117-2012. *Economic Journal* 128(608).

Miguel, E. 2005. Poverty and Witch Killing. *Review of Economic Studies* 72(4).

Miguel, E. and G. Roland. 2011. The Long-Run Impact of Bombing Viet Nam. *Journal of Development Economics* 96(1).

Mobarak, A. M. and M. R. Rosenzweig. 2013. Informal Risk Sharing, Index Insurance, and Risk Taking in Developing Countries. *American Economic Review* 103(3).

Mohan, P. and E. Strobl. 2017. The Short-Term Economic Impact of Tropical Cyclone Pam: An Analysis Using VIIRS Nightlight Satellite Imagery. *International Journal of Remote Sensing* 38(21).

Munshi, K. 2003. Networks in the Modern Economy: Mexican Migrants in the US Labor Market. *Quarterly Journal of Economics* 118(2).

Nakagawa, M., M. Saito, and H. Yamaga. 2007. Earthquake Risks and Housing Rents: Evidence from the Tokyo Metropolitan Area. *Regional Science and Urban Economics* 37(1).

Nakata, H., Y. Sawada, and N. Wakamori. Forthcoming. Robustness of Production Networks Against Economic Disasters: Thailand Case. In Anbumozhi, V., F. Kimura, and S. Thangavelu, eds. *Supply Chain Resilience: Reducing Vulnerability to Economic Shocks, Financial Crises, and Natural Disasters*. Springer.

Noy, I. 2015. *A New Non-Monetary Global Measure of the Direct Impact of Natural Disasters: Country Case Studies*. Paper prepared for the 2015 Global Assessment Report on Disaster Risk Reduction. United Nations Office for Disaster Risk Reduction.

———. 2016a. Tropical Storms: The Socio-Economics of Cyclones. *Nature Climate Change* 6.

———. 2016b. Natural Disasters in the Pacific Island Countries: New Measurements of Impacts. *Natural Hazards* 84(1).

———. 2017. To Leave or Not to Leave? Climate Change, Exit, and Voice on a Pacific Island. *CESifo Economic Studies* 63(4).

Noy, I. and C. Edmonds. 2019. Fiscal Resilience to Disasters in the Pacific. Working Paper. Asian Development Bank.

NRA. 2016. *Nepal Earthquake 2015 Post Disaster Recovery Framework 2016–2020*. National Reconstruction Authority. https://reliefweb.int/report/nepal/nepal-earthquake-2015-post-disaster-recovery-framework-2016-2020.

———. 2018. Reconstruction Progress in Numbers. 2 May. National Reconstruction Authority. http://www.nra.gov.np/en/map-infograhics/AllInfographics/0.

Obstfeld, M. and K. Rogoff. 1996. *Foundations of International Macroeconomics*. MIT Press.

Pacific Catastrophic Risk Assessment and Financing Initiative. Explore Documents, Country Profiles. http://pcrafi.spc.int/documents/?limit=100&offset=0&doc_type_in=presentation (accessed 23 November 2018).

Park, A. and S. Wang. 2017. Benefiting from Disaster? Public and Private Responses to the Wenchuan Earthquake. *World Development* 94.

Ranger, N. and S-L. Garbett-Shiels. 2012. Accounting for a Changing and Uncertain Climate in Planning and Policymaking Today: Lessons for Developing Countries. *Climate and Development* 4(4).

Rigaud, K. K., A. de Sherbidin, B. Jones, J. Bergman, V. Clement, K. Ober, J. Schewe, S. Adamo, B. McKusker, S. Heuser, and A. Midgley. 2018. *Groundswell: Preparing for Internal Climate Migration.* World Bank Group.

Robalino, J., J. Jimenez, and A. Chacon. 2015. The Effect of Hydro-Meteorological Emergencies on Internal Migration. *World Development* 67.

Sakai, Y., J. Estudillo, N. Fuwa, Y. Higuchi, and Y. Sawada. 2017. Do Natural Disasters Affect the Poor Disproportionately? Price Change and Welfare Impact in the Aftermath of Typhoon Milenyo in the Rural Philippines. *World Development* 94(C).

Sawada, Y. 2007. The Impact of Natural and Manmade Disasters on Household Welfare. *Agricultural Economics* 37(s1).

——. 2017. Disasters, Household Decisions, and Insurance Mechanisms: A Review of Evidence and a Case Study from a Developing Country in Asia. *Asian Economic Policy Review* 12.

Sawada, Y. and Y. Kuroishi. 2015a. How Does a Natural Disaster Affect People's Preference? The Case of a Large Scale Flood in the Philippines Using the Convex Time Budget Experiments. In Sawada, Y. and S. Oum, eds. *Disaster Risks, Social Preferences, and Policy Effects: Field Experiments in Selected ASEAN and East Asian Countries.* Economic Research Institute for ASEAN and East Asia. ERIA Research Project Report FY2013, No. 34.

——. 2015b. How to Strengthen Social Capital in Disaster Affected Communities? The Case of the Great East Japan Earthquake. In Sawada, Y. and S. Oum, eds. *Disaster Risks, Social Preferences, and Policy Effects: Field Experiments in Selected ASEAN and East Asian Countries.* Economic Research Institute for ASEAN and East Asia. ERIA Research Project Report FY2013, No. 34.

Sawada, Y. and M. Lokshin. 2008. Obstacles to School Progression in Rural Pakistan: An Analysis of Gender and Sibling Rivalry Using Field Survey Data. *Journal of Development Economics* 88(2).

Sawada, Y., H. Nakata, and T. Kotera. 2017. Self-Production, Friction, and Risk Sharing Against Disasters: Evidence from a Developing Country. *World Development* 94.

Sawada, Y., H. Nakata, K. Sekiguchi, and Y. Okuyama. 2018. Land and Real Estate Price Sensitivity to a Disaster: Evidence from the 2011 Thai Floods. *Economics Bulletin* 38(1).

Sawada, Y. and S. Shimizutani. 2008. How Do People Cope with Natural Disasters? Evidence from the Great Hanshin-Awaji (Kobe) Earthquake in 1995. *Journal of Money, Credit and Banking* 40(2–3).

Sawada, Y. and Y. Takasaki. 2017. Natural Disaster, Poverty, and Development: An Introduction. *World Development* 94(C).

Sawada, Y., M. Tatsujiro, N. Hiroyuki, and S. Kunio. 2017. Natural Disasters: Financial Preparedness of Corporate Japan. *RIETI Discussion Paper Series* No. 17-E-014. The Research Institute of Economy, Trade and Industry. Tokyo. https://www.rieti.go.jp/jp/publications/dp/17e014.pdf.

Sekhri, S. and A. Storeygard. 2014. Dowry Deaths: Response to Weather Variability in India. *Journal of Development Economics* 111.

Sen, A. 2000. *Development as Freedom*. Anchor Books.

Spencer, N., S. Polachek, and E. Strobl. 2016. How Do Hurricanes Impact Scholastic Achievement? A Caribbean Perspective. *Natural Hazards* 84.

Strobl, E. 2011. The Economic Growth Impact of Hurricanes: Evidence from US Coastal Counties. *Review of Economics and Statistics* 93(2).

Surminski, S. and T. Tanner, eds. 2016. Realising the "Triple Dividend of Resilience": A New Business Case for Disaster Risk Management. *Climate Risk Management, Policy and Governance Series*. Springer International Publishing.

Timar, L., A. Grimes, and R. Fabling. 2018a. That Sinking Feeling: The Changing Price of Disaster Risk Following an Earthquake. *International Journal of Disaster Risk Reduction* 31.

———. 2018b. Before a Fall: Impacts of Earthquake Regulation on Commercial Buildings. *Economics of Disasters and Climate Change* 2(1).

UN. 2015. Sendai Framework for Disaster Risk Reduction 2015–2030. United Nations.

———. 2016. Report of the Open-Ended Intergovernmental Expert Working Group on Indicators and Terminology Relating to Disaster Risk Reduction. United Nations.

UNOCHA. 2015. *Note on Migration and Remittances*. United Nations Office for the Coordination of Humanitarian Affairs. https://reliefweb.int/report/nepal/note-migration-and-remittances-24072015.

UNISDR. 2009. *2009 Global Assessment Report on Disaster Risk Reduction. Risk and Poverty in a Changing Climate: Invest Today for a Safer Tomorrow.* United Nations Office for Disaster Risk Reduction.

———. 2013. 2013 Global Assessment Report on Disaster Risk Reduction. From Shared Risk to Shared Value: The Business Case for Disaster Risk Reduction. In *Global Assessment Report on Disaster Risk Reduction.* United Nations Office for Disaster Risk Reduction.

———. 2015. *2015 Global Assessment Report on Disaster Risk Reduction. Making Development Sustainable: The Future of Disaster Risk Management.* United Nations Office for Disaster Risk Reduction.

———. 2017. *Build Back Better in Recovery, Rehabilitation and Reconstruction—Consultative Version.* United Nations Office for Disaster Risk Reduction.

Waldinger, M. 2016. Migration and Climate-Resilient Development. In Fankhauser, S. and T. K. J. McDermott, eds. *The Economics of Climate Resilient Development.* Edward Elgar.

Watkiss, P. 2016. Adaptation Experience and Prioritisation. In Fankhauser, S. and T. K. J. McDermott, eds. *The Economics of Climate Resilient Development.* Edward Elgar.

Wilde, O. 2009. *The Soul of Man Under Socialism.* Book Jungle.

Winsemius, H., B. Jongman, T. Veldkamp, and S. Hallegatte. 2018. Disaster Risk, Climate Change, and Poverty: Assessing the Global Exposure of Poor People to Floods and Droughts. *Environment and Development Economics* 23(3).

Wong, G. 2008. Has SARS Infected the Property Market in Hong Kong? *Journal of Urban Economics* 63.

World Bank. 2012. *Thai Flood 2011: Rapid Assessment for Resilient Recovery and Reconstruction Planning.* https://openknowledge.worldbank.org/handle/10986/26862.

———. 2017. *Bank Guidance: Contingent Emergency Response Components.*

World Bank and United Nations. 2010. *Natural Hazards, UnNatural Disasters: The Economics of Effective Prevention.*

Yang, D. and H. Choi. 2007. Are Remittances Insurance? Evidence from Rainfall Shocks in the Philippines. *World Bank Economic Review* 21(2).

3

ECONOMIC TRENDS AND PROSPECTS IN DEVELOPING ASIA

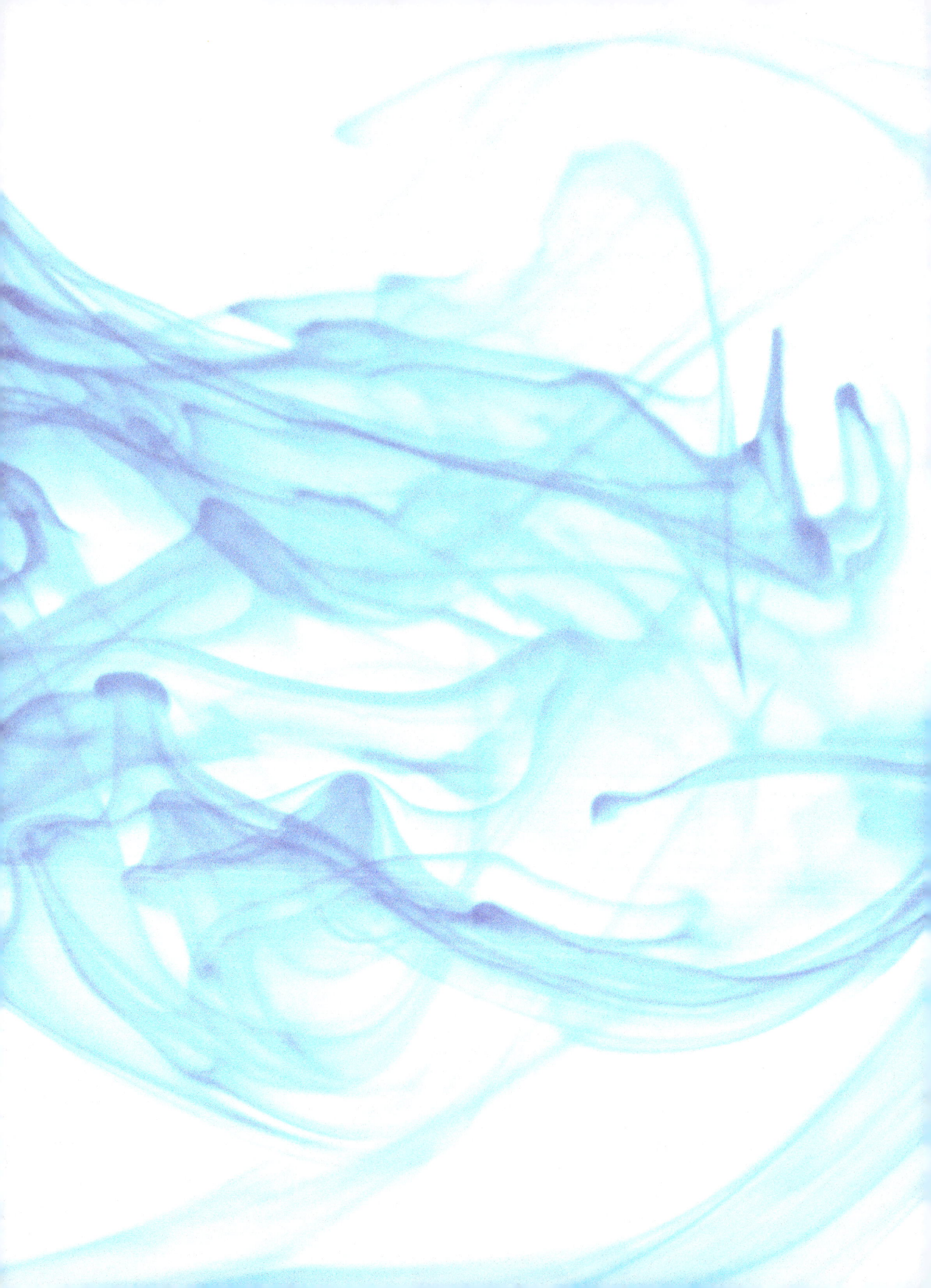

CENTRAL ASIA

- ARMENIA
- AZERBAIJAN
- GEORGIA
- KAZAKHSTAN
- KYRGYZ REPUBLIC
- TAJIKISTAN
- TURKMENISTAN
- UZBEKISTAN

Armenia

Growth slowed across sectors in 2018, with agriculture contracting further. Inflation accelerated somewhat, and a larger trade deficit and lower remittances widened the current account deficit. Continued fiscal consolidation will mean slower growth in 2019 and 2020. Higher import duties and excise taxes will bring more inflation. A wider trade deficit is expected to keep the current account deficit sizable despite gains in income and service exports. Innovation is critical to ensure growth.

Economic performance

Growth slowed from an exceptionally strong 7.5% in 2017 to 5.2% in 2018. On the supply side, services and industry drove growth as agriculture contracted. Services, providing more than half of output, expanded by 9.6% on improvements in trade, finance, insurance, recreation, transportation, and health care, though growth was less than the 12.1% rise in 2017. Growth in industry excluding construction slackened from 6.6% in 2017 to 4.1% as mining and quarrying output plunged by 14.1% because of low international prices for copper, uncertainties surrounding a gold mining project, and the closure of Armenia's second largest copper and molybdenum mine. However, growth in manufacturing almost doubled from 5.9% to 10.1%, supported by strong gains in processed foods, beverages, tobacco, textiles, and nonferrous metal products. Growth in construction slowed from 2.5% in 2017 to 1.6% as private construction slumped. Adverse weather caused agriculture to contract by 8.5%, compounding a 5.3% drop in 2017 (Figure 3.1.1).

On the demand side, private consumption and investment were the main sources of growth. Private consumption slowed from 8.9% in 2017 but still expanded by 5.7%, benefiting from low inflation, increased consumer lending, and a government initiative in July 2018 to write off fines and penalties on overdue personal loans. Public consumption declined by 6.4%, reversing 13.1% growth in 2017. Despite lower public investment, total investment expanded by 28.5% on much higher inventories, which were likely motivated by disruptions and business uncertainty stemming from political events in 2018, and on a 5.0% rise in gross fixed capital formation. The deficit in net exports widened further as imports grew faster than exports.

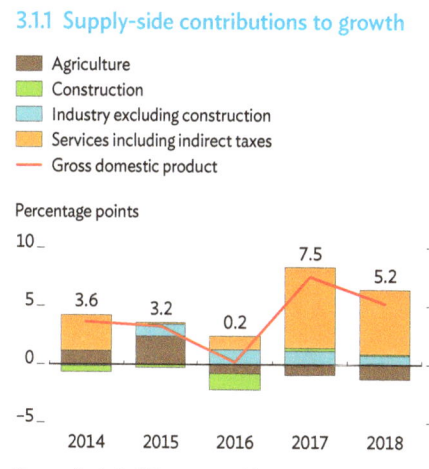

3.1.1 Supply-side contributions to growth

Source: Statistical Committee of Armenia. http://www.armstat.am (accessed 25 February 2019).

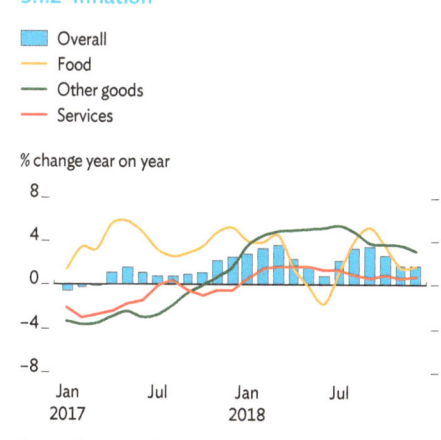

3.1.2 Inflation

Source: Statistical Committee of Armenia. http://www.armstat.am (accessed 25 February 2019).

This chapter was written by Grigor Gyurjyan of the Armenia Resident Mission, ADB, Yerevan.

Average annual inflation rose from 1.0% in 2017 to 2.5% in 2018, reflecting higher excise taxes on fuel, liquefied gas, beverages, and cigarettes, as well as increased customs duties since January 2018 for about 200 items under the Customs Code of the Eurasian Economic Union. Prices increased by 2.5% for food, 4.5% for other goods, and 1.2% for services. Inflation at 1.8% year on year in December 2018 was still well below the target band of 2.5%–5.5% set by the Central Bank of Armenia (Figure 3.1.2).

Monetary policy remained steady throughout the year, with the policy rate unchanged at 6.00% from February 2017 to the end of 2018. As inflation, while rising, stayed moderate, the central bank trimmed the policy rate to 5.75% in January 2019.

Monetary expansion slowed sharply from 18.5% in 2017 to 7.4% last year as net foreign assets tumbled by three-quarters, and despite a 12.0% rise in net domestic assets. Credit to the private sector rose significantly, pushing total credit higher by more than 17% in 2018, including an increase of 45.3% for consumers.

In a 2018 assessment, the International Monetary Fund found Armenia's financial system stable and noted significant progress in strengthening oversight of the sector, with improved regulation and supervision contributing to financial deepening along with additional capital from shareholders and several mergers. Despite improved financial soundness indicators, vulnerabilities remain. A high 47.1% of loans and 60.4% of bank deposits were in foreign currency at the end of 2018, and liquidity cushions were inadequate, with foreign currency loans four times higher than deposits.

Fiscal policy remained consistent with the government's medium-term consolidation objectives of reducing the deficit and the high ratio of public debt to GDP. The budget deficit narrowed sharply from 4.8% of GDP in 2017 to 1.8% in 2018, greatly outperforming the budget's 2.7% target (Figure 3.1.3). Domestic sources provided two-thirds of budget financing. Revenue rose by 8.3% to equal 22.3% of GDP, reflecting better tax collection, a new tax code with higher excise taxes and customs duties, and increased nontax revenue. Outlays declined by 3.9 percentage points to equal 24.1% of GDP as capital spending fell 12.2% short of the budget target. The ratio of public debt to GDP eased from 58.9% in 2017 to 55.8%, the first drop since 2013, as GDP grew faster than debt. External public debt grew by only 1.8% to $5.0 billion, equal to 44.6% of GDP, while domestic public debt rose by 8.6% to $1.4 billion (Figure 3.1.4).

The estimated current account deficit more than doubled from 2.4% of GDP in 2017 to 6.6% as a much larger trade deficit and weaker remittances outweighed gains in service exports and income flows (Figure 3.1.5). Problems in mining slashed annual growth in exports from 26.2% in 2017 to 8.5% last year,

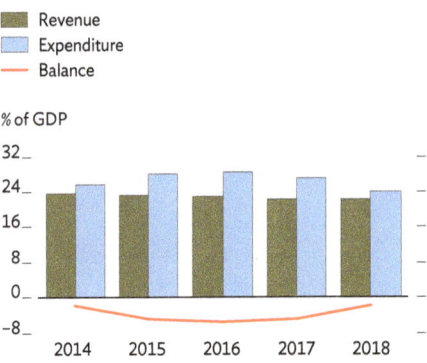

3.1.3 Fiscal indicators

Sources: Ministry of Finance. http://www.minfin.am; Statistical Committee of Armenia. http://www.armstat.am (accessed 25 February 2019).

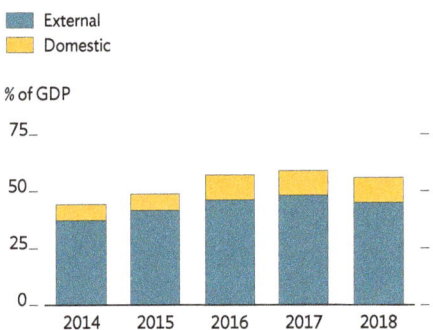

3.1.4 Public debt

Sources: Ministry of Finance. http://www.minfin.am; Statistical Committee of Armenia. http://www.armstat.am (accessed 25 February 2019).

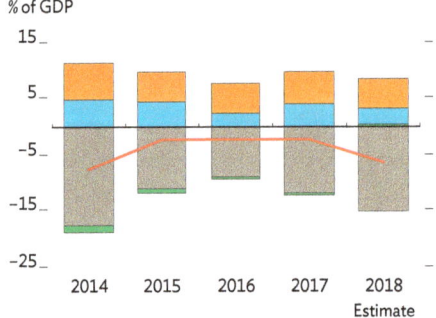

3.1.5 Current account components

Sources: Central Bank of Armenia. http://www.cba.am (accessed 25 February 2019); ADB estimates.

while slackening domestic demand cut import growth from 32.6% to 18.5%. Remittances, measured as net inflow of private noncommercial transfers through banks, fell by 22.1% to $600 million in 2018. Ruble depreciation cut remittances from the Russian Federation by 16.1%, and remittances from other countries plunged even further (Figure 3.1.6).

Gross international reserves slumped by 2.8% to $2.2 billion at the end of 2018, estimated to cover 4.3 months of imports. The Armenian dram remained relatively stable in real effective terms but appreciated by 6.0% in nominal effective terms (Figure 3.1.7).

3.1.1 Selected economic indicators (%)

	2019	2020
GDP growth	4.3	4.5
Inflation	3.5	3.2
Current account balance (share of GDP)	-6.9	-6.1

Source: ADB estimates.

Economic prospects

Growth is projected to slow to 4.3% in 2019 then recover slightly to 4.5% in 2020 (Figure 3.1.8).

Risks to the outlook are broadly balanced. Growth could strengthen with improved political stability, following an eventful 2018, and as a new government pledges to promote competition, combat corruption, enhance public services, and encourage entrepreneurship and innovation. Major downside risks stem from any growth slowdown in 2019 in the Russian Federation, Armenia's main trade partner and destination for migrant workers; weaker mining output and diminished exports from lower prices for nonferrous metals; and preparations to repay a $500 million eurobond coming due in September 2020.

On the supply side, services should be the main driver of expansion, with lesser support from agriculture, industry, and construction. Services are projected to grow by 6.0% in 2019 and 5.5% in 2020, reflecting gains in wholesale and retail trade, finance, insurance, recreation, and transport and communications. Agriculture is projected to rebound by 2.5% in 2019 and 3.3% in 2020, assuming more normal weather but also continued government-subsidized loans to farmers for hail nets, drip irrigation, intensive gardening, and leasing, as well as the success of a pilot agricultural insurance program that promises to encourage planting. Expansion in industry excluding construction will likely slow to 2.9% in 2019 before recovering to 3.6% in 2020. While low international copper prices and problems in mining will again weigh on the output and export of minerals, growth could benefit from higher demand for processed foods, pharmaceuticals, textiles, and footwear from Eurasian Economic Union partners and the Middle East. Tepid capital spending will likely keep growth in construction modest.

On the demand side, growth is expected to slow further for both investment and consumption. Fiscal consolidation including low capital outlays will likely limit gains in public consumption and investment, though private consumption and investment should find support in expected increases in remittances and tax changes to be implemented in 2019: the introduction of a

3.1.6 Remittances by source

Source: Central Bank of Armenia. http://www.cba.am (accessed 25 February 2019).

3.1.7 Reserves and effective exchange rates

Sources: Central Bank of Armenia. http://www.cba.am; International Monetary Fund. International Financial Statistics online database (accessed 25 February 2019).

flat personal income tax at 23% and lower profit taxes on small firms. The deficit in net exports is expected to widen further as exports grow more slowly than imports.

Monetary policy will aim to support economic growth while curbing inflation. Despite slower growth, average annual inflation is projected to accelerate to 3.5% in 2019, boosted by higher customs duties for about 560 items imported from countries outside the Eurasian Economic Union, a 10% price rise for imported gas beginning in January 2019, and expected increases in excise taxes for fuel, beverages, and cigarettes in the second half of 2019. Inflation is seen moderating to 3.2% in 2020 as the effects of these factors abate.

Fiscal policy will remain tight under fiscal consolidation that includes planned government restructuring and the rationalization of some agencies that will likely trim employment in several ministries. The 2019 budget projects a fiscal deficit equal to 2.2% of GDP as revenue rises by 14.4% and expenditure by only 12.5%. Planned revisions to the tax code in the second half of the year should boost revenue collection by strengthening tax administration and enlarging the tax base, but preparations to repay the $500 million eurobond in September 2020 will pose a serious fiscal challenge. In addition, public debt engaged in 2018 but drawn down in 2019 will likely raise total public debt to about 58% of GDP.

The current account deficit is projected to widen slightly to 6.9% of GDP in 2019 before narrowing to 6.1% in 2020 as higher income and service exports offset continued expansion of the trade deficit (Figure 3.1.9). Export growth is projected to slip further to 6.0% in 2019 and then recover to 8.5% in 2020 on higher exports of agricultural products, textiles, precious stones, and metal products, even as mineral earnings remain weak. Import growth will likely moderate to 8.2% in 2019 and 6.5% in 2020 but continue to outpace growth in exports as demand grows for consumer and capital goods. Gains in tourism and information technology (IT) will buoy net service inflows, while rising remittances are expected to boost net income and current transfers. International reserves are projected at $2.2 billion in 2019, rising in 2020 to $2.4 billion.

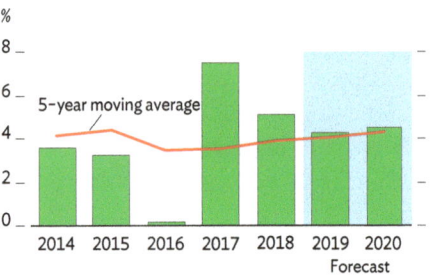

3.1.8 GDP growth

Sources: Statistical Committee of Armenia. http://www.armstat.am (accessed 25 February 2019); ADB estimates.

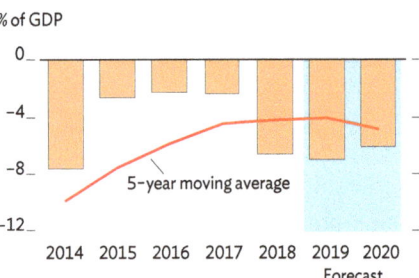

3.1.9 Current account balance

Sources: Central Bank of Armenia. http://www.cba.am; Statistical Committee of Armenia. http://www.armstat.am (both accessed 25 February 2019); ADB estimates.

Policy challenge—ensuring growth through innovation and a knowledge economy

Growth averaged a respectable 4.1% from 2010 to 2018 but faces an uncertain future. Remittances and exports of commodities may fuel growth, but they are vulnerable to external shocks. Armenia has responded by diversifying its export base, yet exports of goods with high value added remain small. To address these problems and ensure stable and more inclusive growth, Armenia's capacity for innovation must be strengthened.

In its *Global Competitiveness Report 2018*, the World Economic Forum ranked innovation capacity in Armenia at 60 out of 135 economies and 14 out of 34 peers in the upper-middle-income category. While Armenia scores well on international co-invention, patent applications, and buyer sophistication, it compares less favorably on workforce diversity, research and development (R&D) spending, the quality of its research institutions, and its use of cluster development. Addressing these issues and promoting a knowledge-based economy depends on the successful implementation of comprehensive education, science, technology, and innovation policies. Among key government objectives are upgrading Armenia's scientific infrastructure, ensuring a steady rise in the number of highly skilled workers, strengthening innovation, and internationalizing science and innovation. Specific targets for certain objectives appear in an innovation concept paper the government approved in 2011 and in other documents, notably *Strategy on Development of Science 2011–2020* and *Science and Technology Priorities 2015–2029*.

Successful policy implementation requires an enabling environment, support for human capital development, aid for R&D and innovation in private firms, and more integrated innovation systems. As human capital is especially important, innovation capacity depends crucially on the quality of education, particularly in science and technology, and the availability of workers with the necessary technical skills. Armenia has made considerable progress, and IT-related services now provide more than 11% of service exports, 16% of all services, and 5% of GDP. Continued rapid expansion in IT depends on enhanced education to meet the industry's growing demand for highly skilled workers. In particular, the quality of science, technology, engineering, and mathematics education must be improved by modernizing teaching and learning materials and by going beyond existing initiatives and projects to develop and promote techno-parks, innovation incubators, R&D centers opened and operated by global companies, IT classes, school engineering labs, and after-school learning platforms.

Though Armenia's skills base is evolving, R&D capacity and efforts still lag. R&D spending equaled only 0.3% of GDP in 2018, or barely one-six of the 1.8% average in upper-middle-income economies. Measures to support innovation must be comprehensively inventoried before they can be streamlined and reoriented. Flexible financing arrangements that include incentives and other cost-effective support could allow firms to improve their performance and become more willing to undertake the risks inherent in developing new products and services. The government is providing R&D and physical facilities for technology-based firms through a program called Engineering City and Engineering Cluster, designed to help firms and universities combine their efforts to commercialize research products and catalyze the growth of high-tech companies.

Azerbaijan

GDP growth strengthened in 2018 as expansion in services and agriculture continued, and as industry contracted less. Exchange rate stability tamed inflation, and higher oil prices widened the current account surplus. Growth is forecast to inch higher in 2019 and 2020 on expanded public spending, gas production, and output aside from petroleum, with inflation rebounding slightly in both years and higher gas exports further widening the current account surplus. Improving infrastructure is a priority.

Economic performance

Growth accelerated from a negligible 0.1% in 2017 to 1.4% on gains of 0.6% in the dominant petroleum sector and 1.8% in the rest of the economy (Figure 3.2.1).

On the supply side, industry contracted by 0.4%, improving considerably on 3.6% decline in 2017 with recovery in mining and 7.9% growth in manufacturing largely offsetting a steep drop in construction. Mining expanded by 0.4%, reversing 4.6% decline in 2017, as the beginning of supply from Shah Deniz 2 field boosted gas production by 7.1%. Lower capital outlays with the completion of major public investment projects deepened contraction in construction from 1.5% in 2017 to 9.0%. Agriculture expanded from 4.2% in 2017 to 4.6%, reflecting government support to farmers, particularly for crop production, which rose by 6.8%. Growth in services remained at 3.5% with gains in tourism and transportation.

On the demand side, 9 months' data show a 12.0% rise in consumption, including 13.0% expansion in private consumption as household incomes increased. Total investment contracted by 0.2%—though an estimate for the full year shows total investment rising. Net exports tripled as exports outgrew imports.

Average annual inflation plunged from 12.9% in 2017 to 2.3%, and core inflation to 1.8%, thanks to higher prices for oil exports and tightened control over the amount of currency in circulation to stabilize the exchange rate (Figure 3.2.2). With a decline in more expensive imported food, price rises for food slowed from 16.4% in 2017 to 1.7%, for other goods from 11.6% to 2.6%, and for services from 9.3% to 2.7% (Figure 3.2.3).

Expansionary fiscal policy saw expenditure increase from the equivalent of 25.1% of GDP in 2017 to 28.5%, mainly for investment (Figure 3.2.4). Revenue rose from 23.5% of GDP

3.2.1 GDP growth by sector

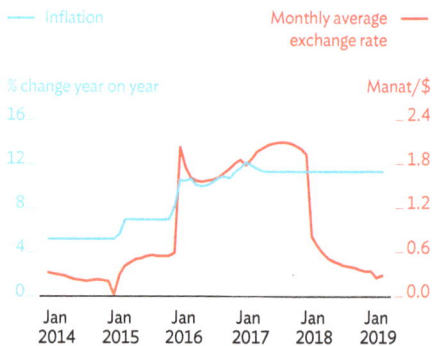

Source: State Statistical Committee of the Republic of Azerbaijan.

3.2.2 Inflation and exchange rate

Source: State Statistical Committee of the Republic of Azerbaijan.

This chapter was written by Nail Valiyev of the Azerbaijan Resident Mission, ADB, Baku.

in 2017 to 28.1% on an 80% rise in transfers from the State Oil Fund of Azerbaijan (SOFAZ), the sovereign wealth fund, and on reform to tax and customs administration that improved tax revenue by 13.3%. Higher revenue trimmed the budget deficit almost to zero, from 1.6% of GDP in 2017 to 0.4%. However, the deficit excluding SOFAZ transfers remained substantial, rising from 10.3% of GDP in 2017 to 14.1%. Debt service payments of both interest and principal soared by 47.0% as the government opted to prepay a portion of more expensive external debt. External public and publicly guaranteed debt consequently fell from the equivalent of 22.8% of GDP at the end of 2017 to 19.0% a year later, partly reflecting a new strategy adopted in 2018 to rein in public debt.

Monetary policy continued to prioritize price stability. Success in reducing inflation nevertheless allowed the Central Bank of Azerbaijan to cut the policy rate from 15.00% to 9.75% in four rounds during 2018 and to 9.25% in January 2019. Broad money growth slowed from 9.0% in 2017 to 5.7% (Figure 3.2.5). Banks continued to face challenges as the percentage of nonperforming loans remained high at 12.2%, though efforts to address the problem brought a reduction from 13.8% a year earlier. Confidence in the Azerbaijan manat continued to firm, as indicated by the share of local currency deposits rising from 27.6% at the end of 2017 to 34.6% a year later, and the share of local currency loans rising from 59.1% to 62.0%. With greater exchange rate stability and more consumer confidence, the supply of credit grew by 10.7%, reversing 28.5% contraction in 2017.

The current account surplus was estimated to have nearly doubled from the equivalent of 3.6% of GDP in the first 9 months of 2017 to 6.9% in the same period of 2018. Higher oil prices raised the full-year trade surplus to 16.0% of GDP and doubled export growth from 17.9% in 2017 to 35.9% as hydrocarbons continued to account for more than 90% of all exports, with other exports expanding as well. Import growth jumped from 1.6% in 2017 to 32.1%. With the completion of hydrocarbon construction projects, the deficit in services fell from $3.4 billion in 2017 to $1.3 billion, even as profit transfers by foreign petroleum investors widened the income deficit from $1.2 billion in 2017 to $1.5 billion. Growth in neighboring countries, particularly the Russian Federation, buoyed remittances by 10.7% to $600 million. Net foreign direct investment in the first 9 months of 2018 was $1.0 billion, up from $800 million in the same period of 2017. Foreign exchange reserves rose by $300 million to $5.6 billion at the end of 2018, which was cover for an estimated 3.8 months of imported goods and services. SOFAZ assets were $38.9 billion at the end of October 2018 (Figure 3.2.6).

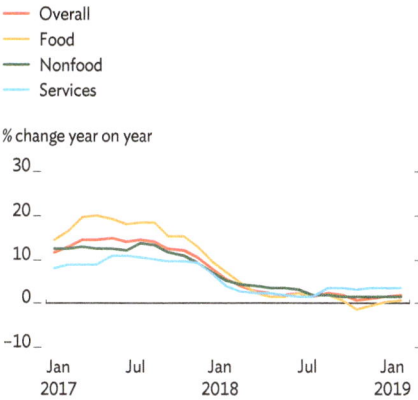

3.2.3 Monthly inflation

Sources: State Statistical Committee of the Republic of Azerbaijan; Haver Analytics (accessed 11 March 2019).

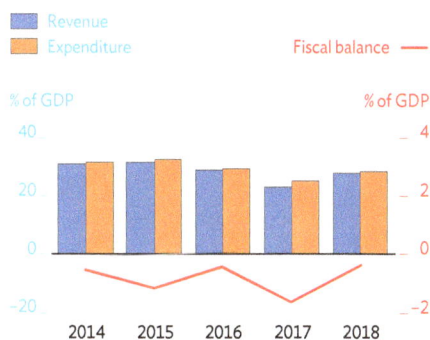

3.2.4 Fiscal balance

Source: Ministry of Finance of the Republic of Azerbaijan.

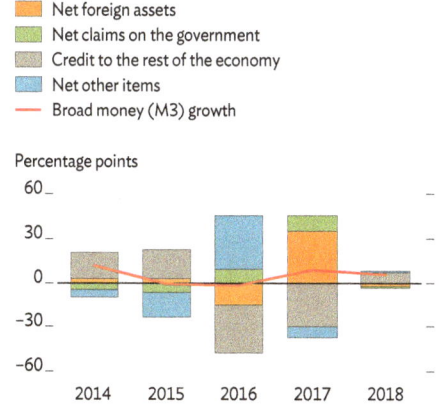

3.2.5 Contributions to money supply growth

Source: Central Bank of the Republic of Azerbaijan.

Economic prospects

Growth is forecast to strengthen to 2.5% in 2019 on higher public investment and increased consumption, reaching 2.7% in 2020 as gas production at the Shah Deniz 2 field accelerates (Figure 3.2.7).

On the supply side, industry is forecast to grow by 1.0% each year, driven by manufacturing and gains in mining from higher gas production. Construction is expected to expand by 3.0% in 2019 to accommodate additional government programs for agriculture and housing and by 2.0% in 2020 with the implementation of regional development programs. Agriculture is projected to expand by 3.0% in 2019 and by 4.0% in 2020 as farmers' access to finance improves. Growth in services is projected at 3.0% in both 2019 and 2020 on gains in transportation, tourism, and retail trade.

On the demand side, a higher government salary bill will boost public consumption, while higher effective household income from growth should fuel private consumption, especially as inflation stays fairly moderate. A stable exchange rate and the implementation of economic reform to improve the business climate are projected to boost private investment, and more expansionary fiscal policy will raise public investment. Net exports will rise on higher hydrocarbon exports and lower imports, particularly in 2019 as higher customs duties suppress imports of machinery and automobiles, which together accounted for 36% of all imports in 2017.

Inflation is projected to accelerate to 4.0% in 2019 in line with higher salaries and, as faster growth boosts domestic demand, reach 5.0% in 2020 (Figure 3.2.8). A relatively stable exchange rate should prevent high inflation.

Over the next 2 years, the central bank is expected to focus on two objectives: maintaining exchange rate stability and limiting inflation to 5.0%. The authorities will therefore closely monitor import demand, foreign exchange movements, and capital flows. A stable exchange rate is expected to boost lending to the private sector. If the inflation target is attained, the central bank can be expected to ease the policy interest rate further.

Fiscal policy is expected to become more expansionary, with the state budget deficit including SOFAZ transfers rising notably to 2.8% of GDP in 2019 before narrowing again to 2.0% in 2020. Deficit financing will come from privatization proceeds, domestic and external borrowing, and unused balances in Treasury accounts. The deficit excluding SOFAZ transfers will equal 18.6% of GDP in 2019 and 16.9% in 2020. Revenue is forecast to reach the equivalent of 32.2% of GDP in 2019 and 33.2% in 2020 as higher gas shipments boost hydrocarbon revenue and increased customs tariffs and other tax changes raise revenue from the rest of the economy.

3.2.1 Selected economic indicators (%)

	2019	2020
GDP growth	2.5	2.7
Inflation	4.0	5.0
Current account balance (share of GDP)	13.6	10.8

Source: ADB estimates.

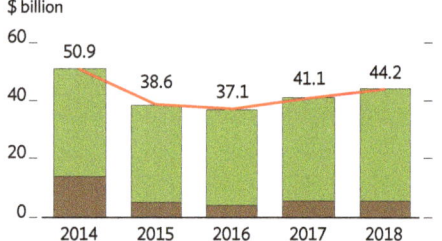

3.2.6 State oil fund assets and central bank reserves

Sources: Central Bank of the Republic of Azerbaijan; State Oil Fund of Azerbaijan. http://www.oilfund.az (accessed 11 March 2019).

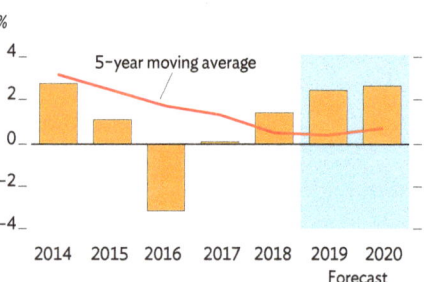

3.2.7 GDP growth

Sources: Central Bank of the Republic of Azerbaijan; ADB estimates.

Expenditure is forecast to equal 35.0% of GDP in 2019 and 35.2% in 2020, reflecting a 38% rise in the minimum wage and minimum pension, general pay increases in 2019, and a new regional development program in 2020 that will expand current and capital outlays alike. With higher growth and the debt management policy adopted in 2018, the government expects to hold public and publicly guaranteed external debt to less than 20% of GDP at the end of 2020.

The current account surplus is projected to double again to equal 13.6% of GDP in 2019 before falling back to 10.8% in 2020 (Figure 3.2.9). Despite higher gas exports, lower average oil prices will cut total exports in 2019 by 7.5%, then further increases in gas production at the Shah Deniz 2 field will boost exports by 1.0% in 2020. However, lower exports will be more than offset by an expected 19.9% decline in imports in 2019 owing to increased customs duties on machinery and cars. Imports are seen recovering by 11.1% in 2020 to meet rising domestic demand as the impact of these tariffs wanes. The deficit in services is projected to narrow further by 6.7% in 2019 and 7.1% in 2020 as construction on Shah Deniz 2 ends. However, the income deficit may widen further in 2019 and 2020 as foreign investors repatriate more of their hydrocarbon earnings.

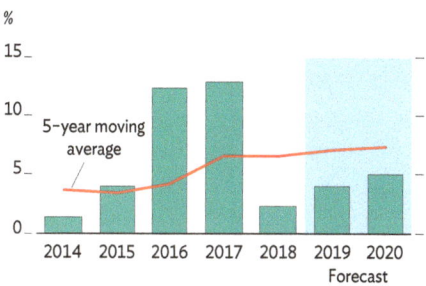

3.2.8 Inflation

Sources: Central Bank of the Republic of Azerbaijan; ADB estimates.

Policy challenge—improving infrastructure

Azerbaijan's oil wealth has fostered considerable social and economic development. While enabling rapid economic growth, hydrocarbon earnings have created an economy overly dependent on the petroleum industry. Toward diversifying the economy, the government has used much of the hydrocarbon earnings, including SOFAZ transfers, to rebuild and modernize Soviet-era infrastructure. From 2003 to 2017, investment in public infrastructure excluding oil and gas averaged the equivalent of 6.6% of non-hydrocarbon GDP. Maintaining and expanding this infrastructure is a continuing challenge.

Capital investments have so far focused on reconstructing and expanding road and railway networks, ports, and electric power plants. Most investment has gone into improving the country's east–west and north–south transport corridors toward fashioning Azerbaijan as a major transit and trade hub. Despite the creation of good transport and electric power networks, along with massive investments in other public utilities, critical gaps in infrastructure remain. Investment is still needed to replace and upgrade infrastructure for agriculture, rail transport, tourism, and information technology, among other needs. The government has estimated that investment of nearly $7 billion, equal to 4.7% of GDP, is required during 2017–2020 for these purposes.

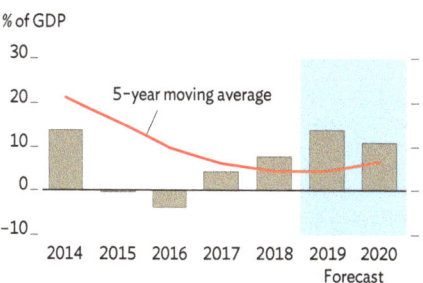

3.2.9 Current account balance

Sources: Central Bank of the Republic of Azerbaijan; ADB estimates.

As state-owned enterprises have limited financial capacity, and as the private sector plays little role in financing and operating infrastructure, most of the costs will fall on the central government budget. However, public investment spending generally tracks hydrocarbon revenue. Capital outlays in the central budget declined from the equivalent of 12% of GDP in 2015 to 7% in 2016 as prices for hydrocarbons fell. They remained near 7% of GDP in 2017 but rose to 11% in 2018 with much higher SOFAZ transfers (Figure 3.2.10). The long-term sustainability of existing assets is a concern, and utility tariffs set by the government should be adjusted to cover operating costs.

The government needs to establish a robust system for managing public investment that will individually appraise the economic and financial viability of proposed projects, strengthen project implementation capacity, improve project monitoring and evaluation, and adopt a framework for comprehensively assessing project results. It has adopted a medium-term expenditure framework to ensure that adequate funds are allocated to maintain infrastructure once it is built. However, due attention will be needed to link the investment program with that framework to ensure that resources are provided in a timely fashion for infrastructure operation and maintenance.

To facilitate private investment in public infrastructure, The National Assembly adopted in 2016 a law on special financing for infrastructure investment projects that promotes the build–operate–transfer model, in which private firms construct infrastructure projects, operate them for a specified period to recoup their investment, and then hand them over to the government. An adequate legal framework is still needed, as is the acquisition of appropriate skills, to develop feasible projects for private financing and management. While state-financed infrastructure projects will remain dominant, private participation in selected areas can make service provision more efficient and competitive.

Enhanced skills will be important as well for maintaining infrastructure. Infrastructure expansion and the mastery of new technology will require better training facilities, curriculum, methods, and certification programs. Stakeholders, especially in agriculture and information technology, will need to adopt technology and comply with quality standards and certification requirements. Strengthened skills can help maintain existing infrastructure and promote investment in worthwhile new projects.

3.2.10 Budget transfers and capital expenditure

Sources: Ministry of Finance. *Annual Statements on Budget Execution, 2014–18*; Central Bank of the Republic of Azerbaijan.

Georgia

Rising external demand in 2018 kept growth unchanged despite lower fiscal spending. Inflation fell by more than half, and rapid tourism and export growth narrowed the current account deficit. Growth is projected to rise in 2019 with higher investment spending, then moderate slightly in 2020. Inflation will be slightly higher. Workforce skills must be improved to attract investment into more diverse and remunerative activities.

Economic performance

Growth continued at 4.8% in 2018 thanks to rising exports and tourism and despite slower expansion in infrastructure projects and worsening regional volatility, notably in neighboring Turkey. On the supply side, growth in industry slowed sharply from 6.4% in 2017 to 2.3% as a 2.5% decline in construction from lower capital spending offset gains of 4.1% in manufacturing and 10.8% in mining. Meanwhile, growth in services accelerated from 5.1% in 2017 to 5.9% on strong gains of 4.5% in trade, 17.9% in finance, and 9.8% in real estate. Agriculture rebounded from 3.8% contraction in 2017 to 0.4% growth as crop production improved with better weather (Figure 3.3.1).

On the demand side, estimated growth in consumption nearly tripled from 0.5% in 2017 to 1.4% as higher incomes increased private consumption by 2.5%, while public consumption fell by 2.5%. Growth in investment is estimated to have risen from 3.8% to 4.8% despite a slowdown in public investment. However, the estimated rise in net exports, while high, slowed from 20.1% to 17.8% as growth in exports diminished and expansion in imports accelerated.

Average inflation fell by more than half from 6.0% in 2017 to 2.6% as the impact of higher excise taxes implemented in 2017 waned and the Georgian lari appreciated against the Turkish lira, easing prices for imported goods, in particular clothing and footwear. Inflation slowed for food from 6.8% in 2017 to 2.2%, for other goods from 5.0% to 1.3%, and for services from 4.7% to 2.4%. Some prices rose more quickly: for health care by 4.8% and, following electricity and water tariff increases in January 2018, for utilities by 4.3% (Figure 3.3.2). Core inflation excluding food and energy slowed from 4.0% in 2017 to 1.7%.

3.3.1 GDP growth by sector

Source: National Statistics Office of Georgia. http://www.geostat.ge (accessed 22 February 2019).

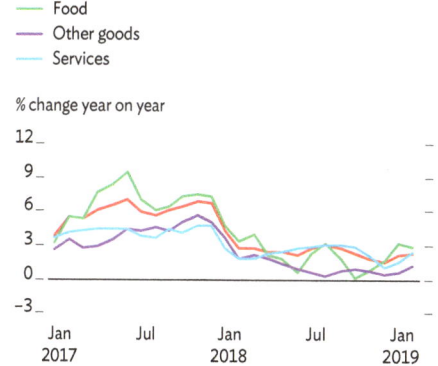

3.3.2 Monthly inflation

Source: National Statistics Office of Georgia. http://www.geostat.ge (accessed 7 March 2019).

This chapter was written by George Luarsabishvili of the Georgia Resident Mission, ADB, Tbilisi.

Prudent fiscal policy in 2018 helped narrow the deficit from the equivalent of 0.9% of GDP in 2017 to 0.8% (Figure 3.3.3). Tax collections were limited by accelerated refunds to firms of value-added tax estimated to equal 1.3% of GDP, causing tax revenue to fall from 25.8% of GDP to 25.4%—a smaller decline than expected—and trimming total revenue from 28.9% of GDP to 28.6%. Capital expenditure rose toward year-end, but current spending was lower as a law on civil service remuneration, adopted in December 2017, helped contain administrative costs. Total expenditure declined from 29.7% of GDP in 2017 to 29.4%. Public debt declined slightly from 44.2% of GDP at the end of 2017 to 43.4% a year later, with domestic public debt down from 9.3% of GDP in 2017 to 9.2%.

Monetary policy aimed to support growth as domestic demand remained moderate. The National Bank of Georgia, the central bank, reduced its policy rate by 0.25 percentage points in July 2018 to 7.0% and further to 6.75% in January 2019 as economic activity slowed, demand pressures on inflation abated, and the lari strengthened in nominal effective terms faster than expected with currency depreciation in the Russian Federation and Turkey. Tighter restrictions on lending contained borrowing, keeping credit growth broadly stable at 22.7% and slowing broad money growth marginally to 14.7% (Figure 3.3.4). Measures launched in 2017 to reverse dollarization held the share of loans in foreign currency at 56.1%, down from 56.3% in 2017.

Banks remained well capitalized, liquid, and profitable with a capital adequacy ratio of 18.4%, return on equity of 23.3%, and return on assets at 3.0%. Nonperforming loans declined slightly from 2.8% of all credit in 2017 to 2.7%. Interest rates on Treasury securities decreased to 7.2%. Corporate debt was stable at 27.9% of GDP in 2018, but household debt continued to climb, reaching 33.7% (Figure 3.3.5).

Rapid export growth narrowed the current account deficit from the equivalent of 8.8% of GDP in 2017 to 8.0% despite higher profit repatriation. Exports of goods and services jumped by 18.5%, with receipts from tourism up by 18.4%, as demand increased from markets other than Turkey, where an economic crisis cut into Georgia's receipts from trade, tourism, and remittances. Imports expanded by 14.6% on rising oil prices earlier in the year. Net remittances increased by 15.1% to a record high of $1.4 billion, reflecting strong inflows from Greece, Israel, Italy, and the US.

Current account financing came mainly from $1.2 billion in foreign direct investment, largely into construction, energy, transport, and finance. The lari appreciated against the US dollar in the first half of 2018 but retreated in the second half, ending up 2.1% weaker by year-end. However, the lari appreciated by 3.7% in nominal effective terms and 1.0% in real effective terms as it strengthened against the currencies of the

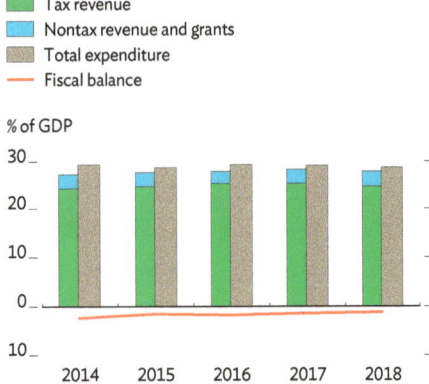

3.3.3 Fiscal indicators

Sources: International Monetary Fund. www.imf.org; Ministry of Finance of Georgia. www.mof.ge (both accessed 22 February 2019).

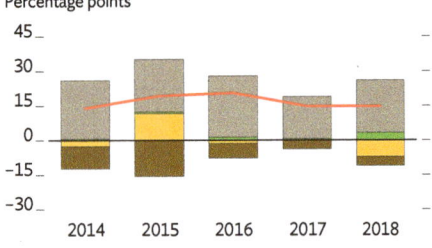

3.3.4 Contributions to broad money growth

Source: National Bank of Georgia. http://www.nbg.gov.ge (accessed 20 February 2019).

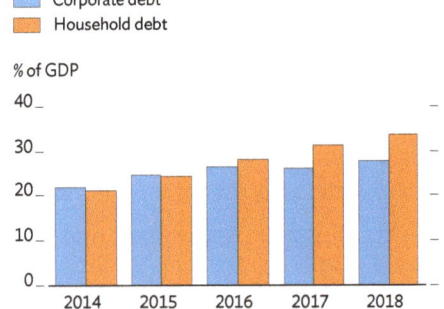

3.3.5 Corporate and household debt

Source: National Bank of Georgia. http://www.nbg.gov.ge (accessed 7 March 2019).

Russian Federation and Turkey (Figure 3.3.6). The central bank purchased $198 million in foreign currency during the year, boosting gross international reserves by 8.2% to $3.3 billion for an adequacy ratio of 93% as defined by the International Monetary Fund. Public and publicly guaranteed external debt declined slightly from the equivalent of 34.9% of GDP at the end of 2017 to 34.2% a year later.

Economic prospects

Growth is forecast to rise to 5.0% in 2019 with higher infrastructure spending and then to slow marginally to 4.9% in 2020 with less growth in investment outlays (Figure 3.3.7). Net exports, consumption, and investment are all expected to support growth in 2019 and 2020, bolstered by higher infrastructure outlays and a new pension system based on beneficiaries' prior contributions that should boost savings. On the supply side, growth in wholesale and retail trade and in finance is expected to expand services by 5.5% in 2019, easing to 5.1% in 2020. A rebound in construction is projected to boost growth in industry to 5.9% this year, easing to 5.4% next year. Higher investment should accelerate growth in agriculture to 2.6% and then 2.8% with favorable weather.

Inflation is projected to accelerate somewhat to 3.2% in 2019 before slowing again to 3.0% in 2020 (Figure 3.3.8). Further tightening of credit standards should cut credit growth to 13.0% in 2019 and 12.5% in 2020. Bread price increases beginning in December 2018 and higher excise taxes on tobacco may add to inflationary pressures. Inflation could also be higher if economic growth or prices for petroleum or food exceed expectations, or if the lari depreciates further because of monetary tightening in the US or Europe.

With little change in growth and less imported inflation as global expansion slows, a gradual transition to an accommodative monetary policy is expected. The central bank is likely to reduce the policy rate gradually to 6.0% at the end of 2020 if inflation remains below 3.0%. Broad money (M3) growth is projected to slow to 12.0% in 2019 and 11.0% in 2020, reflecting a decline in net foreign assets and less growth in private sector credit, particularly to households, but also with tighter control of state enterprise balance sheets. Continuing efforts should succeed in rolling back dollarization and mitigating borrowers' exposure to foreign exchange risks, in part by developing a local capital market regulated to prevent excessive credit growth. Foreign exchange intervention will likely be limited to smoothing exchange rate volatility and augmenting international reserves.

Over the next 2 years, fiscal policy will become more expansionary and reallocate spending toward infrastructure and education. The fiscal deficit is expected to rise slightly to

3.3.1 Selected economic indicators (%)

	2019	2020
GDP growth	5.0	4.9
Inflation	3.2	3.0
Current account balance (share of GDP)	−7.9	−7.8

Source: ADB estimates.

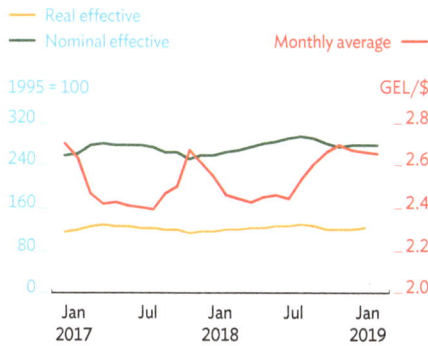

3.3.6 Exchange rate

Source: National Bank of Georgia. https://www.nbg.gov.ge (accessed 7 March 2019).

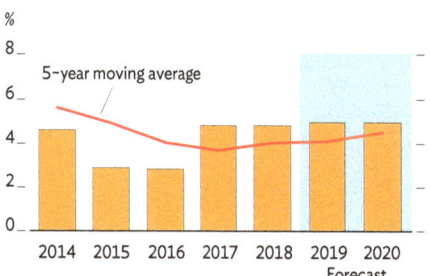

3.3.7 GDP growth

Sources: National Statistics Office of Georgia; ADB estimates.

equal 1.0% of GDP in both 2019 and 2020 to enable additional capital spending. While the wage bill and most other current outlays will be contained, social spending is expected to rise by the equivalent of 0.4% of GDP in both years to cover higher pensions and salaries for teachers. By promoting private investment, a public–private partnership law enacted in 2018 is expected to moderate contingent liabilities, off-budget operations, and the balance sheet of the public sector while strengthening the framework for managing public investment projects. Public debt is nevertheless expected to reach the equivalent of 43.6% of GDP in 2019 before easing to 43.3% in 2020 as foreign debt declines (Figure 3.3.9).

The current account deficit is forecast to continue to narrow to 7.9% of GDP in 2019 and 7.8% in 2020 as strong growth endures in exports, tourism, and remittances (Figure 3.3.10). Exports of goods and services are projected to rise by 6.1% in 2019 and 11.3% in 2020 with growth in Georgia's trade partners. Despite continued expansion, import growth is projected to plunge by two-thirds to 4.7% in 2019, reflecting slower growth in petroleum and pharmaceuticals, before recovering to 8.6% in 2020. Growth in remittances is projected to diminish to 1.3% in 2019 with slower growth in the Russian Federation and further afield in Greece and Italy, then rise by 6.9% in 2020 as the external environment strengthens. Continued recovery in Azerbaijan and, to a lesser extent, the Russian Federation is expected to offset risks posed by a deeper slowdown in Turkey. Gross reserves are projected to increase to $3.5 billion in 2019 and $3.8 billion in 2020 (Figure 3.3.11).

Downside risks to the forecast could emerge from external shocks and escalating trade tensions, tighter credit, rising global interest rates, difficulties in financial markets, or reduced capital spending. However, growth could be higher than forecast if the outlook improves for key trade partners such as Azerbaijan and the Russian Federation.

Policy challenge—improving skills to mobilize foreign direct investment into high-value sectors

Despite its relatively attractive business climate, Georgia's economy remains poorly diversified, its exports concentrated in few products and providing only a small share of GDP. Foreign direct investment (FDI), an important source of capital for Georgia because of low domestic investment and limited savings, nearly tripled from 2005 to 2018. However, FDI goes mainly into existing labor-intensive activities, rather than more complex sectors of the economy that add more value, such as manufacturing (Figure 3.3.12).

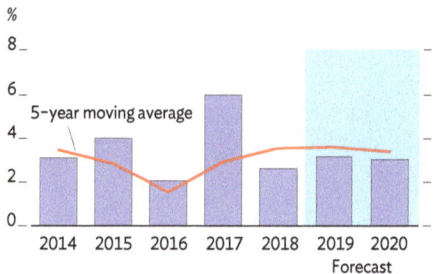

3.3.8 Inflation

Sources: National Statistics Office of Georgia; ADB estimates.

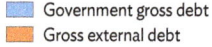

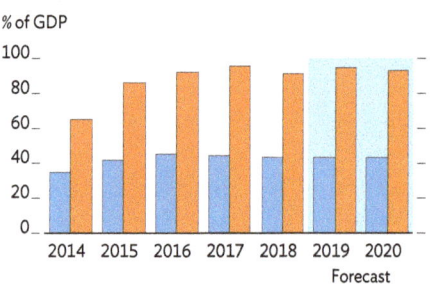

3.3.9 Government gross debt and total external debt

Sources: Ministry of Finance of Georgia. www.mof.ge; International Monetary Fund. www.imf.org (both accessed 7 March 2019).

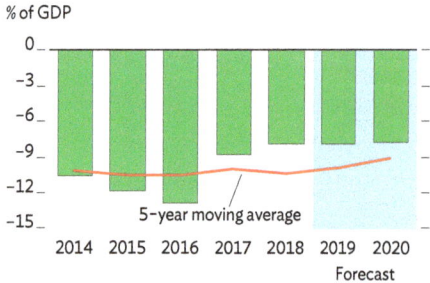

3.3.10 Current account balance

Sources: National Bank of Georgia; ADB estimates.

An obstacle to attracting FDI for diversification is the shortage of qualified workers graduating from Georgia's educational system. With limited education and training, most of the workforce remains in sectors with low productivity such as subsistence agriculture, leaving a shortage of skilled workers for manufacturing and other activities with greater product complexity. Also inhibiting diversification are the relatively high cost of logistics and documenting compliance for imports.

While Georgia has done much to develop an attractive business environment, it lags in supporting research and development, training workers, and promoting innovation. In the World Economic Forum's *Global Competitiveness Report 2018*, Georgia ranked 66 of 140 economies in the quality of its education system and 85 in innovation capability. An inadequately educated workforce was among the key constraints for doing business.

The government has taken steps to address skills mismatch in the workforce. In 2018, it announced a new and comprehensive strategy covering all levels of schooling to boost the quality of education. In addition, the Ministry of Education, Science, Culture, and Sport has implemented a number of reforms aiming to integrate general and vocation education by creating associate degree programs and promoting professional training. It has instituted a work-based learning model and offers state accreditation for privately provided certificate programs. A program called Digital Society assesses labor market trends and the ability of the education management information system to provide analysis and suggestions for change. Further, the government is developing occupational safety standards for institutions offering technical and vocational education and training, and it seeks to outsource the management of technical colleges.

Georgia's Innovation and Technology Agency strives to improve workforce skills by promoting information, computer, and digital technology and training in science, technology, engineering, and mathematics. It supports the development of innovative products with startup funding for creative projects and promotes collaboration between universities and businesses in research and development. These reforms are helping to develop electronic business and e-commerce to support diversification.

Stronger private sector involvement in training for entrepreneurship would help, as would efforts to encourage more women to enter business.

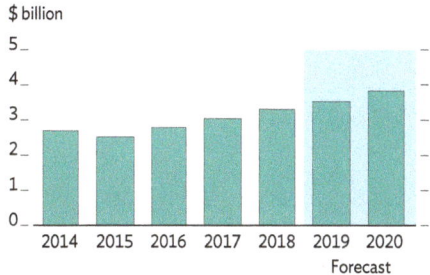

3.3.11 Gross international reserves

Sources: National Bank of Georgia. www.nbg.gov.ge; International Monetary Fund. www.imf.org (both accessed 7 March 2019); ADB estimates.

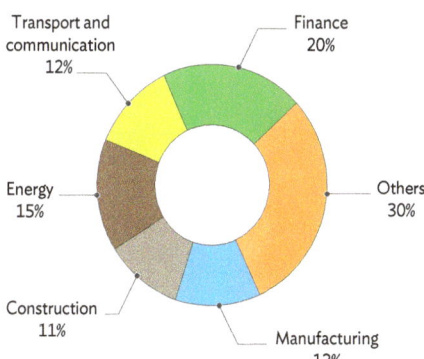

3.3.12 Foreign direct investments by sector

Source: National Statistics Office of Georgia. http://www.geostat.ge (accessed 7 March 2019).

Kazakhstan

The growth rate was unchanged in 2018 as a slowdown in industry offset gains elsewhere. Tight monetary policy trimmed inflation, and higher petroleum exports created a small current account surplus. Growth will slow in 2019 with lower petroleum exports and in 2020 under less expansionary fiscal policy. The current account will return to deficit, but continued monetary restraint should contain inflation. Restoring bank sector health depends on reducing nonperforming loans.

Economic performance

Growth remained at 4.1% in 2018 (Figure 3.4.1). Expansion in industry decelerated from 7.7% in 2017 to 4.2%, however, as manufacturing slowed from 6.1% to 4.0% and mining from 9.5% to 4.6%, though increased output at the major oil fields raised oil production by 4.8%. State support for housing boosted growth in construction from 2.8% in 2017 to 4.1%. Services accelerated by 4.0%, up from 2.4% in 2017 with gains in wholesale and retail trade. Growth in agriculture increased slightly from 3.2% in 2017 to 3.4% on rising livestock and crop production.

On the demand side, comparisons are for the first 9 months of both years. Growth in consumption remained at 1.6% as high consumer lending and lower inflation boosted private consumption growth from 1.4% to 5.1%, offsetting a 13.9% drop in public consumption. Growth in investment accelerated from 2.5% in 2017 to 2.8%, with fixed capital formation, mainly for mining, rising by 4.6%. Net exports also increased as exports of goods and services rose by 8.9 and imports by only 3.7%.

Despite significant local currency depreciation in the second half of 2018 and heightened inflationary expectations, average inflation slowed from 7.4% in 2017 to 6.0% as the National Bank of Kazakhstan, the central bank, issued state-backed securities to absorb liquidity and bring inflation within its target range of 5%–7%. Price increases for food slowed from 8.6% in 2017 to 5.1%, and for other goods from 8.4% to 7.8%, though increases for services edged up from 5.1% to 5.3%. In December 2018, inflation was 5.3% year on year, near the lower bound of the central bank's target range (Figure 3.4.2).

3.4.1 Supply-side contributions to growth

Source: Republic of Kazakhstan. Ministry of National Economy. Statistics Committee.

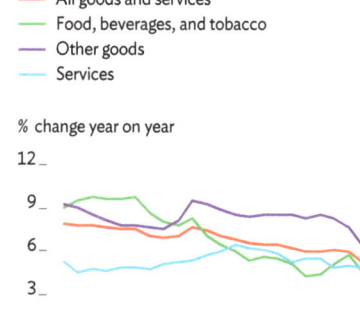

3.4.2 Monthly inflation

Source: Republic of Kazakhstan. Ministry of National Economy. Statistics Committee.

This chapter was written by Genadiy Rau of the Kazakhstan Resident Mission, ADB, Astana.

Appreciation of the Kazakh tenge in the first quarter of 2018, however brief, helped slow inflation and enabled the central bank to lower its key policy rate gradually from 9.75% at the start of the year to 9.00% in June. After currency depreciation resumed, however, the central bank sold foreign exchange worth $520.6 million in September, its first intervention since 2017, and increased the policy rate to 9.25% in October. Despite these moves, the tenge depreciated by nearly 16% against the US dollar in 2018 to reach an all-time low of T384.2 per dollar at the end of the year. During this period, the tenge moved in line with the ruble and the currencies of neighboring economies, which depreciated in response to worsening geopolitical tensions and rising US interest rates.

Broad money (M3) expanded by 7.0% as deposits grew by 16.1% and credit by 3.1%, reversing 1.7% contraction in 2017, when deposits fell by 3.0% and credit by 0.2% (Figure 3.4.3). Credit to households rose by 16.8% in 2018, but loans to firms declined by 4.6%. Currency fluctuation helped raise the share of foreign currency deposits from 47.7% of all deposits in December 2017 to 48.4% a year later, though the share of foreign currency loans dropped from 26.3% of the loan portfolio to 22.9% (Figure 3.4.4).

The state budget recorded a deficit equal to 1.4% of GDP, down from 2.7% in 2017 (Figure 3.4.5). Higher petroleum earnings and improved tax administration boosted tax revenue by 15.8% to equal 13.4% of GDP, and total revenue to 18.4% of GDP, well above projections. Expenditure fell by 9.1% to equal 19.3% of GDP as government outlays for bank recapitalization declined from 4.0% of GDP in 2017 to 1.7%. The non-oil state budget deficit narrowed from 10.4% of GDP in 2017 to 9.0%. Government and government-guaranteed debt rose from 26.3% of GDP at the end of 2017 to 27.3%. Meanwhile, state-owned enterprises cut their debt from 27.0% of GDP in 2017 to an estimated 22.1% as oil and gas enterprises made major debt repayments during the year.

The current account recorded a surplus, equal to 0.5% of GDP, for the first time since 2014, reversing a 3.3% deficit in 2017. Rising oil prices and volumes boosted merchandise exports by 25.2% from the equivalent of 30.3% of GDP in 2017 to 36.3%, while imports rose by 7.5%, climbing from 19.7% of GDP in 2017 to 20.2% as private consumption rose and demand increased for capital goods to supply oil and gas projects and state development programs. The service balance improved slightly, but primary income deteriorated as profit repatriation by foreign investors rose by 29.6% to $20.2 billion. Net foreign direct investment, mainly into oil and mining, rose by 9.8% to $4.1 billion, while net outflows of portfolio investment reached $5.8 billion, reflecting repayment of eurobonds by resident oil and gas companies.

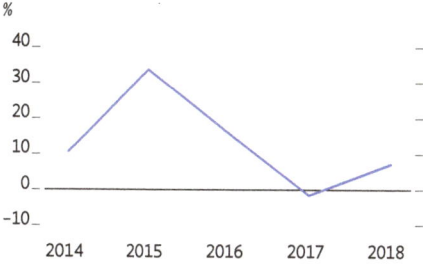

3.4.3 Growth in broad money

Source: National Bank of the Republic of Kazakhstan.

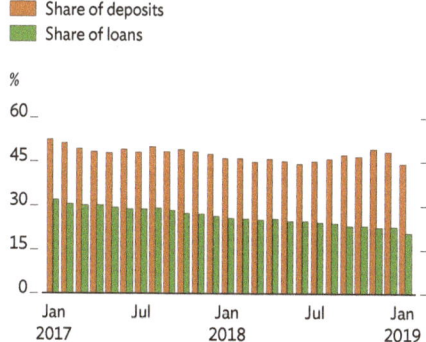

3.4.4 Dollarization in the banking system

Source: National Bank of the Republic of Kazakhstan.

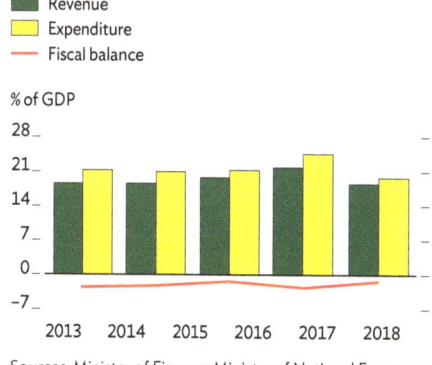

3.4.5 Fiscal indicators

Sources: Ministry of Finance; Ministry of National Economy.

With net central bank sales of $520.6 million in foreign exchange in September 2018 to support the tenge, gross international reserves declined by $70 million during the year to $30.9 billion, or cover for 8.1 months of imports (Figure 3.4.6). Assets in the National Fund of the Republic of Kazakhstan (NFRK), the sovereign wealth fund, declined by 1.1% to $57.7 billion, and external debt—63.4% of which is private intercompany debt—eased from the equivalent of 102.7% of GDP at the end of 2017 to an estimated 94.7% a year later (Figure 3.4.7). In November, investors bought €1.05 billion in euro-denominated Kazakh bonds, half paying 1.550% over 5 years and half paying 2.375% over 10 years. Demand for the bonds was three times the amount offered.

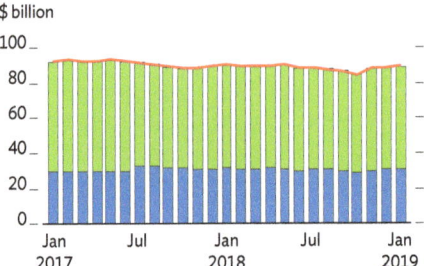

3.4.6 Foreign currency reserves and oil fund assets

Source: National Bank of the Republic of Kazakhstan.

Economic prospects

Growth is forecast to slow to 3.5% in 2019 and 3.3% in 2020, reflecting mainly lower oil prices and slower growth in the People's Republic of China and the Russian Federation (Figure 3.4.8). State investment is expected to become a key source of growth aside from oil in the coming years.

On the supply side, industry is forecast to expand by 4.3% in 2019 and 4.4% in 2020 as state-led investment in manufacturing and utilities partly offsets slower gains in oil production. Oil production will likely decline in the first half of 2019 to meet Kazakhstan's commitments under production constraints agreed with the Organization of the Petroleum Exporting Countries, and to accommodate planned maintenance on the country's three major oilfields, then recover in the second half and expand in 2020 despite lower average oil prices.

Government housing and infrastructure modernization programs will support construction, which is forecast to expand by 3.4% in 2019 and 3.5% in 2020. Services are projected to grow by 3.2% and then 2.7%, buoyed by a 50% rise in the minimum wage in January 2019 that should boost household income in 2019 but have limited effect in 2020. Agriculture is forecast to expand by 3.0% in 2019 and 2.5% in 2020 on strong state support for livestock expansion, crop diversification, and measures to boost agricultural productivity and exports, with substantial nonperforming loans (NPLs) in agriculture limiting further expansion. In 2018, Kazakhstan's Unified Pension Savings Fund bought $1.2 billion in NPLs from KazAgro, the state agency that promotes agricultural development.

On the demand side, growth in consumption is projected to slow to 1.3% this year and 1.0% next as continued declines in public consumption more than offset gains in private consumption spurred by higher household income.

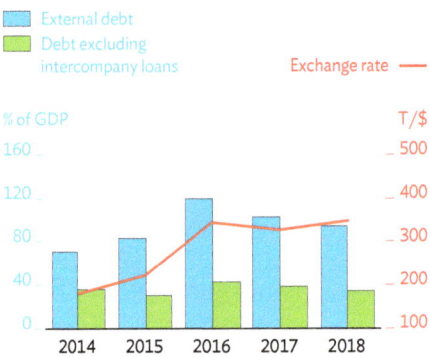

3.4.7 External debt

Sources: National Bank of Kazakhstan; ADB estimates.

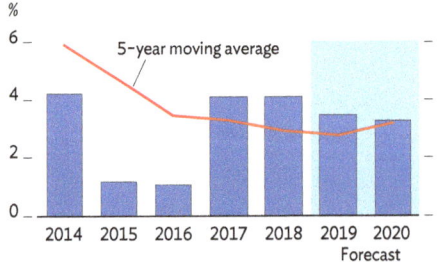

3.4.8 GDP growth

Source: Asian Development Outlook database.

Expansion in investment is similarly projected to slow, to 1.8% in 2019 and 1.6% in 2020, as further reductions in transfers from the NFRK constrain government capital spending. Net exports are forecast to rise gradually, by 1.0% in 2019 and 2.0% in 2020, as moderate increases in oil production beginning in the second half of 2019 outpace rising imports for industrialization programs and higher household purchases of imported services.

Average inflation is projected to remain in 2019 at 6.0%, the upper end of the central bank's target range for the year, then moderate to 5.5% in 2020 (Figure 3.4.9). The central bank will likely raise the policy rate and maintain measures to absorb excess liquidity to counter inflationary pressures imposed by higher import prices as the tenge depreciates. Food price inflation is projected to slow from 5.2% in 2019 to 5.0% in 2020 as the government promotes domestic food production, institutes stabilization funds for critical foodstuffs, and imposes selective price controls. A review of utility prices ordered by the President in November 2018 prompted considerable reductions in 2019 utility charges. Further government intervention in utilities, and in the gasoline market, should trim inflation for goods other than food to 7.3% in 2019 and 6.5% in 2020. Price rises for services will slow from 5.8% in 2019 to 5.2% in 2020.

Fiscal policy is expected to remain slightly expansionary in the next 2 years. State budget deficits are projected to equal 1.5% of GDP in 2019 and 1.3% in 2020, with the non-oil deficit narrowing to 7.0% of GDP in 2019 and 6.5% in 2020 (Figure 3.4.10). Revenue is projected to fall to 17.0% of GDP in 2019 and 17.7% in 2020. This reflects a policy to reduce NFRK transfers to the budget to $6.7 billion in 2019 and $6.0 billion in 2020, as well as a tax amnesty for small and medium-sized enterprises (SMEs) intended to get more firms to start reporting income. A separate effort aims to improve tax administration. Expenditure is forecast to fall to 18.5% of GDP in 2019 and then recover to 19.0% in 2020 on modest civil service pay increases as programs continue to support industrialization, infrastructure, housing, and agriculture. Economic growth will trim government and government-guaranteed debt to 26.0% of GDP in 2019 and 25.0% in 2020.

Broad money is projected to increase by only 5.0% annually in 2019 and 2020 as the central bank continues to drain excess liquidity. A relatively high NPL rate, officially 7.9% at the end of 2018 but possibly higher because of underreporting, will constrain credit growth despite efforts to resolve NPLs through mergers and closures of problem banks. Although Kazakhstan has a floating exchange rate, the central bank may intervene in the market to smooth exchange rate volatility and limit opportunities for cross-currency arbitrage with the ruble, which historically has been closely linked with the tenge.

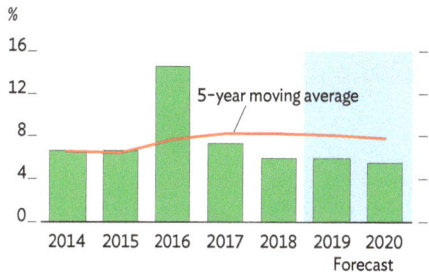

3.4.9 Inflation

Source: Asian Development Outlook database.

3.4.1 Selected economic indicators (%)

	2019	2020
GDP growth	3.5	3.3
Inflation	6.0	5.5
Current account balance (share of GDP)	-0.8	-1.2

Source: ADB estimates.

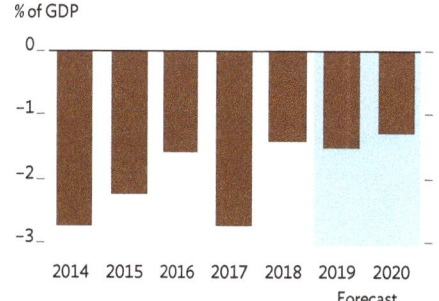

3.4.10 Fiscal balance

Source: Asian Development Outlook database.

The current account is forecast to revert to a deficit in 2019, equal to 0.8% of GDP and then 1.2% in 2020, with lower global petroleum prices and higher profit repatriation by foreign investors (Figure 3.4.11). Despite a slowdown in the first half of the year, exports are projected to grow by 6.0% in 2019 and 7.0% in 2020 after oilfield modernization boosts production. Growth in imports will slow to 5.0% in 2019 and 2020, reflecting measures to promote import substitution and, as the tenge depreciates, weaker domestic purchasing power. Currency depreciation will also trim the service deficit in 2019 and 2020 by reducing demand for imported services and facilitating service exports, especially after the completion of major road construction projects intended to strengthen Kazakhstan's position as a transport and logistics hub.

International reserves are projected to turn around and reach $31.5 billion this year and then $32.4 billion, or cover for 10 months of imports. With smaller transfers to the budget and a reasonable projection for commodity exports, NFRK assets are forecast to rise to $59.5 billion at the end of 2019 and $60.7 billion a year later, with external debt at the equivalent of 98.0% of GDP at the end of 2019 and 95.0% a year later.

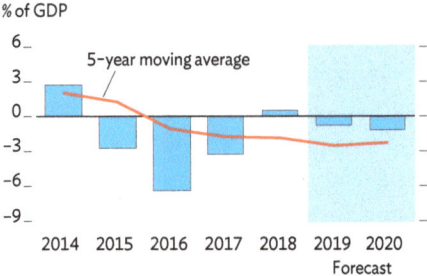

3.4.11 Current account balance

Source: Asian Development Outlook database.

Policy challenge—addressing nonperforming loans

A healthy banking system is a prerequisite for expanding private enterprise and ensuring sustainable economic development in Kazakhstan. Before the global financial crisis, when the economy was expanding rapidly, the bank sector was considered an engine of dynamism, innovation, and economic growth. A decade later, numerous bank failures and a proliferation of mainly underreported NPLs have left the sector's survival dependent on state support and continuous injections of liquidity.

Kazakhstan's massive NPL problem stems largely from fraud and loans to connected parties. The leading case in the past decade saw the prosecution of senior and middle management at Bank Turan Alem, then the largest domestic bank. It was nationalized in 2009 and sold to Kazkommertsbank in 2014, with net government support estimated at $10 billion. In mid-2018, that bank was merged with Halyk Bank, a deal made possible by additional government capitalization of $7 billion. In addition, the Problem Loans Fund purchased $1.3 billion in troubled assets from Tsesnabank in September 2018 and an additional $1.6 billion in agricultural loans in February 2019.

A policy to limit NPLs to 10% of the commercial banks' total loan portfolios may have contributed to underreporting.

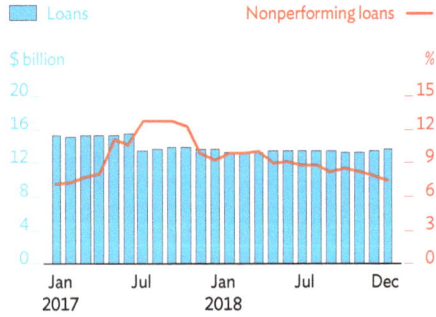

3.4.12 Lending portfolio and share of nonperforming loans

Source: National Bank of Kazakhstan.

In May 2018, the central bank acknowledged that NPLs in 2017 were actually 23% of the loan total, two and a half times the officially reported 9.3% (Figure 3.4.12). The underreporting of NPLs appears to have continued in 2018. For example, the central bank reported Eximbank NPLs at 3.6% in April 2018, but only 5 months later determined that they were 53.7% and revoked Eximbank's license.

Extensive NPLs, along with the restructuring of loan portfolios and the closure of several banks, have severely limited lending to firms, especially SMEs, despite substantial state support to banks, hindering private investment. Loans to SMEs fell by 12.2% in 2018, following a 1.1% decline in 2017, while the share of loans to SMEs declined to 33.6% in December 2018, well below the average of 44.0% in member countries of the Organisation for Economic Co-operation and Development (Figure 3.4.13). This happened despite government subsidies of up to 50% on interest for business loans made within the framework of the Business Road Map approved in 2010. The central bank's tight monetary policy, which kept average rates for business loans at 12.5% in 2018, has also hindered new lending. The National Chamber of Entrepreneurs (Atameken) estimates that only 20% of the country's 1.2 million or more entrepreneurs use credit.

In January 2019, the government acknowledged that the lack of an efficient bankruptcy procedure and lax supervision have exacerbated difficulties among commercial banks. The central bank and the government aim to streamline the bankruptcy law, and the central bank to adopt a risk-based approach to bank regulation. However, inadequate transparency, accountability, and integrity remain fundamental problems that need to be addressed. Resolving them will require a comprehensive overhaul of the regulatory framework, not least to limit the influence of insiders and connected interests, and a rethinking of loan subsidies. Further, constraints impeding the work of the Problem Loans Fund should be addressed.

Independent portfolio reviews and bank stress tests are also critical. In April 2018, a deputy central bank chairman declared that large discrepancies had been identified between audited statements and central bank assessments of bank assets for fiscal year 2017. Because the underreporting of NPLs undermines the credibility of official statistics and confidence in bank regulation, the central bank needs to strengthen macroprudential policies to ensure that commercial banks comply with rules and standards. In addition, it needs to take steps to level the playing field for SME access to credit.

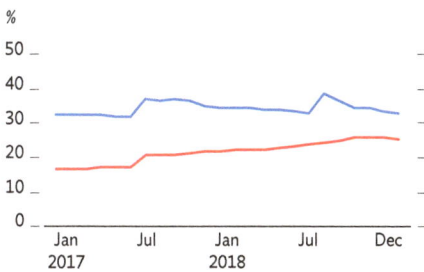

3.4.13 Shares of SME and consumer credit in the lending portfolio

SMEs = small and medium-sized enterprises.
Source: National Bank of Kazakhstan.

Kyrgyz Republic

Growth slowed in 2018 in tandem with smaller gains in mining and manufacturing. Inflation decelerated by half, and the current account deficit widened sharply. Growth is projected to recover in 2019 and continue accelerating in 2020 on recovery in gold production and slower but continued growth in the region. Inflation will be higher and the current account deficit wider. Reducing risks from flooding and associated disasters has become urgent with climate change.

Economic performance

Growth declined from 4.7% in 2017 to 3.5% in 2018 as slower growth in the large gold mining industry outweighed gains in textiles and apparel.

On the supply side, growth in industry slowed from 8.6% in 2017 to 6.2% as expansion in mining plunged from 58.4% to 8.1% and that of manufacturing fell less dramatically from 6.7% to 5.0% (Figure 3.5.1). Gold production in the first half of 2018 was 40% lower than in the same period a year earlier because of the poor quality of ore, but it recovered substantially in the second half of the year as ore quality improved. Construction expanded by 7.8%, decelerating marginally from 7.9% in 2017 as slower growth in investment into mining, energy generation, and transport offset acceleration elsewhere. Growth in agriculture rose from 2.2% in 2017 to 2.7% on gains in horticulture and animal husbandry. Growth in services slowed from 3.3% in 2017 to 2.1% as expansion in retail and wholesale trade diminished from 7.1% to 5.1%.

On the demand side, growth found support from higher public investment into energy and transport infrastructure projects, and from higher public and private consumption, the latter reflecting a 5.5% rise in remittances, with all remittances equal to a quarter of GDP (Figure 3.5.2).

Average annual inflation slowed from 3.2% in 2017 to 1.5% last year as a good harvest and substantial imports of food from Uzbekistan cut food prices by 2.6%. Prices rose by 1.1% for goods other than food and by 4.1% for services. Inflation in December 2018 year on year was only 0.5%, down sharply from 3.7% a year earlier (Figure 3.5.3). In the course of 2018, the Kyrgyz som depreciated only slightly, by 1.5%, against the US dollar (Figure 3.5.4).

3.5.1 GDP growth by sector

Source: National Statistics Committee of the Kyrgyz Republic. http://www.stat.kg (accessed 8 March 2019).

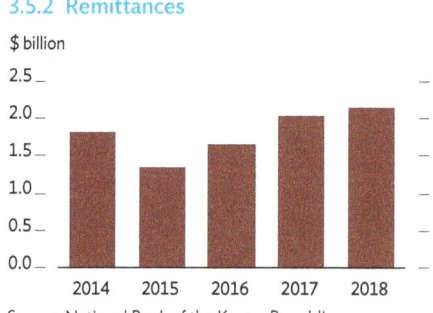

3.5.2 Remittances

Source: National Bank of the Kyrgyz Republic. http://www.nbkr.kg (accessed 13 March 2019).

This chapter was written by Gulkayr Tentieva of the Kyrgyz Resident Mission, ADB, Bishkek.

The fiscal deficit narrowed from the equivalent of 3.3% of GDP in 2017 to 1.2% despite higher spending on infrastructure projects. Revenue slipped from 25.4% of GDP in 2017 to 24.3%, while expenditure fell more steeply from 28.7% of GDP to 25.5%. The smaller deficit and higher GDP trimmed external government debt from 53.1% at the end of 2017 to 48.0% at the end of 2018. Domestic government debt equaled less than 8.0% of GDP.

Monetary policy remained cautious as the National Bank of the Kyrgyz Republic, the central bank, limited its currency interventions to simply smoothing excess exchange rate volatility. It reduced the policy interest rate from 5.00% at the end of 2017 to 4.75% in May 2018 and further to 4.50% in February 2019. The average deposit interest rate declined by 0.2 percentage points to 4.1%, while the average lending rate fell by 1.0 percentage point to 15.0%. Deposits rose by 10.4% and credit by 13.1%, while growth in broad money slowed from 17.9% in 2017 to 5.5%. At the end 2018, nonperforming loans were stable at 7.5% of the total. Dollarization remained extensive, with the share of loans in foreign currency at the end of 2018 unchanged at 38.0% and the share of deposits at 44.5%, down from 48.7% at the end of 2017.

The current account deficit is estimated to have widened by half from the equivalent of 6.5% of GDP in 2017 to 10.0%. Trade increased by 6.6%, with exports stagnant, as gains in cement, metals, cotton, and textiles could not offset lower gold shipments, and with imports rising by 9.2% on increases for oil products, construction materials, textiles, and consumer goods. Growth in remittances was estimated at 5.5%, down sharply from 24.3% in 2017. International reserves remained at $2.2 billion at the end of 2018, providing cover for 3.8 months of imports. External debt, including government-guaranteed and private debt, is estimated to have fallen from the equivalent of 92.4% of GDP at the end of 2017 to 83.9% at the end of the third quarter of 2018 (Figure 3.5.5). External government and government-guaranteed debt stood at 48.0% of GDP.

Economic prospects

Growth is expected to recover to 4.0% in 2019 and 4.4% in 2020 with some improvement in the domestic economy, especially gold production, and despite adverse effects from a slowdown in the region, especially in Kazakhstan and, in 2019, the Russian Federation, the country's two main regional partners (Figure 3.5.6).

On the supply side, gains in industry from recovery in gold production—and, less importantly, in agro-processing, light industry development, and, to some extent, construction—should support growth over the next 2 years. On the demand side, continued increase in remittances will raise household

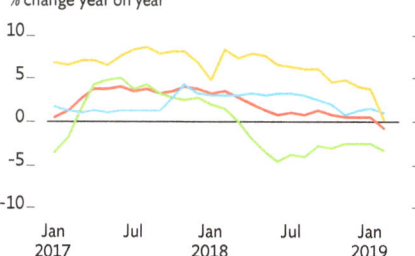

3.5.3 Monthly inflation

Source: Bulletin of the National Bank of the Kyrgyz Republic. http://www.nbkr.kg (accessed 13 March 2019).

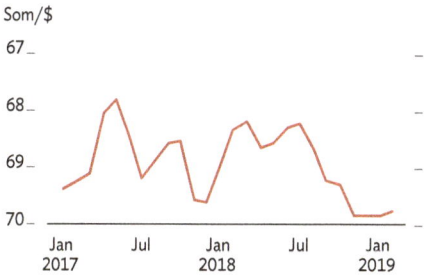

3.5.4 Exchange rate

Source: National Bank of the Kyrgyz Republic. http://www.nbkr.kg (accessed 14 March 2019).

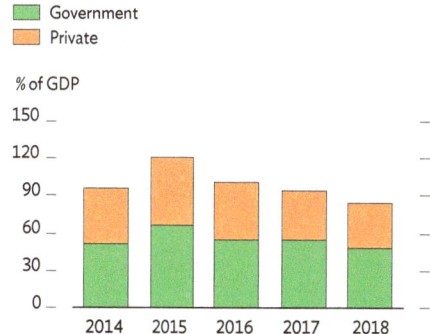

3.5.5 External debt

Note: Government debt is both government and government-guaranteed debt. Data for 2018 are as of the end of the third quarter.
Sources: The Ministry of Finance; National Statistics Committee. http://www.stat.kg; National Bank of the Kyrgyz Republic. http://www.nbkr.kg (both accessed 20 February 2019).

incomes, bolstering private consumption. Over the longer term, membership in the Eurasian Economic Union (EEU) should catalyze growth through increased foreign trade and freer movement of labor, capital, and services within the EEU.

Inflation is expected to accelerate to 3.0% in 2019 and 3.5% in 2020 on higher growth (Figure 3.5.7). The forecast factors in the risk of greater depreciation of the Kyrgyz som against the US dollar if the currencies of the country's main regional partners weaken.

The central bank is expected to continue to permit a flexible exchange rate and limit its interventions to smoothing excessive volatility. In view of the expected rise in inflation, monetary policy will likely remain focused on maintaining price stability. The central bank aims to establish a policy of inflation targeting over the medium term, using an inflation target of 5%–7%.

The fiscal deficit is projected to widen again to 1.7% of GDP in 2019 on higher current and capital spending. As the government aims to restrain expenditure on low-priority items while improving tax policy and administration, the fiscal deficit is seen easing to 1.2% in 2020 (Figure 3.5.8). Fiscal consolidation remains a major concern, the goal being to rebuild fiscal space for later accommodation as needed and to ensure debt sustainability. Consolidation efforts will focus on rationalizing expenditure by reforming public wages, cutting subsidies, and improving the targeting of social benefits. The government intends to raise revenue as well by broadening the tax base and strengthening tax and customs administration. The aim is to keep external public debt below 50% at least to the end of 2020.

The current account deficit is expected to widen to 12.0% in both 2019 and 2020 (Figure 3.5.9). Higher gold exports are projected to raise export growth above 10.0% in both years, while infrastructure spending is projected to boost imports by 14.0% in 2019, subsiding a bit to 12.0% in 2020. However, growth in exports other than gold may continue to be constrained—and the current account deficit large—as Kyrgyz products struggle to comply with EEU veterinary and agricultural standards and if demand from EEU trade partners is weaker than expected. Remittances will likely rise by a further 5%–10% over the course of 2019 and 2020, reflecting the continuing advantages to Kyrgyz migrant workers of membership in the EEU since 2015 and continued, if modest, growth in the Russian Federation. International reserves are forecast to remain at $2.2 billion in 2019 and 2020 (Figure 3.5.10).

While debt sustainability has improved in the Kyrgyz Republic, the International Monetary Fund assesses the country as facing moderate risk of debt distress because of continuing vulnerability involving currency stability and

3.5.1 Selected economic indicators (%)

	2019	2020
GDP growth	4.0	4.4
Inflation	3.0	3.5
Current account balance (share of GDP)	–12.0	–12.0

Source: ADB estimates.

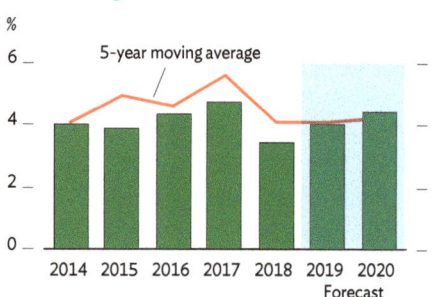

3.5.6 GDP growth

Sources: National Statistics Committee of the Kyrgyz Republic. http://www.stat.kg (accessed 8 March 2019); ADB estimates.

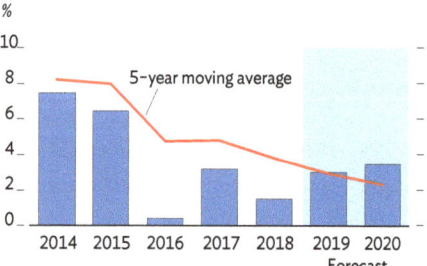

3.5.7 Inflation

Sources: National Bank of the Kyrgyz Republic; ADB estimates.

possible deterioration in the fiscal balance. Barring shocks, and assuming that public external debt stays below 50% of GDP as intended, total external debt could remain below 90% of GDP for at least the next few years.

Policy challenge—reducing risks from flooding and associated disasters

The Kyrgyz Republic is at high risk from extreme weather events, a situation that is likely to worsen under climate change. The country's vulnerability to harm from climate change is ranked at 68 of 181 countries in the Notre Dame Global Adaptation Index in 2017. Moreover, the Kyrgyz Republic is located in a seismically active mountainous region prone to earthquakes, floods, mudslides, avalanches, snowstorms, and mountain lake spills. Disasters from natural hazards such as floods and earthquakes occur frequently and are estimated to cost the equivalent of 1.0%–1.5% of GDP annually. Water resources are particularly vulnerable, particularly in the southwestern districts, where droughts, landslides, flooding, and other water-related disasters are frequent. Landslides comprise a quarter of all disasters and cause half of disaster-related fatalities. Risk is heightened by a lack of investment in preventive works, inadequate risk management, and the limited amount of state and local government resources available to address risks.

Efforts to strengthen resilience under climate change and extreme weather events are guided by the government's national development, climate change, and sector strategies. The national development program for 2018–2022 includes proactive management of disaster and climate change risks and prioritizes building and rehabilitating irrigation infrastructure to achieve greater water-use efficiency. A comprehensive strategy introduced in 2018 for protecting the land and its people in emergencies to 2030 seeks to reduce disaster losses through, among other measures, improved monitoring and forecasting and the construction of protective structures. The strategy will require funding from 2018 to 2022 equal to 1.8% of annual GDP. A state program to develop irrigation from 2017 to 2026 seeks to use water resources more productively by constructing and modernizing infrastructure and by introducing improved technology. It requires funding equal to 10% of annual GDP.

Development partners support government efforts through projects that emphasize modernizing irrigation systems and that target optimized and resilient agricultural production, as well as improved water productivity. One project is pilot testing a new system of hydrological monitoring and forecasting that uses satellite data.

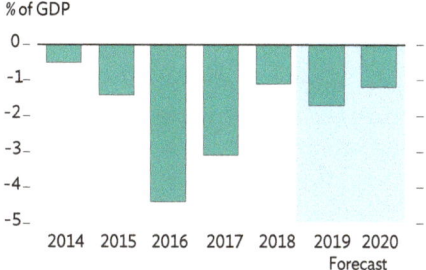

3.5.8 Fiscal balance

Sources: Ministry of Finance of the Kyrgyz Republic; ADB estimates.

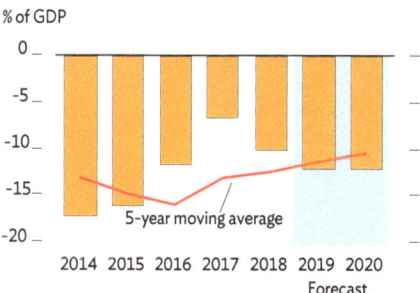

3.5.9 Current account balance

Sources: National Bank of the Kyrgyz Republic. http://www.nbkr.kg (accessed 13 March 2019); ADB estimates.

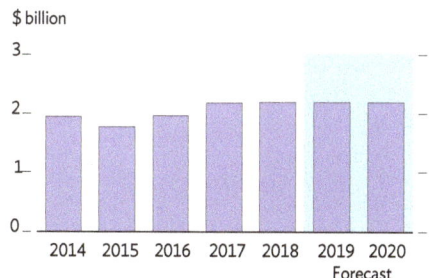

3.5.10 Gross international reserves

Sources: National Bank of the Kyrgyz Republic; ADB estimates.

Other projects focus more on system rehabilitation rather than modernization, using a holistic approach to irrigation infrastructure, management, operation, and maintenance. Existing water-user associations deliver agricultural advisory services to their members, and smaller projects employ community-oriented approaches to improve water productivity and water management on farms.

The government is developing a pilot program to enhance climate resilience by coordinating various projects, avoiding overlap in investments and target areas, and incorporating lessons from earlier projects into later efforts. A system of forecasting mudflows for better protection of vulnerable settlements is being developed. In addition, the current Central Asia Hydromet Modernization Program supports capacity building in Kyrgyz Hydromet and equipment modernization to improve data collection and weather forecasting. Finally, several projects aim to strengthen climate resilience and cross-border management of water resources in the lower Syr Daria and Chu river basin.

To better coordinate and cost-effectively augment these efforts, the government needs to prioritize its goals and improve project implementation, as the Kyrgyz Republic has large infrastructure investment needs, to ensure the sustainable and effective management of efforts to reduce disaster risk. In the coming years, extreme weather events will likely become more frequent and severe with climate change, rising temperatures, and intensifying precipitation and snowmelt. Water availability is likely to decline even as demand increases—a situation that would only be aggravated by inefficient water resource infrastructure and insufficient resources to improve hydro-meteorological capacity. The government needs to continue its efforts to improve institutional capacity to manage climate and disaster risk and thereby strengthen resilience.

Tajikistan

Growth accelerated in 2018 on continued public investment and an improved external environment. Inflation slowed, but the current account slipped back into deficit as exports shrank and imports grew. Economic expansion is projected to slow in 2019 and again in 2020 as capital spending moderates. Inflation may accelerate under more exchange rate flexibility, but rising electricity exports should narrow the current account deficit. Diversifying exports could improve incomes and economic resilience.

Economic performance

Growth increased marginally from 7.1% in 2017 to 7.3% as large public investment projects continued, remittances remained high, and relations improved with Uzbekistan, boosting bilateral trade. Improvement came despite weak private investment and persistent problems in banking.

On the supply side, growth in industry fell by almost half from 21.3% in 2017 to 11.8% as aluminum production plunged by 7.1% because of delays in importing ore and ongoing renovation of production facilities—and despite gains of 16.3% in mining, 12.5% in manufacturing, and 7.8% in electricity generation (Figure 3.6.1). Gold production rose by 16.9% to a new record. Growth in agriculture slowed from 6.8% in 2017 to 4.0% as drought cut cotton production by 22.3%. Despite fruit and vegetable production higher by more than 10%, agriculture's share in GDP slipped from 21.1% in 2017 to 18.7% (Figure 3.6.2). Growth in services accelerated from 1.8% to 2.1% as an 11.0% rise in disposable income from higher remittances and government salaries boosted retail trade by 9.8%. Expansion in construction, fueled by infrastructure and private building, rose from 4.1% in 2017 to 7.8%.

On the demand side, growth in investment accelerated from 4.1% in 2017 to 7.8% on higher public outlays. Despite improved trade with Uzbekistan, net exports plunged by 40.2% as continued heavy infrastructure spending drove a 13.5% rise in imports, in particular of capital goods, and weak demand for minerals cut exports by 10.4% even as electricity exports rose.

Inflation decelerated from 6.7% in 2017 to 5.4% (Figure 3.6.3). This reflected prudent monetary policy, the introduction of inexpensive food imports from Uzbekistan and a cut in that country's transit fees, flat global food prices, lower railroad tariffs, and moderate credit growth at 6.5%.

This chapter was written by Muhammadi Boboev of the Tajikistan Resident Mission, ADB, Dushanbe.

3.6.1 GDP growth by sector

- Industry
- Agriculture
- Construction
- Services
- Gross domestic product

Source: Tajikistan State Statistical Agency.

3.6.2 Production structure

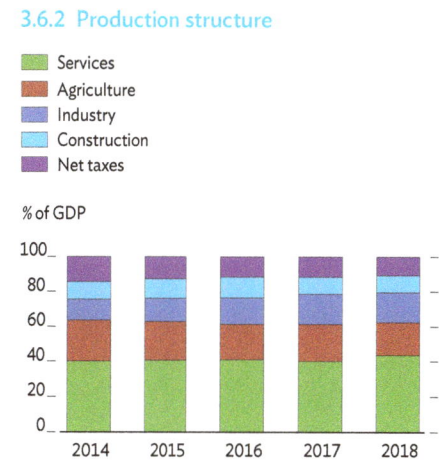

- Services
- Agriculture
- Industry
- Construction
- Net taxes

Source: Tajikistan State Statistical Agency.

These factors more than compensated for a 15.0% hike in government salaries and pensions in September, a 10.0% rise in utility prices in October, a further 15.0% rise in electricity tariffs in November, and 6.9% depreciation of the somoni against the US dollar. Prices rose by 4.9% for food, 6.4% for other goods, and 4.9% for services.

The budget deficit narrowed from the equivalent of 5.1% of GDP in 2017 to 4.8% as revenue slipped from 30.6% of GDP to 30.0% with shortfalls in corporate profits and value-added taxes, though higher imports and improved tax administration boosted excise and customs duties (Figure 3.6.4). Expenditure declined from 35.7% of GDP in 2017 to 34.8% under fiscal consolidation and despite continued large infrastructure outlays for the Rogun hydropower project, the first unit of which came online in November. Repayment of external debt and limited new borrowing reduced public and publicly guaranteed external debt from the equivalent of 44.5% of GDP at the end of 2017 to 38.9%, with total public debt declining from 54.7% of GDP to 48.8% (Figure 3.6.5).

Monetary policy aimed to maintain currency stability and limit inflation. The National Bank of Tajikistan, the central bank, continued moving toward an inflation target of 5%–9% by expanding sales of Treasury bills and central bank securities to slow monetary expansion even as it extended significant credit to the government budget. Growth in broad money tumbled from 21.8% in 2017 to 5.1%, though private credit reversed a 1.3% decline in 2017 to rise by 6.5% (Figure 3.6.6). Reserve money growth slowed sharply from 21.0% to 7.0%. With less inflation, the central bank cut the refinancing rate from 16.00% to 14.75% in January 2018 and further to 14.00% in March, but returned the rate to 14.75% in February 2019 to cool the economy. Tightened foreign exchange controls and other efforts to combat dollarization trimmed the share of foreign currency deposits from 60.3% at the end of 2017 to 53.2% a year later, and of loans in foreign currency from 61.0% to 57.2%.

Higher remittances and more careful screening of new borrowers helped cut the rate of nonperforming loans from 36.5% of all lending at the end of 2017 to 31.1% a year later. The return on bank assets improved from 0.5% in 2017 to 1.9%, and on bank equity from 1.7% to 7.0% (Figure 3.6.7). Two large banks remained troubled, however, with no resolution plan for them yet approved. The government established in June 2018 the National Financial Stability Council, chaired by the minister of economic development and trade, to facilitate information sharing and crisis management and to recommend how to reduce risk in the financial sector.

The current account slid back into deficit estimated at the equivalent of 4.4% of GDP, reversing a 2.1% surplus in 2017. The trade deficit widened from $1.6 billion to $2.1 billion

3.6.3 Sources of inflation

Source: Tajikistan State Statistical Agency.

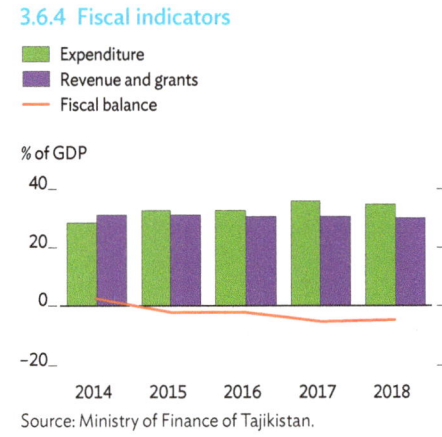

3.6.4 Fiscal indicators

Source: Ministry of Finance of Tajikistan.

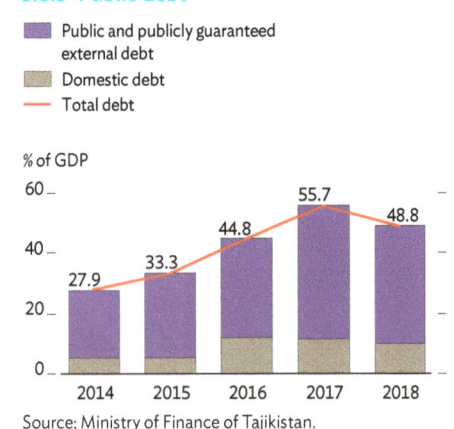

3.6.5 Public debt

Source: Ministry of Finance of Tajikistan.

as weak global demand for minerals cut exports by 10.4% after a 9.4% rise in 2017, and as capital inputs for the Rogun hydropower project boosted imports by 13.5%, reversing 8.5% contraction in 2017 (Figure 3.6.8). With economic recovery in the Russian Federation, remittances in the first 9 months of 2018 rose to $1.9 billion, equal to 36.5% of GDP, from $1.7 billion in the same period of 2017. Gross international reserves at the end of September 2018 slightly exceeded $1.2 billion, providing cover for 4.7 months of imports. The improvement came from purchases of domestically produced gold and a $500 million eurobond issue (Figure 3.6.9).

Economic prospects

Growth is forecast to slow to 7.0% in 2019 and 6.5% in 2020 as capital spending moderates following the completion of the second phase of the Rogun project in April 2019. Support for expansion will continue from higher remittances under positive growth in the Russian Federation, an expected pickup in private credit, increased production across sectors, and export expansion with additional electricity generation and improving economic relations with neighboring countries (Figure 3.6.10). Downside risks stem from weakness at two large banks and several state-owned enterprises.

On the supply side, industry is forecast to expand this year and next as the completion of the second turbine of the Rogun hydropower plant and accelerated industrialization boost electricity generation, mining, and manufacturing. Ongoing construction of the Tajikistan segment of a gas pipeline from Turkmenistan to the People's Republic of China should boost construction. Agriculture is expected to rise modestly with additional area under cultivation. Higher remittances will expand services and enhance demand for private lending.

On the demand side, public investment will remain the main growth driver as private investment languishes in a weak business climate. Private consumption will rise moderately on higher remittances. Exports are forecast higher as electricity exports expand with Rogun coming online and the construction of a new transmission line reconnecting Tajikistan's electricity system to the Central Asian power grid. Abundant electricity will also facilitate the domestic production of import substitutes.

Inflation is projected to accelerate to 7.5% in 2019 with expected exchange rate flexibility, higher consumer demand from increased remittances, and possibly faster monetary expansion from a second round of bank recapitalization (Figure 3.6.11). In 2020, inflation will likely remain within the targeted range of 5%–9%. It could go higher, however, if somoni depreciation exceeds expectations or fiscal spending spurs growth in the money supply.

3.6.6 Contributions to money supply growth

Source: National Bank of Tajikistan.

3.6.7 Banking system soundness indicators

Source: National Bank of Tajikistan.

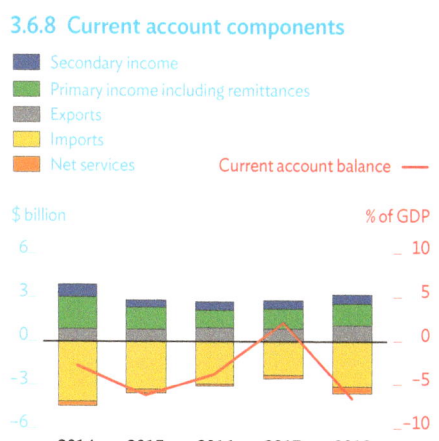

3.6.8 Current account components

Sources: National Bank of Tajikistan; ADB estimates.

Over the next 2 years, fiscal policy will be less expansionary despite significant financing needs for the Rogun project. The budget deficit is forecast to narrow to the equivalent of 4.0% of GDP in 2019 and 3.3% in 2020—both higher than approved in the fiscal strategy for 2017–2020. Revived business activity and higher imports are projected to boost revenue to 30.5% of GDP in 2019 and 30.8% in 2020. Expenditure is forecast equal to 34.5% of GDP in 2019 and 34.1% in 2020 on stepped-up repayment of external debt, currently equal to 1.5% of GDP, and domestic debt, now 0.3% of GDP. Expenditure could turn out higher with additional recapitalization of troubled banks, a clearing of arrears at state-owned enterprises, or faster currency depreciation. With foreign assistance now entirely through grants because of high debt risk, commercial borrowing is expected to cover gaps in financing for infrastructure, raising external debt to $3.3 billion, or 42.2% of GDP, by the end of 2020.

Monetary policy will likely tighten liquidity to contain inflation, including raising the refinancing rate if necessary, and to limit somoni depreciation. Gradual recovery in the banking system may increase resources available for private lending.

The current account deficit is forecast to narrow to 4.0% of GDP in 2019 and 3.8% in 2020 despite continued heavy imports of capital goods (Figure 3.6.12). Exports are projected to grow by 5.0% in 2019 and 10.0% in 2020 with higher electricity generation, including substantial exports of electricity to Afghanistan and Uzbekistan. With continued, if slow, growth in the Russian Federation, remittances are projected to rise by an additional 10% annually in 2019 and 2020. Despite higher remittances, imports are expected to contract by 5.0% in 2019 and stabilize in 2020 as efforts continue to replace food imports with local alternatives and to manufacture more import substitutes.

3.6.9 Gross international reserves

Q = quarter.
Source: National Bank of Tajikistan.

3.6.1 Selected economic indicators (%)

	2019	2020
GDP growth	7.0	6.5
Inflation	7.5	7.0
Current account balance (share of GDP)	-4.0	-3.8

Source: ADB estimates.

Policy challenge—diversifying production and exports

Tajikistan has traditionally had an agrarian-industrial economy that produces few exports, with services, fueled mainly by remittances, comprising more than half of GDP. This has made it vulnerable to external economic shocks that emanate largely from the Russian Federation, the main source of remittances, as occurred in the global financial crisis of 2008–2009 and in 2014–2015, when global oil prices tumbled. To reduce its vulnerability, Tajikistan needs to diversify its economy and in particular its export base.

Work on the Rogun hydropower project, the second generator of which is due to come online in April 2019, has diversified the economy both directly and indirectly.

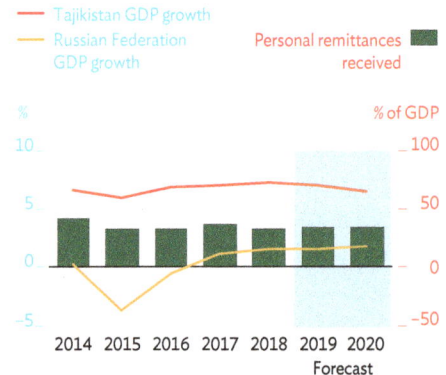

3.6.10 Remittances and GDP growth

Sources: World Bank. *World Development Indicators online database*; National Bank of Tajikistan; ADB estimates.

More electricity generation—along with the construction of a new power transmission line and Tajikistan's reconnection to the Central Asian power grid—will boost electricity exports and provide additional power for domestic manufacturing and other activities. However, more could be done to promote diversification.

First, Tajikistan would benefit from strengthening information technology to provide better commercial support services. This would require education and training to enhance computer skills in the population while making internet access cheaper and better. In December 2018, the Speedtest Global Index ranked Tajikistan the worst in the world for mobile internet speed and at 113 of 177 countries for the quality of its fixed broadband. Tajikistan could reap significant economic dividends by strengthening its information technology infrastructure—improving internet connections and encouraging private investment in data and voice services, both domestic and international—and by training a cohort of young developers in programming and technology applications.

Second, Tajikistan should explore opportunities to export products for which it likely enjoys a comparative advantage, such as high-value agricultural products. With appropriate branding and marketing, it could sell in nearby countries and potentially beyond. Yet agriculture remains largely subsistence, according to a 2014 survey by the World Bank, with only one-third of crop producers selling their output and more than half of this group doing so at the farm gate. Giving farmers technical support in marketing, and establishing marketing associations to attain economies of scale and reduce transaction costs, could help boost production, sales, and ultimately exports, which would raise rural incomes.

Third, Tajikistan should address other shortcomings in its investment climate. In *Doing Business 2019*, the World Bank ranked Tajikistan at 148 of 189 countries in cross-border trade, a deficiency it could address by improving customs, transport, and logistics procedures and by upgrading its rail and road connections with neighboring countries. Tajikistan similarly ranks at 136 of 189 countries in tax policy and collection. Its effective tax rate on company profit is, at 67.3%, more than double the 32.3% national average in Europe and Central Asia. Lower tax rates could be made feasible by reviewing tax policy to see whether some of the corporate tax burden could be shifted to other sources and by eliminating tax exemptions that fail to promote investment and innovation while distorting markets. Simplifying procedures for starting a business could potentially expand the tax base. Finally, Tajikistan could explore how to improve access to credit, another area where it ranks low, at 124 of 189 countries. Reducing the rate of nonperforming loans would help, as would creating more equitable access to loans for private firms.

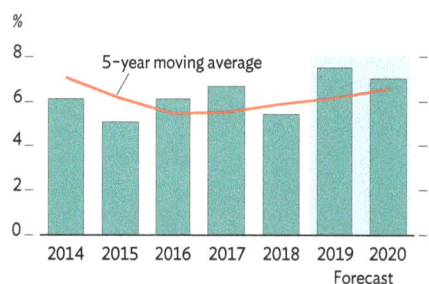

3.6.11 Inflation

Sources: Tajikistan State Statistical Agency; ADB estimates.

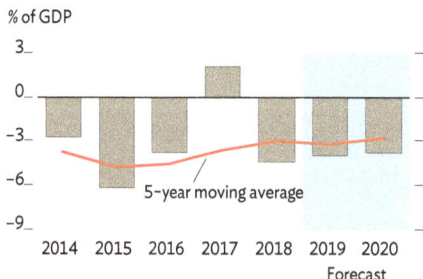

3.6.12 Current account balance

Sources: National Bank of Tajikistan; ADB estimates.

Turkmenistan

Growth reportedly moderated as expansion apart from hydrocarbons slowed with fiscal consolidation. Inflation accelerated, and the current account deficit narrowed. Continued fiscal consolidation will slow growth further in 2019 and 2020. Inflation will likely ease but remain near double digits, and higher hydrocarbon export volumes will further narrow the current account deficit. The government needs to evaluate and mitigate the social impact of subsidy reform.

Economic performance

The government reported GDP growth at 6.2% in 2018, down from 6.5% a year earlier (Figure 3.7.1). On the supply side, the hydrocarbon industry expanded by 6.0%, well up from 1.7% in 2017. However, growth in the larger non-hydrocarbon economy slowed from 7.5% in 2017 to 6.2% last year.

From preliminary estimates, industry growth accelerated from 5.4% in 2017 to 6.0%. Gains in hydrocarbons were partly offset by slower expansion in construction. Growth in services slowed from 7.9% to 6.8% with less expansion in construction and despite strong performances in trade, transport, and communications. Agriculture growth is estimated to have slowed from 5.9% in 2017 to 4.8% as adverse weather affected harvests of strategic crops, notably cotton and wheat.

On the demand side, investment continued to drive growth despite a cut in government capital spending. The International Monetary Fund (IMF) estimated gross investment in 2018 down from the equivalent of 41.0% of GDP in 2017 to 37.0%, of which 3.4 percentage points was foreign direct investment (FDI), mainly for gas, oil, and chemical processing (Figure 3.7.2). Growth in consumption weakened, especially private consumption, as inflation and a widening gap between the official and parallel market exchange rates eroded real household incomes despite a nominal 10.0% rise in public sector salaries, pensions, and stipends in January 2018.

No official estimate is available for inflation in 2018, but in November 2018 the IMF estimated inflation at 9.4%, up from 8.0% in 2017 (Figure 3.7.3). Actual inflation may have been higher, as estimated by other foreign sources, with pressures on the foreign exchange market driving up prices for imported goods. Adding to inflation were subsidy cuts and consequent

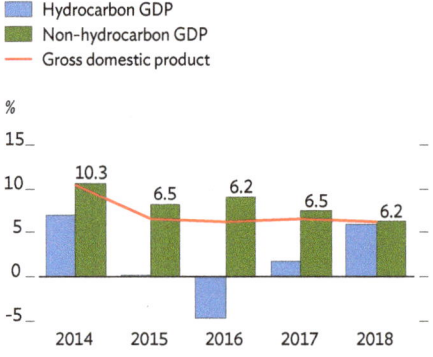

3.7.1 GDP growth by sector

Sources: International Monetary Fund. 2018. *Regional Economic Outlook, Middle East and Central Asia*; ADB estimates.

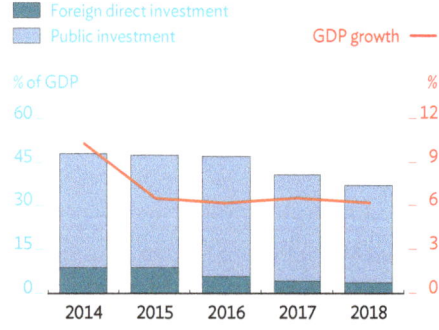

3.7.2 Gross investment including foreign direct investment

Sources: International Monetary Fund. 2018. Press release following a staff visit; ADB estimates.

This chapter was written by Jennet Hojanazarova of the Turkmenistan Resident Mission, ADB, Ashgabat.

increases in prices for utilities, public transportation, food, and services. To stem even larger increases, the government instituted price controls for selected foods and services.

Monetary policy focused on containing inflation as the Central Bank of Turkmenistan kept strict control of cash in circulation, promoted noncash payments instead, and imposed restrictions on foreign exchange transactions. Although credit growth slowed from 17.0% in 2017 to 12.0%, lending remained sizable at the equivalent of 60% of GDP, mostly subsidized credit to state-owned enterprises in priority sectors to facilitate import substitution and promote exports (Figure 3.7.4).

The state budget deficit is estimated to have narrowed from the equivalent of 2.8% of GDP in 2017 to 0.9%, reflecting fiscal consolidation that reduced capital spending and cut subsidies under major subsidy reform (Figure 3.7.5). Revenue was estimated at 14.4% of GDP, down from 14.9% last year, with expenditure falling from 17.7% of GDP in 2017 to 15.3%. Budget financing came mainly from central bank purchases of Treasury securities. The government reported that over 70% of outlays were for social spending and a 10.0% rise in salaries, pensions, and stipends. The non-hydrocarbon fiscal deficit narrowed from 7.7% of GDP in 2017 to 5.5%. Extra-budgetary operations remained large, however, and should be incorporated into the budget to improve transparency and accountability in public finance. Public debt incurred by both the government and state enterprises was estimated to equal 30.9% of GDP at the end of 2018, up from 28.8% a year earlier.

Export revenue rose in 2018 on recovery in global hydrocarbon prices and increased demand for gas from the People's Republic of China. This and import restrictions narrowed the current account deficit from 11.5% of GDP in 2017 to an estimated 8.2%. Estimated growth in exports soared from 6.3% in 2017 to 26.0%, while imports expanded by 9.3% following an 18.0% drop in 2017. FDI inflows in 2018 were estimated at $1.5 billion, most of them for oil, gas, and chemical production. Besides FDI, external borrowing remained significant, risking debt accumulation and the eventual need to draw down the central bank's international reserves, a concern in a period of rising loan repayments and low global energy prices. External debt rose from the equivalent of 25.1% of GDP in 2017 to 26.7% last year.

Economic prospects

Continued fiscal consolidation is projected to slow growth to 6.0% in 2019 and 5.8% in 2020. On the supply side, further recovery in hydrocarbons is expected to help industry expand by 6%–7%, supported by gains in agricultural processing, light industry and food products, construction materials, and chemicals, which are all targets for import substitution.

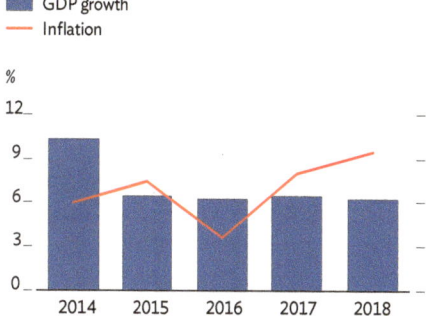

3.7.3 GDP growth and inflation

Sources: International Monetary Fund. 2018. *Regional Economic Outlook, Middle East and Central Asia*; ADB estimates.

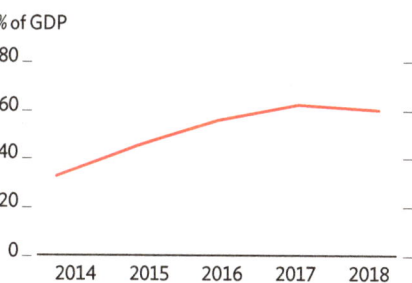

3.7.4 Credit

Sources: International Monetary Fund. 2018. Press release following a staff visit; ADB estimates.

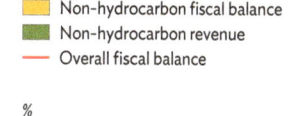

3.7.5 Government fiscal balance

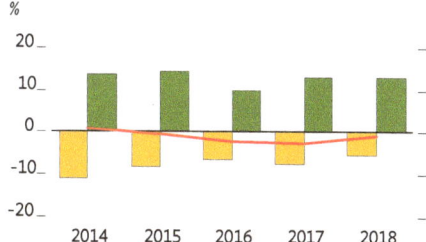

Note: Fiscal data refer to the general government. Nonhydrocardon fiscal balance and revenue are percentages of non-oil gross domestic product, and the overall fiscal balance is a percentage of total gross domestic product.

Sources: International Monetary Fund. 2018. *Regional Economic Outlook, Middle East and Central Asia*; ADB estimates.

With announced government support for farmers, agriculture is forecast to expand by 4% in both years, while services are projected to grow by 5%–6% annually.

With slower growth, inflation is likely to decelerate slightly but remain near double digits, given the likelihood of further price adjustments and foreign exchange shortages. The government is expected to continue its efforts to curtail inflation by maintaining a fixed exchange rate and administrative price controls, supporting import substitution, and limiting foreign exchange conversion. Banks will continue to direct their lending to state-owned enterprises in priority sectors.

The state budget envisages further cuts to capital spending, continued subsidy reform, and improved tax administration to better mobilize revenues. The government plans to develop a medium-term fiscal framework with technical assistance from the IMF, which should include a path for annual reductions in public investment. The state budget is projected to incur deficits equal to 1.3% of GDP in 2019 and 0.9% in 2020 (Figure 3.7.6). The government aims to continue support for social services, with over 70% of budget expenditure going for such outlays plus wages, pensions, and stipends. Treasury bonds in local currency are expected to provide budget financing equal to 4.2% of GDP and allow some existing domestic debt to be refinanced.

Contracts for larger gas shipments are forecast to lift merchandise exports by 14.0% in 2019 and 10.0% in 2020, outpacing projected merchandise import growth of 6.2% in 2019 and 0.5% in 2020. With the completion of large projects that require imports of advanced equipment and services, the current account deficit is expected to narrow to 5.7% of GDP in 2019 and 3.4% in 2020 (Figure 3.7.7). As financing other large investments would require further accumulation of external debt, which is already projected to equal 29.4% of GDP in 2019 and 31.0% at the end of 2020, a sound debt-management strategy is required, especially given low hydrocarbon prices and a sizable external deficit (Figure 3.7.8).

Policy challenge—assessing and mitigating the social impact of subsidy reform

In response to the adverse impact of lower global hydrocarbon prices on budget revenue, the government has taken significant measures to rationalize public spending. Besides trimming capital spending, it has initiated comprehensive subsidy reform.

Since 1991, generous subsidies have been a key element of Turkmenistan's effort to distribute to citizens benefits from the country's resource wealth and ensure the well-being of low-income households. Along with petroleum products,

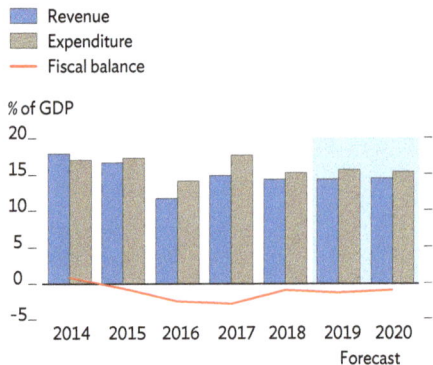

3.7.6 Fiscal indicators

Sources: International Monetary Fund. 2018. *Regional Economic Outlook, Middle East and Central Asia*; ADB estimates.

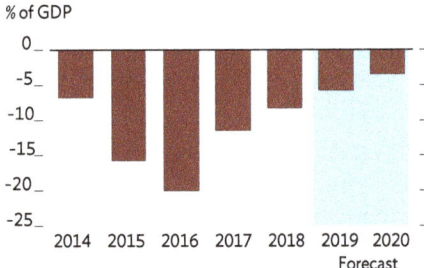

3.7.7 Current account balance

Sources: International Monetary Fund. 2018. *Regional Economic Outlook, Middle East and Central Asia*; ADB estimates.

3.7.1 Selected economic indicators (%)

	2019	2020
GDP growth	6.0	5.8
Inflation	9.0	8.2
Current account balance (share of GDP)	-5.7	-3.4

Source: ADB estimates.

some health-care services and basic public utilities such as electricity, gas, water, and heating have historically been provided at very low prices. In addition, large subsidies were given for 17 other types of products: certain foods, medicines, public transportation, housing, telephone, kindergarten, and other services. The IMF reports that Turkmenistan has maintained some of the largest energy subsidies in the Commonwealth of Independent States.

The government began to reform subsidies in 2014, liberalizing prices to various degrees on regulated goods and services. In January 2019, it ended free electricity, gas, and water allotments for households. As the government aims to achieve cost recovery in its provision of services, further cuts in subsidies are envisaged, with consequent price increases for many products and services. These and future price increases will have important social consequences that need to be properly assessed and addressed.

The World Bank's *Macro Poverty Outlook 2018* suggests that rising inflation and further cutbacks in social subsidies have eroded living standards and households' real purchasing power. As income disparities are large, low-income households may have been affected substantially (Figure 3.7.9).

A comprehensive review of existing social protection programs is needed to inform efforts for their improvement, taking into account households' real income, purchasing power, and rates of unemployment and poverty. Improving data bases and strengthening the capacity of state institutions to conduct periodic assessments using best international practices can help maintain adequate social safety nets, to cushion the negative effects of subsidy cuts and rising inflation on income and living standards. In tandem with such programs, macroeconomic policies should aim to sustain growth, control inflation, and create more productive jobs. A gradual and phased-in approach to subsidy cuts and price liberalization would provide time to strengthen social safety nets.

Apart from enhancing social protection, Turkmenistan could do more to improve other aspects of social development. Despite high subsidies and social spending, many health and education indicators lag those of economies with high human development, according to the latest United Nations' human development report. Thus, savings from subsidy reform should be used to improve the quality of health care and education services, and targeted support for low-income households.

Subsidy reform can be more successful when it is part of a larger agenda encompassing institutional reform to improve public finances and economic efficiency while maintaining adequate living standards. The government thus needs to ensure that measures to preserve living standards are an integral part of its subsidy reform program.

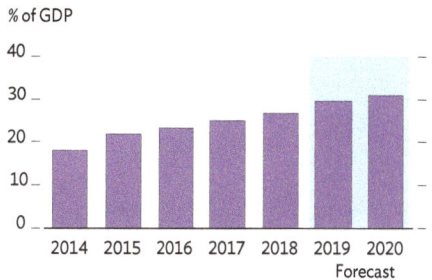

3.7.8 External debt

Sources: International Monetary Fund. 2018. *Regional Economic Outlook, Middle East and Central Asia*; ADB estimates.

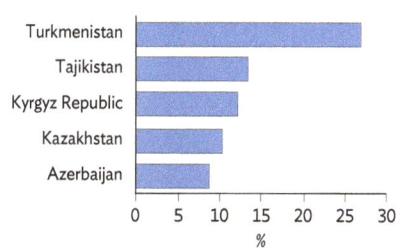

3.7.9 Inequality in income, 2017

Note: The Atkinson inequality index, used here, indicates heightened inequality as a higher percentage.
Source: United Nations Development Program. 2018. *Human Development Indices and Indicators: 2018 Statistical Update*.

Uzbekistan

Growth reportedly accelerated in 2018, inflation jumped, and the current account slipped from surplus into a deep deficit. Growth is projected higher in 2019 and 2020 on expansion in industry and services. Tighter monetary policy is expected to slow inflation in 2019 and 2020 despite upward adjustments to utility tariffs. The current account deficit will persist but shrink slightly in 2020. Irrigation reform is essential to agricultural sustainability and climate proofing.

Economic performance

The government reported that growth accelerated from 4.5% in 2017 to 5.1% in 2018 on faster expansion in industry, construction, and investment. The figure for 2017 has been revised down as the government revisited GDP data, including growth rates, dating back to 2010.

On the supply side, growth in industry excluding construction doubled from 5.2% in 2017 to 10.6%, driven by increases of 6.4% in manufacturing and 28.2% in mining and quarrying (Figure 3.8.1). Construction expanded by 9.9%, up from 6.0% in 2017, with gains in housing and production facilities. Growth in services slowed from 6.4% to 5.4% last year, with smaller increases in transport and trade. Expansion in agriculture dropped from 1.2% in 2017 to 0.2% as poor rainfall cut cereal harvests by 12.5% and crop production more broadly by 4.7%.

Investment was the main driver of growth on the demand side. Expansion in gross fixed capital formation jumped from 7.1% in 2017 to 18.1% largely on higher investment in manufacturing, housing, energy, and mining fueled by a 36.6% surge in foreign investment and lending for fixed capital. In real terms, public consumption rose by an estimated 4.0%, as did private consumption by 3.0% on nominal wage increases that averaged 25.0% (6.4% in real terms) and nominal pension increases that averaged 22.6%.

Average inflation accelerated from 13.7% in 2017 to 17.9%, reflecting the continuing impact of foreign exchange liberalization in the last quarter of 2017 and the first half of 2018 (Figure 3.8.2). Adding to inflation were utility price increases, price liberalization for bread and other basic goods, higher wages and pensions, and rapid credit growth, all occurring in 2018. Inflation rose despite exchange rate

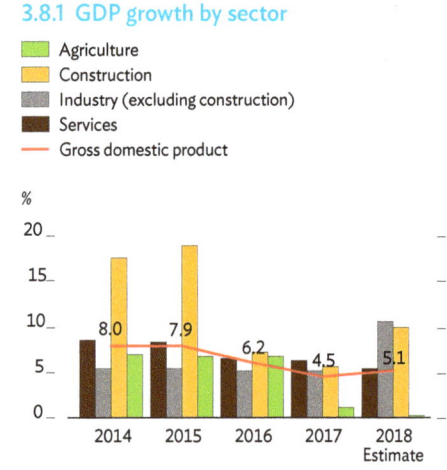

3.8.1 GDP growth by sector

Sources: State Statistics Committee; ADB estimates.

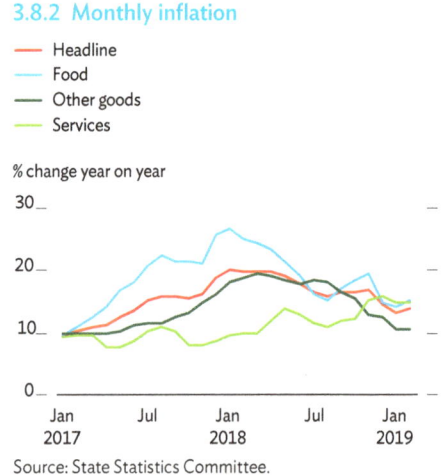

3.8.2 Monthly inflation

Source: State Statistics Committee.

This chapter was written by Begzod M. Djalilov of the Uzbekistan Resident Mission, ADB, Tashkent.

stability, monetary tightening, the cancellation of customs duties on imports of basic foodstuffs, and better logistics and facilities for fruit and vegetables.

The consolidated budget surplus, reflecting balances of the state budget and specialized public funds, narrowed from 0.7% of GDP in 2017 to 0.5%. Ambitious development spending for social programs raised expenditure from 23.0% of GDP in 2017 to 26.2%, while tax reform is estimated to have raised revenue from 23.7% to 26.7%. The augmented government balance—combining the consolidated budget and policy-guided operations such as on-lending by the Uzbekistan Fund for Reconstruction and Development and recapitalization for state-owned enterprises and banks—is expected to record a deficit equal to 2.5% of GDP.

Responding to inflationary pressures, the Central Bank of the Republic of Uzbekistan raised the refinancing rate from 14.0% to 16.0% in September and subsequently adopted new instruments to manage liquidity, including auctions of deposits and government securities. These measures helped slash broad money growth from 40.2% in 2017 to 14.4%. Bank assets expanded by 28.7% in 2018, and credit jumped by 51.4% as the government channeled credit at preferential rates to selected sectors such as housing (Figure 3.8.3). The assets of banks with state ownership expanded by 32.0%, and their lending by 52.2%.

The Uzbek sum depreciated by 2.5% against the US dollar in 2018 despite the central bank selling $3.8 billion in US dollars during the year. Demand for foreign exchange reached $10.4 billion, mainly for imports to supply manufacturing and construction.

The current account balance recorded a deficit equal to 7.0% of GDP, reversing a surplus of 2.9% in 2017 (Figure 3.8.4). Exports of goods and services grew by 13.6%, with exports of services rising by 22.4% and of hydrocarbons by 65.8%. Imports of goods and services jumped by 39.6%, reflecting a 64.6% increase in imports of machinery and equipment to modernize industry and infrastructure. The resulting trade deficit was $5.3 billion. Remittances in the first 9 months of 2018 were $3.8 billion, 80% of which came from the Russian Federation.

Lower foreign investment into hydrocarbons cut foreign direct investment by 14.2% in 2018. Foreign reserves slipped from $28.1 billion at the end of 2017 to $27.1 billion a year later, still providing cover for 17 months of imports (Figure 3.8.5). Higher foreign borrowing hiked external debt from 26.5% of GDP in 2017 to 34.7%. This prompted the Ministry of Finance to strengthen its management of external debt. In December 2018, it adopted the Debt Management and Financial Analysis System of the United Nations Conference on Trade and Development to monitor government debt obligations and grants, as well as private external debt that it does not guarantee.

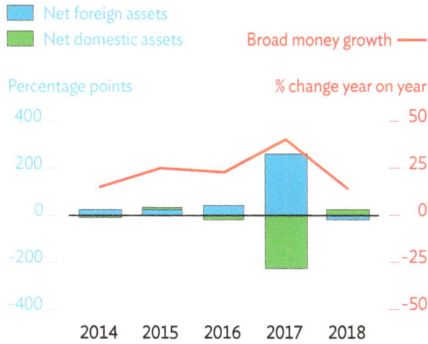

3.8.3 Contributions to money supply growth

Source: The Central Bank of the Republic of Uzbekistan.

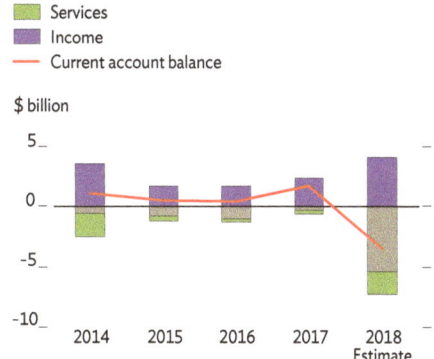

3.8.4 Current account components

Sources: International Monetary Fund; ADB estimates.

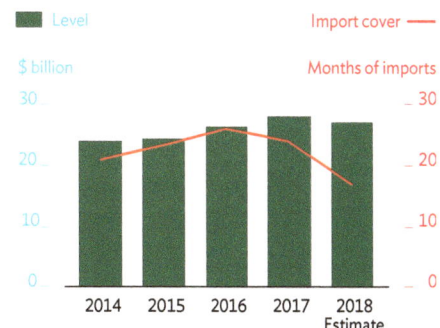

3.8.5 Gross international reserves

Sources: International Monetary Fund; ADB estimates.

Economic prospects

Growth is forecast to improve further to 5.2% in 2019 and 5.5% in 2020, boosted by higher infrastructure spending, an improved investment climate, expected gains in exports, and a pickup in agriculture (Figure 3.8.6). The main risk to macroeconomic stability stems from persistent credit expansion, which could revive inflationary pressure and push the current account further into deficit.

On the supply side, growth in industry is expected to slow to 5.5% in 2019, reflecting slower expansion in the production of machinery and petrochemicals for agriculture, and in mining and quarrying primarily for export and construction. Industrial sector growth is forecast to recover to 6.0% in 2020. Construction is forecast to expand by 9.0% each year, sustained by government expansion of urban infrastructure and services. Periodic increases in wages and pensions, and of spending for social assistance, are projected to expand services by 5.5% each year by boosting trade and transport. Growth in agriculture is forecast to accelerate to 4.0% in 2019, thanks to ample rain and structural reform in cotton and wheat, and 4.5% in 2020. Ongoing farm and agro-processing reform should boost exports.

On the demand side, growth will come mainly from investment as gross fixed capital formation rises on further improvement in the investment climate and government-led investment to modernize manufacturing, mining, power generation, transportation, and housing. Private consumption is expected to benefit from wage growth. Net exports are anticipated to remain a drag on growth in 2019 and 2020.

Inflation is projected to decelerate to 16.0% in 2019 and further to 14.0% in 2020 as lending growth under state programs slows and as further streamlining of customs procedures facilitates imports (Figure 3.8.7). Inflationary pressure will persist, however, from the lagged effects of a November 2018 rise in energy prices, further hikes to electric power and natural gas prices planned for June 2019, consequent adjustments to wages and pensions, and upward revisions to customs duties on imports. The central bank will pursue a phased transition to inflation targeting, aiming to reduce it to single digits by 2021. To contain inflationary pressure, monetary and fiscal authorities must coordinate their actions to mitigate the impact of liberalized prices for agricultural products and of protracted growth in credit.

Growth in broad money is forecast to slow to 13.0% in 2019 and 12.0% in 2020 as growth in credit falls by half to 25.0% and then drops to 15.0% (Figure 3.8.8). In 2019, the central bank will limit preferential lending under state programs and further modify capital requirements for commercial banks when extending credit. Considering the continued impact of hikes in 2018 on utility tariffs and further tariff adjustments

3.8.1 Selected economic indicators (%)

	2019	2020
GDP growth	5.2	5.5
Inflation	16.0	14.0
Current account balance (share of GDP)	-7.0	-6.5

Source: ADB estimates.

3.8.6 GDP growth

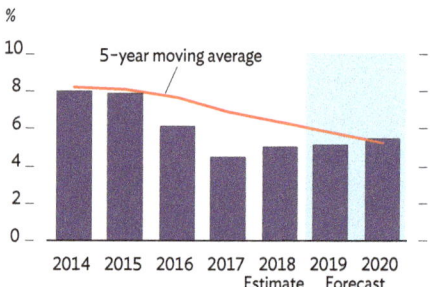

Source: *Asian Development Outlook* database.

3.8.7 Inflation

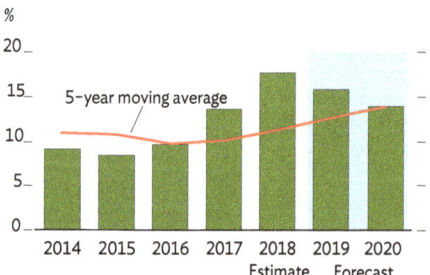

Source: *Asian Development Outlook* database.

planned for 2019, the central bank has set its inflationary target at 13.5%–15.5% in 2019 and kept its refinancing rate at 16.0% in January 2019. It envisions developing money market instruments such as short-term deposits, swaps, and repo auctions—and issuing bonds that pay in 1, 3, 6, and 12 months—to manage liquidity in 2019 and 2020 while expanding its sterilization of foreign exchange inflows to keep monetary policy tight.

The consolidated fiscal balance is forecast to remain at the equivalent of 0.5% of GDP in 2019 and 2020 (Figure 3.8.9). The augmented fiscal deficit is projected to narrow to 2.0% of GDP in 2019 and 2020, reflecting the planned reduction in policy-guided lending, in particular on-lending by Uzbekistan Fund for Reconstruction and Development, to curb inflationary pressure from credit growth. As a part of tax reform, the government adopted in January 2019 a flat 12.0% individual income tax, introduced value-added tax on companies with revenue above SUM1 billion, and reduced the corporate income tax rate from 14.0% to 12.0%. Revenue in the consolidated budget is forecast to reach the equivalent of 30.0% of GDP in 2019 and 2020 as expenditure, mainly capital spending on infrastructure, remains at 29.5%. The restructuring of state-owned enterprises, the major contributors to the state budget, will create challenges for revenue, which the government plans to address through tax reform that brings more private firms into the tax base.

The current account deficit is expected to remain high at 7.0% of GDP in 2019 before narrowing slightly to 6.5% in 2020 (Figure 3.8.10). Exports of goods are forecast to grow by 10.0% in 2019 and 12.0% in 2020, reflecting expectations of higher gold prices, stable demand for natural gas from the People's Republic of China, expanded agricultural exports to the Russian Federation and other neighbors including Kazakhstan, and further processing of cotton fiber into textiles. Imports of goods are projected to rise by 25.0% in 2019 and 20.0% in 2020 as demand generated by infrastructure projects and the continued modernization of industry boost imports for these sectors. The risk of wider current account deficits persists as credit growth may further encourage imports of capital goods.

External borrowing for state-led development programs is projected to push external debt to the equivalent of 35.0% of GDP in 2019 and 2020 (Figure 3.8.11). Foreign investment will likely increase as well. Uzbekistan received a sovereign rating in December 2018 and issued its first eurobond in February 2019, providing for Uzbek corporations a benchmark for access to international capital markets.

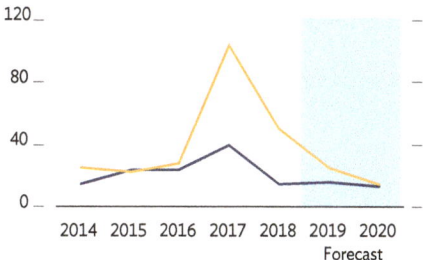

3.8.8 Broad money and credit growth

Sources: The Central Bank of the Republic of Uzbekistan; ADB estimates.

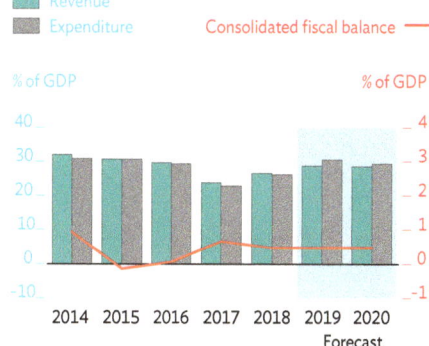

3.8.9 Fiscal components

Sources: International Monetary Fund; ADB estimates.

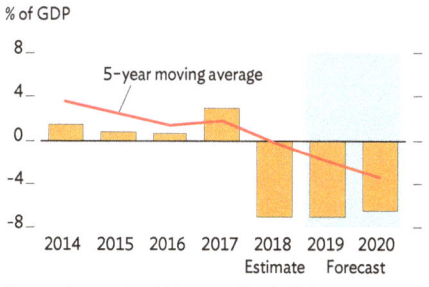

3.8.10 Current account balance

Sources: International Monetary Fund; ADB estimates.

Policy challenge—reforming irrigation

Agriculture is critical to the livelihoods of the half of Uzbeks who live in rural areas. It provides 27.3% of all jobs and contributes nearly one-third of GDP. Rapid population growth averaging 1.9% per year from 2005 to 2019 has put stress on the country's limited environmental resources, exacerbating land degradation and water shortages that constrain agricultural output.

A study by the International Food Policy Research Institute and the Center for Development Research estimated that over half of cropland suffers soil salinization caused by extensive irrigation, and that the resulting ecosystem changes and suppressed agricultural output cost Uzbekistan about 4% of GDP annually. In this arid climate, drought and water shortages are a constant threat. Precipitation in most areas averages less than 600 millimeters per year, and high temperatures can reach 49° Celsius in some areas, requiring river-fed irrigation. According to the Ministry of Water Resources, available water resources declined from 64 billion cubic meters (m^3) in 1991 to 59 billion m^3 in 2018, and population growth almost halved per capita availability from 3,048 m^3 to 1,589 m^3. In 2018, agriculture received nearly 90% of the water supply.

To address salinization and diminished water resources, the government is rehabilitating the irrigation system with investments worth $350 million last year and this year. It is providing incentives to adopt more water-efficient technologies. Suppliers of imported drip and sprinkler irrigation systems are exempted from customs duties for 5 years, and farmers that adopt them are similarly exempted from land tax. At the end of 2018, farmers were applying water-efficient technologies on more than 328,000 hectares. Drip irrigation currently supplies only 43,000 hectares, though, because of the high cost of introducing it. To encourage adoption, the government decided this year to award drip-adopting cotton farmers a one-time payment of $950 per hectare.

Despite their benefits, measures implemented in an ad hoc fashion allocate resources inefficiently. Over the next 2 years, the government should accelerate the creation of long-term strategies for agriculture and water resource management and develop an even broader plan for mitigating and adapting to climate change. These strategies should prioritize farmers' access to extension services and finance for machinery, and strengthen the security of their land tenure, to promote more efficient use of land and water resources. In addition, as water resource management cannot be undertaken on a national scale in isolation from the broader regional context, Uzbekistan should promote water resource management and climate proofing across borders through collaboration with its neighbors.

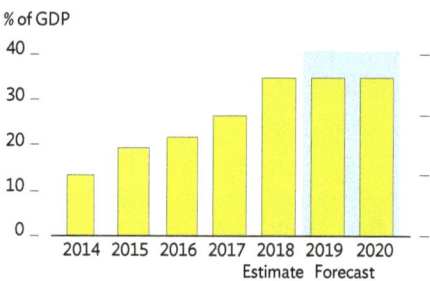

3.8.11 External debt

Sources: The Central Bank of the Republic of Uzbekistan; ADB estimates.

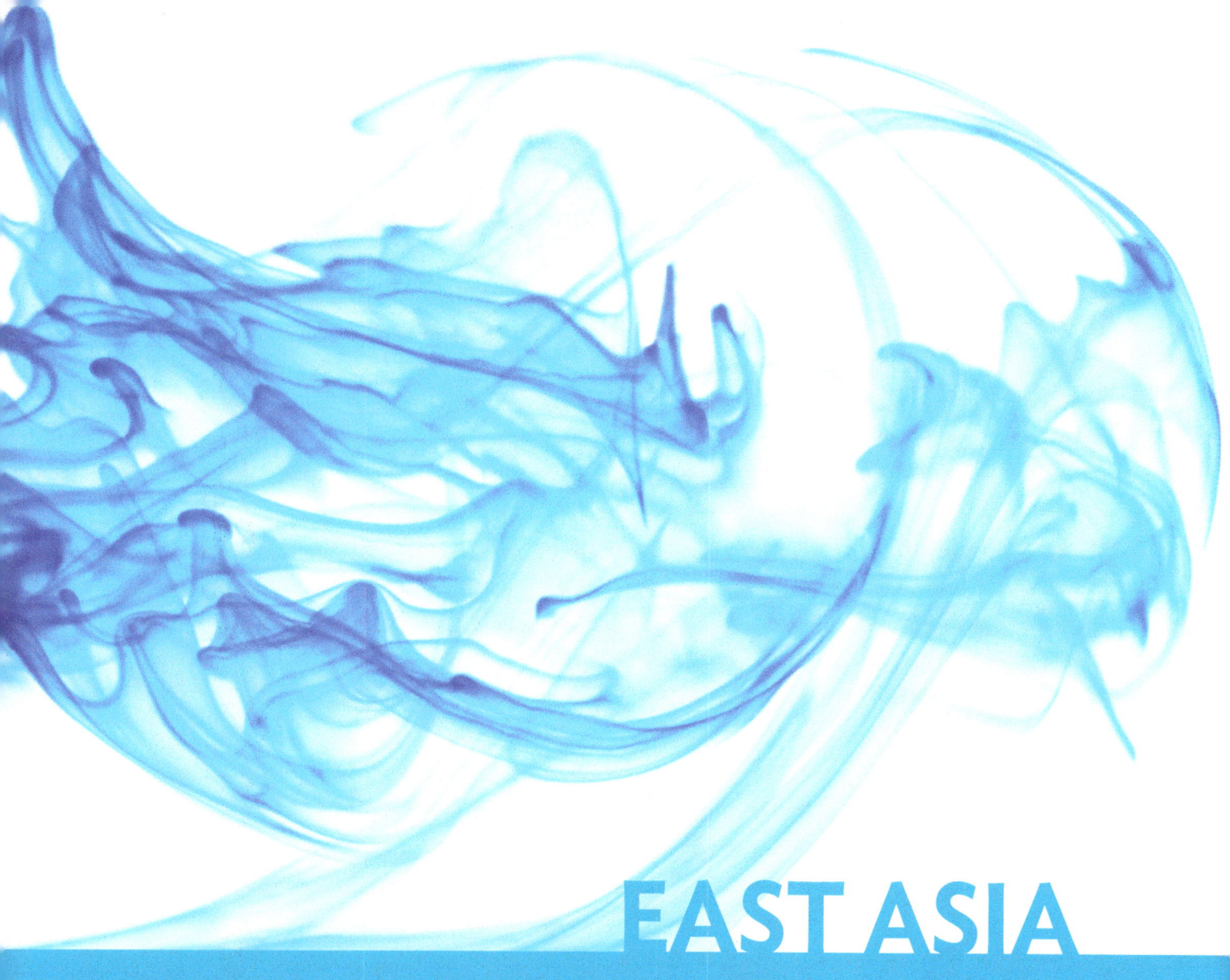

EAST ASIA

- HONG KONG, CHINA
- MONGOLIA
- PEOPLE'S REPUBLIC OF CHINA
- REPUBLIC OF KOREA
- TAIPEI,CHINA

Hong Kong, China

Growth slowed in 2018 as the external environment became more challenging. Moderate growth should continue this year and next with domestic demand still resilient and the labor market tightening. Inflation will remain subdued, and the current account surplus will narrow further on weaker trade. Innovative policies are needed to raise the rate of labor force participation among women and older workers, toward alleviating the economic challenges posed by a rapidly aging population.

Economic performance

GDP growth moderated to 3.0% in 2018 from 3.8% in 2017 as downward pressure came from sluggish global trade, tightening external financial conditions, and persistent global trade friction (Figure 3.9.1). Domestic demand nevertheless remained resilient and served as the source of growth in 2018. Spurred by favorable job and income conditions, private consumption expenditure expanded by 5.6% in real terms and contributed 3.8 percentage points to GDP growth. Government spending also expanded, by 4.2%, adding 0.4 points to growth. Machinery and equipment acquisition picked up significantly, but building and construction saw a marginal decline, dragging down the investment contribution to growth to 0.3 points. Both export and import growth edged down, with net exports shaving 1.5 points off growth (Figure 3.9.2).

On the supply side, services remained the primary driver of economic growth, expanding by 3.4% last year. Manufacturing grew by 1.3%, while construction deteriorated by 0.2%. The residential property market remained buoyant in the first half of 2018 but began to cool in the second half as trade conflicts, global stock market corrections, and hikes in mortgage and lending rates dampened market sentiment (Figure 3.9.3).

Consumer price inflation accelerated from 1.5% in 2017 to 2.4% in 2018, mainly because food prices increased by 3.4% (Figure 3.9.4). External price pressures edged up in the first half—fueled by robust global conditions, a depreciating local dollar, and higher oil prices—but largely held steady in the second half in light of subdued international prices and a

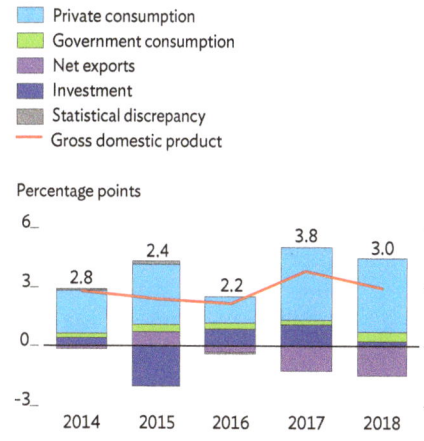

3.9.1 Demand-side contributions to growth

Source: Census and Statistics Department, https://www.censtatd.gov.hk/home/ (accessed 14 March 2019).

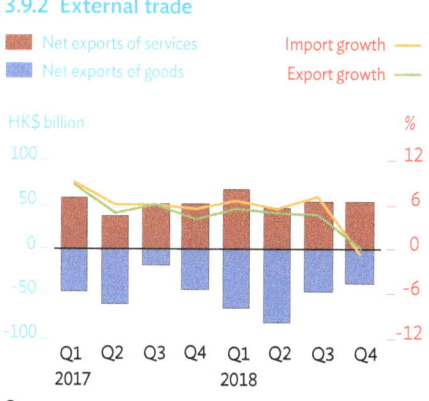

3.9.2 External trade

Q = quarter.
Source: Census and Statistics Department, https://www.censtatd.gov.hk/home/ (accessed 14 March 2019).

This chapter was written by Benno Ferrarini of the Economic Research and Regional Cooperation Department, ADB, Manila, and Michael Timbang, consultant, Economic Research and Regional Cooperation Department, ADB, Manila.

strengthening US dollar, to which the local dollar is linked. Netting out the effects of government one-off relief measures, underlying consumer price inflation rose from 1.7% in 2017 to 2.6% in 2018 as the economy sustained a growth rate above trend. Average residential property prices retreated from their peak in July but still rose by 1.8% in 2018, while newly let residential rents increased by 3.3%.

The current account surplus narrowed from the equivalent of 4.7% of GDP in 2017 to 4.3% in 2018. This reflected a higher goods trade deficit, albeit partly offset by rising net inflows of primary income and a higher surplus in services trade. Meanwhile, the overall balance of payments surplus narrowed sharply from 9.4% of GDP in 2017 to 0.3% in 2018 as net capital flows turned negative. Gross official reserves fell to $424.7 billion at the end of 2018, or cover for 7.5 months of imports.

The government revised its budget surplus estimate for fiscal year 2018 (FY2018, ending 31 March 2019) from 1.2% of GDP to 2.1%, mainly because expenditure was 5.6% less than budgeted (Figure 3.9.5). Revenue was also lower than the original estimate, by 1.3%, because of lower-than-expected receipts from land premium and stamp duties, which tend to be highly sensitive to market fluctuations.

Monetary conditions remained broadly accommodative in 2018. In tandem with the interest rate hike by the US Federal Reserve in December, the Hong Kong Monetary Authority raised its base rate by 25 basis points to 2.75%, marking its fourth adjustment in 2018. Domestic credit grew by 5.4%, and the broad money supply (M2) rose by 4.3%. The local stock market—the sixth largest in the world and the third largest in Asia—underwent a sharp correction last year amid trade conflicts and concern over US interest rate hikes that outpaced expectations. In December, the Hang Seng Index closed 13.6% lower than a year earlier and a sharp 22.0% down from its all-time high in January 2018 (Figure 3.9.6).

Hong Kong, China has been ranked the world's freest economy for 25 years in a row by the Heritage Foundation and, since 1996, by the Fraser Institute. Its economy was named in 2018 the most competitive in Asia, and the second most competitive globally, by the International Institute for Management Development. The economy ranked seventh in the *Global Competitiveness Report 2018* of the World Economic Forum and fourth in the World Bank's *Doing Business 2019*. Hong Kong, China has maintained its favorable business environment and its status as a regional and global trading hub, positioned among the world's top-ranked economies.

3.9.3 Property market indicators

ᵃ = 3-month moving averages.
Source: CEIC Data Company (accessed 14 March 2019).

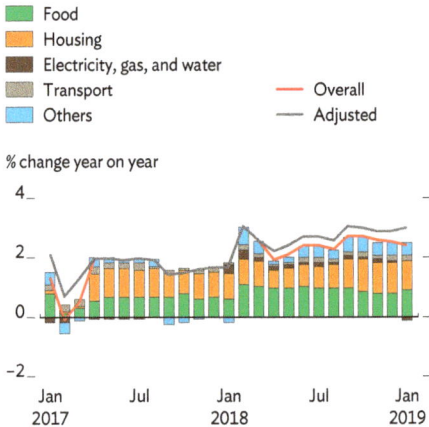

3.9.4 Monthly inflation

Note: Adjusted inflation is the rate once the effects of temporary government subsidies are removed.
Source: CEIC Data Company (accessed 14 March 2019).

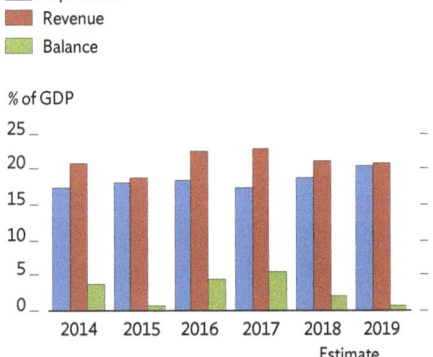

3.9.5 Fiscal indicators

Note: Years are fiscal years ending on 31 March of the next year.
Sources: The Government of the Hong Kong Special Administrative Region of the PRC. The 2019–2020 Budget, and other years. http://www.budget.gov.hk; CEIC Data Company; *Asian Development Outlook* database.

Economic prospects

GDP growth is projected to slow to 2.5% in 2019 and 2020 (Figure 3.9.7). Growth moderation in the People's Republic of China (PRC) and several other key partners will weigh on exports from Hong Kong, China, such that net exports will add little to growth this year and next. Consumption will remain the engine of growth, supported by continued stable employment and strong incomes, though recent economic developments both at home and abroad have dampened confidence in the economy, reflected in softer asset prices and declines in retail sales. Private investment could weaken further this year, after a sharp decline in the fourth quarter of 2018, on deteriorating local business sentiment. The composite purchasing managers' index inched up slightly in January but remains in contraction territory. Business surveys saw sharp deterioration in sentiment, particularly in import/export trade and wholesale, reflecting the impact of ongoing trade conflict, and in real estate, mirroring the recent cooling in the property market.

On the supply side, services will continue to be the main driver of growth, supported by trade-related and professional services. Business sentiment in the sector fell markedly in mid-January, but retail, accommodation, and food services will likely be buttressed by continued strength in inbound tourism.

Inflation is forecast to decelerate slightly to 2.3% in 2019 and 2020 (Figure 3.9.8). The rising trend in rents starting early last year will continue to feed through, but recent consolidation in property markets will have a mitigating effect on consumer prices. Cost increases will be restrained as well by slower economic growth, higher interest rates at home, and the strong US dollar, while soft international commodity prices will keep external price pressures at bay.

The FY2019 budget surplus is forecast to dip to the equivalent of 0.6% of GDP. Budgetary revenue is slated to rise by 5.0% on higher expected receipts from land premiums. Budgetary expenditure is also projected to increase, by 13.0%, on higher outlays for social welfare, education, health care, family allowances, tourism, and infrastructure, as well as increased investment in land resource utilization, environmental protection, and promoting innovative and creative industries. Fiscal reserves are forecast to equal 39.4% of GDP by the end of March 2020.

Trade is likely to offer little support to growth this year as slower increase in demand from the PRC and uncertainty spawned by escalating trade conflict with the US will dampen export growth. A strengthening US dollar could further limit export gains. Imports are also likely to be restrained by weakening domestic demand. The resulting goods trade deficit will be offset by an improving surplus in the services account as tourist numbers grow and demand for professional and

3.9.1 Selected economic indicators (%)

	2019	2020
GDP growth	2.5	2.5
Inflation	2.3	2.3
Current account balance (share of GDP)	3.5	3.3

Source: ADB estimates.

3.9.6 Stock market

Source: Bloomberg (accessed 14 March 2019).

3.9.7 GDP growth

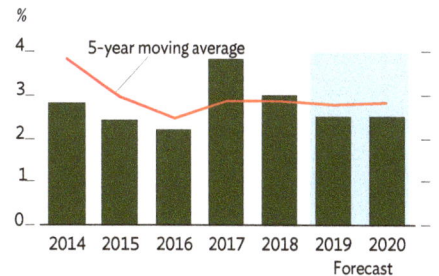

Source: Asian Development Outlook database.

financial services increases with new opportunities arising in the development of the Guangdong–Hong Kong–Macao Bay Area. Further, several trade and investment agreements, including those signed with the PRC and other key trade partners, may come into force this year. On balance, the current account surplus is forecast to narrow to 3.5% of GDP this year and further to 3.3% in 2020 (Figure 3.9.9).

The main risk to the outlook would be spillover from worsening trade friction. Full-blown escalation of the US–PRC trade conflict seems to mean the imposition by both economies of 25% blanket tariffs on all merchandise imports and, between the US and its trade partners globally, additional 25% tariffs on trade in automobiles and their parts and components. If this worse-case scenario occurs—and if Hong Kong, China sees half of its trade affected by the conflict—export growth is likely to fall by 0.2 percentage points, and GDP growth could lose an estimated 0.1 percentage points. Further, domestic demand, while still solid, may eventually succumb to heightened external uncertainties and weaker asset markets this year and next.

The other main risk would be an abrupt and steep increase in US interest rates, which could push up local interest rates. Tighter local monetary conditions would deepen the fall in residential property prices, which is already a downside domestic risk, and add to the debt burden, thus further weakening domestic demand. Nevertheless, Hong Kong, China remains well positioned to withstand external headwinds and counter these risks, buffered by ample fiscal reserves and benefiting from prudent economic management and a sound financial system.

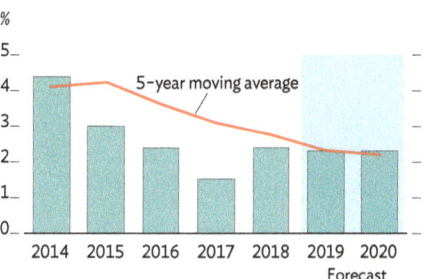

3.9.8 Inflation

Source: *Asian Development Outlook* database.

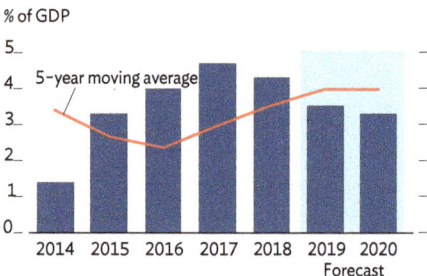

3.9.9 Current account balance

Source: *Asian Development Outlook* database.

Policy challenge—sustaining labor supply as the population ages

Hong Kong, China has a population that is aging more rapidly than in many other developed economies, including Japan, as fertility remains low and life expectancy rises. The Census and Statistics Department projects the share of the elderly in the population to nearly double from 17.9% in 2018 to 31.9% in 2038, while the shares of those aged 18–64 and under 18 both decrease (Figure 3.9.10). According to the International Monetary Fund, the rapidly increasing old age dependency ratio—defined as the ratio of residents drawing retirement benefits to working-age residents—can double public health spending, from the equivalent of 2.9% of GDP in 2016 to 6.0% in 2050, and spending on pensions, from 1.8% of GDP in 2015 to 3.9% in 2050. These projections indicate that population aging threatens to lower potential GDP growth by 0.75 percentage points annually, on average, during 2020–2050, putting further pressure on revenue and the fiscal balance.

Given the social implications, there is limited scope to gradually consolidate spending or raise adequate additional revenue to stem the demographic push toward structural deficits. The other main policy instruments available to the authorities for this purpose are to raise the rate of labor force participation and support innovation that keeps the elderly healthy and productive. There is certainly scope for raising female participation in the labor force, which, at 65% for ages 15–64 in 2017, was about 15 percentage points lower than for males. This gap can be narrowed through a range of actions: increased support for child care, more affordable child and after-school care, and the promotion of flexible work arrangements and part-time employment. The government has already embarked on policies that aim to retain older workers and thereby slow labor force depletion. As part of this policy, the Labor Department expanded its employment program for the middle aged by providing subsidies to employers that hire the unemployed or retirees aged above 60. In addition, the authorities are studying interventions successfully undertaken in Japan and Singapore: employer subsidies, support for creating short-term and flexible jobs, and statutory protection against age discrimination.

The government should also consider adaptive technologies that help counter the downside effects of an aging workforce. Such technologies allow people to work from home, help make the workplace more ergonomically correct and supportive, and facilitate medical advances that contribute to longevity and working lives that are longer and more productive. Yet other channels—through which technology can help seniors adapt and build their job skills, allowing them to be retained or brought back into the workforce—are advances in cloud-based job matching services and customized interactive training services, such as remote and virtual education and training for the elderly. Training programs should be developed for businesses to improve their management of age diversity and human resources.

The government should actively embrace labor market technological innovations more broadly and support them by funding research and development. The aim should be to develop human capital and resources with better skills, particularly in science, technology, engineering, and mathematics, especially in industries attuned to the current demographic shifts. With the work dependency ratio in steep ascent, now is the time to act decisively to accommodate these demographic changes and mitigate their negative impacts on the economy.

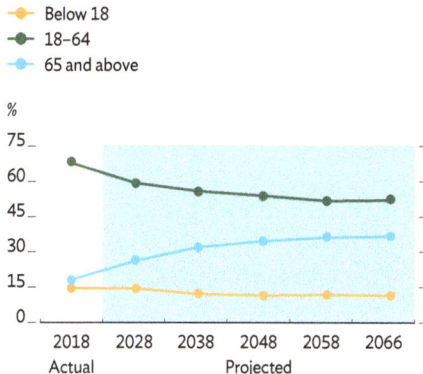

3.9.10 Population share by age group

Sources: Demographic Statistics Section, Census and Statistics Department; Wong, K. and M. Yeung. 2019. Population Ageing Trend of Hong Kong. *Economic Letter 2019/02*. Office of the Government Economist.

Mongolia

Economic recovery continued in 2018, buoyed by mining investment and higher output in services and industry. Growth should extend into 2019 and 2020, albeit at a declining rate, on strong domestic demand. Inflation will accelerate in 2019 before slowing again in 2020, and the current account deficit will narrow in 2019 before widening in 2020. The use of natural resource revenue can be enhanced, and sustainable development assured, through better financial management.

Economic performance

Growth quickened from 5.3% in 2017 to 6.9% in 2018 on expansion in manufacturing and services and strong investment in mining (Figure 3.10.1). Benefiting from a 55.8% rise in credit and rising demand for transport services to carry mineral exports, services contributed 3.2 percentage points to growth. Industry added 2.8 points, boosted by 15.7% growth in manufacturing and despite a slump in residential construction. Growth recovered in mining on stronger gold and coal production but remained moderate. Agriculture recovered from drought in 2017 to add 0.9 percentage points to growth as crop harvests improved sharply and livestock production rose moderately.

On the demand side, investment—buoyed by a 29.2% increase in foreign direct investment (FDI), mainly into mining—increased by 27.2%, contributing 10.0 percentage points to growth (Figure 3.10.2). Consumption contributed a more modest 2.3 points, almost entirely derived from an increase in private consumption driven by rising credit. Exports rose by 15.3% as coal shipments grew despite logistical bottlenecks at the border with the People's Republic of China (PRC). However, as imports rose by 21.4%, driven by increased FDI-financed mining inputs and a surge in car imports to beat anticipated credit tightening in 2019, net exports subtracted 5.4 points from growth.

Average consumer price inflation rose from 4.3% in 2017 to 6.8%, driven mostly by tight supply (Figure 3.10.3). Food prices increased because drought affected crop production in 2017, and meat exports increased substantially despite lower meat production. Prices for heating coal rose sharply in anticipation of a ban on the sale of raw coal in May 2019, and a higher excise tax pushed up prices for alcoholic beverages and tobacco.

This chapter was written by Declan Magee of the Mongolia Resident Mission, ADB, Ulaanbaatar.

3.10.1 Supply-side contributions to growth

Source: National Statistics Office of Mongolia. 2019. *Monthly Statistical Bulletin.* February. http://www.nso.mn.

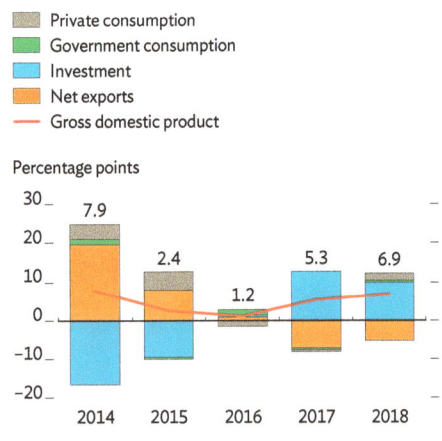

3.10.2 Demand-side contributions to growth

Source: National Statistics Office of Mongolia. 2019. *Monthly Statistical Bulletin.* February. http://www.nso.mn.

Budget revenue surged to equal 31.3% of GDP on increased receipts from value-added tax and social insurance, while expenditure increased modestly to 28.7%, yielding a surplus equal to 2.6% of GDP after 5 straight years of deficits (Figure 3.10.4). Interest payments on government bonds fell from 12.9% of expenditure in 2017 to 11.4% thanks to debt clearance and concessional lending from development partners. Public debt including the foreign liabilities of the Bank of Mongolia, the central bank, fell from the equivalent of 99.2% of GDP in 2017 to 86.2% as fiscal policy tightened and included a freeze on the issuance of government domestic bonds (Figure 3.10.5).

Broad money surged by 22.8% in 2018 as credit to households grew by 52.6% in anticipation of tighter credit controls in 2019 and as interest rates on loans continued to slide along with a 1.0 percentage point cut in the central bank base rate in early 2018, which followed a 2.0-point cut in 2017. In response to mounting pressure on the Mongolian togrog, the central bank hiked its base rate by 1.0 point in November 2018. Concerns about rising household indebtedness further prompted the central bank to impose restrictions on the granting of bank loans, effective in 2019. The nonperforming loan ratio jumped from 8.5% of all loans in December 2017 to 10.4% a year later, bringing the capital shortfall in the banking sector to 3.1% of GDP (Figure 3.10.6).

The current account deficit widened to 14.6% of GDP in 2018 as deficits in services and net income—reflecting higher transport and insurance costs for imports and dividend payments to foreign investors—outweighed the merchandise trade surplus (Figure 3.10.7). Gross reserves rose by $500 million in 2018 to equal 5 months of imports, boosted by international bond issues and FDI inflows. The togrog depreciated against the US dollar by 1.1% on average in 2018 and by 8.9% in the year to the end of 2018.

Economic prospects

Growth is forecast to slow to 6.7% in 2019 and 6.3% in 2020 (Figure 3.10.8). Domestic demand fueled by a more accommodative fiscal policy will support growth in 2019. After 2 years of fiscal consolidation, government spending will increase by 19.0% under the 2019 budget. FDI into mining will remain important, but will not increase as much as last year, making its contribution to growth statistically less pronounced. Net exports will continue to drag on growth but at a declining rate as export growth outpaces import growth. Coal exports will benefit from a gradual switch in the PRC away from more expensive processed coal from Australia, while high gold inventories in Mongolia are expected to encourage higher exports in 2019.

On the supply side, services will be key to growth, with transport expected to gain from growth in mining exports. Manufacturing will also benefit from mining growth and from

3.10.3 Inflation and exchange rate

Source: Bank of Mongolia. http://www.mongolbank.mn.

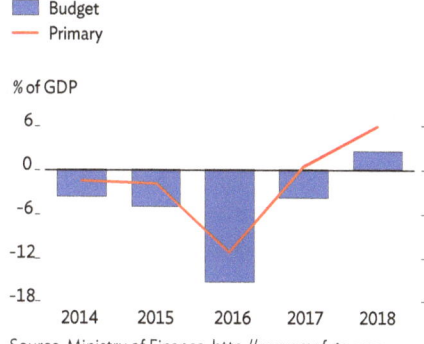

3.10.4 Fiscal balance

Source: Ministry of Finance. http://www.mof.gov.mn.

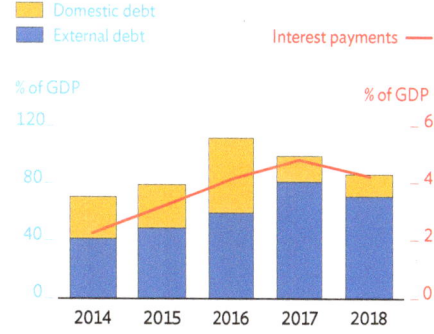

3.10.5 Public debt

Note: Includes Bank of Mongolia foreign liabilities.
Sources: Ministry of Finance. http://www.mof.gov.mn; Bank of Mongolia. http://www.mongolbank.mn.

expanded processing of meat for export. Construction growth will recover, boosted by a large public investment program in 2019, but moderate in 2020 with some retrenchment expected in public investment. Agriculture will continue to recover in 2019, assuming adequate rainfall and mild winter weather, but will expand more slowly in 2020.

Average inflation will reach 8.5% in 2019 on rising domestic demand supported by higher government expenditure, as well as the effects of togrog depreciation and higher fuel prices in the second half of 2018 (Figure 3.10.9). These effects will be less pronounced in 2020 as public expenditure eases and the pass-through of depreciation wanes, allowing inflation to stabilize at 7.5%.

The 2019 budget is expected to record a primary surplus equal to 1.0% of GDP and an overall deficit at 1.4% of GDP because of a large increase in government capital and election-related spending. Revenue growth, which was high in 2017 and 2018, is expected to moderate but could benefit from any of the upside risks to the growth outlook. The budget deficit is likely to shrink in 2020 as expenditure subsides in the aftermath of the elections.

The current account deficit will narrow to equal 9.6% of GDP in 2019 as exports grow, in particular on anticipated large increases in gold shipments, and as car imports slow under tighter credit. The deficit in services will remain elevated in both years. The current account deficit will widen again to 13.0% of GDP in 2020 as export growth slows and import demand remains steady.

Mongolia is vulnerable to exogenous shocks owing to a depleted Fiscal Stability Fund and low official international reserves. Slower growth in the PRC caused by trade tensions with the US could squeeze Mongolia's mineral exports with lower prices and perhaps reduced volume. Further, continuing logistical challenges at the PRC border may slow mineral exports. Domestically, the 2020 parliamentary elections could apply political pressure to loosen fiscal and monetary policies, which would weigh on the exchange rate and put the country's scant reserves at risk, though a program agreed with the International Monetary Fund (IMF) would act as a counterbalance. Despite progress in bank recapitalization, continuing bank fragility poses a risk to economic health. As always, commodity price fluctuations present risks to the forecast in both directions, while rising FDI for new projects presents an upside risk.

Policy challenge—better use of natural resource revenue through improved financial management

Mongolia derives almost a quarter of its fiscal revenue directly from mining, with other revenue streams closely correlated with it. To strengthen its management of the sector, Mongolia

3.10.1 Selected economic indicators (%)

	2019	2020
GDP growth	6.7	6.3
Inflation	8.5	7.5
Current account balance (share of GDP)	-9.6	-13.0

Source: ADB estimates.

3.10.6 Banking indicators

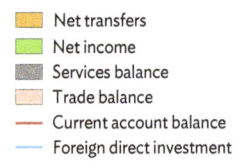

Q = quarter.
Source: Bank of Mongolia. http://www.mongolbank.mn.

3.10.7 External indicators

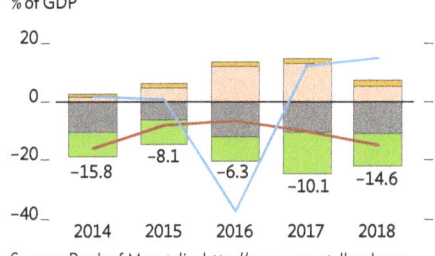

Source: Bank of Mongolia. http://www.mongolbank.mn.

has established state-owned enterprises, enacted fiscal rules, created several extra-budgetary funds to manage mineral revenues (the Fiscal Stability Fund, the Future Heritage Fund, and, soon to close, the Human Development Fund), and established a system of distributing mineral revenue to subnational governments.

However, the original intent of these initiatives has not always been honored, and fiscal rules were abandoned when commodity prices fell after 2012. The Human Development Fund was used for universal social transfers and accumulated large debts. The Law on Government Special Funds was amended in 2016 and 2017 to allow withdrawals from the Fiscal Stability Fund to cover the budget deficit until 2023. The Fiscal Stability Law, enacted in 2010 to smooth fiscal expenditure and create precautionary savings, has been undermined by 12 amendments to allow larger deficits as off-budget and quasi-fiscal spending rose substantially. Further, fiscal expenditure has been pro-cyclical, fluctuating in line with coal and copper prices, running up public debt and proliferating public investment projects that are not always viable (Figure 3.10.10).

Under the program with the IMF, public finances have stabilized and growth has recovered. However, the recovery is fragile, debt-servicing costs are still high, and Mongolia remains vulnerable to fluctuations in commodity prices. The government should respond to these challenges and set the stage for more effective use of mineral resources, not by creating new funds, but by strengthening public financial management more broadly. This will become even more crucial as major mining investments advance toward their production stage, mineral revenues consequently rise, and debt service payments moderate with the implementation of the IMF stabilization program.

Crucial steps toward better public financial management include bringing all spending on budget and creating a stronger fiscal base that reduces dependence on commodity prices by, for example, amending excise and income taxes. The government should implement the recommendations of a 2015 World Bank report on public financial management performance, notably requiring all government entities to follow budgetary procurement procedures. It should also ensure the effective functioning and independence of the new Fiscal Stability Council, which is tasked with ensuring compliance with the Fiscal Stability Law and fiscal sustainability rules, by providing security of tenure to its members, sufficient staff and financing, and the political independence of its members. To enhance accountability, revenue projections should be strengthened and budgetary information better disseminated to the public. Investment plans should be closely aligned with national development plans, and project evaluation should be improved, to ensure that projects offer value for money and are properly implemented.

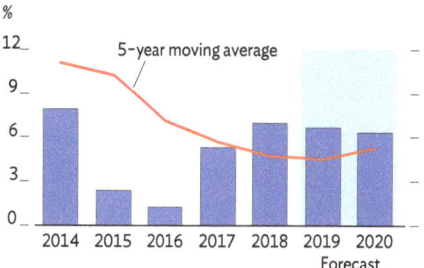

3.10.8 GDP growth

Source: Asian Development Outlook database.

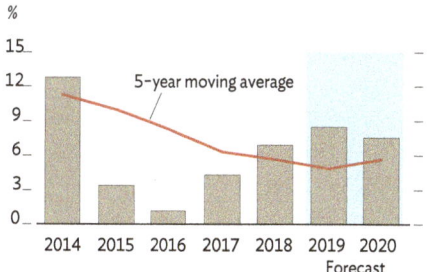

3.10.9 Inflation

Source: Asian Development Outlook database.

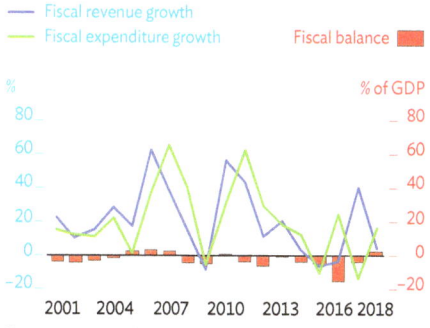

3.10.10 Fiscal indicators

Source: National Statistics Office. NSO Annual Yearbook. December NSO Bulletin.

People's Republic of China

Growth decelerated in 2018, weighed down by efforts to control risk in the financial sector, a tighter fiscal policy in the first half of the year, housing market restrictions, and uncertainty in the global trade environment. Growth will moderate further in 2019 and 2020 as global growth slows. Inflation will remain benign as the current account edges into deficit. Social security reform can help rebalance the economy toward consumption.

Economic performance

The People's Republic of China (PRC) saw growth slow from 6.8% in 2017 to 6.6% in 2018, in line with the government's growth target of around 6.5% (Figure 3.11.1). On the demand side, consumption confirmed its role as the main driver of growth by contributing 5.0 percentage points, up from 3.9 points in 2017 (Figure 3.11.2). Consumption found support in a rapid increase in government social spending, a cut in personal income tax, and solid growth in household disposable income, though it softened somewhat in the fourth quarter (Q4). Real growth in household consumption expenditure accelerated from 5.4% in 2017 to 6.2% in 2018. However, while spending on services such as tourism and information technology kept increasing rapidly, real growth in retail sales of consumer goods decelerated from 8.5% in 2017 to 6.9% in 2018, owing mostly to a slump in car sales, but edged up in early 2019. Rural households' real income and consumption expenditure increased faster than those of urban residents thanks to growth in online shopping in rural areas and the government's Rural Vitalization Strategy, which boosts support for agricultural modernization, land reform, and financial services (Figure 3.11.3).

The contribution of investment to growth slipped to 2.1 percentage points in 2018 from 2.3 points in 2017 because of an infrastructure investment downturn as local governments tightly controlled expenditure, both on budget and off budget, in the first 9 months of 2018 (Figure 3.11.4). Growth in infrastructure investment plummeted from 19.0% in 2017 to 3.8% in 2018, though its declining trend reversed in Q4 of 2018, and growth continued in early 2019 as more projects were rolled out, financed mainly by a sharp increase in special bond issues by local governments. Growth in manufacturing investment doubled from 4.8% in 2017 to 9.5% in 2018 as supply side reform, notably industrial upgrades, continued and as

3.11.1 Economic growth

Q = quarter.
Sources: National Bureau of Statistics; ADB estimates.

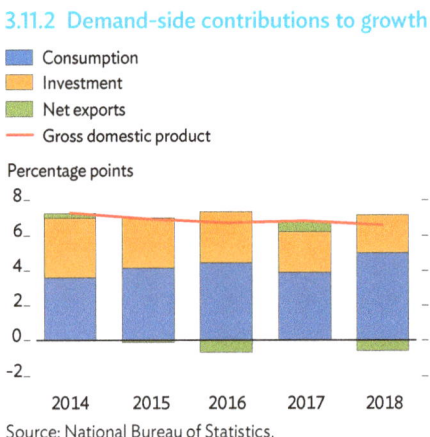

3.11.2 Demand-side contributions to growth

Source: National Bureau of Statistics.

This chapter was written by Dominik Peschel and Jian Zhuang of the People's Republic of China Resident Mission, ADB, Beijing.

exports grew quickly. Investment in high-tech manufacturing such as medical, electrical, and communication equipment kept growing at double-digit rates. Meanwhile, growth in real estate investment, comprising land purchases and new construction, increased from 7.0% in 2017 to 9.5% in 2018. This trend persisted in early 2019 as property sales continued to exceed new property completed and as floor space waiting for sale declined. Net exports dragged growth down by 0.6 percentage points in 2018, reversing a 0.6-point contribution in 2017, as merchandise imports outgrew exports.

On the supply side, services remained the main driver of growth, despite slowing from 7.9% growth in 2017 to 7.6% last year. Services contributed 3.9 percentage points to GDP growth, lifting the sector's share in GDP from 51.9% to 52.2% (Figure 3.11.5). Growth was strong in transport, leasing and commercial services, and information technology services, while financial and real estate services remained weak. The contribution to growth of industry including construction and mining remained unchanged at 2.4 percentage points as real growth in the sector moderated marginally from 5.9% in 2017 to 5.8% in 2018. Strong increases in consumer, high-tech, and export-oriented manufacturing partly offset deceleration in mining and raw materials, where retrenchment targets reined in production. Robust service sector growth helped edge down the unemployment rate in cities, determined using a recently instituted survey, from 5.0% in January to 4.9% in December 2018; as fluctuation continued, unemployment rose again to 5.3% in February 2019. At the same time, media reports pointed to a weakening job market for fresh graduates and migrant workers in line with decelerating growth. A poor grain harvest and the spread of pig disease decelerated agriculture growth from 4.0% in 2017 to 3.5% in 2018, but the sector's contribution to GDP growth remained unchanged at 0.3 percentage points given its small share in GDP.

In 2018, consumer price inflation averaged 2.1%, up from 1.6% in 2017 but softened at the beginning of 2019 (Figure 3.11.6). Spikes in food prices, mostly caused by weather, and pricier health care, education, and rent, were key drivers of inflation. Core consumer inflation, excluding food and energy, stayed modest at 1.9%, suggesting a steady underlying trend. Prices for newly constructed homes in the 70 largest cities were on average 7.0% higher than a year earlier as inventories continued to shrink, with price increases more pronounced in the second and third tiers of this group (Figure 3.11.7). Average housing prices accelerated further in early 2019. Producer price inflation softened significantly to 3.5% from 6.5% in 2017. While this reflected a base effect following an index spike in 2017 owing to substantial supply-side reform, the decline in the second half of 2018 derived as well from weaker industrial activity. With further moderation in industry, producer prices stayed virtually flat in January and February 2019.

3.11.3 Real growth in urban and rural household income and consumption expenditure

Q = quarter.
Sources: National Bureau of Statistics; ADB estimates.

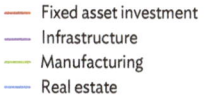

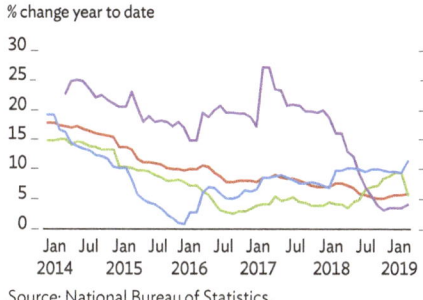

3.11.4 Growth in fixed asset investment

Source: National Bureau of Statistics.

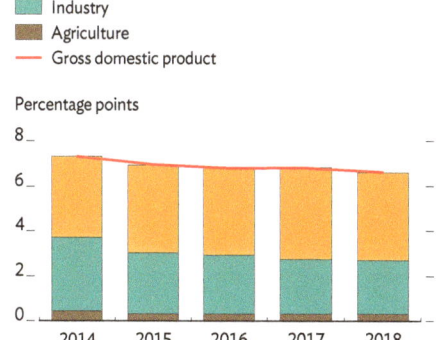

3.11.5 Supply-side contributions to growth

Sources: National Bureau of Statistics; ADB estimates.

Monetary policy became more accommodative in mid-2018 to temper and smooth the growth slowdown. Through cuts in the reserve requirement ratio and liquidity injections via medium-term lending facilities, the People's Bank of China, the central bank, lowered interbank interest rates in the second half of 2018 (Figure 3.11.8), while leaving unchanged benchmark 1-year lending and deposit rates. It eased the reserve requirement in several steps from April 2018 to January 2019, lowering it for large banks from 17.0% to 13.5%. Nevertheless, broad money (M2) growth remained at 8.1% in 2018, as in 2017.

Continued tightening of regulations on shadow banking caused it to contract, while outstanding bank loans were 12.7% higher by the end of 2018. The contraction in shadow bank financing slowed growth in outstanding social financing—a broad measure of credit that includes elements of shadow banking—from 13.4% in 2017 to 9.8% (Figure 3.11.9). Despite a rising corporate default rate and declining profits, bond issuance recovered in 2018 from a low base in 2017, and the value of corporate bonds outstanding grew by double digits.

Fiscal policy was tight in the first half of 2018 but loosened in the second half. Besides increases in special bond issues in August and September 2018, the government revised the personal income tax law to ease the tax burden on low- and middle-income earners. This cushioned moderation in private consumption in Q4 of 2018. Expansionary fiscal policy continued in Q4 as the revised personal income tax law went into effect on 1 October 2018 and the government strongly increased spending on rural infrastructure, employment, social security, and environmental protection. Growth in consolidated central and local government revenue slowed to 1.0% in second half of 2018, sharply down from 10.6% in the first half, while growth in consolidated fiscal budget expenditure increased from 7.8% to 9.5%. The on-budget deficit thus rose from the equivalent of 3.7% of GDP in 2017 to 4.2%, contributing to a rise in outstanding government debt (Figure 3.11.10). Actual government support to the economy should have been recorded as larger, as these figures exclude off-budget expenditure, which has been large in the past and was unlikely to have declined substantially in 2018.

External trade expanded in 2018. With exports to the US having profited from frontloaded orders in mid-2018, and despite some deceleration in both export and import growth in Q4, merchandise exports grew by 9.1% in 2018, or 7.1 percentage points less than import growth. The merchandise trade surplus shrank in 2018, and data for January–February 2019 signaled further trade deceleration. As the deficit in the service balance widened further in line with the rising trend in outgoing tourism in recent years, the current account surplus narrowed to 0.4% of GDP in 2018 from 1.4% in 2017 (Figure 3.11.11). At the same time, encouraged

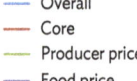
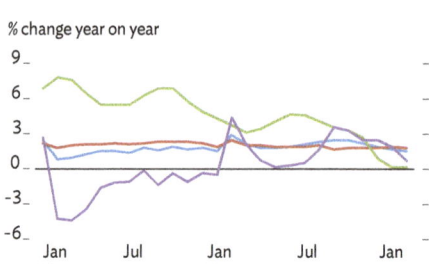

3.11.6 Monthly inflation

Source: National Bureau of Statistics.

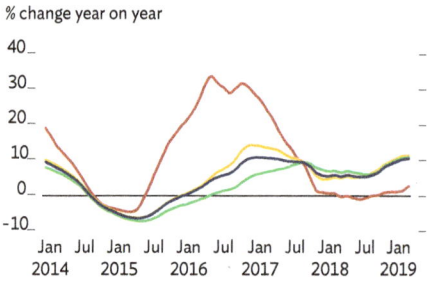

3.11.7 Price inflation for newly constructed residences

Note: Tier I includes 4 cities: Beijing, Guangzhou, Shanghai, and Shenzhen; Tier II includes 31 provincial capital cities, municipalities, and sub-provincial cities; Tier III includes 35 other cities.
Sources: National Bureau of Statistics; ADB estimates.

3.11.8 Policy and interbank interest rates

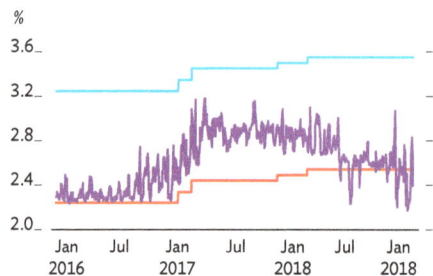

Sources: People's Bank of China; National Interbank Funding Center.

by more attractive investment conditions, inward foreign direct investment (FDI) increased by 21.0% in 2018, while FDI outflows declined owing to tighter controls. Net capital outflows excluding FDI but including errors and omissions are estimated to be virtually unchanged because the central bank reintroduced regulatory measures to curb them, as described in *ADO 2018 Update*. Official gross international reserves fell by $68 billion to stand at $3.2 trillion at the end of 2018.

The renminbi strengthened in 2018 by 1.2% in nominal effective terms (against a trade-weighted basket of currencies) and by 0.9% in real effective terms (taking inflation into account), while it weakened in nominal terms by 5.0% against the US dollar (Figure 3.11.12). Depreciation had multiple causes, including lost momentum in the domestic economy, uncertainty related to the trade conflict, a smaller current account surplus, and, as domestic interest rates declined while US rates rose, a narrower yield spread that had favored PRC bonds over US Treasuries. Amid ongoing trade talks, the renminbi rallied against the dollar in early 2019.

3.11.9 Growth of broad money, total social financing, bank loans, and shadow banking

— Broad money (M2)
— Total social financing
— Bank loans
— Shadow banking

Note: Shadow banking = entrusted loans + trust loans + banker's acceptance bills.
Sources: People's Bank of China; ADB estimates.

Economic prospects

The downward trend in GDP growth is expected to continue in 2019 and 2020 as uncertainty pertaining to trade tensions with the US continues to weigh on domestic consumption and investment, and as restrictions on shadow banking remain in place. Growth is expected to slow to 6.3% in 2019 and, reflecting ongoing efforts to contain risk in the financial sector, moderate a bit further to a more sustainable 6.1% in 2020 (Figure 3.11.13). Monetary and fiscal policy are expected to remain supportive, but no major stimulus is expected. The policy, which in the second half of 2018 aimed to prevent a sharp deceleration in growth but not to raise the growth rate, should continue. An agreement with the US in 2019 would limit adverse effects from the trade conflict and help revive consumer and investor sentiment. However, growth will be lower as ongoing restrictions on shadow banking continue to limit expansion in credit to the economy, albeit partly compensated by fiscal support.

On the demand side, consumption will remain the main driver of growth, though consumption growth is expected to moderate slightly in line with slowing growth in household income. Consumer staples are expected to hold up well, but discretionary consumer spending will likely remain subdued in the short run before recovering later in 2019. The expected gradual loosening in 2019 of local housing market restrictions will boost property-related consumer spending, supporting retail sales in late 2019 and 2020. Growth in disposable income will likely slow because the economic slowdown has started to affect the labor market. In this respect, cuts to personal income tax in October 2018 and higher allowances from January 2019

3.11.1 Selected economic indicators (%)

	2019	2020
GDP growth	6.3	6.1
Inflation	1.9	1.8
Current account balance (share of GDP)	0.0	−0.1

Source: ADB estimates.

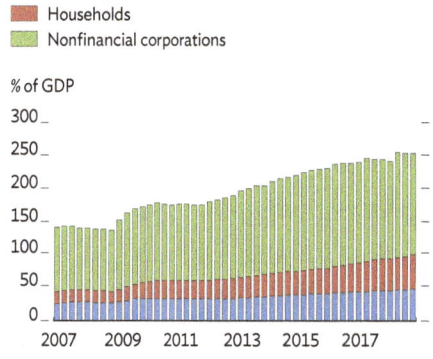

3.11.10 Debt structure

Sources: Bank of International Settlements; ADB estimates.

were timely policy measures to alleviate the adverse effect of anticipated weaker wage growth. Public spending in 2019 and 2020 is expected to be higher than in 2018, to support the economy.

Investment growth recovered in Q4 of 2018 on a sharp increase in infrastructure investment, which will continue under a higher quota for special bond issues in 2019. Government support for high technology and continued industrial upgrading should ensure that investment in manufacturing keeps growing but at a reduced rate as manufacturing profits decline, growth slows, and external trade loses its luster. Investment in real estate is expected to hold up well as housing market restrictions gradually loosen. Net exports are projected to continue to drag on growth in 2019 as the current account surplus wanes and edges into deficit in 2020.

On the supply side, services are expected to outgrow industry. Value added in financial services should grow solidly, driven by solid bank profits from expanded lending, while construction and services related to real estate will benefit from expected recovery in the housing market. Headwinds will likely moderate manufacturing growth, especially as trade growth slows in 2019, though government support will help high-tech manufacturing and innovative industries continue to grow rapidly. Mining is expected to suffer under lower commodity demand, given slower domestic and global growth, while upstream industries, especially steel and cement, are set to profit from rising construction of both infrastructure and housing. Agriculture is expected to grow steadily as in previous years.

The outlook for the labor market is less robust. Moderation in consumption growth and less dynamic foreign trade are expected to dampen demand for low-skilled and blue-collar workers. However, some companies, especially state-owned ones, may find it difficult to lay off workers, affecting their profitability. This could increase corporate debt in the form of bank credit and bond issues, as access to alternative financing, especially from shadow banks, will remain difficult (Figure 3.11.10).

Under declining domestic growth, lower global oil prices, a largely stable renminbi against the US dollar, and sharply lower producer prices, consumer price inflation will remain moderate, edging down from 2.1% in 2018 to 1.9% in 2019 and 1.8% in 2020 (Figure 3.11.14). Apart from potentially volatile food prices, spending on health remains the main driver of inflation. At the same time, reform to pharmaceutical procurement, currently planned on a trial basis, may be rolled out on a broader scale to contain medical costs. Producer prices may fall a bit further from their high base and even decline briefly, but they will stabilize as demand for construction materials rises under continued high infrastructure investment and the pickup in housing construction later in 2019.

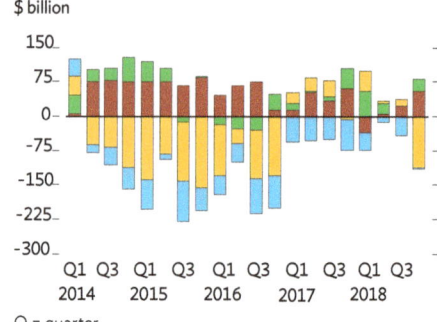

3.11.11 Balance of payments

Sources: State Administration of Foreign Exchange; ADB estimates.

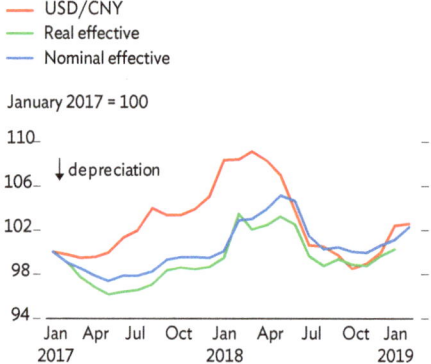

3.11.12 Renminbi exchange rates

Sources: Bank for International Settlements; People's Bank of China; ADB estimates.

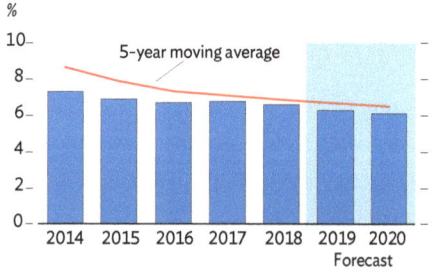

3.11.13 GDP growth

Source: Asian Development Outlook database.

Monetary policy is expected to become more accommodative. Data on new bank loans in January–February 2019 suggest a slight pickup in bank credit. At the same time, the monetary policy transmission mechanism has been undermined by banks' reluctance to lower lending rates as long as deposit rates remain unchanged. The central bank will continue to cut the reserve requirement ratio to ensure sufficient bank liquidity and keep interbank interest rates low, which should enable banks to lend on favorable terms to companies. In Q4 of 2018, following guidance from the central bank and the regulator, fewer loans were priced above the benchmark rate, driving down the weighted average of interest rates charged by banks (Figure 3.11.15). However, as long as deposit rates remain unchanged, banks will likely shy away from lowering their lending rates much further, partly because credit demand remains high as financing alternatives are drying up and partly because the risk of corporate default has increased as the economy slowed. Going forward, the central bank has room to lower benchmark 1-year lending and deposit rates, thereby reducing financing costs for the real economy while preserving banks' interest margin. Such loosening would benefit in particular highly indebted enterprises by lowering their interest payments.

State-owned and other larger companies enjoy better access to bank loans than do private small- and medium-sized enterprises (SMEs) because they generally offer better collateral, more transparency, and lower default rates. The central bank and financial regulator may therefore find it necessary to lean on banks to ensure that SMEs obtain credit at a reasonable cost. At the same time, while restrictions on shadow banking, the main alternative financing vehicle for SMEs, are expected to continue through 2019 and 2020, they may be relaxed to allow the volume of outstanding shadow credit to be reduced more gradually. While both measures support growth in the short run, they come at the potential cost of continued accumulation of risk pertaining to shadow banks and more nonperforming loans for banks.

Fiscal policy became more expansionary in the second half of 2018, especially with increased special bond issues, but any large fiscal stimulus remains unlikely as the government continues to try to stabilize debt. Going forward, some support will come from the government. A cut in the highest value-added tax rate from 16% to 13%, and in the next highest rate from 10% to 9%, was approved at the National People's Congress in March 2019. The direct effect of the tax cut on growth will likely be modest as only companies in markets with fierce competition will pass on the lower rates to customers. Further, given slowing economic growth, most firms are expected to save the extra revenue instead of investing it. However, as growth in tax revenue slows along with the economy, these cuts will

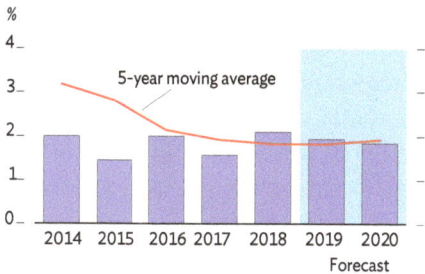

3.11.14 Inflation

Source: Asian Development Outlook database.

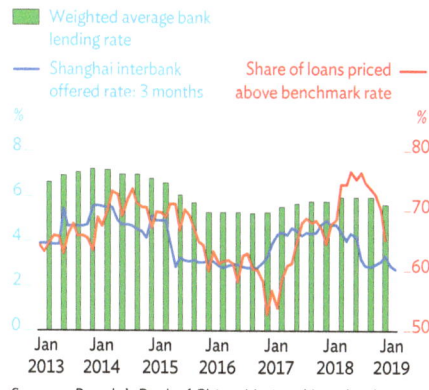

3.11.15 Bank loan and interbank interest rates

Sources: People's Bank of China; National Interbank Funding Center.

put additional pressure on the budget, limiting the increase in public spending, especially for local governments, which receive half of the value-added tax collected but are not allowed to raise taxes or issue public debt without central government approval. The deficit in the consolidated budget, at 4.2% in 2018, is expected to be higher in both 2019 and 2020. Local and central government debt alike are expected to increase in both years.

To sustain a revival in infrastructure investment that started in Q4 of 2018, local governments have been authorized to continue issuing special bonds to finance infrastructure before the 2019 budget is finalized. The annual special bond quota will rise from CNY1.35 trillion in 2018 to CNY2.15 trillion. This quota will likely remain high in 2020 to enable local governments to reduce their off-budget financing for infrastructure.

The current account is forecast to be in balance in 2019. Merchandise exports are expected to decelerate in 2019 in the aftermath of frontloaded exports to the US in mid-2018, and in light of forecast slower growth in Europe, which will weaken demand for PRC exports. At the same time, imports are projected to grow much less than in 2018 with decelerating growth in domestic demand, and the widening of the service trade deficit is expected to slow in line with lower import growth and only a moderate rise in outbound tourism. In 2020, the current account is expected to cross into deficit as declining global growth hampers export demand while the service deficit persists.

Notwithstanding recent government steps to improve investment opportunities for foreigners, FDI inflows are projected to moderate slightly in the shadow of the trade conflict with the US and as supply chains consequently reorganize somewhat away from the PRC. FDI outflows will also be lower owing to tight capital controls and greater scrutiny of FDI inflows in the advanced economies. Inflows of capital will pick up as foreign investors continue to acquire PRC bonds and stocks to diversify their portfolios despite the narrowing spread between PRC and US bond yields (Figure 3.11.16). These inflows will help compensate for deterioration in the current account, while unregistered capital outflows are expected to remain moderate under strict capital controls.

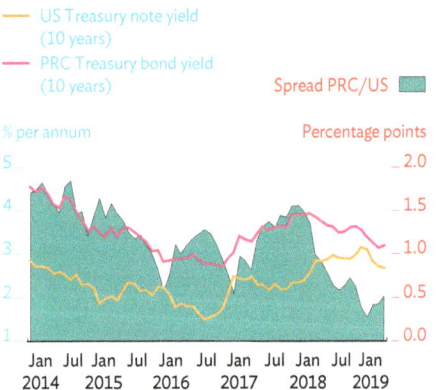

3.11.16 Spread between PRC and US treasury bond and note yields

PRC = People's Republic of China, US = United States.
Note: Yields are period average of monthly yields.
Sources: National Interbank Funding Center; Federal Reserve Board; ADB estimates.

The forecast is subject to external uncertainties and domestic risks. The main downside international risk is any intensification of the trade conflict with the US in the absence of a durable deal. This could have spillover effects, damaging investor and consumer sentiment. On the upside, a comprehensive trade deal that covers intellectual property rights protection, technology transfer, market access, and the role of state-owned enterprises, though unlikely, would assuage uncertainty and provide a more stable external environment. A domestic downside risk is that policy makers see measures to stabilize growth as insufficient, abandon efforts to stabilize lending, and/or loosen restrictions on shadow banking, thereby allowing nonbank financing to reaccelerate and debt to balloon. Such measures would boost growth in the short run but endanger financial stability over the longer term. Sustaining growth in the PRC depends instead on continued efforts to control financial leverage and on accelerated structural reform.

Policy challenge—reforming social security contributions

Since the PRC shifted its growth model toward higher domestic consumption during the global financial crisis of 2008–2009, consumption has become the main contributor to growth, fueled by solid increases in household income (Figure 3.11.17). However, private consumption is likely to face headwinds as the economy slows, the job market weakens, and wage growth decelerates. The government reinforced its support for private consumption when it introduced personal income tax reform comprising new tax brackets and a higher standard allowance effective on 1 October 2018, with more specific additional deductions effective on 1 January 2019. It is debatable, though, that such policies can sustainably raise household consumption to support growth and bring about economic rebalancing. The potential for more consumer spending in the PRC is limited by a high savings rate largely necessitated by a social safety net that is much weaker than in the advanced economies.

In the medium term, enhancing the social security system remains pivotal to lowering households' precautionary savings, provided that it is carried out in a manner that avoids causing unemployment and strengthens job growth. Higher unemployment would undermine consumption, especially because the social safety net remains weak. With this concern in mind, the National People's Congress approved in March 2019 a rate cut for employers' contributions to pension funds, lowering it from 19%–20% of the wage bill to 16%. While this was a step in the right direction, other anomalies remain. First, pension contribution rates are set by each province and vary from 14% in Zhejiang and Guangdong to 19%–20% in most other provinces (though capped at 16% from May 2019, following the recent decision). Moreover, these contributions are pooled within provinces. These features limit the transferability of pensions nationwide and probably hinder labor mobility. According to the Thirteenth Five-Year Plan, 2016–2020, pension contributions should be pooled nationwide by 2020. Attaining this goal may prove challenging. Pooling has been hampered by slow progress in standardizing contribution rates and because richer provinces see national pooling as redistribution. Yet addressing the problems of underreporting and nationwide pooling are essential to enhance efficiency and create room to lower nominal contribution rates.

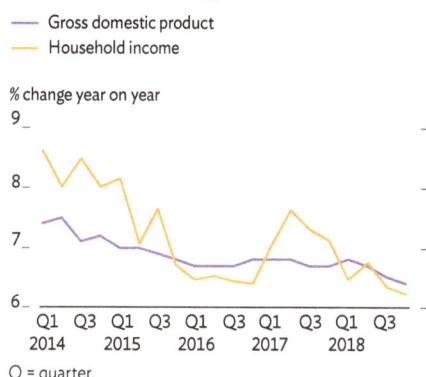

3.11.17 Real household income growth and real GDP growth

Q = quarter.
Sources: National Bureau of Statistics; ADB estimates.

A second important step toward improving the social security system as a whole would be to address the following inefficiencies in the collection of social security contributions (SSCs), which include contributions not only to pensions but also to cover medical care, unemployment, maternity, and work-related injury (Figure 3.11.18). High statutory SSC rates and the way they are determined create incentives for employers to underpay contributions by underreporting salaries. PRC social security law requires both employers and employees to make SSCs. Employers, though, bear the significantly larger share. A flat SSC contribution rate, slightly different by province and locality, is applied to employees' gross salaries. With the latest cut to the pension component of SSCs, the national average rate for employers has dropped to 30%—still nearly double the 16% average in the 10 advanced economies in the Group of 20. The average contribution rate for employees is 11%, similar to the average in the same comparator group. Though an employee's salary in the previous year serves as the basis for SSCs, those employees earning below a threshold must pay a fixed minimum amount, and those earning above a threshold pay a fixed maximum amount. The lower threshold is generally set at 60% of the previous year's average local wage, and the top threshold at 300%.

To reduce their contributions, companies often underreport employee salaries to the social security administration, which cannot check the reports because it has no access to tax data. According to a 2018 white paper on social security, only 27% of surveyed enterprises paid the full SSC based on employees' actual salaries. Others either based payments on underreported employee salaries or paid the minimum contribution per employee. These practices suppress the effective rate of SSCs, including for pensions. To consolidate the SSC base before lowering the contribution rate, the government decided to transfer authority for SSC collection from the Ministry of Human Resources and Social Security to the State Taxation Administration, to which salaries are reported for tax purposes. This promised to make systematic underreporting more difficult. However, the transfer, which was to occur on 1 January 2019, was postponed in response to resistance from employers that feared having to pay higher contributions as a result. Despite such resistance, the transfer of authority should be pursued and speeded up to streamline the collection of SSCs.

Finally, the government should pay legacy costs that arise from obligations to retirees who became eligible for state pensions when the pension system was modified in 1997. To raise pension fund revenues toward financing these payments, the government should implement its plans to raise both the share of state-owned enterprise equity transferred to the pension fund, which currently stands at 10%, and the dividends state-owned enterprises pay out to their shareholders.

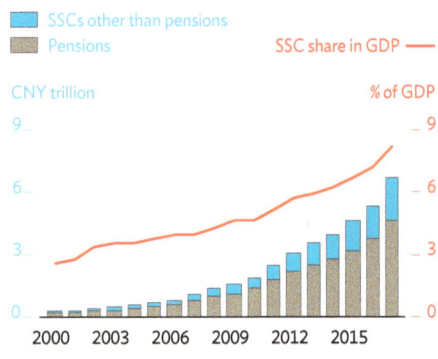

3.11.18 Social security contributions as a share of GDP

SSC = social security contribution.
Sources: Ministry of Human Resources and Social Security; ADB estimates.

Republic of Korea

Despite strong consumption and net exports, growth slowed in 2018. Contracting investment and moderating export growth, though countered by significant fiscal stimulus to sustain domestic demand and consumption, will pare GDP growth a bit further in 2019 and 2020. Inflation will remain tame, and the current account surplus will shrink slightly in both years but remain sizable. Invigorating youth entrepreneurship can address youth employment and spur broader economic dynamism.

Economic performance

GDP grew by 2.7% in 2018, down from 3.1% a year earlier and the slowest expansion in the past 6 years. Consumption and net exports each contributed 1.4 percentage points to GDP growth (Figure 3.12.1). Expenditure grew by 5.6%, propping up government consumption and providing the biggest impetus to growth. Private consumption rose by 2.8% as a 16.4% hike in the minimum wage outweighed the impact of a 3.8% increase in the unemployment rate as job creation plunged from 316,000 in 2017 to 97,000 last year.

Export growth in real terms doubled from 1.9% in 2017 to 4.0%, backed by strong sales of semiconductors, information technology products, and petrochemicals. Meanwhile, real growth in imports slowed from 7.0% in 2017 to 1.5% as demand softened for manufacturing inputs and as oil prices fell. Investment slumped, subtracting 0.1 percentage points from growth as the uncertain trade environment weighed on firms' investment plans and the government took measures to rein in speculative property development. Machinery investment plunged from 14.6% growth in 2017 to 1.7%, and construction investment shrank by 4.0% as capital gains taxes on multiple homes and property taxes were raised, and as plans were announced to establish anti-speculation zones in Seoul.

On the supply side, services drove economic expansion as the sector growth rate accelerated from 2.2% in 2017 to 2.9% and contributed 1.7 percentage points to GDP growth in 2018 (Figure 3.12.2). Growth in industrial output slowed sharply from 4.6% in 2017 to 2.5% as demand softened globally and locally, industries outside of semiconductors such as shipping restructured, input costs rose, and construction slowed.

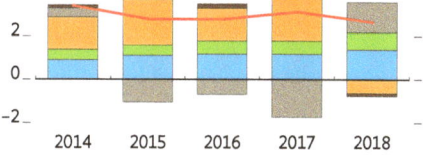

3.12.1 Demand-side contributions to growth

Source: Bank of Korea, Economics Statistics System. http://ecos.bok.or.kr (accessed 5 February 2019).

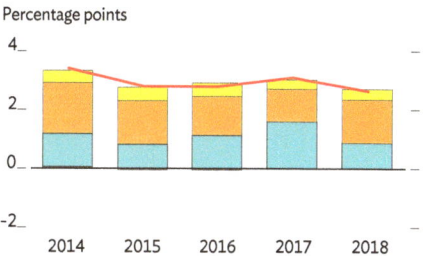

3.12.2 Supply-side contributions to growth

Source: Bank of Korea, Economics Statistics System. http://ecos.bok.or.kr (accessed 5 February 2019).

This chapter was written by Cindy Castillejos-Petalcorin and Donghyun Park of the Economic Research and Regional Cooperation Department, ADB, Manila.

The contribution of industry to growth fell to 1.0 percentage point. Agriculture recovered to 1.4% growth with favorable weather and higher livestock production.

Inflation was subdued by weak domestic demand and a dismal job market. Reflectingr slower economic activity, consumer price inflation decelerated from 1.9% in 2017 to 1.5% last year, falling further below the official target of 2.0% set by the Bank of Korea, the central bank (Figure 3.12.3). Inflation climbed to 2.0% year on year in September, mainly on higher food prices, and remained stable in the following 2 months, but decelerated again to 1.3% in December as food prices stabilized and housing prices retreated when policies to cool an overheating property market came into effect. Core inflation, which excludes food and energy prices, remained stable at 1.2%.

The central bank maintained an accommodative monetary stance in 2018, motivated by tepid inflation and weakening domestic demand. However, it did raise its benchmark interest rate once, by 25 basis points to 1.75% on 30 November 2018, in response to an increase in the US federal funds rate. Broad money (M2) growth accelerated from 5.1% in 2017 to 6.7% even as household credit expansion slowed with the cooling of the property market (Figure 3.12.4).

Fiscal policy also remained largely accommodative in 2018. A $3.6 billion supplementary budget was introduced that boosted business subsidies and aimed to reduce youth unemployment. Budgetary revenue decreased, however, as a tax on car purchases was lowered from 5.0% to 3.5% and as fuel taxes were cut by 15% in November. The budget and the supplementary budget together recorded a deficit equal to 0.1% of GDP, compared with a deficit of 1.1% in 2017, and sovereign debt rose from the equivalent of 38.2% of GDP in 2017 to 38.6%.

Following a 20-year trend, the current account registered a surplus in 2018, but the surplus fell to 4.6% of GDP from 4.9% the year before as merchandise exports grew less strongly than merchandise imports. Inbound foreign direct investment increased by 14.2% to a record high of $38.9 billion in 2018, and the surplus in the overall balance of payments boosted official foreign reserves to $404.6 billion at the end of the year. The won appreciated by 2.6% on average against the US dollar in nominal terms and by 1.4% in real effective terms (against a trade-weighted basket of currencies and taking inflation into account).

Economic prospects

Growth will slow to 2.5% in 2019 and 2020 in line with lower export growth (Figure 3.12.5). Waning confidence is indicated by declines in the Nikkei purchasing managers' index for 4 consecutive months to 47.2 in February 2019 (Figure 3.12.6).

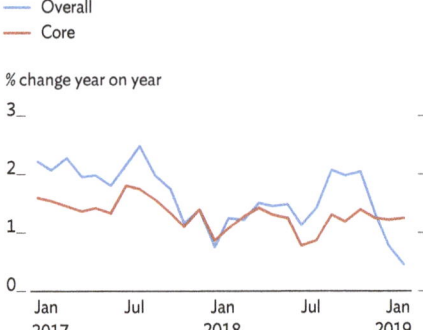

3.12.3 Monthly inflation

Source: CEIC Data Company (accessed 14 February 2019).

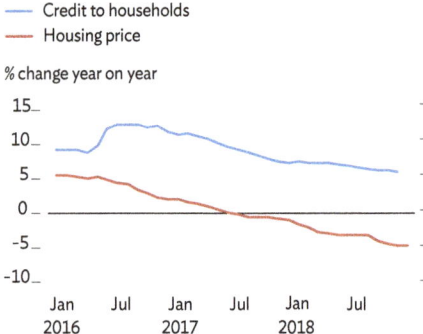

3.12.4 Credit to households and household price

Note: Housing price is the deposit for a 2-year lease on an apartment under the *jeonse* system.
Source: CEIC Data Company (accessed 14 February 2019).

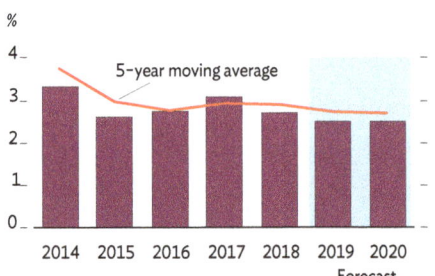

3.12.5 GDP growth

Source: *Asian Development Outlook* database.

Progress in trade negotiations between the US and the People's Republic of China (PRC) is seen to help stabilize falling consumer and business confidence in the coming months but may not restore export momentum as growth in the PRC continues to moderate and as world trade growth decelerates. Any positive impact from a renegotiated free trade agreement between the US and the Republic of Korea (ROK) is similarly overshadowed by global trends.

The strong performance by exports in 2018 will not be repeated this year or next because of softening external demand. The global information technology business cycle is heading into a slowdown and could undermine semiconductor exports, the largest ROK export category, accounting for nearly 21% of merchandise exports. Shipments of semiconductors are already falling, as have new export orders from Germany, Japan, and the PRC. Import growth will be lower this year and next, reflecting weaker domestic demand and lower world oil prices. However, the deficit in the service account will narrow on higher tourist arrivals. On balance, the sizeable current account surplus will shrink slightly in the next 2 years to equal 4.1% of GDP in 2019 and 3.9% in 2020.

Growth in private consumption, which provides almost half of GDP, will likely falter under weak employment growth coupled with pessimism regarding economic prospects and rising household debt, which equaled 95% of GDP as of September 2018 (Figure 3.12.7). On the other hand, the government's target to create 150,000 jobs this year will, if achieved, improve household incomes. Public consumption will receive a boost from additional spending in the run-up to general elections in April 2020. Investment will likely remain subdued this year but recover slightly next year. Construction investment will continue to decline, albeit at a slower pace, as the government's efforts to cool the property market constrain growth. Public spending on the 5G telecommunications network and transport infrastructure should spur moderate growth in fixed investment.

Consumer price inflation remained tepid, rising by only 0.5% year on year in February 2019 as transport and communications prices declined. Headline inflation is forecast to edge down to 1.4% in 2019 and 2020, held down by falling international oil prices and softening domestic demand.

Monetary policy will remain broadly accommodative in 2019 and 2020, supporting growth while mitigating risks in the finance and property sectors. As the US Federal Reserve is planning interest rate hikes at a slower pace this year (with only two hikes now expected in 2019, down from three hikes projected earlier), and in the absence of any major shock, there will be no need for the central bank to increase interest rates. That should be welcomed in the ROK in light of the low growth rate forecast and high household debt.

3.12.6 Purchasing managers' index

Note: Nikkei, Markit.
Source: Bloomberg (accessed 14 March 2019).

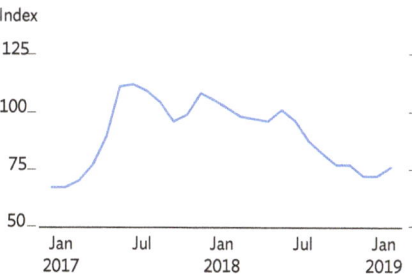

3.12.7 Consumer confidence

Note: A reading below 100 means that fewer consumers answered positively than negatively.
Source: Bank of Korea, Economics Statistics System. http://ecos.bok.or.kr (accessed 14 February 2019).

3.12.1 Selected economic indicators (%)

	2019	2020
GDP growth	2.5	2.5
Inflation	1.4	1.4
Current account balance (share of GDP)	4.1	3.9

Source: ADB estimates.

Indeed, given the sluggish job market, and the expected completion of the US monetary tightening cycle, monetary policy is likely to become more accommodative toward the end of 2019.

In a renewed effort to revitalize the economy, the 2019 budget authorizes $420 billion in expenditure—equal to 24.8% of GDP, 11.6% higher than in the 2018 budget and the biggest increase since 2009—to fund health, welfare, and education programs and lend support to local governments (Figure 3.12.8). Revenue will expand by 6.3% with corporate and other tax hikes. This will leave budget deficits equal to 1.8% of GDP in 2019 and 2.3% in 2020, nudging up government debt to the equivalent of 40.2% of GDP at the end of next year.

Upside risks to the outlook include growth in the global economy and the PRC that exceeds expectations, a successful resolution of the US–PRC trade dispute, and an improving relationship with the Democratic People's Republic of Korea. However, most risks are on the downside. Moderating growth globally—and especially the slowdown in the PRC, the largest trade partner of the ROK—will weigh on growth. Worsening protectionism and the unresolved trade dispute between the PRC and the US will hurt ROK exports, given their place in Asian supply chains. Another risk could be unexpected financial instability in emerging markets in response to monetary tightening in major economies as central banks continue to normalize their policies throughout 2019 and 2020. The principal domestic risks to the outlook are high household debt, which may dampen consumption more than forecast, and the possibility that with the higher minimum wage and a shorter work week, local companies may be unwilling to hire new workers, worsening unemployment from its already high rate in January (Figure 3.12.9).

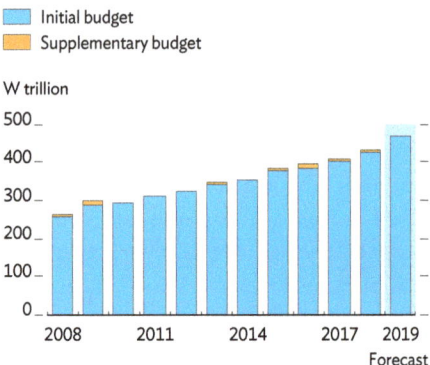

3.12.8 Fiscal spending, 2008–2019

Source: Ministry of Economy and Finance.

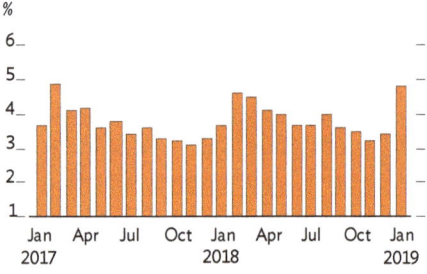

3.12.9 Unemployment rate

Source: CEIC Data Company (accessed 14 February 2019).

Policy challenge—revitalizing youth entrepreneurship

Weak entrepreneurship is viewed as contributing to the recent slowdown of growth in the ROK. Considered together with a rapidly aging population, this trend raises concern over the prospects for economic growth in the long term. However, demographic change aside, the ROK retains an abundance of youthful energy. As recent research by Edward Lazear shows, youthful countries tend to be entrepreneurial. Fostering youth entrepreneurship is therefore key to catalyzing growth and to reducing youth unemployment, which has emerged in recent years as a major economic and social issue.

According to surveys by the Korea Institute of Startup & Entrepreneurship Development, entrepreneurship among those 29 years old and under is anemic. While the number of startups in the ROK rose by 6.4% in 2013–2015, youth startups plunged by 40.5%, and their share of the total dropped from 3.0% to 0.9%. The rate at which youth startups survive is significantly lower than the overall rate. Further, according to the Global Entrepreneurship Monitor, youth entrepreneurship in the ROK as a share of all startups nationally substantially lags behind other innovative economies such as Israel, the PRC, and the US (Figure 3.12.10). The Hyundai Research Institute reports that youth entrepreneurship in the ROK tends to be skewed toward wholesale and retail trade, accommodation, and restaurants, where entry barriers such as technological knowhow requirements are low but the potential to create high-quality jobs is limited. More broadly, self-employment in the ROK is trending down as a share of all youth employment.

These surveys reveal that limited access to finance remains the biggest challenge to youth entrepreneurship. The government has established various funds, including policy funds for youth entrepreneurship, to facilitate more access. It has taken other steps to create an environment that encourages private firms and financial institutions to discover, nurture, and invest in or acquire promising startups. These steps facilitated an increase by more than 10% per year in new private venture capital investments from 2011 to 2015, enabling more startups. Going forward, any initiatives and fiscal incentives that the government offers should be directed, to the extent possible, to the more innovative industries and activities, and to those that promise to create the most jobs.

Excessive regulation remains another major impediment to innovative entrepreneurship. In stark contrast with the US and the PRC, which enforce negative lists of activities and technologies closed to startups, the ROK has a more restrictive positive list that specifies only a few business activities and areas open to them. Without a fundamental overhaul of this stifling regulatory framework, innovative entrepreneurship is unlikely to put down roots in the ROK.

Regulations could be relaxed to allow, in particular, the establishment of "sandbox zones," in which youth entrepreneurs are free to develop new products and services and to experiment with fresh ideas, constrained by only minimal regulation. Policy support can be extended for youth entrepreneurs to venture abroad at an early stage of their enterprise development to get a sense of the global marketplace. Meanwhile, the successful transformation of science and technology universities in the US into vibrant cradles of youth entrepreneurship, such as the Martin Trust Center for Entrepreneurship at the Massachusetts Institute of Technology, can provide models for enhancing education in the ROK.

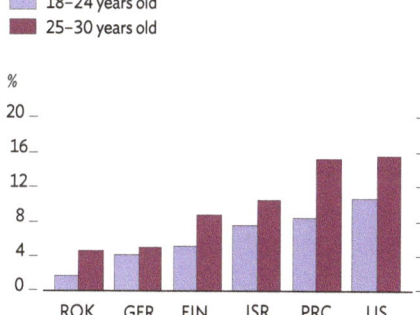

3.12.10 Total early stage entrepreneurial activity, 2016

ISR = Israel, FIN = Finland, GER = Germany, PRC = People's Republic of China, ROK = Republic of Korea, US = United States.

Note: Total entrepreneurial activity is the percentage of members of an age group that own or manage a business that is less than 42 months old.

Source: *Global Entrepreneurship Monitor 2017*.

Taipei,China

Softer external demand tamped down growth in 2018, and inflation remained low even as it doubled with higher food and transportation prices. Growth is expected to moderate further in 2019 and 2020 as global growth slows and business sentiment wanes. Inflation should trend down as oil prices moderate, and the current account surplus will shrink as export growth slows. Improving export competitiveness is essential for diversifying exports in terms of both products and destinations.

Economic performance

GDP growth moderated from 3.1% in 2017 to 2.6% in 2018 as export growth decelerated with softer external demand. Growth in exports to the People's Republic of China (PRC), which accounted for 28.8% of the total, slowed sharply from 20.4% in 2017 to 8.8%, while growth in exports to the US, the second biggest market, slowed to 7.5%, dragging total export growth down by more than half to 5.9%. Exports of manufactured goods and of machinery and transport equipment were especially hit, rising by only a fraction of their 2017 growth rate. As the decline in import growth was more moderate, from 12.5% in 2017 to 10.6% last year, net exports deducted 0.5 percentage points from GDP growth (Figure 3.13.1).

Domestic demand, in particular investment, was the engine of growth. Gross capital formation expanded by 6.1% in 2018, reversing a decline in 2017 and adding 1.3 percentage points to GDP growth as public infrastructure investment accelerated and spurred private investment. Consumption added 1.6 points to growth as government consumption recovered from a decline of 0.6% in 2017 to increase by 3.5% on election-related spending, but private consumption grew less than in 2017. The unemployment rate edged down from 3.8% in 2017 to 3.7%.

On the supply side, growth in services improved from 2.5% in 2017 to 2.6%, adding 1.6 percentage points to growth. It was sustained by tourist arrivals that rose by 3.0% in 2018 as a decline in arrivals from the PRC was offset by increases from Southeast Asia, Japan, and the US (Figure 3.13.2). Industry growth slowed as production for export moderated but still added 1.1 points to growth, while the contribution of agriculture was minimal.

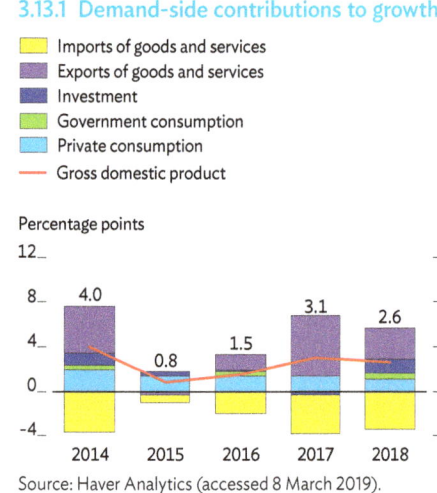

3.13.1 Demand-side contributions to growth

Source: Haver Analytics (accessed 8 March 2019).

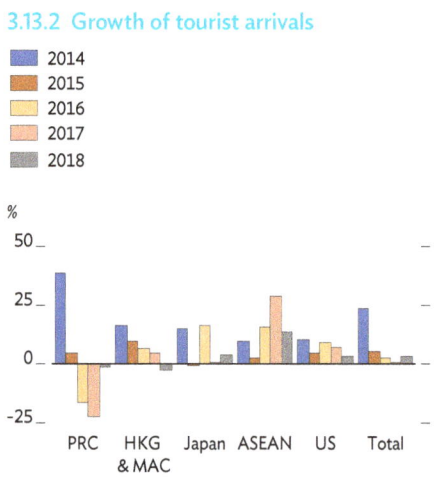

3.13.2 Growth of tourist arrivals

ASEAN = Association of Southeast Asian Nations, HKG = Hong Kong, China, MAC = Macau, China, PRC = People's Republic of China, US = United States.
Source: Haver Analytics (accessed 8 March 2019).

This chapter was written by Irfan Qureshi and Nedelyn Magtibay-Ramos of the Economic Research and Regional Cooperation Department, ADB, Manila.

Average inflation more than doubled to 1.3% in 2018 on rising prices for food, transportation, and communication (Figure 3.13.3). Core inflation, which excludes food and energy, also increased, from 0.7% in 2017 to 1.0%, and wholesale price inflation averaged 3.6%, pushed up from 2017 by higher prices for petroleum and wooden products, with sizable fluctuations during the year reflecting exchange rate movements.

The budget recorded a deficit equal to 0.3% of GDP in 2018, reversing a surplus of 0.1% of GDP in 2017 and pushing government debt to the equivalent of 31.0% of GDP. Revenue growth decelerated to 0.5%, while expenditure rose by 2.1%, mainly government investment under its Forward-looking Infrastructure Development Program, which is entirely debt financed.

The central bank kept its policy rate unchanged at 1.375% in 2018 as inflation remained moderate and economic growth slowed. Outstanding credit to the private sector rose by 5.4%, and net foreign assets in the banking system grew by 1.0%, but broad money growth slowed from 3.6% in 2017 to 2.7%.

The current account surplus narrowed from the equivalent of 14.4% of GDP in 2017 to 11.6% in 2018 as the trade surplus narrowed and net income receipts declined, and despite lower net service payments. Gross foreign exchange reserves grew by 2.3% in 2018. The local dollar appreciated by 0.9% against the US dollar, by 0.5% in nominal effective terms (against a trade-weighted basket of currencies), and by 0.7% in real effective terms (taking inflation into account) (Figure 3.13.4).

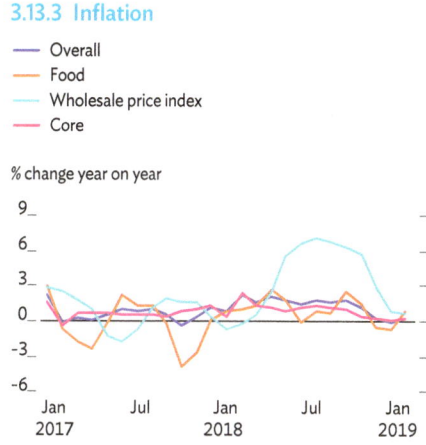

Source: CEIC Data Company (accessed 8 March 2019).

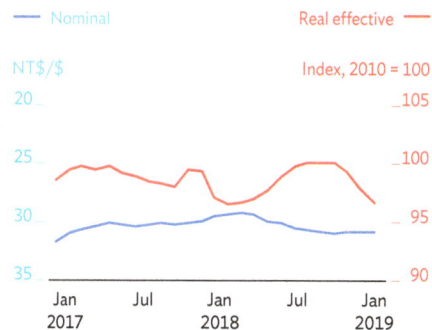

Source: Haver Analytics (accessed 8 March 2019).

Economic prospects

Economic expansion is expected to moderate this year and next, reflecting the impact of the global economic slowdown, trade tensions, and deteriorating business sentiment. The Nikkei manufacturing purchasing managers' index tumbled in January 2019 at its fastest pace in more than 3 years. GDP growth is therefore forecast at 2.2% in 2019 and 2.0% in 2020. Services will make the largest contribution to growth this year and next on the growing strength of tourism. Planned cuts to individual income tax may also boost consumption. Meanwhile, substantial investment growth in 2018 is expected to become tepid this year and next, though kept positive by outlays under the Forward-looking Infrastructure Development Program and recent government incentives for investors, such as income tax credits for 5G mobile networks and smart machinery investments.

Export growth is projected to moderate primarily in response to weakening global economic conditions and US–PRC trade tensions. Exports of semiconductors to the PRC, used as inputs for PRC products exported to the US, are particularly likely to be adversely affected. Imports of capital and intermediate goods are likely to remain modest, considering weakness in export demand, and overall import growth will slow further. On balance, net exports are expected to contribute little to GDP growth this year and next. The trade surplus is projected to trend downward, narrowing the current account surplus to the equivalent of 6.0% of GDP in 2019 and 2020, despite a likely increase in net receipts from services on continuing strength in inbound tourism.

Inflation is forecast to slow to 1.1% in 2019 in line with a gradual decline in oil prices and then edge up to 1.2% in 2020 as the currency weakens along with the current account. Given the tame inflation forecast, the central bank will likely keep its policy rate unchanged at least until the end of 2019.

The budget deficit is projected to shrink from the equivalent of 0.3% of GDP in 2018 to a mere 0.03% as revenue grows more than expenditure despite planned income tax reform. The outstanding debt of the central government has declined in recent years and is projected to equal 32.2% of GDP at the end of 2019, which is well below the 40.6% ceiling mandated by the Public Debt Act. As the debt is entirely domestic, there is little exchange rate risk.

Downside risks to the outlook are external threats, such as further worsening of global trade tensions or a deeper slowdown in the advanced economies and the PRC, which might reduce demand for exports. Tighter global financial conditions, in particular unexpectedly high interest rates in the US, could reduce capital flows into Taipei,China. Possessing ample fiscal reserves, however, Taipei,China is in a position to address threats as they materialize.

3.13.1 Selected economic indicators (%)

	2019	2020
GDP growth	2.2	2.0
Inflation	1.1	1.2
Current account balance (share of GDP)	6.0	6.0

Source: ADB estimates.

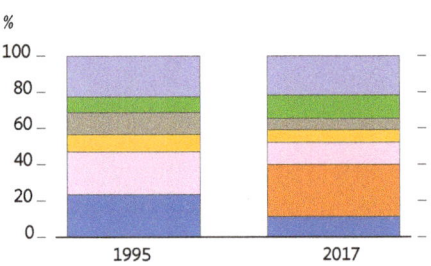

3.13.5 Main exports destinations, Taipei,China

ASEAN-5 = Indonesia, Malaysia, the Philippines, Thailand, and Viet Nam.
Source: Haver Analytics (accessed 8 March 2019).

Policy challenge—diversifying exports by raising competitiveness

Rising global trade tensions and the slowdown in the major industrial economies and the PRC pose significant risks for an export-oriented economy like Taipei,China. These vulnerabilities are accentuated by high concentration of exports in terms of both products and destinations. Data on export concentration in 1995 and 2017 show more than half of exports going to the top three export destinations: the PRC and then the US and Hong Kong, China (Figure 3.13.5). Data further show that the top five exported goods occupy a larger portion of total exports than in peer economies (Figure 3.13.6). Moreover, the number of products exported by Taipei,China has increased only marginally and has yet to catch up with the major industrial economies (Figure 3.13.7). To reduce vulnerability to external shocks, the government seeks to diversify exports by generating comparative advantage in a wider range of products, which should also help to expand the scope of export destinations.

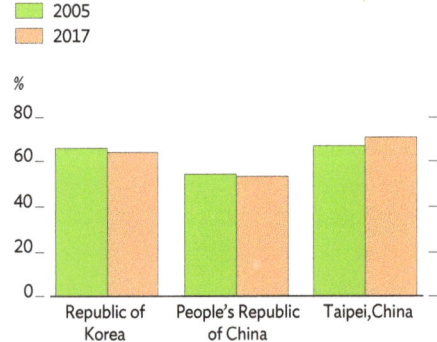

3.13.6 Export share of top 5 commodities

Source: Haver Analytics (accessed 8 March 2019).

To diversify export destinations more directly, the government has introduced its New Southbound Policy to deepen economic ties with Australia, New Zealand, and countries in Asia. The policy aims to encourage industrial collaboration, conduct outreach sessions, provide strategic guidance, and organize trade promotions to gauge demand in nascent markets. The government also looks to sign multilateral and bilateral free trade agreements. However, for these initiatives to expand the operations of existing export-oriented companies and encourage new export industries to emerge, exports need to become competitive in overseas markets. The first steps toward enhancing competitiveness are to improve exporters' emissions footprints and, more importantly, ensure the adequacy of skilled labor supply.

Owing to reliance on fossil fuels as a primary source of energy, a number of products are reportedly unable to meet the emissions standard for world trade, making them less competitive. Possible approaches to reducing emissions include phasing out energy subsidies and offering financial incentives to develop low-carbon technology or switch to renewable energy.

A shortage of skilled workers in Taipei,China was documented in a recent manpower survey. Alleviating this shortage requires a multipronged approach, which should include the following: First, planned income tax reform can be amended to improve compensation for skilled workers, which has not kept pace with inflation even in major export industries and is not internationally competitive. Second, female workforce participation, which is low at 51%, should be raised by offering special pensions, longer working years, and flexible parental leave. Third, the government should operate training programs for local labor or extend incentives for companies to do so.

Finally, overcoming barriers to forging new export destinations requires innovation and entrepreneurship. In 2006 and 2016, Taipei,China lagged behind its peers in the number of newly registered firms (Figures 3.13.8). The indicator of new business density, which measures the number of newly registered firms per 1,000 working-age people per calendar year, also shows Taipei,China lagging behind its peers (Figure 3.13.9). While this shortcoming may have multiple causes, providing a healthier entrepreneurial ecosystem will be an important step toward alleviating it. To this end, the government can help by encouraging research and development, funding business incubators in colleges and universities, and relaxing regulations to encourage the launch of new industries and products.

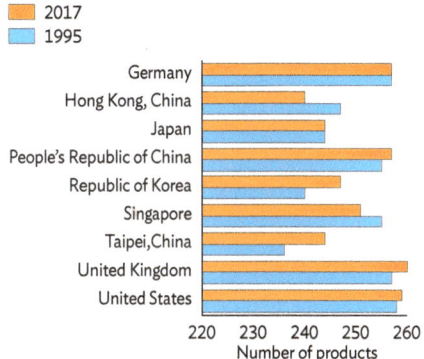

3.13.7 Number of export products

Source: UNCTADstat. https://unctadstat.unctad.org (accessed 19 January 2019).

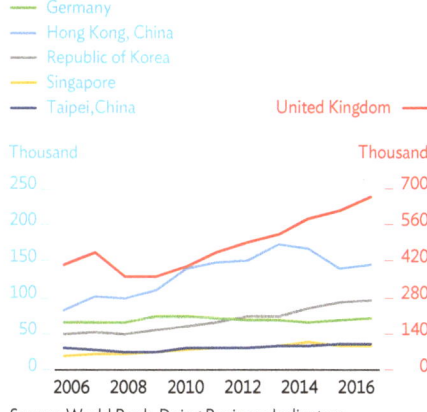

3.13.8 Number of new limited liability companies

Source: World Bank. Doing Business Indicators. https://www.worldbank.org/.

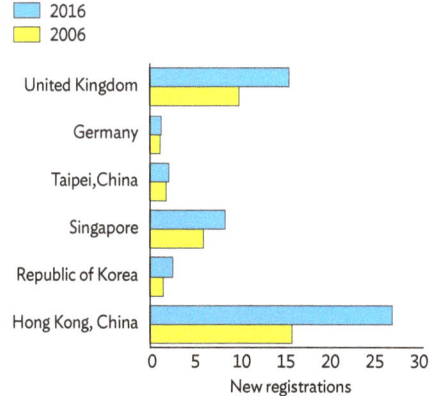

3.13.9 New business density

Source: World Bank. Doing Business Indicators. https://www.worldbank.org/.

SOUTH ASIA

- AFGHANISTAN
- BANGLADESH
- BHUTAN
- INDIA
- MALDIVES
- NEPAL
- PAKISTAN
- SRI LANKA

Afghanistan

Growth slowed in 2018, weighed down by a devastating drought, continuing security challenges and political uncertainty, and negative spillover from neighboring economies. Inflation slowed despite currency depreciation throughout 2018. The outlook for growth is only modest improvement in light of continuing security concerns, upcoming elections, and declining foreign assistance. Infrastructure development promises to be the foundation of economic growth and job creation.

Economic performance

Growth is estimated to have slowed from 2.7% in 2017 to 2.2% in 2018, largely because of a severe drought (Figure 3.14.1). On the supply side, growth in agriculture shrank from 3.8% to 2.0% as drought affected more than half of the country, causing wheat production to fall by 71% in rainfed fields and by 6% in the much smaller irrigated area. Industry picked up to grow by 2.0%, and services expanded by 2.5%, unchanged from the previous year.

According to estimates by the United Nations Office on Drugs and Crime, opium production decreased by 29% to 6,400 tons in 2018 after record-high production the year before, reflecting decreasing yield because of prolonged drought and less area under poppy cultivation due to significantly lower market prices following the glut in 2017. The farm gate value of opium fell by more than half to $604 million in 2018, equal to 3% of Afghanistan's licit GDP.

Public consumption and investment both increased slightly on higher government budget expenditure in 2018. Private consumption is estimated to have contracted as continued drought squeezed rural incomes, while business uncertainty caused private investment to decelerate. Net exports continued to weigh on growth, probably aggravated by the reimposition of international sanctions on neighboring Iran, one of Afghanistan's main trade partners.

Inflation slowed considerably from 5.0% in 2017 to average 0.6% in 2018 as food inflation fell steeply in the course of the year to average 1.0%, and as food imports outweighed the shortfall in domestic food production (Figure 3.14.2). Nonfood inflation was quite moderate at 2.3%, especially considering large increase in global oil prices during the year and substantial currency depreciation.

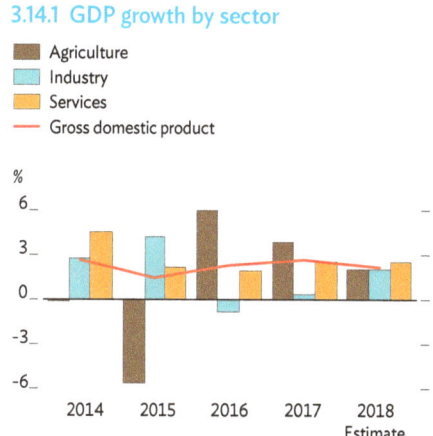

3.14.1 GDP growth by sector

Sources: World Development Indicators, World Bank (accessed 22 February 2019); ADB estimates.

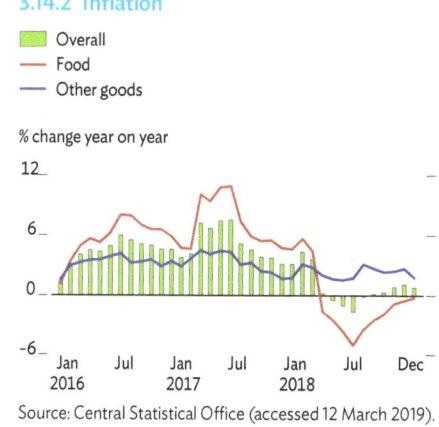

3.14.2 Inflation

Source: Central Statistical Office (accessed 12 March 2019).

This chapter was written by Abdul Hares Halimi of the Afghanistan Resident Mission, ADB, Kabul.

Amid regional currency pressures, informal outflows of US dollars to Iran, and global strengthening of the US currency, the afghani depreciated by 8.6% against the US dollar in 2018, reaching a record low in November (Figure 3.14.3). Sharp depreciation that started on 11 September was the result of speculation on the money market that led Da Afghanistan Bank, the central bank, to stabilize the currency by boosting sales of US dollars in the final months of the year by some 30% above sales a year earlier.

Domestic revenue is estimated to have reached 11.7% of GDP in 2018 thanks to enhanced tax administration and compliance, as well as measures against corruption in the customs department. Foreign aid comprised 56.3% of budget revenue, or 15.1% of GDP, to bring total revenue and grants to the equivalent of 26.4% of GDP. Government expenditure increased to equal 26.8% of GDP, with development expenditure at 7.8% of GDP. The operating budget deficit excluding grants increased to equal 6.1% of GDP because of higher security requirements and spending on pensions and civil service wages. The overall budget balance was estimated to be a deficit equal to 0.4% of GDP. Public debt was up slightly from 7.0% of GDP in 2017, estimated to equal 7.2% of GDP in 2018.

Growth in broad money supply (M2) accelerated from 4.1% in 2017 to 9.0% in 2018 (Figure 3.14.4). Credit to the private sector grew by 3.5% in 2018, but lending risks under the difficult security situation and poor macroeconomic conditions keep outstanding credit to the private sector very low at the equivalent of only 3.5% of GDP. Most transactions are in cash, with currency in circulation amounting to about 17% of GDP. Nonperforming loans declined slightly to 12% of total loans. Dollarization is high, with the share of foreign-denominated loans at about 60%.

The current account surplus including official grants rose from the equivalent of 5.0% of GDP in 2017 to an estimated 5.3% as official grants increased from 38.0% of GDP to an estimated 39.7% (Figure 3.14.5). Excluding grants, the current account deficit widened from 33.0% of GDP in 2017 to 34.5%. The merchandise trade deficit widened from 31.2% of GDP in 2017 to 32.4% as imports increased by 4.3%. Import growth more than offset 11.9% expansion in exports supported by currency depreciation and improved market access to India by air. Merchandise exports remained low at only 4.4% of GDP.

Gross international reserves rose from $8.1 billion in 2017 to $8.3 billion, or cover for 11.2 months of imports, as development partners financed large trade and current account deficits (Figure 3.14.6). The country's weak external position has necessitated government policy that strictly limited external borrowing, with external debt in 2018 estimated at only 6.7% of GDP.

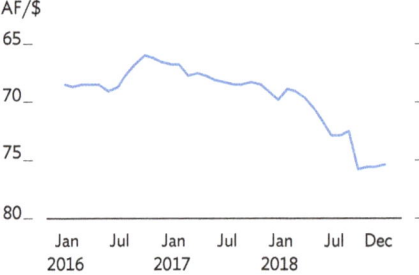

3.14.3 Nominal exchange rate

Source: Da Afghanistan Bank (accessed 22 February 2019).

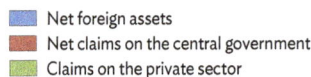

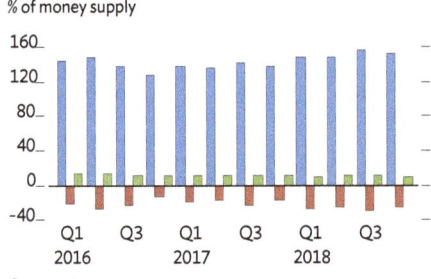

3.14.4 Monetary indicators

Q = quarter.
Source: Haver Analytics (accessed 12 March 2019).

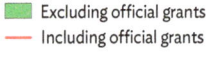

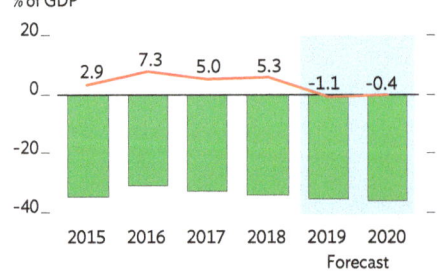

3.14.5 Current account balance

Note: Years are fiscal years ending on 21 December of the same year.
Source: International Monetary Fund Country Report 18/359, December 2018.

Economic prospects

GDP growth is expected to recover to 2.5% in 2019 and 3.0% in 2020 (Figure 3.14.7). Political and security uncertainties cloud the outlook, however, as Afghanistan approaches elections in September 2019 for president, provincial councils, and district councils. At the Geneva Ministerial Conference on Afghanistan in November 2018, the international community reaffirmed its commitment to continued collaboration to further Afghanistan's socioeconomic development.

Agriculture is expected to pick up with better weather, fostering in turn expansion in industry and services. The International Monetary Fund agreed to renew its Extended Credit Facility for Afghanistan until 31 December 2019, and the consequent implementation of additional reform should support economic activity. Business confidence stands to improve if peace talks begun in late 2018 between the US and the Taliban prove to be productive. Public investment will become more challenging as inflows from development partners trend downward. New air corridors to the People's Republic China and India—and the Lapis Lazuli route to Europe inaugurated on 13 December 2018—promise to boost exports and improve the trade balance.

Inflation will accelerate to 3.0% in 2019 and 4.5% in 2020 with the lagged impact of 2018 currency depreciation and further depreciation expected in 2019 and 2020 as inflows of assistance slow. However, food prices are expected to remain low as agriculture recovers.

The 2019 budget presented a medium-term expenditure framework that foresees a less expansionary role for fiscal policy. Domestic revenue is budgeted to increase to the equivalent of 12.0% of GDP in 2019 and 12.3% in 2020. Grants are projected to fall to 51.4% of budget revenue in 2019 and 45.5% in 2020. Expenditure is budgeted to fall back to the equivalent of 25.5% of GDP in 2019 and 24.7% in 2020—considered necessary even though it will entail budget deficits equal to 0.6% of GDP in 2019 and 1.5% in 2020. In this scenario, the policy response to achieve fiscal sustainability requires an intense focus on reform to tax policy and administration and more efficient allocation of financial resources.

The current account balance including grants is expected to move into deficit equal to 1.1% of GDP in 2019 with an anticipated decline in grants. The deficit is forecast to narrow to 0.4% of GDP in 2020 as exports benefit from various trade connectivity initiatives.

3.14.1 Selected economic indicators (%)

	2019	2020
GDP growth	2.5	3.0
Inflation	3.0	4.5
Current account balance (share of GDP)	-1.1	-0.4

Source: ADB estimates.

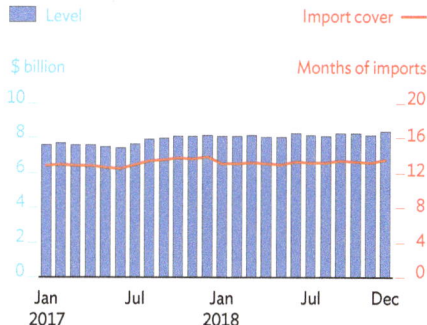

3.14.6 International reserves

Sources: International Financial Statistics, IMF; Da Afghanistan Bank (both accessed 12 March 2019).

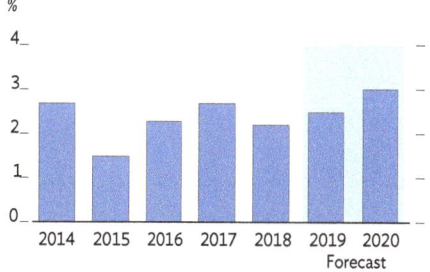

3.14.7 GDP growth

Sources: World Development Indicators, World Bank (accessed 22 February 2019); ADB estimates.

Policy challenge—accelerating infrastructure development

Afghanistan's growth prospects continue to be constrained by a number of factors beyond security, such as poor connectivity, poor access to limited energy supply, low agricultural productivity, and heavy reliance on overseas development partners. Better infrastructure can strengthen economic growth, enlist improved mobility to energize commerce and agriculture, and thereby boost government revenue available for development spending. Addressing infrastructure gaps can improve opportunities for trade as well and enhance regional economic cooperation and integration, the better to realize Afghanistan's potential as a transit hub connecting Central Asia with South Asia and beyond.

Despite some improvements to infrastructure, Afghanistan endures a severe infrastructure deficit, with disparity between urban and rural areas particularly high. According to the Afghanistan Living Conditions Survey, conducted in 2016 and 2017, only 36% of the population has access to safe drinking water nationally, including 75% of urban households but only 25% of rural households. Only 31% of the population is connected to the electric grid, the primary source of electrical power in urban areas with penetration at 92%, but reaching only 13% in rural areas. Only 63% of the rural population lives within 2 kilometers of an all-season road, and road density is estimated at a low 15 kilometers per 100 square kilometers of territory, below densities achieved by Afghanistan's neighbors. Further, the quality of infrastructure is generally poor. According to the World Bank's Logistics Performance Index, Afghanistan has consistently ranked in the bottom quintile for the quality of its infrastructure for trade and transport.

Regulatory and administrative reforms have attempted to provide a safer and more enabling environment for infrastructure investment. The government should accelerate its implementation of ongoing construction projects and upgrade its capacity to design, implement, and monitor investment projects. Moreover, the government should address skills shortages and stimulate private sector investment in infrastructure development.

Finally, the government should seek sustainable infrastructure financing and look at innovative approaches to increase access to funding. Financing needed for the National Infrastructure Plan, 2017–2021 of about $1 billion annually exceeds available resources from development partners, and domestic fiscal resources for new investment are limited. High security costs greatly add to project costs. Debt-financed infrastructure investment carries risks and would require adequate monitoring and macroeconomic management. Attracting private capital for infrastructure requires further efforts to create an enabling legal and institutional environment. Addressing fiscal risks is necessary to develop a strong public–private partnership framework. Finally, closing the infrastructure gap should be pursued in tandem with developing strong institutions and an agenda for regional cooperation.

Bangladesh

Growth accelerated in fiscal 2018 on higher public investment and stronger consumption demand with a revival in exports. Inflation remained moderate. The current account deficit widened with surging imports despite revived remittances. Growth is expected to be slightly higher in both fiscal 2019 and 2020 on slowing in major trading partners. The current account deficit is forecast to shrink, and inflation to stay in check. To sustain higher investment and growth, the banking system requires strengthening reform.

Economic performance

GDP growth accelerated to 7.9% in fiscal year 2018 (FY2018, ended 30 June 2018) from 7.3% in the previous year, as rising growth in total demand found support in higher consumption, investment, and exports (Figure 3.15.1). Continued political calm, improved power supply, and higher growth in private sector credit facilitated the fastest economic expansion in Bangladesh since 1974.

On the supply side, growth was lifted by improved expansion in industry and agriculture. Industry grew by 12.1% on strong production in large and medium-sized industries and higher investment. Agriculture grew by 4.2% as quick policy response to flood-induced crop losses in the summer facilitated a good winter harvest and buoyant horticulture output. Growth in services moderated to 6.4% as expansion slowed in transport, finance, education, and health care services.

On the demand side, strong private consumption that was buoyed by a recovery in remittances provided the main lift to growth. Public investment also contributed, reflecting substantial progress in implementing large infrastructure projects, notably the Padma Bridge and Dhaka Metro Rail. Investment increased from the equivalent of 30.5% of GDP in FY2017 to 31.2% in FY2018 as public investment rose from 7.4% of GDP to 8.0% and private investment increased slightly to 23.3%. A surge in imports made net exports a larger drag on growth than a year earlier despite the revival in exports.

Average inflation edged up from 5.4% in FY2017 to 5.8%. Headline inflation year on year decelerated from 5.9% in June 2017 to 5.5% as food inflation eased from 7.5% to 6.0%, benefiting from the good winter harvest and large rice imports (Figure 3.15.2). Nonfood inflation rose by just over 1 percentage

3.15.1 Supply-side contributions to growth

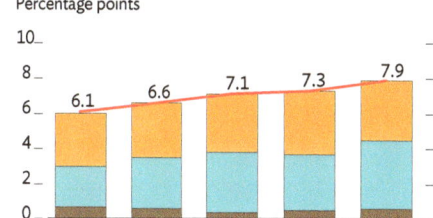

Note: Years are fiscal years ending on 30 June of that year.
Sources: Bangladesh Bureau of Statistics. http://www.bbs.gov.bd; ADB estimates.

3.15.2 Monthly inflation

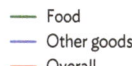

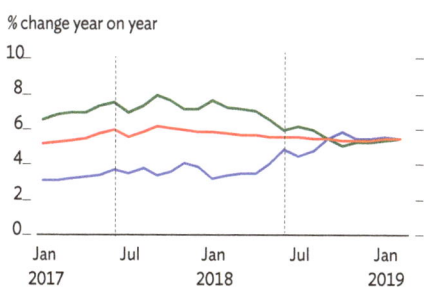

Note: Dotted lines denote ends of fiscal years.
Source: Bangladesh Bank. 2019. *Monthly Economic Trends.* February. https://www.bb.org.bd.

This chapter was written by Jyotsana Varma, Soon Chan Hong, Md. Golam Mortaza, and Barun K. Dey of the Bangladesh Resident Mission, ADB, Dhaka.

point to 4.9% in June 2018 on higher global oil prices, upward adjustments in domestic administered gas and electricity prices, and depreciation of the Bangladesh taka against the US dollar.

Growth in broad money slowed to 9.2% in FY2018, well below the monetary program target of 13.3%, with a decline in net foreign assets (Figure 3.15.3). This was despite strong growth in private credit at 16.9%, notably for investment and import financing. Net bank credit to the government declined by 2.5% as sales of national savings certificates provided much of the domestic financing of the budget deficit.

With declining net foreign assets pressuring bank liquidity, Bangladesh Bank, the central bank, reduced the required cash reserve ratio by 1.0 percentage point to 5.5% and lowered the repo rate by 75 basis points to 6.00% in April. This reduced pressure on the call money rate and forestalled any marked increase in bank lending rates, thereby supporting private sector growth. Banks' weighted average lending rate was nonetheless somewhat higher at 9.9% at the end of June 2018 than a year earlier, when it was 9.4%. The weighted average deposit rate also increased, from 4.7% to 5.5%, slightly narrowing banks' interest rate spread (Figure 3.15.4).

Budget revenue underperformed its target and declined from the equivalent of 10.2% of GDP in FY2017 to 9.6% with slower growth in value-added tax and supplementary duty collection at the import stage, while nontax revenue collection also underperformed. Government spending was lower than budgeted and declined marginally to the equivalent of 13.5% of GDP, curbing current spending from 8.3% of GDP in FY2017 to 7.8%. The annual development program and other capital spending strengthened from 5.3% of GDP to 5.7% with the implementation of the government's priority development projects. The fiscal deficit increased from 3.4% of GDP in FY2017 to 3.9% in FY2018, well within the budget target of 5% (Figure 3.15.5).

Export growth surged from 1.7% in FY2017 to 6.4% as garment exports, accounting for over 80% of the total exports, recovered from only 0.2% growth in FY2017 to 8.8% on stronger demand in the euro area. Other exports declined by 7.0% on lower demand for a number of other manufactured products. Import payments surged from 9.0% growth in FY2017 to 25.2%, reaching $58.9 billion. Imports of capital goods, food grains, and intermediate goods grew strongly. Remittances rebounded to grow by 17.3% to $15.0 billion, reflecting an increase in the number of workers going abroad in the past few years, a more favorable exchange rate, and measures to foster money transfer through official channels.

Despite larger remittances, the current account deficit grew abruptly from $1.3 billion in FY2017 to $9.8 billion, equal to 3.6% of GDP, as the surge in imports doubled the trade deficit, and deficits in services and primary income widened

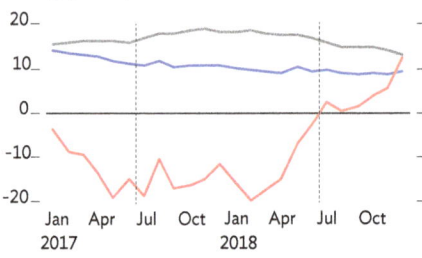

3.15.3 Growth of credit and money supply

Note: Dotted lines denote ends of fiscal years.
Source: Bangladesh Bank. 2019. *Major Economic Indicators: Monthly Update*. February. https://www.bb.org.bd.

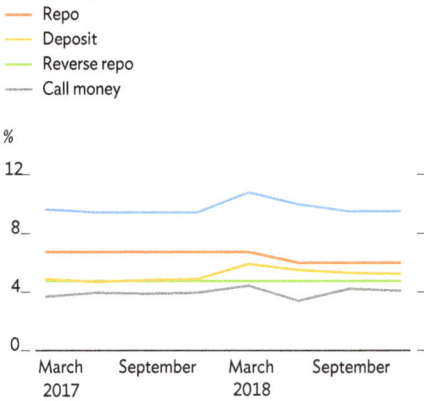

3.15.4 Interest rates

Source: Bangladesh Bank. 2019. *Major Economic Indicators: Monthly Update*. January. https://www.bb.org.bd.

3.15.5 Fiscal indicators

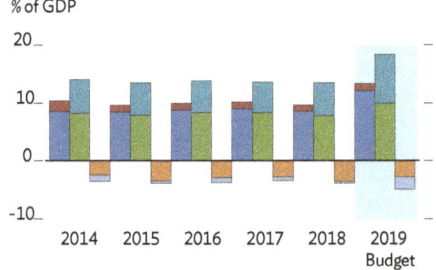

Note: Years are fiscal years ending on 30 June of that year.
Source: Ministry of Finance. http://www.mof.gov.bd.

(Figure 3.15.6). While financing inflows nearly doubled to $9.4 billion, a financing gap of nearly $1 billion remained for the central bank to fill. Gross foreign exchange reserves at the end of June 2018 were still substantial at $32.9 billion, providing cover for nearly 6 months of estimated imports. The Bangladesh taka depreciated by 3.7% against the US dollar in FY2018, but it appreciated by 1.8% in real effective terms (Figure 3.15.7).

The ratio of government debt to GDP increased from 27.0% in FY2017 to 27.9% in FY2018. The government continues to prefer concessional external borrowing, especially to finance infrastructure projects, raising external debt from 11.3% of GDP to 12.1%. Domestic debt increased only marginally, from 15.7% of GDP to 15.8%, as the issuance of national savings certificates slowed.

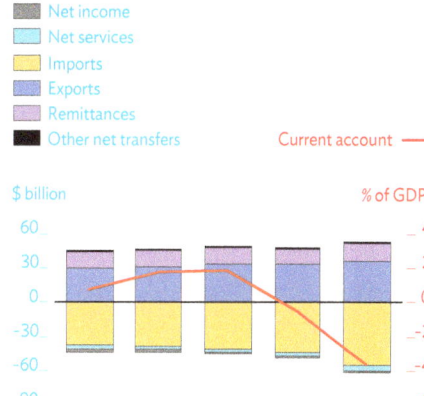

3.15.6 Current account components

Note: Years are fiscal years ending on 30 June of that year.
Sources: Bangladesh Bank. *Annual Report 2017–2018*. http://www.bb.org.bd; ADB estimates.

Economic prospects

GDP growth is expected to edge up to 8.0% in FY2019 on robust private consumption aided by continued recovery in remittances (Figure 3.15.8). Public investment will remain strong as the government continues to expedite the implementation of large infrastructure projects and other big projects receiving overseas support. Private investment is expected to rise, supported by measures to increase private sector credit, reform initiatives to improve the ease of doing business, and plans to make several hundred industrial plots available in special economic zones. Despite a weaker growth outlook in key exports markets, earnings from apparel exports are expected higher as new destinations strengthen. Tariff tensions between the People's Republic of China and the US make Bangladesh an attractive alternative source of manufactures. Consequently, the trade deficit will narrow as growth in exports outpaces imports. GDP growth in FY2020 is expected to remain solid at 8.0% as momentum from the previous year broadly continues.

On the supply side, further expansion in industry is expected to drive growth in FY2019 as export growth accelerates. Growth in agriculture is expected to moderate, considering the high base set last year. Growth in services is likely to remain unchanged, restrained in part by slower growth in agriculture. In FY2020, agriculture is projected to edge up as government policy support continues. However, with global growth continuing to slow, growth in industry is expected to moderate slightly, and expansion in services is likely to follow that trend.

Inflation is expected to ease from 5.8% last year to a FY2019 average of 5.5%, contained by a good harvest and lower global food and oil prices (Figure 3.15.9). Inflation declined to 5.5% year on year in February 2019 from 5.7% a year before.

3.15.7 Exchange rates

Note: Dotted lines denote ends of fiscal years.
Source: Bangladesh Bank. 2019. *Monthly Economic Trends*. February. http://www.bb.org.bd.

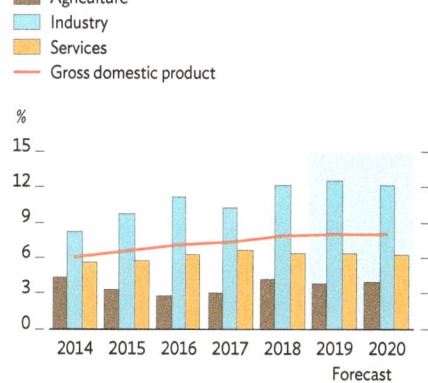

3.15.8 GDP growth by sector

Note: Years are fiscal years ending on 30 June of that year.
Sources: Bangladesh Bureau of Statistics. http://www.bbs.gov.bd; ADB estimates.

Inflation is projected to edge up to 5.8% in FY2020 on further upward adjustments likely for natural gas and electricity prices, as well as currency depreciation.

The monetary policy statement for the second half of FY2019 aims to balance inflation and output risks by providing an adequate supply of credit to productive economic sectors while implementing monetary and macroprudential policies to ensure domestic and external financial stability. The central bank kept the main policy rates unchanged: the repo at 6.00% and the reverse repo at 4.75%. It set target ceilings for broad money growth at 12.0% and domestic credit at 15.9%, which is expected to both accommodate the GDP growth target and contain inflation. Government borrowing appears on track while leaving adequate liquidity for private sector credit to grow within the target ceiling of 16.5%. The central bank will regularly monitor bank adherence to guidelines to better align their lending with deposit mobilization.

Exports increased by 13.4% in the first 7 months of FY2019, doubling 6.6% growth in the year-earlier period (Figure 3.15.10). Growth in readymade garment exports accelerated from 7.6% to 14.5%, benefiting from strong new orders from retailers that are partly attributable to global trade tension elsewhere. Given high demand for low-end products and acknowledged improvement in factory safety standards, exports are expected to increase by 14.0% in FY2019 and a further 15.0% in FY2020.

In the first 6 months of FY2019, import growth slowed steeply from the year-earlier rate of 25.2% to 5.7%. Although imports of intermediate and capital goods increased strongly in this period, imports of food grains and consumer goods markedly declined in the wake of high inventory building and food grain restocking in FY2018. On balance, imports are forecast to grow by 10.0% in FY2019 and 12.0% in FY2020.

Remittance growth moderated from 16.6% in the first 8 months of FY2018 to 10.0% in the same period this year after the large improvement in FY2018 set a high base (Figure 3.15.11). Government efforts have continued to reduce the cost of transferring remittances and to sideline unauthorized intermediaries. Remittances are expected to grow by 11.0% in FY2019 and by 10.0% in FY2020. With growth in exports and remittances expected to outpace growth in import demand, the current account deficit is expected to narrow to the equivalent of 2.3% of GDP in FY2019 and 2.5% in FY2020 (Figure 3.15.12).

The taka depreciated by 1.4% against the US dollar in the 12 months to February 2019 and is expected to depreciate a bit more in the remaining months of FY2019 as imports rise somewhat higher. To avoid excessive volatility in the foreign exchange market, the central bank sold about $1.3 billion up to 27 January 2019 to meet demand for foreign exchange.

3.15.1 Selected economic indicators (%)

	2019	2020
GDP growth	8.0	8.0
Inflation	5.5	5.8
Current account balance (share of GDP)	-2.3	-2.5

Note: Years are fiscal years ending on 30 June of that year.
Source: ADB estimates.

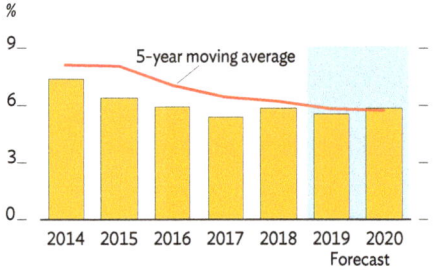

3.15.9 Inflation

Note: Years are fiscal years ending on 30 June of that year.
Sources: Bangladesh Bank. 2019. *Monthly Economic Trends*. February. http://www.bb.org.bd; ADB estimates.

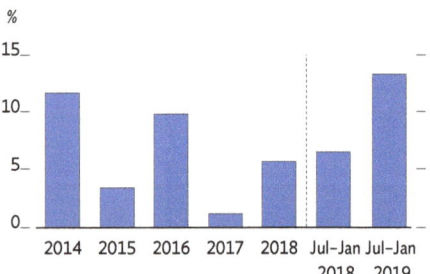

3.15.10 Export growth

Note: Years are fiscal years ending on 30 June of that year.
Sources: Export Promotion Bureau, Bangladesh. *Export performance*, various issues.

The FY2019 budget targets 30.8% growth in revenue to bring the ratio of revenue to GDP to 13.4%. Total spending is set to grow by 25.1% to equal 18.3% of GDP, with current spending equal to 9.9% of GDP and the annual development program and other capital spending at 8.4%.

Attaining these high targets will be challenging in light of recent developments. In the first 6 months of FY2019, growth in revenue collection by the National Board of Revenue plunged from 20.4% in the year-earlier period to 6.1%. Import taxes and domestic indirect taxes have both been lower than expected with import demand weaker. Achieving the high investment spending planned in the budget will demand concerted effort, considering that only 27.4% of the annual development program was implemented in the first half of FY2019. However, as in the past, shortfalls on both sides of the ledger are likely to be managed to yield a fiscal deficit within the budget target, equal to 5.0% of GDP.

The outlook is subject to downside risks. Failure to boost revenue could crimp expenditure pledged for implementing priority projects. Global oil prices rising above expectations could stoke inflationary pressure. Failure to improve governance, the investment climate, and infrastructure could undermine other development achievements. Finally, adverse weather is a perennial risk.

Policy challenge—promoting an efficient banking system

Banks play a key role in mobilizing and allocating resources for investment, especially as Bangladesh lacks a mature capital market. As of June 2018, the country had 57 commercial banks with 10,114 branches and combined assets of Tk13.9 trillion, equal to 62% of GDP. Loans and advances amount to about two-thirds of total assets.

Banks fall into four categories: 6 state-owned commercial banks (SCBs), 2 state-owned development financial institutions (DFIs), 40 domestic private commercial banks (PCBs), and 9 foreign commercial banks (FCBs). They operate under the regulation and supervision of the central bank. The SCBs once dominated the system with a large market share, but that share shrank over time as PCBs and FCBs gained market share, reflecting increased competition in banking. The asset share of SCBs declined from about 55% of the total in 1993 to 26.1% in June 2018, though the decline in deposit share was slightly smaller (Table 3.15.2).

SCBs and DFIs have small market shares, but they face major issues such as high nonperforming loans (NPLs), low profitability, weak governance, widening capital shortfalls, operational inefficiencies, scant automation, inadequate credit

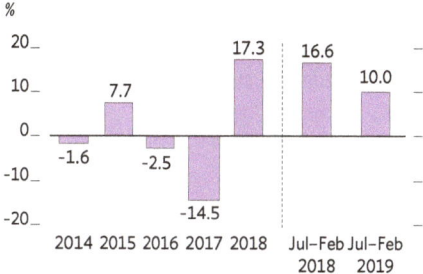

3.15.11 Remittance growth

Note: Years are fiscal years ending on 30 June of that year.
Source: Bangladesh Bank. http://www.bb.org.bd.

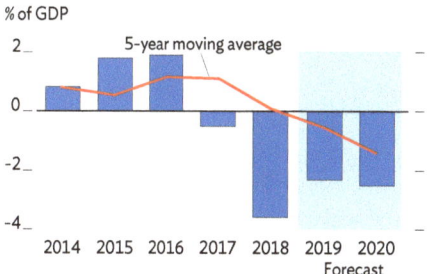

3.15.12 Current account balance

Note: Years are fiscal years ending on 30 June of that year.
Sources: Bangladesh Bank. *Annual Report 2017–2018*. https://www.bb.org.bd; ADB estimates.

3.15.2 Banking system structure, assets, and deposits, June 2018

Bank type	Number of banks	Number of branches	Share of industry assets (%)	Share of deposits (%)
SCB	6	3,741	26.1	27.4
DFI	2	1,411	2.4	2.8
PCB	40	4,888	67.0	65.8
FCB	9	74	4.6	4.0
Total	57	10,114	100.0	100.0

DFI = development financial institution, FCB = foreign commercial bank, PCB = domestic private commercial bank, SCB = state-owned commercial bank.

Source: Bangladesh Bank. 2018. *Annual Report 2017–2018*. http://www.bb.org.bd.

monitoring and internal risk management, and an ineffective legal framework.

NPLs have gone up for all classes of banks (Table 3.15.3). SCBs are burdened, however, with much higher NPLs than are PCBs or FCBs, which weak management allowed them to accumulate over time. The ratio of gross NPLs to total loans peaked at 41.1% at the end of 1999—the upshot of loans granted after only weak appraisal, directed lending programs during 1970s and 1980s, weak follow-up on repayment, and reluctance to write off long-standing bad loans because of the poor quality of underlying collateral and fear of possible legal complications. However, the ratio of NPLs steadily decreased to 6.1% at the end of 2011 with provisioning, write-offs, and a sharp reduction in new bad debt. NPLs rebounded, with some fluctuation, to 10.3% at the end of December 2018, partly reflecting a tightening of loan classification standards. The NPL ratio at SCBs then was about five times that of PCBs and FCBs.

Profitability at SCBs, measured as bank return on assets and return on equity, has been negative and below the industry average since 2014 because of higher provision requirements and operational inefficiency. The authorities were therefore required to inject capital into them on several occasions, still leaving the SCB capital adequacy ratio at only 2.0% as of June 2018 (Table 3.15.4). It will be a challenge for them to meet the Basel III requirement by 2019 of a capital adequacy ratio at 12.5% of risk-weighted assets. PCBs and FCBs, by contrast, have maintained stronger capital positions and enjoyed higher return on equity.

Better governance is required in the banking sector. Indications of weak governance are a high ratio of expenditure to income, high administrative and operating expenses, lending with scant appraisal, weak credit monitoring, a lack of integrity and compliance with applicable laws and regulations, and inefficient appointments in management.

To address banking sector issues, the authorities have taken a number of measures under past reform programs: enforcing stronger regulations, introducing a bankruptcy law, establishing money loan courts and a credit information bureau, corporatizing SCBs, applying a uniform guideline for writing off loans, changing loan classification and loan-loss provision, restructuring policy for large loans above Tk5 billion, the phased introduction of Basel III, and promoting a number of measures for good corporate governance. Although these initiatives have brought some improvements, they have not turned around weak performance in the sector.

The government is planning various measures to impose greater discipline on the financial sector through amendments to the Bank Company Act of 1991, Bankruptcy Act of 1997, and Money Loan Court Act of 2003. It is planning as well a special audit for banks to probe irregularities in the sector.

3.15.3 Gross nonperforming loans to total loans by type of bank (%)

Bank type	2011	2016	2017	2018
SCB	11.3	25.1	26.5	30.0
DFI	24.6	26.0	23.4	19.5
PCB	2.9	4.6	4.9	5.5
FCB	3.0	9.6	7.0	6.5
Total	6.1	9.2	9.3	10.3

DFI = development financial institution, FCB = foreign commercial bank, PCB = domestic private commercial bank, SCB = state-owned commercial bank.
Source: Bangladesh Bank. 2018. *Annual Report 2017-2018*. http://www.bb.org.bd.

3.15.4 Indicators of banking sector performance, FY2018 (%)

Bank type	SCB	DFI	PCB	FCB	Total
Share of assets	26.1	2.4	67.0	4.6	100.0
Gross nonperforming loan ratio	28.2	21.7	6.0	6.7	10.4
Provision adequacy	64.1	111.6	103.2	104.3	84.9
Ratio of capital to risk-weighted assets	2.0	-31.9	12.2	23.0	10.0
Return on assets	-0.7	-1.6	0.6	2.8	0.3
Return on equity	-12.3	-8.4	8.2	13.7	4.4
Net interest margin	2.1	0.9	3.5	4.6	3.2
Ratio of expenditure to income	83.9	149.9	78.4	44.3	80.3

DFI = development financial institution, FCB = foreign commercial bank, PCB = domestic private commercial bank, SCB = state-owned commercial bank.
Source: Bangladesh Bank. 2018. *Annual Report 2017-2018.* http://www.bb.org.bd.

Meanwhile, the central bank launched a new guideline on credit risk management, the Internal Credit Risk Rating System, effective on 1 July 2019. When revising the Bankruptcy Act, it is important to ensure that it sets time-bound procedures for Money Loan Courts to speed up the resolution of cases being settled.

Further, to improve governance, appointment to SCB boards of directors could be limited to competent professionals who possess operational knowledge of banking and finance, avoiding political appointments. Moreover, SCB management should be given full operational independence to conduct operations day to day, with both the board and management accountable to the central bank.

The authorities should ensure strict enforcement of existing bank rules and regulations. They might consider consolidation, merger, or divestment for SCBs, or even privatization to reduce their number. Alternatively, restructuring SCBs could be considered before divestment. The authorities could also consider establishing a national asset management company to take over NPLs from ailing banks. The government might decide to compensate SCBs in some efficient way or provide budgetary support for their mandated social services, such as providing financial services to underserved areas of the economy.

Bhutan

Growth slipped for a second year running as construction at hydropower projects slowed and low water temporarily undermined electric power generation. Inflation trended downward with declines in import prices, and the current account deficit narrowed on stronger exports. The outlook is for growth to strengthen moderately. With the country's expected graduation from least-developed status, the government plans reform to strengthen domestic resources toward better funding development.

Economic performance

Provisional estimates indicate GDP growth in fiscal year 2018 (FY2018, ended 30 June 2018) slowed further from 6.3% in FY2017 to 5.5% on weaker performance in industry (Figure 3.16.1). Construction remained an important driver of growth despite decelerating by nearly half from 9.8% expansion in FY2017 to 5.0%, mainly because of slower construction on hydropower projects. Moreover, hydropower generation, the other large component of industry, declined by 2.9% because of weak water flows. Services grew at a rapid 8.0% on robust expansion in wholesale and retail trade, hotels and restaurants, and transportation and communications. Revenue from international tourism rose by 5.0%. Agriculture expanded by 4.5%, partly on greater access to credit under the priority sector lending policy adopted by the government in December 2017, which requires banks to increase the share of credit granted to qualifying loan proposals from cottage and small industries, including agriculture.

On the demand side, capital formation increased only marginally as construction slowed (Figure 3.16.2). Growth in consumption expenditure was a major contributor to sustaining growth as private consumption markedly revived and government current spending remained robust. The trade and current account balances, though still in deficit, improved markedly again in FY2018, keeping net exports an important contributor to growth.

Inflation moved lower throughout FY2018, the monthly average falling from 4.3% the previous year to 3.6%. Food inflation was elevated for much of the year as adverse weather hurt domestic supply and import restrictions limited imports from India, but food prices trended much lower starting in March 2018 (Figure 3.16.3). Nonfood inflation fell notably

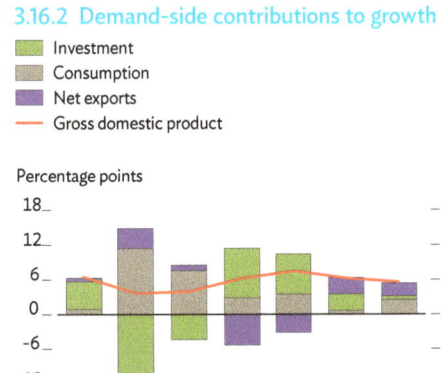

3.16.1 Supply-side contributions to growth

Sources: National Statistics Bureau. National Accounts Statistics 2018. http://www.nsb.gov.bt; ADB estimates.

3.16.2 Demand-side contributions to growth

Sources: National Statistics Bureau. National Accounts Statistics 2018. http://www.nsb.gov.bt; ADB estimates.

This chapter was written by Kanokpan Lao-Araya and Tshewang Norbu of the Bhutan Resident Mission, ADB, Thimphu, and Danileen Parel, consultant, South Asia Department, ADB, Manila.

from November 2017, reflecting the impact of India's adoption of a goods and services tax (GST) from July that reimburses exporters for all indirect taxes on production, thus lowering prices for goods imported from India. Although gasoline and diesel were not included in the GST, India waived central government excise taxes on these products, which eased food and nonfood inflation alike. Improved access to housing loans caused home rents to decline. From the beginning of FY2019, inflation began to rise as the 1-year impact of the change to a GST faded, and it once again tended to track inflation in India and developments in domestic demand.

Monetary policy remains oriented to maintaining price stability and supporting employment growth by channeling credit to productive sectors of the economy. Broad money growth slowed to 10.4% in FY2018 with net foreign assets, a main driver, declining by 3.2% (Figure 3.16.4). Growth in domestic credit reflected mainly a 15.7% increase in credit to the private sector, marginally higher than a year earlier. The expansion in credit largely benefited transportation, services, and housing, while credit to manufacturing slowed. Credit to the government was slight as its budget deficit shrank to near balance.

Government expenditure increased in FY2018 by 17.3% to reach 34.0% of GDP, providing a lift to domestic demand (Figure 3.16.5). Current expenditure grew by 18.6%, mainly on account of a higher bill for salaries and allowances, increase in government staff, an electricity subsidy to low-income consumers, and provisions for national elections. Capital expenditure rose by 16.1% to complete projects under the Eleventh Five-Year Plan, 2013–2018. Government revenue increased by about 27.8% in FY2018, three times average growth over the previous 5 years, driven by a 23.6% rise in tax revenue on buoyant domestic demand while nontax and other revenue was up by 39.2%. Grants also expanded markedly by 34.2%. On balance, the budget deficit declined from 3.4% of GDP in FY2017 to only 0.7%.

The current account deficit, though still high, continued to narrow in FY2018, falling by 5.0 percentage points to equal 18.2% of GDP (Figure 3.16.6). Most of the improvement came in the trade account, with the bulk of that coming from a 7.6% increase in exports as larger mineral exports overwhelmed the fall in electricity exports. Imports again declined, by 1.2% in FY2018 as construction slowed, but remained equal to nearly 40% of GDP, reflecting the country's small manufacturing base.

External debt rose from $2.5 billion in FY2017 to $2.6 billion as debt unconnected to hydropower rose with the drawing down of about $100 million from a swap line with the Reserve Bank of India to build up Indian rupee reserves (Figure 3.16.7). Hydropower debt increased only marginally. The external debt position deteriorated slightly from the equivalent of 103.0% of GDP to 105.4%. The risk of debt distress is assessed

3.15.1 Selected economic indicators (%)

	2019	2020
GDP growth	5.7	6.0
Inflation	3.8	4.0
Current account balance (share of GDP)	-16.9	-13.4

Source: ADB estimates.

3.16.3 Monthly inflation

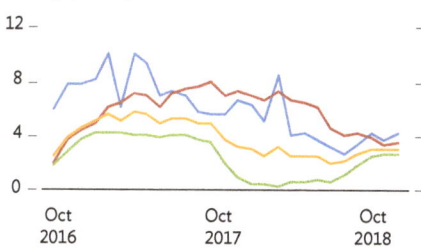

Source: National Statistics Bureau. Monthly Consumer Price Index Bulletin. December 2018. http://www.nsb.gov.bt.

3.16.4 Monthly trend in monetary indicators

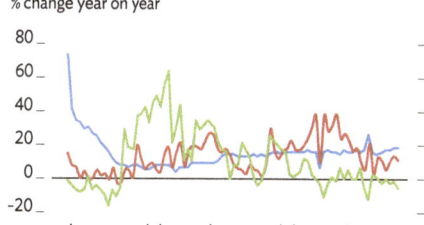

Source: Royal Monetary Authority of Bhutan. Monthly Statistical Bulletin February 2019. http://www.rma.org.bt.

to be moderate because hydropower debt is associated with long-term export sales arrangements. Debt servicing was less than a quarter of export earnings.

Gross international reserves increased slightly by 0.6% to $1.1 billion in FY2018, providing cover for 13 months of merchandise imports (Figure 3.16.8). Indian rupee reserves, which are the working balances for settling about 85% of import transactions, declined slightly from cover for 4.4 months of imports to 3.3.

Economic prospects

Growth will likely accelerate slightly to 5.7% in FY2019 with electricity generation normalized in the rainy winter season and production higher at existing plants. Barring further delays to the commissioning of the Mangdechhu Hydropower Plant, a full year of operation in FY2020 will help lift growth to 6.0% in that year. Private spending is anticipated to strengthen following parliamentary elections and the formation of a new government in November 2018. Government spending is expected to see a major increase only in FY2020, however, after the new government begins implementing programs and projects under the Twelfth Five-Year Plan, 2018–2023. Services, particularly wholesale and retail business and tourism, will continue to underpin the economy. After resolving export clearance issues that prevented sales of certain crops to India for several months, agriculture is expected to grow moderately with continued improvement in access to credit.

Inflation is forecast to increase to 3.8% in FY2019 and edge up further to 4.0% in FY2020 as the initial benefits from India's GST change taper and Indian inflation trends higher. Prices for export crops, particularly cardamom, will normalize following the resolution of the export clearance issue. Lower international oil prices forecast for 2019 and 2020 will help keep inflation at bay. Planned revisions to civil servant salaries and the minimum day wage will, once implemented, generate some inflationary pressure.

Following established practice in an election year, the outgoing government had Parliament pass an interim budget for FY2019 that covered current expenditure for the year and capital appropriations for ongoing projects but did fund any new projects. As a result, capital expenditure in FY2019 is estimated to be about half that of FY2018. Government revenue is projected to drop by a third from a year earlier with the discontinuation of excise tax refunds from India under the GST, loss of revenue from a delay in commissioning of the Mangdechhu plant, and grants expected to be only a third of those a year earlier, mainly to support uncompleted projects. With India's GST affecting the competitiveness of Bhutan exports, India has committed to a Nu4 billion grant over 5 years

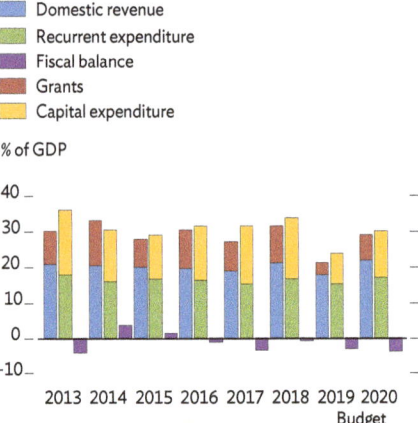

3.16.5 Fiscal indicators

Source: National Budget Financial Year 2018/19. Ministry of Finance. http://www.mof.gov.bt.

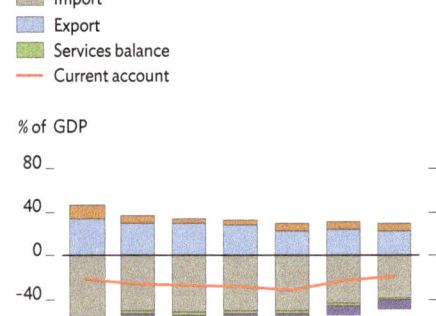

3.16.6 Current account components

Sources: Royal Monetary Authority. *Monthly Statistical Bulletin*, February 2019; *Annual Report FY2017/18*. http://www.rma.org.bt.

toward Bhutan making its products more trade competitive. On balance, the budget deficit is expected to increase to 2.8% of GDP and be financed by external and domestic borrowing.

The fiscal policy framework projects a sharp increase in budget revenue in FY2020 on Bhutan introducing its own GST to replace most indirect taxes, revenue transfers from full operation of the Mangdechhu Hydropower Plant, and a near tripling of grants from the previous fiscal year as the implementation of the Twelfth Five-Year Plan picks up. Expenditure is similarly projected to surge on large capital spending to implement new projects under the plan and on a pickup in current expenditure buoyed in part by expected recommendations of the Fourth Pay Commission to increase salaries for civil servants and contractors. On balance, the budget deficit is projected to increase to 3.6% of GDP.

The current account deficit is expected to shrink further in the forecast period. The deficit is forecast at 16.9% of GDP in FY2019, narrowing mainly on declining imports with further slowing of hydropower construction and a 6-month hiatus in new government capital expenditure in the transition to a new administration. The FY2020 current account deficit is estimated to fall to 13.4% of GDP even as the lower import trend reverses as government investment starts to pick up. This is because export revenue from full-year operation of Mangdechhu is forecast to be much larger.

A downside risk to growth forecasts would be any further delay in commissioning the Mangdechhu Hydropower Plant toward the end of FY2019.

Policy challenge—responding to fiscal pressures

Bhutan has made significant progress in improving its economy and reducing poverty over the past 3 decades, primarily driven by the public sector. Expenditure outlays, including current and capital expenditures in the Twelfth Five-Year Plan, have increased substantively from the previous plan by 38%, while foreign grants and domestic resource mobilization have not kept pace. As Bhutan prepares for graduation from United Nations least-developed-country status in 2023, the country will have limited access to concessional overseas development assistance. In addition, India will stop remitting an excise duty refund to Bhutan as part of the change to a GST regime from FY2019. Facing the fiscal pressures, over the next 5 years Bhutan aims to strengthen its tax system to mobilize larger domestic revenues to fund development expenditure.

The existing tax regime features low rates, a narrow base, and numerous incentives. Tax revenue, amounting to of 15.6% of GDP in FY2018, depends mainly on hydropower sales, which provide

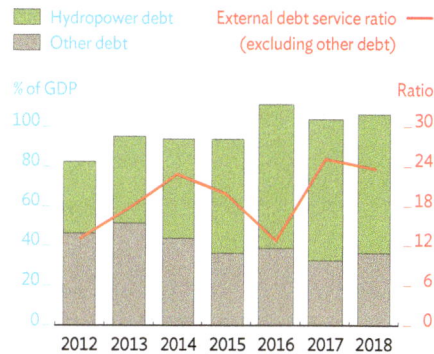

3.16.7 External debt

Source: Royal Monetary Authority of Bhutan. Monthly Statistical Bulletin February 2019. http://www.rma.org.bt.

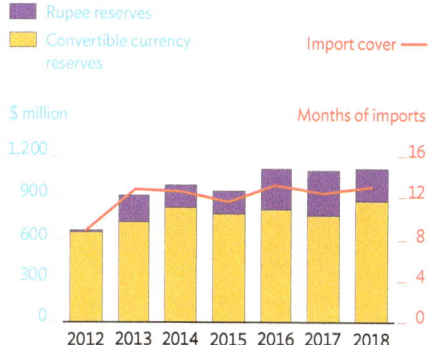

3.16.8 Gross international reserves

Source: Royal Monetary Authority. Monthly Statistical Bulletin February 2019. http://www.rma.org.bt.

the bulk of corporate taxes (Figure 3.16.9). The ratio of tax to GDP is expected to decline for several years, however, owing to major delays in commissioning two large hydropower projects.

Hydropower development entails large fiscal swings, from very heavy expenses during construction to robust revenue flows upon commissioning. To accommodate such swings, a stabilization fund was established in November 2017 for setting aside at least 5% of hydropower revenue annually to be used during subsequent periods to smooth budgetary volatility and ensure more even distribution of expenditure. The completion of two large hydropower projects after FY2020 promises to sharply boost export revenue and contributions to the fund.

Toward comprehensive reform of the tax system, a GST regime is being planned for adoption in 2020. It will replace all indirect taxes with a tax rate that is uniformly applied to goods and services, allowing only a limited list of exemptions and items bearing higher tax rates. A standard value-added tax system is being considered, with tax crediting for inputs and mandatory business registration based on turnover. Such reform would be a major step forward for Bhutan, as it is one of only six economies in Asia and the Pacific that has not yet adopted a value-added tax.

Although fiscal incentives may encourage investors and stimulate private sector growth, they have been costly for the government. In 2017, foregone revenue amounted to about 17% of tax collected, mainly from indirect taxes, in particular on sales and from customs duty (Figure 3.16.10). The Fiscal Incentives Act, 2017 removed from the Ministry of Finance the authority to grant exemptions and tax holidays, making them subject instead to parliamentary debate and approval. Parliament would benefit from the establishment of a technical group to make assessments of requests to evaluate their net benefit to the country according to prescribed criteria. Counsel from the group would inform parliamentary debate and decisions on requests for tax incentives.

The large number of existing exemptions should be reduced to enable more revenue to be raised. Steering clear of tax holidays would likely be beneficial because, despite their ease of implementation, they lack transparency and invite tax avoidance. Removing tax holidays would not deter investors who see solid business opportunities but would discourage the entry of footloose opportunists ready to exit the market when the holiday ends. Further, the provision and administration of incentives should be simplified without compromising investment.

As a complement to revenue reform, public financial management needs further strengthening to ensure the proper collection and administration of revenue. A fully electronic system for government payments is currently being rolled out. However, room exists to improve the quality of reporting by making it more frequent and informative.

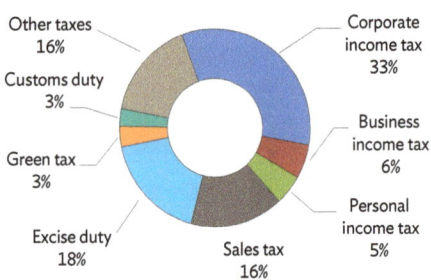

3.16.9 Tax revenues, FY2018

Source: Ministry of Finance, National Revenue Reports.

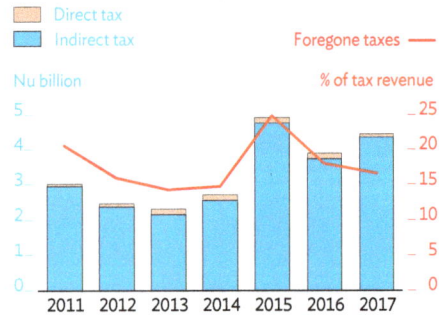

3.16.10 Foregone revenue from fiscal incentives

Source: Ministry of Finance, National Revenue Reports.

India

Growth slowed slightly in fiscal 2018 as expansion in agriculture and services slipped, even though industry and investment strengthened. The current account deficit widened but remained modest, while inflation continued to be benign. The outlook is for growth to edge up on strengthened domestic demand and bank and corporate fundamentals. Inflation and the current account deficit should remain tame. Export performance can be enhanced by improving conditions for participation in global value chains.

Economic performance

Economic growth slowed to 7.0% in fiscal year 2018 (FY2018, ended 31 March 2019) according to preliminary official estimates, slightly down from 7.2% in FY2017 (Figure 3.17.1). Growth slowed progressively during the year, partly from a base effect. The slowdown reflected subdued agriculture, which grew by only 2.7%, the lowest in 3 years. Food grain production was robust but slightly below the harvest in the previous year, mainly with a shortfall in cereals and pulses. Production from livestock rearing, fisheries, and forestry is estimated to have grown at a healthy rate.

Growth in industry sharply increased to 7.7% in FY2018, owing to strong manufacturing, construction, and utilities. Manufacturing expanded by 8.1%, helped by strong expansion in corporate earnings. The index of industrial production grew solidly, reflecting robust demand for capital equipment, construction goods, and consumer durables. Construction clocked robust growth at 8.9%, aided by government spending on affordable housing and new infrastructure, especially roads. However, mining grew by a meager 1.2% as contraction in crude oil and natural gas production offset strong growth in the output of coal.

Services slowed to 7.4%, their lowest growth rate in 7 years. Growth in trade, hotels, transportation, and communication remained sluggish with only subdued growth in the freight and passengers carried by railways, and in cargo handled by ships. Small and medium-sized enterprises, which account for a large part of this sector, may have struggled to comply with new regulations under the goods and services tax (GST), undermining the sector's performance. An uptick in credit and deposit growth helped financial, real estate,

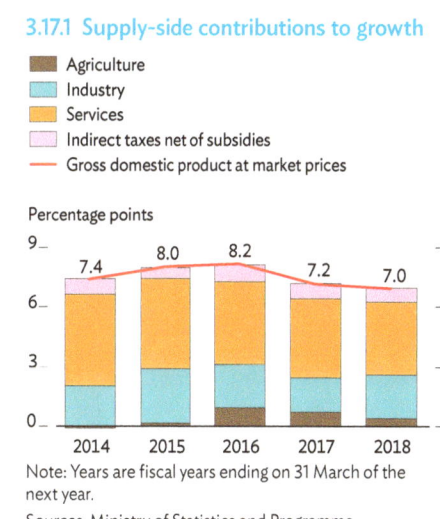

3.17.1 Supply-side contributions to growth

Note: Years are fiscal years ending on 31 March of the next year.
Sources: Ministry of Statistics and Programme Implementation. http://www.mospi.nic.in; CEIC Data Company (accessed 1 March 2019).

This chapter was written by Abhijit Sen Gupta of the India Resident Mission, ADB, New Delhi.

and professional services grow at marginally higher rates than in the previous year, though stress on shadow banks likely dented growth somewhat. Government steps to reduce GST rates for some real estate activities are thought to have provided a boost to this industry. Finally, a government slowdown in current spending slowed growth in government services including public administration, defense, and the "other services" category.

On the demand side, private consumption was the main driver of growth in FY2018 (Figure 3.17.2). It grew by 8.3%, the highest rate in 7 years, despite rural consumption remaining sluggish under subdued crop prices, slow growth in rural wages, and stress on nonbank lenders. Consumption is likely to have received impetus from reduced GST rates across a wide range of commodities during the year and a cut in key monetary policy rates. Government consumption slowed, as expected, because of tightened finances.

Gross fixed capital formation grew by a robust 10% in FY2018 despite coming off a high base. It was sustained by growth in central government capital expenditure by a robust 20.3% as investment in roads, railways, and urban infrastructure remained strong. Private investment is estimated to have increased a bit, reflecting a pickup in lending to industry, an uptick in capacity utilization, and increased production of capital goods.

Headline retail inflation averaged 3.5%, the lowest since a new metric was introduced in 2011. It declined steadily, especially from the second quarter of FY2018 (Figure 3.17.3). The headline number masks, however, a lot of heterogeneity. Much of the decline can be explained by muted food prices, which occupy 46% of the consumer price basket, as their average annual increase in FY2018 was only 0.7%. Prices for vegetables, sugar, and pulses fell significantly during the year as robust production created a supply glut, and as prices for cereals, fruit, milk products, and edible oil increased only modestly. Slow growth in rural wages squelched purchasing power in rural areas, reducing demand for food and pushing food inflation down further.

By contrast, core inflation remained elevated at 5.6% on price increases for housing, education and recreation services, and health care. Fuel inflation also remained strong on account of both higher global oil prices and Indian rupee depreciation.

Muted headline inflation prompted the Reserve Bank of India, the central bank, to reduce key policy rates by 75 basis points in FY2018, taking the repo rate to 6.25% (Figure 3.17.4). The most recent cut, in February 2019, was prompted by a drop in household inflation, a reduction in the output gap, and the general assumption that fiscal deficit targets would be met. The central bank also indicated a change in monetary policy away from calibrated tightening, under which policy rates

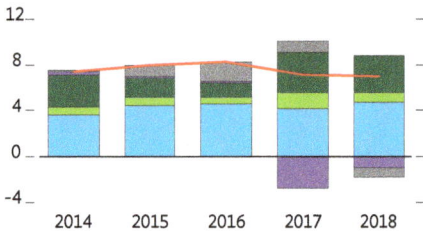

3.17.2 Demand-side contributions to growth

- Private consumption
- Government consumption
- Gross capital formation
- Net exports
- Statistical discrepancy
- Gross domestic product

Note: Years are fiscal years ending on 31 March of the next year.
Sources: Ministry of Statistics and Programme Implementation. http://www.mospi.nic.in; CEIC Data Company (accessed 1 March 2019).

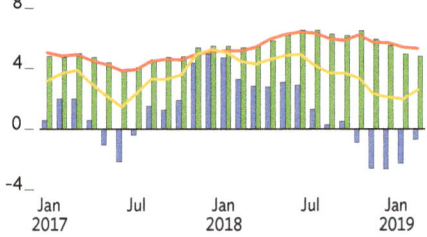

3.17.3 Inflation

- Food
- Other goods
- Core
- Headline

Sources: CEIC data company (accessed 13 March 2019); ADB estimates.

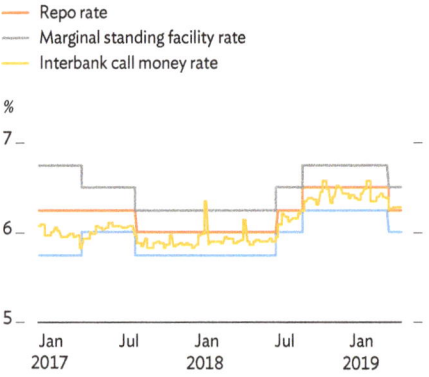

3.17.4 Policy interest rates

- Reverse repo rate
- Repo rate
- Marginal standing facility rate
- Interbank call money rate

Sources: Bloomberg; CEIC Data Company (accessed 8 March 2019).

could be only raised or kept unchanged, to a neutral stance, allowing rates to be changed in either direction.

Growth in bank credit rose from 7.0% in FY2017 to 11.9% in FY2018 largely on higher credit to services and personal loans (Figure 3.17.5). Within the service sector, credit to nonbank financial companies enjoyed the biggest increase, aiming to restore liquidity to this troubled business segment. Professional services and wholesale trade also benefited. Credit to industry inched up a bit over FY2017. Credit to infrastructure has picked up over the past few months, albeit from a low base.

Initial results are heartening, after various steps were taken to improve the health of the bank sector, including a review of stressed assets in 2015, the introduction of new guidelines for resolving insolvency and bankruptcy in 2016, and the recapitalization of selected banks. The share of nonperforming loans in all loans declined from 11.5% in March 2018 to 10.8% in September 2018 (Figure 3.17.6). This first decline in nonperforming loans since 2016 was broad-based, with public, private, and foreign banks all experiencing declines.

The nonbank financial sector, which has played a vital role in meeting credit needs, has been under stress since a default by a large player. This likely tightened financial conditions, raising the cost of capital.

The government fell marginally short of its fiscal deficit target for FY2018, the deficit finally equaling 3.4% of GDP, above the 3.3% target (Figure 3.17.7). One reason was the introduction of an agricultural income support program under which small farmers received ₹6,000 per year. The scheme will be implemented retroactively from December 2018 and is expected to cost the equivalent of 0.1% of GDP in FY2018.

Direct tax revenue remained buoyant in FY2018 as improved compliance boosted the collection of personal income tax and healthy earnings bolstered corporate tax collections. GST collection fell short of its target, mainly because tax rates on various commodities were reduced during the year. Revenue growth from customs and excise taxes was flat for goods that remain outside of the GST. Central government revenue received a fillip from strong growth in dividends from the central bank and receipts from charges for telecommunication spectrum use. The government's disinvestment targets are estimated to have been met for a second year in a row.

Central government capital expenditure grew by a robust 20.3% in FY2018 on increased outlays for roads, railways, and defense. In addition, capital spending by public sector enterprises grew by 5.5%. Growth in current expenditure was more modest at 13.9%. Apart from income support to small farmers, other contributors to mounting current expenditure were higher food subsidies, interest payments, and outlay on pensions.

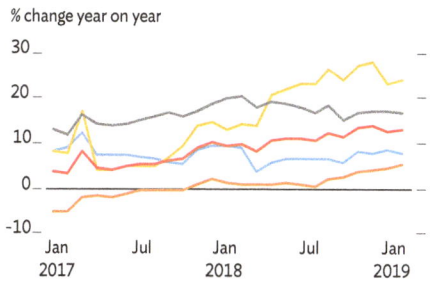

3.17.5 Bank credit

Source: Bloomberg (accessed 8 March 2019).

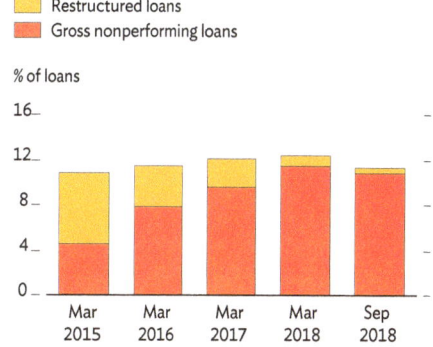

3.17.6 Stressed loan ratio

Source: Reserve Bank of India (accessed 8 March 2019).

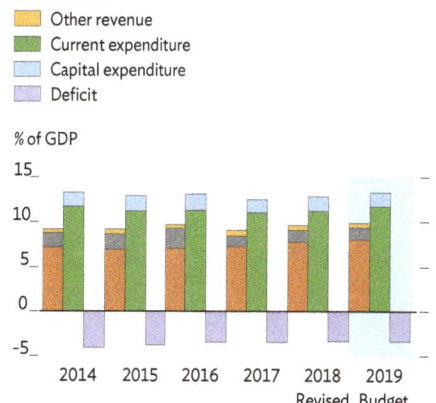

3.17.7 Federal budget indicators

Note: Years are fiscal years ending on 31 March of the next year.
Source: Ministry of Finance Union Budget 2016–2018. http://indiabudget.nic.in.

After rebounding in FY2017, import growth slowed to 9.8% in FY2018, reflecting sluggishness in imports other than oil (Figure 3.17.8). Growth in imports of capital goods declined in the second half of FY2018 in line with weakening economic activity. Gold imports contracted from the previous year, possibly indicating subdued rural demand. In contrast, higher oil prices and domestic consumption propelled oil import growth by more than 32.0%.

Exports grew by 8.9%, slightly slower than in the previous year. Export growth was buoyed by strong growth for refined petroleum exports, aided by the rise in global prices. Non-oil exports grew by a meager 6.0% despite a low base. Healthy growth in exports of electronics, chemicals, pharmaceuticals, machinery, and textiles was countered by contraction in exports of metals and leather products.

The surplus in services grew by only 3.0% in FY2018 even though software exports revived after 3 years of stagnation. Exports of transportation, travel, and business services also increased, though financial service exports dipped. Remittances grew robustly as higher oil prices boosted growth prospects in oil-producing countries, where many Indian migrants work. On balance, the FY2018 current account deficit is estimated to equal 2.3% of GDP.

Net foreign direct investment inflows were, at $32 billion in FY2018, slightly higher than in the previous year. By contrast, net portfolio investment flows turned negative with strong outflows from India in the first half of FY2018 as investor sentiment dampened in response to rate hikes in the US, rising oil prices, a worsening current account deficit, and uncertainty over India meeting its fiscal deficit target (Figure 3.17.9). Despite the withdrawal of foreign portfolio investors, the stock market climbed by over 10% in FY2018, substantially outperforming other emerging markets in Asia and the rest of the world as domestic investors upped their stakes (Figure 3.17.10).

The Indian rupee depreciated by 7.2% against the US dollar during FY2018, reflecting the widening current account deficit and tepid foreign investment flows (Figure 3.17.11). It depreciated by about 3% in real effective terms. India's international reserve holdings declined by $22 billion in FY2018 to $398 billion (Figure 3.17.12).

Economic prospects

Domestic demand is expected to remain the main driver of growth. Steps to alleviate agriculture distress such as income support to farmers and strong hikes to procurement prices for food grains are expected to bolster rural demand. The implementation of farmer income support will face some start-up challenges because it demands accurately linking

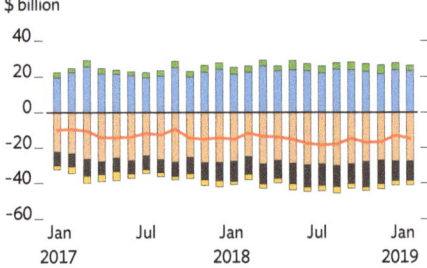

3.17.8 Trade indicators

Sources: CEIC Data Company (accessed 6 March 2019); ADB estimates.

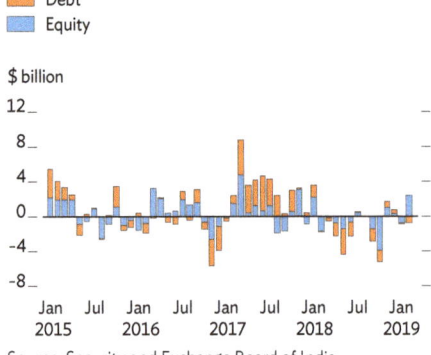

3.17.9 Portfolio capital flows

Source: Security and Exchange Board of India.

3.17.10 Stock price indexes

Source: Bloomberg (accessed 8 March 2019).

land records with farmers' bank accounts. In urban areas, consumption demand is expected to receive a boost from interest rate cuts, continued low prices for food, and declining fuel prices. The central bank's index of consumer confidence reached in December 2018 its highest reading in nearly 2 years (Figure 3.17.13).

The recent pickup in investment growth is expected to continue, albeit at a slow pace. The improvement in nonperforming loans held by banks, and the resulting easing of credit restrictions on certain banks, are expected to boost lending to industry. The central bank's industrial outlook survey showed business expectations in the last quarter of 2018 reaching their highest in more than 4 years (Figure 3.17.14). Similarly, the share of respondents expecting capacity utilization to improve in the coming quarters was the highest in 6 years, which is likely to spur private investment. Public sector capital formation is likely to be muted, with capital expenditure by the central government and its public enterprises forecast to decline from an estimated 5.1% of GDP in FY2018 to 4.5% in FY2019. Any investment revival will be dampened a bit by a decline in new project announcements in FY2018, even as the number of stalled projects increased.

Current weather points to a normal monsoon, suggesting healthy growth in agriculture, helped by a low base in FY2018 and steps to improve agricultural productivity.

Surveys provide a mixed outlook for manufacturing. The Nikkei purchasing managers' index indicates steady improvement in recent months for manufacturing, given strong growth in new orders (Figure 3.17.15). In contrast, a downward trend in the Nomura composite leading index indicates some moderation in growth outside of agriculture. Manufacturing is likely to benefit from lower borrowing costs and rising demand for consumer goods, aided by government measures to boost disposable incomes. The purchasing managers' index for services has inched up since from the middle of 2017, though dipping a bit in the most recent months. Moderating growth prospects in the advanced economies hurt tradeable services, though this was mitigated by a more competitive currency.

In sum, growth is forecast to pick up modestly to 7.2% in FY2019 on revived rural consumption, continued growth in private investment in response to improved bank and corporate balance sheets, more competitive domestic firms and products under the GST, and less drag from net exports. Growth in public investment is likely to be modest for lack of funds. Growth is expected to edge up further to 7.3% in FY2020 on dividends reaped from recent reforms to improve the business climate, strengthen banks, and alleviate agricultural distress.

The forecast has some downside risks. Exports could suffer if the following threats exceed expectations: moderation in global demand as financial conditions tighten, uncertainty

3.17.1 Selected economic indicators (%)

	2019	2020
GDP growth	7.2	7.3
Inflation	4.3	4.6
Current account balance (share of GDP)	-2.4	-2.5

Source: ADB estimates.

3.17.11 Exchange rates

Source: Bloomberg (accessed 8 March 2019).

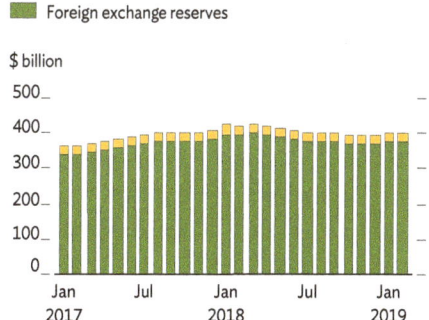

3.17.12 International reserves

Source: CEIC Data Company (accessed 8 March 2019).

arising global trade tensions, and weakness in the economic outlook in the industrial countries. On the domestic front, growth could suffer if tax revenue falls short or any disruption affects the ongoing resolution of the twin problems of bank and corporate balance sheets.

Inflation, remaining largely benign in FY2018, is expected to inch up in FY2019. Food inflation is likely to experience a mild uptick as some of the increase in procurement prices passes on to retail prices. Any increase in input costs such as wages and fertilizers could also push up food prices. Mistimed or misdirected rainfall could damage harvests and stoke food inflation. Average global oil prices are expected to be 13% lower in 2019 than last year. However, retail prices for deregulated fuels like gasoline and diesel are unlikely to decline by this much because the government is likely to raise taxes on them to boost revenue, as it has done in the past. Core inflation is expected to persist at current rates as proposed budget measures to raise disposable income would bolster aggregate demand. The lagged impact of the recent depreciation of the rupee will force up prices for imported goods. In sum, inflation is likely to average 4.3% in FY2019, rising to 4.6% in FY2020 as market prices firm up and domestic demand strengthens.

Inflation below expectations in FY2018 opened some space for monetary policy stimulus. With inflation expected to average below 4.0% in the first half of FY2019, the central bank could further lower policy rates. However, the extent of any easing would be restrained by fiscal concerns and the risk of stoking food inflation.

The central government put fiscal consolidation on hold in FY2019 by targeting a deficit equal to 3.4% of GDP, close to the FY2018 outcome, and higher than the earlier target of 3.1% of GDP. Part of the divergence was on account of the agricultural income support scheme and tax relief to people earning up to ₹500,000. Central government tax revenue is forecast to grow by 14.9%, an ambitious follow-on from high 19.5% growth in FY2018. Improved compliance and measures to broaden the tax base will help personal income tax to grow, but the 17.2% growth target may be a bit ambitious given tax concessions in the budget. Similarly, the growth target of 18.2% in GST revenue seems a bit optimistic. Nontax revenue is forecast to grow by 11.2%, aided by strong growth in dividends from the central bank and other financial institutions. Divestiture and strategic sales are expected to raise ₹900 billion, equal to 0.4% of GDP, which is ambitious but achievable.

Current expenditure growth, forecast at 14.3%, is more than growth in capital expenditure, which is budgeted at 6.2%. Further, as in the previous years, a significant part of capital expenditure will be undertaken by public enterprises, though as a percentage of GDP it is lower than in the previous year. Higher current expenditure is predicated on increased outlays

3.17.13 Consumer confidence

Source: Reserve Bank of India (accessed 8 March 2019).

3.17.14 Industry outlook survey of manufacturing

Q = quarter.
Source: CEIC Data Company (accessed 20 March 2019).

of committed expenditure. Subsidies are budgeted 11.7% higher, primarily to raise the cooking gas subsidy. Interest payments are also budgeted higher by 13.2%.

Exports of refined petroleum products are expected to grow at a slower rate as oil prices dip and growth slows in the industrial economies and the People's Republic of China (PRC). Part of this will be offset by improved exports other than oil or gold, which will benefit from a more competitive currency. Overall merchandise exports in FY2019 are expected to grow by 8.0%, slightly slower than in FY2018. Import growth is also expected to slow with lower oil prices and weakening currency. A revival in rural income could bolster gold imports. Similarly, an uptick in investment could draw in more imports of capital goods. On balance, import growth is expected to slow to 8.0% in FY2019.

The surplus in services could narrow a bit with weaker growth in the industrial economies. Growth in remittances is similarly expected to moderate for this reason—and with slower growth in oil-exporting countries—as both groups employ large numbers of workers from India. On balance, the current account deficit is expected to equal 2.4% of GDP in FY2019.

Recent gains in the ease of doing business and a healthy growth outlook are likely to attract strong inflows of foreign direct investment. Portfolio debt flows may weaken a bit with policy rates lowered in FY2019, reducing the interest rate differential with industrial economies. Portfolio equity flows are expected to remain robust. Overall capital flows are expected to finance the current account deficit, though a shortfall may require a modest drawdown of reserves.

In FY2020, export growth is expected to remain modest at 7.0% as growth in the industrial economies slows further. Stable oil prices will help moderate import growth, though non-oil imports are likely to grow at a slightly faster pace as growth inches up. Overall import growth is projected to be 8.0%. The current account deficit is forecast to widen slightly to the equivalent of 2.5% of GDP in FY2020.

Policy challenge—enhancing participation in global value chains

India's merchandise exports have grown from $35.7 billion in 2000 to $298 billion in 2017, at an average annual rate of 12.2%, nearly double growth in global exports. This has raised India's share of global exports from 0.7% in 2000 to 1.7% in 2017. Despite improvement, India's share in global exports trails that of other large Asian economies like the PRC at 12.7%, Japan at 3.9%, and the Republic of Korea at 3.2%. It is similar to the shares of smaller economies like Thailand at 1.3%,

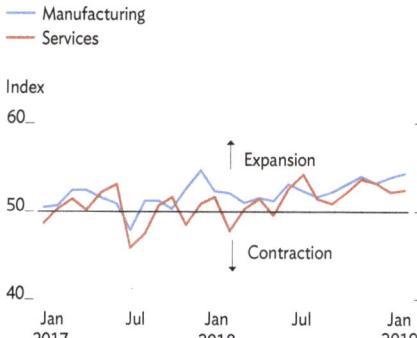

3.17.15 Purchasing managers' indexes

Note: Nikkei, Markit. Years are fiscal years ending on 31 March of the next year.
Source: Bloomberg (accessed 6 March 2019).

Malaysia at 1.2%, and Viet Nam at 1.2%. Recently, policy makers have delineated numerous strategies to improve India's export performance in strategy documents like *Foreign Trade Policy 2015–20, Strategy for New India @75*, and *Unlocking the Potential of Micro Small and Medium Enterprise Exports*.

India could improve its export performance by enhancing its participation in global value chains (GVC), as GVC exports account for more than 70% of global exports over the past 8 years. India's GVC exports in 2017 came to only $241 billion (62.7% of overall exports), significantly below $1,314 billion for the PRC, $577 billion for Japan, $533 billion for the Republic of Korea, $329 billion for Singapore, and $318 billion for Taipei,China (Figure 3.17.16). Sectors that dominate India's GVC exports include coke and petroleum, chemicals, basic and fabricated metals, textiles, and electrical and optical equipment.

Economies that have the highest increase in GVC participation, measured as the ratio of GVC exports to all exports, also experience the sharpest rise in all exports measured as a percentage of GDP (Figure 3.17.17). Enhanced GVC participation is similarly associated with other development goals for India: a higher share for manufacturing in GDP, faster job creation, and faster economic growth.

GVC participation benefits from low trade barriers. As GVCs depend on goods crossing international borders multiple times, high trade costs from high tariffs or nontariff barriers are passed on to the downstream firms, raising the cost of the finished goods. This affects the production and investment decisions of firms involved in GVCs. According to the Global Competitiveness Index compiled by the World Economic Forum, India's tariffs remain significantly higher than average in emerging markets. Lowering them would improve GVC participation. International trade costs depend as well on the time and cost involved in complying with customs and border procedures. Although India has made substantial progress in this regard, as evidenced by a sharp improvement in recent years in its World Bank rank for trading across borders, its rank at 80 out of 190 in 2018 shows that there is still scope for improvement. Improvement in trade across borders was one of the factors that helped India jump 23 places to 77th position in overall ease of doing business.

A country's ability to connect with GVCs depends crucially on the quality of its infrastructure. One of the main reasons for geographic fragmentation of production under GVCs is to take advantage of varying production costs across countries and produce each component at its cheapest location. Firms' production costs depend crucially on the quality of infrastructure. Poor electricity supply and frequent outages force a firm to restart the assembly line to restore production, clean up and repair damage to facilities, and dispose of faulty

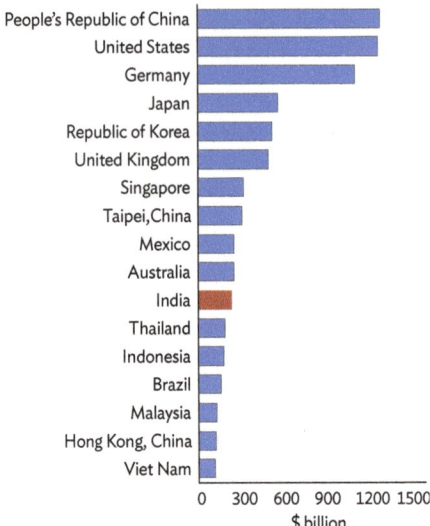

3.17.16 Cross-country comparison of global value chain exports

Source: ADB Multi-regional Input-Output database.

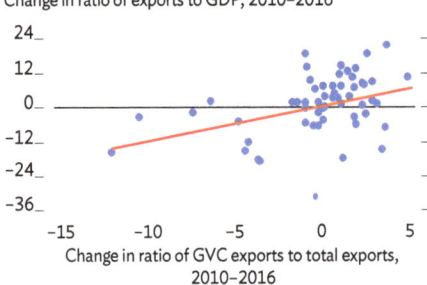

3.17.17 GVC participation and export performance

GDP = gross domestic product, GVC = global value chain.
Sources: ADB Multi-regional Input-Output database; World Bank. World Development Indicators.

products, all of which substantially raise costs and undermine competitiveness. Similarly, underdeveloped road and rail transport infrastructure impedes connectivity between ports and production centers, slowing production and making it more expensive. While India has substantially improved the quality of its roads, according to the Global Competitiveness Index, the quality of its electricity supply trails that of other emerging markets. Sectors like electrical and optical equipment, transport equipment and chemicals, and rubber and plastics have the potential to be further integrated into GVCs if these impediments are resolved.

Limitations on the finance available for infrastructure argue for concentrating investments in industrial zones. Infrastructure can be developed within such zones with costs shared by the firms present in them, reducing the infrastructure investment required of individual firms. These zones can be strategically located near transport hubs and linked with ports and airports that have better road and rail infrastructure.

Finally, skills development can help countries enhance their productivity gains from participation in GVCs. It allows countries and industries to specialize in higher and medium technology production and in complex business services like chemicals, electrical and optical equipment, and finance and insurance with potential to foster innovation and productivity growth. India faces a formidable challenge in this area, as only an estimated 4.7% of its workforce has received formal training, much lower than in other large economies of Asia: Japan at 80%, the PRC at 24%, and the Republic of Korea at 96%. To close this gap, policies on skills development need to be designed to meet the requirements of both low- and high-technology manufacturing and complex services. It would be prudent to design policies that improve skills across different segments of industries and not focus on too narrow a selection, to avoid misallocation.

Maldives

Despite slippage in tourist arrivals, growth strengthened in 2018 on higher construction and services underpinned by greater government expenditure. The current account deficit remained large, and inflation trended sharply lower as food subsidies resumed. With slower growth in tourism markets, the outlook is for growth to moderate and the current account deficit to stay large. A rapid buildup of government debt calls for careful management to keep the economy on a sustainable growth track.

Economic performance

Expansion in tourism, construction, and supporting services boosted growth from 6.9% in 2017 to an estimated 7.6% in 2018, despite bouts of political unrest that ended in September with the election of a new president and government administration (Figure 3.18.1).

Growth in tourist arrivals slowed from 8.0% in 2017 to 6.8% in 2018, reaching almost 1.5 million. Fewer scheduled flights from Asian markets were offset by new flights and higher frequencies from Europe, bringing growth in arrivals from Europe to 12.4%, with that market accounting for 84.5% of the increase in arrivals and maintaining the largest market share at 48.9%. Arrivals from Asia, the second largest market, fell by 1.0%, to a 39.2% market share, as arrivals from the People's Republic of China declined by 7.6%, continuing a persistent trend as the market share of this single largest national market fell from 30.2% in 2014 to 19.1% in 2018. Meanwhile, the share of all other Asian countries increased only moderately over this period, from 17.0% to 20.1%.

Despite slower growth in tourist arrivals, travel receipts grew by 10.3% as the average stay lengthened to 6.4 days (Figure 3.18.2). Moreover, growth in collections of goods and services taxes on tourists accelerated to 11.4%, reflecting strong growth in income not only for the government but also for resorts.

Construction growth remained robust in 2018, underpinned by credit growth and rising demand from infrastructure projects both public and private. The Public Sector Investment Program (PSIP) increased, with spending 20.3% higher than in 2017. Similarly, strong growth continued in bank loans to the private sector for construction and real estate, albeit

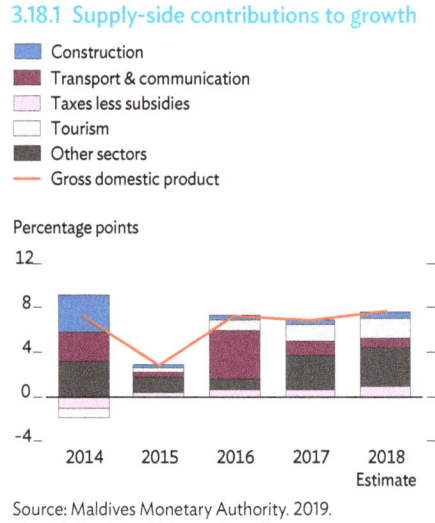

3.18.1 Supply-side contributions to growth

Source: Maldives Monetary Authority. 2019. Monthly Statistics. February. http://www.mma.gov.mv.

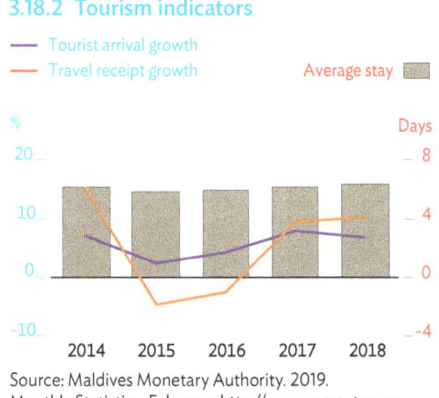

3.18.2 Tourism indicators

Source: Maldives Monetary Authority. 2019. Monthly Statistics. February. http://www.mma.gov.mv.

This chapter was written by Masato Nakane of the South Asia Department, ADB, Manila; and Abdulla Ali, Anthony Baluga, and Macrina Mallari, consultants, South Asia Department, ADB, Manila.

slowing from 34.1% in 2017 to 22.1% as the government offered competing loans with more favorable terms. Notably, growth in imports of construction materials markedly accelerated from 24.2% in 2017 to 37.7%.

Fish exports contracted by 10.2% on weak demand and lower global prices for skipjack and yellowfin tuna, the main export species. Growth remained strong in other sectors such as financial services, transportation and communications, and wholesale and retail trade.

Average inflation fell from 2.8% to 0.1% deflation in 2018 (Figure 3.18.3). This reflected government efforts starting in the second quarter of 2017 to reduce food prices, which had ballooned earlier after subsidies on staples were removed. The measures included imposing price cuts and controls on major staples, cutting import duties on fuel to counter higher global prices, and setting lower prices for electricity and transportation. In April 2018, the government harmonized utility rates across the country to the lower urban rate and fully reversed its earlier policy to remove subsidies, which essentially restored 2016 food prices.

With inflationary pressure low, the Maldives Monetary Authority has maintained the accommodative policy in force since it lowered the indicative monetary policy rate in 2014 and again in 2015. In 2018, credit to the private sector increased by 11.2%, mainly through large loans for tourism, construction, and real estate.

Spending reprioritization helped to bring the budget deficit down to 3.0% of GDP in 2017 from 9.9% in 2016 (Figure 3.18.4). Fiscal policy for 2018 turned expansive with reacceleration of the PSIP, which raised capital expenditure by 16.0%, and with a new pay structure for civil servants that swelled recurrent spending by 14.8%. Total expenditure thus rose from 30.1% of GDP in 2017 to 31.3%. Revenue rose by 5.3% to equal 25.8% of GDP, though this reflected a weaker tax performance than in 2017 as collections of goods and services tax slumped and capital revenue declined. Accordingly, the estimated budget deficit climbed from 3.0% of GDP in 2017 to 5.5% in 2018, with financial data indicating a rather higher deficit in 2018 at 9.3% of GDP.

Government external debt, including Rf10.5 billion in state loan guarantees, nearly doubled to Rf30.8 billion in 2018, or the equivalent of 37.4% of GDP (Figure 3.18.5). State-owned enterprises' use of guarantees was the main factor pushing debt higher. Government external debt increased, by 21.9% of GDP, mainly from the private placement in May 2018 of a $100 million sovereign bond with a 5-year maturity and a 5.5% coupon, and a $130 million increase in commercial buyers credits. Government domestic debt, including a notional amount of domestic guaranteed debt, rose by 1.7% in 2018 to Rf28.7 billion but became a smaller percentage of GDP at 34.7%,

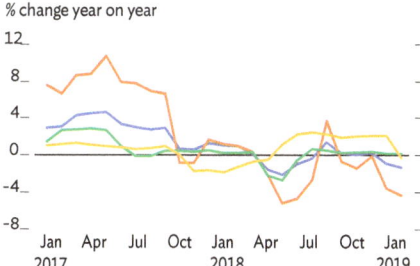

3.18.3 Inflation

Source: Maldives Monetary Authority. 2019. Monthly Statistics. February. http://www.mma.gov.mv.

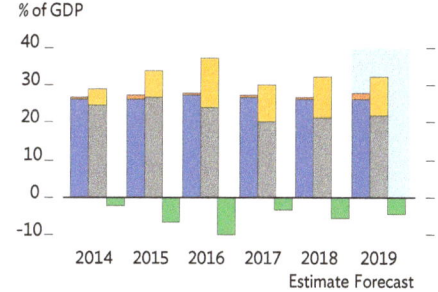

3.18.4 Fiscal indicators

Source: Maldives Monetary Authority. 2019. Monthly Statistics. February. http://www.mma.gov.mv.

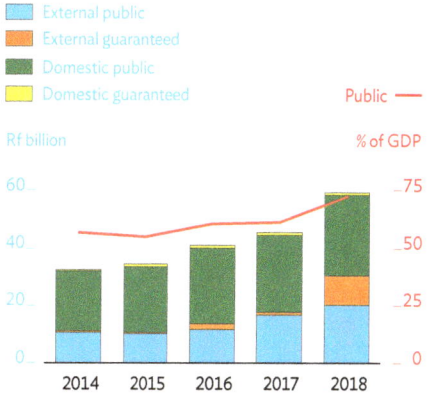

3.18.5 Public debt including guarantees

Source: Ministry of Finance, http://www.finance.gov.mv/.

down by 2.9 percentage points from 2017. At the end of 2018, total public debt including state guarantees was estimated at Rf59.5 billion, rising sharply to the equivalent of 72.1% of GDP from 61.0% a year earlier.

Provisional estimates indicate an 19.0% increase in the trade deficit and an almost 10% rise in foreign workers' outbound remittances, which pushed the 2018 current account deficit from 22.1% of GDP in 2017 to 23.7%, despite higher receipts from tourism. Imports rose by 25.6% on increased demand for construction goods, machinery, and electrical equipment, while exports rose by only 0.1%, with fuel reexports offsetting the drop in fish exports (Figure 3.18.6). The current account deficit was amply financed by large net financial inflows of direct and portfolio investment, including the $100 million government bond placement, and a marked increase in inflows of other investment liabilities facilitated by state guarantees.

A $100 million currency swap facility between the Maldives Monetary Authority and the Reserve Bank of India helped gross international reserves climb from $586.1 million in 2017 to $757.8 million. Usable reserves—gross international reserves less commercial banks' foreign currency deposits—amounted to $280.9 million, or cover for only about 1 month of imports (Figure 3.18.7).

3.18.6 Balance of payments

Goods exports
Services exports
Goods imports
Service imports
Primary income balance
Secondary income balance
Current account balance

Source: Maldives Monetary Authority. 2019. Monthly Statistics. February. http://www.mma.gov.mv.

Economic prospects

Tourism and construction will continue to underpin growth in 2019 and 2020. The new government plans an aggressive approach to developing tourism that targets 2.5 million arrivals in 2023, or 1.0 million more than in 2018. An augmented promotional budget of $10 million for 2019 will fund intensified marketing campaigns to further enhance Maldives' exposure in foreign markets. To extend tourism beyond several selected atolls to the whole country, the government plans to develop tourist destinations on each atoll and to prioritize the development of guesthouses.

The outlook for construction is positive. The new government has pledged to continue the infrastructure projects initiated by the previous administration and to start new capital projects throughout the country. Although the PSIP allocation in the approved budget for 2019 is 2.0% lower than a year ago, the budget targets larger PSIP financing in succeeding years. Toward increasing private sector participation in infrastructure projects, the government plans to set up the Government Fund Management Corporation, which will extend funding to facilitate national development projects initiated by private firms.

Fiscal policy is slated to be slightly less expansionary in 2019 as the government aims to increase revenue by about 10% on higher tax collections and hold expenditure

3.18.1 Selected economic indicators (%)

	2019	2020
GDP growth	6.5	6.3
Inflation	1.0	1.5
Current account balance (share of GDP)	−21.8	−22.0

Source: ADB estimates.

5.8% above revenue in 2018. The share of capital spending in total expenditure is programmed to ease from 33.8% in 2018 to 32.2% with lower PSIP allocations, while the recurrent expenditure share will increase by 1.5 percentage points to 67.8%. The deficit is set to narrow to 4.4% of GDP in 2019, though it could reach 5.5% with higher capital investment and pressure to deliver on election pledges such as lower domestic airfares, lower electricity prices, and tuition-free higher education in Maldives to the first degree earned.

Fisheries will get much-needed policy attention intended to increase output and earnings by developing fish products with high value added for premium markets and expanding the capacity of Maldives Industrial Fisheries Company, a state-owned processer and exporter of fish products. The government intends to explore the potential of mariculture, aquaculture, and reef fishing.

Despite good prospects domestically, signs of a global economic slowdown in the next 2 years, especially in Maldives' main tourist markets in Europe and the People's Republic of China, will weigh on tourism and the economy. GDP growth is thus projected to moderate to 6.5% in 2019 and further to 6.3% in 2020.

Forecasts of subdued global prices for oil and food should keep average inflation low. Also holding down price pressures will be government policies to contain the prices of basic commodities and several newly announced policies, notably removing duty on farming and fishing equipment, tuition free education, lower airfares and electricity prices, and harmonizing staple food prices across the country by April 2019. On balance, inflation is forecast at 1.0% in 2019, rising to 1.5% in 2020.

The high trade deficit will shrink slightly as large imports required to supply construction ease a bit on the projected marginal cut in the infrastructure program, and as investments to lift fishing capacity enable fish exports to recover. Sustained growth in tourism will maintain the service surplus. On balance, the current account deficit is expected to narrow to 21.8% of GDP in 2019 before widening again slightly to 22.0% in 2020 as capital expenditure picks up.

Threats to the outlook include the government's continuing unstable finances and the country's high ratio of debt to GDP and low foreign exchange reserves.

Policy challenge—managing the buildup of public debt

Maldives has increased its borrowing over the past few years to support a massive program to scale up infrastructure, and this has fueled a rapid buildup in public debt. Moreover, debt will mount further in the years ahead as large undisbursed balances

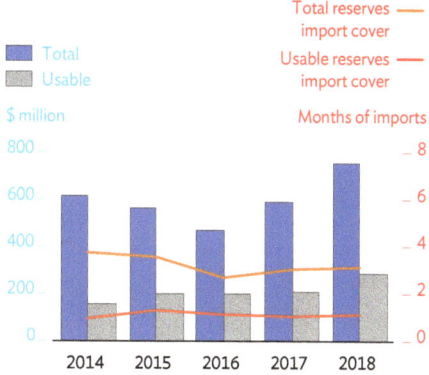

3.18.7 Gross international reserves

Source: Maldives Monetary Authority. 2019. Monthly Statistics. February. http://www.mma.gov.mv.

in contracted debt materialize and from leaders' commitments to fund new projects. Moreover, the introduction of a sovereign guarantee scheme in 2017 has bound the government to additional debt obligations. Under the scheme, state-owned enterprises and private parties are both eligible for sovereign guarantees on projects that the government chooses to support, though so far only one private party has received a guarantee.

In 2018, public debt including government-guaranteed debt increased markedly by 30.4% to Rf59.5 billion, equal to 72.1% of GDP (Figure 3.18.8). According to an International Monetary Fund Article IV mission statement in 2019, Maldives is at high risk of debt distress. A challenge to the country is to balance infrastructure development with long-term debt sustainability in light of limited repayment capacity. To remain eligible for grants under the International Development Association, Maldives must comply with its Non-Concessional Borrowing Policy (NCBP). However, non-concessional loans to Maldives signed from 2015 to 2017 prompted the NCBP committee to find it in breach of this policy because a number of the loans did not meet the 35% minimum required for the grant component. This prompted a change starting in 2018 for allocations to Maldives to be half grant, half International Development Association credit.

The new government intends to borrow on more concessional terms in the future and has recently secured $1 billion in concessional financing from the Government of India, of which $50 million is grants, $150 million is concessional budgetary assistance, and $800 million is a line of credit with the Export-Import Bank of India. Moreover, the government plans to refinance high-cost debt with more concessional financing and is currently looking for options to do so. It has expressed its intention to renegotiate unfavorable loan and project agreements signed in recent years, and it is strengthening the process it uses to issue sovereign guarantees. To create a sufficient reserve buffer toward paying off external debt, the government will continue building up its Sovereign Development Fund. Meanwhile, it is requesting a waiver on the NCBP change in its funding allocation as it seeks to comply with the NCBP going forward.

Fiscal consolidation and proper debt management of government and government-guaranteed debt are critical to long-term fiscal and debt sustainability. This requires Maldives to prioritize capital expenditure in line with its National Development Strategy, improve public finance management, and reform state-owned enterprises. Further, the government needs to be mindful of the implications of it pledges and find ways to restrain the fiscal deficit in the near term. External pressures would be lower under more manageable fiscal deficits in the near term than are projected in the baseline scenario of the fiscal framework.

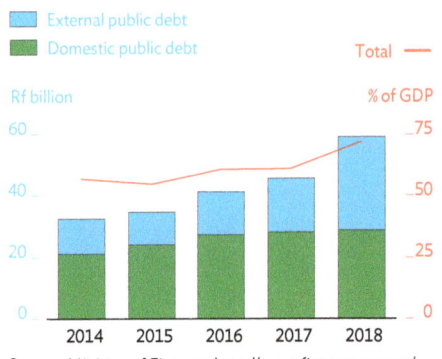

3.18.8 Public debt including guarantees

Source: Ministry of Finance, http://www.finance.gov.mv/.

Nepal

The economy remained healthy in fiscal 2018, though growth moderated. The outlook is for stable growth fueled by buoyant domestic demand as the government improves infrastructure and the investment climate. The current account deficit will widen on an expected increase in imports coupled with weak export competitiveness, building pressure on external stability. The authorities can smooth the transition to federalism by developing institutional capacity, clarifying legislation, and ensuring sufficient resources to subnational governments.

Economic performance

GDP growth moderated to an estimated 6.3% in fiscal year 2018 (FY2018, ended 16 July 2018) as economic activity recovered and normalized after earlier devastating earthquakes and trade disruptions (Figure 3.19.1). A continued expansive fiscal policy underpinned robust domestic demand. This kept industry growth high at 8.8% as construction expanded by 10.6%, bolstered by government capital spending and accelerated earthquake reconstruction, and manufacturing expanded by 8.0%, benefiting from more and better electricity supply. Services, the largest sector, grew by 6.6% as tourism increased and economic activity normalized. Floods early in the year crimped rice production to limit growth in agriculture to only 2.8%.

On the demand side, high consumption expenditure induced by faster growth in remittances dominated spending in FY2018. Fixed investment soared by 15.7% on higher private investment in manufacturing, energy, and tourism, to provide nearly one-third of GDP. Strong growth in construction spurred higher imports of building materials and capital goods, widening the trade deficit and making net exports a drag on growth.

Inflation eased from 4.5% in FY2017 to average 4.2% in FY2018, mainly tracking subdued inflation in India, the main source of supplies and to whose currency the Nepalese rupee is pegged (Figure 3.19.2). Despite a spike in domestic oil prices, the supply of goods improved, inflation for health care and education services moderated, and prices for clothing and footwear and housing and utilities remained subdued.

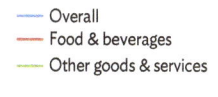

3.19.1 Supply-side contributions to growth

Note: Years are fiscal years ending in mid-July of that year.
Sources: Central Bureau of Statistics. 2018. *National Accounts of Nepal 2017/18*. http://cbs.gov.np/; ADB estimates.

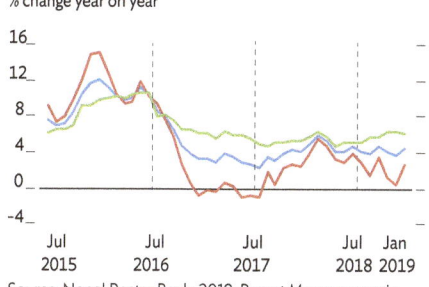

3.19.2 Monthly inflation

Source: Nepal Rastra Bank. 2019. *Recent Macroeconomic Situation*. http://www.nrb.org.np.

This chapter was written by Manbar Singh Khadka and Neelina Nakarmi of the Nepal Resident Mission, ADB, Kathmandu.

Budget policy continued to be expansionary with higher recurrent and capital expenditure. The fiscal deficit doubled from the equivalent of 3.2% of GDP in FY2017 to 6.7% in FY2018 (Figure 3.19.3). Capital expenditure rose by 28.0% with reform to budget implementation, and recurrent expenditure climbed by 34.3% on transfers to subnational governments (SNGs) equal to about 8.0% of GDP, as well as election expenses. Reflecting buoyant tax revenue from high import growth, revenue increased by 19.1% to equal 24.2% of GDP.

Broad money (M2) supply increased by 19.4% in FY2018 as rising net domestic assets pushed growth in supply above 15.5% in the previous year (Figure 3.19.4). Credit to the private sector grew by 22.3%, with a significant share going to wholesale and retail trade, manufacturing, and construction. Nepal Rastra Bank, the central bank, sought to tighten credit by forcing banks to maintain their ratio of loans to core capital plus deposits at 80% and lowering the ratio of mortgages and consumer loans to purchase value, which moderated lending for real estate and vehicle purchases.

Continued rapid growth in imports, particularly of construction materials and capital goods, reached 27.5% in FY2018, pushing the trade deficit to $10.9 billion and taking it as a percentage of GDP from 34.5% in FY2017 to 37.7%. Despite healthy remittance growth at 10.5%, the current account deficit ballooned from $95.4 million in FY2017 to $2.3 billion, equal to 8.2% of GDP (Figure 3.19.5). The deficit was partly financed by government borrowing.

Financial inflows could not fully offset this deficit, so gross foreign exchange reserves fell slightly to $10.1 billion, still providing 9.4 months of cover for imports of goods and services (Figure 3.19.6). The Nepalese rupee depreciated by 6.0% against the US dollar in FY2018, in line with Indian rupee depreciation. In real effective terms, the currency has been appreciating in recent years, indicating erosion of export competitiveness, but the trend reversed in FY2018 with slight depreciation.

Economic prospects

Economic growth is anticipated marginally down in FY2019 at 6.2%. A normal monsoon is expected to boost rice production to 5.5 million tons, for an 8.4% rise from a year earlier. The production of maize, the other important summer crop, is projected to rise by only 1.8%. Winter rainfall has been timely and will likely boost the production of cash crops like potatoes, vegetables, and fruit to boost agriculture growth overall to 4.5%.

Industry will likely grow by 7.1% in FY2019, buoyed by higher expectations for political stability. With no major electric power cuts since May 2018, more manufacturing firms have launched operations, and capacity utilization has

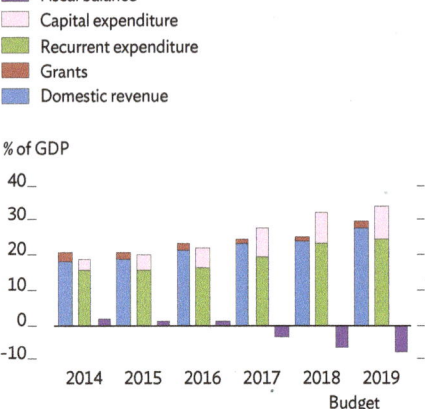

3.19.3 Fiscal indicators

Note: Years are fiscal years ending in mid-July of that year.
Source: Ministry of Finance. FY2019 Budget Speech.

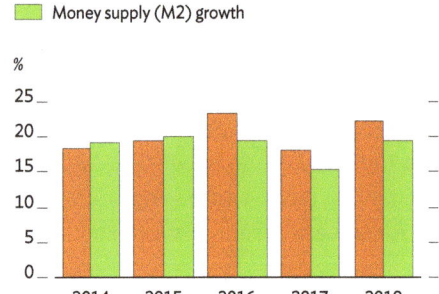

3.19.4 Credit to the private sector and money supply growth

Note: Years are fiscal years ending in mid-July of that year.
Source: Nepal Rastra Bank. 2019. *Recent Macroeconomic Situation*. http://www.nrb.org.np.

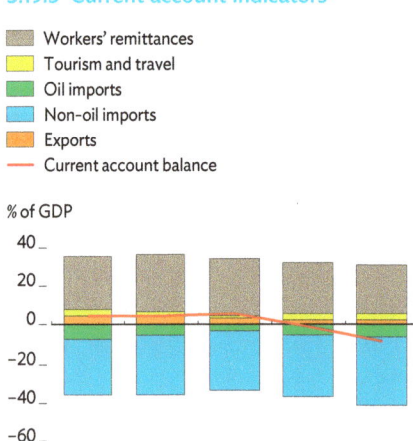

3.19.5 Current account indicators

Note: Years are fiscal years ending in mid-July of that year.
Source: Nepal Rastra Bank. 2019. *Recent Macroeconomic Situation*. http://www.nrb.org.np.

improved at existing plants. Construction gained momentum in the first half of FY2019, to mid-January 2019, and will continue to do so in the whole year in light of development needs, larger budget allocations made to SNGs, and accelerated reconstruction. Growth in services will edge up to 6.4% on expansion in wholesale and retail trade, hotels and restaurants, and finance.

Growth in FY2019 will find support in private investment, public infrastructure spending, and buoyant government recurrent spending. Data for the first half of FY2019 show capital expenditure up by 14.7% over the year-earlier period. SNG spending will similarly stimulate growth in FY2019. The budget for the year envisages a deficit equal to 8.0% of GDP, but it will likely be lower as capital expenditure underperforms allocation. Private consumption will likely remain strong with robust growth in remittances (Figure 3.19.7).

The trade deficit will widen further in FY2019 as domestic demand pushes up imports of oil and other products, and as the economy continues to struggle with its low manufacturing base and weak export competitiveness. The current account deficit is projected to deepen from 8.2% in FY2018 to 9.3% with increased imports of capital and consumer goods and services, and despite lower oil prices and healthy growth in remittances.

Average annual inflation will edge up from 4.2% in FY2018 to 4.4% in FY2019, having averaged 4.2% in the first 6 months of FY2019. Inflationary pressure will be kept largely in check by increased crop production, better supplies of goods and electricity, subdued oil prices, and expected moderation of inflation in India.

GDP growth is envisaged at 6.3% in FY2020, assuming a normal monsoon and no untoward circumstances such as floods devastating crops. Support for growth will come from the ongoing mechanization of agriculture, efforts to accelerate the implementation of large infrastructure projects, and the likely implementation of proposed legal reform to promote investment.

Average annual inflation will stay moderate at 5.1% in FY2020, assuming a better harvest, subdued oil prices, and only modestly higher inflation in India. The current account deficit is expected to narrow to the equivalent of 8.1% of GDP as import growth moderates thanks to fuel imports for generators replaced by better hydroelectricity supply. Remittances will continue to grow robustly.

Downside risks to the FY2020 outlook center on the challenges pertaining to the smooth implementation of fiscal federalism. SNGs face uphill tasks in program and project development, project implementation, and grant utilization. Separately, financial institutions may be vulnerable to risk from the recent buildup of credit to real estate and construction in the absence of strong risk management.

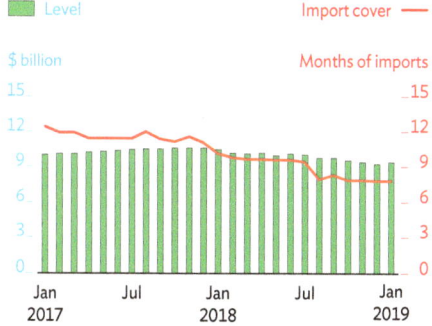

3.19.6 Gross international reserves and foreign exchange adequacy

Source: Nepal Rastra Bank. 2019. *Recent Macroeconomic Situation*. http://www.nrb.org.np.

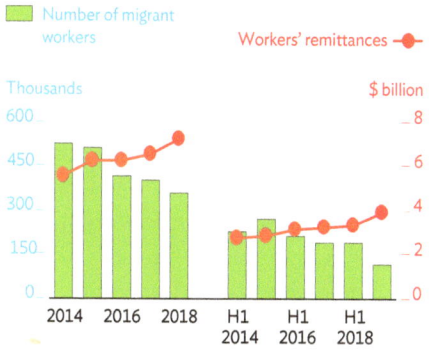

3.19.7 Migrant workers and remittances

H = half.
Note: Years are fiscal years ending in mid-July of that year.
Sources: Department of Foreign Employment; Nepal Rastra Bank.

3.19.1 Selected economic indicators (%)

	2019	2020
GDP growth	6.2	6.3
Inflation	4.4	5.1
Current account balance (share of GDP)	-9.3	-8.1

Source: ADB estimates.

Policy challenge—smoothly implementing fiscal federalism

Nepal transitioned from a unitary system of government to a federal one after the successful conclusion of federal, provincial, and local elections in 2017 and the subsequent formation in 2018 of government in three tiers. The first year of the implementation of federalism yielded mixed results, full of challenges and learning experiences. While the Constitution broadly specifies the rights and responsibilities of the three tiers, the smooth implementation of federalism stumbled over ambiguities in enabling legislation and a lack of capacity and appropriate human resources and capacity in SNGs.

The central government found it a challenge to quickly realign the existing national civil service with a federal system. A lack of requisite staff, both technical and administrative, affected the delivery of services and project execution. However, legislation passed in early 2019 set favorable promotion and pay grades for staffers who meet specified criteria, encouraging thousands of civil servants to apply for transfer to SNG positions. Additional legislation now in the works addresses other administrative staffing constraints on SNGs.

The budget for FY2019 apportioned fiscal transfers to SNG units in four modes: fiscal equalization grants, conditional grants, complementary grants, and special grants (Table 3.19.2). SNG budget execution in the first 6 months of FY2019 was low, mainly owing to a lack of staff capacity to carry out programs and project implementation.

Responsibility for expenditure has been decentralized (Figure 3.19.8). However, revenue mobilization remains with the national government, which collects the major revenue streams like income tax, value-added tax, and customs and excise duties to fund intergovernmental transfers to SNGs to cover their spending. Alternatively, though, local constituencies would have more choice in prioritizing local government services, and spending efficiency would likely improve, if SNGs had their own clearly defined sources of revenue.

Ensuring greater coordination among the tiers of government is key to effective service delivery and project execution, as are legislation and directives to further clarify the mandates and responsibilities of the different tiers of government.

To make expenditure more efficient, SNGs should augment their own revenue collection by improving taxpayer databases and accountability. The success of federalism hinges on maintaining cooperation, transparency, accountability, and fiscal discipline at all three tiers of government. And, finally, so does macroeconomic stability.

3.19.2 Fiscal transfers to subnational governments (% of GDP)

	FY2019
Transfer to provincial governments	3.6
Fiscal equalization grant	1.5
Conditional grant	1.8
Complementary grant	0.1
Special grant	0.1
Transfer to local governments	6.0
Fiscal equalization grant	2.5
Conditional grant	3.2
Complementary grant	0.1
Special grant	0.1

Note: Percentages may not total 100% because of rounding.
Source: Ministry of Finance. FY2019 Budget Speech.

3.19.8 Functional expenditure

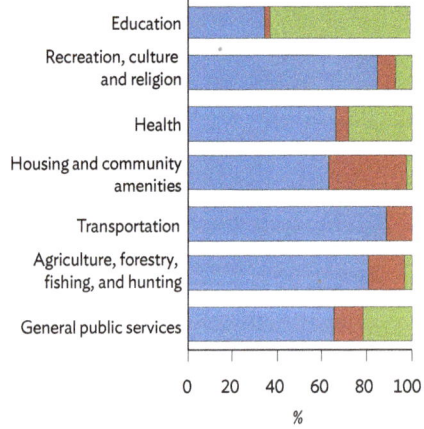

Source: Ministry of Finance. FY2019 Budget Speech.

Pakistan

Growth decelerated in fiscal 2018 despite revived agriculture. Expansionary fiscal policy markedly widened the budget and current account deficits and drained foreign exchange. Until macroeconomic imbalances are alleviated, the outlook is for slower growth, higher inflation, pressure on the currency, and heavy external financing needed to maintain even a minimal cushion of foreign exchange reserves. Recurrent crises in the balance of payments require that firms become more export competitive.

Economic performance

For fiscal year 2018 (FY2018, ended 30 June 2018), the estimated GDP growth rate has been revised downward from earlier 5.8% to 5.2%. Growth therefore slowed from 5.4% a year earlier, with revisions indicating slowdowns in industry and services (Figure 3.20.1). Lower growth in industry mirrored weaker growth in large-scale manufacturing, which is almost half of the sector, from 5.4% in FY2017 to 5.0%, as well as a slowdown in construction despite a strong revival in mining and quarrying. Growth in services decelerated from 6.5% in FY2017 to 5.8% last year. Growth in agriculture accelerated, by contrast, from 2.1% in FY2017 to 3.7% on an uptick in minor crops and cotton ginning.

On the demand side, growth in private consumption—which provides on average 81% of GDP and was the largest contributor to growth in FY2018—found support in low inflation and interest rates. Fixed investment in FY2018 reflected higher public investment in infrastructure and energy, especially under the China–Pakistan Economic Corridor (CPEC) project, including electric power projects. Meanwhile, private investment declined slightly despite low interest rates. Net exports weighed on growth as imports grew considerably faster than exports to meet rising demand for oil and capital products, notably to support infrastructure projects.

Average consumer price inflation decelerated from 4.2% in FY2017 to 3.9% as food inflation fell from 3.8% to 1.8%, and despite other inflation accelerating from 4.4% to 5.4% on strong domestic demand, rising global commodity prices, and a lagged effect of exchange rate adjustment (Figure 3.20.2). To counter rising inflation expectations, the State Bank of Pakistan, the central bank, gradually raised from January to May 2018 its policy rate by 75 basis points to 6.50%.

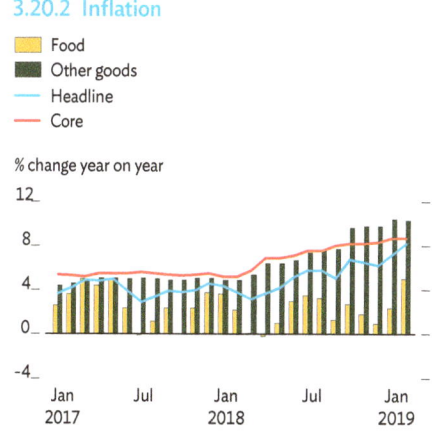

3.20.1 Supply-side contributions to growth

Note: Years are fiscal years ending on 30 June of that year.
Source: Ministry of Finance. *Pakistan Economic Survey 2017–18*. http://www.finance.gov.pk.

3.20.2 Inflation

Note: Inflation snapshot (FY2008 = 100).
Source: State Bank of Pakistan. Economic Data. http://www.sbp.org.pk (accessed 14 March 2019).

This chapter was written by Guntur Sugiyarto and Farzana Noshab of the Pakistan Resident Mission, ADB, Islamabad.

With expansionary fiscal policy, the consolidated federal and provincial budget deficit surged from the equivalent of 5.8% of GDP in FY2017 to 6.6% in FY2018, which was higher than expected (Figure 3.20.3). Revenue declined slightly from 15.4% of GDP in FY2017 to 15.2% last year, despite tax revenues rising to equal 13.0% of GDP. Nontax revenues fell by 0.8 percentage points to 2.2% of GDP in FY2018 as receipts from the Coalition Support Fund declined and despite higher central bank profits. Expenditure rose from 21.3% of GDP in FY2017 to 21.8% on higher interest payments, defense spending, and federal government subsidies, as well as a sizable increase in provincial current expenditure, which was expected in an election year. To contain the rising budget deficit, development expenditure, equal to 5.3% of GDP in FY2017, was cut to 4.6%.

Gross public debt rose from the equivalent of 67.0% of GDP at the end of FY2017 to 72.5% a year later, above the 60% threshold stipulated in the Fiscal Responsibility and Debt Limitation Act (Figure 3.20.4). The fiscal deficit was financed largely by borrowing from the central bank and external sources. Domestic borrowing for budgetary support was, at 4.2% of GDP in FY2018, twice the amount borrowed from external sources. External financing comprised multilateral and bilateral loans, as well as inflows from the issuance of a $2.5 billion eurobond in November 2017. External public debt including liabilities increased by $9.2 billion to $75.4 billion in FY2018, rising from 21.7% of GDP in FY2017 to 26.6%.

Private sector credit expanded by PRs775.5 billion, or 14.9% in FY2018, as lower government borrowing from commercial banks left more liquidity available to the private sector (Figure 3.20.5). This was despite credit to state-owned enterprises sustained at PRs254.7 billion, slightly above the FY2017 amount, reflecting their weak finances and need for continued government support.

A large trade deficit drove the current account deficit to $19 billion, equal to 6.1% of GDP in FY2018 and significantly above the 4.1% deficit a year earlier (Figure 3.20.6). Exports rebounded from near stagnation at only 0.1% growth in FY2017 to 12.8% in FY2018 on rising exports of textiles, chemicals, leather, and food—and are benefiting from currency depreciation. Import growth slowed from the equivalent of 18% of GDP in FY2017 but, at 15% in FY2018, still outpaced export growth on higher imports of metal, vehicles, machinery, and petroleum, Pakistan's major imported commodities. The service account balance worsened by another 32%, following a 27% decline in FY2017, reflecting in part discontinued receipts under the Coalition Support Fund. Growth in remittances reversed a 2.8% decline in FY2017, but weak 1.4% growth had little impact against the persistent trade deficit (Figure 3.20.7).

3.20.1 Selected economic indicators (%)

	2019	2020
GDP growth	3.9	3.6
Inflation	7.5	7.0
Current account balance (share of GDP)	–5.0	–3.0

Source: ADB estimates.

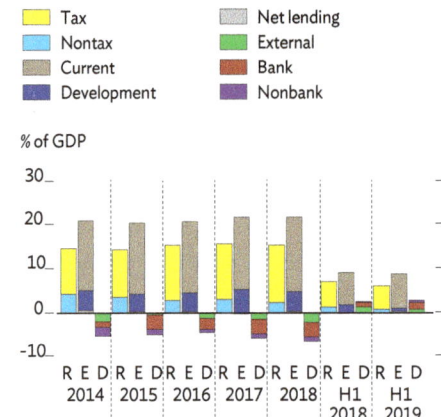

3.20.3 Government budget indicators

D = deficit financing, E = expenditure, H = half, R = revenue.
Note: Years are fiscal years ending on 30 June of that year.
Sources: Ministry of Finance. *Pakistan Economic Survey 2017–2018; Pakistan Summary of Consolidated Federal & Provincial Budgetary Operations, July–September 2018.*

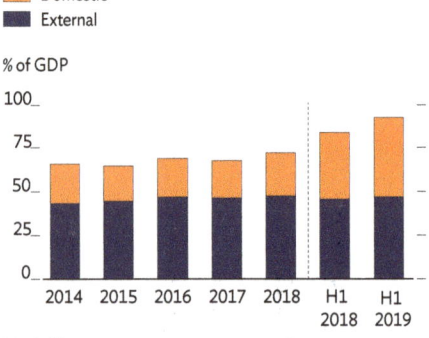

3.20.4 Public debt

H = half.
Note: Years are fiscal years ending on 30 June of that year.
Source: State Bank of Pakistan, Economic Data. http://www.sbp.org.pk (accessed 14 March 2019).

Also contributing to the current account deficit were a higher income deficit with increased repatriation of profits by foreign firms and rising interest payments.

Financial inflows increased by $3.1 billion to $13.3 billion in FY2018, mainly under portfolio investment despite a fall in loan disbursements and near stagnation in foreign direct investment (Figure 3.20.8). Foreign exchange reserves, under pressure, declined by $6.3 billion to $9.9 billion at the end of FY2018, sufficient to finance less than 2 months of imports of goods and services. These external pressures caused the Pakistan rupee to depreciate by 11.7% against the US dollar from December 2017 to the end of June 2018, when the exchange rate was PRs121 per $1 (Figure 3.20.9).

Economic prospects

GDP growth is forecast to decelerate further to 3.9% in FY2019 as macroeconomic challenges continue and despite steps to tighten fiscal and monetary policies to rein in high and unsustainable twin deficits. To meet its large financing needs, the government is discussing a macroeconomic stabilization program with the International Monetary Fund in addition to arranging financial assistance and oil credit facilities from bilateral sources. Continued fiscal consolidation in FY2020 will keep growth subdued at 3.6%.

The supply side is already showing signs of slowdown. Agriculture is expected to underperform the 3.8% growth target for FY2019 after water shortages struck as wet season crops were being sown. Large-scale manufacturing reversed 6.6% growth in the first half of FY2018 to decline by 1.5% in the same period of FY2019 as domestic demand contracted and rising world prices crimped demand for raw materials. Contraction hit all key categories, including a 0.2% decline in textiles. A slowdown in agriculture and industry as domestic demand shrinks will keep growth in services subdued. A government structural reform package announced in January 2019 is expected to support agriculture, facilitate new business openings, and continue to expand capacity in some industries to the forecast horizon. Stabilization policies and rising inflation are likely to contain growth in private consumption and investment, while public sector development spending has already slackened. With exchange rate flexibility and declining imports, net exports are expected to contribute to growth.

Average inflation accelerated sharply from 3.8% in the first 8 months of FY2018 to 6.5% in the same period of FY2019, led by a surge in nonfood inflation to 9.1% that reflected currency depreciation and a significant increase in gas tariffs for consumers and industry in the first half. Food inflation remains relatively moderate at 2.6% thanks to

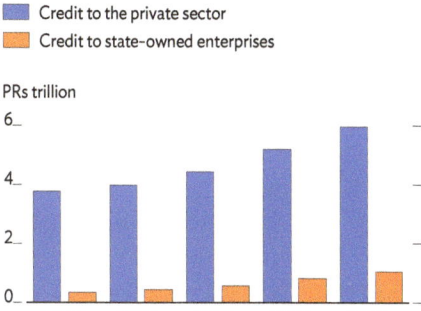

3.20.5 Credit to the nongovernment entities

Note: Years are fiscal years ending on 30 June of that year.
Sources: State Bank of Pakistan, *Monetary Policy Compendium*, Jan 2019; *Monthly Statistical Bulletin*, Jan 2019 (Table 2.6 Monetary Aggregates).

3.20.6 Current account components

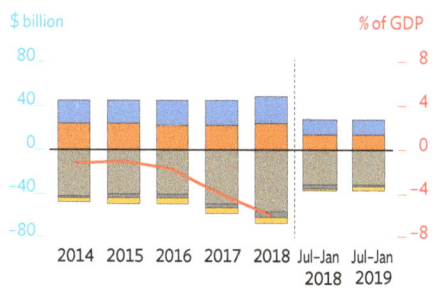

Note: Years are fiscal years ending on 30 June of that year.
Source: State Bank of Pakistan. Economic Data. http://www.sbp.org.pk (accessed 25 February 2019).

3.20.7 Remittances

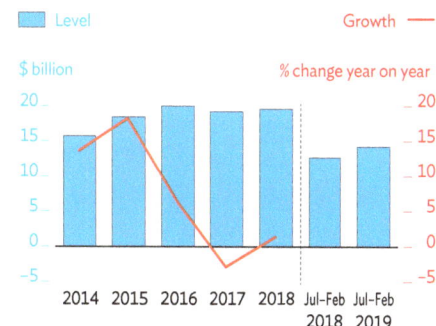

Note: Years are fiscal years ending on 30 June of that year.
Source: State Bank of Pakistan. Economic Data. http://www.sbp.org.pk (accessed 14 March 2019).

sufficient stocks of food staples. In response to intensifying inflationary pressures, the central bank gradually raised, in four rounds from July 2018 to January 2019, its policy rate by 375 basis points to 10.25%. Despite tighter monetary policy and lower international oil prices, inflation is expected to rise sharply to average 7.5% in FY2019, driven up by continued heavy government borrowing from the central bank, hikes to domestic gas and electricity tariffs, further increases in regulatory duties on luxury imports, and the lagged impact of currency depreciation by more than 10.7% since July 2018. Inflation will remain elevated at 7.0% in FY2020.

A supplementary consolidated government budget for FY2019, adopted in September 2018, envisages a decline in the budget deficit to 5.1% of GDP in FY2019, mainly by cutting development expenditure excluding CPEC projects, but it also included measures to enhance revenue and extend relief to the poor. Growth in tax collection weakened from a robust 16.4% in the first half of FY2018 to only 2.7% a year later. The Federal Board of Revenue targets tax collection equal to only 11.6% of GDP in FY2019, taking into account reduced sales taxes on major petroleum products, drag on the collection of withholding tax from contracts, contraction in general sales tax revenue as imports slow, and the overall slowdown in the economy. Including nontax revenue, total revenue declined by nearly 2.4% in the first half of FY2019.

Budget expenditure increased by 5.5% in the first half of FY2019 over the same period a year earlier as current spending rose for interest payments and defense. Lower revenue collection and higher current expenditure pushed the budget deficit from the equivalent of 2.3% of GDP in the first half of FY2018 to 2.7% a year later. This situation will make it a challenge for the government to achieve the reduction in the budget deficit it targets for FY2019. A second supplementary budget, adopted on 6 March 2019 without information on the projected deficit, focuses on an economic reform package envisaging incentives and measures to encourage investment and exports, enhance the ease of doing business, and strengthen export-oriented activities.

In the first 8 months of FY2019, the government borrowed more from the central bank and less from commercial banks, freeing up liquidity with which commercial banks boosted credit to the private sector by 18.9% over the same period of FY2018. This sharply increased net domestic assets and nearly doubled broad money growth to 2.8%.

The current account deficit is expected to ease in FY2019 but will remain high at the equivalent of 5.0% of GDP because of the large trade deficit. It will narrow further to 3.0% in FY2020 with easing macroeconomic pressures on the external accounts. Export growth plunged from double digits in the first 7 months of FY2018 to 1.6% in the same period of FY2019.

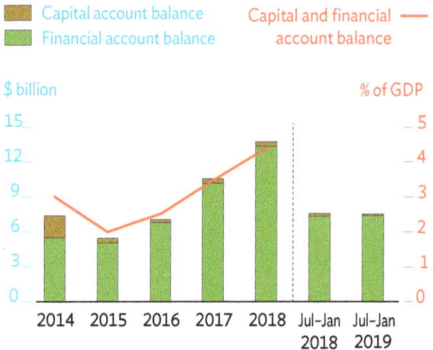

3.20.8 Capital and financial account balance

Note: Years are fiscal years ending on 30 June of that year.
Source: State Bank of Pakistan. Economic Data. http://www.sbp.org.pk (accessed 14 March 2019).

3.20.9 Exchange rates

Source: State Bank of Pakistan, Economic Data. http://www.sbp.org.pk (accessed 14 March 2019).

It is expected, however, to strengthen in the remaining months of this fiscal year and further in FY2020 as the lagged impact of currency depreciation kicks in, along with the incentive package for export-oriented industries announced in January 2019. Imports fell by 0.8% in the first 7 months of FY2019 from the same period of FY2018, with imports other than oil 5.7% lower because of slower domestic economic activity, currency depreciation, and an increase in import duties for nonessential items. Remittances are expected to revive—having already risen by 10% in the first 7 months of FY2019 over the same period of FY2018—as the Pakistan rupee depreciate further, economic activity holds broadly steady in the Middle Eastern oil-exporting countries (major destinations for Pakistani migrants), and the government takes measures to facilitate remittances through official channels.

The government's diaspora bonds—issued in January 2019 with terms of 3 and 5 years and an attractive return of over 6%—aim to tap resources from overseas Pakistanis. Inflows that do not incur debt, such as foreign direct investment, are expected to be lower in FY2019 as several CPEC energy projects near completion. Financing a high current account deficit in FY2019 will require substantial borrowing, as in the first 7 months of the year, and use much of the bilateral lending support announced in the early months of 2019 to finance the deficit in the balance of payments. Foreign exchange reserves, depleted to $8.1 billion in February 2019, will likely remain stressed at the end of FY2019.

Policy challenge—improving business competitiveness

Pakistan ranks 107 of 140 economies on the Global Competitiveness Index 2018. It is classified as inhabiting the first stage of development among 35 factor-driven economies—that is, economies heavily reliant on unskilled labor and natural resources. The country's persistently low score and ranking on the index is reflected in its companies' struggles to compete in international markets and in weak export opportunities, which spark recurring crises in the balance of payment.

Pakistan lags behind the South Asia regional average on most index indicators (Figure 3.20.10). Business competitiveness in Pakistan suffers under a challenging macroeconomic environment and adverse terms of trade, significantly eroding production and exports. Pakistan's exports, such as they are, remain largely primary products whose lack of sophistication and diversification condemn them to declining shares in world markets (Figure 3.20.11). Agricultural commodities, textiles, and other manufactures with little value added comprise over 80% of exports.

3.20.10 Pakistan vs. South Asia: GCI Scores 2018

Source: Global Competitiveness Index 2017–2018, World Economic Forum.

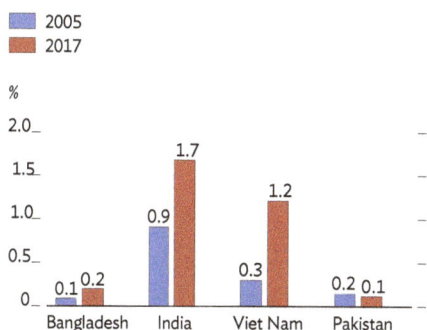

3.20.11 Share in total world exports

Source: WTO Annual Reports. http://www.wto.org.

The high cost of doing business is a key factor limiting firms' ability to compete. Access to affordable capital is constrained by a shallow and underdeveloped capital market. Manufacturing firms face high corporate tax rates, taxes on dividends and retained earnings, cascading taxes levied on intercorporate dividends, and a super tax levied on retained reserves. The effective corporate tax rate of up to 49% is significantly higher than taxes on international competitors. High custom duties on machinery imports raise the cost of investment, and high tariffs on raw materials and intermediate inputs erode the price competitiveness of both exporters and domestic industries facing stiff competition from imports. Similarly, high tariffs and undependable electric power add to production costs.

Pakistan's cumbersome customs and clearance procedures, and the poor quality of its logistics and infrastructure, remain constraints on its capacity for just-in-time supply chain management. Investing in infrastructure and improving trade facilitation could boost participation in world markets, but the absence of industry-wide facilities to test and certify compliance would still leave many exporters disadvantaged.

Macroeconomic stability is needed to create an environment that inspires business confidence and is conducive to investment and trade. Facing twin deficits in fiscal and current accounts, the government has long been bedeviled by difficult policy choices that pit improved tax revenues against enhanced competitiveness. Moreover, with an anti-export bias in tax and exchange rate policies, and high government borrowing that crowds out private investment, firm competitiveness erodes even though recent currency depreciation supports exports.

The government is currently preparing its 5-year Strategic Trade Policy Framework with the objective of boosting export competitiveness. All elements of a competitiveness framework are under consideration, including measures taken at the border and others behind it. The framework will address issues that hinder not only export competitiveness but also the creation of a more competitive domestic industry. As a first step, the Prime Minister announced in March 2019 a more liberal e-visa policy for foreign visitors from 175 countries.

Sri Lanka

Despite recovery in agriculture and improved services performance, growth remained subdued in 2018 as industry slowed. Inflation softened as food inflation eased, but core inflation picked up. Fiscal and structural reforms continued and remain critical to averting repeated macroeconomic stress. Growth is projected to recover moderately in 2019 and 2020, but with a downside risk stemming from upcoming elections. Sri Lanka is highly vulnerable to climate change and needs to become more disaster resilient.

Economic performance

Growth in 2018 edged lower to 3.2% (Figure 3.21.1). Political uncertainties in 2018 weighed on economic sentiment and worsened in the last quarter, affecting Sri Lanka's risk perception and prompting all three major agencies to downgrade its rating.

On the supply side, a turnaround in agriculture and a pickup in services supported growth. However, growth was held back by a slowdown in industry with contraction in construction and weaker manufacturing.

Agriculture grew by 4.8% in 2018 as rice production increased by 33.9%, reversing sharp contraction in 2017, and production expanded as well for a number of other crops. However, a dip in tea production by 0.8% following excessive rain and lackluster performance of fisheries, both sizeable contributors to agriculture, slowed the sector's recovery.

As growth in fixed investment slipped lower in 2018, construction shrank by 2.1%, pulling down industry growth from 4.1% in 2017 to 0.9%. Manufacturing growth remained moderate at 3.0% despite a turnaround in food and beverages, the largest category. Other important areas such as garments, rubber products, basic metals, and nonmetallic mineral products slowed, while some others contracted. Services grew by 4.7%, with finance expanding by 11.8% and wholesale and retail trade up by 5.0%. Transportation, the largest service industry, continued to be weak, growing by only 2.8%. Public administration shrank by 0.6%.

On the demand side, consumption expenditure remained subdued and dropped to 1.6% growth as government consumption contracted for the second straight year. Private consumption growth slowed to 2.3% from 2.5% in 2017.

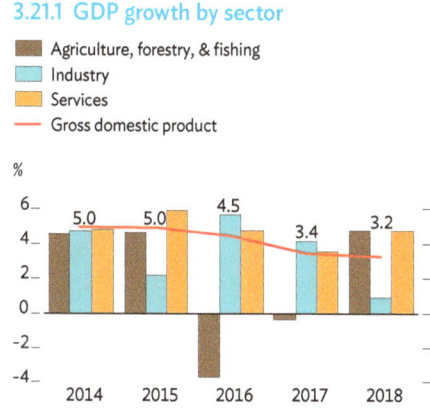

3.21.1 GDP growth by sector

Source: Department of Census and Statistics of Sri Lanka. http://www.statistics.gov.lk/ (accessed 20 March 2019).

This chapter was written by Nimali Hasitha Wickremasinghe and Savindi Jayakody of the Sri Lanka Resident Mission, ADB, Colombo.

Gross fixed capital formation experienced a marginal decline in the face of fiscal consolidation and political uncertainty, while 29.6% expansion in inventories meant growth in gross capital formation (Figure 3.21.2).

Headline inflation, driven by food price deflation with recovery in agriculture, trended lower in 2018 to average 2.1% for the year (Figure 3.21.3). Headline inflation decelerated during 2018 from 5.4% year on year in January 2018 to 0.1% in October and then picked up to 2.4% in February 2019. Average food prices fell by 0.2% in 2018, while nonfood inflation averaged 4.1%. Nonfood inflation trended higher from 2.5% year on year in January 2018 to 6.7% in February 2019, while core inflation was broadly stable in the first half of 2018 but picked up in the second half and reached 5.5% year on year in February 2019. These movements reflect currency depreciation and the pass-through of fuel prices to production costs.

Revenue collection, mostly of domestic indirect taxes, improved by 4.8% in 2018 over 2017, but the ratio of revenue to GDP still declined, to 13.4% (Figure 3.21.4). Expenditure increased by 4.7% on higher current expenditure, with interest payments increasing by 15.8%, while public investments declined by 4.9%. A primary surplus, equal to 0.6% of GDP, was recorded for a second consecutive year in 2018 as fiscal adjustment continued under an International Monetary Fund (IMF) program, but the budget deficit for 2018, estimated at 5.3% of GDP, missed the 4.8% target. As the Sri Lanka rupee sharply depreciated, the ratio of central government debt to GDP spiked, from an estimated 76.9% in 2017 to a provisional 84.0% in 2018, illustrating the need to sustain fiscal consolidation (Figure 3.21.5).

As inflation eased and growth slowed, the Central Bank of Sri Lanka lowered its standing lending facility rate by 25 basis points in April 2018 to 8.50%, leaving the standing deposit facility rate unchanged at 7.25% (Figure 3.21.6). In response to liquidity constraints, and with call rates hovering near the upper end of the policy rate corridor, the central bank reduced the statutory reserve ratio in November 2018 by 1.5 percentage points to 6.0% to bolster liquidity, and at the same time it increased the standing deposit facility rate by 75 basis points to 8.0% and the standing lending facility rate by 50 basis points to 9.0% to neutralize any potential effect on inflation from excess liquidity. Despite increased lending rates, credit to the private sector accelerated marginally after September (Figure 3.21.7). The central bank further lowered the statutory reserve ratio to 5.0% in February 2019 to address liquidity deficits, while leaving policy rates unchanged.

Export earnings expanded by 4.7% in 2018 as industrial exports grew by 8.4% and agricultural exports fell by 6.8% with declines across all major agriculture export categories. Garment export growth accelerated moderately from 3.0%

3.21.2 Demand-side contributions to growth

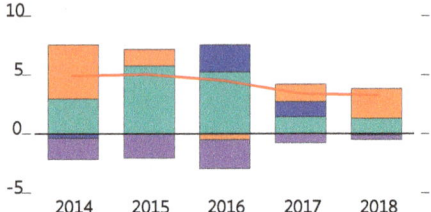

Sources: Department of Census and Statistics of Sri Lanka. http://www.statistics.gov.lk (accessed 19 March 2019); ADB estimates.

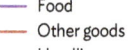

3.21.3 Inflation

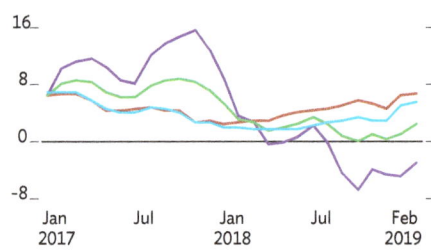

Source: Department of Census and Statistics of Sri Lanka. http://www.statistics.gov.lk (accessed 19 March 2019).

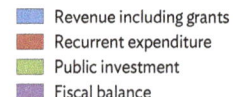

3.21.4 Government finance

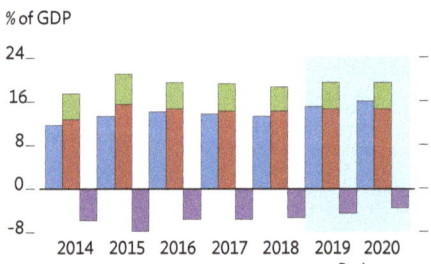

Note: Figures exclude revenue and expenditure transfers to provincial councils.
Sources: Central Bank Annual Report various years, Ministry of Finance; ADB estimates.

in 2017 to 4.7%, while tea exports reversed 20.5% growth in 2017 to contract by 6.6% with both lower volume and lower prices. Imports expanded by 6.0%, driven by large increases for vehicles, fertilizer, and fuel, causing the trade deficit to widen even as rice imports shrank on recovery in agriculture and gold imports declined following the imposition of customs duty. Motor vehicle imports increased sharply in the first 9 months but showed declines month on month in the last 2 months of 2018. This followed the imposition of import controls in September 2018 that included a 200% cash margin on letters of credit for motor vehicles, suspension of vehicle imports by all state institutions for 1 year, and disallowing government employees concessionary duty rates on car imports for 6 months.

A decline in outmigration since 2015 meant a second consecutive year of lower worker remittances, falling by 2.1% in 2018 (Figure 3.21.8). Earnings from tourism increased by 11.6% in 2018 to reach $4.4 billion as tourist arrivals increased by 10.3% to reach 2.3 million. With service account and income net outflows, the current account deficit widened from the equivalent of 2.6% of GDP in 2017 to an estimated 3.0% in 2018 (Figure 3.21.9).

Capital outflows brought the rupee under significant pressure in 2018, causing it to depreciate against the US dollar by 19.6% year on year to the end of December 2018 (Figure 3.21.10). Global conditions precipitated capital outflows and pressure on exchange rates in many emerging markets, with some recovering by the end of the year. However, in Sri Lanka, the pressure on the currency continued as a political crisis unfolded in the last quarter.

Foreign currency reserves rose from $8.0 billion at the end of December 2017, or cover for 4.6 months of imports, to an all-time high of $9.9 billion in April 2018 as Sri Lanka successfully raised $2.5 billion in international markets. By the end of December 2018, reserves had fallen again to $6.9 billion, or 3.7 months of imports (Figure 3.21.11). A month later, reserves had fallen further to $6.2 billion after the government repaid debt using $1.0 billion from its reserves. As the political crisis reached resolution and discussions with the IMF restarted, pressure on the rupee eased.

The government continued a raft of reforms in 2018: opening the Single Window Investment Facilitation Taskforce, a web portal to streamline and fast-track investment approval; setting up as a one-stop shop and portal with trade information for exporters and importers; and simplifying business procedures to obtain online construction permits, as well as property registration and other information. Sri Lanka's rank in the World Bank's ease of doing business index improved from 111 in 2017 to 100 in 2018. Major reforms to support fiscal operations were the passage of the Active Liability Management Act, which enables the government to raise funds for debt repayment, and the implementation of the new Inland Revenue Act.

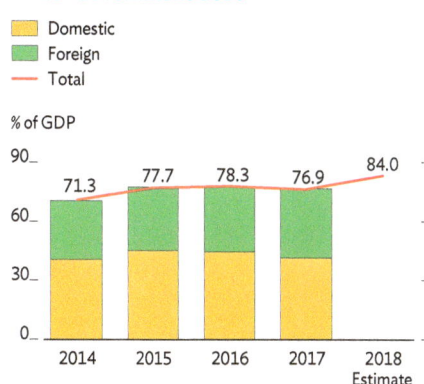

3.21.5 Government debt

Sources: Central Bank of Sri Lanka, *Monthly Economic Indicators*, Ministry of Finance (accessed 20 March 2019); ADB estimates.

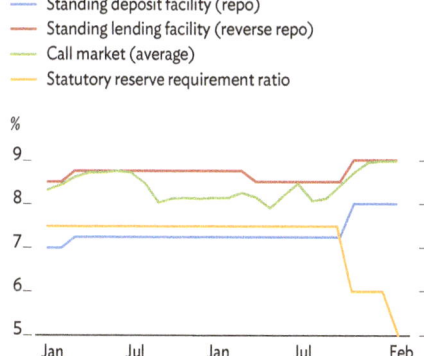

3.21.6 Policy rates

Source: Central Bank of Sri Lanka.

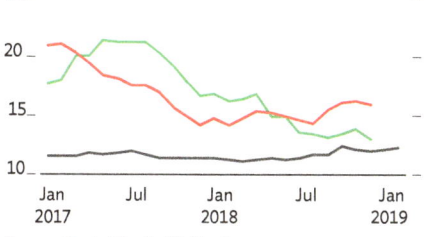

3.21.7 Interest rate, credit, and money growth

Source: Central Bank of Sri Lanka.

May 2018 saw the introduction of a fuel pricing formula that revises prices to align with global prices every 2 months. However, electricity pricing reform, a key component of energy pricing reform, could not be completed in 2018.

Economic prospects

Growth is expected to pick up to 3.6% in 2019 and then to 3.8% in 2020. Having normalized in 2018, agriculture is expected to continue to grow at about the same rate in the next 2 years, assuming normal weather. Tea and marine fishing, both large contributors to agriculture, will turn around in 2019 from the dip experienced in 2018. Industry will pick up gradually over the 2-year period, reversing the slowdown in 2018. Construction is expected to reverse contraction last year with marginal growth this year thanks to a base effect but also a higher budget for public investment. Services will continue moderate growth at 4.6% in 2019, picking up marginally to 4.8% in 2020 with support from trade and financial services, as well as from accommodation and food and beverage services, which will benefit from continued expansion in tourism.

On the demand side, the 2019 budget includes proposals to increase public sector salaries and allowances and to address pension anomalies. This will support private expenditure and thereby growth. The government continues to consolidate its finances, but the primary surplus target of 1.5% in 2019 is downgraded from the original target of 2.0%. This may provide an impetus to public investment as the 2019 budget includes several capital expenditure projects. Uncertainties surrounding an upcoming election will affect private investor sentiment. The Colombo Port City Project is expected to bring in new investment, but the pace may depend on the passage of supporting laws.

Headline inflation is expected to be higher coming off a low base in 2018 and fueled by rising economic activity in 2019 and 2020. Food inflation, which slowed throughout 2018 and was negative toward the end of 2018, will pick up from the low base. A weak currency will exert upward pressure on prices and may offset anticipated lower fuel prices. Inflation is expected to edge up to 3.5% in 2019 and then reach 4.0% in 2020.

Agriculture exports will turn around from contraction in 2018 with improved performance from tea exports. Garment exports will continue to grow only moderately as export markets expand more slowly over the next 2 years. Downside risks to garments arise from a scenario of a no-deal Brexit and tariff escalation between Sri Lanka and UK (Box 1.1.4). The introduction of an excise duty and a luxury tax on motor vehicles will keep vehicle imports in check. After shrinking in 2018, remittances will remain more or less the same over the next 2 years under a structural decline in outmigration

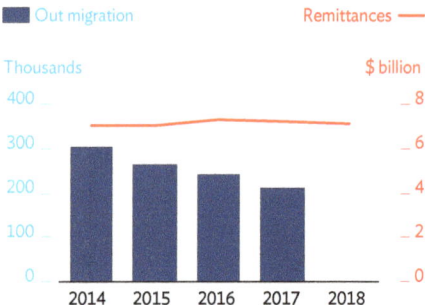

3.21.8 Labor migration and remittance earnings

Note: The number of out migrants in 2018 is not available.
Source: Central Bank of Sri Lanka.

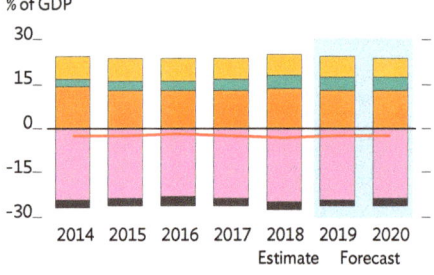

3.21.9 Current account components

Sources: Central Bank of Sri Lanka, *Annual Report 2017*; ADB estimates.

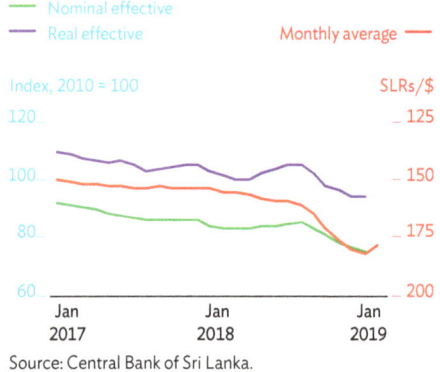

3.21.10 Exchange rates

Source: Central Bank of Sri Lanka.

and lower oil prices affecting economic activity in key host countries. The current account deficit will shrink to 2.5% in 2019, widening marginally to 2.6% in 2020.

The 2019 budget aims to reduce the budget deficit to the equivalent of 4.4% of GDP, mainly with higher revenue collection. The revenue ratio is expected to improve to 15.1%, a large portion of the increase coming from tax revenue. Expenditure is budgeted to increase marginally to equal 19.5% of GDP with public investment increasing to 4.8% of GDP. The budget deficit is projected to fall to 3.5% of GDP in 2020. The primary surplus is targeted to increase progressively to 1.5% of GDP in 2019 and 2.4% in 2020. From an election year perspective, the budget was a positive development, signaling commitment to restoring fiscal order. To support export growth, the budget announced accelerated reduction in the cess on intermediate goods used in key sectors. To encourage women to participate in the labor force, corporate tax deductions were announced for companies that grant 3–4 months of maternity leave.

In February 2019, the IMF completed its fifth review of the program, and a staff-level agreement was reached to extend the program for an additional year until June 2020. This will allow more time for the government to complete the economic reform agenda.

Political uncertainty and large payments to service external debt may affect market sentiment and exert pressure on the rupee. In January 2019, Sri Lanka entered into a swap arrangement worth $400 million with India through the South Asian Association for Regional Cooperation swap facility. Soon after the conclusion of the IMF review and the presentation of the 2019 budget, Sri Lanka issued a 5-year $1.0 billion bond and a 10-year $1.4 billion bond, both of which were oversubscribed. Together, these measures promise to shore up reserves and support the currency.

Downside risks to the forecast emanate from political developments connected to elections and the ensuing policy direction, as well as weather uncertainties. International risks would be a deeper slowdown in the advanced economies, fuel prices or import volume above expectations, or fallout from Brexit that is difficult to fully assess at this point.

Policy challenge—building disaster resilience

Sri Lanka is susceptible to weather-related hazards partly because of climate change. These hazards, from severe floods to extreme droughts, are recurrent events in Sri Lanka, with greater frequency in the recent past, with heavy rain in May 2016 and May 2017 causing flooding and landslides, and drought striking in late 2016 (Table 3.21.2). The Global Climate Risk Index ranked Sri Lanka among the top four countries globally most affected by adverse weather in 2016 and 2017 in terms of fatalities and economic losses.

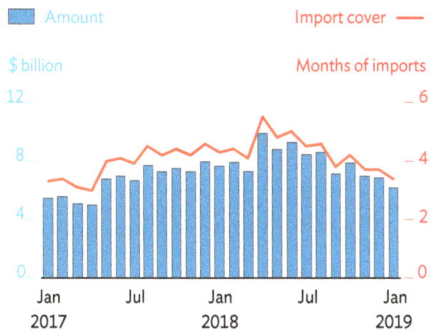

3.21.11 Gross official reserves

Source: Central Bank of Sri Lanka. http://www.cbsl.gov.lk.

3.21.1 Selected economic indicators (%)

	2019	2020
GDP growth	3.6	3.8
Inflation	3.5	4.0
Current account balance (share of GDP)	-2.5	-2.6

Source: ADB estimates.

3.21.2 Hazard consequence in Sri Lanka, 1965–2018

Hazard	Number of occurrences	Number of deaths	Number of people affected	Damage ($ million)
Flood	67	1,977	16,418,587	2,574
Drought	11		10,756,000	45
Storm	8	810	1,709,457	503
Tsunami	1	35,399	1,019,306	1,317
Landslide	6	360	1,927	
Epidemic[a]	10	1,015	440,537	
Total	103	39,561	30,345,814	4,438

[a] Bacterial, viral, and parasite diseases.
Sources: Emergency Events Database (EM-DAT). http://www.emdat.be; ADB estimates.

Disasters have multiple impacts on the economy. With two rice cultivation cycles disrupted since 2016, agricultural GDP contracted by 3.7% in 2016 and 0.4% in 2017, domestic food prices surged by 14.4% in December 2017, and food imports increased in 2017 by about 13%, or $214 million, to equal 0.2% of GDP. The extended dry spell in 2016 affected large swathes of land across the country, reducing yields and causing other crop losses. The drought forced power generation to shift from hydro to more expensive thermal production, raising oil imports by 40%, or $950 million, equal to 1.1% of GDP. Government spending to repair the damage wrought by disasters amounted to 3% of government expenditure in 2016, or 0.4% of GDP, and 2% of expenditure in 2017, or 0.5% of GDP. The cost of damage caused by disasters in 2016 and 2017 was more than twice as high in rupee terms as the worst disaster years in the past (Figure 3.21.12). Disasters were felt disproportionately by the poor, upending the livelihoods of more than 2 million people. Rising food prices and falling production can deny food to the most vulnerable households, aggravating the malnutrition prevalent in hazard-prone areas as the poor limit the number and size of meals they consume each day. They may cope by prioritizing feeding their children, limiting expenditures on education and health care. Financial instruments to mitigate the impact of weather-related hazards, such as insurance, are not readily available for the vulnerable, including women.

Quick government action through higher imports, public food distribution, and increased fiscal spending on an expanded social safety net mitigated the hardship inflicted on the disaster-struck poor. However, the recurrence of disasters signals the need to develop a preemptive strategy to deal with similar shocks in the future.

The government has started to build disaster resilience by emphasizing environment protection and disaster management in its strategy document Vision 2025 and in the 2019 budget. It is developing national targets for disaster risk reduction based on the Sendai Framework for Disaster Reduction 2015–2030, proposing a national disaster reserve fund for reconstruction after disasters, strengthening disaster insurance and increasing mitigation spending, ratifying nationally determined contributions to achieve the objectives of the Paris Agreement on climate change, and developing its National Disaster Master Plan with balanced investment to implement its Comprehensive Disaster Management Program.

The government can further improve disaster risk management by articulating a policy for the near term and expediting its implementation. It is important to prevent disasters and mitigate the consequences of those that occur through risk-informed investment planning and effective risk management enabled by timely financing.

The economic consequences of recent disasters would not have been as bad as they were if the economy had been robust in general and more diversified in terms of employment. Recurrent weather-related disasters may threaten significant gains in poverty reduction made over the past 20 years. Further efforts to reduce poverty will be sustainable over the longer term only if they successfully incorporate disaster risk reduction and climate change adaptation into development planning.

The focus needs to shift to areas prone to disaster and to determining how to make people, assets, and infrastructure more resilient. Measures to mitigate disasters include formulating risk management action plans and early warning systems, especially localized warnings to vulnerable communities, through community-based disaster risk management, holding community education sessions and emergency drills, and assembling evacuation plans and kits. Reliable risk profiles and timely hydrometeorological data and information on disasters are core inputs for many disaster risk management initiatives. This requires effective capacity building in data-generating agencies and a comprehensive mechanism for sharing data and information among all users.

Major efforts need to be mounted to mobilize funds for risk reduction and adaptation, establish correct policy frameworks, and build institutional capacity. Beyond the near term is a need to develop a comprehensive disaster risk financing strategy that is consistent with debt sustainability. It should use a risk-layering approach to promote the use of instruments to retain and transfer risk, as well as build up infrastructure and implementation capacity.

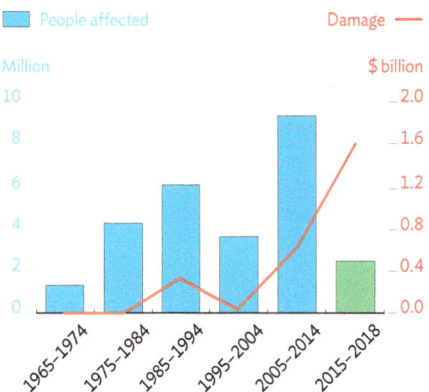

3.21.12 Impact of weather-related hazards

Sources: Emergency Events Database (EM-DAT). http://www.emdat.be; ADB estimates.

SOUTHEAST ASIA

- BRUNEI DARUSSALAM
- CAMBODIA
- INDONESIA
- LAO PEOPLE'S DEMOCRATIC REPUBLIC
- MALAYSIA
- MYANMAR
- PHILIPPINES
- SINGAPORE
- THAILAND
- VIET NAM

Brunei Darussalam

Even as oil prices rose in 2018, this energy exporter saw oil and gas production decline because of unplanned repairs and maintenance. Inflation stirred, and the current account shrank. As refineries resume normal production this year, growth will likely return and inflation edge up, though the current account surplus will continue to shrink. With global demand for energy increasingly favoring renewables, this hydrocarbon-dependent economy should exploit its solar potential.

Economic performance

GDP is estimated to have contracted by 1.0% in 2018, reversing 1.3% growth in the previous year (Figure 3.22.1). Oil and gas output, accounting for close to two-thirds of GDP, likely contracted. Crude oil production fell by 1.5%, while the production of natural gas and liquefied natural gas each shrank by more than 3.0%. The rest of the economy contracted as well, by 0.8%, in the 3 quarters of 2018 for which data are available.

On the demand side, lower exports and domestic consumption drove down GDP growth, more than offsetting a strong rise in domestic investment (Figure 3.22.2). The decline in oil and gas production dragged volume growth in exports of goods and services to less than 1.0% in the first 3 quarters of 2018. Domestic consumption contracted by 0.4% as government consumption declined by 1.3%. Meanwhile, domestic investment rose by a whopping 23.1%, largely reflecting continued work on the Hengyi refinery, the Temburong Bridge, and a fertilizer plant for Brunei Fertilizer Industries.

Even as GDP contracted, the deflationary trend of the previous 4 years reversed because of higher global commodity prices and depreciation of the Brunei dollar against the US dollar. Consumer prices rose by 0.1% last year, with prices for food and beverages, hotels and restaurants, education and health care services posting modest increases (Figure 3.22.3).

The rise in international oil prices meant that, despite near stagnation in the volume of exports, the US dollar value of merchandise exports rose by a solid 17.8% in 2018 (Figure 3.22.4). This was, however, barely more than half of the rise in the US dollar value of merchandise imports, which exceeded 35.0%. The trade surplus for the year thus narrowed, moderating the current account surplus from the equivalent

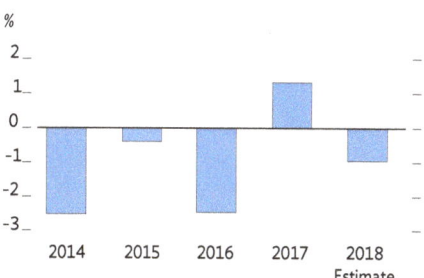

3.22.1 GDP growth

Sources: CEIC Data Company (accessed 8 March 2019); ADB estimates.

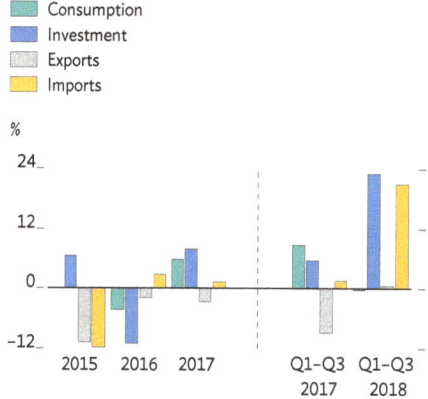

3.22.2 Demand-side growth

Q = quarter.
Source: CEIC Data Company (accessed 8 March 2019).

This chapter was written by Pilipinas Quising of the Economic Research and Regional Cooperation Department, ADB, Manila, and Thiam Hee Ng of the Southeast Asia Department, ADB, Manila.

of 16.7% of GDP in 2017 to an estimated 15.5% last year. With capital and financial accounts posting substantial deficits, international reserves likely declined from $3.5 billion in December 2017 to $3.4 billion a year later—still cover for 10 months of imports.

The government budgeted a fiscal deficit of B$1.54 billion for fiscal year 2018 (FY2018, ended 31 March 2019), but in the first 10 months of the fiscal year, revenues were driven higher than budgeted by rising international oil prices, keeping the actual fiscal deficit smaller than budgeted. Monetary policy continued to focus on maintaining exchange rate parity with the Singapore dollar. Broad money (M2) grew by 2.8% in calendar 2018, while credit to the private sector contracted by 2.9%.

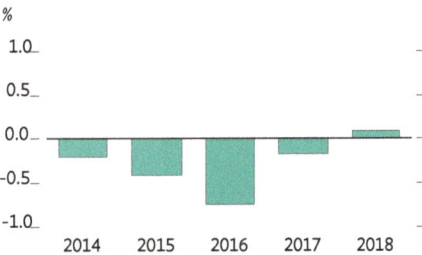

3.22.3 Inflation

Source: CEIC Data Company (accessed 8 March 2019).

Economic prospects

Hopes for growth in the near term are tempered by a weakening external environment and lower prospects for international oil prices. A modest boost to energy production is likely, though, with the start of downstream production at the new Hengyi refinery. Further, construction on the Brunei Fertilizer Industries plant and the $1.3 billion Temburong Bridge is expected to stimulate growth until scheduled completion near the end of 2019. The economy is thus expected to return to growth, with GDP expansion forecast at 1.0% this year and 1.5% in 2020.

Net exports will continue to drag on the economy as an expected increase in the volume of exports will be more than offset by higher imports to supply investment projects. Last year's decline in domestic consumption may begin to reverse, however, and domestic investment may continue to grow, especially in construction as various economic diversification projects proceed and as the government streamlines regulations and procedures toward improving the business environment (Figure 3.22.5). An anticipated increase in oil and gas revenue should enable higher government consumption but will be tempered by government efforts to consolidate its finances.

Inflation is expected to edge up as the economy improves but only minimally, to 0.2% in both years, as global commodity prices stay subdued, the government continues to subsidize consumer needs including fuel, and the Brunei dollar remains stable.

Export earnings will be constrained by lower international oil prices even as the import bill keeps rising in tandem with domestic investment that will require higher imports of construction materials, machinery, and equipment. The current account surplus is thus expected to narrow to the equivalent of 13.0% of GDP both this year and next.

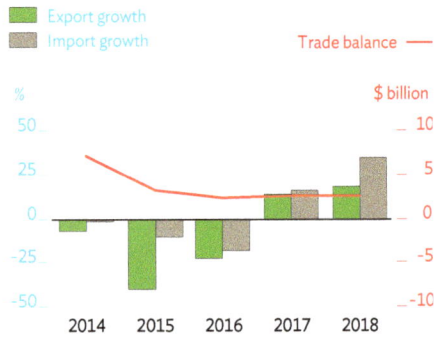

3.22.4 Merchandise trade

Source: CEIC Data Company (accessed 18 March 2019).

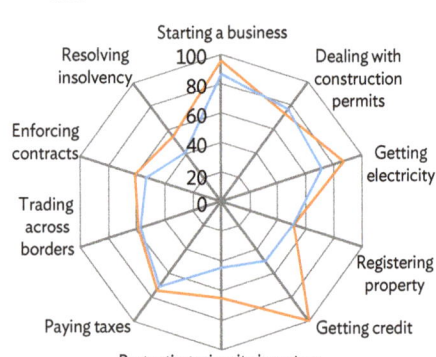

3.22.5 Doing business scores

Note: An economy's ease of doing business score is reflected on a scale from 0 to 100, where 0 is the lowest performance and 100 the best.
Source: World Bank. *Doing Business 2019, 2017.*

Key external risks to the outlook would be a global slowdown that is steeper than expected or a sharp fall in international oil prices. A critical domestic risk would be possible failure of the government to sustain the timely implementation of domestic investment projects.

Policy challenge—exploiting solar energy potential

Brunei Darussalam has substantial reserves of oil and gas that will last for decades (Figure 3.22.6). However, the composition of global demand for energy is expected to shift significantly away from conventional nonrenewable sources toward renewable ones. The International Energy Agency predicted in 2018 that growth in global demand for oil and gas would slow as energy users sought other sources. The Association of Southeast Asian Nations now aims to source 23% of its primary energy from renewable sources by 2025. For its part, Brunei Darussalam aims by 2035 to reduce its energy intensity by 45% and, by the same deadline, increase the share of renewables in electric power generation to at least 10.0%.

Most electricity in Brunei Darussalam currently comes from oil and gas. The sole solar energy plant, Tenaga Suria Brunei, produces 1,700 megawatt-hours of solar energy per year, or 0.05% of domestic electricity supply. A recent study estimated that from January 2011 to August 2017 the plant saved the government $1.7 million and reduced carbon dioxide emissions by 8,000 tons. Given the proven value of solar plants such as this and the improving affordability of solar panels, solar power has significant potential as an additional source of energy, even in a country as rich in hydrocarbons as Brunei Darussalam.

In 2014, the Energy Department—since reorganized as the Ministry of Energy, Manpower, and Industry—published its *Energy White Paper*, which outlines several initiatives to develop renewable energy. Progress on these initiatives has been slow, however, with no regulatory framework or renewable energy policy yet formulated. Work is not yet complete on a program to apply a feed-in tariff, which has encouraged the use of solar power globally by allowing users of renewable energy to sell energy back to the electric utility.

Much remains to be done toward educating the public on the benefits of solar power. One way to do this would be to introduce small standalone solar systems to replace the noisy, polluting generators used to power lights and fans in night markets. More broadly, the government should support research and development on ways to reduce the cost of solar energy.

3.22.1 Selected economic indicators (%)

	2019	2020
GDP growth	1.0	1.5
Inflation	0.2	0.2
Current account balance (share of GDP)	13.0	13.0

Source: ADB estimates.

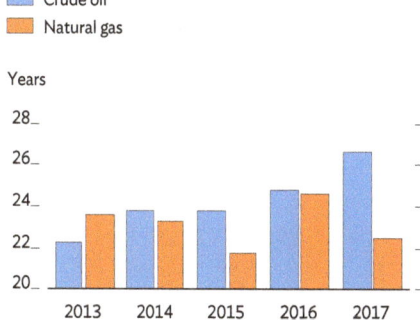

3.22.6 Ratio of reserves to production

Note: The ratio of reserves to production is the number of years the remaining reserves at year-end would last given the production rate of the particular year.
Source: *BP Statistical Review of World Energy*, various years.

Cambodia

Accelerating exports, tourism, and investment fueled strong GDP growth in 2018. Inflation nevertheless slowed. The current account deficit widened, but rising foreign direct investment drove currency reserves higher. A weaker external environment will likely soften growth this year and next, with inflation remaining subdued and the current account deficit narrowing. A skills gap must be closed to extend high GDP growth beyond Cambodia's waning phase of cheap labor before its demographic dividend expires.

Economic performance

Economic expansion last year hit 7.3% on a hefty increase in exports, buoyant tourism, and continuing strong foreign direct investment (FDI) inflows (Figure 3.23.1). Growth in the dollar value of exports of goods and services rose from 10.7% in 2017 to an estimated 18.3% in 2018. The value of merchandise exports alone jumped by the same estimated 18.3%, almost doubling a 9.3% rise in 2017. International tourist arrivals rose by 10.7%, with those from the People's Republic of China building on a 45.9% increase in 2017 with a further 70.0% surge last year (Figure 3.23.2). Growth in FDI inflows edged up from 12.6% in 2017 to an estimated 13.0%.

By sector, agriculture likely grew by 1.8%, and growth in industry accelerated to an estimated 10.8%, up by more than a percentage point from 2017 thanks to impressive growth in garments and footwear. Construction was also brisk, with growth rising from 18.0% in 2017 to 19.0%. Services maintained growth at 6.9%.

Even as growth accelerated, inflation slowed from 2.9% in 2017 to 2.5% last year. Stable food prices and government measures to contain fuel price increases tamped down inflation, as did appreciation of the Cambodian riel along with the US dollar, which is widely used in Cambodia for all but the smallest purchases.

Stronger growth was accompanied by a widening of the current account deficit as growth in imports outpaced that of exports. Growth in merchandise imports more than doubled in dollar terms from 9.8% in 2017 to an estimated 20.0% last year, driven largely by rising imports of materials and components for export-oriented garment and footwear production and higher imports of construction materials.

3.23.1 Supply-side contributions to growth

FISM = financial intermediation services indirectly measured.
Sources: National Institute of Statistics; ADB estimates.

3.23.2 Tourist arrivals by region

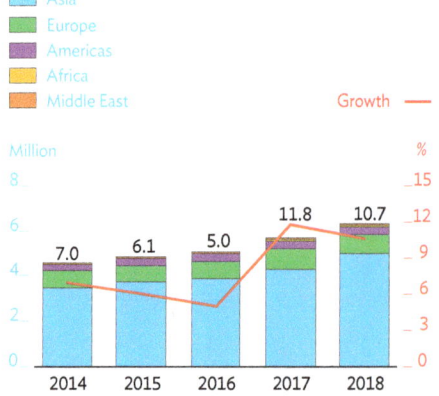

Sources: Ministry of Tourism, ADB estimates.

This chapter was written by Poullang Doung of the Cambodia Resident Mission, ADB, Phnom Penh.

The current account deficit excluding official transfers likely widened from the equivalent of 10.5% of GDP in 2017 to 13.6% (Figure 3.23.3).

Continued strength in FDI inflows more than offset the current account deficit, enabling gross foreign exchange reserves to rise to about $10 billion at the end of 2018, or cover for 5.6 months of imports. Reserves exceeded external public debt.

Based on the government's table of financial operations, the 2018 budget was expansionary, with a deficit equal to 5.1% of GDP, somewhat higher than a 3.1% budget deficit realized in 2017 (Figure 3.23.4). Expenditure was budgeted to equal 22.9% of GDP and revenue 17.8%. By December, though, actual revenue had exceeded the budget target, but expenditure seemed to have lagged.

Monetary policy continued to be anchored on maintaining a stable exchange rate between the riel and the US dollar and on ensuring that ample credit availability continued to support growth. Credit to the private sector grew by 23.2% in 2018, nudging up the ratio of private sector credit to GDP to 83.3% by year-end.

Economic prospects

A growth slowdown that is now forecast for the advanced economies and the People's Republic of China—major destinations for Cambodian exports—will likely soften prospects for growth in exports and tourism arrivals. GDP growth is thus seen to moderate to 7.0% this year and 6.8% in 2020 (Figure 3.23.5).

By sector, industry and construction are expected to feel the adverse effects of the weakening external environment the most. Growth in industry is likely to slow to 10.1% in 2019 and 9.4% in 2020, and construction to 17.0% this year and 16.0% next year. Growth in services will slow but only marginally to 6.8% in 2019, as will growth in agriculture to 1.7%.

With slowing growth, lower international oil prices, and stable food prices, inflation should remain subdued, the average staying at 2.5% both this year and next.

Moderating growth and subdued inflation should narrow the country's current account deficit, as shown in particular by imports of raw materials for export production. The current account deficit is seen narrowing to the equivalent of 12.7% of GDP this year and 11.8% next year. Robust FDI inflows should more than offset the current account deficit, pushing gross international reserves to $12 billion in 2019, or cover for about 6 months of imports—and, again, more than external debt. The ratio of external debt to GDP should thus remain at a sustainable 30.0%.

With growth softening, fiscal policy is targeting a narrower budget deficit this year, equal to 4.5% of GDP, according to the government's table of financial operations.

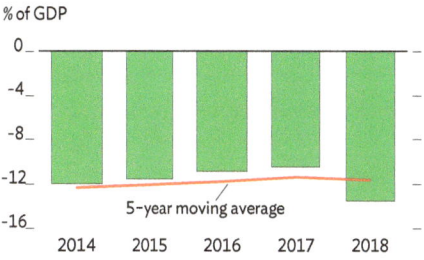

3.23.3 Current account balance

Source: Asian Development Outlook database.

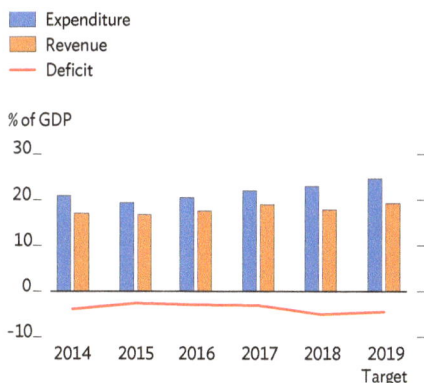

3.23.4 Fiscal indicators

Source: Ministry of Economy and Finance.

3.23.1 Selected economic indicators (%)

	2019	2020
GDP growth	7.0	6.8
Inflation	2.5	2.5
Current account balance (share of GDP)	–12.7	–11.8

Source: ADB estimates.

Monetary policy will continue to maintain the value of the riel against the dollar. The government aims to gradually wean the economy of dollarization with greater use of the riel and is slowly but steadily pushing banks' prudential norms toward international benchmarks.

A key external risk to the outlook would be a global economic slowdown steeper than currently anticipated. Another is the European Union carrying through with its plan to suspend trade preferences for Cambodia under the Everything But Arms program that it extends to least-developed countries. Notable domestic risks are a rising ratio of credit to GDP and possible drought this year.

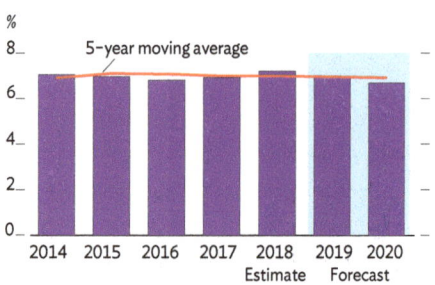

3.23.5 GDP growth

Source: Asian Development Outlook database.

Policy challenge—closing a skills gap

Cambodia has achieved high growth by offering low-cost labor, but this phase of its development is drawing to a close. Sustaining strong growth in the future will increasingly require the country to build a skilled workforce that can easily adapt to rapid technological changes sweeping the global economy, including automation and robotics.

Over the years, Cambodia has achieved notable progress in education, but a number of recent surveys and studies highlight that investors and businesses are constrained by a widening gap between the skills the workforce possesses and those it needs. Reflecting this, the World Bank Human Capital Index 2018—a composite measure of enrollment and dropout rates, average number of years of schooling, and learning quality while in school—ranks Cambodia just above the Lao People's Democratic Republic and Myanmar, among its peers in the Association of Southeast Asian Nations, but its index score of 0.49 falls far short of Viet Nam's 0.67 (Figure 3.23.6). A worsening mismatch between the skills demanded by industry and business and those imparted to youth in school, including in institutions that specialize in technical and vocational education and training (TVET), is the most important factor causing this skills gap. Unless it can be closed expeditiously, Cambodia will squander the demographic dividend it enjoys in having a young and expanding workforce.

The government recognizes the urgency of closing the skills gap. It recently announced its National TVET Policy, 2017–2025, which focuses on forging much closer collaboration between educational institutions and private businesses. This collaboration promises to make education more market driven. Regular information flows between private firms and TVET institutions, and collaboration in developing and operationalizing TVET curricula, promise to ensure that the skills imparted align with those in demand. To help keep students in school and learning the skills needed for the digital age, Cambodia needs more and better teachers and financial support for poor children and outstanding students.

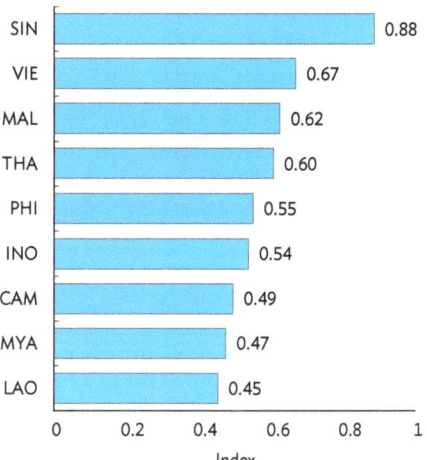

3.23.6 Human capital index, 2018

CAM = Cambodia, INO = Indonesia, LAO = Lao People's Democratic Republic, MAL = Malaysia, MYA = Myanmar, PHI = Philippines, SIN = Singapore, THA = Thailand, VIE = Viet Nam.
Source: World Bank. https://datacatalog.worldbank.org/dataset/human-capital-index (accessed 13 March 2019).

Indonesia

Growth edged up last year on stronger domestic investment and consumption. Inflation was lower, but the current account deficit widened under higher imports for large infrastructure projects. As it strengthens further, domestic demand should counter weaker exports to sustain growth in the near term, with inflation and the current account little changed. Harnessing technology, as called for in the recently announced Indonesia 4.0 development strategy, is key to realizing national growth potential.

Economic performance

GDP growth accelerated marginally from 5.1% in 2017 to 5.2% last year. Stronger domestic investment and robust domestic consumption more than offset weaker export growth, enabling the economy to grow at its fastest pace since 2013 (Figure 3.24.1). While exports of goods and services expanded more slowly than in 2017, down from 8.9% to 6.5% last year, fixed investment increased from 6.2% in 2017 to 6.7% (Figure 3.24.2). Strong investment was driven largely by public infrastructure projects in transportation and energy. Private investment into plantation agriculture recovered somewhat after slower growth in 2017, in response to the government's Biodiesel 20 program, which requires all diesel vehicles and heavy machinery to use blends that are at least 20% biofuel.

Meanwhile, domestic consumption improved slightly on growth in 2017 at about 5%, helped by higher public consumption, sustained momentum in private spending, and low and stable inflation. A continuing rise in household incomes thanks to a robust increase in formal employment underpinned growth in private consumption and a decline in the incidence of poverty to single digits, at 9.7% in September. Last year saw continued improvement in household welfare, as evidenced by gains in access to better-quality housing.

Growth last year spanned economic sectors. While agriculture maintained its 2017 growth rate, industry and services improved upon theirs (Figure 3.24.3). Industry growth accelerated from 4.1% in 2017 to 4.3%, and services edged up from 5.7% growth in 2017 to 5.8%. Within industry, mining output rose from 0.7% expansion in 2017 to 2.2% last year as growth in manufacturing remained steady at 4.3% and growth in construction moderated from 6.8% in 2017 to 6.1%.

This chapter was written by Emma Allen and Priasto Aji of the Indonesia Resident Mission, ADB, Jakarta.

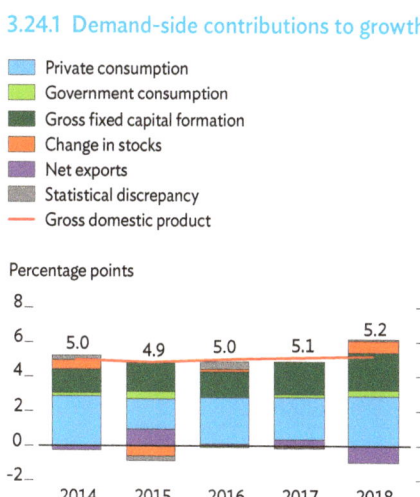

3.24.1 Demand-side contributions to growth

Source: CEIC Data Company (accessed 8 March 2019).

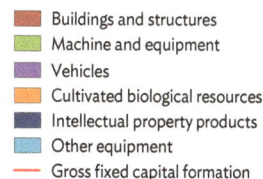

3.24.2 Contributions to fixed investment growth

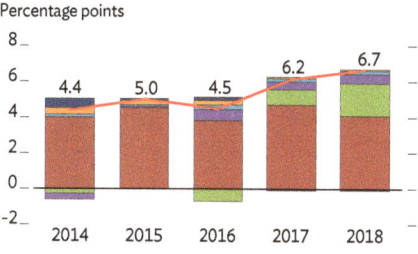

Source: CEIC Data Company (accessed 8 March 2019).

Mining benefited from a sustained rise in coal prices along with increases in production quotas and 2017 policies to allow more metal ore exports. Manufacturing growth was buoyed by stronger exports of manufactures such as apparel and footwear, as well as higher production of food and beverages mostly for domestic consumption. Strong expansion in information and communication technology—and in transport and storage, which grew by 7.0%—underpinned expansion in services, the sector supplying roughly half of GDP growth last year.

Even as growth edged up, inflation moderated from an average of 3.8% in 2017 to 3.2% with ample food supplies owing to sustained agricultural production, deft food supply management, limited pass-through from currency depreciation, and fuel and electricity prices kept stable by government subsidies (Figure 3.24.4). Core inflation remained subdued as monetary policy steadily tightened. Average inflation hovered around the lower end of the 2.5%–4.5% target range set by Bank Indonesia, the central bank.

Strong domestic demand saw merchandise imports expand last year by 20.7% in US dollar terms, up from 16.2% growth in 2017, while growth in the dollar value of merchandise exports slowed from 16.9% in 2017 to 7.0%. The trade balance thus declined from a surplus of $18.8 billion in 2017 to a small deficit of $0.4 billion (Figure 3.24.5). Improvement in net service exports—driven by rising tourism revenues, telecommunication service receipts, and remittances from workers overseas—partly offset the deterioration in the trade balance. The current account deficit rose from the equivalent of 1.6% of GDP in 2017 to 3.0% last year.

Meanwhile, the surplus in the financial account narrowed. Although portfolio investment recovered ground in the last quarter of 2018, the year as a whole witnessed higher outflows as the US Federal Reserve raised its federal funds rate. Net foreign direct investment (FDI) similarly weakened as Indonesians invested more abroad. The overall balance of payments thus fell into a deficit of $7.1 billion, causing foreign exchange reserves to slip from an all-time high of $132.0 billion in January 2018 to $120.7 billion by the end of the year (Figure 3.24.6). Reserves were still sufficient to cover 6.5 months of imports and repayment of government external debt.

Pressure on the balance of payments and foreign currency reserves saw the Indonesian rupiah depreciate by 5.7% in the course of 2018. It fell to a low of Rp15,253 to the US dollar on 11 October and recovered to Rp14,481 by the end of the year (Figure 3.24.7). In response to currency depreciation, the central bank raised its policy interest rate, the 7-day reverse repo rate, five times last year by a total of 175 basis points, taking the rate to 6.00% by the end of the year.

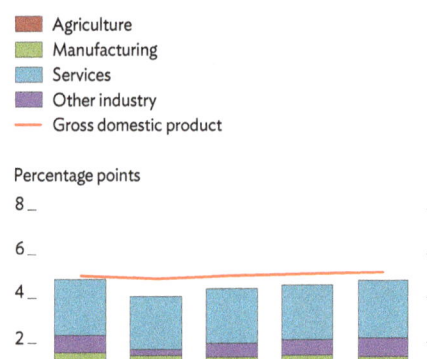

3.24.3 Supply-side contributions to growth

Source: CEIC Data Company (accessed 8 March 2019).

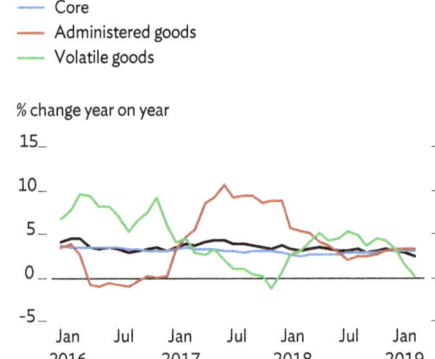

3.24.4 Inflation

Source: CEIC Data Company (accessed 8 March 2019).

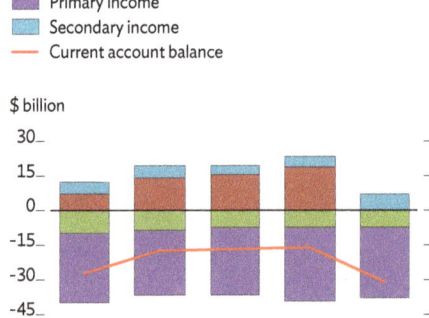

3.24.5 Current account components

Source: CEIC Data Company (accessed 8 March 2019).

Meanwhile, the fiscal deficit as a share of GDP narrowed from 2.5% in 2017 to an estimated 1.7% last year, the lowest since 2011. Fiscal deficit reduction was achieved last year by both raising revenue and containing expenditure growth. Revenue was equal to 13.2% of GDP, surpassing the original budget target, while expenditure was contained at 14.9%. Revenue was boosted by previous gains from the tax amnesty program and higher commodity prices. Subsidies for energy increased from the equivalent of 0.7% of GDP in 2017 to 1.0%, but infrastructure spending was unchanged from 2017 at 2.8%.

Economic prospects

Weakening global growth and world trade may pull down Indonesian exports and hence economic growth in the near term. Yet this effect is likely to be offset by continued strength in domestic demand. Fiscal and monetary policies have some room to maneuver to support growth. GDP growth is thus seen being sustained at 5.2% this year and edging up to 5.3% in 2020.

With key public infrastructure projects such as the Trans-Java Toll Road now approaching completion, strong foundations are laid for private investment. In addition, recent reforms to improve the business environment, such as streamlining tax administration and simplifying business licensing, should give a fillip to private investment. Coupled with these reforms, improved macroeconomic management saw the three major international credit rating agencies upgrade Indonesia's sovereign credit rating to investment grade in 2017 and reaffirm that higher rating last year. Positive investor sentiment is reflected in steady improvement in the amount of new capital raised and in the number of companies listed (Figure 3.24.8). Recent initiatives to strengthen shareholder protection should further boost private investment.

Private consumption should remain robust in the near term as formal employment continues to expand, the government scales up its social assistance programs, and inflation remains modest. In the first half of 2019, consumption is likely to get an additional boost from spending in the run-up to a national election in April. Yet another boost to private consumption is likely from sustained improvement in household access to credit, as evidenced by a near quadrupling in the percentage of households that report having business loans from 8.2% in 2014 to 28.7% in 2018 (Figure 3.24.9).

Growth this year and next is likely to span sectors, with agriculture, industry, and services all forecast to sustain 2018 growth rates in 2019 and agriculture and industry to accelerate in 2020. Continued strength in footwear and apparel manufacturing is expected yield robust industrial growth in 2019 and 2020. Trends in investment registrations reported

3.24.6 Balance of payments

Source: CEIC Data Company (accessed 8 March 2019).

3.24.7 Gross international reserves and exchange rate

Sources: Bloomberg, CEIC Data Company (both accessed 8 March 2019).

3.24.8 New capital raised and number of listed companies

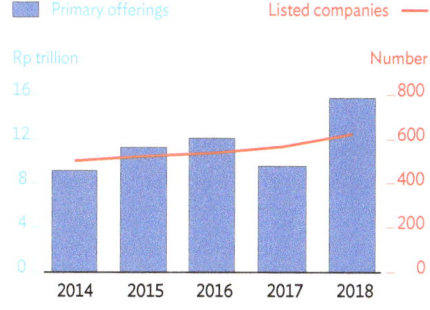

Source: CEIC Data Company (accessed 13 March 2019).

by the Indonesia Investment Coordinating Board indicate sustained growth in industry, as does the purchasing managers' index (Figure 3.24.10). The service sector is similarly likely to maintain last year's growth pace, with strong performances from wholesale and retail trade, hotels and restaurants, and information and communications. Transportation and storage will benefit from improved transport logistics, customs regulations, and warehousing.

With growth sustained this year and edging up next year, inflation is similarly likely to remain unchanged at 3.2% this year and edge up to 3.3% in 2020, in both years near the middle of the central bank target range of 2.5%–4.5%. As international oil prices decline, the government is unlikely to change administered prices of domestic fuel. A new pricing formula for unsubsidized fuels is expected to keep prices contained.

Merchandise exports are expected to grow more slowly in US dollar terms as economic growth in Indonesia's trading partners weakens and as international commodity prices subside for coal, rubber, and palm oil. At the same time, import growth will be lower as well as global oil prices soften and demand for capital goods ease with the completion of large infrastructure projects. Growth in imports will likely continue to outpace that of exports. Net service receipts should grow robustly, however, as gains from tourism revenue look set to continue. The current account deficit is thus expected to narrow to the equivalent of 2.7% of GDP both this year and next.

Improvement in portfolio investment seen in the last quarter of 2018 is expected to continue. FDI should remain robust with manufacturing again, as last year, receiving a dominant share of inflows, followed by trade. In addition, investors have already provided Indonesian startups with fresh capital injections this year. The government recognizes the need to attract more FDI by improving the business and investment climate, and thereby improve the balance of payments.

Fiscal policy is likely to remain supportive. The 2019 budget sets a fiscal deficit equal to 1.8% of GDP, as in 2018. Public infrastructure spending is higher at 17% of total expenditure and is more focused on investments with high returns. Additional allocations have been made for disaster risk management and mitigation. The budget prioritizes making conditional cash transfers to poor and vulnerable households in the countryside more effective. Depending on how the macroeconomic situation unfolds in the near term, the central bank may adjust policy to sustain steady growth, keep inflation low, and maintain a stable exchange rate.

Risks to the outlook tilt downwards. Any escalation of current trade tensions between the US and the People's Republic of China is a major external risk. Domestic risks could

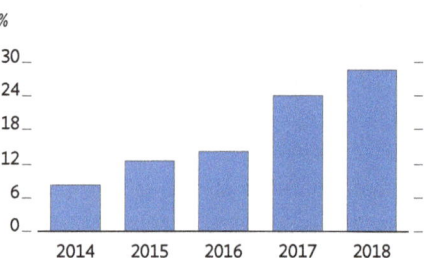

3.24.9 Households receiving business loans

Source: Statistics Indonesia. 2018. Welfare Statistics, Jakarta. https://www.bps.go.id.

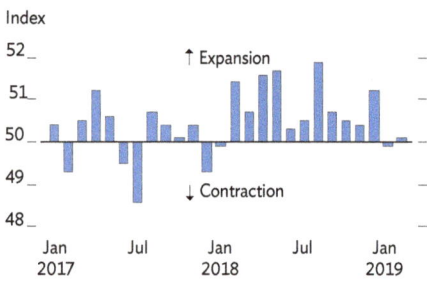

3.24.10 Manufacturing purchasing managers' index

Note: Nikkei, Markit.
Source: Bloomberg (accessed 8 March 2019).

3.24.1 Selected economic indicators (%)

	2019	2020
GDP growth	5.2	5.3
Inflation	3.2	3.3
Current account balance (share of GDP)	-2.7	-2.7

Source: ADB estimates.

stem from dry weather under El Niño or from any newly imposed nontariff restrictions on imports that cause uncertainty for investors and businesses.

Policy challenge—harnessing new technologies to accelerate growth

Estimates of Indonesia's potential GDP growth rate in 2020–2024 range from 5.5% to 6.3%. For the country to bring actual growth more in line with potential growth, manufacturing has to expand to create more and better jobs. However, any transformation of the manufacturing sector in Indonesia faces a key constraint: More than 99% of manufacturing firms are micro and small enterprises (MSEs) (Figure 3.24.11). Such firms suffer low productivity and have little capability to expand and adopt emerging technologies.

Given MSE predominance in manufacturing, the sector makes very little use of the digital technologies—cloud computing, big data, artificial intelligence, machine learning, and the internet of things—that enable manufacturers elsewhere to streamline logistics, develop new products quickly, and grow. Global technological rankings for 2018–2022 compiled by the Economist Intelligence Unit place Indonesia near the bottom among Asian economies for technological readiness, reflecting limited internet access and the low quality of digital services (Figure 3.24.12). In a similar vein, the World Economic Forum ranks Indonesia behind many other countries in the region in its *Readiness for the Future of Production Report 2018*.

Encouragingly, the government, recognizing the constraints that hamper faster adoption of new technologies in manufacturing, recently announced a medium- to long-term development strategy called Making Indonesia 4.0. Abbreviated as I.4.0, the strategy focuses on technology and productivity upgrades in five manufacturing subsectors: food and beverages, textiles and garments, automobiles, electronics, and chemicals. To ramp up performance in these subsectors, 10 priority areas that cut across them are identified: improving upstream capabilities, optimizing industrial zones, embracing sustainability, empowering small enterprises, building digital infrastructure, improving human capital, adopting technology, attracting FDI, establishing an innovation ecosystem, and ensuring policy coherence.

I.4.0 is an ambitious strategy for faster and more efficient industrialization. However, as is common with ambitious development strategies, it announces long-term goals but is short on implementation details. In particular, I.4.0 does not articulate how the government will address the intertwined problems of MSE predominance and the low use of new

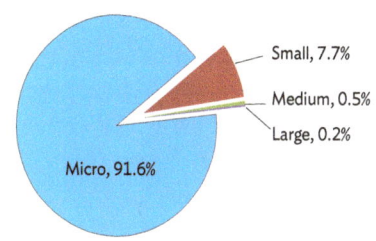

3.24.11 Distribution of manufacturing firms in Indonesia by size, 2015

Source: Badan Pusat Statistik. http://www.bps.go.id (accessed 27 March 2019).

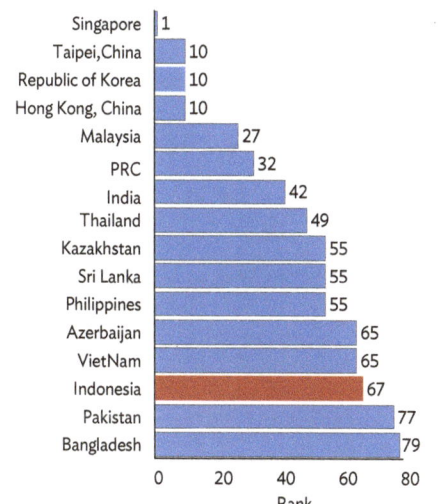

3.24.12 Technological readiness ranking, selected developing Asian economies

PRC = People's Republic of China.
Note: Many economies share a rank because of identical scores.
Source: The Economist Intelligence Unit. 2018. *Preparing for disruption: Technological Readiness Ranking*.

technologies in manufacturing. For I.4.0 to make headway in achieving its goals, it would be useful to develop a policy roadmap, in consultation with industry and business to ease these twin constraints.

The policy roadmap should focus on, among other things, how to help MSEs grow and expand so they can reap benefits of scale when adopting new technologies. It needs to pay special attention to improving MSE access to finance, investing in digital infrastructure, and enhancing technology diffusion across firms. One in four manufacturing MSEs in Indonesia cites inadequate finance as the main constraint on expansion. Policies to ease this constraint could aim to lower the cost of finance and simplify the cumbersome procedures required of businesses for obtaining bank loans.

To enable businesses to take advantage of the opportunities offered by new technologies, higher investment in digital infrastructure is crucial. Public efforts are needed as well to adopt advanced technology offered by foreign firms and to foster indigenous innovation. This may require the establishment of knowledge forums at which foreign and local companies exchange information and experiences, as well as forums at which domestic firms raise their awareness of the benefits of the technologies emerging.

Lao People's Democratic Republic

The economy slowed last year as floods suppressed growth in agriculture and decelerating growth in electricity generation dragged down industry growth. GDP growth should hold up this year and next as agriculture and electricity generation recover. Inflation is likely to accelerate a little but remain modest, and the current account deficit is forecast to ease. Substantial public finance reform is needed to rein in stubborn fiscal deficits and rapidly rising public debt.

Economic performance

GDP growth slowed from 6.9% in 2017 to 6.5% last year as severe floods hit agriculture and slower hydropower generation drove down industrial growth (Figure 3.25.1). Growth in agriculture and allied activities, comprising 15% of the economy, slowed from 2.9% in 2017 to 2.0% as production was disrupted by floods in August and September 2018.

Even as construction maintained rapid growth and mining climbed almost completely out of contraction, industry growth slowed from 11.6% in 2017 to 7.9% last year. Electricity generation, accounting for 20% of industrial output, decelerated from a 33.0% rise in 2017 to 8.3% last year as no new power plants were added to enhance existing annual production capacity (Figure 3.25.2). Meanwhile, buoyed by an 8.2% increase in international tourist arrivals, growth in services accelerated from 4.5% in 2017 to 7.4% (Figure 3.25.3).

Even as GDP growth slowed, higher food prices caused by weaker farm production and higher international oil prices pushed average inflation from 0.8% in 2017 to 2.0% last year. Inflation peaked in July 2018 at 2.4% year on year but fell back to 1.5% in December (Figure 3.25.4).

The steep growth slowdown in electricity generation slowed growth in the volume of electricity exports from 19.8% in 2017 to 7.2% last year. As a result, growth in merchandise exports fell by almost half in US dollar terms from 19.8% in 2017 to 10.0%. Meanwhile, despite higher international oil prices, softening demand for imports held growth in imports to less than 3.0% in dollar terms, narrowing the trade deficit from the equivalent of 11.4% of GDP in 2017 to 9.0% last year.

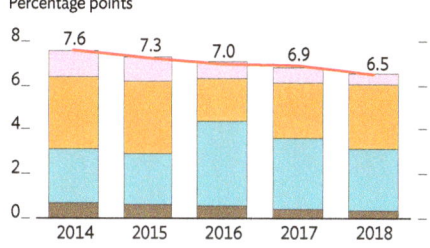

3.25.1 Supply-side contributions to GDP growth

Sources: Lao Statistics Bureau; *Asian Development Outlook* database.

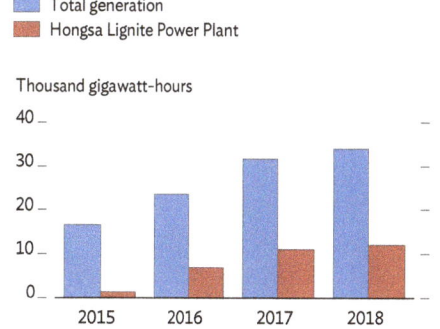

3.25.2 Electricity generation

Source: Lao PDR Ministry of Energy and Mines.

This chapter was written by Rattanatay Luanglatbandith and Soulinthone Leuangkhamsing of the Lao PDR Resident Mission, ADB, Vientiane.

Despite a strong rise in international tourist arrivals, net service receipts worsened last year. In sum, the current account deficit narrowed from the equivalent of 11.2% of GDP in 2017 to 8.6% in 2018. With foreign direct investment rising, the overall balance of payments posted a small surplus, and international reserves edged up from $1.0 billion at the end of 2017 to $1.1 billion a year later. Despite this improvement, reserves remained perilously low, providing cover for only 1.5 months of imports.

The government's efforts to consolidate its finances brought the fiscal deficit down from the equivalent of 5.6% of GDP in 2017 to 4.6% last year as public expenditure, equal 21.8% of GDP in 2017, was contained at 20.3%. Meanwhile, revenue slipped from 16.2% of GDP in 2017 to 15.7% last year. Monetary policy aimed to keep the Lao kip–US dollar exchange rate within a narrow daily trading band of 5% or less, as well as contain growth in credit and the supply of money (Figure 3.25.5).

Economic prospects

Slowing growth in the advanced economies—and closer to home in the People's Republic of China (PRC), Thailand, and Viet Nam—does not augur well for the growth prospects of the Lao People's Democratic Republic (Lao PDR). However, growth in agriculture should edge up, and electricity generation should accelerate with the expected addition of 1,500 megawatts to capacity. The construction of the Vang Vieng–Vientiane Expressway and the ramping up of work on a railway linking the PRC and the Lao PDR, to be completed by 2021, should boost GDP growth, as should likely continued buoyancy in international tourist arrivals. GDP growth should thus sustain last year's pace of 6.5% both this year and next (Figure 3.25.6).

By sector, growth in industry is forecast to edge up slightly to 8.1% in 2019 on solid construction and as growth in electricity generation resumes. Agriculture is expected to grow by 2.5% both this year and next. Meanwhile, the government's promotion of the PRC and the Lao PDR as twin tourist destinations is seen to help services maintain growth at 6.7%.

Inflation is forecast to remain at 2.0% this year and next, with global oil prices forecast lower and food prices subdued as agriculture recovers.

Electricity exports will edge up this year with new generating capacity. Total exports are thus seen rising by 12.0% in US dollar terms this year and next. Meanwhile, import growth will accelerate by 13.5% this year and 12.0% next year on imports of capital goods for hydropower, expressway, and rail projects. The current account deficit is thus forecast to widen to 9.5% of GDP in 2019 and 10.0% in 2020 (Figure 3.25.7). International reserves are forecast to fall to just under $1.0 billion, providing cover for 1.3 months of imports.

3.25.1 Selected economic indicators (%)

	2019	2020
GDP growth	6.5	6.5
Inflation	2.0	2.0
Current account balance (share of GDP)	-9.5	-10.0

Source: ADB estimates.

3.25.3 Tourist arrivals

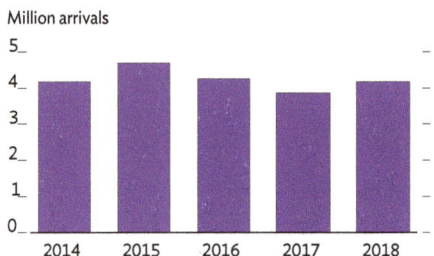

Source: CEIC Data Company (accessed 19 March 2019).

3.25.4 Inflation

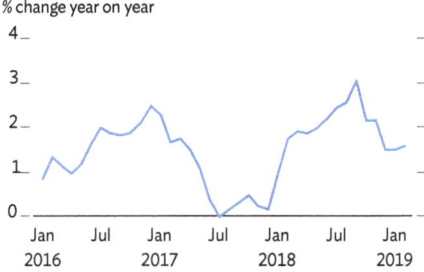

Sources: Bank of Lao; CEIC Data Company (both accessed 12 March 2019).

3.25.5 Monetary indicators

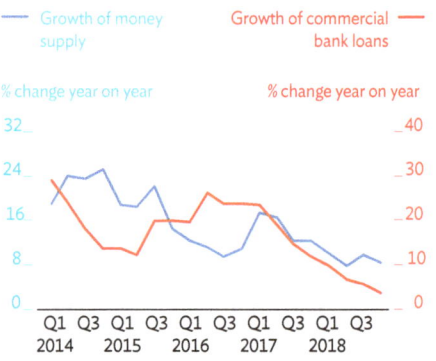

Q = quarter.
Sources: Bank of Lao; CEIC Data Company (both accessed 12 March 2019).

Progress in consolidating government finances is expected to gradually yield better results. The fiscal deficit is likely to subside to the equivalent of 4.3% of GDP this year and 3.7% in 2020. Expenditure is forecast to equal about 20% of GDP this year and next, while revenue including grants is forecast to hover at around 16% of GDP. The government has withheld a salary increase for civil servants and halved the annual intake of new civil servants to 1,500 in 2019.

Although inflation remains low, monetary policy has little room to ease credit conditions because of constant pressure on the exchange rate and the need to shield the country's fragile balance of payments, which poses the major domestic risk to the outlook. Another domestic risk is vulnerability to natural hazards. An uncertain global trading environment poses the main external risk.

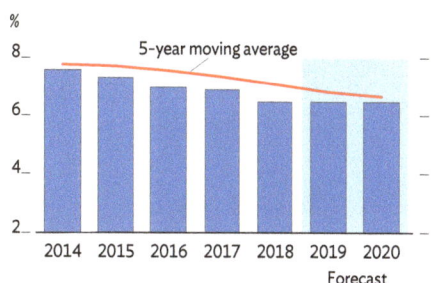

3.25.6 GDP growth

Source: *Asian Development Outlook* database.

Policy challenge—reforming public finances

Strong economic growth in the Lao PDR over the years has been shadowed by unsustainable fiscal deficits and rising public debt. Including publicly guaranteed debt, public debt now equals about 65% of GDP (Figure 3.25.8). About 80% of the public debt is in foreign currency. The ratio of debt service to GDP has increased in the last 4 years as the government relied more on capital markets and less on concessional bilateral sources in recent years.

Continued high fiscal deficits and high public debt threaten macroeconomic and financial stability. A 2018 analysis of debt sustainability by the International Monetary Fund places the Lao PDR at high risk of debt distress. Containing fiscal deficits is critical to reaching a more sustainable ratio. This demands in turn further containing government expenditure and raising revenue.

Toward strengthening public debt management and instituting tax reform, the government adopted a law on public debt management in 2018 that establishes a ceiling for public debt at 60.0% of GDP. Any public investment project exceeding $50 million must now seek approval from the National Assembly. The government aims to reduce the fiscal deficit by more than a third, to less than 3.0% of GDP by 2025. The government has delayed a salary increase for civil servants. Its Public Finance Development Strategy 2025 and Vision to 2030 announce reforms that will improve public debt management and medium-term fiscal planning and budgeting.

Successful implementation depends on strong political will and leadership in the Ministry of Finance to effectively collaborate and coordinate with other ministries. Only then will the Lao PDR be able to gradually restore fiscal and public debt sustainability.

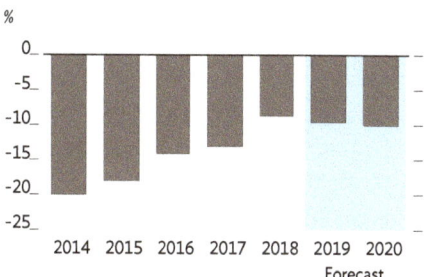

3.25.7 Current account balance forecast

Source: *Asian Development Outlook* database.

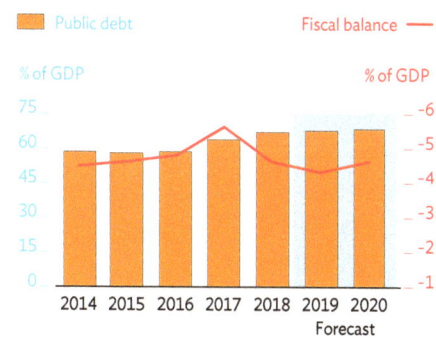

3.25.8 Fiscal indicators

Note: Fiscal balance is on an inverted axis.
Sources: *Asian Development Outlook* database; IMF estimates.

Malaysia

Growth slowed last year as external demand softened and global trade tensions mounted. Inflation remained subdued, and the current account surplus widened. As demand continues to weaken this year, growth is forecast to slow further. Inflation will quicken back to trend as the effect of a temporary tax holiday fades. With the public sector role in investment shrinking, policies and programs are needed to boost private investment.

Economic performance

Despite softer exports and slowing domestic investment shaving 1.2 percentage points off the 2017 growth rate, growth in 2018 held up at 4.7% (Figure 3.26.1). Growth in exports of goods and services by volume plunged from 9.4% in 2017 to 1.5% as foreign demand weakened for electronics, palm oil, and refined petroleum products.

Domestic investment reversed 6.4% expansion in 2017 to contract by 4.4%. Public investment sank from stagnation in 2017 to a 5.2% decline as a new government suspended several public infrastructure projects that had been approved by the previous administration. Growth in private investment fell by more than half from 9.3% in 2017 to 4.5% last year with investors uncertain about the new government's policy direction, concerned about the trade conflict between the People's Republic of China and the US, and gloomy at the outlook for the global semiconductor market. Investment in residential construction fell as measures to curb the real estate market included shortened mortgage maturities and lowered loan-to-value ratios.

Continued strength in domestic consumption partly offset the slump in investment. Growth in private consumption surged from 7.0% in 2017 to a 6-year high of 8.1% thanks to modestly higher wages and expanded employment in the first half of the year, a temporary tax holiday, and higher government cash transfers to low-income households. The abolition of the goods and services tax ahead of the imposition of a new sales and services tax created a 3-month tax-free window in June–August that consumers and businesses used to generate substantial increases in retail sales (Figure 3.26.2). Growth in public consumption moderated, meanwhile, from 5.4% in 2017 to 3.3%.

3.26.1 Demand-side contributions to growth

Sources: Haver Analytics; Bank Negara Malaysia. 2019. Monthly Statistical Bulletin. February. http://www.bnm.gov.my (accessed 25 February 2019).

3.26.2 Consumption indicators

Source: Haver Analytics (accessed 8 March 2019).

This chapter was written by Thiam Hee Ng of the Southeast Asia Department, ADB, Manila, and Valerie A. Mercer-Blackman and Shiela Camingue-Romance of the Economic Research and Regional Cooperation Department, ADB, Manila.

By sector, agriculture, industry, and construction slowed, but services improved on its growth rate in 2017. Agriculture reversed 7.2% expansion in 2017 to contract by 0.4% last year, largely because of softening palm oil prices internationally. Industry growth slowed from 4.9% in 2017 to 3.4% as external demand for electronics weakened and pipeline repairs disrupted production and drove down natural gas output. Construction growth slowed from 6.7% in 2017 to 4.2% last year as the new government decided to suspend several infrastructure projects. Meanwhile, services, providing more than half of GDP, improved on growth at 6.2% in 2017 with 6.8% expansion on buoyance in wholesale and retail trade and in finance and business services.

As growth slowed, inflationary pressures eased not only because of lower aggregate demand, but also reflecting the partial reintroduction of fuel subsidies and the windfall from the temporary tax holiday. Inflation thus fell from 3.8% in 2017 to 1.0% last year (Figure 3.26.3).

Growth in merchandise exports slowed in US dollar terms from 13.3% in 2017 to 10.5% in 2018. Merchandise imports also experienced slower growth, decelerating from 13.8% to 10.4%, largely because the slump in domestic investment cut demand for imports of capital and intermediate goods. On balance, the trade surplus rose by 10.8% to $30.1 billion last year. Net service receipts declined, however, as net payments to foreign service providers exceeded tourism receipts, and as foreign workers boosted their outward remittances. The current account surplus thus shrank from the equivalent of 3.0% of GDP in 2017 to 2.3% (Figure 3.26.4).

Meanwhile, the financial account registered net inflow for the first time in 7 years, at $4.7 billion. Portfolio capital net outflow of $11.0 billion was more than offset by larger net inflow of foreign direct investment and other inflows in the second half of the year. The overall balance of payments was thus a small surplus last year, and by December 2018 foreign exchange reserves stood at $99.8 billion, providing cover for 7.4 months of imports.

The budget deficit widened from the equivalent of 3.0% of GDP in 2017 to 3.7% in 2018, more than the 2.8% deficit originally targeted under the *2018 Budget Report*. The temporary reintroduction of fuel subsidies and the removal of the goods and services tax drained government coffers even as oil-related revenues picked up. The government had hoped to keep the budget deficit close to target by raising oil-related revenues and cutting nonessential spending, but government expenditure nevertheless grew by 9.6%, more than double the 2017 rate, on higher government transfers, debt service payments, and operating expenditure. Meanwhile, Bank Negara Malaysia, the central bank, maintained a neutral monetary policy, its overnight policy rate unchanged at 3.25%.

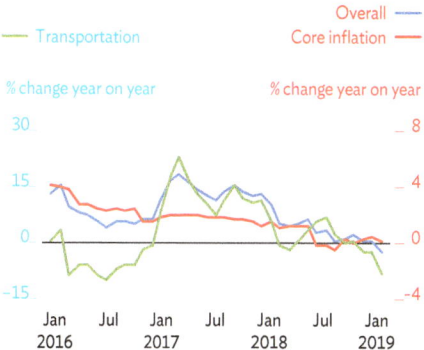

3.26.3 Monthly inflation

Sources: Haver Analytics; Bank Negara Malaysia. 2018. Monthly Highlights and Statistics. February. http://www.bnm.gov.my (accessed 8 March 2019).

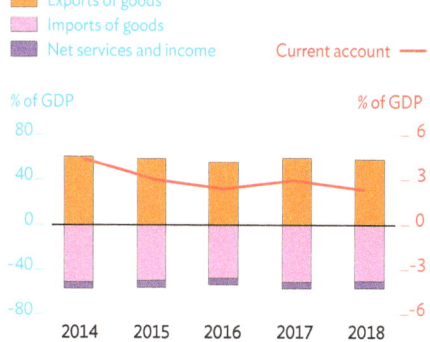

3.26.4 Current account balance and components

Sources: Haver Analytics; Bank Negara Malaysia. 2019. Monthly Highlights and Statistics. February. http://www.bnm.gov.my (accessed 11 March 2019).

Economic prospects

With slower growth in the advanced economies and moderation in the global electronics trade, export growth is expected to remain weak. Domestic demand will continue to slow this year but is expected to pick up in 2020 with a recovery in private investment. GDP growth will likely slow this year to 4.5% and pick up to 4.7% in 2020 (Figure 3.26.5).

Private consumption growth is expected to pull back somewhat from last year's strong performance. Although the recent introduction of an income tax refund may boost consumption to some extent, the end of the temporary tax holiday last year with the introduction of the sales and service tax should moderate growth in private consumption to a still robust pace of 6.0% this year and next, underpinned as it is by low unemployment and rising wages. Growth in public consumption will continue to slow in both years as the government cuts costs.

Public investment is likely to slow in both years as well, with the government continuing to reconsider and reprioritize its investment program. With several large infrastructure projects already deferred, the government is looking at options to reduce costs on other projects currently in the works. Its renegotiation of several large investment projects has unsettled some private investors, adding to their concerns about weakening export prospects. The RAM business confidence index showed sagging sentiment in the initial months of 2019 (Figure 3.26.6).

Private investment is therefore likely to remain subdued this year. It is poised for recovery next year, though, with the implementation of a large backlog of projects with foreign direct investment. Historical trends show 60%–80% of investment approvals implemented after 2 years (Figure 3.26.7 and Table 3.26.2). A giant new refinery and petrochemical complex at Pengerang, on the southern coast of Peninsular Malaysia, is scheduled to become operational by the end of 2019 with the capacity to process 300,000 barrels of crude per day. The complex is expected to attract additional private investment to the Pengerang area as investors take advantage of enhanced feedstock availability and well-developed infrastructure, including a power plant, liquefied natural gas terminal, and deepwater port. This should help offset the lull in manufacturing investment.

Agriculture will rebound this year from contraction last year, but growth will moderate again in 2020 as it returns to trend. Industry growth will slow to 3.1% this year, mainly because of weakness in manufacturing, but is expected to pick up to 3.8% in 2020 as private investment recovers. Some of the new investment into manufacturing may start kicking in with new production next year. Construction will stagnate this year and next as real estate remains weak and fewer construction permits are issued. Growth in services will moderate to 5.8%

3.26.1 Selected economic indicators (%)

	2019	2020
GDP growth	4.5	4.7
Inflation	2.0	2.7
Current account balance (share of GDP)	2.4	2.4

Source: ADB estimates.

3.26.5 GDP growth

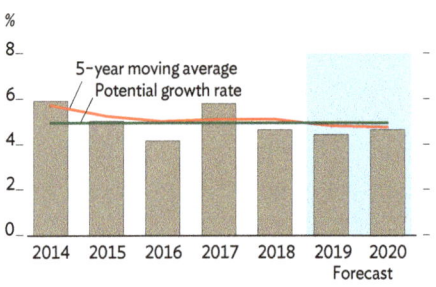

Source: *Asian Development Outlook* database.

3.26.6 Consumer and business confidence indexes

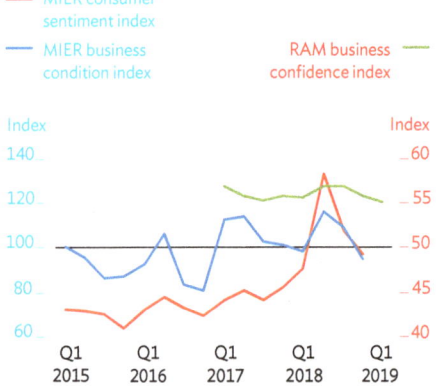

MIER = Malaysia Institute of Economics Research.
Note: Above 100 indicates improvement in business conditions and rising consumer confidence.
Sources: Haver Analytics (accessed 11 March 2019); RAM Rating Services Berhad.

this year and next, returning to trend after the boost it got last year from temporary exemption from the goods and services tax.

Inflation is expected to rebound from its dip last year to 2.0% this year and 2.7% next year, despite slowing growth and lower global oil prices, with the fading of last year's downward pressure on prices from the tax holiday. In 2020, inflation should return to its medium-term trend (Figure 3.26.8).

Export growth is expected to continue to slow in line with weaker global economic conditions. Import growth should also remain subdued with slowing economic growth at home. Although exports may get a small boost from resumed natural gas exports after last year's disruption, as well as some pickup from the redirection of manufacturing production with the trade conflict between the US and the People's Republic of China, export prospects remain muted. As the Pengerang petrochemical and refining complex hits full production in 2020, though, it will likely provide some impetus to exports. The suspension of infrastructure projects will reduce imports of construction materials and machinery, though these imports may revive in 2020 as private investment recovers. On balance, the current account surplus is forecast to widen marginally to the equivalent of 2.4% of GDP in 2019 and 2020. With foreign direct investment inflows more than offsetting portfolio outflows, the financial account is expected to remain in surplus. The external payments position should therefore remain comfortable.

Despite slowing growth, the government will consolidate its finances and pursue institutional reform to strengthen public finance and the fiscal management system. In line with consolidation, the government is adopting zero-based budgeting, which requires that all expenses be justified for each new period; improving government procurement systems; and moving away from cash to accrual accounting, counting income when it is earned and liabilities when they are billed, not when cash changes hands. The government is further committed to greater transparency in reporting contingent liabilities and off-budget investments.

Monetary policy is expected to be accommodative. The central bank is unlikely to raise its policy interest rate with inflation not forecast to breach the official target. The financial system remains strong, with banks well capitalized and sufficiently liquid to provide ample credit and to ride out any financial volatility. The resulting policy space allows the central bank to respond quickly and effectively as macroeconomic conditions evolve.

Risks to the outlook tilt downward. Any escalation of trade tensions between the US and People's Republic of China could derail Malaysia's highly trade-dependent economy. The new government's continuing reexamination of many large

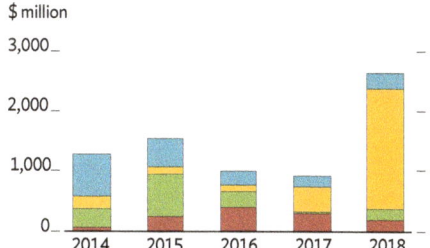

3.26.7 High-tech manufacturing FDI approvals by country, Q1–Q3 2014–2018

Note: High-tech manufacturing includes machinery & equipment, electronics and electrical products, transport equipment, and scientific and measuring equipment.
Source: Malaysian Investment Development Authority. http://www.mida.gov.my/home.

3.26.2 Investment approvals, 2018

Sector	Foreign (% total approvals)	Growth (% year on year)	
		Foreign	Domestic
Primary	56.0	11.0	65.1
Manufacturing	83.0	24.0	43.5
Services	14.0	−25.0	10.5
Total	**46.0**	**−7.0**	**20.7**

Source: Malaysian Investment Development Authority. http://www.mida.gov.my/home.

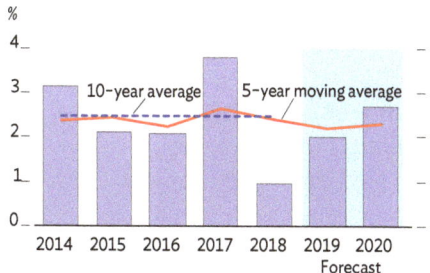

3.26.8 Inflation

Source: Asian Development Outlook database.

infrastructure projects approved by the previous administration creates uncertainty for foreign and domestic investors alike. Finally, persistent oversupply in the housing market could trigger housing price declines and dampen confidence.

Policy challenge—boosting private investment to take up slack in public investment

Malaysia's export-led growth model has succeeded in establishing a strong manufacturing base, and its investment climate continues to be one of the most attractive in Asia. The model has enabled the country to raise the ratio of investment to GDP significantly over 25%, which is high by international standards. Almost half of domestic investment in 2000 to 2015 has been public (Figure 3.26.9).

The new government's decision to cancel or postpone investment projects is a tacit admission that the return on many public projects is low and will only add to the nation's indebtedness. It is thus highly likely that public investment will continue to slow in the coming years. As the government winds down many investment projects, it needs to consider how it can catalyze private investment.

As policy makers strive to foster a new "entrepreneurial economy," to echo a phrase used in the 2019 budget, they need to pay attention to both the scale and the quality of private investment. This will be best achieved with policy measures that improve the business and investment climate in ways that attract private investors. This requires concerted action in three areas:

First, the government should minimize policy uncertainty by better communicating its capital spending priorities and enhancing transparency in its fiscal accounts, particularly on contingent liabilities and tax expenditure. The government is adopting some of these policies but should broaden their application to the rest of the public sector.

Second, the government should invest in strengthening workforce skills to attract private investment in high technology. Such investments align with the vision of making Malaysia—as articulated in the Industry 4.0 development strategy unveiled in November 2018—a strategic partner in smart manufacturing, a primary destination for high-technology industries, and a provider of total tech solutions for the region (Figure 3.26.10).

Finally, the government should minimize tax incentives for investors, which studies have shown are costly but tend to do little to sustain private investment over the long term. Rather than undermine fiscal revenue through tax incentives, the government can use the revenue it collects from investors for vocational training and enhancing workforce skills, among other priorities.

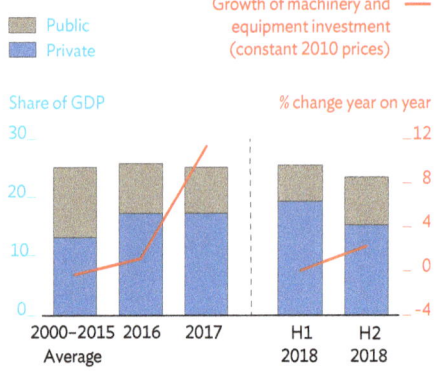

3.26.9 Share of investment in GDP and growth in machinery and equipment investment

H = half.
Source: Haver Analytics (accessed 8 March 2019).

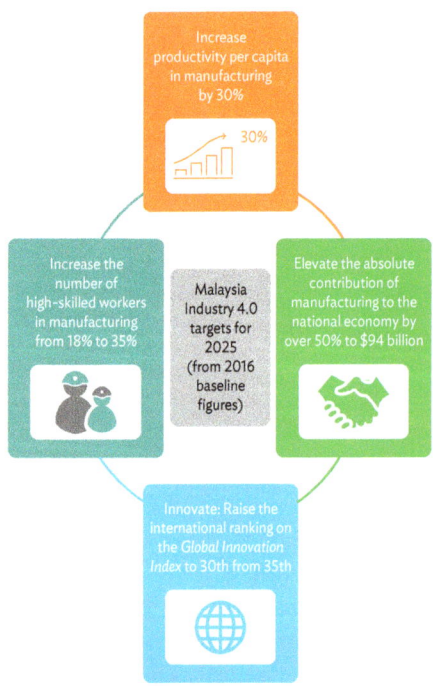

3.26.10 National goals and targets under Industry 4.0

Source: ADB estimates based on Industry 4WRD: National Policy on Industry 4.0.

Myanmar

Growth slowed in the 6-month transition to a new fiscal year. The current account deficit narrowed, and inflation rose. Growth is projected to pick up in the near term on an expected turnaround in tourism-related businesses and foreign direct investment. Inflation will ease this year and accelerate next year, and the current account will widen in both years. Expediting economic reform promises to sustain robust growth over the medium term.

Economic performance

Despite stronger exports, weaker domestic demand likely caused GDP growth to slow from 6.8% in fiscal year 2017 (FY2017, ended 31 March 2018) to 6.2% year on year in the transitional fiscal year 2018 (TFY2018, from 1 April 2018 to 30 September 2018) (Figure 3.27.1). Helped partly by depreciation of the Myanmar kyat, merchandise exports rose sharply in US dollar terms from 10.5% growth in FY2017 to 19.0% year on year in TFY2018.

Domestic consumption was likely weakened by slowing income growth and higher inflation. International tourist arrivals from January to August 2018 rose by about 1% from the same period a year earlier as a steady increase in Asian tourists offset a drop in visitors from the Americas, Europe, and Oceania. Domestic investment was sluggish, possibly reflecting slower disbursement of government expenditure, weaker investor sentiment, and a decline in foreign direct investment (FDI) approvals. These approvals plunged from $4.1 billion in April–September 2017 to $1.8 billion in TFY2018.

By sector, while agriculture posted higher growth with favorable weather in most of TFY2018, growth in industry and services slowed. Agriculture and allied activities, providing a quarter of GDP, accelerated from 1.3% growth in FY2017 to 2.0% year on year in TFY2018. Sluggish domestic consumption and investment dragged down industry growth to 8.7% year on year and services growth to 6.8% year on year in TFY2018.

Even as growth moderated, higher international oil prices and kyat depreciation against the US dollar fueled inflation at 7.1% year on year in TFY2018, up from 4.0% in FY2017. From April to September 2018, the kyat depreciated from MK1,330 to MK1,552 per dollar (Figure 3.27.2), losing 16.7% of its value. Some of this depreciation is attributed to the removal in August 2018 of a foreign exchange trading band for the currency.

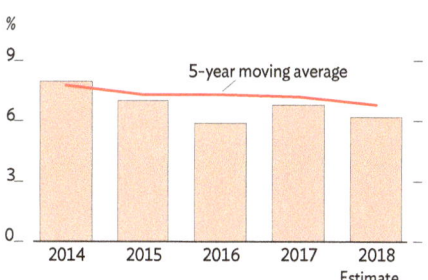

3.27.1 GDP growth

Note: From 2014 to 2017, years are fiscal years ending 31 March of next year; 2018 covers April to September.
Sources: Central Statistical Organization; Central Bank of Myanmar; ADB estimates.

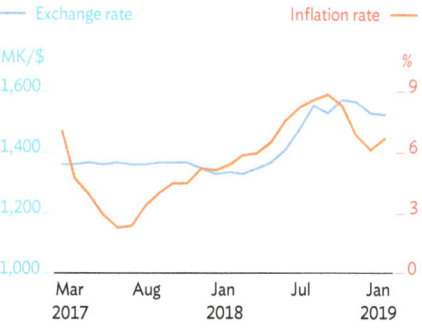

3.27.2 Exchange rate and inflation rate

Sources: Central Statistical Organization; Central Bank of Myanmar; CEIC database (accessed 19 March 2019).

This chapter was written by Yumiko Tamura of the Myanmar Resident Mission, ADB, Nay Pyi Taw.

Sluggish domestic demand slowed growth in imports in US dollar terms from 9.3% in FY2017 to 5.5% year on year in TFY2018, significantly narrowing the trade deficit. Robust net service receipts and the narrowing trade deficit slashed the current account deficit by more than half, from the equivalent of 4.7% of GDP in FY2017 to 2.0% in TFY2018. In September 2018, international reserves provided cover for slightly more than 3 months of imports.

The government budget for TFY2018 indicated an expansionary fiscal stance through more ambitious public spending targets despite no projected improvement in revenue. The budgeted fiscal deficit was equal to 6.2% of GDP, much higher than in previous years. As TFY2018 was only in the wet season, though, when difficult weather interferes with project implementation, the actual fiscal deficit was likely lower, equal to about 4.5% of GDP.

Monetary policy continued to focus on instituting a more flexible exchange rate regime and improving banks' compliance with prudential regulations and credit risk management. As of June 2018, growth in broad money (M2) was 18.2% year on year and growth in credit to the private sector was 23.7% year on year.

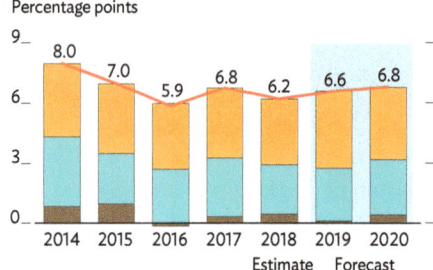

3.27.3 Supply-side contributions to growth

Note: From 2014 to 2017, years are fiscal years ending 31 March of next year; 2018 covers April to September; in 2019 and 2020, fiscal years end 30 September of the year.
Sources: Central Statistical Organization; Central Bank of Myanmar; ADB estimates.

Economic prospects

A weakening external environment, notably a continuing slowdown in the People's Republic of China, dims export prospects for Myanmar. However, domestic and foreign investment should improve in response to the opening up to FDI of retail and wholesale trade and the insurance business, as well as from the continued implementation of the Companies Act, which clarifies procedures for setting up businesses. Growth is forecast higher at 6.6% year on year in FY2019 (a full year ending 30 September 2019) and 6.8% in FY2020.

FDI approvals already show signs of revival. From October 2018 to January 2019, FDI approvals nearly doubled to about $1.5 billion from $823 million in the same period a year earlier as investors from Singapore and elsewhere in Asia took higher stakes in manufacturing and services. A recent policy measure to standardize FDI application and implementation procedures should further strengthen prospects for FDI inflows in the near term.

By sector, growth in services is likely to accelerate to 9.0% if tourism revives at the beginning of the dry season in October, coupled with solid growth in other sectors. Growth in agriculture is projected to slow to 0.5% in FY2019 following floods in mid-2018 that likely affected harvests, especially of rice in November. Weakening export prospects and slowing agriculture will hold back industry growth to 8.2% in FY2019 (Figure 3.27.3).

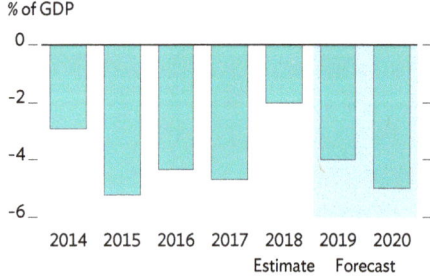

3.27.4 Current account balance

Note: From 2014 to 2017, years are fiscal years ending 31 March of next year; 2018 covers April to September; in 2019 and 2020, fiscal years end 30 September of the year.
Sources: Central Bank of Myanmar; ADB estimates.

3.27.1 Selected economic indicators (%)

	2019	2020
GDP growth	6.6	6.8
Inflation	6.8	7.5
Current account balance (share of GDP)	-4.0	-5.0

Source: ADB estimates.

Strengthening growth should sustain inflationary pressures, as will further depreciation of kyat against the US dollar. However, inflation may ease to 6.8% in FY2019 as international oil prices soften but is forecast to revive to 7.5% in FY2020.

The trade deficit is expected to widen this year and next as export earnings weaken and imports strengthen on stronger investment, particularly by the government. Even if net service receipts improve with a pickup in trade and tourism-related business, the current account deficit is forecast to widen to 4.0% in FY2019 and 5.0% in FY2020 (Figure 3.27.4).

Fiscal and monetary policies will likely strive to remain supportive of growth while maintaining macroeconomic stability. The fiscal deficit is forecast unchanged at the equivalent of 4.5% of GDP this year and next, with the Central Bank of Myanmar funding a fifth of it (Figure 3.27.5). The government is planning to end central bank financing of the fiscal deficit by FY2022, freeing the bank up to conduct monetary and exchange rate policies to maintain financial stability.

An external risk to the outlook would be the European Union withdrawing Myanmar's privileges under the Generalized System of Preferences, affecting 10% of exports from Myanmar. A domestic risk would be lackluster progress on economic reform, as would communal tensions flaring in conflict-affected areas.

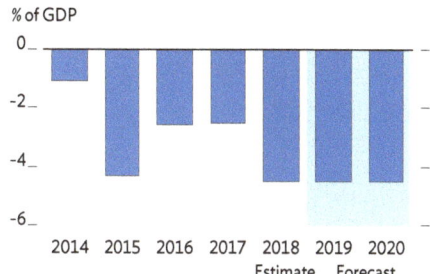

3.27.5 Fiscal balance

Note: From 2014 to 2017, years are fiscal years ending 31 March of next year; 2018 covers April to September; in 2019 and 2020, fiscal years end 30 September of the year.
Sources: Central Bank of Myanmar; ADB estimates.

Policy challenge—accelerating economic reform

Wide-ranging reform initiated in 2011 has continued under the democratically elected government that took office in April 2016. Elements of the government's development strategy have recently been announced in a number of strategic planning documents such as the Myanmar Sustainable Development Plan, 2018–2030; National Education Strategic Plan, 2016–2021; Myanmar National Health Plan, 2017–2021; and Myanmar National Social Protection Strategic Plan, 2014.

Building on these initiatives, the country needs to accelerate reform, which will contribute to inclusive development.

Reform to public financial management should aim for greater fiscal prudence, transparency, and efficiency. It should include strengthened Treasury functions, more systematic public investment planning and implementation, and the adoption of appropriate accounting and auditing standards to make public spending more productive.

Myanmar could become more competitive by further strengthening its legal and regulatory framework toward improving the business and investment climate, which would also spur integration into regional and global value chains (Figure 3.27.6). Stronger governance and accountability would help optimize the use of scarce financial resources, including official development assistance, and maximize their impact.

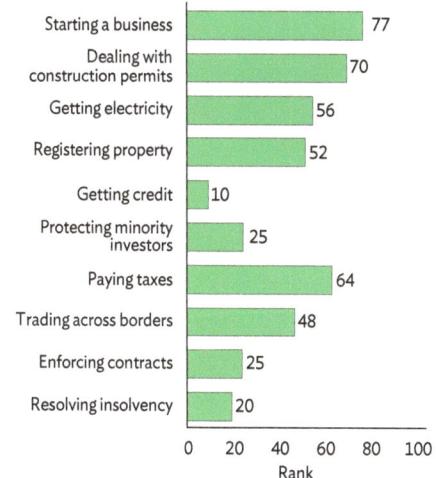

3.27.6 Ease of doing business score, 2019

Note: An economy's ease of doing business score is reflected on a scale from 0 to 100, where 0 is the lowest performance and 100 is the best.
Sources: World Bank. Doing Business 2019. http://www.doingbusiness.org.

Philippines

Growth moderated in 2018 but remained strong, buoyed by domestic investment. Even as the external environment weakens in 2019 and 2020, growth is expected to pick up in both years on strong domestic demand. Inflation surged last year but is forecast to be within the government's target range this year and next. The current account deficit will persist under investment-led growth. Agricultural reform to lift productivity and promote off-farm livelihoods promises to foster inclusive growth.

Economic performance

GDP growth moderated from 6.7% in 2017 to 6.2% in 2018, largely in line with average annual growth of 6.3% since 2010. Higher domestic investment and consumption partly offset a slowdown in growth of exports of goods and services.

Investment rose by 13.9% last year, improving on a 9.4% increase in 2017 and making in 2018 the largest demand-side contribution to GDP growth (Figure 3.28.1). Growth in public investment in construction rose from 12.7% in 2017 to 21.2% last year (Figure 3.28.2). Private investment remained robust as well, with a 12.9% rise in private construction and higher purchases of machinery and equipment. Consequently, fixed investment rose to equal 27.0% of GDP in 2018, its highest since the mid-1980s (Figure 3.28.3).

Private consumption growth softened from 5.9% in 2017 to 5.6%, finding support from a relatively low unemployment rate of 5.3%, steady remittances from overseas Filipinos, and a cut in the personal income tax rate for most workers. Remittances rose by 3.0% in 2018 to reach $32.2 billion, equal to 9.7% of GDP. Growth in government consumption quickened to 12.8%, with higher spending on social services and a hike in salaries for government employees. Meanwhile, growth in exports of goods and services slowed in real terms from 19.5% in 2017 to 11.5% last year, while imports rose rapidly in response to higher demand for investment and consumer goods.

By sector, services and industry were the drivers of growth, despite slowing a bit from 2017 (Figure 3.28.4). Growth in services reached 6.6% in 2018, only slightly down from 6.8% in 2017, and generated nearly two-thirds of GDP growth last year. Sustained gains were posted in retail trade, tourism, business process outsourcing, real estate, and finance.

3.28.1 Demand-side contributions to growth

Source: CEIC Data Company (accessed 12 March 2019).

3.28.2 Growth in construction

Source: CEIC Data Company (accessed 12 March 2019).

This chapter was written by Teresa Mendoza of the Philippines Country Office, ADB, Manila.

Industry expansion eased from 7.2% in 2017 to 6.8%, with construction and manufacturing the main growth drivers. Construction contributed 16% of the increase in GDP, and manufacturing provided nearly a fifth, despite slowing from 8.4% in 2017 to 4.9% as growth in external demand slackened. Agriculture was stagnant as crop damage caused by several typhoons compounded long-term structural and policy impediments to the sector's productivity and growth.

Inflation quickened to 5.2% in 2018, exceeding the target range of 2%–4% set by the government. Inflation was driven by constraints on food supply and by higher global oil prices. Increases in excise taxes on fuel, sugar-sweetened beverages, and cigarettes in January 2018 added to inflationary pressure last year. To ease food price inflation, the government removed administrative barriers to agricultural imports. Complementing this measure, Bangko Sentral ng Pilipinas, the central bank, raised its policy rate by a cumulative 175 basis points from May to November 2018 to address demand-side pressures and quell inflation expectations. These measures quickly eased inflation, which slowed from a peak of 6.7% year on year in October 2018 to 3.8% in February 2019. Core inflation also slowed, from a high of 5.1% in November 2018 to 3.9% in February 2019 (Figure 3.28.5). The higher policy rate reined in growth in broad money (M3) from 13.0% year on year in January 2018 to 7.6% a year later, as well as credit to the private sector from 17.1% to 13.7% over the same period.

The current account deficit widened from the equivalent of 0.7% of GDP in 2017 to 2.4% in 2018. In response to strong domestic investment, imports of machinery and equipment and of construction materials increased sharply. Imports thus rose by 9.4% in US dollar terms, while export earnings shrank by 0.3%, widening the trade deficit. Higher remittances and earnings from exports of services partly cushioned the merchandise trade deficit (Figure 3.28.6).

In the financial account, net inflows of foreign direct investment moderated from a high of $10.3 billion in 2017 to $9.8 billion in 2018, while net outflows of portfolio investment declined (Figure 3.28.7). The overall balance of payments deficit widened from the equivalent of 0.3% of GDP in 2017 to 0.7%. Foreign exchange reserves stood at $82.8 billion at the end of February 2019, providing cover for 7.3 months of imports of goods and services and income payments. The country's external payments position improved further as a broad downtrend in external debt brought it from the equivalent of 59.7% of GDP in 2005 to 23.9% last year.

Fiscal policy was expansionary, with the fiscal deficit widening from the equivalent of 2.2% of GDP in 2017 to 3.2% last year. This took the deficit slightly above the government's ceiling of 3.0%, reflecting its higher infrastructure and social investments and also improved budget execution as

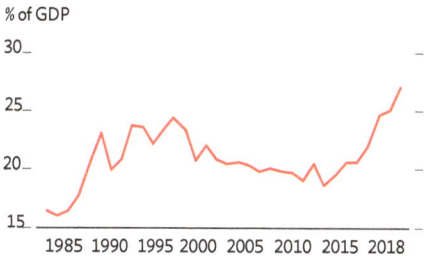

3.28.3 Fixed investment

Sources: World Development Indicators online database; CEIC Data Company (both accessed 12 March 2019).

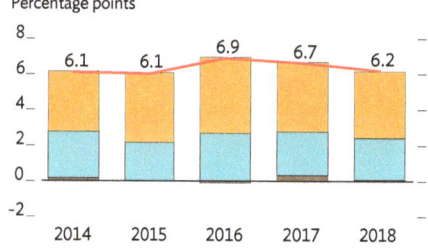

3.28.4 Supply-side contributions to growth

Source: CEIC Data Company (accessed 12 March 2019).

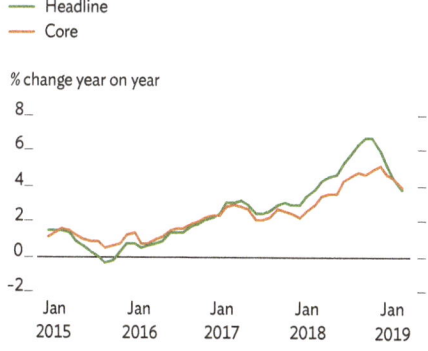

3.28.5 Monthly inflation

Source: CEIC Data Company (accessed 12 March 2019).

government disbursements slightly exceeded the budget program—a reversal of underspending in the past, by 13% on average in 2014 and 2015 and by 3% in 2016 and 2017. On the revenue side, the ratio of tax collection to GDP improved from 14.2% in 2017 to 14.7% in 2018, supported by revenue increments from the Tax Reform for Acceleration and Inclusion (TRAIN) Law. Despite the higher fiscal deficit, national government debt stood at 41.9% of GDP in December 2018, in line with government objectives for fiscal sustainability (Figure 3.28.8).

Economic prospects

GDP growth is projected to pick up to 6.4% this year and next as strengthening domestic investment and consumption more than offset weakening external demand (Figure 3.28.9).

Private consumption should pick up with a low unemployment rate, growth in formal sector employment, a continued rise in remittances, and lower inflation. The unemployment rate fell to 5.2% in January 2019 with the creation of an additional 1.4 million jobs for wage-earners and salaried employees. Also boosting consumption is increased public expenditure on social services. The Universal Health Care Law, passed in February 2019, automatically enrolls all citizens in the national health insurance program and thus promises to expand health care services, which should give an impetus to consumption. Election-related spending ahead of a May 2019 midterm poll will modestly lift aggregate demand.

Public investment will drive domestic investment with the implementation of major public infrastructure projects such as bridges, expressways, ports, and railways. The government aims to raise public infrastructure outlays from a 2017–2018 average equal to 6.3% of GDP to 7% by 2022 under its Build Build Build infrastructure program. Efforts to improve budget execution continue with a focus on project preparation and implementation including procurement.

Prospects for private investment remain favorable. Imports of capital goods and credit to businesses have continued to grow. Momentum in private construction is sustained by continuing strong demand for office and retail space and for housing. Building permit approvals rose by 20.7% year on year in the fourth quarter of 2018. Recent reform, such as the Ease of Doing Business Act approved in 2018, streamlines procedures for government transactions, including for local governments. Additional reform approved in the first quarter of 2019 includes revision of the Corporation Code that relaxes certain provisions for setting up businesses, and another law establishing a one-stop shop for processing permits for energy projects including power generation, transmission, and distribution. The new Central Bank Act strengthens the

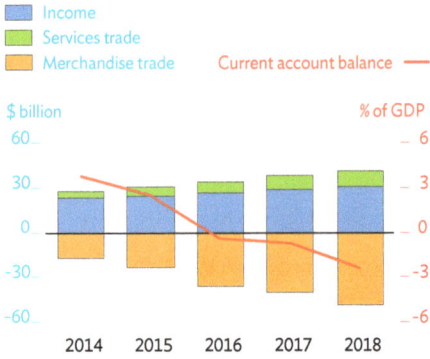

3.28.6 Current account components

Source: CEIC Data Company (accessed 15 March 2019).

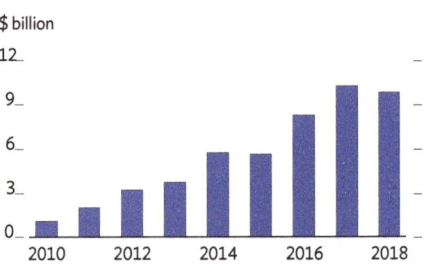

3.28.7 Foreign direct investment net inflows

Source: CEIC Data Company (accessed 12 March 2019).

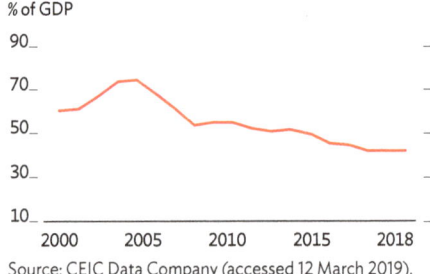

3.28.8 National government debt

Source: CEIC Data Company (accessed 12 March 2019).

policy framework for promoting price stability, prudential regulation, and systemic risk management in the financial system. The effective implementation of these reforms should further boost private sector confidence and investment.

Agriculture will likely continue to languish—especially as El Niño weather disturbances are expected to prolong dry spells this year—but services, construction, and manufacturing will all drive growth higher in the near term. Within services, retail trade will continue to benefit from strong consumption. International tourist arrivals, having risen by 7.7% to 7.1 million in 2018, are projected to rise further to 8.2 million this year, the increase supported by airport modernization in the provinces and other infrastructure improvement. Business process outsourcing will continue to expand, particularly outside Manila. Growth in manufacturing is expected to hold up well, supported by domestic demand, with a modest expansion indicated in the February 2019 manufacturing purchasing managers' index. Steady foreign direct investment inflows to manufacturing bode well for the sector's growth prospects in the near term. Spurred by public infrastructure projects, construction is forecast to remain buoyant.

Despite strengthening GDP growth and a tightening labor market, inflation is projected to moderate to 3.8% in 2019 and 3.5% in 2020 as global oil prices decline and last year's monetary tightening continues to be effective (Figure 3.28.10). A second round of excise tax rises on fuels in 2019 and a possible decline in agricultural output this year may add to inflationary pressure, though food supply should improve following the approval in February 2019 of a law that replaces quantitative restrictions on rice imports with tariffs.

As prospects for export growth soften, accelerating domestic investment and consumption should continue to draw in imports, keeping the merchandise trade and current account in deficit. However, continued strength in net service exports and lower international prices for oil should cushion the deficit somewhat. On balance, the current account deficit is forecast at 2.3% of GDP in 2019 and 2.4% in 2020.

As inflation stays within the government's target range of 2%–4%, monetary policy is likely to remain unchanged for some time. The fiscal deficit, meanwhile, has a ceiling set at the equivalent of 3.2% of GDP for 2019 and 3.0% for 2020. Legislating the government's proposed tax reform is vital to sustaining higher public infrastructure and social investments.

Risks to the growth outlook tilt to the downside. External risks would stem from an unexpectedly deep slowdown of economic growth in the advanced economies, which are major export markets and sources of foreign direct investment for the Philippines (Figure 3.28.11). Uncertainties from global trade tensions and potential heightened volatility in international financial markets pose another set of

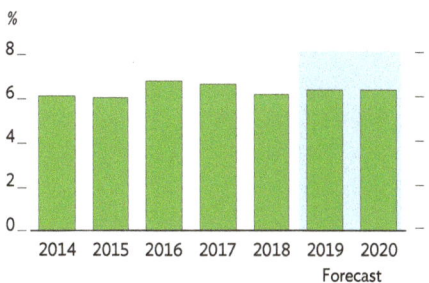

3.28.9 GDP growth

Source: *Asian Development Outlook* database.

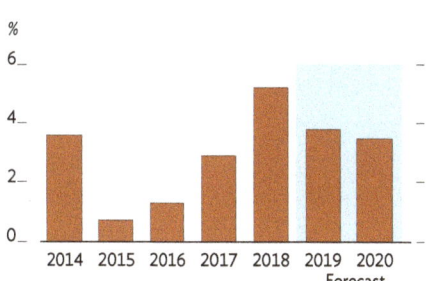

3.28.10 Inflation

Source: *Asian Development Outlook* database.

3.28.1 Selected economic indicators (%)

	2019	2020
GDP growth	6.4	6.4
Inflation	3.8	3.5
Current account balance (share of GDP)	-2.3	-2.4

Source: ADB estimates.

external risks. Domestic risks to growth would be severe or prolonged El Niño dry spells and a delay in approving the 2019 budget, which could slow the implementation of new large infrastructure projects and social programs this year.

GDP growth prospects for this year and next are supported by recent government reform to lay the foundation for raising growth potential in the medium term. Besides a massive infrastructure program, the government has implemented the TRAIN Law, the first package of comprehensive reform to make the tax system more equitable and efficient. Other recent reforms aim to improve the ease of doing business in the Philippines. Social protection reform and universal health care will support human capital development and help narrow wide household income disparities. The rollout of a national identification system that unifies all government identification cards into one will help facilitate financial inclusion and improve access to social services by the poor.

Another reform, the Bangsamoro Organic Law in 2018, creates an autonomous area on the large southern island of Mindanao and could spur development over the long term.

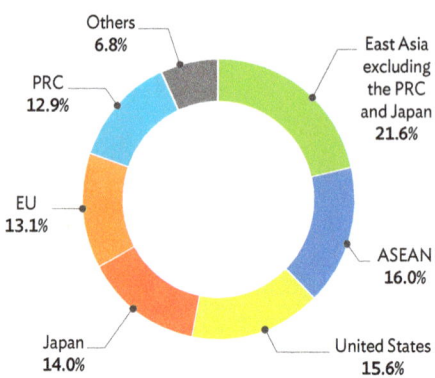

3.28.11 Merchandise export markets, 2018

ASEAN = Association of Southeast Asian Nations, EU = European Union, PRC = People's Republic of China.
Source: CEIC Data Company (accessed 12 March 2019).

Policy challenge—pursuing agricultural reform and off-farm incomes

The rapid rise in food price inflation in 2018 reflected, at least in part, structural and policy impediments to agriculture growth. Annualized food price inflation reached a high of 9.7% year on year in September 2018 and averaged 6.8% in 2018. Growth in agriculture value added was essentially stagnant in 2018. Indeed, agriculture has been underperforming for the past 2 decades. It grew by an average of 2.9% annually from 2000 to 2010, then growth slowed by half to 1.5% from 2011 to 2018. Improvement in labor productivity in Philippine agriculture compares poorly with that of its regional peers (Figure 3.28.12).

Notwithstanding its lackluster performance, agriculture remains the livelihood of many rural families. Half of the population resides in rural areas, and nearly one quarter of all employment is in agriculture. Poverty in rural areas is higher than the national average and especially high for farm households. According to a 2015 family income and expenditure survey, almost 35% of farmers and fisherfolk live below the national poverty line. As such, both farm and off-farm income-generating activities are critical for fostering inclusive growth.

While typhoons and droughts have played a role in erratic growth in agriculture and periodic food price instability, policy shortcomings have also weighed on the sector's development.

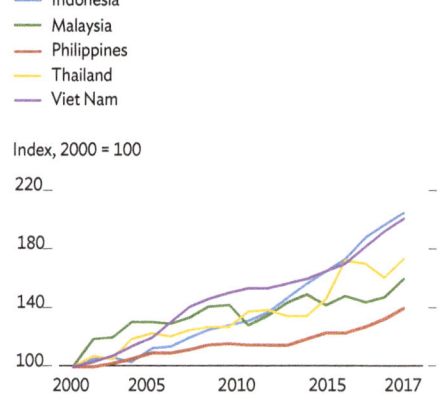

3.28.12 Labor productivity in agriculture

Note: Data are based on constant 2010 $.
Source: ADB estimates using data from World Development Indicators online database (accessed 15 March 2019).

These include trade restrictions on some agricultural products, notably rice; inadequate extension services to farmers; poor water resource management; and underinvestment in rural infrastructure.

The implementation of the 2019 law liberalizing the trading of rice is a major first step toward improving farm productivity and incomes. The law replaces quantitative restrictions on rice imports with tariffs, which should help stabilize domestic rice prices. It also restructures the National Food Authority, notably by transferring its main functions to other government agencies, and establishes the Rice Competitiveness Enhancement Fund, financed with revenue from tariffs on rice imports. The fund aims to raise farm productivity by, among other strategies, financing the modernization of farm practices, developing high-quality rice seed, beefing up extension services, and enhancing credit to rice farmers.

The law and the Rice Competitiveness Enhancement Fund together provide a unique opportunity to lift rural incomes by enhancing farm productivity and helping marginal rice farmers to switch to cultivating higher-value crops. But more can be done to enhance productivity. These include increasing investments in rural infrastructure that connect farm communities and urban growth centers, better irrigation, crop insurance against typhoons and droughts, and innovation that will engage the support of private sector providers of extension services to farmers in the transition to higher-value crops.

At the same time, it is important for the government to support emerging growth industries in rural areas that generate sustainable off-farm income. Tourism could be a catalyst as it has significant links with agriculture, construction, and retail services. Such a transition would require further improvement of rural tourism infrastructure and the business climate in rural areas, as well as investment in skills development.

Singapore

Growth decelerated in 2018 on softening demand, both external and internal. Further moderation is expected in 2019 and 2020 as slowdowns in major trade partners and lingering trade tensions tamp down expansion in export-oriented industries and erode business sentiment. Inflation will pick up slightly but remain tame, and the current account surplus will edge higher on rising net service receipts. The introduction of a carbon tax demands policies to keep affected companies competitive.

Economic performance

Growth moderated from 3.9% in 2017 to 3.2% in 2018 as expansion in manufacturing and services slowed and domestic demand weakened. Services remained the main driver of economic activity, contributing 2.1 percentage points to growth. Growth in manufacturing slowed from 10.4% in 2017 to 7.2% as demand for electronics softened but still contributed 1.3 points to growth. Construction contracted by 3.4%, shaving 0.1 points from growth, owing to weakness in public construction (Figure 3.29.1).

Consumption contributed 1.2 percentage points to growth, less than in 2017, as private expenditure growth slowed in line with spending on transportation, and public expenditure also rose modestly in line with spending on social services. Investment shaved 0.4 points from growth on faltering public and private construction and investment in transport equipment. Exports of goods and services grew by 5.2% in real terms, driven largely by higher shipments of machinery and transport equipment. Meanwhile, imports of goods and services rose by only 4.5%, leaving net exports to add 2.6 percentage points to GDP growth (Figure 3.29.2).

Consumer price inflation eased to 0.4% in 2018 with a decline in accommodation costs as rebates to households rose, bus and train transport costs dropped, and car prices moderated. However, core inflation, which excludes accommodation and private transportation on land, rose by 1.7% on steady price increases for food and for education and health care services (Figure 3.29.3).

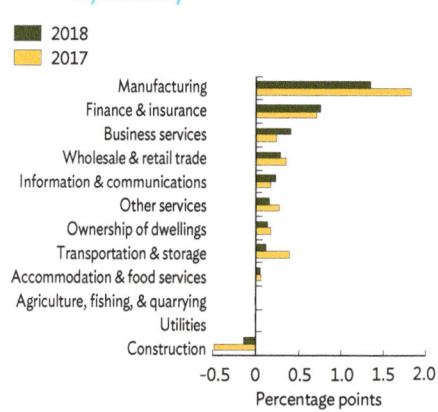

3.29.1 Supply-side contributions to growth, by industry

Source: Ministry of Trade and Industry. Economic Survey Singapore 2018 (accessed 18 February 2019).

3.29.2 Demand-side contributions to growth

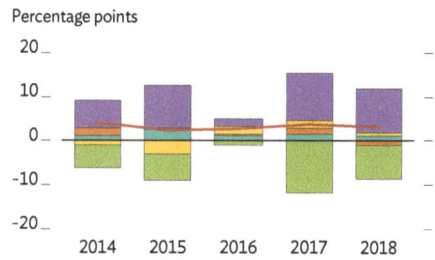

Source: Ministry of Trade and Industry. Economic Survey Singapore 2018 (accessed 18 February 2019).

This chapter was written by Shu Tian and Mai Lin Villaruel of the Economic Research and Regional Cooperation Department, ADB, Manila.

In April 2018, the Monetary Authority of Singapore tightened monetary policy, allowing the Singapore dollar to appreciate by 0.8% in nominal effective terms and by 2.3% against the US dollar in nominal terms (Figure 3.29.4). The interbank overnight rate increased by 0.4 basis points following movement in the US federal funds rate. Loans and advances rose by 3.0%, less than in 2017, and money supply grew by 3.9% (Figure 3.29.5).

Merchandise exports increased by 12.7% in 2018 as prices for petroleum product exports increased, though export volume fell. Merchandise imports rose by 14.3%, but the trade surplus still widened. As the deficit in services also narrowed on higher net receipts from financial services, the current account surplus rose to equal 17.7% of GDP. Nevertheless, the overall balance of payments surplus narrowed from the equivalent of 8.1% of GDP in 2017 to 3.5% as net capital outflows widened to $50.3 billion, equal to 13.9% of GDP (Figure 3.29.6).

The budget for fiscal year 2018 (FY2018, ended 31 March 2019) recorded a surplus equal to 0.4% of GDP, though a small deficit had been planned. Revenue declined by 0.5%, less than originally budgeted, with lower receipts from vehicle quota premiums and stamp duties and reduced contributions from statutory boards. Expenditure including special transfers grew by 10.4%, also less than originally planned, on higher transport, security, and defense outlays (Figure 3.29.7).

Economic prospects

GDP growth is expected to moderate further to 2.6% in 2019 and 2020. Manufacturing and export-oriented services will grow at a slower pace than last year, tamped down by a global growth slowdown and lingering trade tensions. According to a business expectation survey in the first quarter of 2019, business conditions are expected to be less favorable in the first half of 2019. The purchasing managers' index for manufacturing edged down in February 2019, and that for electronics dipped into contraction territory (Figure 3.29.8). Nevertheless, modern services—which include business services, finance, and information and communication technology—will continue to drive growth this year and next, buttressed by government support for digitalization. Construction looks likely to recover in 2019, as public sector contracts rose substantially in late 2018.

Investment growth will accelerate in 2019 on recovery in construction and plans by the Economic Development Board of Singapore to attract more than S$10 billion in fixed asset investment. Low unemployment and tightening supply of foreign workers will push up real wages and encourage household spending, while government consumption will

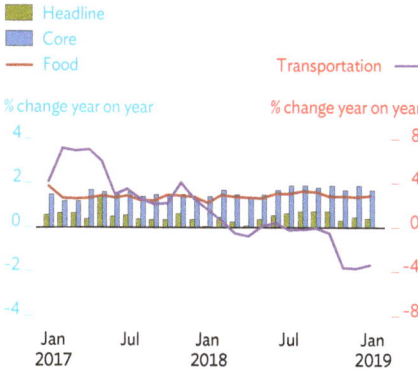

Source: CEIC Data Company (accessed 5 March 2019).

Source: CEIC Data Company (accessed 5 March 2019).

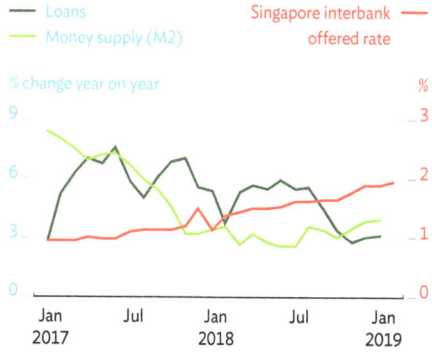

Source: CEIC Data Company (accessed 8 March 2019).

rise with more spending on social services and security. January 2019 data show exports of both oil and other products, notably machinery and transport equipment, declining in real terms, though lower exports were cushioned by increased re-exports. Imports too are expected to grow at a slower pace in 2019, generating a modest rise in net exports.

A budget deficit equal to 0.7% of GDP is planned for FY2019. If implemented as planned, expenditure will increase by 1.6% on spending in social services, and revenue will grow by 1.7% on higher receipts from fees and charges.

Inflation is projected to edge up to 0.7% in 2019 and 0.9% in 2020. In January 2019, headline inflation eased to 0.4% year on year and core inflation to 1.7% year on year. However, inflationary pressure will intensify this year and the next. A higher private residential property price index in the fourth quarter of 2018 indicated rising accommodation costs. A carbon tax will come into effect, wages could rise as reliance on foreign workers becomes more restricted, and education and health care costs and license fees on car ownership are set to increase. However, with core inflation still within the forecast range of the Monetary Authority of Singapore, monetary policy will likely be unchanged at least for the remainder of 2019.

The trade account is forecast in surplus in both 2019 and 2020, though imports are expected to grow faster than exports. In January 2019, export growth softened to 1.0% year on year, while imports grew by 8.0%, but the trade balance remained in surplus. The deficit in services is expected to narrow as net payments for imports of business and transport services fall, and as net receipts from the use of intellectual property and financial services increase. On balance, the current account surplus is projected to remain stable at the equivalent of 17.8% of GDP in 2019 and 2020.

An external risk to the outlook is global growth slowing more than expected. Singapore's highly open economy is vulnerable to protectionist policies elsewhere, and the trade conflict between the People's Republic of China and the US could further erode business confidence. Separately, increases in US interest rates that are higher or more abrupt than expected could reduce capital flows and raise local interest rates. The main domestic downside risks arise from tightening in the labor market and slower productivity growth than experienced in recent years. Singapore enjoys substantial financial buffers to mitigate the impact of these risks, however, if they materialize.

3.29.1 Selected economic indicators (%)

	2019	2020
GDP growth	2.6	2.6
Inflation	0.7	0.9
Current account balance (share of GDP)	17.8	17.8

Source: ADB estimates.

3.29.6 Balance of payments

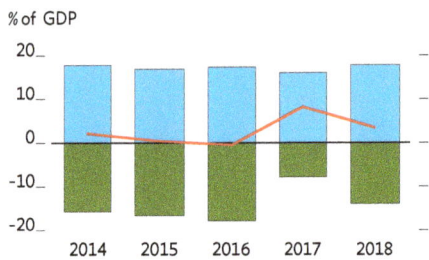

Source: Ministry of Trade and Industry. Economic Survey Singapore 2018 (accessed 18 February 2019).

3.29.7 Fiscal indicators

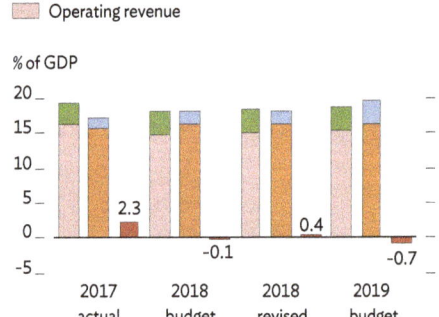

Note: Years are fiscal years ending on 31 March of the next year.
Source: Ministry of Finance (accessed 22 February 2019).

Policy challenge—balancing competitiveness and low-carbon development

Singapore's carbon emissions relative to GDP rank low in the world, but its emissions per capita ranked 24 out of 204 in 2014. Under the 2015 Paris Agreement, Singapore pledged to reduce by 2030 its carbon emission intensity by 36% from its 2005 level. To this end, Singapore introduced a carbon tax on carbon dioxide emissions, effective from 2019, making it the first economy in the Association of Southeast Asian Nations to do so.

The carbon tax applies to large emitters and has directly affected the businesses, as many as 40 of them, that contribute more than 80% of emissions (Figure 3.29.9). The tax is expected to encourage the transition to energy-efficient operations, set the stage for future platforms for emissions trading, and generate revenues estimated at $1 billion in the first 5 years, which the government intends to use to help companies innovate and improve their energy efficiency. Meanwhile, though, there is a risk that the carbon tax could make affected businesses less competitive than peers that are not subject to the tax—a risk exacerbated by volatile oil prices. The authorities now face the challenge of balancing objectives for controlling emissions with those for sustaining competitiveness and economic growth.

Reflecting this concern, the carbon tax is scheduled to increase gradually, starting at S$5 per ton of carbon dioxide during the transition phase of 2019–2023, then rising to S$10–S$15 per ton following an assessment in 2023 of its impact. Gradual implementation and intense competition among energy supply companies should make it unlikely that the carbon tax will be passed on to consumers through higher electricity prices.

To ensure that the carbon tax is effective in the subsequent phase of implementation—when more information on energy emissions will be available and more companies will become subject to the tax—a carbon emissions trading system can be introduced. For this purpose, the government should set gradually stricter annual ceilings both for aggregate pollution from all industries and for company-specific emissions. Companies can then be allowed to trade their emissions. This will provide more flexibility to larger polluters, as they strive to bring down their emissions in an orderly fashion, while ensuring that the aggregate emission ceiling is not breached. During this phase, the carbon tax can be extended to the transportation industry, which the government forecasts will be second only to industry as a source of carbon pollution by 2020.

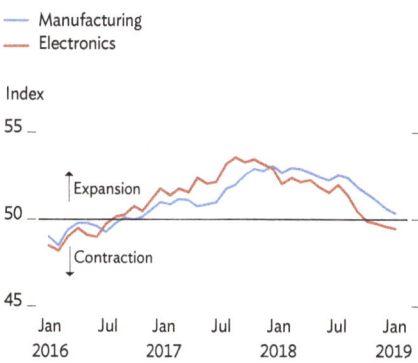

3.29.8 Purchasing managers' index

Source: CEIC Data Company (accessed 8 March 2019).

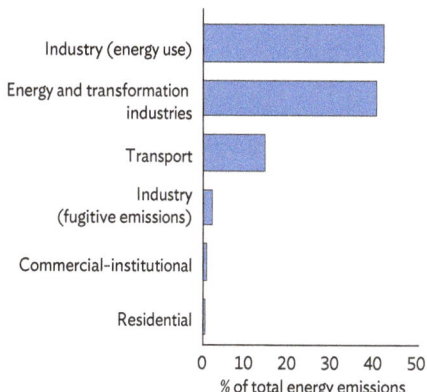

3.29.9 Emissions by sector, 2014

Source: National Environment Agency. 2018. Fourth National Communication and Third Biennial Update Report (accessed 1 March 2019).

Thailand

Higher domestic demand more than offset moderation in exports to drive economic growth higher in 2018. In a weakening external environment, growth is likely to fall back to its 2017 rate this year and a bit lower next year. Inflation will continue to be benign, and current account surpluses will remain substantial even as they shrink. Strengthening Thailand's economic links with its close neighbors can add impetus to growth in the medium term.

Economic performance

GDP growth rose from 4.0% in 2017 to 4.1% in 2018 on higher domestic demand and despite weaker export growth, as volume growth in exports of goods and services moderated from 5.4% in 2017 to 4.2% last year (Figure 3.30.1). Growth in the US dollar value of merchandise exports slipped from 9.8% in 2017 to 7.7% as external demand softened. While lower prices caused a 23.6% reduction in earnings from rubber exports, a slowdown in global electronics trade dragged manufacturing export growth down from 10.2% in 2017 to 8.4%.

On the domestic front, both consumption and investment picked up. Buoyed by improved domestic conditions, low inflation, and continued government support for low-income households, private consumption grew by 4.6% in 2018, more than half again the 3.0% rise in 2017. Retail sales continued to be robust, with the retail sales index rising from 6.3% in 2017 to 10.8%. Domestic investment rose by a hefty 16.9% on top of a 14.1% increase in 2017. In tandem with a recovery in private investment that began in 2017 and gathered strength last year, public investment, buoyed by the implementation of several public infrastructure projects, grew by 3.3%, reversing a decline in 2017.

Excepting services, growth in 2018 improved on 2017 across the board. Favorable weather helped growth in agriculture improve from 3.7% in 2017 to 5.0% (Figure 3.30.2). Industry growth rose from 2.2% in 2017 to 2.7%, and construction staged a turnaround from 2.8% contraction in 2017 to 2.7% growth last year on accelerated implementation of public infrastructure projects. Meanwhile, softening international tourist arrivals slowed growth in services from 5.8% in 2017 to 5.1% in 2018, when the service sector nevertheless provided almost three-fourths of GDP growth.

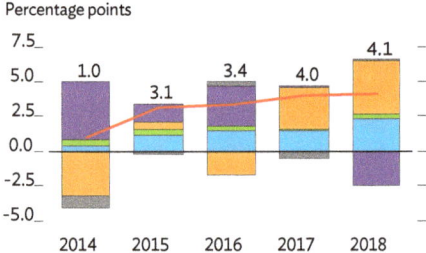

3.30.1 Demand-side contributions to growth

Source: Office of the National Economic and Social Development Council. http://www.nesdb.go.th (accessed 1 March 2019).

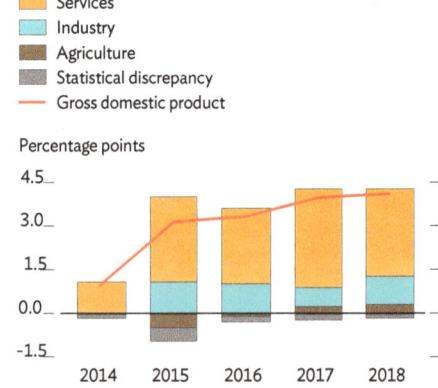

3.30.2 Supply-side contributions to growth

Source: Office of the National Economic and Social Development Council. http://www.nesdb.go.th (accessed 1 March 2019).

This chapter was written by Thiam Hee Ng of the Southeast Asia Department, ADB, Manila.

Tourism took some hits in 2018. In July, bad weather caused a ferry carrying tourists from the People's Republic of China (PRC) to capsize near Phuket, killing all 47 passengers on board. The World Cup in June and July is blamed for diverting European tourists away from Thailand and to the Russian Federation. In any case, tourist arrivals slumped in the third quarter, prompting the government to step up tourism promotion and grant a temporary waiver, to the end of April 2019, on the fee for visa on arrival. International tourist arrivals showed signs of recovery in the fourth quarter and grew by 7.9% in the whole year to reach 38.3 million (Figure 3.30.3).

As growth picked up and international oil prices rose last year, inflation accelerated from 0.7% in 2017 to 1.1%, though it began to ease again in the fourth quarter as international oil prices softened (Figure 3.30.4). Food price inflation remained muted as higher agriculture growth ensured ample supply.

The trade surplus narrowed sharply from the equivalent of 7.5% of GDP in 2017 to 4.7% (Figure 3.30.5). While growth in merchandise exports slowed in US dollar terms from 9.8% in 2017 to 7.7%, that of merchandise imports accelerated from 13.2% to 14.3%, mostly on higher imports of consumer goods to meet demand as private expenditure rose. Net export receipts for services were marginally lower as well. The result was a smaller current account surplus, equal to 7.5% of GDP.

The financial account recorded a deficit of $21.6 billion, reflecting mostly rising investment overseas by investors based in Thailand. The surplus in the overall balance of payments thus plunged by three-quarters, from the equivalent 5.7% of GDP in 2017 to 1.4% last year. International reserves continued to climb, reaching $205.6 billion at the end of 2018, which was cover for 8.7 months of imports or 3.3 times the country's short-term foreign debt. With a still-comfortable balance of payments and ample international reserves, the Thai baht appreciated by 4.8% against the US dollar in 2018.

The Bank of Thailand, the central bank, raised its policy rate in December 2018, for the first time in 11 years, by 25 basis points to 1.75%. This was primarily a preemptive measure to maintain financial stability and to build space in the rate for any reductions needed later if global economic conditions deteriorate.

Fiscal policy remained broadly supportive to growth as the deficit for fiscal year 2018 (FY2018, ended 30 September 2018) equaled 2.5% of GDP, only slightly down from 2.7% in FY2017 (Figure 3.30.6). Actual government expenditure came to 94.5% of the budget, while revenue lagged at 82.4% of the budget. Public debt remained sustainable at the equivalent of 41.9% of GDP, of which foreign debt accounted for less than 2%.

3.30.3 Tourism indicators

Source: Bank of Thailand. http://www.bot.or.th (accessed 13 March 2019).

3.30.4 Inflation and policy interest rate

Sources: Bank of Thailand. http://www.bot.or.th; CEIC Data Company (both accessed 13 March 2019).

3.30.5 Trade indicators

Source: Bank of Thailand. http://www.bot.or.th (accessed 1 March 2019).

Economic prospects

Slowing global growth and a lingering trade conflict between the PRC and the US will dim export prospects. Following bumper harvests in 2018, growth in agriculture and allied businesses is likely to return to the long-term trend. Although domestic consumption and investment should hold up, GDP growth is expected to revert to 3.9% in 2019 and slow a bit more to 3.7% in 2020 (Figure 3.30.7).

Domestic consumption is forecast to stay robust as upbeat consumer sentiment endures, as reflected in the consumer confidence index. Low unemployment—at 0.9% most recently, in the last quarter of 2018—should buttress consumer spending, as will continued government assistance to low-income households. That said, high household debt and a recent tightening of macroprudential policy will likely hold consumer spending back from significant acceleration.

Domestic investment is projected to sustain last year's growth rate as the implementation of large public infrastructure projects proceeds. Budgetary capital outlays in FY2019 have so far increased by 19.9%. As of February 2019, 20 public infrastructure investment projects with a combined budget of nearly $23 billion had reached their construction phase. With construction in progress, budgetary disbursements are expected to smooth out. Moreover, several new infrastructure projects connected to the Eastern Economic Corridor—a massive government-led development program in the provinces of Chachoengsao, Chonburi, and Rayong—have recently received cabinet approval and could begin implementation by the middle of 2019.

Private investment also looks positive, buoyed by broadly stable business sentiment. Thailand is expected to benefit from the US–PRC trade dispute if it lasts long enough to prompt some manufacturing to relocate outside of the PRC. In 2018, the value of all applications placed before the Thailand Board of Investment rose by 42.8%, promising higher private investment in the near term.

All the major productive sectors—agriculture, industry, and services—are nevertheless seen to experience slower growth this year and next. Growth in agriculture will moderate from a high base in 2018. Growth in industry will slow as manufacturing expansion weakens in tandem with external demand, though accelerating implementation of infrastructure projects should give a boost to construction. Growth in services will slow further from last year's pace but nevertheless still be robust.

Inflation is projected to remain stable at a low 1.0% in 2019 and 2020 as the economy slows, international fuel prices weaken, and the exchange rate sees little change (Figure 3.30.8).

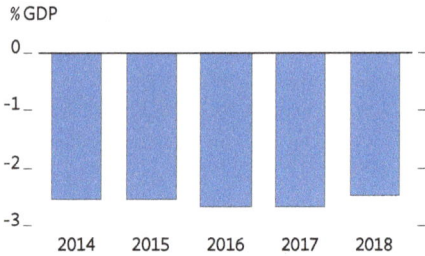

3.30.6 Fiscal balance

Note: Years are fiscal years ending on 30 September of that year.
Source: Bank of Thailand. http://www.bot.or.th (accessed 1 March 2019).

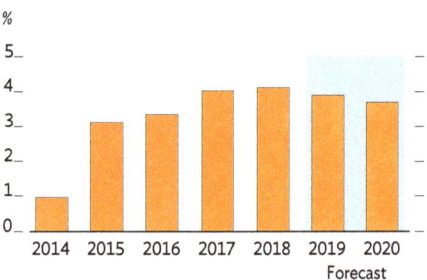

3.30.7 GDP growth

Source: *Asian Development Outlook* database.

3.30.1 Selected economic indicators (%)

	2019	2020
GDP growth	3.9	3.7
Inflation	1.0	1.0
Current account balance (share of GDP)	7.0	7.0

Source: ADB estimates.

Merchandise exports are likely to slow as external demand softens with slowdowns in the industrial economies and the PRC. Recent bilateral tariff hikes between the PRC and the US could adversely affect exports from Thailand, given its role as a major supplier of intermediate goods in global value chains. Separately, the downturn in the global electronics cycle may hinder exports of electronics and electrical appliances.

Growth in merchandise imports is forecast to outpace exports as imports rise to support the rollout of the large infrastructure projects. The merchandise trade surplus is thus expected to narrow. Net exports of services should continue in surplus as growth in international tourist arrivals returns to trend following last year's temporary setback. The net result is likely to be a somewhat narrower current account surplus equal to 7.0% of GDP in 2019 and 2020 (Figure 3.30.9). With foreign direct investment and portfolio inflows both remaining stable, the overall balance of payments should remain comfortable, as should international currency reserves.

As growth slows, fiscal policy is expected to stay accommodative this year and next, with spending on public infrastructure continuing to accelerate and project implementation requiring faster budgetary disbursement. The budget for FY2019 calls for a fiscal deficit of B450 billion, equal to 2.6% of GDP, with a similar fiscal deficit planned for FY2020.

With slower growth, low and stable inflation, and a comfortable balance of payments, monetary policy will continue to be accommodative. The central bank is unlikely to raise rates in 2019. In fact, after the increase in December 2018, it has room to ease monetary policy if the economy slows more than expected and deemed tolerable.

The main external risk to the outlook is any escalation in the trade conflict between the PRC and the US. An unexpected delay in implementing infrastructure investment projects is a domestic risk, as are adverse weather that could affect farm production and damage the rural economy.

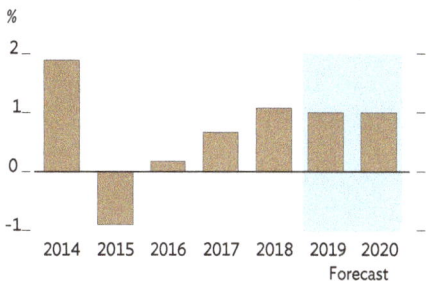

3.30.8 Inflation

Source: *Asian Development Outlook* database.

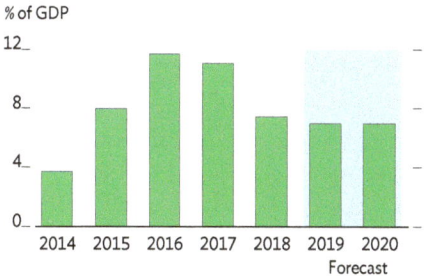

3.30.9 Current account balance

Source: *Asian Development Outlook* database.

Policy challenge—strengthening economic links with close neighbors

Thailand has long benefited from being an open economy. It has prospered as a hub in the regional production network and in global value chains, making foreign trade a major contributor historically to its economic growth. Building on this success, Thailand can benefit by further strengthening its economic links with its close neighbors through trade, investment, and technology transfer. This would allow it to shift to a higher position in the regional production network and in global value chains—an ambition enunciated under the Thailand 4.0 development strategy.

Encouragingly, Thailand is surrounded by dynamic, fast growing neighbors: Cambodia, the Lao People's Democratic Republic, Myanmar, and Viet Nam. These countries are quickly climbing the development ladder, and their demand for consumer goods is likely to accelerate. Thailand is well placed to meet this demand. Already, recent trends reveal the growing importance of these neighbors as trade partners for Thailand, with their share of Thai exports nearly quadrupling from about 3% in 1995 to almost 12% in 2018 (Figure 3.30.10). These exports are expected to continue to grow as trade ties further strengthen.

These four economies have been destinations not just for Thai exports but also for Thai private investment (Figure 3.30.11). Such investment has grown quickly, concentrated in energy and transportation infrastructure.

Looking ahead, potential exists for Thailand to invest more in its neighbors' manufacturing sectors. Channeling foreign direct investment into its neighbors could be one solution to Thailand's worsening shortage of skilled workers at home as its population ages, even as investment augments the capital supply and technological knowhow available to its neighbors. In contrast with Thailand's shrinking pool of young workers able and willing to take factories jobs, Thailand's neighbors boast young and growing populations eager to enter the workforce.

Thailand can use its long experience in global value chains to guide the integration of its neighbors into these production networks. Improving transport links can further cement closer trade ties and better integrate these economies with the regional production network and global value chains. The main hurdles to further integration are bottlenecks and delays at border crossings. A recent study for the Organisation for Economic Co-operation and Development found that Southeast Asia could reap large gains by expeditiously implementing trade facilitation. By improving transportation links and streamlining border formalities, Thailand could better integrate itself and its neighbors into the regional production network and global supply chains.

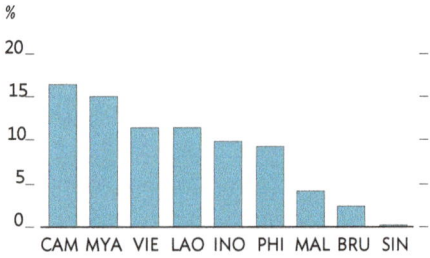

3.30.10 Average annual growth of Thai exports, 2007–2018

BRU = Brunei Darussalam, CAM = Cambodia, INO = Indonesia, LAO = Lao People's Democratic Republic, MAL = Malaysia, MYA = Myanmar, PHI = Philippines, THA = Singapore, VIE = Viet Nam.
Source: CEIC Data Company (accessed 14 March 2019).

3.30.11 Average annual growth in outward FDI stock, 2007–2017

BRU = Brunei Darussalam, CAM = Cambodia, FDI = foreign direct investment, INO = Indonesia, LAO = Lao People's Democratic Republic, MAL = Malaysia, MYA = Myanmar, PHI = Philippines, THA = Singapore, VIE = Viet Nam.
Source: CEIC Data Company (accessed 14 March 2019).

Viet Nam

Strong exports and domestic demand pushed GDP growth higher in 2018 than in more than a decade. Inflation was stable, and the current account surplus widened. This year and next, though, a weaker external environment will likely moderate growth and narrow the current account surplus, while inflation remains stable in 2019 but rises somewhat in 2020. Small and medium-sized enterprises need to upgrade their capacity to benefit from better integration into global value chains.

Economic performance

The economy experienced another year of strong growth as it accelerated from 6.8% in 2017 to 7.1% in 2018, the highest in 11 years. Solid growth in exports of goods and services and continued strength in domestic demand underpinned last year's expansion. Private consumption, the largest component of GDP, accounted for most of GDP growth last year (Figure 3.31.1).

Although growth in exports of goods and services moderated from 16.7% in 2017 to 14.3% last year, net exports expanded by 9.2%. Strong external demand thus gave a big boost to Viet Nam's highly trade-dependent economy. Merchandise exports rose by 13.8%, with exports of telephones and accessories, which now account for a fifth of merchandise exports, rising by 11.0%.

Domestic demand held up well, though moderating from 7.3% in 2017 to 7.2% last year. Rising incomes and stable inflation underpinned a strong rise in private consumption. Growth in gross investment slowed from 9.8% in 2017 to 8.2%. Buoyant foreign direct investment (FDI) was up by 9.1% in 2018, and investment from the state budget rose by 12.5% (Figure 3.31.2).

By sector, growth in agriculture, industry, and construction accelerated while growth in services moderated. Agriculture and agribusiness improved on 2.9% expansion in 2017 with growth at 3.8% last year. Fisheries were the best performer within the sector, achieving 6.5% growth. More broadly, agriculture profited from recent government initiatives to update farm technology.

Benefiting from strong export orders and domestic demand, growth in industrial production accelerated from 7.8% in 2017 to 8.8% last year, with construction,

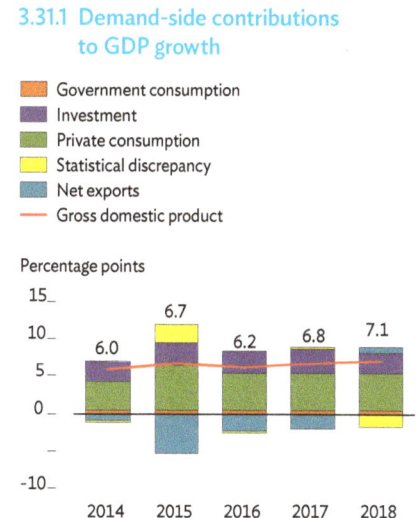

3.31.1 Demand-side contributions to GDP growth

Source: General Statistics Office of Viet Nam.

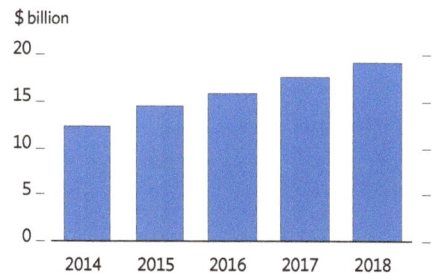

3.31.2 Disbursement of foreign direct investment

Sources: General Statistics Office of Viet Nam; State Bank of Viet Nam.

This chapter was written by Cuong Minh Nguyen, Chu Hong Minh, and Nguyen Luu Thuc Phuong of the Viet Nam Resident Mission, ADB, Ha Noi.

up by 8.7% in 2017, improving to 9.2% growth. Industry and construction contributed nearly half of GDP growth last year with improved mining output and continued momentum in manufacturing driven by increases in the export-oriented sectors: telecommunications, electronics, and textiles. Growth in services moderated from 7.4% in 2017 to 7.0%, with wholesale and retail trade the strongest segment, up by 8.5%. International tourist arrivals rose by a fifth (Figure 3.31.3).

Encouragingly, stronger growth did not cause much inflationary pressure. Inflation averaged 3.5% in 2018, as in 2017 and below the official target of 4.0% (Figure 3.31.4). Core inflation averaged 1.5%, little changed from the previous year. While higher costs for medical services, education, and transportation contributed to inflationary pressure in the first 10 months of the year, pressure was eased by a decline in international oil prices, the government's decision to postpone a planned hike in electricity tariffs, and tighter monetary conditions.

The external position strengthened. The current account continued to post a surplus, up from the equivalent of 2.9% of GDP in 2017 to an estimated 3.0%, supported by a $7 billion trade surplus and stable service receipts. Sizeable FDI and portfolio capital inflows pushed the estimated surplus in the capital account to the equivalent of 6.0% of GDP. Data from the General Statistics Office show that registered foreign investment reached $35.5 billion in 2018, including an estimated $25.5 billion in new FDI commitments. Inflows of foreign equity investment reached an estimated $10 billion, reflecting positive sentiment among foreign investors.

Surpluses in the current and capital accounts added up to an overall balance of payments surplus estimated to equal 5% of GDP. The strengthened external position improved foreign reserves from a low 2.7 months of import cover at the end of 2017 to an estimated 3.0 months a year later.

Budgetary expenditure growth was sharply down from 17.1% in 2017 to an estimated 10.5% last year. Growth in current expenditure slowed from 11.6% in 2017 to 8.7% as discretionary spending was contained. Budget revenue growth slowed from 11.9% in 2017 to 9.6% in 2018. The on-budget fiscal deficit expanded marginally from the equivalent of 3.5% of GDP in 2017 to an estimated 3.7% (Figure 3.31.5). Strong economic growth helped the government to contain public debt at the equivalent of 61.4% of GDP at the end of 2018, down from its peak of 63.7% in 2016 and comfortably below the statutory cap of 65.0%.

Inflationary pressures eased at year-end, but as they built in the first 10 months of 2018, growth in credit and the money supply (M2) was controlled with stricter limits applied on commercial banks' credit growth and stricter regulations on lending in high-risk areas such as real estate and securities.

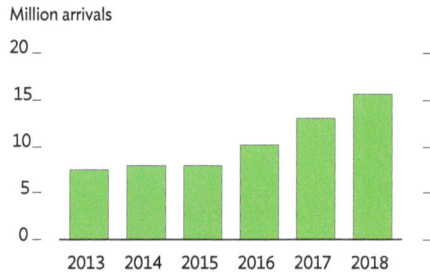

3.31.3 Tourist arrivals

Source: General Statistics Office of Viet Nam.

3.31.4 Monthly inflation

Source: General Statistics Office of Viet Nam.

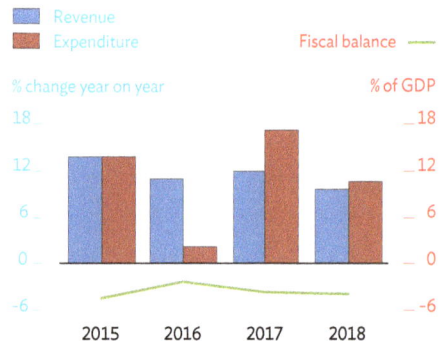

3.31.5 Fiscal balance

Note: Data exclude off-budget spending and on-lending.
Source: Ministry of Finance.

Estimated growth in credit was contained at 14.0% and in money supply at 12.0%, the lowest growth for both since 2015 (Figure 3.31.6). Despite volatility in international financial markets, the Viet Nam dong stabilized against the US dollar, depreciating by only 1.8% in the whole year (Figure 3.31.7).

Economic prospects

With growth in the global economy and world trade forecast to slow, growth in Viet Nam is forecast to moderate but remain strong at 6.8% in 2019 and 6.7% in 2020 (Figure 3.31.8). Growth will continue to be broad-based, underpinned by export-oriented manufacturing, inward FDI, and sustained domestic demand.

Ongoing reform to improve the business environment should encourage private investment, as should efforts to forge stronger ties with partners around the world through various trade agreements. Viet Nam's ratification of the Comprehensive and Progressive Agreement for Trans-Pacific Partnership in 2018, and its expected free trade agreement with the European Union, may stimulate investment in the near term as foreign enterprises explore the expanding business opportunities that Viet Nam offers.

These trade agreements signify the government's continued commitment to liberalizing the economy. The government targets the establishment of 140,000 new businesses in 2019, which bodes well for exports, FDI inflows, and private investment more generally. The outlook for private consumption remains robust as households enjoy rising incomes and stable inflation. Investment should find support in accelerated public capital expenditure this year and next to meet the target of the country's 2016–2020 socioeconomic development plan.

By sector, manufacturing and construction will slow but still maintain solid expansion, with substantial FDI likely to flow into export-orientated manufacturing. The purchasing managers' index points to rising orders in manufacturing (Figure 3.31.9). Services will benefit in 2019 from continued growth in retail and wholesale trade, and in banking and finance. An expected 16.0% annual increase in tourist arrivals this year and next, though slowing from growth in 2018, should support tourism-related businesses such as hotels, restaurants, and transportation. Meanwhile, agriculture will likely expand at near the government's target of 3.0% per year.

Inflation is expected to continue to average 3.5% in 2019 but accelerate to 3.8% in 2020 (Figure 3.31.10). The announcement that the US Federal Reserve will no longer raise its policy rate in 2019 is likely to relieve pressure on the Viet Nam dong and inflation, as will lower international oil prices. Upward adjustments to administered fees for public

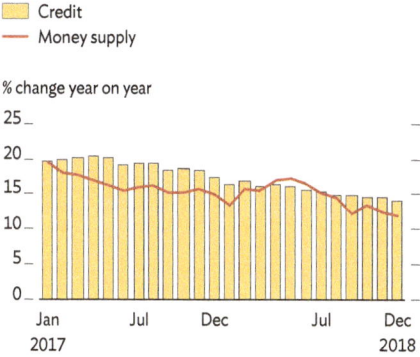

3.31.6 Growth in credit and money supply

Sources: State Bank of Viet Nam; ADB estimates.

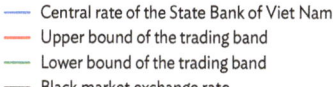

3.31.7 Exchange rates

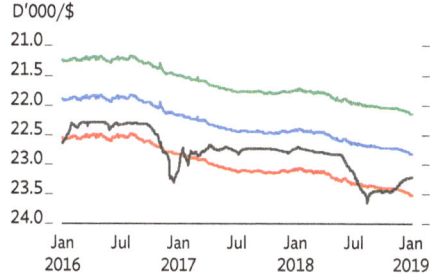

Sources: State Bank of Viet Nam; ADB observations.

3.31.1 Selected economic indicators (%)

	2019	2020
GDP growth	6.8	6.7
Inflation	3.5	3.8
Current account balance (share of GDP)	2.5	2.0

Source: ADB estimates.

education, health care, and electricity may add to inflationary pressures, however, as may a higher minimum wage.

The current account surplus is expected to narrow to the equivalent of 2.5% of GDP this year and 2.0% in 2020 as exports decelerate under softening global demand but imports slow less because of robust domestic consumption and investment. Remittances may also suffer from slower global growth. If trade tensions between the People's Republic of China (PRC) and the US drag on, Viet Nam may benefit as trade and production shift from the PRC to its regional neighbors, with as much as 2.0% of GDP accruing over the medium to long term, mostly beyond the forecast horizon.

The government will continue to pursue fiscal consolidation even as it supports growth. It targets holding the fiscal deficit to the equivalent of 3.6% of GDP this year and reducing it in 2020. To spur investment and support economic growth, the 2019 budget plans to raise capital expenditure by 7.4%. Current expenditure is set to rise by 7.2%.

With slower GDP growth and stricter control of credit in high-risk areas such as real estate, credit growth will likely be contained in 2019 below last year's 14.0%. The resolution of banks' nonperforming loans is expected to continue in 2019 and 2020. Nonperforming loans—including those warehoused at the Viet Nam Assets Management Company and other problem loans not yet classified as nonperforming—are to be reduced to below 5% of banks' outstanding loan portfolio in 2019 and to 3% in 2020. This should make the banking sector more stable and efficient, as should Viet Nam's implementation of Basel II standards and its easing of restrictions on foreign ownership of banks.

An external risk to the outlook would be a sharper slowdown in the major economies, including the European Union, the US, Japan, and the PRC, Viet Nam's key trade partners. Domestic risks could stem from lackluster progress in reforming state-owned enterprises. The equitization of state-owned enterprises in 2018 fell far short of the government's target of at least 85 enterprises. The establishment of the Committee for Management of State Capital in 2018 is expected to ensure that the use of state capital is more effective so that conflicts that arise from the state having dual roles as owner and regulator are minimized. By leveling the playing field for the private sector and reducing market distortion, the government hopes to encourage more private enterprise.

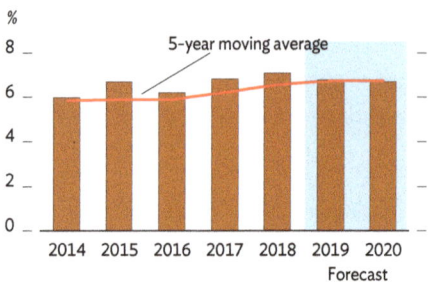

3.31.8 GDP growth

Source: Asian Development Outlook database.

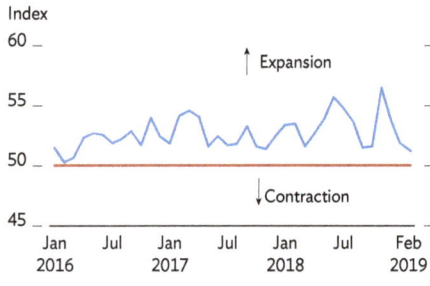

3.31.9 Purchasing managers' index

Note: Nikkei, Markit.
Source: Bloomberg.

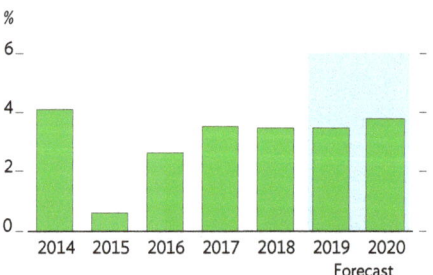

3.31.10 Inflation

Source: Asian Development Outlook database.

Policy challenge—integrating private firms into global value chains

Since the beginning of economic reform in 1986, Viet Nam has rapidly integrated with the global economy. The value of all trade to and from Viet Nam is now twice its GDP, and FDI inflow in 2018 equaled 8% of GDP. Viet Nam is a signatory to 12 free trade agreements that integrate the economy into global value chains (GVCs). However, participation in GVCs has been driven largely by foreign-owned firms. Domestic private firms in Viet Nam are predominantly small and medium-sized enterprises (SMEs). In 2017, more than half a million domestic SMEs contributed nearly half of GDP, but hardly any participated in GVCs (Figure 3.31.11).

The uneven quality of products and services offered by domestic SMEs is the main constraint on their integration into GVCs. This is particularly problematic as international markets tighten their technical, quarantine, environmental, and health standards. SMEs have little access to new technologies that would help them overcome these barriers. A World Bank Enterprise Survey found that SMEs in Viet Nam approached product innovation primarily as a way to reduce costs, not to improve product quality. In addition, few SMEs purchase or license newer technologies developed elsewhere.

Indeed, SMEs in Viet Nam suffer many constraints. Their capacity to purchase and adapt newer technologies is restricted by limited access to finance and a shortage of workers with the necessary skills. Affordable financing is often out of reach because of banks' stringent collateral requirements and complicated procedures, and because capital markets are insufficient, despite the existence of multiple mechanisms to provide finance to SMEs: the SME Development Fund, commercial banks, credit guarantee funds, and the Viet Nam Development Bank, among others. Regarding the shortage of skills, a recent survey by ManpowerGroup showed that only 11% of firms in Viet Nam can provide the skills required for GVC participation. Yet the "low cost, low skills" era of Viet Nam's development is over, and Viet Nam must become a higher-skilled economy.

To address the underlining causes of uneven product quality, policy should encourage and support the adoption of new technology and, eventually, domestic innovation. SMEs need credit for purchasing and leasing capital equipment and new technologies. Developing the necessary skills requires comprehensive and integrated solutions that bring together governments, schools, and the private sector to provide technical and vocation training that responds to demand. Without better access to finance and skills, SMEs will continue to lag in their integration into GVCs.

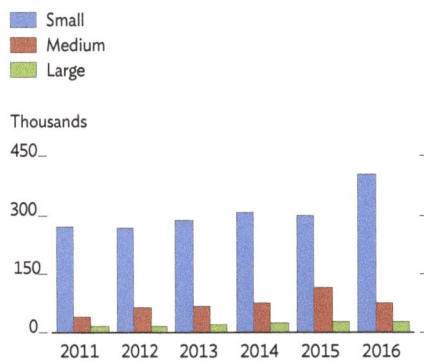

3.31.11 Number of enterprises, 2011–2016

Source: Enterprise Census 2017, General Statistics Office of Viet Nam.

THE PACIFIC

- FIJI
- PAPUA NEW GUINEA
- SOLOMON ISLANDS
- TIMOR-LESTE
- VANUATU
- NORTH PACIFIC ECONOMIES
- SOUTH PACIFIC ECONOMIES
- SMALL ISLAND ECONOMIES

Fiji

Estimated growth in 2018 is unchanged from 2017, sustained by continued expansion in visitor arrivals, increased agricultural production, and continuing reconstruction of cyclone damage incurred in 2016. Inflation rose, and the current account deficit expanded. Growth will accelerate further in 2019 and 2020 as inflation and the current account deficit ease. Government policies supporting tourism growth need to ensure that development is appropriate and sustainable.

Economic performance

The economy grew by 3.0% in 2018 with contributions from agriculture, forestry, and construction, and particularly with continued growth in tourist arrivals (Figure 3.32.1). Despite two cyclones that caused flooding, sugarcane production increased to 1.7 million tons, up by 4.0% from 2017, though cane quality suffered and milling efficiency declined. Timber harvested from pine and mahogany plantations increased substantially for higher forestry output. Gold production declined, but food, beverages, tobacco, sawmilling, and the manufacture of wood products all experienced growth.

Private construction grew strongly in 2018 with increased new construction augmenting maintenance and repair. Visitor arrivals grew by 3.3%, bringing tourism earnings to the equivalent of 20% of GDP and boosting employment in the industry (Figure 3.32.2). Japan contributed the most to this increase with the resumption of direct flights. Visitor arrivals were higher as well from Europe, New Zealand, and other parts of Asia, notably the People's Republic of China.

Despite frequent disasters, economic growth in Fiji has been uninterrupted since 2010. In 2018, the national statistics office increased its estimate of growth for 2016 but reduced the estimate for 2017.

Consumption continued to grow in 2018, with new vehicle sales up by 7.2%, second-hand vehicle sales up by 11.5%, and collections of value-added tax up by 6.1%. Commercial bank lending for consumption grew by 9.2%.

Inflation rose to 4.1% in 2018, the largest category increase being beverages, tobacco, and other intoxicants mainly because of higher duties on alcohol and tobacco but also because production of kava declined. Prices for food and nonalcoholic beverage rose by 3.4%. Prices fell for household goods and health care.

This chapter was written by Shiu Raj Singh of the Pacific Subregional Office, ADB, Suva.

3.32.1 GDP growth

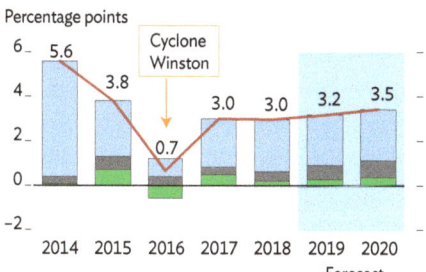

Sources: Fiji Bureau of Statistics; ADB estimates.

3.32.2 Visitor arrivals

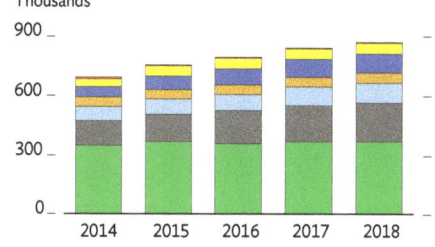

Source: Fiji Bureau of Statistics.

The fiscal deficit in fiscal year 2018 (FY2018, ended 31 July 2018) was equal to 5.3% of GDP, more than double the deficit of 2.3% in FY2017, as operating and investment expenditures both rose (Figure 3.32.3). Government debt increased from the equivalent of 46.4% of GDP in FY2017 to 50.0%.

Monetary policy remained accommodative, with the policy interest rate unchanged at 0.5%. Financial system liquidity declined in 2018 along with foreign exchange reserves as imports expanded, but liquidity remains adequate because the Reserve Bank of Fiji, the central bank, eased controls on external flows. Broad money increased by 3.1%. Average rates for time deposits of more than 36 months remained stable at 3.73%, just 1 basis point lower than 12 months earlier. The weighted average lending interest rate charged by commercial banks was also stable despite lower liquidity, increasing only marginally from 5.66% to 5.68%.

The current account deficit fell from the equivalent of 5.8% of GDP in 2017 to an estimated 5.2% as the surplus in services expanded on record visitor arrivals. Foreign currency reserves stood at $1.0 billion at the end of the year, sufficient to cover 4.5 months of retained imports of goods and nonfactor services.

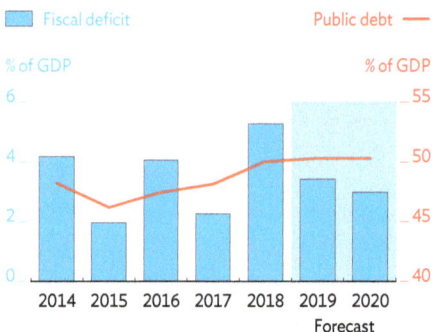

3.32.3 Fiscal deficit and public debt

Note: Calendar year data for 2014; from 2015, years are fiscal years ending on 31 July of that year.
Source: Fiji Ministry of Economy.

Economic prospects

Growth is projected to improve to 3.2% in 2019. All sectors are expected to grow, with tourism in the lead, but construction will likely contribute substantially, considering high bank lending for real estate and the number of projects in progress. Tourism will continue to drive growth higher to 3.5% in 2020, with other contributors also strong. Growth forecasts assume that public resources will go into productive investments in infrastructure, but growth is unlikely to reach the trend that existed before Cyclone Winston in 2016 because the government plans to ensure that public debt does not exceed the government-set ceiling equal to 50.0% of GDP.

Planned investments in transportation and in water supply and sanitation in the greater Suva area are expected to contribute to growth in construction over the medium term. In addition, public investment in flood control structures in urban areas of Nadi should improve confidence in the tourism industry and encourage more investment.

Agriculture and forestry are important suppliers of exports with significant domestic value added. They are expected to continue growing, assuming no weather shocks, and contribute to economic growth. Fiji's largest sawmill has undertaken significant upgrades that promise to boost timber and woodchip production. Government policies supporting the sugar industry and mill improvements should encourage sugar output. Mining and quarrying are also expected to contribute to growth. A new iron sand mine slated to become operational

3.32.1 Selected economic indicators (%)

	2019	2020
GDP growth	3.2	3.5
Inflation	3.5	3.0
Current account balance (share of GDP)	-4.7	-4.2

Source: ADB estimates.

this year has invested in dredgers and port facilities toward extracting 750,000 tons of magnetite concentrate annually to be sold to steel mills in the People's Republic of China. Tourism is on track for another record year and likely to benefit from reduced travel costs as fuel prices fall. Expanded private investment in tourism will contribute to continued growth in construction. Inward remittances are expected to continue growing in 2019 on increased seasonal employment in Australia and New Zealand.

Inflation is expected to ease to 3.5% in 2019 and 3.0% in 2020 as international prices remain low, but domestic tax measures and strengthening demand will prevent further deceleration (Figure 3.32.4).

Exports of goods are expected to grow as shipments of magnetite concentrate commence, and as the sugar and timber industries continue to recover. This development and higher earnings from tourism are expected to narrow the current account deficit by 0.5 percentage points in 2019 and again in 2020 (Figure 3.32.5).

3.32.4 Inflation

Sources: Fiji Bureau of Statistics; ADB estimates.

Policy challenge—ensuring a sustainable tourism industry

Like many other Pacific island nations, Fiji depends increasingly on tourism to drive growth and provide employment. Visitor arrivals in Fiji have increased from 2010 to 2018 at an average annual rate of 5.5%. With tourism earnings now providing a fifth of GDP, the business is central to employment, incomes, and poverty reduction. More tourists now insist on authentic cultural experiences and pristine nature, which is likely to continue benefiting Fiji in the future.

As Fiji's tourism industry depends crucially on the environment, any degradation threatens to undermine it. Tourism growth needs to be managed to minimize its environmental impacts. As the industry matures and moves into a more complex phase of development, greater coordination of policy and the regulatory environment will become necessary to ensure both maximal development impact and continuing sustainability. Fijian Tourism 2021, which provides a cohesive tourism strategy and plan, is a step in the right direction. However, the formulation and implementation of a broader sustainable development framework is still critically needed, as is the implementation of Fiji's Green Growth Framework and better compliance with existing environmental laws and policies.

In addition to public sector efforts to improve planning and regulations, Fiji needs an environment conducive to appropriate private investment and commitment to sustainable tourism initiatives. Finally, public infrastructure must do more than facilitate private investment. It must be able to withstand the impacts of climate change and heightened weather variability.

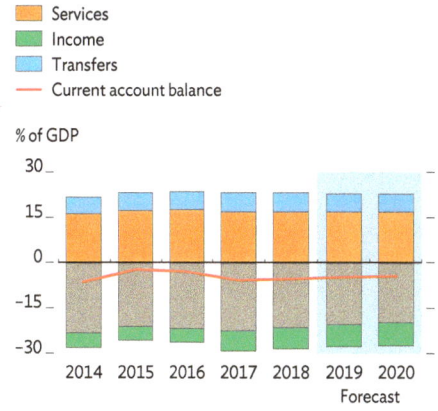

3.32.5 Current account balance

Source: Reserve Bank of Fiji.

Papua New Guinea

An earthquake disrupted production from major resource projects in 2018, slowing growth. However, economic circumstances improved with higher commodity prices, easier access to foreign exchange, and the government's continued commitment to fiscal consolidation. Inflation eased, and the current account posted another large surplus. Sustained adoption of market-orientated policies and ongoing structural reform are needed to attract foreign capital.

Economic performance

A large earthquake in February 2018 undermined growth, estimated at 0.2%, but the impact was somewhat mitigated by higher commodity prices, activity associated with the Asia-Pacific Economic Cooperation (APEC) summit in Port Moresby in November 2018, and reconstruction in the earthquake-affected zone. Credit to the private sector picked up by about 7% in 2018, and employment ceased to decline. The availability of foreign currency improved with greater inflows, though private businesses continued to be stymied by delays in accessing it.

The oil and gas industry, which constitutes 20.2% of GDP, contracted in 2018 primarily because of damaged facilities and lost output caused by the earthquake. Output of liquefied natural gas (LNG), which provides an estimated 14.9% of GDP, fell by 8.8% in 2018. Production of oil and condensate, which together account for more than 4% of GDP, were also lower (Figure 3.33.1).

Gold production from Porgera, a large mine in the highlands, was hit by the earthquake, but this loss was largely offset by increased production from the country's largest gold mine on the island of Lihir, New Ireland. Production from the Lihir mine, which has the third-largest reserves of gold in the world, grew by 6.2% in 2018, with total output equal to 5.0% of GDP. Production from some medium-sized mines, including the Kainantu gold mine, was also higher in 2018. An estimated 80,000 small-scale alluvial miners increased production by over 7% in 2018, earning combined revenues of about $120 million.

The economy apart from mining and petroleum is estimated to have grown by 3.1% in 2018. The APEC summit in 2018 boosted growth to some extent, channeling business

3.33.1 Contributions to growth

Sources: Papua New Guinea national budget documents, various years; ADB estimates.

This chapter was written by Edward Faber of the Papua New Guinea Resident Mission, ADB, Port Moresby.

to hotels, restaurants, and transportation providers, and accelerating growth in construction. Higher government spending and the improved availability of foreign exchange also supported growth.

The agriculture, forestry, and fisheries sector, which makes up about 17.0% of GDP, had mixed results in 2018. Farm production, including vegetables and fruit for the domestic market, continued to expand steadily on increased demand from population growth and with improved access to markets thanks to new infrastructure such as roads and bridges. Palm oil is the largest agricultural export, providing 1.3% of GDP, but export volume in 2018 fell below that of 2017 because of a carryover effect from the 2016 El Niño event. Cocoa production was lower in 2018, but coffee production was higher. Forest products, largely logs for export, increased in 2018.

Inflation eased to 4.5% in 2018 as foreign exchange became more readily available and the money supply contracted (Figure 3.33.2). Prices for food, betel nut, and beverages, which had earlier spiked under drought, increased only slightly in 2018. However, higher oil prices pushed up transportation costs. Prices for health care increased by 9.0% in 2018, and for clothing and footwear by 8.3%. Hotel and restaurant prices rose by 8.2%, largely because of the APEC summit.

The Bank of Papua New Guinea, the central bank, maintained a neutral monetary policy in 2018, with the main policy rate, called the kina facility rate, maintained at 6.25%, a slight premium over the rate of inflation. There is no transmission of the policy rate to banks' lending or deposit rates because commercial banks can source cheap local currency deposits. This largely reflects excess liquidity arising in part from a tough lending environment. Although there is ample liquidity in the system, broad money contracted by 8% in 2018 as statutory authorities transferred their deposits from banks into government coffers in accordance with revenue reform measures.

The current account posted a large surplus in 2018 equal to 26.7% of GDP (Figure 3.33.3). Oil and gas prices lifted the surplus and helped to overcome the effects of the earthquake. LNG exports were the largest contributor to the surplus. Foreign currency reserves increased by 33.6% to $2.3 billion at the end of 2018, providing cover for 11.6 months of imports. The main source was $940 million in new external sovereign borrowing.

Government revenue increased by 16.3% in 2018, benefiting from improved tax compliance and higher collections of mining and petroleum taxes and dividends with the rise in commodity prices (Figure 3.33.4). Taxes and dividends from the Papua New Guinea (PNG) LNG project were $267 million, according to the Department of Treasury, equal to 1.1% of GDP.

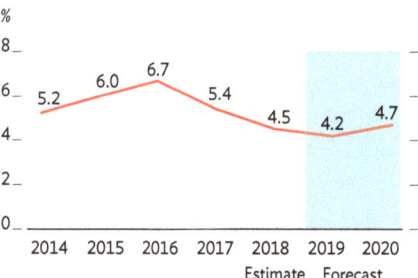

3.33.2 Inflation

Sources: Bank of Papua New Guinea Quarterly Statistical Tables; ADB estimates.

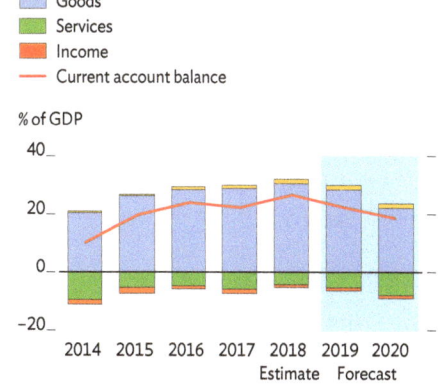

3.33.3 Current account balance

GDP = gross domestic product.
Sources: Bank of Papua New Guinea Quarterly Statistical Tables; ADB estimates.

Expenditure almost kept pace with revenue growth, however, increasing by about 15% in 2018 as it was brought higher by arrears carried over from 2017 and a steeper public sector wage bill. In its supplementary budget, the Department of Treasury projected the 2018 fiscal deficit at the equivalent of 2.3% of GDP, in line with the government's strategy to reduce the fiscal deficit, but the final outcome is expected to be slightly higher.

Economic prospects

Growth is projected to rebound in 2019 with a return to a full year of production of gold, LNG, oil, and condensate. LNG production is forecast to expand by 9%–16% in 2019. If production reaches the higher end of this range, the growth forecast may need to be revised upward. Condensate and oil production are similarly expected to rebound in 2019, though oil production is on a declining trend and condensate production is forecast to start falling by 2020. Gold output should expand in 2019 as the Porgera mine enjoys a full year of uninterrupted production.

Agriculture should also expand in 2019 assuming oil palm rebounds to the kind of output achieved in 2017. Fisheries are expected to grow steadily, and forestry may also expand, though a proposed ban on log exports may be introduced in 2020, causing production to fall. Coffee, cocoa, and copra will continue to experience volatility in production year on year because of weather variation and changes in global commodity prices.

A number of major resource projects are set to drive growth in the medium term. The Papua LNG project and the PNG LNG expansion project together are forecast to attract foreign direct investment in excess of $10 billion, with construction expected to commence in 2020. The forecast period should also see construction start on the $2.8 billion Wafi-Golpu gold and copper mine project. A telecommunication fiber optics cable connecting Port Moresby with Sydney is scheduled for completion toward the end of 2019 and has the potential to significantly increase internet speed and reduce costs, which should facilitate business growth.

Inflation is expected to ease slightly in 2019 as foreign exchange becomes more available and following the recent contraction in the money supply. In 2020, inflation is expected to pick up again with the commencement of new resource projects.

The current account surplus is expected to shrink somewhat as oil and gas prices sink below those of 2018. Imports should pick up with the greater availability of foreign exchange. In 2020, imports should rise even more rapidly as construction begins on new projects, further shrinking the current account surplus. The new resource projects will attract

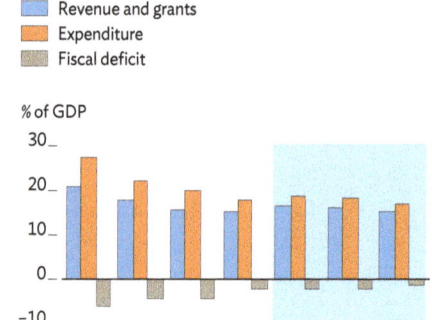

3.33.4 Fiscal performance

GDP = gross domestic product.
Sources: Papua New Guinea national budget documents, various years.

3.33.1 Selected economic indicators (%)

	2019	2020
GDP growth	3.7	3.1
Inflation	4.2	4.7
Current account balance (share of GDP)	22.5	18.5

Source: ADB estimates.

significant inflows of foreign exchange, finally ending the era of foreign currency shortages.

The 2019 budget targets a fiscal deficit equal to 2.1% of GDP, which aligns with the government's fiscal consolidation strategy. Targets become progressively lower, with the 2022 deficit intended to equal 1.0% of GDP. Revenue including grants is forecast at 16.1% of GDP in the 2019 budget and is seen to increase by 6.5% largely through ongoing reform, including the recent establishment of an office dedicated to handling large tax payers. Mining and petroleum taxes and dividends, which are forecast to equal 2.1% of GDP, assume an oil price of $68 per barrel, meaning that a lower average oil price would cause revenue to fall below expectations, possibly widening the fiscal deficit or forcing cuts to expenditure, which is forecast to equal 18.2% of GDP. The government's expenditure strategy would reallocate spending from current to capital expenditure, which aligns with the government's Medium Term Development Plan 3, 2018–2022 to increase spending on infrastructure. The 2019 budget seeks to reduce current expenditure, including the public sector wage bill, but this may prove to be challenging.

The deficit will be financed by external borrowing, including budget support loans from multilateral institutions and proceeds from a 2018 sovereign bond. External debt has been on the rise in recent years, projected by the Department of Treasury to reach the equivalent of 13.6% of GDP by 2020, when it will be 44.8% of total central government debt (Figure 3.33.5).

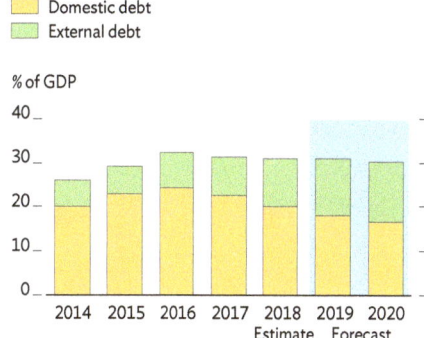

3.33.5 Public debt outstanding

Sources: Papua New Guinea national budget documents, various years.

Policy challenge—resolving foreign currency shortages

Shortages of foreign currency have been a key constraint on the private sector in recent years, with importers having to queue to receive foreign currency, sometimes for several weeks until it becomes available. These circumstances have dragged on the economy. Business surveys found foreign currency shortages to be among the worst impediments to doing business.

From January 2010 to June 2012, during the construction of PNG LNG and a period of buoyant commodity prices, large inflows of foreign currency caused significant appreciation of the kina, by 33% in real terms (Figure 3.33.6). Central bank reserves grew accordingly, from $2 billion in 2007 to over $4 billion in 2012.

This trend reversed in 2012 as PNG LNG construction ended and commodity prices began to slide. This put significant downward pressure on the kina and on international currency reserves. The central bank intervened to stem the pace of depreciation by introducing in July 2014 a trading band and

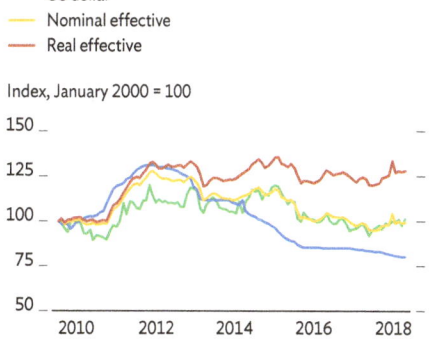

3.33.6 Real and nominal kina exchange rates

Sources: Bank of Papua New Guinea; International Monetary Fund.

a policy of rationing foreign exchange. These interventions prevented the exchange rate and currency trading from adjusting to market conditions, finally appearing as shortages of foreign exchange.

Managing the foreign exchange imbalance has been a challenge for the authorities, who fear that significant inflation could result if the market determined the exchange rate.

The foreign currency environment improved in 2018. Whereas there was only minimal kina depreciation in 2017, in 2018 the kina depreciated about 4% against the US dollar, which is seen as having helped to ameliorate the foreign exchange imbalance. The central bank intervened further in 2018, supplying $695.2 million to the market, more than three times the $227.0 million it supplied in 2017. This was enabled by higher commodity prices that improved earnings in the form of taxes, dividends, and royalties from resource projects, including from PNG LNG. In addition, a portion of foreign currency was released from the $940 million of new sovereign borrowing in 2018. The central bank reported that the waiting time to clear foreign exchange orders was shortened in 2018 as pending foreign exchange orders fell by 48% from K2.5 billion in January 2018 to K1.3 billion in January 2019.

In 2019, the foreign currency backlog should continue to shrink as the central bank injects more foreign exchange into the system at the same rate as in 2018 or higher thanks to proceeds from its 2018 sovereign borrowing and up to $450 million of new sovereign borrowing planned for 2019 (Figure 3.33.7). The central bank has increased its monthly allocations to up to $60 million in recent months. Continued allocations will allow the rolling up of another backlog, this one composed of undeclared dividends estimated by market participants at about $500 million. These are retained profits held by foreign companies operating in PNG and heretofore unable to remit currency overseas. In the longer term, observers predict, new plans for large resource projects expected to begin in 2020 will bring significant inflows of foreign exchange, helping to restore the market to equilibrium.

While a market-determined exchange rate allows equilibrium that puts an end to foreign exchange shortages and removes distortions that can hurt exporters and industries that compete with imports, ongoing structural reform is just as critical for attracting foreign capital and helping to build an economy that is more diversified and shock resilient. Many such reforms are outlined in the Medium Term Development Plan 3, 2018–2022, recently released by the government. They include increasing investment in infrastructure to facilitate business and trade, expanding access to investable land, continuing revenue-raising reform, and improving the management of public finances.

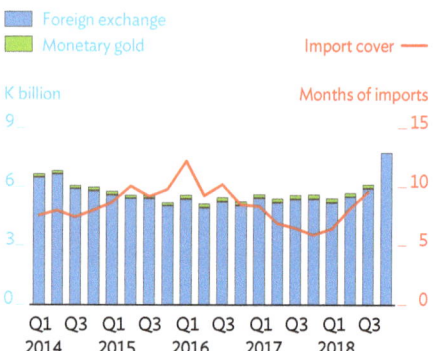

3.33.7 Gross international reserves

SDR = special drawing rights.
Note: Data on monetary gold, SDR holdings, and imports in the December 2018 quarter are not yet available. Imports are free-on-board values.
Source: Bank of Papua New Guinea. *Quarterly Statistical Bulletins*.

Solomon Islands

Despite rising exports of timber, fish, and minerals, growth decelerated in 2018 as government spending slowed and cash crop yields declined. Inflation rose on higher taxes but will ease this year and next. Growth will likely slow in 2019 and 2020 as new construction only partly offsets lower logging output. The current account deficit is expected to return to deficit, reversing last year's surplus. A tax review shows progress, but broadening the revenue base remains a challenge.

Economic performance

Economic growth is estimated to have slowed slightly to 3.0% in 2018 (Figure 3.34.1). Log output continued to outperform expectations and increased by 2.6% in 2018 to a record 2.7 million cubic meters (Figure 3.34.2). Higher volume and global prices sent the value of log exports up by more than 25.0%. Exports of minerals, notably bauxite and nickel, rose by 29.9%. Fish exports grew 15.1%, in line with growth in the previous year. However, the export value of most crops declined in 2018, with copra and coconut oil falling the most. The exception was cocoa, which reversed a plunge by 47.5% in 2017 with a rebound by 42.7% in 2018.

Growth in services slowed to 3.5% in 2018. Wholesale and retail trade decelerated with lower cash crop output and higher taxes, and as growth in government spending slowed. Industry expanded 1.2% in 2018, mainly on higher mining.

The government made a concerted effort to restore fiscal stability after several years of widening deficits, which had significantly reduced its cash reserves, undermining their usefulness as a buffer against shocks. The fiscal deficit narrowed from the equivalent of 3.8% of GDP in 2017 to 0.6% in 2018 (Figure 3.34.3). Growth in government spending slowed with substantial reductions in development expenditure. Revenue rose on higher log export duties, estimated to be up from 2017 by more than a fifth, and budget support from development partners. A domestic development bond helped to capitalize a new state-owned enterprise to lay an undersea telecommunications cable.

A new price index introduced in 2018 showed inflation accelerating to 3.3% in 2018, mainly on higher prices for domestic goods; partly reflecting hikes in the goods tax, excises on alcohol and tobacco, and import duties on fuel.

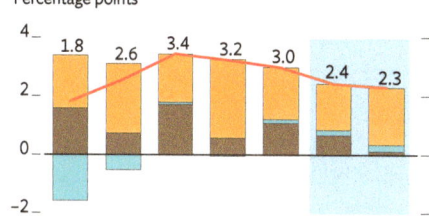

3.34.1 Supply-side contributions to growth

Sources: Solomon Islands National Statistics Office; ADB estimates.

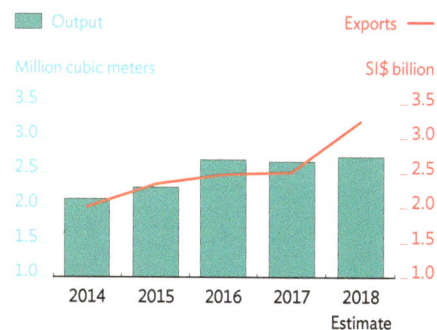

3.34.2 Logging output and exports

Sources: Solomon Islands National Statistics Office; ADB estimates.

This chapter was written by Jacqueline Connell of the Pacific Liaison and Coordination Office and Prince Cruz, consultant, of the Pacific Department, ADB, Manila.

The new price index lowered the share for food mostly in favor of alcohol and tobacco, based on the results of the 2012–2013 Household Income and Expenditure Survey (Figure 3.34.4).

The current account turned into a surplus equal to 3.9% of GDP in 2018, mainly on a 21.2% rise in exports of goods that exceeded import growth at only 8.8%. Tourism receipts jumped by a fifth. Arrivals by air grew by about 10% in 2018, and the average length of stay rose from 13 days in 2017 to 15 days in 2018. Fewer cruise ships visited, though, dragging down arrivals by sea to a fifth of 2017 arrivals (Figure 3.34.5).

Gross international reserves rose by 8.3%, providing import cover for 15 months. Monetary policy remained relatively accommodative in 2018 as the money supply rose by 6.0% and bank loans by 7.8%

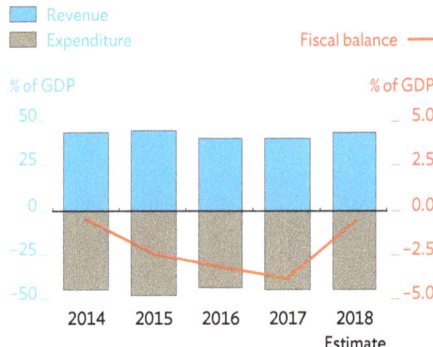

3.34.3 Fiscal balance

Sources: Solomon Islands Ministry of Finance and Treasury budget documents; ADB estimates.

Economic prospects

Growth is projected to slow to 2.4% in 2019 as logging tapers but is partly offset by construction on large infrastructure projects, with growth slowing a bit more to 2.3% in 2020. The Forestry Sustainability Policy, approved in 2018, aims to reduce log production to a more sustainable rate by introducing export caps. The economic impact is potentially large, given that logging supplied some 72% of exports in 2018 and is the country's largest employer after the government. With El Niño weather disturbances expected in 2019, the fish catch will likely suffer, and recovery in cash crops may sputter.

Growth will depend on infrastructure investments in roads, airports, and the undersea telecommunications cable financed by development partners. Construction of the Tina River Hydropower Project is expected to commence in 2020, after delays in signing the electric power purchase agreement.

The government aims to balance the budget in 2019 by further cutting government development expenditure by about a third compared with 2018. Partly offsetting this, the payroll budget is projected to increase by 15% from 2018 to accommodate new staff positions and increased allowances, including a 3.5% boost to cost-of-living allowances for all public servants. A national election scheduled for April 2019 may put additional pressure on government spending and the budget, including an increase for police security.

The Forestry Sustainability Policy is expected to weigh on government revenues in the medium term. The government projects logging export duties to fall in 2019 by 16% from 2018. It hopes to claw back some revenue by raising logging license fees and improving compliance, while recent amendments to the withholding tax and the goods tax should also increase collections. The fiscal deficit is expected to widen in 2020 as government investment in the Tina River Hydropower Project begins.

3.34.4 Components of the consumer price index basket

Q = quarter.
Source: Central Bank of Solomon Islands.

3.34.1 Selected economic indicators (%)

	2019	2020
GDP growth	2.4	2.3
Inflation	2.5	2.5
Current account balance (share of GDP)	-1.4	-2.6

Source: ADB estimates.

Lower inflation is expected as a base effect from higher taxes in 2018 dissipates and as global commodity prices fall, in particular for oil. However, the increased cost-of-living allowances for public servants threaten to stoke inflation in 2019.

As logging exports taper and imports for construction projects rise, the current account balance is expected to fall back into deficits equal to 1.4% of GDP in 2019 and 2.6% in 2020. On the other hand, visitor arrivals by air are expected to continue to grow, boosting exports of services.

The reopening of the country's sole gold mine, Gold Ridge, poses an upside risk to the forecast. Rehabilitating the mine, which closed in 2014 following flashfloods, could spur growth. This prospect is a reminder that the government needs to continue strengthening its regulation and taxation of mining to maximize its benefits and encourage inclusive growth.

Any delays in infrastructure projects, particularly Tina River, would weigh on growth. The only domestic bank in Solomon Islands provides key services to the logging industry but lost its correspondent bank relationship for US dollars in 2018. The problem was resolved by year-end, but it highlights the challenge to the economy and government financing posed by heavy reliance on revenue from the logging industry.

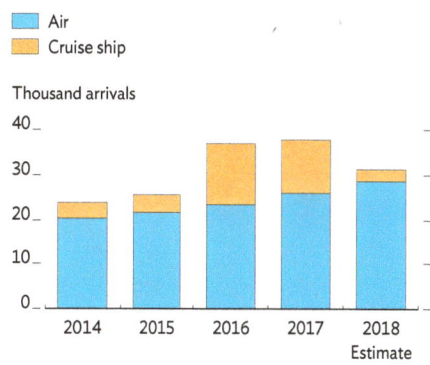

3.34.5 Visitor arrivals by mode of transport

Sources: Solomon Islands National Statistics Office; ADB estimates.

Policy challenge—sustaining tax reform

The current tax structure of Solomon Islands is complex, outdated, and expensive to administer. It is heavily biased toward consumption taxes, partly reflecting dependence on imports and the relatively small proportion of people in formal employment and business (Figure 3.34.6). By relying on high rates applied to a narrow base, the tax system discourages compliance.

Getting the tax system right is important in light of expected declines in logging revenue in the medium term. In November 2017, the Ministry of Finance and Treasury began a system review with the aim of making revenue collection more efficient, fair, and equitable.

The first phase of the tax review has focused on tax administration and consumption taxes. The next phase will address income tax with the aim of lowering marginal tax rates and expanding the tax base. Currently, the highest marginal tax rate is 40% for taxable annual incomes higher than SI$60,000, which is five times GDP per capita in 2017. In 2016, only 4.6% of registered income tax payers filed an income tax return.

In 2018, Parliament enacted amendments to the Goods Tax Act that increased excise taxes on alcohol and tobacco and changed procedures for collecting withholding taxes to improve compliance and bring them in line with international practice. These measures will generate more revenue and fiscal space with which to respond to shocks.

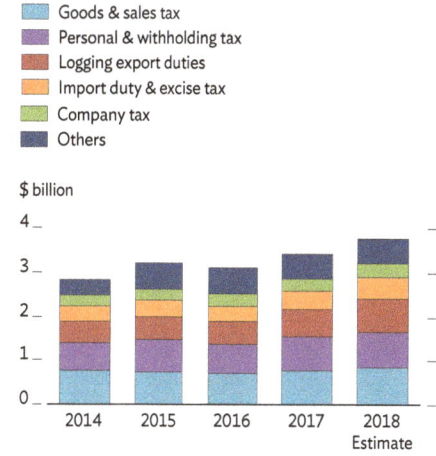

3.34.6 Domestic revenue

Sources: Solomon Islands Ministry of Finance and Treasury budget documents; ADB estimates.

Timor-Leste

The economy contracted as political uncertainty disrupted and reduced public spending. Inflation revived, and the current account deficit narrowed. The formation of a new government and approval of the 2019 budget pave the way for fiscal stimulus that will drive growth in 2019 and 2020. While the government plans to play a more active role in developing onshore oil and gas processing, diversification into hardwood forestry could, if sustainably managed, offer valuable benefits.

Economic performance

Reductions in public spending caused GDP excluding the large offshore petroleum sector (hereafter GDP) to contract by 0.5% in 2018 (Figure 3.35.1). Following a sharp decline in 2017, public expenditure excluding grants from development partners, which are off budget, fell by a further 2.8% in 2018 to $1.16 billion. While public capital investment increased significantly, it was more than offset by lower recurrent spending. Payments for salaries and wages fell by 2.2%, purchases of goods and services by 9.3%, and transfer payments by 23.9%, reflecting lower payments to the Special Administrative Region of Oe-Cusse Ambeno (Figure 3.35.2).

Public spending problems reflected political uncertainty that continued through much of 2018. Parliament was dissolved in March without approving a budget. This left the government to operate in the first part of the year under a duo-decimal budget regime, which allowed monthly budget appropriations of up to one-twelfth of the 2017 budget. In September, a budget for the remainder of 2018 was approved. It called for rapidly scaling up expenditure, but implementation was constrained by its late approval. The resulting decline in public spending was compounded by a reported 10.3% drop in grants from bilateral and multilateral development partners to $156.0 million, equal to 9.5% of GDP (Figure 3.35.3).

Tighter fiscal policy constrained demand for a range of consumption and investment goods. Merchandise imports declined by 11.5% on lower imports of food, consumer goods, construction materials, and equipment and machinery. With new vehicle registrations down by 19.4%, the value of vehicle imports fell by 48.1%. Shifts in the aviation market saw a reduction in the number of international flights and large increases in ticket

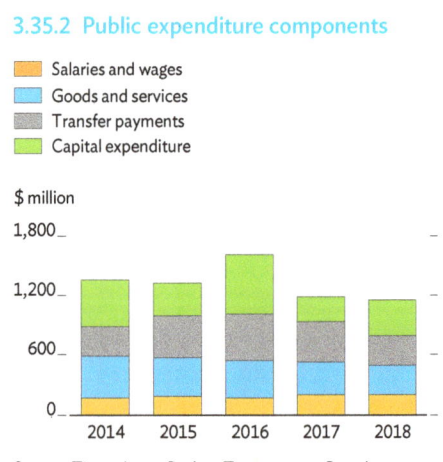

3.35.1 Supply-side contributions to growth

- Agriculture
- Services
- Industry
- Gross domestic product

Sources: Statistics Timor-Leste; ADB estimates.

3.35.2 Public expenditure components

- Salaries and wages
- Goods and services
- Transfer payments
- Capital expenditure

Source: Timor-Leste Budget Transparency Portal.

This chapter was written by David Freedman of the Timor-Leste Resident Mission, ADB, Dili.

prices on key routes. These developments and reduced demand from business travelers saw growth in international visitor arrivals plunge from 12.0% in 2017 to 1.1% in 2018.

Production of maize and rice, the two largest staple crops, posted large gains in 2018 on expanded planting area and a modest increase in productivity. Cash crop production was also strong, with coffee exports up by 34.3% and rising exports of niche products such as cloves and vanilla.

The consumer price index rose by 2.1% in 2018 despite weak consumer demand, with food up by 1.5%, tobacco up by 17.1%, and transportation up by 3.9% because of higher fuel prices. While inflation was driven largely by higher prices for imported goods, prices for non-tradable items also increased, by 2.0%. Conditions in the financial sector reflected the challenges caused by tighter fiscal policy. Bank deposits reversed average growth of 20.5% per annum during 2013–2017 to fall by 1.6% in 2018. Separately, one bank closed its retail operations. Lending to the private sector increased by 3.6%, with reduced lending to construction firms and private individuals being offset by increased lending to businesses in other sectors.

Tasi Mane, a government project to develop oil and gas processing on the south coast, gained momentum in 2018. The government has agreed to purchase the equity of two existing stakeholders in the Greater Sunrise gas field. This will give the government a 56.6% majority share in the joint venture, which may remove key obstacles to developing the field and the onshore processing of gas at a new liquefied natural gas plant at Beacu, a town on the south coast. Investments to support this plan moved forward in 2018 with the opening of a new international airport in Suai and the completion of the first phase of a new highway linking Suai to Beacu.

Taxes and royalties from the Bayu-Undan oil field rose by 21.0% in 2018 and accounted for 48.2% of government revenues. Petroleum Fund investments generated $365.1 million in cash income, but overall return on assets posted a loss of 2.6%, largely because of a sharp decline in the fund's equity portfolio in the final quarter. The fund ended the year with a balance of $15.8 billion, or $12,500 per capita (Figure 3.35.4).

Income from petroleum production that beat expectations, and a narrowing of the trade deficit in goods and services, narrowed the current account deficit from the equivalent of 17.5% of GDP in 2017 to 11.8%.

Economic prospects

The economy is projected to grow by 4.8% in 2019 and 5.4% in 2020 on fiscal stimulus and renewed investor confidence. Inflation is projected to accelerate to 3.0% in 2019 as domestic demand recovers and to 3.3% in 2020 with higher prices for imported food (Figure 3.35.5).

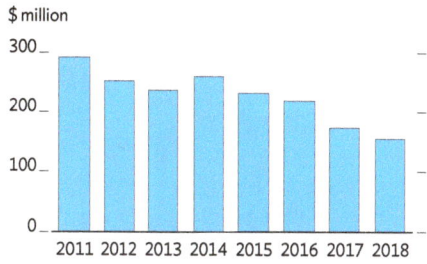

3.35.3 Grant inflows

Source: Timor-Leste Budget Transparency Portal.

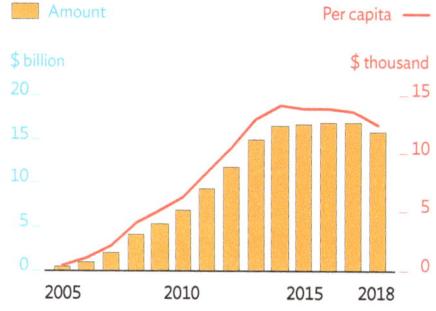

3.35.4 Petroleum fund balance

Source: Timor-Leste national budget documents, various years.

The 2019 state budget will provide strong fiscal stimulus. Approved in February 2019, the budget plans $1.48 billion in expenditure, and a further $162.6 million in grants from development partners spent off budget. Full execution would see public spending rise by 22.3% over 2018. Planned increases are concentrated in recurrent spending, budgeting 6.8% more for salaries and wages, 13.4% more for goods and services, and 35.6% more for transfer payments. These increases are partly driven by a budgeted 17.8% increase over the 2015–2018 average allocated for health programs and a 32.1% increase allocated for education (Figure 3.35.6).

The budget includes $2.0 billion for capital investment from 2019 to 2023, with 82.9% of it implemented through the Infrastructure Fund, an autonomous agency mandated to coordinate the preparation and financing of major projects. Public capital investment is set to increase by 27.6% in 2019 and a further 64.5% in 2020. Upgrading roads and bridges accounts for 59.4% of capital investment in 2019 and 2020, with investment in the Tasi Mane project accounting for a further 16.2% (Figure 3.35.7). Several other large investment projects are expected to move forward this year and next with government support. Construction on the new Tibar Bay port formally commenced in August 2018 and will ramp up in 2019. The initial investment to develop the project is estimated at $280 million, of which the government contributed $129.5 million. Separately, the government has contributed $50 million for equity investment and other support to develop limestone mining and cement manufacturing in the Baucau region.

Rising capital investment will stimulate demand for construction services and boost employment. In agriculture, coffee production is expected to increase in 2019 with favorable weather so far, and the government will seek to consolidate recent increases in the area planted with maize and rice. Prospects for further growth in tourism hinge on a sustained reduction in the cost of travel to and from Timor-Leste, which rose sharply in 2018. Two separate groups of investors are developing plans for hotel and resort complexes close to Dili, and these projects will move ahead in 2019 and 2020 if they can secure the required financing and government support.

The revenue the government collects from domestic sources is projected to grow by an average of 5.0% annually during 2019–2023, but the bulk of public spending will be financed using withdrawals from the Petroleum Fund. The fund is currently invested in relatively low-risk foreign assets, with 60% invested in high-quality bonds and the remaining 40% in equities. The investment strategy is expected to change in 2019 following equity investment in the Greater Sunrise gas joint venture. In February the government adjusted the Petroleum Fund's investment rules to enable up to 5% to be invested in new petroleum operations in Timor-Leste.

3.35.5 Inflation

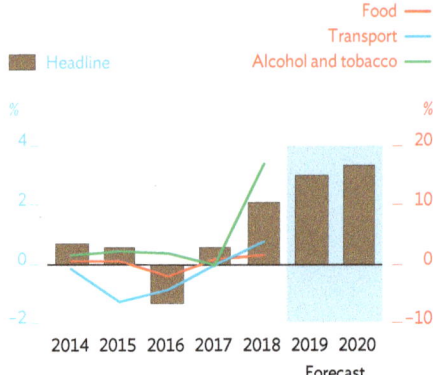

Sources: Statistics Timor-Leste; ADB estimates.

3.35.6 Expenditure on education and health

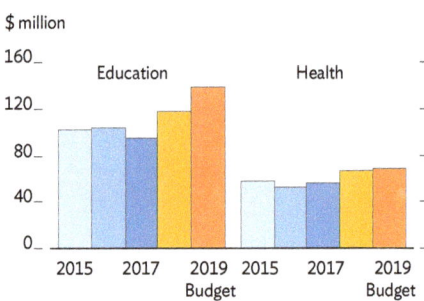

Source: Timor-Leste national budget documents, various years.

3.35.1 Selected economic indicators (%)

	2019	2020
GDP growth	4.8	5.4
Inflation	3.0	3.3
Current account balance (share of GDP)	–12.0	–12.0

Source: ADB estimates.

These investments will be channeled through the national oil company, Timor Gap, and be structured as interest-bearing debt securities with a yield of 4.5% per annum. Once implemented, these changes will reduce to 35% the share of the portfolio that is allocated to international equities.

The Petroleum Fund's sustainable income, or the amount that can be withdrawn from the fund each year without depleting it, is estimated at $529.0 million in 2019. Given planned spending, actual withdrawals are projected at $1.19 billion in 2019 and $1.24 billion in 2020. Inflows to the fund from taxes and royalties from the Bayu-Undan field are projected to fall to $343.7 million in 2019 (equal to 19.3% of GDP), rise modestly in 2020, and come to an end in 2023. Planned withdrawals in 2019 and 2020 mean that the Petroleum Fund balance is now projected to decline to $15.1 billion at the end of 2020.

The fiscal stimulus that is planned for 2019 and 2020 will affect the current account balance. Increased imports of goods and services offset gains from higher petroleum income and grants, leaving the current account deficit at the equivalent of 12.0% of GDP in 2019 and 2020.

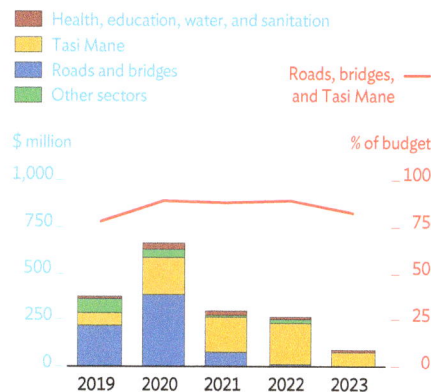

3.35.7 Infrastructure fund budget

Sources: Timor-Leste State Budget 2019; ADB estimates.

Policy challenge—developing a sustainable forestry industry

The development of forestry could make an important contribution to growth and job creation in the medium term. However, this would be sustainable only with well-coordinated policies to strengthen forest management and encourage tree planting.

The climate and soils in Timor-Leste are well suited to growing a range of valuable tropical hardwoods, and forests still cover an estimated 58% of Timor-Leste's land area (Figure 3.35.8). Sandalwood, which is prized for its fine fragrance, was the largest export for much of the colonial period. However, the overharvesting of wild stocks in the years before independence steadily undermined production, prompting a current moratorium on exports. Deforestation from population growth and the expansion of subsistence farming is an issue and one of the largest emitters of greenhouse gases in the country.

The government is committed to halting deforestation and developing new plantation forests. It has begun to establish sandalwood plantations in some areas, and many households plant small numbers of trees close to their homes. Recent analysis of satellite data found 2,400 hectares of teak growing in stands of 0.1 hectares or larger. These stocks support a local furniture industry, but current production volumes would not support significant exports.

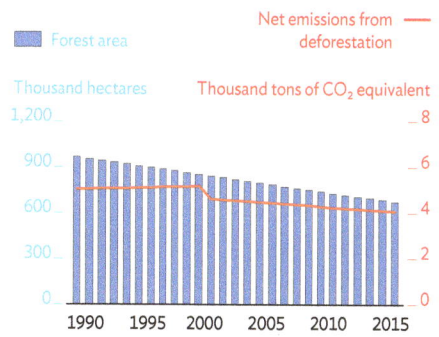

3.35.8 Forest area

CO_2 = carbon dioxide.
Source: Food and Agriculture Organization.

Developing forestry exports would require a significant increase in the area that is planted with teak and other valuable tree species. Analysis of satellite data has identified around 32,500 hectares of suitable land that is not currently forested, protected, or used to grow food. Preliminary estimates suggest that the development of a 30,000 hectare plantation estate could support the production of $100 million worth of teak per year, equal to 6.3% of current GDP. The bulk of this production would be exported, and the establishment, maintenance, and harvesting of tropical hardwoods could create employment equal to 2,000 full-time jobs. Potential also exists to increase the value of wood generated in and harvested from natural forests by restocking selected native species such as sandalwood.

Developing a successful plantation sector is a long-term undertaking, requiring first the strengthening of forest management. In the short term, the key priorities include building human resources, developing an integrated forest information management system, and establishing long-term research and trial plots across the main agroecological zones. While some stakeholders may wish to see tree planting increased very rapidly, doing so without first establishing a strong knowledge base would pose an unnecessary risk that new plantations perform poorly or fail.

New plantations could be established using various models focused on smallholders and communities, or ranging up to government-managed planting on state land or larger-scale private investment. Uncertain land tenure is likely to deter private investment, but the government should try to leverage private sector capacity by developing a model for public–private partnership or using other mechanisms to mitigate risks and incentivize tree planting.

Vanuatu

Strong growth in construction and tourism sustained economic expansion in 2018 despite a disaster-induced contraction in agriculture. Inflation slowed, and the current account moved into surplus. Growth is expected to remain stable in 2019 and 2020 as tourism benefits from the completion of major infrastructure projects. Inflation will ease further, and the current account will remain in surplus. With increased tourist arrivals, policies must ensure that benefits are broadly enjoyed and sustainable.

Economic performance

Economic recovery continued in 2018 as growth in services and industry supported expansion at 3.2% (Figure 3.36.1). This was down, however, from 4.4% growth in 2017 because of a sharp decline in the large agriculture sector caused by Cyclone Hola in March 2018 and a volcanic eruption on Ambae Island in Penama Province (Figure 3.36.2). Low prices for copra exacerbated a decline in output.

Growth in services increased from 2.9% in 2017 to 3.6% as tourism accelerated. Visitor arrivals rose by 7.8% to 358,000 visitors. This topped the previous record of 357,400 set in 2013. Arrivals by air rose by 4.7% in 2018, while cruise ship arrivals almost doubled that rate with growth of 9.2% (Figure 3.36.3). Slightly more than half of air travelers were from Australia, 13% from New Caledonia, and 12% from New Zealand. Travel and tourism are estimated to have contributed 45% of GDP in 2018.

Growth in industry remained strong as construction continued on major infrastructure projects: facilities to complement newly upgraded wharves in Port Vila and Luganville, rehabilitation of the main airport in Port Vila and other airports on outer islands, and road projects on multiple islands. Government capital expenditure doubled from 2017, most of it financed by development partners. Renewable energy projects and private investment into tourist-oriented facilities and other businesses contributed to industry growth.

Government recurrent expenditure fell by 2.8% despite employee compensation rising by more than a quarter following a Government Remuneration Tribunal ruling in favor of higher public service salary scales. Although grants from development partners declined by 39.4% with the completion of major projects, total revenue rose by 9.5%. Nontax revenue, derived mainly from the sale of secondary passports, rose by 79.5%

3.36.1 Supply-side contributions to GDP growth

- Agriculture
- Industry
- Services
- Gross domestic product

Sources: Vanuatu National Statistics Office; ADB estimates.

This chapter was written by Jacquelline Connell of the Pacific Liaison and Coordination Office, ADB, Sydney, and Prince Cruz, consultant, Pacific Department, ADB, Manila.

from 2017 and now provides a third of all revenue. Nontax revenue has surpassed the value-added tax (VAT) as the biggest single source of domestic revenue despite a higher VAT following a rate increase in January 2018. Excise taxes and taxes on international trade were also higher (Figure 3.36.4). With expenditure rising by only 4.4%, the fiscal surplus expanded from the equivalent of 5.1% of GDP in 2017 to 6.8%. This allowed for early repayment of approximately 6% of government debt at the end of 2018.

The higher VAT rate notwithstanding, inflation eased from 3.1% in 2017 to 2.2% last year. While food prices rose by 4.1%, prices for clothing and for housing and utilities increased by less than 2.0%. The price index for education fell by 11.1%.

A fall in merchandise exports was offset by higher exports of services in the form of tourism and lower imports of goods and services, allowing the current account to climb to a small surplus equal to 0.5% of GDP. Higher exports of kava and cocoa only partly offset large drops in the export value of fish, copra, beef, and timber. Meanwhile, higher fuel imports only partly offset lower imports by value of food, basic manufactured products, and machinery and transport equipment.

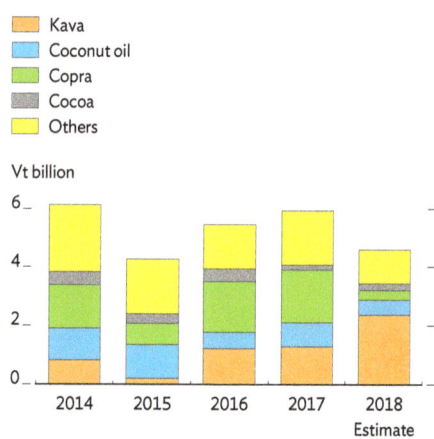

Economic prospects

Growth is expected to moderate to 3.0% in 2019 and 2.8% in 2020. Tourism looks set to remain strong, but construction will likely contract with the completion of major infrastructure projects. The performance of agriculture is anticipated highly uneven because it will take several years to grow replacements for livestock and damaged coconut trees and other crops.

After several years of rapid growth fueled by reconstruction and infrastructure upgrading in the aftermath of Cyclone Pam, construction is expected to return to levels prevailing in earlier years. However, this reduction should be partly offset by expansion in retail trade, transportation, and accommodation and restaurants as these service areas benefit from higher tourist arrivals. Growth in public administration is expected to continue as the government implements various projects to promote education and tourism, enhance disaster resilience, and implement higher wages mandated by the Government Remuneration Tribunal.

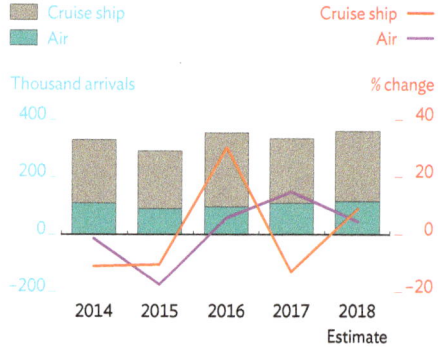

Spending under the 2019 budget is 40.9% higher than actual expenditure in 2018, though realizing expenditure in 2019 depends on large grants from development partners. The government anticipates a fiscal deficit equal to 6.4% of GDP in 2019.

Inflation is expected to ease slightly to 2.0% in 2019 and 2020 as supply constraints caused by the recent disasters are resolved, bringing price stability for food and beverages (Figure 3.36.5). Transport inflation is also forecast to remain subdued with the completion of roads and other major infrastructure projects,

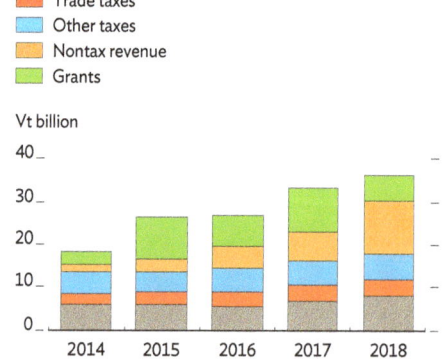

and as international oil prices remain low. The current account surplus is expected to widen to the equivalent of 1.0% of GDP in 2019 and 1.5% in 2020 as tourism continues to grow and imports of goods and services decline with the completion of reconstruction projects (Figure 3.36.6).

There are several risks to the forecast. As in most Pacific island economies, disasters pose an ever-present threat. The sustainability of secondary passport sales also poses a risk to fiscal sustainability.

Policy challenge—tourism as a driver of sustainable, inclusive growth

Visitor arrivals are expected to continue rising in Vanuatu with the completion of major infrastructure projects geared for tourism, including airport rehabilitation, wharf upgrades, and waterfront development in Port Vila and Luganville. Air Vanuatu is exploring prospects for increasing flight frequency and introducing new destinations in Australia and New Zealand. The increase in flights is part of a tourism plan called Shared Vision 2030, which targets visitor arrivals by air reaching 450,000 by 2030, a fourfold increase from 2018.

As a key generator of employment and income in Vanuatu, tourism is pivotal to poverty reduction. However, the industry is vulnerable to disaster and is currently concentrated in Port Vila and Luganville. Vanuatu faces a challenge in maximizing the positive benefits of tourism toward creating jobs and supporting inclusive, sustainable growth.

The government has made some progress in climate proofing new public infrastructure. This enhances the resilience of a tourism industry confronting frequent disasters and climate change. Improving facilities for water supply and sewage treatment outside Port Vila may encourage more tourists to venture into new areas, while providing benefits to local communities from improved water and sanitation. The expansion of technical and vocational training could help increase local employment in better-paid positions in growing hospitality and transport industries. Preserving Vanuatu's cultural and environmental assets will be crucial to the sustainability of tourism.

The benefits of tourism could be made more inclusive by enhancing links with suppliers in local communities of agriculture goods and services. Around 80% of the population depends on agriculture for livelihood, and an established network of farmers and traders already exists to provide services to hotels and other tourism facilities. The capacity and scope of these networks are limited, however, and many hotels and restaurants favor imported produce over local supplies. Ways to address these issues are proposed in the Vanuatu Agritourism Action Plan, which the government finalized in 2016.

3.36.1 Selected economic indicators (%)

	2019	2020
GDP growth	3.0	2.8
Inflation	2.0	2.0
Current account balance (share of GDP)	1.0	1.5

Source: ADB estimates.

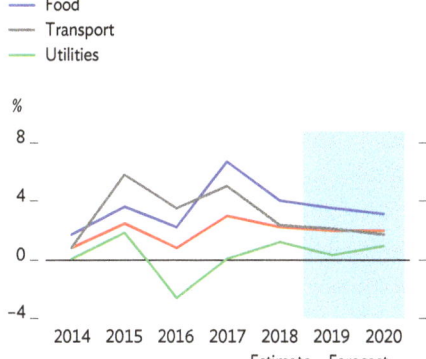

3.36.5 Inflation

Sources: Vanuatu National Statistics Office; ADB estimates.

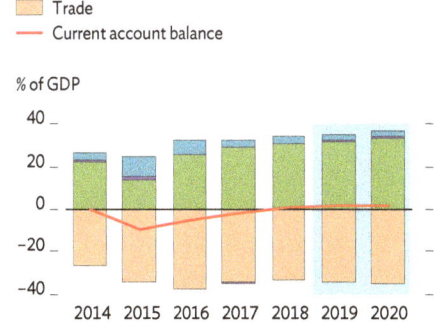

3.36.6 Current account balance

Sources: Reserve Bank of Vanuatu; ADB estimates.

North Pacific economies

Growth last year weakened in the storm-hit Federated States of Micronesia and in the Marshall Islands as construction slowed, but Palau achieved modest recovery on higher public and private investment. Reconstruction of damaged infrastructure is expected to boost growth this year in the Federated States of Micronesia, as is recovering tourism in Palau, but capacity constraints will continue to slow expansion in the Marshall Islands. Trust funds can provide necessary fiscal buffers, smooth government expenditure, and minimize growth volatility.

Economic performance

Although GDP growth trajectories diverged, fiscal year 2018 (FY2018, ended 30 September 2018) generally saw weak expansion across the North Pacific (Figure 3.37.1). The Federated States of Micronesia (FSM) weathered a disaster that temporarily slowed growth, which is resuming under subsequent reconstruction and recovery. The Marshall Islands grew more slowly as capacity constraints impeded infrastructure construction. In Palau, public and private investments drove recovery from steep contraction in FY2017.

In March 2018, Tropical Depression Jelawat brought flooding and landslides to Pohnpei State in the FSM, damaging roads and other critical infrastructure. A state of emergency was declared, and following a joint damage assessment, the US approved in July disaster funding under its Compact of Free Association with the FSM.

Stimulus from reconstruction partly offset the adverse economic impact of the disaster, keeping FY2018 growth fairly solid at 2.0%, albeit down from 2.4% in FY2017. Administrative support from the US helped to overcome some constraints on implementation capacity. This assistance supplements transitional arrangements that have been in place since July 2017, with the US Army Corps of Engineers supporting compact-funded projects and helping to resolve project implementation issues.

In the Marshall Islands, growth slowed from 3.6% in FY2017 to 2.5%, and the economy remains dependent on infrastructure investment projects funded by development partners and US compact grants. Continuing capacity constraints in the Marshall Islands have stifled project implementation. As projects nevertheless reach completion, economic stimulus diminishes.

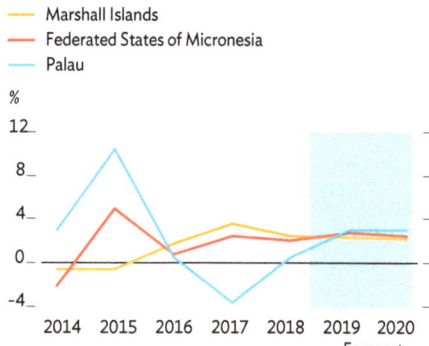

3.37.1 GDP growth in the North Pacific economies

Note: Years are fiscal years ending on 30 September of that year.
Sources: ADB estimates using data from the Republic of the Marshall Islands, Federated States of Micronesia, and Republic of Palau FY2017 *Economic Briefs*.

This chapter was written by Rommel Rabanal and Cara Tinio of the Pacific Department, ADB, Manila.

Palau's economy recovered to 0.5% growth FY2018, reversing 3.7% contraction in FY2017. Growth would have been stronger if a nascent rebound in tourism had not been cut short when two flight services were discontinued. Visitor arrivals grew by a solid 6.6% in the first half of FY2018 following a cumulative 29.9% drop in tourist numbers over the previous 2 years. However, the termination of Delta Airlines flights from Tokyo in May and the indefinite suspension of Palau Pacific Airways charter flights from Hong Kong, China in July drove visitor arrivals sharply down in the second half. For the whole year, tourist arrivals from Palau's two main sources dropped, from Japan by 5.4% and from the People's Republic of China (PRC) by 9.5% after it restricted tour groups transiting to Palau through Hong Kong, China. Consequently, total visitor arrivals fell by 5.0% in FY2018, the third consecutive year of decline (Figure 3.37.2).

Robust construction nevertheless supported economic growth. Public infrastructure projects funded by development partners proceeded in earnest, and some private hotel projects were completed.

Fiscal positions continued to weaken across the North Pacific in FY2018. Preliminary estimates show that the FSM consolidated fiscal surplus eroded from the equivalent of 15% of GDP in FY2017 to 10%. Revenue from fishing license fees fell from their historic high but still equaled 17% of GDP (Figure 3.37.3). However, public wages continued to expand along with government expenditure on services it contracts to implement projects funded by development partners. Capital expenditure built on increases recorded in FY2017, when several project management bottlenecks were cleared.

Likewise, the Marshall Islands is estimated to have realized a smaller fiscal surplus, equal to 3.0% of GDP. The 4.5% surplus in FY2017 reflected record fishing license fee revenues worth 19.4% of GDP that came, not from significantly higher collections in the period, but mostly from a large, one-time appropriation of receipts previously undisbursed by the agency responsible for collecting them. In FY2018, fishing license revenues plunged by 37.7%, reverting to the norm before FY2017 and driving total revenue down by 16.5%.

Palau also saw its fiscal surplus narrow, from 4.8% of GDP in FY2017 to 4.3%, as expenditure increased to fund transfers, including to the civil service pension fund. Steady deterioration in the government's fiscal position also reflected continuing delays in implementing much-needed tax reform that would facilitate higher domestic revenue mobilization.

Inflation in the North Pacific is driven largely by import costs. Higher international prices for food and fuel, and their spillover on prices for other consumer goods, stirred inflation in two of the three economies but were countered by subdued economic activity. Inflation therefore remained very low in

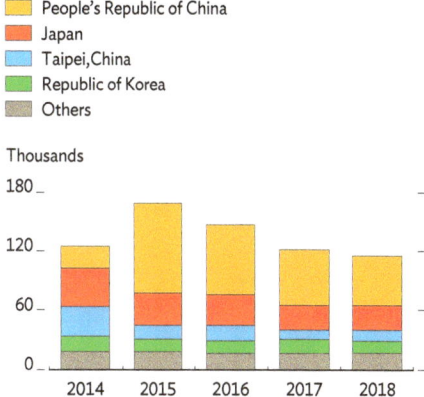

3.37.2 Visitor arrivals in Palau by source

Note: Years are fiscal years ending on 30 September of that year.
Source: Palau Bureau of Labor and Immigration.

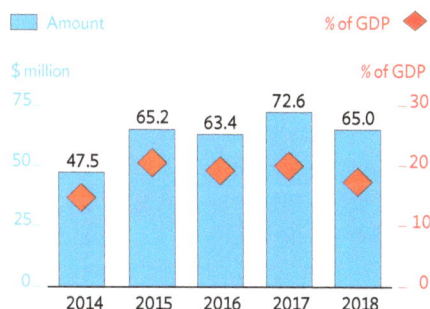

3.37.3 Fishing license revenue in the Federated States of Micronesia

Note: Years are fiscal years ending on 30 September of that year.
Sources: Federated States of Micronesia Department of Finance and Administration and Division of National Statistics.

FY2018, rising from 0.1% to 1.0% in the FSM, from 0.0% to 0.7% in the Marshall Islands, and from 0.9% to 1.1% in Palau.

Higher import bills and lower fishing license revenue in the primary income account further narrowed the FSM current account surplus from the equivalent of 7.5% of GDP in FY2017 to 2.0%. Palau's large current account deficit narrowed only slightly, from 17.9% of GDP to 17.5%, as a larger surplus in the transfers account offset lower tourism receipts. The Marshall Islands current account surplus widened from 3.7% of GDP to 7.0% as, despite higher international commodity prices, imports slowed in line with project implementation delays.

Economic prospects

The outlook for the North Pacific economies is mostly positive. In the FSM, growth is projected to rise to 2.7% in FY2019 as recent steady progress in ramping up capital spending is seen to continue in the near term. Current arrangements for managing and implementing compact-funded projects appear to address capacity constraints. The capital spending program will proceed in accordance with the Infrastructure Development Plan, FY2016–FY2025, which prioritizes energy, water supply and sanitation services, and broader climate change adaptation. More growth promises to stem from potentially greater consumption stirred by expectations of lower fuel prices and stable prices for imported food. Growth is projected to taper slightly to 2.5% in FY2020 as some capital projects near completion.

Growth in Palau is similarly projected to increase with expectations of some recovery in tourism and further increases in capital expenditure thanks to greater financial assistance from the US. Visitor arrivals last year were already below the number recorded in FY2012—before the influx of tourists from the PRC gathered momentum—so no further sharp reductions are likely. Skymark, a low-cost airline in Tokyo, plans to commence regular flights to Palau by mid-2019, which should stem recent declines in arrivals from Japan, Palau's highest-spending tourist market. A recent rebound in tourist numbers from Taipei,China—the fourth-largest tourist market—also bodes well for a recovery in tourism.

In September 2018, Palau and the US agreed to amend their Compact of Free Association. The agreement offers Palau more than $120 million in financial assistance to FY2024. Although most funds are allocated to Palau's Compact Trust Fund, $20 million will be available to finance agreed infrastructure projects that could boost annual capital spending by a quarter—plus $2 million annually for infrastructure maintenance. A further $22 million in direct economic assistance promises further economic stimulus. Growth is thus seen to accelerate to 3.0% in FY2019 and FY2020.

3.37.1 Selected economic indicators (%)

Federated States of Micronesia	2019	2020
GDP growth	2.7	2.5
Inflation	0.7	1.5
Current account balance (share of GDP)	1.0	1.5
Marshall Islands		
GDP growth	2.3	2.2
Inflation	0.5	1.0
Current account balance (share of GDP)	8.0	7.5
Palau		
GDP growth	3.0	3.0
Inflation	0.5	1.5
Current account balance (share of GDP)	-16.3	-16.0

Source: ADB estimates.

Growth in the Marshall Islands, by contrast, is projected to continue slowing to 2.3% in FY2019 and 2.2% in FY2020 as project completion and persistent implementation constraints spell less stimulus from infrastructure investment. The outcome of national elections at the end of 2019 will better shape economic projections for FY2020 and beyond.

The Government of the Marshall Islands plans to issue a cryptocurrency called the sovereign in mid-2019, posing potentially significant downside risks to growth: inflationary pressures if the sovereign causes excessive growth in the money supply, observed volatility in cryptocurrency values, and the threat of quarantine from the international financial system.

Inflation in all three economies is projected to ease slightly in FY2019 before reaccelerating in FY2020 in line with international food and fuel price trends (Figure 3.37.4). Commodity prices are likewise expected to be reflected in import bills, but other factors are seen to drive divergent trends in current account positions in the North Pacific. The FSM current account surplus will likely narrow further to the equivalent of 1.0% of GDP in FY2019 and recover somewhat to 1.5% in FY2020, reflecting the effect of El Niño on tuna migration and thus on fishing license revenue. By contrast, the Marshall Islands current account surplus is expected to widen to 8.0% of GDP in FY2019 as capital equipment imports decline with project completion, and then narrow by half a percentage point in FY2020 with rising commodity import prices. In Palau, the current account deficit is projected to narrow to 16.3% of GDP in FY2019 and 16.0% in FY2020 as tourism receipts recover from the recent slump.

With fishing license revenue in the FSM at risk of falling, the fiscal surplus is forecast to narrow to the equivalent of 7.0% of GDP in FY2019 before bouncing back to 10.0% in FY2020.

In the Marshall Islands, fiscal surpluses are forecast to narrow further to the equivalent of 2% of GDP in FY2019 and then edge back to 3% in FY2020. High recurrent spending, including subsidies to state-owned enterprises and continued social security transfers, will remain unchecked if necessary reform is not implemented (Figure 3.37.5). Tax reform languished, stifling domestic revenue collection.

In Palau, the fiscal surplus is expected to increase to the equivalent of 8.9% of GDP in FY2019 with a surge in grants and then fall back to 1.9% in FY2020 as grant inflows ease.

The parties to the Nauru Agreement, which together manage fishing rights in most of the Pacific, have announced plans to expand their vessel day scheme to cover other forms of fishing. If successful, this could boost fishing license fee revenue for the Marshall Islands and the FSM.

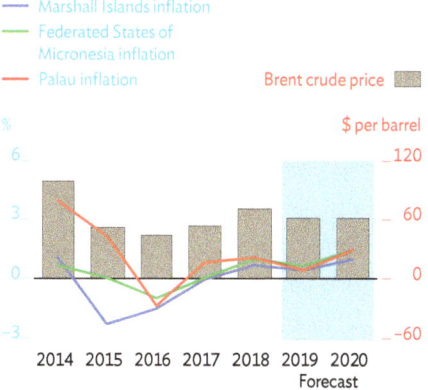

3.37.4 Inflation in the North Pacific economies

Note: Years are fiscal years ending on 30 September of that year.
Sources: ADB estimates using data from the Republic of the Marshall Islands, Federated States of Micronesia, and Republic of Palau FY2017 Economic Briefs.

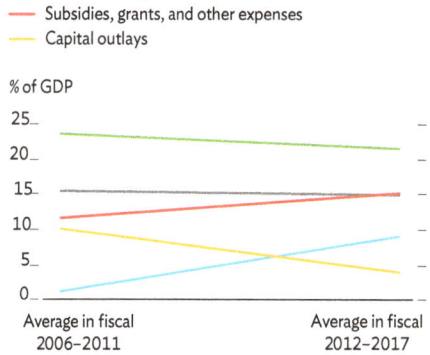

3.37.5 Fishing license revenues and components of public spending in the RMI

Source: ADB estimates using data from the Republic of the Marshall Islands FY2016 Economic Review.

Policy challenge—managing volatility

Like most of their island peers, the North Pacific economies are subject to large growth swings year to year stemming from narrow economic bases and vulnerability to external shocks (Figure 3.37.6).

In the FSM, stagnant growth in the private sector has left economic activity determined largely by public infrastructure construction. To illustrate, growth accelerated from FY2009 to FY2011 on a series of airport upgrades, then contracted for 3 consecutive years as public investment stagnated. Economic growth in the Marshall Islands has similarly depended on public investment projects, as well as on grant-supported government operations. Fiscal constraints caused by variation in grant inflows contributed to contractions in FY2008 and FY2009, then the airport upgrade in Majuro drove expansion from FY2010 until its completion in FY2013. Contractions in the next few years reflected delays in implementing new projects, and subsequent recovery accompanied project resumption.

In recent years, fishing license fees have stimulated finances and growth in both the FSM and the Marshall Islands. However, ADB analysis has shown volatility driven by El Niño weather patterns, as detailed in the December 2017 *Pacific Economic Monitor*. In Palau, volatility derives mainly from tourism peaks and troughs that often mirror global financial and economic crises or even more localized events, such as a collapse in arrivals from Taipei,China caused by a downturn there in FY2013, or an influx of tourists from the PRC in FY2015 followed by the recent policy-induced decline.

Trust funds can help minimize economic volatility by smoothing government revenue otherwise subject to large fluctuations. Higher revenues earned during peak periods can be stored in these instruments to build fiscal buffers for use in subsequent downturns. This allows governments to smooth their annual expenditure and, given the public sector's outsize impact on economic activity in the North Pacific, tamp down volatility in GDP growth.

Further, as disasters and extreme weather can exacerbate volatility, disaster risk management and climate change adaptation need to be emphasized. Climate-proofing can be incorporated into comprehensive strategies to strengthen public investment planning and implementation, yielding more sustainable infrastructure development.

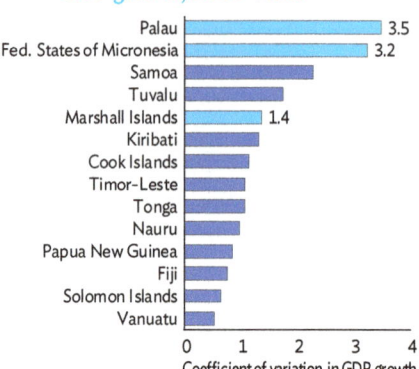

3.37.6 Coefficient of variation in GDP growth, 2009–2018

Note: The coefficient of variation is the ratio of the standard deviation to the mean, where values exceeding 1.0 indicate high variance.
Source: *Asian Development Outlook* database.

South Pacific economies

The South Pacific economies of the Cook Islands, Samoa, and Tonga all grew in 2018. The Cook Islands expanded strongly on record visitor arrivals. Samoa also saw strong growth in visitor arrivals but slower GDP growth because of substantial declines in manufacturing and fishing. Tonga was severely affected by Cyclone Gita in February. South Pacific economies must keep tourism sustainable to ensure that this remains an important source of growth into the future.

Economic performance

The Cook Islands economy grew by 7.0% in fiscal year 2018 (FY2018, ended 30 June 2018), supported by continued strong growth in tourism (Figure 3.38.1). Visitor arrivals increased by 6.2% with a notable 23.4% increase from Canada and 23.7% from French Polynesia. Benefiting from expansion in tourism were related sectors: retail trade, hotels and restaurants, and transport and communications. Aside from these sectors, the implementation of projects for renewable energy on outer islands and water supply and sanitation pushed growth in construction to 25.0%. Small declines were recorded in fishing, finance, and health care.

Growth in Samoa at 0.9% in FY2018 was considerably slower as a large manufacturing enterprise closed and fishing declined. A steep fall in nonfood manufacturing was, however, offset by growth in hotels and restaurants, construction, and communications and business services. Visitor arrivals grew by 11.5%, a sixfold improvement on average annual tourism growth in FY2010–FY2017 at 1.9%. Agriculture, transport, and finance all declined.

The vulnerability of Tonga to disasters was evident from damage inflicted on the economy by Cyclone Gita in February 2018. The destruction of crops, public infrastructure, and buildings limited growth to 0.4% in FY2018, well below the 3.2% average posted from FY2015 to FY2017. Only rapid recovery efforts soon after the cyclone saved the Tongan economy from contraction.

In the Cook Islands, prices rose in FY2018 by 0.4% as increases for food and transportation more than offset falling prices for housing and household operation (Figure 3.38.2).

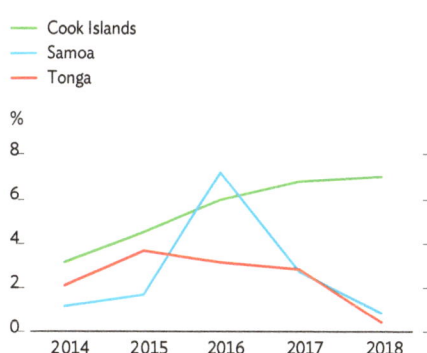

3.38.1 GDP growth in the South Pacific economies

Note: Years are fiscal years ending on 30 June of that year.
Sources: Cook Islands Ministry of Finance & Economic Management; Samoa Bureau of Statistics; Tonga Department of Statistics; ADB estimates.

This chapter was written by Shiu Raj Singh of the Pacific Subregional Office, ADB, Suva; and Noel Del Castillo, consultant, Pacific Department, ADB, Manila.

In Samoa, higher domestic and import prices in FY2018 pushed inflation to 3.7%, with substantially higher prices for food and nonalcoholic beverages and for education and lesser rises for alcoholic beverages and for transport and communications. Somewhat offsetting these higher prices were price declines for housing and household operation. Tonga's inflation averaged higher by 5.3% in FY2018, with food prices increasing substantially as a result of the damage and losses caused by Cyclone Gita. Contributing to inflation were higher prices for transportation and beverages, including kava, a local relaxant.

The Cook Islands' fiscal surplus shrank by more than half from the equivalent of 9.2% of GDP in FY2017 to 4.1% a year later. Although revenue increased in FY2018, even higher operating and capital expenditure narrowed the surplus. Net public debt, all of it external, fell from the equivalent of 17.3% of GDP in FY2017 to 16.8% only because of strong GDP growth, as debt was higher in nominal terms. In any case, debt remains comfortably below the government ceiling of 35% of GDP. The government maintained a debt-service reserve equal to 3.6% of GDP in FY2018 and held additional cash reserves equal to 20.6% of GDP.

Samoa had a small fiscal surplus in FY2018, reversing a deficit equal to 1.1% of GDP in FY2017. This first surplus in 9 years was achieved through rigorous expenditure control and higher external grants received after the International Monetary Fund assessed Samoa to be at high risk of debt distress because of its exposure to disasters. At the end of FY2018, external debt equaled 49.4% of GDP, slightly higher than a year earlier because exchange rate movements were unfavorable and contracted loans continued to be disbursed for ongoing projects.

Tonga's fiscal balance ended FY2018 in a surplus equal to 1.6% of GDP as budget support from development partners, and the postponement of investment projects following Cyclone Gita, more than offset higher spending on emergency response and rehabilitation. External debt increased from the equivalent of 39.5% of GDP at the end of FY2017 to 41.8% a year later.

The Cook Islands updated and substantially revised in FY2018 data on the balance of payments. The result was sharply lower estimates for past current account surpluses, which followed from revised estimates for tourism inflows. The surplus in FY2017 was revised down from the equivalent of 25.5% of GDP to 1.6%, rising in FY2018 to 2.2% on a higher surplus in trade in services. In Samoa, a current account surplus equal to 4.7% of GDP in FY2018 reversed a 1.8% deficit in the previous year thanks to strong growth in visitor arrivals and a 24.3% increase in remittances. In Tonga, higher imports offset huge grant flows from development partners for cyclone relief to narrow the current account surplus to the equivalent

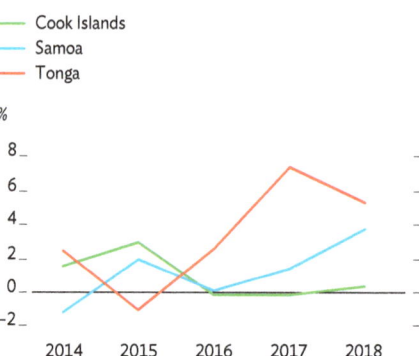

3.38.2 Inflation

Note: Years are fiscal years ending on 30 June of that year.
Sources: Cook Islands Ministry of Finance & Economic Management; Samoa Bureau of Statistics; Tonga Department of Statistics; ADB estimates.

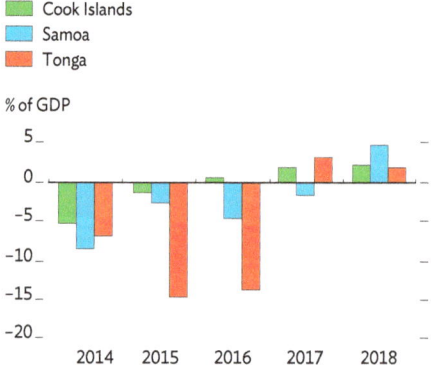

3.38.3 Current account balance

Note: Years are fiscal years ending on 30 June of that year.
Sources: Cook Islands Ministry of Finance & Economic Management; Samoa Bureau of Statistics; Tonga Department of Statistics; ADB estimates.

of 1.8% of GDP in FY2018 (Figure 3.38.3). Meanwhile, remittances remained robust as Tongans living overseas provided support to their families back home, particularly after the disaster, with inward private transfers rising by 8.9%.

Economic prospects

Growth is seen to moderate in the Cook Islands and pick up in Samoa and Tonga during the forecast period.

The Cook Islands economy is projected to grow by 6.0% in FY2019. Tourism and large infrastructure projects for water supply and sanitation, renewable energy, and improved internet connectivity will continue to contribute significantly to economic expansion. Growth is projected to slow further in FY2020 as tourism is constrained by low availability of accommodation.

In Samoa, growth is expected to accelerate in FY2019, driven up as higher visitor arrivals boost growth in commerce, hotels, transport, and other activities ancillary to tourism. Growth is forecast to increase further to 3.0% in FY2020 on continued growth in tourism but also strengthening growth in communications. The 2019 Pacific Games, which Samoa will host in July 2019, are expected to provide further impetus.

Following slow growth in FY2018 as a result of losses from Cyclone Gita, Tonga is expected to enjoy higher economic growth in FY2019 and FY2020 thanks to reconstruction and infrastructure projects in the pipeline.

Inflation expectations are mixed across the three economies in the forecast period. Prices are seen to grow by 1.0% in the Cook Islands and 2.0% in Samoa in FY2019, and inflation in both will converge at 1.5% in FY2020 as higher global food prices affect these import-dependent island economies. In Tonga, inflation is expected to continue to hover at 5.3% in both FY2019 and FY2020 as the government ramps up construction projects.

The Government of the Cook Islands projects a fiscal deficit equal to 1.9% of GDP in FY2019 to pay for an ambitious investment plan for water supply, renewable energy, and communications (Figure 3.38.4). In FY2020, these projects will have progressed substantially, so a surplus equal to 1.0% of GDP is projected. With improved tax collection and a growing economy, the government does not intend to finance projects with loans except when it needs technical assistance for implementation. Continued economic growth and available cash balances should keep net public debt below target. Cash reserves are expected to continue rising over the forecast years.

Samoa's fiscal deficit is budgeted to equal 3.5% of GDP in both FY2019 and FY2020, in line with the government's fiscal strategy to stimulate the economy with expansionary fiscal and

3.38.1 Selected economic indicators (%)

Cook Islands	2019	2020
GDP growth	6.0	4.5
Inflation	1.0	1.5
Current account balance (share of GDP)	2.8	3.4
Samoa		
GDP growth	2.0	3.0
Inflation	2.0	1.5
Current account balance (share of GDP)	-3.5	-3.0
Tonga		
GDP growth	2.1	1.9
Inflation	5.3	5.3
Current account balance (share of GDP)	-12.2	-11.2

Note: Years are fiscal years ending in 30 June of that year.
Source: ADB estimates.

monetary policies. Meanwhile, it intends to keep its focus on revenue collection through measures to improve compliance.

Tonga is forecast to post a deficit in both FY2019 and FY2020 on increased spending on infrastructure and reconstruction, which are expected to remain substantial components of expenditure. Higher projected tax revenue in FY2020 is expected to narrow the fiscal deficit slightly.

Cook Islands current account surpluses are expected to expand to the equivalent of 2.8% of GDP in FY2019 and 3.4% in FY2020. Growing tourism earnings are likely to offset higher imports of goods and services for public investment projects implemented during the period. Samoa's current account is expected to fall into deficit equal to 3.5% of GDP in FY2019, in part because of imports for the 2019 Pacific Games, the deficit easing to 3.0% in FY2020. Increased imports of goods for reconstruction are projected to push Tonga's current account into deficit in FY2019. The deficit is expected to persist in FY2020 with the forecast resurgence in global food prices.

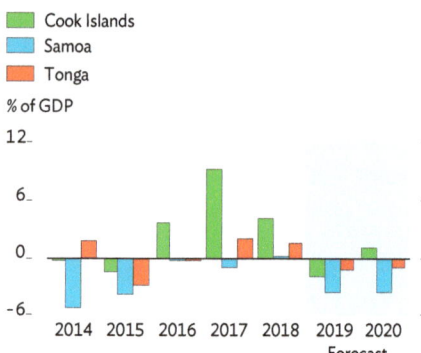

3.38.4 Fiscal balance

Note: Years are fiscal years ending on 30 June of that year.
Sources: Cook Islands Ministry of Finance & Economic Management; Samoa Ministry of Finance; Tonga Ministry of Finance and National Planning.

Policy challenge—ensuring sustainable growth in tourism

The South Pacific economies depend on tourism to drive economic growth (Figure 3.38.5). Cook Islands exports of services, largely tourism receipts, provided 49.6% of GDP on average from FY2012 to FY2018. Growth in the Cook Islands economy mirrors visitor arrivals. In Samoa as well, tourism is growing in importance despite challenges encountered in the aftermath of a tsunami in September 2009. Tourism earnings in Samoa averaged 18.1% of GDP from FY2012 to FY2018, the latter of which was a record year for tourism in Samoa with earnings rising to 20.6% of GDP. The contribution of tourism in Tonga has grown steadily, albeit from a small base of only 7.0% in FY2010, reaching 11.5% in FY2017. All three economies face similar issues in their tourism industries: First is a need to improve infrastructure to ensure that the benefits of tourism spread across the country. Second is to ensure that infrastructure for tourism is sufficiently resilient, able to withstand the cyclones to which these economies are prone. Third is to keep tourism environmentally friendly and sustainable.

Tourism is constrained in the South Pacific economies by underdeveloped infrastructure, which confines and concentrates these industries in accessible areas. Consideration should be given to policies that use infrastructure development to encourage industry diversification. Appropriate infrastructure development will catalyze private sector investment as it is attracted to new locations around the country. The Cook Islands in particular

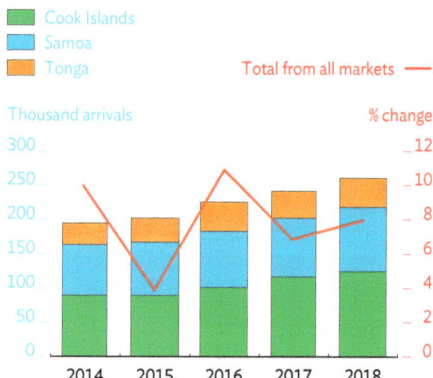

3.38.5 Visitor arrivals from Australia and New Zealand to the South Pacific

Note: Years are fiscal years ending on 30 June of that year.
Sources: Australian Bureau of Statistics; Statistics New Zealand.

is in a favorable fiscal position to support infrastructure development to spread tourism to outer islands. Samoa and Tonga should incorporate facilitative infrastructure investments in their longer-term tourism development plans.

Although diversification supports resilience in industry, long-term sustainability across the South Pacific economies demands additional considerations, notably factoring disaster resilience into investments in buildings and other infrastructure. The Cook Islands has not had a major disaster recently, but Samoa struggled to expand its tourism industry after the 2009 tsunami, which pushed earnings to as low as the equivalent of 16.6% of GDP in the years that followed. This highlights the country's vulnerability to natural disasters and the need for tourism to remain sustainable over the long run. Tourism was the industry second most affected in Tonga after the onslaught of Cyclone Gita. The government intends to adopt the policy in its reconstruction and recovery plan to "build back better" with the emphasis on resilient physical infrastructure.

The growing importance of tourism and its expanding scale mean that its environmental and social impacts should not be overlooked. Here, too, there is a need to embrace opportunities for sustainability. Governments can consider enhancing legislation to better address issues that threaten the sustainability of the tourism industry and policies promoting sustainable tourism practices. The Vava'u island group in Tonga, for example, is one of the country's popular destinations, well known for watching whales and swimming with them. While the government has passed laws regulating these activities, rising demand has greatly increased the number of whale-watching operators. Industry leaders have expressed concern over the increase in activity as noise and other environmental pollutants adversely affect whale populations.

Small island economies

Economic performance in the three small island economies diverged, with growth accelerating in Tuvalu and stable in Kiribati as GDP contracted in Nauru. Infrastructure projects will play a dominant role in economic activity in Nauru and continued growth in Kiribati and Tuvalu. Inflation is expected to be fairly stable while current accounts weaken, with Tuvalu going into deficit. Improving public service delivery while stemming fiscal drain is necessary as reform to state-owned enterprises continues.

Economic performance

The economy of Kiribati grew by 2.3% in 2018 but at a bit less than half the average growth rate of 5.2% from 2015 to 2017 (Figure 3.39.1). Public spending and projects financed by development partners continue to be the main drivers of economic growth. And, while growth in fishing revenue slowed from 10.0% in 2017 to 0.7% in 2018, fisheries remain an important source of national revenue, providing 71.7% of total revenue in 2018.

In Nauru, the economy is estimated to have contracted as the Regional Processing Centre (RPC), an Australian-funded facility for asylum seekers, scaled down and an overseas refugee resettlement program commenced. Meanwhile, phosphate exports remained weak. The RPC scale-down was, however, slower than initially expected. The facility has been the principal source of economic activity in recent years, driving revenue growth, including from visa fees and income taxes paid by expatriate workers, and from consequent demand for local services, as well as infrastructure investment.

Growth in Tuvalu accelerated to 4.3% in 2018, driven by higher government spending on large infrastructure projects and new housing in preparation for hosting the Polynesian Leaders Group Summit, which was held in June 2018, and the upcoming Pacific Islands Forum, to be held in September 2019. Increased spending was supported by recovery in fishing license revenue, which posted an 84.8% jump in 2018 with the receipt of a one-off payment from a subregional pooling scheme last year.

Inflation rose in Kiribati in 2018 on a pickup in economic activity brought about by sustained public spending and higher wages. However, muted global food prices have kept price

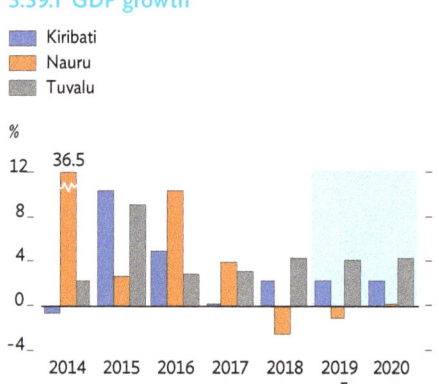

3.39.1 GDP growth

Note: Years are fiscal years ending on 30 June of that year in Nauru and coinciding with the calendar year in Kiribati and Tuvalu.
Sources: Kiribati budget documents; Nauru budget documents; Tuvalu budget documents; *Asian Development Outlook* database; ADB estimates.

This chapter was written by Jacqueline Connell of the Pacific Liaison and Coordination Office, ADB, Sydney; and Prince Cruz and Noel Del Castillo, consultants, Pacific Department, ADB, Manila.

growth in check. Meanwhile, inflation in Nauru continued to slow under economic contraction. Inflation in Tuvalu also decelerated to 1.8% in line with global food price movements.

The current account surplus in Kiribati narrowed further as imports rose and fishing revenue moderated. The current account balance of Tuvalu also remained in surplus in 2018. Higher inflows of fishing license fees offset increased imports of goods to supply government infrastructure investments (Figure 3.39.2).

The fiscal balance in Kiribati posted a deficit in 2018 equal to 20.1% of GDP (Figure 3.39.3). Increased spending on wages by 33.9% and the acquisition of aircraft for Air Kiribati more than offset higher revenue from fishing licenses and 4.2% higher revenue from taxes, which showed up as a surplus in the recurrent budget.

In Nauru, total revenues collected in fiscal year 2018 (FY2018, ended 30 June 2018) were 1.2% higher than in the previous year, mainly reflecting higher tax and nontax revenue collected from operations associated with the RPC. This contrasted with earlier government projections of lower revenue based on the assumed faster scaling-down of RPC operations. This income supported higher expenditure, including capital spending, as well as contributions to the Nauru Intergenerational Trust Fund. The fiscal surplus nevertheless shrank by half from the equivalent of 19.3% of GDP in FY2017 to 8.8%, including trust fund contributions. By year-end, the government's cash buffer was above the International Monetary Fund recommendation of cover for 2 months of spending not associated with the RPC.

Tuvalu saw tax revenue decline by 20.5% from 2017 but still had a fiscal surplus equal to 33.9% of GDP in 2018 thanks to strong recovery in fishing license revenue and lower operating expenditure.

Economic prospects

The pace of growth in Kiribati is expected to be sustained in the next 2 years as continued infrastructure spending offsets the slowdown in fishing revenue. In October 2018, Kiribati secured a grant from development partners that will provide to South Tarawa, the capital, a seawater desalination plant and a solar photovoltaic plant, as well as rehabilitate and expand the water supply network.

Nauru is expected to experience less severe economic contraction in FY2019 than in FY2018, with the Nauru Port project having commenced construction in January 2019 and able to cushion the slowdown caused by the continued scaling down of the RPC and resettlement of refugees. Growth will remain stagnant in FY2020. The government has approved three supplementary budgets so far in FY2019 because higher

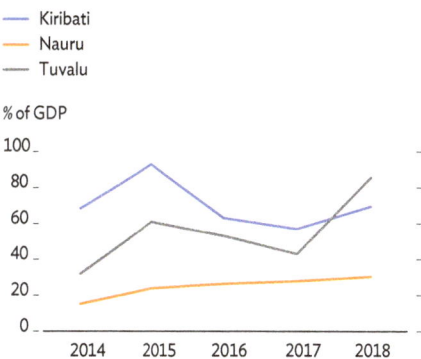

3.39.2 Fishing license revenue

Sources: Kiribati budget documents; Nauru budget documents; Tuvalu budget documents; Asian Development Outlook database

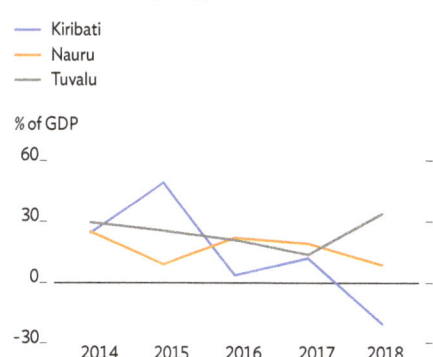

3.39.3 Fiscal balance

Note: Years are fiscal years ending on 30 June of that year in Nauru and coinciding with the calendar year in Kiribati and Tuvalu.
Sources: Kiribati budget documents; Nauru budget documents; Tuvalu budget documents; Asian Development Outlook database.

revenue, including windfall fishing license revenue from pooled days in prior years, allowed for increases in expenditure alongside the building up of cash buffers. Fiscal discipline will be critical in FY2020 as RPC-derived revenue is uncertain and revenue from fishing license fees is projected to drop from the exceptionally elevated receipts in FY2019.

Tuvalu's economy is projected to accelerate in the next 2 years with the implementation of infrastructure projects supported by development partners. In September 2018, it received additional grant for an ongoing project to climate-proof a harbor in Niutao, a reef island in the north.

Inflation is forecast to accelerate in Kiribati in 2019 and 2020 with expected increases in food prices (Figure 3.39.4). It is likewise projected higher in Tuvalu over the next 2 years, pushed up by increased public sector wages and by ongoing and future infrastructure projects. In Nauru, inflation is expected to continue easing as the economy contracts and global commodity prices, especially for oil, remain low.

The fiscal deficit in Kiribati is expected to persist, equal to 23.2% of GDP in 2019 and 20.8% in 2020, as recent unexpected bounty from fishing revenue is expected to revert to slower growth or decline under less favorable weather. Further, the government's commitment to support Air Kiribati as it establishes its own international operations will incur substantial fiscal costs. Tuvalu will fall into a fiscal deficit equal to 1.1% of GDP in 2019 as spending continues on infrastructure for the regional summit and as fishing revenue declines significantly, as projected. However, higher tax revenue and lower spending in 2020 are expected to restore government finances to a surplus equal to 1.4% of GDP.

The volatility in fishing license revenues will be significant for the current account balance of Kiribati, with the surplus shrinking further in 2019 and 2020 (Figure 3.39.5). Similarly in Tuvalu, weaker fishing revenue inflows in the next 2 years and sustained growth in imports of goods will push the current account into deficit in 2019 and widen the deficit in 2020.

Risks to the outlook include delays in implementing infrastructure projects. For Nauru, any change in expected arrangements for the RPC could significantly affect economic activity in either direction. Fiscal sustainability remains a challenge as the main sources of revenues remain narrow and are highly volatile.

3.39.1 Selected economic indicators (%)

Kiribati	2019	2020
GDP growth	2.3	2.3
Inflation	2.3	2.2
Current account balance (share of GDP)	7.6	4.0
Nauru		
GDP growth	-1.0	0.1
Inflation	2.5	2.0
Current account balance (share of GDP)	...	...
Tuvalu		
GDP growth	4.1	4.4
Inflation	3.4	3.5
Current account balance (share of GDP)	-0.9	-11.0

Note: Years are fiscal years ending on 30 June of that year in Nauru, and coinciding with the calendar year in Kiribati and Tuvalu.
Source: ADB estimates.

3.39.4 Inflation

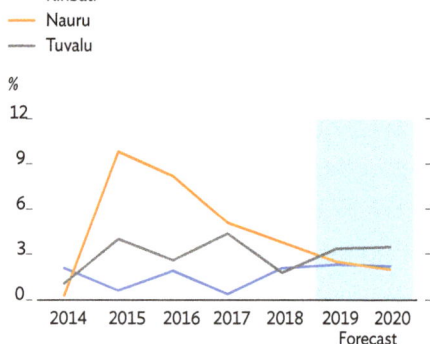

Note: Years are fiscal years ending on 30 June of that year in Nauru, and coinciding with the calendar year in Kiribati and Tuvalu.

Sources: Kiribati budget documents; Nauru budget documents; Tuvalu budget documents; *Asian Development Outlook* database; ADB estimates.

Policy challenge—pursuing reform to state enterprises

State-owned enterprises (SOEs) provide essential services such as water supply and energy utilities, especially in remote areas. However, the high operating costs of SOEs typical in small island economies pose serious concerns for their fiscal sustainability, especially as some SOEs rely heavily on continuous subsidies and repeated capital infusions from the national government. SOE reform to promote fiscal sustainability and responsiveness must ensure the continued provision of essential services while minimizing the fiscal burden on the government.

Maintaining fiscal sustainability is a longstanding challenge for Kiribati. Part of the recent increase in recurrent government expenditure has been to fund higher subsidies for SOEs. The government has made strides in consolidating and downsizing SOEs involved in copra production and trade, and it managed to sell its telecom SOE, but there is a need to continue pursuing improvement in the quality and relevance of SOE financial reports. Further, the government should lay out a plan to enhance the sustainability of its SOEs by improving SOE governance and also, for example, recalibrating tariffs for water supply and sanitation services. Finally, SOEs should not be exempted from the value-added tax to better level the playing field for the private sector and encourage its growth.

In Nauru, SOEs play important roles in the economy and are significant employers. However, weak SOE governance puts at risk the sustainability of the large portion of public assets and infrastructure that SOEs manage. Poorly performing SOEs can absorb large amounts of scarce capital and divert government resources away from critical social investments into health care and education. The government has started to tackle these challenges. Reform to the state-owned power utility has reduced fiscal costs and made electricity supply more reliable. The cabinet approved an SOE policy in 2018 that establishes a framework for SOE reporting, provides guidelines on director appointments and community service obligations, and calls for the establishment of a central monitoring unit to oversee SOE performance. Comprehensive SOE legislation is planned.

Although Tuvalu's outlook remains generally optimistic, the weak balance sheets of its SOEs pose risks to the fiscal balance because SOEs rely heavily on government subsidies (Figure 3.39.6). The latest forecast from the International Monetary Fund indicates that fiscal support to SOEs will increase to equal about 4% of GDP in the medium term. This makes it imperative that SOEs strengthen their financial performance and so mitigate their drag on the national budget. Specific reforms would require the government to pay its outstanding obligations to SOEs; introduce differential electricity tariffs for public and commercial entities to increase the revenue of Tuvalu Electricity Corporation, an SOE; adopt a more transparent approach to annual fiscal transfers to SOEs; and closely monitor any joint ventures that SOEs join.

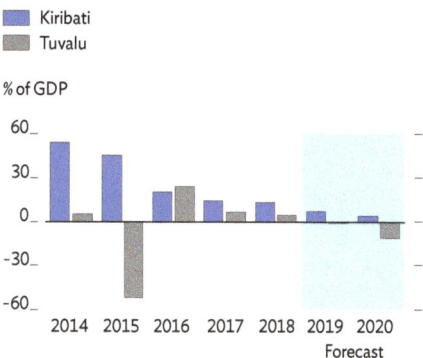

3.39.5 Current account balance

Sources: *Asian Development Outlook* database; ADB estimates.

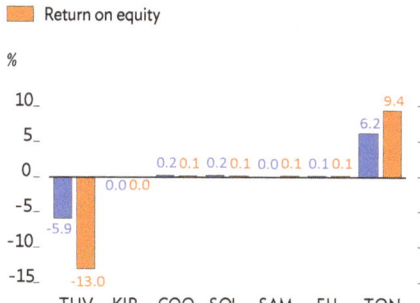

3.39.6 Returns on state-owned electricity enterprises, 2015

COO = Cook Islands Te Aponga Uira O Tumu-Te Varovaro (power authority), FIJ = Fiji Electricity Authority, KIR = Kiribati Public Utilities Board, SAM = Samoa Electric Power Corporation, SOL = Solomon Power, TON = Tonga Power Limited, TUV = Tuvalu Electricity Corporation.

Note: The figures for Solomon Islands and Tonga are 2016 data.

Source: Pacific Power Association. 2015 and 2016. Pacific Power Utilities: Power Benchmarking 2015 and 2016 Fiscal Years.

STATISTICAL APPENDIX

Statistical notes and tables

The statistical appendix presents selected economic indicators for the 45 developing member economies of the Asian Development Bank (ADB) in 18 tables. The economies are grouped into five subregions: Central Asia, East Asia, South Asia, Southeast Asia, and the Pacific. Most of the tables contain historical data from 2014 to 2018; some have forecasts for 2019 and 2020.

The data were standardized to the degree possible to allow comparability over time and across economies, but differences in statistical methodology, definitions, coverage, and practices make full comparability impossible. The national income accounts section is based on the United Nations System of National Accounts, while the data on balance of payments use International Monetary Fund (IMF) accounting standards. Historical data were obtained from official sources, statistical publications, and databases, as well as the documents of ADB, the IMF, and the World Bank. For some economies, data for 2018 were estimated from the latest available information. Projections for 2019 and 2020 are generally ADB estimates made on the bases of available quarterly or monthly data, though some projections are from governments.

Most economies report by calendar year. The following record their government finance data by fiscal year: Brunei Darussalam; Fiji; Hong Kong, China; the Kyrgyz Republic; the Lao People's Democratic Republic (Lao PDR); Singapore; Tajikistan; Thailand; and Uzbekistan. South Asian countries (except for Maldives and Sri Lanka), the Cook Islands, the Federated States of Micronesia, Myanmar, Nauru, Palau, the Republic of Marshall Islands, Samoa, and Tonga report all variables by fiscal year. In Myanmar, there is a statistical break in 2018 caused by a change in the fiscal year, with fiscal 2017 ending 31 March 2017, transitional fiscal year 2018 lasting only 6 months to 30 September 2018, and fiscal 2019 ending 30 September 2019.

Regional and subregional averages or totals are provided for seven tables (A1, A2, A6, A11, A12, A13, and A14). For tables A1, A2, A6, A11, A12, and A14, averages were computed using weights derived from gross national income (GNI) in current US dollars following the World Bank Atlas method. The GNI data for 2014–2017 were obtained from the World Bank's World Development Indicators online. Weights for 2017 were carried over through 2020. The GNI data for the Cook Islands and Taipei,China were estimated using the Atlas conversion factor. For Table A13, the regional and subregional totals were computed using a consistent sum, which means that if country data were missing for a given year, the sum excluded that country.

Tables A1, A2, A3, A4, and A5. These tables show data on output growth, production, and demand. Changes to the national income accounts series for some countries were made to accommodate a change in source, methodology, and/or base year. The series for Afghanistan, Bhutan, India, Myanmar, and Pakistan reflects fiscal year data, rather than calendar year data, while those for Timor-Leste reflect GDP excluding the offshore petroleum sector. In Myanmar, fiscal 2018 growth rates were computed in reference to April–September 2017, and growth rates for 2019 onward were computed in reference to the full 12 months preceding the fiscal year.

Table A1: Growth rate of GDP (% per year). The table shows annual growth rates of GDP valued at constant market prices, factor costs, or basic prices. GDP at market prices is the aggregation of value added by all resident producers at producers' prices including taxes less subsidies on imports plus all nondeductible value-added or similar taxes. Constant factor cost measures differ from market price measures in that they exclude taxes on production and include subsidies. Basic price valuation is the factor cost plus some taxes on production, such as property and payroll taxes, and less some subsidies, such as for labor but not for products. Most economies use constant market price valuation. Pakistan use constant factor costs, while Fiji and Maldives use basic prices.

Table A2: Growth rate of per capita GDP (% per year). The table provides the growth rates of real per capita GDP, which is defined as GDP at constant prices divided by the population. Data on per capita gross national income in US dollar terms (Atlas method) for 2017 are also shown, sourced from the World Bank's World Development Indicators online. The data for the Cook Islands and Taipei,China were estimated using the Atlas conversion factor.

Table A3: Growth rate of value added in agriculture (% per year). The table shows the growth rates of value added in agriculture at constant prices and agriculture's share of GDP in 2017 at current prices. The agriculture sector comprises plant crops, livestock, poultry, fisheries, and forestry.

Table A4: Growth rate of value added in industry (% per year). The table provides the growth rates of value added in industry at constant prices and industry's share of GDP in 2017 at current prices. This sector comprises manufacturing, mining and quarrying, and, generally, construction and utilities.

Table A5: Growth rate of value added in services (% per year). The table gives the growth rates of value added in services at constant prices and services' share of GDP in 2017 at current prices. Subsectors generally include trade, banking, finance, real estate, and similar businesses, as well as public administration. For Malaysia, electricity, gas, water supply, and waste management are included under services.

Table A6: Inflation (% per year). Data on inflation rates are period averages. The inflation rates presented are based on consumer price indexes. The consumer price indexes of the following economies are for a given city only: Cambodia is for Phnom Penh, the Marshall Islands is for Majuro, and Solomon Islands is for Honiara. For Uzbekistan, data from 2016 onwards reflect the IMF fixed weight method of estimating the consumer price index, as adopted by the government, which has not revised annual average inflation data for 2014–2016; for the earlier period, IMF average consumer price data are used.

Table A7: Change in money supply (% per year). This table tracks the annual percentage change in the end-of-period supply of broad money as represented by M2 for most countries. M2 is defined as the sum of M1 and quasi-money, where M1 denotes currency in circulation plus demand deposits, and quasi-money consists of time and savings deposits including foreign currency deposits. For Georgia and India, broad money is represented by M3, which adds longer-term time deposits.

Tables A8, A9, and A10: Government finance. These tables give the revenue and expenditure transactions and the fiscal balance of the central government expressed as a percentage of GDP in nominal terms. For Cambodia, Georgia, India, Kazakhstan, the Kyrgyz Republic, Mongolia, the People's Republic of China, and Tajikistan, transactions are those reported by the general government.

Table A8: Central government revenue (% of GDP). Central government revenue comprises all nonrepayable receipts, both current and capital, plus grants. These amounts are computed as a percentage of GDP at current prices. For the Republic of Korea, revenue excludes social security contributions. For Singapore, revenue includes the contribution from net investment returns. For Kazakhstan, revenue includes transfers from the national fund. Grants are excluded in Cambodia, the Lao PDR, Malaysia, and Thailand; revenue from disinvestment is included for India; and only current revenue is included for Bangladesh.

Table A9: Central government expenditure (% of GDP). Central government expenditure comprises all nonrepayable payments to both current and capital expenses, plus net lending. These amounts are computed as a share of GDP at current prices. For Thailand, expenditure refers to budgetary expenditure excluding externally financed expenditure and borrowing. For Tajikistan, expenditure includes externally financed public investment programs. One-time expenditures are excluded for Pakistan.

Table A10: Fiscal balance of central government (% of GDP). Fiscal balance is the difference between central government revenue and expenditure. The difference is computed as a share of GDP at current prices. Data variation may arise from statistical discrepancy when, for example, balancing items for both central and local governments, and from differences in the concept used in the individual computations of revenue and expenditure as compared with the calculation of the fiscal balance. For Fiji, the fiscal balance excludes loan repayment. For Georgia, fiscal balance is calculated according to the Government Finance Statistics Manual 2001 of the IMF. For Thailand, the fiscal balance is the cash balance of the combined budgetary and nonbudgetary balances. For Uzbekistan, the augmented fiscal balance includes the Fund for Reconstruction and Development. Some off-budget accounts are included in the computation of the fiscal balance for Turkmenistan.

Tables A11, A12, A13, and A14: Balance of payments. These tables show annual flows of selected international economic transactions of countries as recorded in the balance of payments.

Tables A11 and A12: Growth rates of merchandise exports and imports (% per year). These tables show the annual growth rates of exports and imports of goods. Data are in million US dollars, primarily obtained from the balance-of-payments accounts of each economy. Export data are reported free on board. Import data are reported free on board except for the following economies, which value them based on cost, insurance, and freight: Afghanistan; Bhutan; Hong Kong, China; Georgia; India; the Lao PDR; Myanmar; Singapore; and Thailand.

Table A13: Trade balance ($ million). The trade balance is the difference between merchandise exports and merchandise imports. Figures in this table are based on the export and import amounts used to generate tables A11 and A12.

Table A14: Current account balance (% of GDP). The current account balance is the sum of the balance of trade for merchandise, net trade in services and factor income, and net transfers. The values reported are divided by GDP at current prices in US dollars. For Cambodia, the Lao PDR, and Viet Nam, official transfers are excluded from the current account balance.

Table A15: Exchange rates to the US dollar (annual average). Annual average exchange rates are quoted as the local currency per US dollar.

Table A16: Gross international reserves ($ million). Gross international reserves are defined as the US dollar value of holdings of foreign exchange, special drawing rights, reserve position in the IMF, and gold at the end of a given period. For Taipei,China, this heading refers to foreign exchange reserves only. In some economies, the rubric is foreign assets and reserves of national monetary authorities and national oil funds, e.g., net foreign reserves of the State Bank of Pakistan. The data for India are as of 10 March 2019.

Table A17: External debt outstanding ($ million). For most economies, external debt outstanding, public and private, includes short-term debt, medium- and long-term debt, and IMF credit. For Cambodia and the Lao PDR, only public external debt is reported. Intercompany lending is excluded in Georgia. For the Kyrgyz Republic, Singapore, Sri Lanka, and Thailand, the figures for 2018 are as of the end of September.

Table A18: Debt service ratio (% of exports of goods and services). This table generally presents the total debt service payments of each economy, which comprise principal repayments (excluding on short-term debt) and interest payments on outstanding external debt, as a percentage of exports of goods and services. For Cambodia and the Lao PDR, debt service refers to external public debt only. For Viet Nam, exports of goods are used as the denominator in the calculation of the ratio; for the Philippines, exports of goods, services, and income are used as the denominator. For Bangladesh, the ratio represents debt service payments on medium- and long-term loans as a percentage of exports of goods, nonfactor services, and workers' remittances. For Azerbaijan, the ratio represents public and publicly guaranteed external debt service payments as a percentage of exports of goods and nonfactor services.

Table A1 Growth rate of GDP (% per year)

	2014	2015	2016	2017	2018	2019	2020
Central Asia	5.1	3.1	2.4	4.2	4.4	4.2	4.2
Armenia	3.6	3.2	0.2	7.5	5.2	4.3	4.5
Azerbaijan	2.8	1.1	-3.1	0.1	1.4	2.5	2.7
Georgia	4.6	2.9	2.8	4.8	4.8	5.0	4.9
Kazakhstan	4.2	1.2	1.1	4.1	4.1	3.5	3.3
Kyrgyz Republic	4.0	3.9	4.3	4.7	3.5	4.0	4.4
Tajikistan	6.7	6.0	6.9	7.1	7.3	7.0	6.5
Turkmenistan	10.3	6.5	6.2	6.5	6.2	6.0	5.8
Uzbekistan	8.0	7.9	6.2	4.5	5.1	5.2	5.5
East Asia	6.6	6.1	6.0	6.2	6.0	5.7	5.5
Hong Kong, China	2.8	2.4	2.2	3.8	3.0	2.5	2.5
Mongolia	7.9	2.4	1.2	5.3	6.9	6.7	6.3
People's Republic of China	7.3	6.9	6.7	6.8	6.6	6.3	6.1
Republic of Korea	3.3	2.8	2.9	3.1	2.7	2.5	2.5
Taipei,China	4.0	0.8	1.5	3.1	2.6	2.2	2.0
South Asia	6.9	7.3	7.5	6.9	6.7	6.8	6.9
Afghanistan	2.7	1.5	2.3	2.7	2.2	2.5	3.0
Bangladesh	6.1	6.6	7.1	7.3	7.9	8.0	8.0
Bhutan	4.0	6.2	7.4	6.3	5.5	5.7	6.0
India	7.4	8.0	8.2	7.2	7.0	7.2	7.3
Maldives	7.3	2.9	7.3	6.9	7.6	6.5	6.3
Nepal	6.0	3.3	0.6	7.9	6.3	6.2	6.3
Pakistan	4.1	4.1	4.6	5.4	5.2	3.9	3.6
Sri Lanka	5.0	5.0	4.5	3.4	3.2	3.6	3.8
Southeast Asia	4.7	4.7	4.8	5.3	5.1	4.9	5.0
Brunei Darussalam	-2.5	-0.4	-2.5	1.3	-1.0	1.0	1.5
Cambodia	7.1	7.0	6.9	7.0	7.3	7.0	6.8
Indonesia	5.0	4.9	5.0	5.1	5.2	5.2	5.3
Lao People's Dem. Rep.	7.6	7.3	7.0	6.9	6.5	6.5	6.5
Malaysia	6.0	5.1	4.2	5.9	4.7	4.5	4.7
Myanmar	8.0	7.0	5.9	6.8	6.2	6.6	6.8
Philippines	6.1	6.1	6.9	6.7	6.2	6.4	6.4
Singapore	4.1	2.5	2.8	3.9	3.2	2.6	2.6
Thailand	1.0	3.1	3.4	4.0	4.1	3.9	3.7
Viet Nam	6.0	6.7	6.2	6.8	7.1	6.8	6.7
The Pacific	9.6	8.0	2.5	2.4	0.9	3.5	3.2
Cook Islands	3.2	4.5	6.0	6.8	7.0	6.0	4.5
Federated States of Micronesia	-2.2	5.0	0.7	2.4	2.0	2.7	2.5
Fiji	5.6	3.8	0.7	3.0	3.0	3.2	3.5
Kiribati	-0.7	10.4	5.1	0.3	2.3	2.3	2.3
Marshall Islands	-0.7	-0.6	1.8	3.6	2.5	2.3	2.2
Nauru	36.5	2.8	10.4	4.0	-2.4	-1.0	0.1
Palau	3.1	10.4	0.5	-3.7	0.5	3.0	3.0
Papua New Guinea	12.5	10.5	2.0	3.0	0.2	3.7	3.1
Samoa	1.2	1.7	7.2	2.7	0.9	2.0	3.0
Solomon Islands	1.8	2.6	3.4	3.2	3.0	2.4	2.3
Timor-Leste	4.1	4.0	5.3	-5.4	-0.5	4.8	5.4
Tonga	2.1	3.7	3.1	2.8	0.4	2.1	1.9
Tuvalu	2.2	9.1	3.0	3.2	4.3	4.1	4.4
Vanuatu	2.3	0.2	3.5	4.4	3.2	3.0	2.8
Developing Asia	6.4	6.0	6.0	6.2	5.9	5.7	5.6
Developing Asia excluding the NIEs	6.8	6.6	6.5	6.6	6.4	6.2	6.1

Note: The newly industrialized economies (NIEs) are Hong Kong, China; the Republic of Korea; Singapore; and Taipei,China.

Table A2 Growth rate of per capita GDP (% per year)

	2014	2015	2016	2017	2018	2019	2020	Per capita GNI, $, 2017
Central Asia	3.6	1.7	1.0	2.9	3.0	3.0	2.8	
Armenia	3.9	3.5	0.6	7.9	5.5	4.6	4.9	3,990
Azerbaijan	1.5	–0.1	–4.3	–1.0	0.5	1.7	1.8	4,080
Georgia	4.4	2.6	2.7	4.7	4.7	5.0	4.9	3,780
Kazakhstan	2.7	–0.3	–0.3	2.7	2.7	2.2	1.9	7,970
Kyrgyz Republic	2.0	1.8	2.2	2.7	1.6	2.3	2.6	1,130
Tajikistan	3.9	3.6	5.2	4.5	4.9	5.3	4.1	990
Turkmenistan	9.0	5.0	4.8	5.1	4.8	4.6	4.4	6,380
Uzbekistan	6.0	6.3	4.5	2.9	3.3	3.4	3.7	2,000
East Asia	6.1	5.6	5.4	5.6	5.5	5.2	5.0	
Hong Kong, China	2.0	1.5	1.5	3.1	2.2	1.8	1.7	46,310
Mongolia	5.6	0.2	–0.9	3.3	4.9	4.7	4.3	3,270
People's Republic of China	6.8	6.4	6.1	6.2	6.1	5.8	5.6	8,690
Republic of Korea	2.7	2.2	2.5	2.7	2.3	2.2	2.2	28,380
Taipei,China	3.8	0.6	1.3	2.9	2.5	2.1	1.9	23,889
South Asia	5.4	5.9	6.1	5.5	5.3	5.3	5.4	
Afghanistan	–0.5	–1.5	–0.5	0.2	0.8	1.1	1.6	560
Bangladesh	4.6	5.1	5.7	6.0	6.6	6.7	6.6	1,470
Bhutan	2.3	4.5	5.7	4.8	4.5	4.7	5.0	2,660
India	6.1	6.6	6.8	5.8	5.6	5.8	5.9	1,800
Maldives	–3.6	–0.9	3.2	2.7	3.3	2.1	1.8	9,760
Nepal	4.5	1.9	–0.8	6.5	4.8	4.7	5.0	800
Pakistan	2.0	2.0	3.3	3.8	3.2	1.5	1.2	1,580
Sri Lanka	4.0	4.0	3.3	2.5	1.8	2.6	2.8	3,850
Southeast Asia	3.3	3.8	3.5	4.2	4.0	3.8	3.8	
Brunei Darussalam	–3.5	–1.6	–3.6	0.4	–1.9	0.0	0.5	29,600
Cambodia	5.9	5.7	5.6	4.5	5.8	4.4	4.2	1,230
Indonesia	3.7	4.5	3.7	3.8	3.9	4.0	4.1	3,540
Lao People's Dem. Rep.	6.1	5.7	5.5	5.4	5.0	5.0	6.5	2,270
Malaysia	3.3	3.5	2.7	4.6	3.6	2.9	3.3	9,650
Myanmar	10.1	6.1	4.9	5.8	5.3	5.6	5.9	1,210
Philippines	4.4	4.9	4.5	5.0	4.5	4.8	4.8	3,660
Singapore	2.8	1.3	1.5	3.8	2.7	1.5	1.2	54,530
Thailand	0.5	2.2	3.0	3.6	3.8	3.5	3.3	5,950
Viet Nam	4.9	5.5	5.1	5.8	6.1	5.8	5.7	2,160
The Pacific	6.9	5.4	0.0	0.0	–1.5	1.1	0.8	
Cook Islands	3.2	3.9	1.7	7.3	7.5	6.6	5.0	15,522
Federated States of Micronesia	–2.2	5.1	0.9	2.6	2.3	2.9	2.7	3,620
Fiji	5.0	3.3	0.1	2.6	2.4	2.6	2.9	4,970
Kiribati	–2.0	8.9	3.9	–0.9	1.1	1.1	1.1	3,010
Marshall Islands	–1.1	–1.0	1.4	3.2	0.2	–1.6	–1.7	4,840
Nauru	34.8	–10.9	5.5	1.0	0.8	–1.0	0.1	10,220
Palau	2.0	9.3	–0.5	–4.7	–0.5	2.0	2.0	12,700
Papua New Guinea	9.1	7.2	–1.0	–0.1	–2.8	0.6	0.0	2,340
Samoa	0.4	0.8	6.2	1.9	0.0	1.2	2.2	4,090
Solomon Islands	–0.7	0.0	1.9	0.4	0.2	–0.4	–0.5	1,920
Timor-Leste	2.3	2.0	3.4	–7.0	–2.3	2.9	3.5	1,790
Tonga	1.6	3.5	2.9	2.5	0.2	1.8	1.6	4,010
Tuvalu	3.9	10.9	4.7	2.7	3.8	3.6	3.9	4,970
Vanuatu	–0.1	–2.1	–0.9	1.9	0.7	0.5	0.3	2,920
Developing Asia	5.5	5.3	5.2	5.4	5.2	5.0	4.9	
Developing Asia excluding NIEs	6.0	5.9	5.7	5.7	5.6	5.4	5.3	

GNI = gross national income.
Note: The newly industrialized economies (NIEs) are Hong Kong, China; the Republic of Korea; Singapore; and Taipei,China.

Table A3 Growth rate of value added in agriculture (% per year)

	2014	2015	2016	2017	2018	Sector share, 2017, %
Central Asia						
Armenia	6.1	13.2	−5.0	−5.3	−8.5	16.3
Azerbaijan	−2.6	6.6	2.6	4.2	4.6	6.1
Georgia	1.6	1.6	0.3	−3.8	0.4	8.0
Kazakhstan	1.3	3.5	5.4	3.2	3.4	4.6
Kyrgyz Republic	−0.5	6.2	2.9	2.2	2.7	14.4
Tajikistan	4.5	3.2	5.2	6.8	4.0	24.0
Turkmenistan	4.2	7.9	9.0	5.9	4.8	11.1
Uzbekistan	6.9	6.8	6.8	1.2	0.2	34.0
East Asia						
Hong Kong, China	−6.0	−6.8	−2.0	−5.2	−1.6	0.1
Mongolia	13.7	10.7	6.2	1.8	4.5	10.3
People's Republic of China	4.1	3.9	3.3	4.0	3.5	7.4
Republic of Korea	3.6	−0.4	−2.8	0.3	1.5	2.2
Taipei,China	0.5	−7.5	−10.1	8.3	2.0	1.8
South Asia						
Afghanistan	−0.1	−5.7	6.0	3.8	2.0	18.9
Bangladesh	4.4	3.3	2.8	3.0	4.2	14.2
Bhutan	2.4	3.7	4.4	3.6	4.5	17.9
India	−0.2	0.6	6.3	5.0	2.7	17.2
Maldives	−0.3	−0.4	1.5	8.3	9.4	6.6
Nepal	4.5	1.1	0.2	5.2	2.8	28.8
Pakistan	2.5	2.1	0.2	2.1	3.8	24.4
Sri Lanka	4.6	4.7	−3.7	−0.4	4.8	8.6
Southeast Asia						
Brunei Darussalam	4.7	6.4	−3.6	−1.7	−2.4	1.1
Cambodia	0.3	0.2	1.3	1.7	1.8	25.0
Indonesia	4.2	3.8	3.4	3.9	3.9	13.7
Lao People's Dem. Rep.	4.1	3.6	2.8	2.9	2.0	18.3
Malaysia	2.0	1.4	−5.2	7.2	−0.4	8.9
Myanmar	2.8	3.4	−0.5	1.3	2.0	23.3
Philippines	1.7	0.1	−1.2	4.0	0.8	9.7
Singapore	7.2	−6.8	−1.9	−12.1	0.1	0.0
Thailand	−0.3	−6.5	−1.3	3.7	5.0	8.3
Viet Nam	3.4	2.4	1.4	2.9	3.8	16.7
The Pacific						
Cook Islands	−29.8	−1.5	−4.5	2.5	0.3	3.2
Federated States of Micronesia	6.0	10.7	...	...	...	...
Fiji	0.7	6.3	−5.1	4.8	2.0	10.9
Kiribati	5.9	−0.8	...	...	...	...
Marshall Islands	−1.5	0.5	−2.4	5.3	...	16.4
Nauru	9.5	5.2	...	...	...	...
Palau	−5.9	−3.6	7.8	8.8	...	3.5
Papua New Guinea	3.3	2.2	3.4	1.8	3.3	17.8
Samoa	9.6	−0.3	8.1	8.9	−10.5	10.9
Solomon Islands	5.8	2.4	5.8	1.9	3.6	26.9
Timor-Leste	−3.1	−4.3	3.0	...	...	...
Tonga	3.1	...	...	...	...	...
Tuvalu	...	...	...	...	...	...
Vanuatu	4.2	−15.8	5.1	0.4	−2.9	23.1

... = data not available.

Table A4 Growth rate of value added in industry (% per year)

	2014	2015	2016	2017	2018	Sector share, 2017, %
Central Asia						
Armenia	-2.3	2.8	-0.3	5.4	3.4	27.6
Azerbaijan	0.5	-1.9	-5.9	-3.6	-0.4	53.5
Georgia	4.6	4.1	6.0	6.4	2.3	26.5
Kazakhstan	1.9	0.3	2.0	6.1	4.2	34.3
Kyrgyz Republic	5.7	2.9	7.1	8.6	6.2	31.4
Tajikistan	5.1	11.2	16.0	21.3	11.8	19.5
Turkmenistan	11.4	3.1	2.5	5.4	6.0	47.0
Uzbekistan	8.0	8.4	5.6	5.4	10.5	27.9
East Asia						
Hong Kong, China	8.1	2.7	3.1	-0.7	0.2	7.5
Mongolia	12.7	9.9	-0.4	0.4	6.2	38.3
People's Republic of China	7.4	6.2	6.3	5.9	5.8	46.5
Republic of Korea	3.1	2.4	3.3	4.6	2.5	39.6
Taipei,China	7.0	-0.2	2.7	4.7	3.3	36.6
South Asia						
Afghanistan	2.8	4.2	-0.8	0.4	2.0	24.4
Bangladesh	8.2	9.7	11.1	10.2	12.1	29.3
Bhutan	3.8	6.0	7.6	4.6	2.6	43.0
India	7.0	9.6	7.7	5.9	7.7	29.3
Maldives	16.2	18.1	12.3	10.9	12.9	14.9
Nepal	7.1	1.4	-6.4	12.4	8.8	14.7
Pakistan	4.5	5.2	5.7	5.4	5.8	19.1
Sri Lanka	4.7	2.2	5.7	4.1	0.9	30.1
Southeast Asia						
Brunei Darussalam	-4.4	0.0	-2.9	1.5	-0.6	58.7
Cambodia	10.1	11.7	10.3	9.7	10.8	32.7
Indonesia	4.2	3.0	3.8	4.1	4.3	41.0
Lao People's Dem. Rep.	7.3	7.0	12.0	11.6	7.9	34.9
Malaysia	6.0	5.3	4.2	4.9	3.4	36.7
Myanmar	12.1	8.3	8.9	9.4	8.7	36.3
Philippines	7.8	6.4	8.0	7.2	6.8	30.5
Singapore	3.6	-2.7	2.7	5.7	5.0	25.2
Thailand	0.0	3.0	2.7	1.8	2.7	35.3
Viet Nam	6.4	9.6	7.6	8.0	8.9	39.5
The Pacific						
Cook Islands	-3.9	19.6	-13.6	11.1	10.9	7.8
Federated States of Micronesia	-28.4	-6.1	...	...	...	...
Fiji	1.9	3.3	2.3	1.8	2.3	18.1
Kiribati	5.6	13.7	...	...	...	...
Marshall Islands	-12.9	-4.0	16.3	13.2	...	13.5
Nauru	-3.6	-17.1	...	...	...	...
Palau	4.7	30.4	13.2	-8.2	...	8.9
Papua New Guinea	36.7	31.2	4.5	6.0	-4.2	40.1
Samoa	3.8	-6.2	7.3	-1.8	-2.5	22.2
Solomon Islands	-13.0	-5.0	0.9	-0.3	1.2	14.3
Timor-Leste	-10.9	22.2	7.6	...	...	...
Tonga	1.3	...	...	...	...	...
Tuvalu	...	...	...	...	...	...
Vanuatu	3.2	35.4	4.2	7.1	7.4	11.0

... = data not available.

Table A5 Growth rate of value added in services (% per year)

	2014	2015	2016	2017	2018	Sector share, 2017, %
Central Asia						
Armenia	6.7	1.0	3.4	12.1	9.6	56.1
Azerbaijan	7.4	4.5	-0.7	3.5	3.5	40.4
Georgia	4.6	3.1	2.4	5.1	5.9	65.5
Kazakhstan	5.7	3.1	0.9	2.4	4.0	61.1
Kyrgyz Republic	4.6	3.7	3.4	3.3	2.1	54.2
Tajikistan	1.0	-7.1	-0.3	1.8	2.1	56.6
Turkmenistan	10.6	10.0	10.8	7.9	6.8	41.9
Uzbekistan	8.5	8.4	6.6	6.4	5.4	38.1
East Asia						
Hong Kong, China	2.5	1.7	2.3	3.6	3.4	92.4
Mongolia	7.8	0.6	1.1	7.9	5.3	51.4
People's Republic of China	7.8	8.2	7.7	7.9	7.6	46.1
Republic of Korea	3.3	2.8	2.5	2.1	2.8	58.3
Taipei,China	2.8	1.7	1.2	2.5	2.6	61.6
South Asia						
Afghanistan	4.5	2.1	2.0	2.5	2.5	56.7
Bangladesh	5.6	5.8	6.2	6.7	6.4	56.5
Bhutan	5.0	8.4	9.2	8.2	8.0	39.1
India	9.8	9.4	8.4	8.1	7.4	53.5
Maldives	7.0	2.4	6.7	5.2	5.6	78.5
Nepal	6.2	4.6	2.4	7.4	6.6	56.6
Pakistan	4.5	4.4	5.7	6.5	6.4	56.5
Sri Lanka	4.8	6.0	4.8	3.6	4.7	61.4
Southeast Asia						
Brunei Darussalam	0.6	-1.2	-1.6	1.1	-1.6	40.2
Cambodia	8.7	7.1	6.8	7.0	6.9	42.3
Indonesia	6.0	5.5	5.7	5.7	5.8	45.4
Lao People's Dem. Rep.	8.1	8.0	4.7	4.5	7.4	46.8
Malaysia	6.6	5.3	5.7	6.2	6.8	54.4
Myanmar	9.1	8.7	8.1	8.3	6.8	40.4
Philippines	6.0	6.9	7.5	6.8	6.6	59.9
Singapore	4.6	3.9	2.4	3.3	3.0	74.8
Thailand	2.0	5.2	4.6	5.8	5.1	56.4
Viet Nam	6.2	6.3	7.0	7.4	7.0	43.8
The Pacific						
Cook Islands	19.2	3.7	7.9	9.5	6.5	89.0
Federated States of Micronesia	-1.4	3.0	...	...	...	...
Fiji	7.4	3.6	1.2	3.1	3.3	71.0
Kiribati	-0.2	6.5	...	...	...	...
Marshall Islands	2.6	1.7	1.0	3.7	...	70.2
Nauru	41.9	11.6	...	...	...	...
Palau	5.8	9.1	-0.7	-2.8	...	87.6
Papua New Guinea	0.2	0.3	0.6	1.2	3.8	42.1
Samoa	-1.1	5.2	6.9	3.4	3.7	66.9
Solomon Islands	3.9	5.0	3.3	5.3	3.5	58.7
Timor-Leste	7.5	4.9	5.9	...	...	...
Tonga	1.6	...	...	...	...	...
Tuvalu	...	...	...	...	...	...
Vanuatu	2.4	2.0	2.9	2.9	3.1	65.9

... = data not available.

Table A6 Inflation (% per year)

	2014	2015	2016	2017	2018	2019	2020
Central Asia	5.9	6.4	10.3	9.0	7.9	7.8	7.2
Armenia	3.0	3.7	-1.4	1.0	2.5	3.5	3.2
Azerbaijan	1.4	4.0	12.4	12.9	2.3	4.0	5.0
Georgia	3.1	4.0	2.1	6.0	2.6	3.2	3.0
Kazakhstan	6.7	6.6	14.6	7.4	6.0	6.0	5.5
Kyrgyz Republic	7.5	6.5	0.4	3.2	1.5	3.0	3.5
Tajikistan	6.1	5.1	6.1	6.7	5.4	7.5	7.0
Turkmenistan	6.0	7.4	3.6	8.0	9.4	9.0	8.2
Uzbekistan	9.1	8.4	8.0	13.7	17.9	16.0	14.0
East Asia	1.9	1.3	1.9	1.6	2.0	1.8	1.8
Hong Kong, China	4.4	3.0	2.4	1.5	2.4	2.3	2.3
Mongolia	12.8	3.3	1.1	4.3	6.8	8.5	7.5
People's Republic of China	2.0	1.4	2.0	1.6	2.1	1.9	1.8
Republic of Korea	1.3	0.7	1.0	1.9	1.5	1.4	1.4
Taipei,China	1.2	-0.3	1.4	0.6	1.3	1.1	1.2
South Asia	6.2	4.9	4.5	3.9	3.7	4.7	4.9
Afghanistan	4.7	-0.7	4.4	5.0	0.6	3.0	4.5
Bangladesh	7.3	6.4	5.9	5.4	5.8	5.5	5.8
Bhutan	9.6	6.6	3.3	4.3	3.6	3.8	4.0
India	5.9	4.9	4.5	3.6	3.5	4.3	4.6
Maldives	2.1	1.0	0.5	2.8	-0.1	1.0	1.5
Nepal	9.1	7.2	9.9	4.5	4.2	4.4	5.1
Pakistan	8.6	4.5	2.9	4.2	3.9	7.5	7.0
Sri Lanka	3.3	3.8	4.0	7.7	2.1	3.5	4.0
Southeast Asia	4.0	2.7	2.0	2.8	2.7	2.6	2.7
Brunei Darussalam	-0.2	-0.4	-0.7	-0.2	0.1	0.2	0.2
Cambodia	3.9	1.2	3.0	2.9	2.5	2.5	2.5
Indonesia	6.4	6.4	3.5	3.8	3.2	3.2	3.3
Lao People's Dem. Rep.	4.1	1.3	1.6	0.8	2.0	2.0	2.0
Malaysia	3.1	2.1	2.1	3.8	1.0	2.0	2.7
Myanmar	5.1	10.0	6.8	4.0	7.1	6.8	7.5
Philippines	3.6	0.7	1.3	2.9	5.2	3.8	3.5
Singapore	1.0	-0.5	-0.5	0.6	0.4	0.7	0.9
Thailand	1.9	-0.9	0.2	0.7	1.1	1.0	1.0
Viet Nam	4.1	0.6	2.7	3.5	3.5	3.5	3.8
The Pacific	3.8	4.2	4.7	4.2	4.0	3.7	4.0
Cook Islands	1.6	3.0	-0.1	-0.1	0.4	1.0	1.5
Federated States of Micronesia	0.7	0.0	-0.9	0.1	1.0	0.7	1.5
Fiji	0.5	1.4	3.9	3.3	4.1	3.5	3.0
Kiribati	2.1	0.6	1.9	0.4	2.1	2.3	2.2
Marshall Islands	1.1	-2.3	-1.5	0.0	0.7	0.5	1.0
Nauru	0.3	9.8	8.2	5.1	3.8	2.5	2.0
Palau	4.0	2.2	-1.3	0.9	1.1	0.5	1.5
Papua New Guinea	5.2	6.0	6.7	5.4	4.5	4.2	4.7
Samoa	-1.2	1.9	0.1	1.4	3.7	2.0	1.5
Solomon Islands	5.2	-0.5	1.1	0.1	3.3	2.5	2.5
Timor-Leste	0.7	0.6	-1.3	0.6	2.1	3.0	3.3
Tonga	2.5	-1.0	2.6	7.4	5.3	5.3	5.3
Tuvalu	1.1	4.0	2.6	4.4	1.8	3.4	3.5
Vanuatu	1.0	2.5	0.8	3.1	2.2	2.0	2.0
Developing Asia	2.9	2.1	2.4	2.2	2.5	2.5	2.5
Developing Asia excluding the NIEs	3.2	2.4	2.6	2.3	2.6	2.6	2.6

Note: The newly industrialized economies (NIEs) are Hong Kong, China; the Republic of Korea; Singapore; and Taipei,China.

Table A7 Change in money supply (% per year)

	2014	2015	2016	2017	2018
Central Asia					
Armenia	8.3	10.8	17.5	18.5	7.4
Azerbaijan	11.8	-1.1	-2.0	9.0	5.7
Georgia	13.8	19.3	20.2	14.8	14.7
Kazakhstan	10.4	33.8	15.6	-1.7	7.0
Kyrgyz Republic	3.0	14.9	14.6	17.9	5.5
Tajikistan	7.1	18.7	37.1	21.8	5.1
Turkmenistan	11.4	16.1	9.4	11.4	8.8
Uzbekistan	14.9	25.2	23.5	40.2	14.4
East Asia					
Hong Kong, China	9.5	5.5	7.7	10.0	4.3
Mongolia	24.7	-1.3	10.5	24.2	26.5
People's Republic of China	11.0	13.3	11.3	8.2	8.9
Republic of Korea	8.1	8.2	7.1	5.1	6.7
Taipei,China	6.1	5.8	3.6	3.6	2.7
South Asia					
Afghanistan	8.1	3.1	9.7	4.1	9.0
Bangladesh	16.1	12.4	16.3	10.9	9.2
Bhutan	26.0	3.8	23.0	17.4	...
India	10.9	10.1	10.1	9.2	10.8
Maldives	14.9	12.1	-0.2	5.2	3.4
Nepal	19.1	19.9	19.5	15.5	19.4
Pakistan	12.5	13.2	13.7	13.7	9.7
Sri Lanka	13.4	17.8	18.4	16.7	13.0
Southeast Asia					
Brunei Darussalam	3.2	-1.8	1.5	-0.4	2.8
Cambodia	29.9	14.7	17.9	23.8	24.0
Indonesia	11.9	9.0	10.0	8.3	6.3
Lao People's Dem. Rep.	23.5	14.7	10.9	12.2	8.4
Malaysia	7.3	3.0	3.2	4.9	8.0
Myanmar	17.6	26.3	19.4	18.0	18.0
Philippines	11.2	9.4	12.8	11.9	9.2
Singapore	3.3	1.5	8.0	3.2	3.9
Thailand	4.6	4.4	4.2	5.0	4.7
Viet Nam	17.7	16.2	18.4	15.0	12.0
The Pacific					
Cook Islands	3.0	9.6	-2.7	12.3	14.8
Federated States of Micronesia	...	...	...	...	...
Fiji	10.6	14.3	4.6	8.5	2.1
Kiribati	...	...	...	...	...
Marshall Islands	...	...	...	...	...
Nauru	...	...	...	...	...
Palau	...	...	...	...	...
Papua New Guinea	3.4	8.1	10.9	-0.7	-8.0
Samoa	18.7	0.6	7.1	7.8	16.5
Solomon Islands	5.5	15.0	13.4	3.5	6.0
Timor-Leste	19.9	7.1	14.2	12.1	3.1
Tonga	7.9	2.4	12.6	...	...
Tuvalu	...	...	...	...	...
Vanuatu	8.6	11.3	10.7	9.3	14.2

... = data not available.

Table A8 Central government revenue (% of GDP)

	2014	2015	2016	2017	2018
Central Asia					
Armenia	23.7	23.2	23.1	22.2	22.3
Azerbaijan	31.2	31.5	29.0	23.5	28.1
Georgia	27.9	28.2	28.4	28.9	28.6
Kazakhstan	18.5	18.7	19.8	21.8	18.4
Kyrgyz Republic	29.8	29.8	27.4	28.2	27.2
Tajikistan	30.9	31.0	30.4	30.6	30.0
Turkmenistan	17.9	16.6	11.7	14.9	14.4
Uzbekistan	32.0	30.7	29.6	23.7	26.7
East Asia					
Hong Kong, China	20.8	18.6	22.6	22.8	21.0
Mongolia	28.4	25.8	24.4	28.5	31.3
People's Republic of China	21.9	22.2	21.6	21.0	20.4
Republic of Korea	17.1	17.3	18.1	18.7	18.3
Taipei,China	10.7	11.3	11.1	11.0	10.8
South Asia					
Afghanistan	24.0	24.6	26.1	25.3	26.4
Bangladesh	10.4	9.6	10.0	10.2	9.6
Bhutan	33.6	28.8	29.9	27.2	32.2
India	19.2	20.3	20.9	20.5	21.3
Maldives	26.7	27.4	27.4	27.1	25.8
Nepal	20.6	20.8	23.1	24.3	25.4
Pakistan	15.8	15.3	16.7	16.6	16.4
Sri Lanka	11.6	13.3	14.1	13.7	13.4
Southeast Asia					
Brunei Darussalam	34.4	21.7	19.5	22.5	21.1
Cambodia	17.1	16.8	17.6	18.9	17.8
Indonesia	14.7	13.1	12.5	12.3	13.2
Lao People's Dem. Rep.	21.0	17.9	16.4	16.2	15.7
Malaysia	19.9	18.9	17.3	16.3	16.5
Myanmar	25.0	21.5	20.3	18.5	21.1
Philippines	15.1	15.8	15.2	15.6	16.4
Singapore	15.3	15.4	15.8	16.3	15.1
Thailand	15.8	16.2	16.8	15.5	15.7
Viet Nam	22.3	23.8	24.6	24.8	24.5
The Pacific					
Cook Islands	41.0	39.0	39.1	47.9	47.2
Federated States of Micronesia	65.7	66.3	69.1	79.0	...
Fiji	27.3	30.0	29.8	27.8	30.6
Kiribati	143.4	151.1	118.2	130.9	123.0
Marshall Islands	52.6	59.8	61.9	70.0	98.8
Nauru	76.8	81.2	107.0	112.2	113.6
Palau	43.4	39.2	41.0	39.5	40.3
Papua New Guinea	21.0	17.7	15.5	15.2	16.3
Samoa	29.8	27.4	29.0	28.9	29.2
Solomon Islands	43.4	44.8	39.8	40.4	43.4
Timor-Leste	175.7	104.0	57.3	66.2	75.0
Tonga	27.5	26.2	40.6	42.5	44.4
Tuvalu	130.7	147.2	176.5	142.5	138.2
Vanuatu	23.2	31.9	30.8	34.8	36.2

... = data not available.

Table A9 Central government expenditure (% of GDP)

	2014	2015	2016	2017	2018
Central Asia					
Armenia	25.6	27.9	28.6	27.0	24.1
Azerbaijan	31.7	32.7	29.4	25.1	28.5
Georgia	29.8	29.3	29.8	29.7	29.4
Kazakhstan	21.2	20.9	21.4	24.5	19.8
Kyrgyz Republic	30.3	31.3	31.8	31.3	28.3
Tajikistan	28.4	32.9	32.7	35.7	34.8
Turkmenistan	17.0	17.3	14.1	17.7	15.3
Uzbekistan	31.0	30.8	29.5	23.0	26.2
East Asia					
Hong Kong, China	17.3	18.0	18.2	17.3	18.9
Mongolia	32.1	30.8	39.8	32.3	28.7
People's Republic of China	23.7	25.6	25.4	24.7	24.5
Republic of Korea	19.1	19.7	19.5	19.8	18.3
Taipei,China	11.5	11.4	11.4	11.0	11.1
South Asia					
Afghanistan	25.7	25.9	26.0	25.9	26.8
Bangladesh	14.0	13.5	13.8	13.6	13.5
Bhutan	29.8	27.3	31.0	30.6	32.9
India	26.3	27.3	27.5	27.5	27.9
Maldives	29.1	34.0	37.3	30.1	31.3
Nepal	20.0	21.8	23.6	29.3	34.0
Pakistan	20.0	19.6	19.9	21.3	21.8
Sri Lanka	17.3	20.9	19.5	19.2	18.6
Southeast Asia					
Brunei Darussalam	35.4	37.1	37.8	35.7	29.8
Cambodia	20.9	19.4	20.5	22.0	22.9
Indonesia	16.8	15.7	15.0	14.8	14.9
Lao People's Dem. Rep.	23.8	22.4	21.5	21.9	20.3
Malaysia	23.3	22.1	20.4	19.3	20.3
Myanmar	26.1	25.7	22.9	21.1	25.6
Philippines	15.7	16.7	17.6	17.9	19.6
Singapore	14.3	16.0	16.2	15.8	16.2
Thailand	18.3	18.5	19.1	18.4	17.9
Viet Nam	26.4	28.2	26.8	28.2	28.2
The Pacific					
Cook Islands	41.1	40.5	35.4	35.4	43.0
Federated States of Micronesia	54.5	55.9	61.8	64.4	...
Fiji	31.5	32.0	33.9	30.1	35.8
Kiribati	118.8	102.1	114.8	119.0	143.1
Marshall Islands	49.4	57.0	57.9	65.5	98.8
Nauru	51.9	72.3	85.0	93.2	105.0
Palau	39.8	34.3	37.5	34.9	36.0
Papua New Guinea	27.3	22.2	20.0	17.6	18.6
Samoa	35.0	31.3	29.4	30.0	29.1
Solomon Islands	43.8	47.3	42.9	44.2	44.0
Timor-Leste	110.5	96.9	104.6	84.4	79.9
Tonga	25.7	29.1	41.1	40.4	42.8
Tuvalu	101.2	121.9	155.9	128.9	104.4
Vanuatu	22.0	24.4	28.4	29.8	29.5

... = data not available.

Table A10 Fiscal balance of central government (% of GDP)

	2014	2015	2016	2017	2018
Central Asia					
Armenia	-1.9	-4.8	-5.5	-4.8	-1.8
Azerbaijan	-0.5	-1.2	-0.4	-1.6	-0.4
Georgia	-2.0	-1.1	-1.4	-0.9	-0.8
Kazakhstan	-2.7	-2.2	-1.6	-2.7	-1.4
Kyrgyz Republic	-0.5	-1.4	-4.4	-3.1	-1.1
Tajikistan	2.5	-1.9	-2.3	-5.1	-4.8
Turkmenistan	0.9	-0.7	-2.4	-2.8	-0.9
Uzbekistan	1.0	-0.1	0.1	0.7	0.5
East Asia					
Hong Kong, China	3.6	0.6	4.4	5.5	2.1
Mongolia	-3.7	-5.0	-15.4	-3.8	2.6
People's Republic of China	-1.8	-3.4	-3.8	-3.7	-4.2
Republic of Korea	-2.0	-2.4	-1.4	-1.1	-1.6
Taipei,China	-0.8	-0.1	-0.3	0.0	-0.3
South Asia					
Afghanistan	-1.7	-1.4	0.1	-0.6	-0.4
Bangladesh	-3.6	-3.9	-3.8	-3.5	-3.9
Bhutan	3.8	1.5	-1.1	-3.4	-0.7
India	-4.1	-3.8	-3.5	-3.5	-3.4
Maldives	-2.4	-6.5	-9.9	-3.0	-5.5
Nepal	1.8	0.8	1.3	-3.2	-6.7
Pakistan	-4.2	-4.3	-3.3	-4.7	-5.4
Sri Lanka	-5.7	-7.6	-5.3	-5.5	-5.3
Southeast Asia					
Brunei Darussalam	-1.0	-15.4	-18.3	-13.2	-8.6
Cambodia	-3.8	-2.6	-2.8	-3.1	-5.1
Indonesia	-2.1	-2.6	-2.5	-2.5	-1.7
Lao People's Dem. Rep.	-2.8	-4.5	-5.2	-5.6	-4.6
Malaysia	-3.4	-3.2	-3.1	-3.0	-3.7
Myanmar	-1.1	-4.3	-2.6	-2.5	-4.5
Philippines	-0.6	-0.9	-2.4	-2.2	-3.2
Singapore	0.1	-1.0	1.4	2.3	0.4
Thailand	-2.5	-2.5	-2.7	-2.7	-2.5
Viet Nam	-4.1	-4.4	-2.2	-3.5	-3.7
The Pacific					
Cook Islands	-0.1	-1.6	3.7	9.2	4.2
Federated States of Micronesia	11.2	10.4	7.3	14.6	10.0
Fiji	-4.2	-2.0	-4.1	-2.3	-5.3
Kiribati	24.6	49.0	3.4	11.9	-20.1
Marshall Islands	3.2	2.8	4.0	4.5	3.0
Nauru	24.9	8.9	21.9	19.0	8.5
Palau	3.6	4.9	3.5	4.6	4.3
Papua New Guinea	-6.3	-4.5	-4.6	-2.4	-2.3
Samoa	-5.3	-3.9	-0.4	-1.1	0.1
Solomon Islands	-0.4	-2.4	-3.2	-3.8	-0.6
Timor-Leste	65.1	7.2	-47.4	-18.2	-4.8
Tonga	1.7	-2.9	-0.4	2.1	1.6
Tuvalu	29.5	25.3	20.6	13.6	33.9
Vanuatu	1.2	7.5	2.5	5.1	6.7

Table A11 Growth rate of merchandise exports (% per year)

	2014	2015	2016	2017	2018	2019	2020
Central Asia	−6.4	−34.6	−15.7	22.4	19.2	6.2	7.8
Armenia	3.8	−4.4	16.4	26.2	8.5	6.0	8.5
Azerbaijan	−11.1	−44.8	−15.2	14.7	13.0	−7.5	1.0
Georgia	−1.7	−22.9	−4.2	29.5	22.9	7.6	7.2
Kazakhstan	−6.2	−42.1	−19.9	32.7	25.2	6.0	7.0
Kyrgyz Republic	−12.4	−34.8	−0.7	12.8	0.8	10.0	10.0
Tajikistan	−16.0	−8.9	0.8	9.4	−10.4	5.0	10.0
Turkmenistan	2.0	−37.1	−38.2	3.6	29.0	14.0	10.0
Uzbekistan	−7.8	−13.3	−5.4	16.3	11.4	10.0	12.0
East Asia	3.6	−5.5	−6.9	11.6	8.9	2.1	2.4
Hong Kong, China	1.6	−2.4	0.0	7.8	5.2	4.8	4.5
Mongolia	44.2	−18.7	8.0	21.4	12.4	19.2	−2.3
People's Republic of China	4.4	−4.5	−7.2	11.4	9.1	1.3	1.8
Republic of Korea	−0.8	−11.5	−5.7	13.4	7.8	6.0	5.5
Taipei,China	−0.8	−11.1	−8.0	12.9	10.2	5.8	5.7
South Asia	0.9	−12.8	3.6	8.8	9.0	7.8	7.5
Afghanistan	26.8	−9.9	6.7	28.6	11.9	7.3	9.6
Bangladesh	12.1	3.1	8.9	1.7	6.4	14.0	15.0
Bhutan	−2.0	8.4	−14.7	12.3	7.6	2.7	5.5
India	−0.6	−15.9	5.2	10.3	8.9	8.0	7.0
Maldives	−9.1	−20.3	6.8	24.3	−1.6	5.0	9.0
Nepal	5.1	−3.9	−28.7	12.1	15.4	7.0	9.2
Pakistan	1.1	−3.9	−8.8	0.1	12.8	3.0	6.0
Sri Lanka	7.1	−5.2	−2.2	10.2	4.7	4.0	5.0
Southeast Asia	1.2	−11.3	−1.8	15.3	8.1	5.4	5.7
Brunei Darussalam	−6.1	−44.9	−21.4	13.8	20.1	5.0	12.2
Cambodia	16.0	14.3	10.0	9.3	18.3	16.0	15.0
Indonesia	−3.7	−14.9	−3.1	16.9	7.0	5.3	5.5
Lao People's Dem. Rep.	22.8	−12.9	9.3	19.5	10.0	12.0	12.0
Malaysia	2.5	−15.9	−5.1	13.3	10.5	2.5	4.0
Myanmar	−7.8	−8.5	−0.4	10.5	19.0	10.0	12.0
Philippines	11.9	−13.3	−1.1	21.2	−0.3	6.3	5.2
Singapore	−2.0	−12.6	−5.4	9.7	12.7	2.8	5.0
Thailand	−0.4	−5.6	0.1	9.8	7.7	5.0	4.5
Viet Nam	13.8	7.9	8.9	21.2	13.8	10.0	10.0
The Pacific	33.3	−5.0	0.2	12.6	6.3	4.5	2.0
Cook Islands	141.8	−17.0	−0.4	−16.4	91.7	−5.8	5.1
Federated States of Micronesia	−23.9	4.4	24.7	11.0	...	...	...
Fiji	5.1	−19.5	−4.4	6.8	2.4	6.0	6.0
Kiribati	42.3	−18.5	15.8	−11.5	23.0	...	...
Marshall Islands	−15.0	−9.0	−27.4	30.2	...	...	...
Nauru	−22.0	−55.2	20.0	−3.0	4.9	−1.7	−1.2
Palau	6.2	−7.3	−3.2	−12.6	13.0	13.5	0.8
Papua New Guinea	48.3	−4.6	−3.1	21.6	1.8	3.2	−0.7
Samoa	−8.8	6.6	42.4	0.2	−3.3	...	...
Solomon Islands	1.6	−7.5	2.6	8.6	20.2	−9.6	1.8
Timor-Leste	−9.5	12.5	11.1	−17.2	48.6	21.9	16.7
Tonga	19.3	8.4	24.2	−56.5	−15.4	...	...
Tuvalu	−2.4	−4.3	3.5	11.5	4.9	...	...
Vanuatu	36.1	−16.6	−0.9	−7.6	−21.8	0.6	3.7
Developing Asia	2.7	−8.0	−4.8	11.8	9.0	3.5	3.7
Developing Asia excluding the NIEs	3.2	−7.6	−4.7	11.8	9.0	3.2	3.5

... = data not available.

Note: The newly industrialized economies (NIEs) are Hong Kong, China; the Republic of Korea; Singapore; and Taipei,China.

Table A12 Growth rate of merchandise imports (% per year)

	2014	2015	2016	2017	2018	2019	2020
Central Asia	-9.1	-15.2	-10.1	6.8	12.0	6.0	8.3
Armenia	-2.0	-25.1	0.9	32.6	18.5	8.2	6.5
Azerbaijan	-16.3	4.7	-7.9	0.4	-6.0	-19.9	11.1
Georgia	7.2	-15.1	-0.1	8.8	14.9	4.3	7.1
Kazakhstan	-13.3	-23.2	-17.1	14.4	7.5	5.0	5.0
Kyrgyz Republic	-5.8	-27.0	-3.0	12.1	8.2	14.0	12.0
Tajikistan	5.3	-20.8	-11.5	-8.5	13.5	-5.0	0.0
Turkmenistan	1.8	-7.5	-6.2	-22.7	-8.6	6.2	0.5
Uzbekistan	-2.5	-10.9	-2.7	7.8	43.8	25.0	20.0
East Asia	0.6	-14.0	-4.6	15.9	15.1	3.5	3.8
Hong Kong, China	2.3	-4.0	-1.2	8.7	6.7	6.3	6.0
Mongolia	-17.5	-26.6	-10.8	25.3	35.1	7.9	6.2
People's Republic of China	1.1	-13.4	-4.2	16.0	16.2	2.9	3.4
Republic of Korea	-2.0	-19.8	-6.5	18.0	10.0	6.5	6.0
Taipei,China	-2.7	-17.2	-9.3	12.4	9.1	6.7	6.6
South Asia	0.4	-10.8	-0.5	18.2	11.5	7.4	7.8
Afghanistan	-19.4	8.2	-13.5	7.8	4.3	2.1	2.3
Bangladesh	8.9	3.0	5.9	9.0	25.2	10.0	12.0
Bhutan	0.5	8.8	5.0	-3.4	-1.2	-7.9	-1.3
India	-1.0	-14.1	-1.0	19.5	9.8	8.0	8.0
Maldives	15.1	-3.4	10.6	6.3	16.1	15.0	18.0
Nepal	14.0	8.0	-7.1	26.8	26.8	18.5	10.7
Pakistan	3.8	-0.7	-0.3	18.0	15.0	1.0	4.0
Sri Lanka	7.9	-2.5	1.3	9.4	6.0	3.0	5.0
Southeast Asia	-1.8	-11.5	-0.4	15.3	15.1	6.3	6.9
Brunei Darussalam	-25.3	-12.3	-17.3	15.5	35.7	8.0	13.3
Cambodia	12.6	10.5	6.3	9.8	20.1	12.5	12.0
Indonesia	-4.5	-19.7	-4.4	16.2	20.7	5.8	6.3
Lao People's Dem. Rep.	9.1	-5.8	-11.4	8.1	2.8	13.5	8.0
Malaysia	0.6	-15.2	-3.7	13.8	10.4	2.2	3.7
Myanmar	-14.5	10.6	2.4	9.3	5.5	8.0	12.0
Philippines	8.0	-1.0	17.7	17.6	9.4	8.2	9.0
Singapore	-4.5	-17.0	-5.6	11.1	14.3	5.2	5.9
Thailand	-7.9	-10.6	-5.1	13.2	14.3	6.5	6.0
Viet Nam	12.0	12.0	7.0	22.3	11.5	10.5	10.7
The Pacific	-18.0	-24.1	-13.2	32.5	-9.9	13.5	29.7
Cook Islands	7.9	-5.8	-4.9	11.4	15.2	-4.9	6.1
Federated States of Micronesia	-13.0	7.8	-4.6	9.6	...	...	...
Fiji	-3.2	-15.8	2.5	7.9	1.0	3.5	4.0
Kiribati	2.8	2.8	7.4	9.7	4.9	...	...
Marshall Islands	-10.4	-9.4	-10.2	14.6	...	...	...
Nauru	42.5	-18.6	-0.2	11.0	3.0	-2.6	1.7
Palau	18.3	-10.6	-1.5	4.0	3.6	6.2	1.5
Papua New Guinea	-25.8	-36.4	-19.2	47.9	-16.3	18.2	41.5
Samoa	9.0	-8.3	2.4	-2.1	0.7	...	...
Solomon Islands	-1.0	-4.9	-4.3	10.4	7.9	4.4	8.0
Timor-Leste	-11.2	5.7	-14.4	12.9	-2.9	4.9	7.3
Tonga	0.1	10.7	-2.4	-21.1	10.5	...	...
Tuvalu	1.8	141.2	-47.0	11.5	16.7	...	...
Vanuatu	-5.6	17.2	7.3	-8.4	-6.1	2.6	2.7
Developing Asia	-0.1	-13.3	-3.5	16.0	14.5	4.5	4.9
Developing Asia excluding the NIEs	0.2	-12.7	-3.1	16.2	15.1	4.2	4.8

... = data not available.

Note: The newly industrialized economies (NIEs) are Hong Kong, China; the Republic of Korea; Singapore; and Taipei,China.

Table A13 Trade balance ($ million)

	2014	2015	2016	2017	2018	2019	2020
Central Asia	44,763	4,733	-3,693	10,206	17,740	19,380	19,472
Armenia	-2,055	-1,186	-944	-1,375	-1,868	-2,079	-2,159
Azerbaijan	18,928	5,812	4,206	6,115	7,335	7,764	7,203
Georgia	-5,741	-5,096	-5,181	-5,204	-5,760	-5,894	-6,309
Kazakhstan	36,246	12,671	9,193	17,348	27,391	29,379	32,161
Kyrgyz Republic	-2,808	-2,241	-2,137	-2,383	-2,713	-3,166	-3,586
Tajikistan	-3,361	-2,544	-2,132	-1,577	-2,076	-1,321	-1,177
Turkmenistan	4,143	-1,887	-5,657	-2,401	732	1,561	2,657
Uzbekistan	-588	-797	-1,041	-316	-5,300	-6,865	-9,317
East Asia	549,195	747,253	660,621	649,186	567,312	539,273	511,230
Hong Kong, China	-32,359	-22,871	-16,708	-22,912	-32,416	-42,991	-54,512
Mongolia	178	563	1,338	1,490	685	1,477	907
People's Republic of China	435,042	576,191	488,883	476,146	395,100	370,000	345,000
Republic of Korea	86,145	120,275	116,462	113,593	111,867	116,011	119,657
Taipei,China	60,190	73,095	70,647	80,869	92,076	94,776	100,178
South Asia	-190,580	-178,508	-161,663	-222,824	-258,241	-275,276	-298,621
Afghanistan	-5,854	-7,036	-5,971	-6,307	-6,517	-6,606	-6,686
Bangladesh	-6,794	-6,965	-6,460	-9,472	-18,258	-18,636	-19,634
Bhutan	-393	-430	-565	-468	-414	-218	-273
India	-144,940	-130,079	-112,263	-159,935	-178,390	-192,661	-211,709
Maldives	-1,660	-1,655	-1,839	-1,908	-2,271	-2,643	-3,148
Nepal	-6,063	-6,669	-6,409	-8,434	-10,870	-12,985	-14,388
Pakistan	-16,590	-17,285	-19,283	-26,680	-31,178	-30,993	-31,722
Sri Lanka	-8,287	-8,389	-8,873	-9,620	-10,343	-10,534	-11,061
Southeast Asia	137,859	134,975	130,069	133,586	100,815	85,750	76,175
Brunei Darussalam	7,443	2,910	2,153	2,403	2,409	2,406	2,650
Cambodia	-3,852	-3,949	-3,846	-4,278	-5,332	-5,533	-5,735
Indonesia	6,983	14,049	15,318	18,814	-431	-1,360	-2,968
Lao People's Dem. Rep.	-3,518	-3,624	-2,257	-2,454	-3,010	-2,694	-2,430
Malaysia	34,626	27,967	24,599	27,152	30,076	31,387	33,209
Myanmar	-1,859	-4,048	-4,409	-4,696	-2,279	-4,302	-4,818
Philippines	-17,330	-23,309	-35,549	-40,215	-49,036	-54,095	-61,050
Singapore	86,039	90,786	86,478	91,130	97,573	91,827	93,074
Thailand	17,201	26,798	36,539	34,161	23,623	21,357	18,647
Viet Nam	12,126	7,396	11,042	11,570	7,223	6,758	5,597
The Pacific	1,932	3,000	3,303	4,029	4,831	5,156	3,706
Cook Islands	-102	-98	-92	-107	-114	-109	-115
Federated States of Micronesia	-117	-128	-110	...	...	...	...
Fiji	-1,027	-911	-1,000	-1,088	-1,084	-1,097	-1,119
Kiribati	-90	-95	-101	-113	-117	...	...
Marshall Islands	-73	-66	-67	-72	...	...	...
Nauru	-32	-43	-39	-46	-47	-46	-47
Palau	-155	-138	-136	-144	-148	-156	-159
Papua New Guinea	4,817	5,879	6,111	6,888	7,564	7,425	6,089
Samoa	-309	-279	-275	-269	-272	...	...
Solomon Islands	-5	-17	13	7	65	-11	-43
Timor-Leste	-602	-635	-539	-615	-589	-613	-655
Tonga	-170	-188	-179	-149	-168	...	...
Tuvalu	-17	-42	-22	-25	-29	...	...
Vanuatu	-187	-239	-261	-238	-231	-238	-244
Developing Asia	543,168	711,453	628,637	574,183	432,457	374,282	311,962
Developing Asia excluding NIEs	343,154	450,168	371,758	311,503	163,357	114,658	53,566

... = data not available.

Note: The newly industrialized economies (NIEs) are Hong Kong, China; the Republic of Korea; Singapore; and Taipei,China.

Table A14 Current account balance (% of GDP)

	2014	2015	2016	2017	2018	2019	2020
Central Asia	2.3	−3.7	−6.3	−2.1	−2.0	−1.7	−1.8
Armenia	−7.6	−2.6	−2.3	−2.4	−6.6	−6.9	−6.1
Azerbaijan	13.9	−0.4	−3.6	5.5	7.9	13.6	10.8
Georgia	−10.6	−11.9	−12.8	−8.8	−8.0	−7.9	−7.8
Kazakhstan	2.8	−2.8	−6.5	−3.3	0.5	−0.8	−1.2
Kyrgyz Republic	−17.0	−15.9	−11.6	−6.5	−10.0	−12.0	−12.0
Tajikistan	−2.8	−6.2	−3.8	2.1	−4.4	−4.0	−3.8
Turkmenistan	−6.7	−15.6	−19.9	−11.5	−8.2	−5.7	−3.4
Uzbekistan	1.7	0.7	0.6	2.9	−7.0	−7.0	−6.5
East Asia	3.0	3.8	2.9	2.3	1.3	0.8	0.6
Hong Kong, China	1.4	3.3	4.0	4.7	4.3	3.5	3.3
Mongolia	−15.8	−8.1	−6.3	−10.1	−14.6	−9.6	−13.0
People's Republic of China	2.3	2.8	1.8	1.4	0.4	0.0	−0.1
Republic of Korea	5.9	7.6	6.9	4.9	4.7	4.1	3.9
Taipei,China	11.4	14.3	13.7	14.4	11.6	6.0	6.0
South Asia	−1.2	−0.8	−0.5	−2.0	−2.8	−2.7	−2.6
Afghanistan	−1.3	2.9	7.3	5.0	5.3	−1.1	−0.4
Bangladesh	0.8	1.8	1.9	−0.5	−3.6	−2.3	−2.5
Bhutan	−26.4	−28.3	−31.1	−23.2	−18.2	−16.9	−13.4
India	−1.3	−1.0	−0.6	−1.9	−2.3	−2.4	−2.5
Maldives	−3.2	−7.4	−23.5	−22.1	−23.7	−21.8	−22.0
Nepal	4.6	5.1	6.2	−0.4	−8.2	−9.3	−8.1
Pakistan	−1.3	−1.0	−1.7	−4.1	−6.1	−5.0	−3.0
Sri Lanka	−2.5	−2.3	−2.1	−2.6	−3.0	−2.5	−2.6
Southeast Asia	3.0	3.1	3.4	3.3	2.2	2.1	2.1
Brunei Darussalam	30.7	16.7	12.9	16.7	15.5	13.0	13.0
Cambodia	−11.9	−11.6	−10.9	−10.5	−13.6	−12.7	−11.8
Indonesia	−3.1	−2.0	−1.8	−1.6	−3.0	−2.7	−2.7
Lao People's Dem. Rep.	−20.0	−18.0	−14.1	−12.2	−8.6	−9.5	−10.0
Malaysia	4.4	3.0	2.4	3.0	2.3	2.4	2.4
Myanmar	−2.9	−5.2	−4.3	−4.7	−2.0	−4.0	−5.0
Philippines	3.8	2.5	−0.4	−0.7	−2.4	−2.3	−2.4
Singapore	17.9	17.0	17.5	16.0	17.7	17.8	17.8
Thailand	3.7	8.0	11.7	11.0	7.5	7.0	7.0
Viet Nam	5.2	0.5	2.9	2.9	3.0	2.5	2.0
The Pacific	13.3	13.5	11.7	12.0	15.6	12.3	9.8
Cook Islands	−5.3	−1.4	0.6	1.9	2.2	2.8	3.4
Federated States of Micronesia	−0.9	1.6	3.9	7.5	2.0	1.0	1.5
Fiji	−6.2	−2.3	−2.8	−5.8	−5.2	−4.7	−4.2
Kiribati	54.0	45.6	20.4	14.5	13.4	7.6	4.0
Marshall Islands	−1.7	14.4	9.7	4.8	7.0	8.0	7.5
Nauru	−13.4	−9.4	1.6	0.5	1.0	0.5	1.5
Palau	−13.8	−6.5	−10.5	−17.9	−17.5	−16.3	−16.0
Papua New Guinea	10.5	19.6	24.0	22.5	26.7	22.5	18.5
Samoa	−8.6	−2.7	−4.5	−1.8	4.7	−3.5	−3.0
Solomon Islands	−5.5	−3.4	−4.6	−3.9	3.9	−1.4	−2.6
Timor-Leste	75.2	14.9	−30.7	−17.5	−11.8	−12.0	−12.0
Tonga	−6.8	−14.8	−13.8	3.1	1.8	−12.2	−11.2
Tuvalu	5.0	−52.0	24.0	6.7	4.8	−0.9	−11.0
Vanuatu	−0.1	−8.9	−4.6	−1.5	0.5	1.0	1.5
Developing Asia	2.4	2.9	2.3	1.7	0.8	0.4	0.3
Developing Asia excluding the NIEs	1.5	1.8	1.2	0.8	−0.2	−0.5	−0.5

Note: The newly industrialized economies (NIEs) are Hong Kong, China; the Republic of Korea; Singapore; and Taipei,China.

Table A15 Exchange rates to the United States dollar (annual average)

	Currency	Symbol	2014	2015	2016	2017	2018
Central Asia							
Armenia	dram	AMD	415.9	477.9	480.5	482.7	483.0
Azerbaijan	Azerbaijan new manat	AZN	0.8	1.0	1.6	1.7	1.7
Georgia	lari	GEL	1.8	2.3	2.4	2.5	2.5
Kazakhstan	tenge	T	179.2	221.7	342.1	326.0	344.7
Kyrgyz Republic	som	Som	53.7	64.5	69.9	68.9	68.8
Tajikistan	somoni	TJS	4.9	6.2	7.8	8.6	9.2
Turkmenistan	Turkmen manat	TMM	2.9	3.5	3.5	3.5	3.5
Uzbekistan	sum	SUM	2,314.9	2,573.5	2,968.9	5,140.3	8,069.0
East Asia							
Hong Kong, China	Hong Kong dollar	HK$	7.8	7.8	7.8	7.8	7.8
Mongolia	togrog	MNT	1,817.9	1,970.3	2,145.5	2,439.8	2,467.5
People's Republic of China	yuan	CNY	6.1	6.2	6.7	6.7	6.6
Republic of Korea	won	W	1,052.2	1,133.1	1,163.3	1,122.3	1,100.6
Taipei,China	NT dollar	NT$	30.4	31.9	32.3	30.4	30.2
South Asia							
Afghanistan	afghani	AF	57.3	61.2	67.9	68.0	72.1
Bangladesh	taka	Tk	77.7	77.7	78.3	79.1	82.1
Bhutan	ngultrum	Nu	61.5	62.1	66.3	66.4	65.1
India	Indian rupee/s	Re/Rs	61.1	65.5	67.1	64.5	69.9
Maldives	rufiyaa	Rf	15.4	15.4	15.4	15.4	15.4
Nepal	Nepalese rupee/s	NRe/NRs	98.2	99.5	106.4	106.2	104.4
Pakistan	Pakistan rupee/s	PRe/PRs	102.9	101.3	104.2	104.8	109.8
Sri Lanka	Sri Lanka rupee/s	SLRe/SLRs	130.6	135.9	145.6	152.0	163.0
Southeast Asia							
Brunei Darussalam	Brunei dollar	B$	1.3	1.4	1.4	1.4	1.3
Cambodia	riel	KR	4,037.5	4,063.0	4,051.3	4,045.0	4,044.1
Indonesia	rupiah	Rp	11,865.2	13,389.4	13,308.7	13,380.8	14,238.0
Lao People's Dem. Rep.	kip	KN	8,108.0	8,156.0	8,181.0	8,299.5	8,345.0
Malaysia	ringgit	RM	3.3	3.9	4.1	4.3	4.0
Myanmar	kyat	MK	995.0	1,218.9	1,259.2	1,355.7	1,412.9
Philippines	peso	P	44.4	45.5	47.5	50.4	52.7
Singapore	Singapore dollar	S$	1.3	1.4	1.4	1.4	1.3
Thailand	baht	B	32.5	34.3	35.3	33.9	32.3
Viet Nam	dong	D	21,148.8	21,675.6	21,931.0	22,370.3	22,602.9
The Pacific							
Cook Islands	New Zealand dollar	NZ$	1.2	1.3	1.5	1.4	1.4
Federated States of Micronesia	US dollar	US$	1.0	1.0	1.0	1.0	1.0
Fiji	Fiji dollar	F$	1.9	2.1	2.1	2.1	2.1
Kiribati	Australian dollar	A$	1.1	1.3	1.3	1.3	1.3
Marshall Islands	US dollar	US$	1.0	1.0	1.0	1.0	1.0
Nauru	Australian dollar	A$	1.1	1.2	1.4	1.3	1.3
Palau	US dollar	US$	1.0	1.0	1.0	1.0	1.0
Papua New Guinea	kina	K	2.4	2.8	3.1	3.2	3.3
Samoa	tala	ST	2.3	2.6	2.6	2.6	2.6
Solomon Islands	Solomon Islands dollar	SI$	7.4	7.9	8.0	7.9	8.0
Timor-Leste	US dollar	US$	1.0	1.0	1.0	1.0	1.0
Tonga	pa'anga	T$	1.8	1.9	2.2	2.2	2.3
Tuvalu	Australian dollar	A$	1.1	1.3	1.3	1.3	1.3
Vanuatu	vatu	Vt	102.4	116.3	110.8	109.0	111.5

Table A16 Gross international reserves ($ million)

	2014	2015	2016	2017	2018
Central Asia					
Armenia	1,489	1,775	2,204	2,314	2,249
Azerbaijan	13,758	5,017	3,974	5,335	...
Georgia	2,699	2,521	2,756	3,039	3,290
Kazakhstan	29,209	27,871	29,710	30,997	30,927
Kyrgyz Republic	1,958	1,778	1,969	2,177	2,200
Tajikistan	511	494	653	1,292	1,284
Turkmenistan	32,400	...	...	...	...
Uzbekistan	24,149	24,300	26,428	28,076	27,100
East Asia					
Hong Kong, China	328,510	358,823	386,241	431,370	424,670
Mongolia	1,650	1,323	1,296	3,008	3,542
People's Republic of China	3,899,285	3,406,112	3,097,845	3,235,895	3,168,000
Republic of Korea	363,593	367,962	371,102	389,267	403,694
Taipei,China	418,980	426,031	434,204	451,500	461,784
South Asia					
Afghanistan	7,311	6,808	7,357	8,139	8,251
Bangladesh	21,508	25,025	30,168	33,407	32,916
Bhutan	998	958	1,119	1,104	1,111
India	341,638	360,176	369,955	424,545	400,190
Maldives	615	564	467	586	758
Nepal	6,939	8,148	9,736	10,494	10,084
Pakistan	9,098	13,525	18,143	16,145	9,789
Sri Lanka	8,208	7,304	6,019	7,959	6,919
Southeast Asia					
Brunei Darussalam	3,648	3,367	3,489	3,488	3,407
Cambodia	4,391	5,093	6,731	8,758	10,143
Indonesia	111,862	105,931	116,362	130,196	120,654
Lao People's Dem. Rep.	890	1,058	884	1,016	1,105
Malaysia	115,937	95,288	94,501	96,421	103,969
Myanmar	5,125	4,764	5,134	5,370	6,307
Philippines	79,541	80,667	80,692	81,570	79,193
Singapore	256,860	247,747	246,575	279,900	287,673
Thailand	157,108	156,514	171,853	202,562	205,641
Viet Nam	34,330	28,298	41,000	54,870	59,375
The Pacific					
Cook Islands	...	...	...	...	...
Federated States of Micronesia	...	...	...	...	...
Fiji	958	926	919	1,098	1,162
Kiribati	...	...	...	...	...
Marshall Islands	...	...	...	...	...
Nauru	...	...	...	...	...
Palau	...	...	...	...	...
Papua New Guinea	2,445	1,865	1,677	1,736	2,477
Samoa	154	132	111	122	143
Solomon Islands	507	529	530	575	623
Timor-Leste	16,850	16,655	16,125	17,344	16,614
Tonga	159	143	166	170	204
Tuvalu	...	...	...	...	...
Vanuatu	185	256	302	369	396

... = data not available.

Table A17 External debt outstanding ($ million)

	2014	2015	2016	2017	2018
Central Asia					
Armenia	3,785	4,316	4,806	5,495	5,533
Azerbaijan	6,478	6,894	6,913	9,398	8,927
Georgia	10,718	11,983	13,083	14,656	14,764
Kazakhstan	157,561	153,422	163,309	167,224	161,461
Kyrgyz Republic	6,371	6,670	6,830	7,026	6,697
Tajikistan	2,098	2,183	2,276	2,833	2,924
Turkmenistan	8,043	8,354	...	...	...
Uzbekistan	8,399	11,800	13,000	15,600	17,500
East Asia					
Hong Kong, China	1,301,032	1,300,365	1,356,411	1,576,560	1,693,506
Mongolia	21,851	22,718	24,625	27,493	27,913
People's Republic of China	1,779,932	1,382,980	1,415,801	1,710,625	...
Republic of Korea	424,325	396,058	382,162	412,028	440,599
Taipei,China	177,945	158,954	172,238	181,938	191,161
South Asia					
Afghanistan	1,299	1,231	1,199	1,168	1,244
Bangladesh	24,388	23,901	26,306	28,337	33,111
Bhutan	1,759	1,855	2,316	2,505	2,642
India	474,675	485,052	471,824	495,686	510,400
Maldives	744	696	849	1,190	1,383
Nepal	3,617	3,391	3,642	4,025	4,794
Pakistan	65,269	65,169	73,945	83,477	95,342
Sri Lanka	42,914	44,839	46,418	51,824	...
Southeast Asia					
Brunei Darussalam	...	...	...	...	...
Cambodia	5,279	5,648	5,860	6,669	7,022
Indonesia	293,328	310,730	320,006	352,469	376,839
Lao People's Dem. Rep.	9,640	11,664	13,524	14,498	...
Malaysia	213,951	195,010	203,848	217,927	223,484
Myanmar	8,800	9,500	9,100	9,600	11,000
Philippines	77,674	77,474	74,763	73,098	78,960
Singapore	1,412,644	1,325,615	1,389,153	1,400,531	1,468,776
Thailand	141,715	131,078	132,158	155,225	158,129
Viet Nam	...	...	...	...	...
The Pacific					
Cook Islands	61	74	77	56	59
Federated States of Micronesia	90	81	80	80	...
Fiji	573	658	605	662	707
Kiribati	14	33	42	43	42
Marshall Islands	95	89	83	78	78
Nauru	44	39	35	37	38
Palau	71	64	80	86	91
Papua New Guinea	1,446	1,469	1,754	2,001	2,696
Samoa	442	422	398	416	423
Solomon Islands	89	83	80	96	96
Timor-Leste	22	46	77	104	166
Tonga	186	195	176	179	188
Tuvalu	22	19	19	19	16
Vanuatu	135	157	246	342	372

... = data not available.

Table A18 Debt service ratio (% of exports of goods and services)

	2014	2015	2016	2017	2018
Central Asia					
Armenia	6.8	4.4	4.7	5.2	6.9
Azerbaijan	...	...	...	...	...
Georgia	20.3	21.4	20.7	21.7	18.3
Kazakhstan	36.6	72.1	71.9	66.4	52.0
Kyrgyz Republic	26.9	42.2	32.1	35.1	26.0
Tajikistan	...	...	...	...	...
Turkmenistan	...	...	...	...	...
Uzbekistan	6.5	10.0	11.3	15.4	16.5
East Asia					
Hong Kong, China	...	...	...	...	...
Mongolia	39.8	41.6	88.5	21.2	22.4
People's Republic of China	2.6	5.0	6.1	6.9	...
Republic of Korea	7.9	8.9	9.0	10.0	11.0
Taipei,China	1.5	1.6	2.1	1.9	2.3
South Asia					
Afghanistan	...	...	...	...	...
Bangladesh	3.9	3.2	2.8	3.0	3.4
Bhutan	27.1	19.7	14.4	24.8	23.4
India	7.6	8.8	8.3	7.9	8.3
Maldives	2.3	2.3	2.6	2.4	3.0
Nepal	8.9	8.1	9.9	10.8	8.3
Pakistan	21.6	18.0	19.4	29.5	24.9
Sri Lanka	21.7	28.2	25.6	23.9	...
Southeast Asia					
Brunei Darussalam	...	...	...	...	...
Cambodia	1.1	1.0	1.3	1.3	1.4
Indonesia	24.0	30.6	35.3	25.5	24.1
Lao People's Dem. Rep.	5.7	6.5	8.1	...	...
Malaysia	10.7	14.3	14.7	6.8	5.2
Myanmar	5.0	4.7	4.7	4.1	4.0
Philippines	6.3	5.6	7.0	6.2	6.3
Singapore	...	...	...	...	...
Thailand	4.9	6.4	5.9	5.7	...
Viet Nam	...	...	...	...	...
The Pacific					
Cook Islands	8.0	8.0	7.4	7.3	6.3
Federated States of Micronesia	8.9	8.0	6.9	6.0	...
Fiji	1.6	1.7	12.7	5.0	3.0
Kiribati	32.2	5.8	4.8	4.8	4.2
Marshall Islands	7.0	11.4	13.0	12.3	...
Nauru	4.9	−6.4	2.9	3.2	3.8
Palau	4.9	4.8	5.6	6.3	5.8
Papua New Guinea	0.5	0.4	0.3	0.5	...
Samoa	8.9	10.8	8.4	10.3	...
Solomon Islands	3.3	6.5	1.9	2.8	1.4
Timor-Leste	0.4	0.4	0.9	1.6	1.8
Tonga	9.2	9.8	7.6	7.5	6.6
Tuvalu	2.9	12.2	12.0	11.6	12.4
Vanuatu	2.3	2.3	1.9	1.7	...

... = data not available.

www.ingramcontent.com/pod-product-compliance
Lightning Source LLC
Chambersburg PA
CBHW061934290426
44113CB00025B/2910